A
GAZETTEER

OF

THE COUNTRIES ADJACENT TO INDIA

ON

THE NORTH-WEST

INCLUDING

SINDE, AFGHANISTAN, BELOOCHISTAN,

THE PUNJAB

AND THE NEIGHBOURING STATES

A
GAZETTEER

OF

THE COUNTRIES ADJACENT TO INDIA

ON

THE NORTH-WEST

INCLUDING

SINDE, AFGHANISTAN, BELOOCHISTAN,

THE PUNJAB
AND THE NEIGHBOURING STATES

EDWARD THORNTON

IN TWO VOLUMES
VOL. I

ISBN : 978-93-5324-383-8 (Set)
ISBN : 978-93-5324-384-5 Vol. 1 (HB)
First Published, London, 1844
Published, 2020
Published by

Facsimile Publisher
12 Pragati Market
Ashok Vihar, Ph-2
Delhi-110052
E-mail: books@facsimilepublisher.com

Printed at: G. Print Process, Delhi.

A
Gazetteer
of
The countries Adjacent to India
On
The North-West
Including
Sinde, Afghanistan, Beloochistan,
The Punjab
And The Neighbouring States

Author: Edward Thornton

A GAZETTEER

OF

THE COUNTRIES ADJACENT TO INDIA

ON

THE NORTH-WEST;

INCLUDING

SINDE, AFGHANISTAN, BELOOCHISTAN,

THE PUNJAB,

AND THE NEIGHBOURING STATES.

COMPILED BY THE AUTHORITY OF

THE HON. COURT OF DIRECTORS OF THE EAST-INDIA COMPANY,

AND

CHIEFLY FROM DOCUMENTS IN THEIR POSSESSION,

BY

EDWARD THORNTON, Esq.

Author of the " History of the British Empire in India."

IN TWO VOLUMES

VOL. I.

LONDON:

Wm. H. ALLEN AND CO

1844.

PREFACE.

To justify the publication of a Gazetteer of the countries adjacent to India on the north-west, it is only necessary to advert to the manifest want of such a work ; more especially, since, from recent events, the countries to which it relates have acquired a new and extraordinary interest. It is obvious that no general Gazetteer can be expected to furnish the minute and varied information which a similar work of more exclusive character may conveniently afford, and it is to be lamented, that the only sources of information accessible to general perusal are, in very many instances, calculated to mislead. To supply that which is wanting, and to correct that which is erroneous, are the objects of the present undertaking. In the preparation of the work, these objects have been steadily kept in view, without regard to labour. Every published book known or supposed to contain information relating to the countries treated of, has been consulted : the examination has not been confined to English works; it has been extended to those written in the languages of the Continent—works never translated, and, in this country, comparatively unknown. Further, as it was

a 2

essential to completeness, that the knowledge possessed by the ancients of those countries should be adverted to, and as the principle adopted throughout is to refer in every instance to original authorities, it became necessary to collect the notices of the subject which are to be found in the Greek and Roman writers.

The Gazetteer is thus an epitome of all that has yet been written and published respecting the countries adjacent to and westward of the Indus. On this ground alone it might support a claim to the character of a convenient and useful compilation, presenting to the reader, within a brief compass, a mass of information which could not otherwise be obtained, except from a multiplicity of volumes in many languages, some of them of high price, and others not easily procurable. But this is not its only, nor even its principal claim. The stores of information derived from books are indeed considerable, but they yield in value, as well as in extent, to the amount of matter hitherto unpublished, and even unexplored, excepting by those whose official duties have led them to the pursuit. Under the authority of the Court of Directors of the East-India Company, the treasures of their vast collections have been opened for the purposes of the present work, and from the researches thus sanctioned, its chief value is derived.

Any minute account of the mode adopted in working up the materials thus available, would be tedious as well as useless. But it may not be improper to refer to the following heads as having been kept in view in framing the account of a country, province, or large territorial division. First, the name or names by which it is known, and the etymology, if ascertainable or important. Secondly, its local situation, the latitude and longitude of the extreme points, length and breadth in English miles, and superficial extent in square miles. Thirdly, its physical characteristics, mountains, rivers, climate, soil, geology, mineralogy, zoology, botany, &c. Fourthly, economic circumstances, agriculture, commerce, mining, and the means of advancing those operations, roads, canals, &c. Fifthly, statistical, social, and political circumstances, not embraced in the foregoing heads, population, language, manners, religion, form of government, civil arrangements, military organization. Sixthly, the principal cities, towns, fortresses, and public establishments. Seventhly, the history and antiquities of the country or district, wherever they may present any points either useful, interesting, or curious. In framing the descriptions of cities, towns, villages, and stations, it has been sought to fix their relative positions with as much precision as possible, and to exhibit, with the greatest practicable brevity, all that is known respecting them. The principal chains of mountains are described with a minuteness which their importance demands, and the chief rivers have received the same degree of attention. In this respect it is confidently hoped that, with reference to the existing state of information, nothing is left to be desired. With a view to simplicity, as well as to avoiding error, the statements of relative position of places is restricted to the eight principal points of the compass, the closer determination of their mutual bearings being left to be collected from their respective latitudes and longitudes, which will invariably be given with the greatest ascertainable accuracy.

It remains only to advert to a point which cannot be approached without some anxiety, in consequence of the contrariety of opinion prevailing among competent judges, and the impossibility of making a choice without apparent presumption.

The mode of spelling the names contained in this work has been a subject of much perplexity. Few Europeans who have had occasion to use Eastern names extensively, and who have been desirous of maintaining consistency, can have been exempt from the same feelings. The difficulty is the result of various causes. Sir Charles Wilkins, in the Preface to his Glossary, observes, " that the confusion has arisen, in some degree, from there being no fixed rules for the notation of oriental terms in the letters of our imperfect alphabet, every one spelling according to his ear; but, in a greater degree, from the ignorance or inattention of the native clerks employed in the public offices in India to copy the transactions of the East-India Company. To give an instance of the confusion occasioned from these circumstances, the word, which, according to its form and sound, in *Arabic*, should be written *mahal* (A. محال), the first vowel short and the last long, occurs under no less than eight different shapes, not one of which is correct on any system of orthography; viz. *mal, maal, mahl, mehal, mehaal, mehaul, mhal*, and *mohaul*." A very fruitful cause of diversity is to be found in the modes resorted to by travellers for exhibiting to the eye words with which they were acquainted only by the ear; in effecting which object they have often been unconsciously influenced by regard to the peculiarities of accent, quantity, and pronunciation prevailing in the countries or provinces of which they were natives. Systems have been devised for putting an end to these irregularities, but they have not altogether escaped the ordinary fate of attempts to give fixity to the ever-varying elements of speech and language. Of such systems, those of Dr. Gilchrist and Sir William Jones are the chief.* The former, characterized by representing the Roman *i* by *ee*, *u* by *oo*, and some other peculiarities; the latter by employing, in place of these double letters, *i* and *u*, with the pronunciation given them in Italian, and distinguishing the long vowels from the short by the use of accents.   After much deliberation as to the choice to be made, it appeared most expedient—as the present work was intended, not for oriental scholars only, but for general perusal—to abstain from any attempt to secure scientific uniformity— to follow not the most regular and analogical mode of spelling, but that most commonly adopted—that with which the civil and military officers of the East-India Company, and all men of business connected with India, are most familiar.   Accordingly, the names in this work will be found scarcely to vary in any instance from those given in Walker's map, drawn up, by order of the Court of Directors, from documents in their possession.

* To these may be added the modification of the system of Sir William Jones by Mr. Trevelyan, with a view of comprehending within it the many alphabets of eastern nations, and of Romanizing the Indian symbols.

It is worthy of observation, that however loud the complaint respecting the corrupt mode of expressing Indian names in English, no such deviations occur with respect to them as we find in regard to the names of many places in Europe; such as Naples for Napoli, Leghorn for Livorno, Munich for München, Moravia for Mähren, Vienna for Wien, Germany for Deutschland, and many others equally glaring which might be quoted from the language of almost every European nation, with reference to places within the territories of their neighbours. Irregularity, indeed, has not been confined to foreign names. In England, the spelling of local names has been subject to much caprice; the vowel employed in the latter syllable of the word Dover is sometimes *e*, sometimes *o*, and the spelling of Brightelmstone has been assimilated to the ordinary pronunciation of the word— Brighton. The most reasonable view of the question is, perhaps, to regard spelling as altogether a matter of usage. Those, however, who take a different view, will find by reference to the Index at the end of the second volume, that in addition to the ordinary spelling of the names of principal places, there is given also that which is most consistent with orthographical regularity.

LIST OF AUTHORITIES.

ABBOTT.
Narrative of a Journey from Heraut to Khiva, Moscow, and St. Petersburgh, by Captain James Abbott, Bengal Artillery. 8vo. 2 vols. Lond. 1843.

ABUL FAZEL.—See AYEEN AKBERY.

ADELUNG MITHRIDATES oder allgemeine Sprachenkunde, Von Johann Christoph Adelung. 8vo., 4 Th. Berlin, 1806.

AFGHANISTAN.
Papers relating to Military Operations in Afghanistan. Presented to both Houses of Parliament by command of her Majesty. ˊ Folio. Lond. 1843.

ALLEN.
Diary of a March through Sinde and Affghanistan, with the troops under command of General Sir William Nott, by the Rev. J. N. Allen, B.A., Assistant Chaplain on the Hon. East-India Company's Bombay Establishment. 8vo. Lond. 1843.

ARIANA ANTIQUA.—See WILSON.

ARRIANI EXPEDITIO ALEXANDRI. 8vo. Amstel. 1757.

ASIATIC ANNUAL REGISTER, or a View of the History of Hindustan, and of the Politics, Commerce, and Literature of Asia. 8vo. 11 vols. Lond. 1798—1807.

ASIATIC RESEARCHES, or Transactions of the Society instituted in Bengal, for inquiring into the History and Antiquities, the Arts, Sciences, and Literature of Asia. 4to. vols. 1—20. Calcutta, 1788—1839.

ASIATIC SOCIETY OF BENGAL, Journal of, in monthly numbers, from January 1832, to December 1843. 8vo. Calcutta.

ASIATIC (ROYAL) SOCIETY of Great Britain and Ireland, Transactions. 4to. 3 vols. 1824—1835. 8vo. 14 Nos. 1834—1843. Lond.

ASIATIC JOURNAL and Monthly Register for British and Foreign India, China, and Australasia. 28 vols. 1815—1829. New Series. 8vo. 39 vols. 1830—1842. Lond.

ATKINSON.
The Expedition into Affghanistan; Notes and Sketches descriptive of the Country, contained in a personal narrative during the campaigns

of 1839 and 1840, up to the surrender of Dost Mahomed Khan. By James Atkinson, Esq., superintending surgeon of the army of the Indus, Bengal Establishment. 8vo. Lond. 1842.

AYEEN AKBERY, or the Institutes of the Emperor Akber; translated from the original Persian, by Francis Gladwin. 4to. 42 vols. Lond. 1800.

BABER.

Memoirs of Zehir-ed-Din Muhammed Baber, Emperor of Hindustan, written by himself in the Jagathai Turki; and translated partly by the late John Leyden, Esq., M.D., partly by William Erskine, Esq. With notes, and a geographical and historical introduction. Together with a map of the countries between the Oxus and Jaxartes, and a memoir regarding its construction, by Charles Waddington, Esq., of the East-India Company's Engineers. 4to. Lond. 1826.

BAPTISTS.

Brief View of the Baptist Missions and Translations, with specimens of various Languages in which the Scriptures are printing at the Mission Press, Serampore. 8vo. Lond. 1815.

BERNIER.

Voyages de François Bernier, Docteur en Médecine de la Faculté de Montpellier, contenant la description des états du Grand Mogol de l'Hindoustan, du Royaume de Kachemire, &c. 12mo. 2 vols. Amsterd. 1699.

BOILEAU.

Personal Narrative of a Tour through the Western States of Rajwara in 1835, comprising Bekaner, Jesulmer, and Jodhpoor, with the Passage of the Great Desert, and a Brief Visit to the Indus and to Buhawulpoor, accompanied by various tables and memoranda, statistical, philological, and geographical. By Lieut. A. H. E. Boileau. Bengal Eng., first assistant Great Trigonometrical Survey. 4to Calcutta, 1837.

BROOME.

Abstract Journals of the Routes of Lieutenants A. Broome and A. Cunningham to the Sources of the Punjab Rivers. Journ. As. Soc. Beng. 1841, pp. 1—6.

BURNES, ALEXANDER.

Travels into Bokhara, being an account of a Journey from India to Cabool, Tartary, and Persia; also a Narrative of a Voyage on the Indus from the Sea to Lahore, with Presents from the King of Great Britain, performed under the orders of the Supreme Government of India in the years 1831, 1832, 1833. By Lieut. Alex. Burnes, of the East-India Company's Service. 8vo. 3 vols. Lond. 1834.

Cabool, a Personal Narrative of a Journey to and Residence in that City, in the years 1836, 7, and 8. By the late Lieut.-Colonel Alexander Burnes, C. B., &c., of the East-India Company's Service. 8vo. Lond. 1843.

BURNES, ALEXANDER—(continued).

On the Political Power of the Sikhs beyond the Indus. By Captain Burnes. Indian Government Reports and Papers, pp. 1—6. Fol. Calcutta, 1839.

On the Trade of the Upper Indus, or Derajat. By Captain Alexander Burnes. Indian Government Reports and Papers, sect. iii. pp. 98 -104.

Report on the Establishment of an Entrepôt, or Fair, for the Indus Trade. By Capt. Alexander Burnes. Indian Government Papers, sect. iii. pp. 108—117.

On the Commerce of Tatta in Sinde. By Capt. Alexander Burnes. Indian Government Papers, sect. iii. pp. 8 -14.

On the Persian Faction in Cabool. Report by Alexander Burnes. Indian Government Papers, pp. 6—13.

On the Siah-Posh Kaffirs, with specimens of their language and costume. By Captain Burnes. Indian Government Papers, sect. ii. pp. 69—77.

Report on Herat, with a Sketch of the State of the surrounding Countries. By Alexander Burnes. Indian Government Papers, pp. 38—48.

Notice on the Wool of Cabool and Bokhara. By Captain Alexander Burnes. Indian Government Papers, sect. iii. pp. 105—108.

Notice of Articles of Commerce in Sinde and Affghanistan. By Alexander Burnes. Indian Government Papers, pp. 164—178.

BURNES, JAMES.

A Narrative of a Visit to the Court of Sinde, with a Sketch of the History of Cutch from its first connection with the British Government in India till the conclusion of the Treaty in 1819. By James Burnes, Surgeon to the Presidency of Bhooj. Bombay, 1829. Edinburgh, 1831.

CARLESS.

Official Report on the State and Navigation of the Indus below Hyderabad. Compiled by Lieut. Carless, I.N., from the Reports of Licuts. Carless and Wood, I.N., and Lieut. Pottinger, Bombay Artillery. With a Report on the Inundation of the Indus. By Lieut. Wood. Published by order of Government, with a Map. 8vo. 1837.

Account of a Journey to Beylah, and Memoir on the Province of Lus. By Lieut. Carless, I.N. Journ. As. Soc. Beng. 1839, pp. 184—202.

CHRISTIE, CAPTAIN.

Journal of a Journey from Nooshky, in Beloochistan, to Isfahan. Appendix to Pottinger's Beloochistan, pp. 402—422.

CONOLLY, ARTHUR.

Journey to the North of India, overland from England, through Russia, Persia, and Affghanistan. By Lieut. Arthur Conolly, 8vo. 2 vols. Lond. 1834.

b 2

CONOLLY, ARTHUR—(*continued*).

Extracts from Demi-official Reports, by Capt. Arthur Conolly, on a Mission into Khorasan. Journ. As. Soc. Beng. 1841, pp. 116—128.

CONOLLY, EDWARD.

Sketch of the Physical Geography of Seistan. By Captain Edward Conolly. Journ. As. Soc. Beng. 1840, pp. 710—726.

Journal kept while travelling in Seistan by the late Captain Edward Conolly. Journ. As. Soc. Beng. 1841, pp. 319—340.

Notes on the Eusofzye Tribes of Afghanistan. By the late Captain Edward Conolly. Journ. As. Soc. Beng. 1840, pp. 924—938.

COURT.

Collection of Facts which may be useful for the comprehension of Alexander the Great's Exploits on the Western Banks of the Indus. With Map. By M. A. Court, ancien Elève de l'Ecole Militaire de Saint Cyr. Journ. As. Soc. Beng. 1839, pp. 304—313.

Extracts translated from a Memoir on a Map of Peshawur, and the country comprised between the Indus and the Hydaspes. By M. A. Court, in the service of Maha Raja Ranjet Singh. Journ. As. Soc. Beng. 1836, pp. 468—482.

Conjectures on the March of Alexander. By M. Court. Journ. As. Soc. Beng. 1836, pp. 387—396.

CUNNINGHAM.

Abstract Journal of the Route of Lieut. A. Cunningham, Bengal Engineers, to the Source of the Punjab Rivers. Journ. As. Soc. Beng. 1841, pp. 106—115.

DE LA HOSTE.

Report on the Country between Kurrachee, Tatta, Scinde, and Sehwan. By Capt. E. P. De la Hoste. Journ. As. Soc. Beng. 1840, pp. 907—916.

Memoranda respecting the Existence of Copper in the Territory of Luz, near Bela. By Capt. De la Hoste. Journ. As. Soc. Beng. 1840, pp. 30—33.

D'HERBELOT.

Bibliothèque Orientale. 4to. 4 tom. A La Haye, 1777.

DORN.—See NEAMET ULLAH.

DRUMMOND.

On the Mines and Mineral Resources of Northern Afghanistan. By Capt. Drummond. Journ. As. Soc. Beng. 1841, pp. 74—93.

EAST-INDIA COMPANY. MANUSCRIPT DOCUMENTS in Collections of the Hon. East-India Company.

Reports and Papers, political, geographical, and commercial, submitted to Government by Sir Alexander Burnes, Bom. N.I.; Lieut.

E.I.C. MS. DOC.—*(continued).*
> Leech, Bombay Eng.; Dr. Lord, Bom. M.S.; and Lieut. Wood, I.N.; employed on Missions in the Years 1835, 36, 37, in Sinde, Afghanistan, and adjacent Countries. Printed by order of Government. Fol. Calcutta, 1839.

EDGEWORTH.
> Grammar and Vocabulary of the Cashmiri Language. By M. P. Edgeworth, Esq. Journ. As. Soc. Beng. 1841, pp. 1038—1064.

ELPHINSTONE.
> An Account of the Kingdom of Caubul and its Dependencies in Persia, Tartary, and India, comprising a View of the Afghan Nation, and a History of the Dooraunee Monarchy. By the Hon. Mountstuart Elphinstone, late Envoy to the King of Caubul. 4to. Lond. 1815.

EYRE.
> The Military Operations at Cabul which ended in the Retreat and Destruction of the British Army, January, 1842; with a Journal of Imprisonment in Affghanistan. By Lieut. Vincent Eyre, Bengal Artillery, late Deputy Commissary of Ordnance at Cabul. 8vo. Lond. 1843.

FALCONER.
> Letter to the Secretary of the Asiatic Society on the recent Cataclysm of the Indus. From Dr. Falconer, Saharunpoor. Journ. As. Soc. Beng. 1841, pp. 615—620.

FERISHTA.
> History of the Rise of the Mahomedan Power in India till the Year A.D. 1612. Translated from the original Persian of Mahomed Kasim Ferishta, by John Briggs, M.R.A.S., Lieut.-Colonel in the Madras Army. 8vo. 4 vols. Lond. 1829.

FORSTER.
> A Journey from Bengal to England through the Northern part of India, Kashmire, Afghanistan, Persia, and into Russia by the Caspian Sea. By George Forster, of the Civil Service of the Hon. East-India Company. 8vo. 2 vols. Lond. 1808.

FRASER.
> Narrative of a Journey into Khorasan in the Years 1821 and 1822. Including some Account of the Countries to the North-east of Persia, with Remarks upon the national Character, Government, and Resources of that Kingdom. By James B. Fraser. 4to. Lond. 1825.

GEOGRAPHICAL SOCIETY.
> Journal of the Royal Geographical Society, 1831—1843. 8vo. Lond.

GERARD, ALEXANDER.
> Account of Koonawur in the Himalaya. By the late Capt. Alexander Gerard. Edited by George Lloyd. 8vo. Lond. 1841.

GERARD, J. G.

Observations on the Spiti Valley and circumjacent Country within the Himalaya. By Surgeon J. G. Gerard, Bengal N.I. Asiatic Researches, xviii. 238—277.

Route of Lieut. A. Burnes and Dr. Gerard from Peshawer to Bokhara. Journ. As. Soc. Beng. 1833, pp. 1—22.

GRANT.

Journal of a Route through the Western Parts of Mackran. By Capt. N. P. Grant. Journal of the Royal Asiatic Society, 1839, pp. 328—341.

GRIFFITH.

Tables of Barometrical and Thermometrical Observations made in Afghanistan, Upper Scinde, and Kutch Gandava, during the Years 1839, 1840. By Dr. Griffith. Journ. As. Soc. Beng. 1842, pp. 49—90.

Extracts from a Report on Subjects connected with Afghanistan. By Dr. Griffith. Journ. As. Soc. Beng. 1841, pp. 797—815, 977—1035.

HAMILTON.

A New Account of the East Indies; being the Observations and Remarks of Capt. Alexander Hamilton, who spent his Time there from the Year 1688 to 1723. 8vo. 2 vols. Edinb. 1727.

HART.

Some Account of a Journey from Kurrachee to Hinglaj, in the Lus Territory, descriptive of the intermediate Country and of the Port of Sonmeanee. Journ. As. Soc. Beng. 1840, pp. 134—154.

HAVELOCK.

Narrative of the War in Afghanistan, in 1838—39. By Capt. Henry Havelock. 8vo. 2 vols. Lond. 1840.

HORSBURGH.

The India Directory; or, Directions for Sailing to and from the East Indies. By James Horsburgh, Hydrographer to the Hon. East-India Company. 4to. 2 vols. Lond. 1841.

HOUGH.

A Narrative of the March and Operations of the Army of the Indus in the Expedition to Affghanistan, in the Years 1838, 1839. By Major W. Hough. 8vo. Lond. 1841.

HÜGEL.

Kaschmir und das Reech der Siekh. Von Carl Freiherrn von Hügel. 8vo. 4 B. Stuttgart, 1840.

HUMBOLDT.

Asie Centrale : Recherches sur les Chaines de Montagnes, et la Climatologie comparée. Par A. de Humboldt. 8vo. 3 tom. Paris, 1843.

HYDE.

Veterum Persarum, et Parthorum, et Medorum Religionis Historia. Autor est Thomas Hyde, S.T.D., Linguæ Hebraicæ in Universitate Oxon. Professor Regius, et Linguæ Arabicæ Professor Laudianus. Editio Secunda. Oxon. 1769.

IBN BATUTA.

The Travels of Ibn Batuta. Translated from the abridged Manuscript Copies preserved in the Public Library of Cambridge. With Notes illustrative of the History, Geography, Botany, Antiquities, &c. occurring throughout the work. By the Rev. Samuel Lee. 4to. Lond. 1829.

IRWIN.

Memoir on the Climate, Soil, Produce, and Husbandry of Afghanistan and the neighbouring Countries. By Lieut. Irwin. Journ. As. Soc. Beng. 1839, pp. 745, 779, 869, 1005 ; 1840, pp. 33, 189.

IZZET ULLAH.

Travels beyond the Himalaya. Oriental Magazine, 1825, p. 103. 8vo. Calcutta.

JACKSON.

Views in Afghaunistaun. By Sir Keith A. Jackson, Bart. Fol. Lond.

JACQUEMONT.

Voyage dans l'Inde, par Victor Jacquemont, pendant les Années 1828 à 1832. Fol. Paris, 1841.

Correspondance de Victor Jacquemont avec sa Famille et plusieurs de ses Amis, pendant son Voyage dans l'Inde. 8vo. 2 tom. Paris, 1835.

JAMESON.

Account of Mineralogy of the Salt Range. Journ. As. Soc. Beng. 1842, pp. 1—4.

JONES, Sir WILLIAM.

On the Descent of the Afghans. Asiatic Researches, pp. 11—76.

KELLY.

Oriental Metrology, comprising the Monies, Weights, and Measures of the East Indies and other trading Places in Asia, reduced to the English Standard by verified Operations. To which is added an Appendix on Oriental Measures of Time, explaining the Calendars, Dates, and Eras of Asiatic Nations. By P. Kelly, LL.D. 8vo. Lond. 1832.

KENNEDY.

Narrative of the Campaign of the Army of the Indus in Sind and Kaubool, in 1838—39. By Richard Hartley Kennedy, M.D. 8vo. 2 vols. Lond. 1840.

KINNEIR.

A Geographical Memoir of the Persian Empire. By John Macdonald Kinneir. 4to. Lond. 1813.

KITTOE.

On Somnath. Journ. As. Soc. Beng. 1838, pp. 883—888.

KLAPROTH, JULIUS.

Asia Polyglotta. 4to. Paris, 1823.

LEECH.

Report on the Sindhian, Khelat, and Daoodpulr Armies, with a Collection of Routes. By Lieut. R. Leech. Indian Government Papers, pp. 65—95.

Short Notice of Leia. By Lieut. R. Leech. Indian Government Papers, sect. iii. pp. 89—92.

Report on the Commerce of Multan. By Lieut. R. Leech. Indian Government Papers, sect. iii. pp. 79—88.

Sketch of the Trade of the Port of Mandavie, in Cutch. By Lieut. R. Leech. Indian Government Papers, sect. iii. pp. 41—54.

Description of the Khyber Pass. By Lieut. R. Leech. Indian Government Papers, sect. ii. pp. 8—14.

Description of the Passes over the Hindoo Coosh Range of Mountains from the Koh Daman of Cabool. By Lieut. R. Leech. Indian Government Papers, sect. ii. pp. 29—43.

Grammars of the Brahooekee, Beloochee, and Punjabee Languages. By Lieut. R. Leech. Indian Government Papers, sect. ii. pp. 80—148.

Grammar of the Pushtoo or Afghanee Language. By Lieut. R. Leech. Journ. As. Soc. Beng. 1839, pp. 1—16.

Description of the Passage of the Indus at Attok by a Bridge of Boats. By Lieut. R. Leech. Indian Government Papers, sect. ii. pp. 15—17.

Commercial Information regarding Bhawal Khan's Country. By Lieut. R. Leech. Indian Government Papers, sect. iii. pp. 55—59.

LLOYD and GERARD.

Narrative of a Journey from Caunpoor to the Boorendo Pass in the Himalaya Mountains. By Major Sir William Lloyd. And Captain Alexander Gerard's Account of an Attempt to penetrate by Bekhur to Garoo, and the Lake Manasarowara. Edited by George Lloyd. 8vo. 2 vols. Lond. 1840.

LORD.

Some Account of a Visit to the Plain of Koh-i-Damun, the Mining District of Ghorbund, and the Pass of Hindu Kush. By Percamt B. Lord, M. D. Indian Government Papers, pp. 45—57.

Medical Memoir of the Plain of the Indus. By Percamt B. Lord, M. D. Indian Government Papers, pp. 58—68.

MACARTNEY.

Memoir on the Construction of the Map of Afghanistan and neighbouring Countries. In Elphinstone's Account of Caubul, Appendix, pp. 631—665.

MACGREGOR.

A Geographical Notice of the Valley of Jullalabad. By Lieut. MacGregor. Journ. As. Soc. Beng. 1842, pp. 117—130.

MACKESON.

Journal of Captain C. M. Wade's Voyage from Lodhiana to Mithankot, by the River Sutlaj. By Lieut. Mackeson. Journ. As. Soc. Beng. 1837, pp. 169—217.

MACMURDO.

An Account of the Country of Sindh, with Remarks on the State of Society, the Government, Manners, and Customs of the People. By the late Captain James Macmurdo. Journ. Royal As. Soc. 1834, pp. 223—257.

Dissertation on the River Indus. By the late Captain James Macmurdo. Journ. Royal As. Soc. 1834, pp. 20—44.

MALCOLM.

The History of Persia from the most early period to the present time ; containing an account of the Religion, Government, Usages, and Character of the Inhabitants of that Kingdom. By Sir John Malcolm. 4to. 2 vols. Lond. 1815.

Sketch of the Sikhs. As. Researches, xi. pp. 197—292.

MARCO POLO.

The Travels of Marco Polo, a Venetian, in the Thirteenth Century. Being a Description, by that early Traveller, of remarkable Places and Things in the Eastern Parts of the World. Translated from the Italian, with Notes. By William Marsden, Esq. 4to. Lond. 1818.

MASSON.

Narrative of Various Journeys in Balochistan, Afghanistan, and the Panjab, including a Residence in those Countries from 1826 to 1838. By Charles Masson, Esq. 8vo. 3 vols. Lond. 1842.

Narrative of a Journey to Kalat, including an Account of an Insurrection in that Place in 1840; and a Memoir on Eastern Balochistan. By Charles Masson, Esq. 8vo. Lond. 1843.

Memoir on the Ancient Coins found at Beghram, in the Kohistan of Kabul. By Charles Masson. Journ. As. Soc. Beng. pp. 153—175.

Second Memoir on the Ancient Coins found at Beghram, in the Kohistan of Kabul. By Charles Masson. Journ. As. Soc. Beng. 1836, pp. 1—28.

Notes on the Antiquities of Bamian. By Charles Masson. Journ. As. Soc. Beng. 1836, pp. 707—724.

Third Memoir on the Ancient Coins discovered at the site called Beghram, in the Kohistan of Kabul. By Charles Masson. Journ. As. Soc. Beng. 1836, pp. 537—554.

MOHUN LAL.

On the Trade of Khairpoor, in Sinde. By Munshi Mohun Lal. Indian Government Papers, sect. iii. pp. 36—39.

On the Trade of Bahawalpur. By Munshi Mohun Lal. Indian Government Papers, sect. iii. 70—78.

A brief Description of Herat. By Munshi Mohun Lal. Journ. As. Soc. Beng. 1834. pp. 9—18.

Further Information regarding the Siah Posh Tribe, or reputed Descendants of Macedonians. By Munshi Mohun Lal. Journ. As. Soc. Beng. 1834. pp. 76—79.

Account of Kala Bagh, on the right Bank of the Indus. By Munshi Mohun Lal. Journ. As. Soc. Beng. 1838. pp. 25—27.

A brief Account of the Origin of the Daud Putras, and of the Power and Birth of Bahawal Khan, their Chief, on the bank of the Ghara and Indus. By Munshi Mohun Lal. Journ. As. Soc. Beng. 1838. pp. 27—33.

MOORCROFT.

A Journey to Lake Manasarovara, in Un-des, a Province of Little Tibet. By William Moorcroft, Esq. As. Res. xii. pp. 375—534.

Travels in the Himalayan Provinces of Hindostan and the Punjab, in Ladakh and Kashmir, in Peshawur, Kabul, Kunduz, and Bokhara. By Mr. William Moorcroft and Mr. George Trebeck. From 1819 to 1825. Prepared for the Press by Horace Hayman Wilson, Esq. F. R. S., Professor of Sanscrit in the University of Oxford. 8vo. 2 vols. Lond. 1839.

NEAMET ULLAH.

History of the Afghans, translated from the Persian of Neamet Ullah. By Bernard Dorn, Professor of Oriental Literature in the Imperial Russian University of Kharkoo. 4to. Lond. 1829.

NOWROZJEE FURDOONJEE.

Description of Articles, mostly Russian, found in the Bazaar of Cabool, and brought to it by way of Bokhara. By Nowrozjee Furdoonjee. Indian Government Papers, sect. iii. pp. 147—154.

Report on the Weights, Measures, and Coins of Cabool and Bokhara. By Nowrozjee Furdoonjee. Indian Government Papers, sect. iii. pp. 155—164.

ORIENTAL MAGAZINE (Quarterly), Review, and Register. 8vo. 1824—1826. Calcutta.

OSBORNE.

The Court and Camp of Runjeet Sing. By the Hon. W. G. Osborne, Military Secretary to the Earl of Auckland. With an Introductory Sketch of the Rise and Origin of the Sikh State. 8vo. Lond. 1840.

OUTRAM.

Rough Notes of the Campaign in Sinde and Afghanistan in 1838-9, being Extracts from a Personal Journal kept while on the Staff of the Army of the Indus. By Major James Outram. 12mo. Lond. 1840.

POSTANS.

Notes of a Journey to Girnar, in the Province of Kattywar, for the purpose of copying the ancient Inscriptions upon the Rock near that place; undertaken by order of the Bombay Government. Journ. As. Soc. Beng. 1838. pp. 865—887.

A few Observations on the Increase of Commerce by means of the River Indus. By T. Postans, Bombay Army. 8vo. Lond. 1843.

Personal Observations on Sindh: The Manners and Customs of its Inhabitants, and its Productive Capabilities, with a Sketch of its History, and a Narrative of Recent Events. By T. Postans, Captain, Bombay Army. 8vo. Lond. 1843.

POTTINGER, HENRY.

Travels in Beloochistan and Sinde, accompanied by a Geographical and Historical Account of those Countries. By Lieut. Henry Pottinger, of the Hon. East-India Company's Service. 4to. Lond. 1818.

POTTINGER, WILLIAM.

On the Present State of the River Indus, and the Route of Alexander. By Lieut. Wm. Pottinger. Journ. Roy. As. Soc. 1834. pp. 199—212.

PRICE.

Chronological Retrospect, or Memoirs of the principal Events of Mahommedan History, from the Death of the Arabian Legislator to the Accession of the Emperor Akbar and the establishment of the Mogul Empire in Hindustaun; from original Persian Authorities. By Major David Price, of the East-India Company's Service. 4to. 3 vols. Lond. 1821.

PRINSEP, JAMES.

Useful Tables, forming an Appendix to the Journal of the Asiatic Society. 8vo. Calcutta, 1834.

PRINSEP, HENRY T.

Origin of the Sikh Power in the Punjab, and Political Life of Runjeet Singh; with an account of the present Condition, Laws, and Customs of the Sikhs. Compiled, by Henry T. Prinsep, from a Report by Captain William Murray. 8vo. Calcutta, 1834.

Notes on the Passes into Hindoostan from the West and Northwest, and the use made of them by different Conquerors. Journ. As. Soc. Beng. 1842, pp. 552—573.

RENNELL.

Memoir of a Map of Hindoostan, or the Mogul Empire; with an Introduction illustrative of the Geography and present Division of that Country. By James Rennell, F. R. S. 4to. Lond. 1788.

RITTER.

Die Erdkunde von Asien, von Carl Ritter. 8vo. B. i.—vii. Berlin, 1832—1843.

ROYLE.

Illustrations of the Botany and other branches of the Natural History of the Himalayan Mountains, and of the Flora of Cashmere. By J. Forbes Royle, Esq., F.L.S. and G. S. Folio. Lond. 1833—1840.

SALE.

A Journal of the Disasters in Affghanistan, 1841, 2. By Lady Sale. 8vo. Lond. 1843.

SAINTE CROIX.

Examen des Anciens Historiens d'Alexandre le Grand. 4to. Paris, 1810.

SINDE.

Correspondence Relative to Sinde, 1838—1843. Presented to both Houses of Parliament by command of Her Majesty. Folio. Lond. 1843.

VIGNE.

Travels in Kashmir, Ladak, Iskardo, the countries adjoining the mountain course of the Indus, and the Himalaya north of the Punjab, with Map, engraved by direction of the Hon. East-India Company. By G. T. Vigne, Esq., F.G.S. 8vo. 2 vols. Lond. 1842.

Personal Narrative of a Visit to Ghuznee, Kabul, and Afghanistan.

VON HAMMER.

Geschichte des Osmanischen Reichs. 8vo. Pesth.

WADE.

Notes taken by Captain C. M. Wade, Political Agent at Lodiana in 1829, relative to the Territory and Government of Iskardoh, from information given by Charagh Ali, an agent who was deputed to him in that year by Ahmed Shah, the Gelpo or Ruler of that country. Journ. As. Soc. Beng, 1835, pp. 589—601.

WADDINGTON.

Map of the Countries between the Oxus and Jaxartes, and a Memoir regarding its Construction. By Charles Waddington, Esq., of the East-India Company's Engineers. Prefixed to Leyden's Translation of Baber's Memoirs.

WARD.

A View of the History, Literature, and Religion of the Hindoos, including a minute Description of their Manners and Customs, and Translations from their Principal Works. By the Rev. W. Ward, one of the Baptist Missionaries at Serampore, Bengal. 8vo. 4 vols. Lond. 1817—1820.

WESTMACOTT.

A Short Account of Khyrpoor and the Fortress of Bukur in North Sind. By Capt. G. E. Westmacott. Journ. As. Soc. Beng. pp. 1090—1113, 1187—1210.

Roree, in Khyrpoor, its Population and Manufactures. By Capt. G. E. Westmacott. Journ. As. Soc. Beng. 1841, pp. 393—479.

WILFORD.

On Mount Caucasus. By Capt. Francis Wilford. As. Res. vi. pp. 455—536.

WILKINS, Sir CHARLES.

Wilkins's Glossary, in Appendix to Reports of the House of Lords. 4to. 1830.

WILSON.

Ariana Antiqua; a descriptive Account of the Antiquities and Coins of Afghanistan; with a Memoir on the Buildings called Topes, by Charles Masson, Esq. By Horace H. Wilson, M.A., F.R.S. 4to. Lond. 1841.

An Essay on the Hindu History of Cashmir. By Horace Hayman Wilson, Esq., Sec. A.S. As. Res. xv. pp. 1—119.

Sketch of the Religious Sects of the Hindus. By Horace Hayman Wilson, Esq., Sec. A.S. Soc. As. Res. xvii. pp. 169—313.

WOOD.

A Personal Narrative of a Journey to the Source of the River Oxus, by the Route of the Indus, Kabul, and Badakshan, performed under the Sanction of the Supreme Government of India in the Years 1836, 1837, 1838. By Lieut. John Wood, of the East-India Company's Navy. 8vo. Lond. 1841.

Report on the River Indus. By Lieut. John Wood, Indian Navy, in Appendix to Burnes' Personal Narrative. Also in Journ. As. Soc. Beng. 1841, pp. 518—569.

A Geographical Notice of the South Side of the Valley of the Cabool River, with the Topography of the Route leading from Khyber to Cabool. By Lieut. John Wood, I.N. Indian Government Papers, sect. ii. pp. 1—7.

Memoir to accompany a reconnoitering Survey of the Road from Cabool to Toorkistan, by the line of Bamian and the Pass of Hajeyuk. By Lieut. John Wood, I.N. Indian Government Papers, sect. ii. pp. 21—28.

ZIMMERMAN.

Geographische Analyse der Karte von Inner-Asien. Von Carl Zimmermann. 4to. Berlin, 1841.

A GAZETTEER,

&c.

A GAZETTEER,

&c.

AAS—ABD.

AASNEE.—A village of Afghanistan, in the district of Hur- E.I.C. Ms. Doc.
rund and close to the south-eastern frontier. Lat. 29° 13′, long.
70° 13′.

ABAD.—A small village of Sinde, on the route from Shi- E.I.C. Ms. Doc.
karpoor to Sukkur, and three miles and a quarter north-west
from this last place. Considerable cultivation is carried on
around it. Lat. 27° 45′, long. 68° 50′.

ABAD.—A village in Beloochistan, twenty-two miles south- Walker's Map of
N.W. Frontier.
east from Gundava. Lat. 28° 17′, long. 67° 49′.

ABASABAD.—A small village in Afghanistan, three miles E.I.C. Ms. Doc.
west of Kandahar, on the road to Giriskh. Lat. 31° 36′, long.
65° 27′.

ABDALLA-I-BOORJ.—A village in Afghanistan, thirty- E.I.C. Ms. Doc.
seven miles north-east of Kabool. Lat. 35° 2′, long. 69° 18′.

ABDOOL. — A village in Afghanistan, thirty-five miles E.I.C. Ms. Doc.
north-east of Kandahar. Lat. 31° 40′, long. 66° 3′.

ABDOORUHMAN. — A village in the Punjab, two miles E.I.C. Ms. Doc.
from the west bank of the Chenaub. Lat. 30° 40′, long. 71° 49′.

ABDULLA AZEER.—A village in Afghanistan, situate six E.I.C. Ms. Doc.
miles east of Kandahar. Lat. 31° 36′, long. 65° 38 .

ABDUL RAHIM KHAN.—A village in Beloochistan, in E.I.C. Ms. Doc.;
Ewd. Map; Jour.
As.Soc. 1842, p.55;
Griffith, Bar. and
Ther. Meas.
the valley of Shawl, two miles and a half north-west of the town
of that name, and on the route to Kandahar. There is a good
supply of water from a running stream, and considerable cultivation. Here commences a gentle ascent towards the Pass of
Koochlak, farther to the north-west. Elevation above the level
of the sea 5,500 feet. Lat. 30° 10′, long. 66° 54′.

E.I.C. Ms. Doc.;
Jour. As. Soc.
1842, p. 54; Grif-
fith, Bar. and Ther.
Meas.; Hough's
Narr. 52; Conol-
ly's Jour. 220;
Atkinson's Afg.
116; Havelock,
War in Afg. i. 128;
Kennedy, Sinde
and Kabool, i. 216.

AB-I-GOOM (" the lost river "), in Beloochistan.—A halting-place in the Bolan Pass, thirty-six miles from its eastern extremity. It is so called because the Bolan stream is here absorbed by the shingly soil of the valley and disappears. Near Beebee Nanee, about nine miles below, it again comes to light. The elevation of Abigoom above the level of the sea is 2,540 feet. Lat. 29° 46′, long. 67° 23′.

E.I.C. Ms. Doc.

AB-I-KOORMEH, a halting-place in Western Afghanistan, is situate about twenty-one miles north of the Furrah Rood (river), on the route from Kandahar to Herat, from which last place it is distant 110 miles south. It lies in a hilly, barren, and uninhabited country, and owes its importance to a spring of indifferent water. The adjacent tract, though at present a desert, bears marks of former irrigation and cultivation. Lat. 32° 53′, long. 62° 26′.

¹ E.I.C. Ms. Doc.

AB-ISTADA LAKE, in Afghanistan,[1] is situate sixty-five miles a little west of south from Ghuznee. The name in Persian signifies standing water. It lies between lat. 32° 30′ and 32° 42′, and long. 67° 50′ and 68° 5′. It is represented to be a little above forty miles in circumference, but this estimate seems to have been founded on observations made when the water was lowest, in which state the dimensions are materially less than in times of inundation. Kennedy[2] says—" We marched fully fifteen miles in length in sight of it, and never saw across it. It looked like an inland sea, and one felt surprised not to see the white sails of commerce or pleasure on its waters." Masson[3] also describes it as stretching as far as the eye could reach. Outram[4] estimates its diameter to be about twelve miles. Baber[5] calls it a wonderfully large sheet of water. Elphinstone,[6] on the contrary, states that in dry weather it is only three or four miles in diameter, and about twice as much after floods. The dimensions[7] given by the author of the estimate of its circumference first quoted are—length, in the direction north-east and south-west, eighteen miles; breadth at right angles to this direction, eight miles; circumference, forty-four. The water is salt,[8] and the banks are deeply incrusted with that production. As the water-fowl with which[9] it abounds may be seen standing on the bottom[1] at a great distance from the margin, the depth is probably not great. Some of Baber's[2] horsemen, in pursuit of the Afghans, rode above a mile into it without the water being higher than the horses' bellies.

² Sinde and Kabool,
ii. 110.

³ Bal. Afg. Panj.
i. 202.
⁴ Rough Notes,
140.
⁵ Baber's Memoirs,
165.
⁶ Account of Ka-
bool, 119.
⁷ E.I.C. Ms. Doc.

⁸ Masson, ut su-
pra.
⁹ Baber's Memoirs,
ut supra.
¹ Masson, ut su-
pra.

² Memoirs, ut
supra.

Its principal feeder is the river of Ghuznee, which flows into it
at the north-eastern part. Outram [3] found the banks of this
river strewed with "thousands of dead fish," perhaps destroyed
by the salt and bitter waters of the lake. Several small streams
fall into the lake from the south-west and west. Its elevation
must be very great: Ghuznee [4] is 7,726 feet above the sea, and
if we allow a fall of ten feet per mile for each of the [5] sixty-five
miles which the river descends from the city to the lake, and
which would cause the current to be a very rapid torrent, the
elevation of Ab-istada would be determined at 7,076 feet. The
surrounding country is very barren and dreary, and has scarcely
any inhabitants.

[3] Rough Notes, ut supra.

[4] Hough's Narr. App. 74.
[5] E.I.C. Ms. Doc.

AB-I-TULK.—A village in Afghanistan, on the road from
Ghuznee to Dera Ismail Khan. Lat. 32° 28', long. 68° 53'.

E.I.C. Ms. Doc.

ABKHANA, in Afghanistan, a post on the Kabool river,
where the Abkhana route from Peshawur to Kabool crosses that
river for the second time. This route commences fifteen miles
north-west of the city of Peshawur, and at Muchnee [1] crosses the
Kabool river to the northward, and thence proceeds in a north-
westerly direction over the mountains for ten miles to the ferry of
Abkhana, where it recrosses the river to the southern side. The
passage of the ferry is represented as very dangerous.[2] Masson,
who crossed it, observes, "I was astonished at its boisterous
state and the frightful scene presented by rocks, whirlpools, and
surges, with the rapidity of the current." From the ferry the
Abkhana route winds upwards at a short distance from the right
bank of the Kabool river, and at Duka joins the route through
the Khyber Pass. Abkhana is in lat. 34° 16', long. 71° 25'.

[1] Leech, Khyber Pass, 12.

[2] Masson, Bal. Afg. Panj. ii. 238 ; Burnes' Bokhara, i. 115; Burnes' Pers. Narr. 277.

ABKHOR-I-ROOSTUM.—A village in Western Afghanistan. Lat. 31° 34', long. 62° 34'.

Walker's Map.

ABOOKHAN.—A village in Afghanistan. Lat. 31° 36',
long. 67° 9'.

E.I.C. Ms. Doc.

ACESINES RIVER.—See Chenaub.

ACORA.—See Akora.

ADAM-KHAN-KA-MAREE.—A village in Sinde, on the
route from Subzulcote to Shikarpoor, and fifty miles north-east
of the latter place. It is situate twelve miles from the left bank
of the Indus, in a low alluvial country under water during the
season of inundation, but traversed by a good road when the
river is low. Lat. 28° 9', long. 69° 34'.

E.I.C. Ms. Doc.

Ms. Survey Map. **ADAMPOORA.**—A village in Sinde, twelve miles west of Khyerpoor. Lat. 27° 33′, long. 68° 35′.

E.I.C. Ms. Doc. **ADAWAON.**—A village in the Punjab, on the road from Mooltán to Bhawlpoor, six miles north of the latter place. Lat. 29° 29′, long. 71° 38′.

E.I.C. Ms. Doc. **ADEEAN.**—A village in the Punjab, on the road from Amritsir to Vazcerabad, thirty miles north-west of the former place. Lat. 31° 54′, long. 74° 23′.

E.I.C. Ms. Doc. **ADHEE BAHR.**—A village in the Punjab, twelve miles south-west of Mooltan. Lat. 29° 57′, long. 71° 22′.

E.I.C. Ms. Doc. **ADREK.**—A village in Afghanistan, forty-six miles east of Kabool. Lat. 34° 29′, long. 69° 56′.

E.I.C. Ms. Doc.; Conolly, A., Jour. to India, ii. 59; Jour. As. Soc.1840, p.713; Conolly,E., Sketch of the Physical Geography of Seistan. **ADRUSCUND, or ROOD-I-ADRUSCUND,** in Western Afghanistan, is a fine stream of clear water, which has been explored upwards as far as the spot where it is crossed by the route from Kandahar to Herat, fifty miles south of the latter place, and in lat. 33° 40′, long. 62° 16′. Its source is not well known, but is probably in the mountainous country, about eighty miles north-west of Ghore. It takes a course generally southerly, flowing by the town and plain of Subzawur, whence it is sometimes called the river of Subzawur. Lower down it is called the Jaya, and subsequently the Haroot. After a course of about 160 miles from the spot where first explored, it falls into the lake of Hamoon, or Zirrah, in lat. 31° 49′, long. 61° 38′.

[1] Elphinstone's Caubul, 151.

[2] Malcolm's Persia, i. 596.

[3] Neamet Ullah, i. 23.

[4] Account of Caubul, ut supra.

AFGHANISTAN,[1] signifying, in Persic, Afghanland, is the name given by the Persians to the northern part of the region lying between their country and India. The name of Afghan is only known to the nation through the Persian language, the vernacular denomination of that people being Pushtoon, in the plural Pushtauneh, or, in some of their dialects, Puktaunch, and hence is derived the appellation Patan, by which they have become so celebrated in Indian politics and history. The word Afghan, signifying, in Persian, 'lamentation,' was, according to some,[2] given to the race on account of their lamenting their expulsion from Judea, and consequently having reference to their alleged descent from the lost tribes of Israel. Many native writers[3] derive the name from a fabulous personage of the name of Afghan, or Afghana, supposed by some to be the son of Japhet, by others the grandson of Saul, King of Israel. Elphinstone[4] observes, that " the origin of the name of Afghan is entirely uncertain, but it is probably modern." The name of Afghanistan has of late been applied not only to the extensive region permanently occupied by tribes speaking Pushtoo vernacularly and of acknowledged Afghan extraction, but also to the large rugged and mountainous tract in the north-west, inhabited by the Huzarehs and Eimauks, as these Tartars have of late been subject to the Afghans and partaken of their fortunes. Taken in this extent, Afghanistan is bounded on the north by Chitral, Kafiristan, and Kunduz, from which last it is separated by the crest of the Hindoo Koosh ;[4] on the [4] Vigne's Kashmir, east by the rugged mountain tracts called Gilgit, Yessen, and some [ii. ch. ix.] others of less note, all governed by independent rajahs ; and south of these the eastern frontier, throughout its whole remaining extent, is formed by the Indus ; on the south it is bounded by Chawlpoor, Sinde, and Beloochistan, and on the west by Persia. It lies between lat. 28° 50′—36° 30′, long. 62°—72° 30′. Its greatest length, which is in a direction nearly from east to west from Torbela to a little beyond Herat, is 660 miles ; its greatest breadth, nearly in a direction from north to south, is 500 miles ; its superficial extent, as ascertained from calculations based on Walker's excellent map of the north-west frontier of India, is, in round numbers, 225,000 square miles. Such a process is necessarily merely an approximation to accuracy, yet a close and safe one, where the map, as in this instance, is laid down with great care from the most authentic data.

The physical aspect of Afghanistan is characterized by the unevenness and great elevation of most of its surface. Much of the more valuable portion of its territory has a very considerable elevation above the sea, and extends over the undulating, yet, in general, gradual slope southwards, from the crest of the Hindoo Koosh to the course of the Kabool river. The great range of Hindoo Koosh[5] is a prolongation of the Mustak and [5] Elphinstone's Karakorum mountains of Tibet, which extend on the north, in [Caubul, 85-88.] some degree parallel to the western part of the Himalaya range, and separated from it[6] by the valley through which the Sing-kha- [6] Moorcroft, Punj. bab, or upper part of the Indus, holds its course. To the north [Bokhara, i. 261;] of this range is the table land of Pamir, elevated between 15,000 [Burnes' Bokhara, ii. 238; Ritter] and 16,000 feet above the sea, and where the line of perpetual [Erd. Kunde von] congelation, in lat. 37°, is of the extraordinary height of 17,000 [Asien, B. v. S. 200; Wood's Oxus,] feet. On the southern side this stupendous range, which has [364, 5, 6; Elphinstone's Caubul, 85,] here a height averaging from 20,000 to 21,000 feet, slopes gra- [637; Trans. of Beng. As. Soc. 1839, viii. 749;]

dually, or rather in ridges diminishing in height as they recede
from the crown. Elphinstone[7] saw four of these ridges, or terraces, rising to the north of the plain of Peshawur, and increas-
ing in height as they approached the summit, which was ascertained by measurement to have an elevation of 20,493 feet.

These[8] subordinate ranges inclose, in succession westward, the
great valleys of Suwat, Panjkora, Chitral, and Kafiristan, drained
by the rivers Lundye, Kooner or Kama, and Alishang. These
districts are deeply secluded and little known, especially
the last, inhabited by the Siah Posh, or black-clad people,
called Kafirs or infidels by the Mahometans, and who, being
persecuted by them, refuse all access to their country. Though
of very uneven surface, these valleys are said to be remarkably fertile and well watered, producing excellent grain, as
well as the finest fruits, and pasturing numerous flocks and
herds.[9] Where not cultivated, they are in many places covered
with dense forests of the most luxuriant growth; below, of oaks
and similar deciduous trees, and in the higher parts, of pine and
birch. South of Chitral, Panjkora, and Kafiristan, a low cross
range extends from east to west, separating them from the
Afghan provinces of Lughman and Jelalabad. Westward of
Kafiristan, a long and high ridge proceeds from the crest of the
Hindoo Koosh in a south-west direction, separating that unexplored country from the valley of Punchshir, and from this part
westward the Hindoo Koosh has been explored until it sinks into
the less elevated Huzareh mountains. The general bearing of
that part of the range dividing Pamir, or the elevated table-land
of Tartary, from the upper valley of the Indus, is in a great measure from north-east to south-west. Nothing is satisfactorily
known of these mountains eastward of the valley of Punchshir,
if we except the ascertained fact that there are passes from Kafiristan to Pamir and Badakshan. But from the Punchshir valley
the crest takes a direction nearly west, and from it[1] proceed a
great number of narrow, rocky, and very high ridges, running
nearly due south, and parallel to each other. Twenty of these
ridges have been observed in a distance of about 150 miles between Punchshir and Bamian, at which last place the Hindoo
Koosh is considered to terminate on the west.

Proceeding to survey in detail the aspect of Afghanistan, we
shall find that the north-western part, inhabited generally by the

Huzarehs, is an extensive maze of lofty mountains (the Paropamisus of classical writers), sending forth rivers in every direction,
feeders of the Helmund to the east, [2] the Adruscund and seve- [2] E.I.C. Ms. Doc.
ral other rivers to the south, the Heri-Rood or Hury river to the [3] Fraser, Jour.
west, the Moorgaub[3] and others to the north; so that in one day, Khorasan,App.57;
according to Baber,[4] it is possible to drink of the waters of the and Khiva, i. 30;
Helmund and the respective rivers of Kabool, of Kunduz, and of ii. 35.
Balkh. The sources of some of these have great elevations; that of [4] Memoirs, 146.
the Helmund[5] has 10,076 feet, that of the Heri-Rood 9,500.[6] The [5] Jour. As. Soc.
whole of the northern part of the western frontier is indeed very Bar. and Ther.
high, as is evident from the great length of time during which [6] Jour. As. Soc.
the snow lies there. Some mountains south-west of Ghore are 1841, p. 118; Co-
computed to have a height of from 12,000 to 14,000 feet.[7] The Khorasan.
extensive tract between the western frontier and the Helmund [7] E.I.C. Ms. Doc.;
has never been explored by Europeans, but is described by Elphin- India, ii. 5.
stone,[8] on native report, as very rugged and mountainous. The [8] Acc. of Caubul,
ridges between Ghuznee[9] and the upper part of the Helmund are [9] E.I.C. Ms. Doc.
even in summer covered extensively with snow. They seem to [1] E.I.C. Ms. Map
be offsets from the celebrated Koh-i-Baba, which rises about of Route from Kalat. 34° 30′, long. 67° 30′,[1] to the height probably of 16,000 feet. tan; Burnes' Bo-
This is connected with the Hindoo Koosh[2] to the north-east by khara, i. 173-196,
several ranges of inferior height, yet attaining an elevation of Wood's Oxus,
from 10,000 to 13,000 feet, and furrowed with the various [2] E.I.C. Ms. Map
gorges which form the passes between Kabool and Bamian. of Route from
At the south-western extremity of the Hindoo Koosh,[3] and sepa- kestan; Moorcroft
rated from it by the long valley of Ghorbund, is the Pughman or ii. 380-397; Ba-
Pamghan range of mountains, rising close to the west of the city ber's Memoirs,146;
of Kabool. These are always covered with snow, and are esti- Panj. iii. 377,422;
mated to have a height of 13,000 feet. From the south-eastern 416-435.
brow flow numerous streams, which water the Koh-i-Damun and [3] Baber's Me-
produce the luxuriant fertility for which it is remarkable. The E.I.C. Ms. Doc.
highest strata of the Hindoo Koosh[4] are nearly vertical and of [4] Lord's Koh-i-
primary formation—granite, gneiss, quartz, slate, and primary
limestone. The general direction of these strata is east and
west. The valley or basin of the Kabool river running on the
south of the Hindoo Koosh is bounded on the south by the high
land of Ghuznee, and by the Sufeid Koh or White Mountain, [5] Jour. As. Soc.
the former 8,500,[5] the latter above 14,000 feet high. [6] The Khy- Bar. and Ther.
ber range stretches across this valley at its eastern extremity, the Meas.
Kurkutcha farther west, and through them the river of Kabool Pass, 2.

makes its way, discharging the water of the entire valley into
the Indus near Attock. The valley of Kabool, nearly 200 miles long,
has a slope to the eastward from the neighbourhood of the city of
Kabool, where the height is between 6,000 and 7,000 feet above
the sea, to the plain of Peshawur, where it is little more than 1,000.
This valley is highly celebrated and important in a military point
of view, as through it lie from west to east the routes from Kabool to Attock. They traverse the Khyber range by two roads or
passes, in some degree parallel; the Kurkutcha is in like manner
traversed by four, which, if not parallel, are at least collateral. In
the most southern of these last, the British army was exterminated
in its attempted retreat in 1842. (See *Kurkutcha* and *Khyber*.)

[7] Wood's Oxus,
131 ; Elphinstone's
Caubul, 108 ;
Burnes' Bokhara,
i. 51.
Southward of the Khyber mountains, the Kala or Salt range[7]
overspreads the country, and being intersected by the course of
the Indus, continues beyond it, and is connected in the Punjab
with the most southern and lower ranges of the Himalaya.
Southward from the Sufeid Koh, the great range of Suliman
extends to the southern frontier. The height of this last range is
very considerable, that of the summit, called Tukht-i-Suliman, or

[8] Wood's Oxus, 89;
Elphinstone's
Caubul, 102 ;
Masson, Bal. Afg.
Panj. i. 47.
Khaisa Ghar, being 11,000 feet.[8] Eastward of the Suliman range,
and between it and the Indus, is the long, low, narrow tract of the
Daman. Westward is the extensive district of Sewestan, unex-
plored by Europeans. It is certainly of no great elevation, as its

[9] Elphinstone's
Caubul, 136 ;
E.I.C. Ms. Doc.
No. 10; Kennedy,
Sinde and Kabool,
ii. 123-140.
heat is proverbial.[9] The march of the British army in 1839, from
Ghuznee to Shawl, has led to the knowledge of the fact, that
the country between those places has an elevation nowhere less
than 5,000 feet, and in many places much exceeding it. The
narrowest part of this elevated tract is eastward of the plain of
Kandahar, at which part it is about sixty miles wide, being bounded
on the west by the Amran mountains, on the east by the Hala
range. West of the Amran, the plain of Kandahar is comparatively depressed, though more than 3,000 feet above the level

[1] Jour. As. Soc.
1842, p. 57; Grif.
Bar. and Ther.
Meas.
[2] Jour. As. Soc.
1840, p. 710; Co-
nolly, E., Sketch of
Physical Geogra-
phy of Seistan.
[3] E.I.C. Ms. Doc.;
Elphinstone's
Caubul, 119-121 ;
Baber's Memoirs,
of the sea.[1] The water system of Afghanistan may be briefly
described as follows. By the Kabool river the country is drained
eastward into the Indus, while the west is drained by the Helmund and its tributaries, flowing into the swamp of Hamoon,[2] in
Seistan. Between these is the Ab-istada Lake,[3] receiving the
river of Ghuznee and some others of less importance. The
elevation here is very considerable, that of Ab-istada being
probably not less than 7,000 feet. The principal mountains,

Hindoo Koosh, Koh-i-Baba, Pughman, Sufeid Koh, Kurkutcha, 165; Kennedy, and Khyber, on the north ; the Kala, or Salt range on the east ; Sinde and Kaboul, ii. 119; Outram's the Toba, Tukatoo, Kurklekkee, and Amran, on the south ; the Rough Notes, 149; Masson, Bal. Afg. Goolkoo and Punjangoosht on the south-east, will be found i. 262. described under their respective names.

TABLE OF HEIGHTS.

	FEET.	
Hindoo Koosh summit,[4] north of Peshawur, lat. 34° 30', long. 71° 40'	20,493	[4] Macartney, in Elphinstone, 637.
Hindoo Koosh summit,[5] north of Jelalabad, in long. 70° 50'	20,248	[5] Wood's Khyber Pass, 2; Wood's Oxus, 161.
Koh-i-Baba,[6] * lat. 34° 30', long. 67° 30', estimated ...	18,000	[6] Burnes' Bokhara, i. 176, ii. 241;
Summit of Koushan Pass,[7] lat. 35° 37', long. 68° 55', estimated	15,000	Sale's Dis. in Afg. 419. [7] Lord, Koh-i-Damun, 48.
Summit of Sufeid Koh,[8] lat. 34° 5', long. 70° 10' ...	14,100	[8] Wood's Khyber Pass, 2; Wood's
Highest accessible point of Koh-i-Baba,[9] lat. 34° 30', long. 67° 30'	13,500	Oxus, 164. [9] Jour. As. Soc. 1841, p.801; Griffith, Bar. and
Khawak Pass, highest part of Punchshir valley,[1] lat. 35° 42', long. 69° 53'	13,200	Ther. Heights in Afg. [1] Wood's Oxus,
Summit in the Huzareh country,[2] visible from Herat, lat. 34°, long. 63° 30', estimated	13,000	416. [2] E.I.C. Ms. Doc.
Pughman,[3] lat. 34° 30', long. 68° 40', estimated ...	13,000	[3] E.I.C. Ms. Doc.
Summit of Erak Pass,[4] lat. 34° 40', long. 68° 5' ...	12,909	[4] Griffith, 71.
Summit of Kaloo Pass,[5] lat. 34° 40', long. 67° 48 ...	12,480	[5] Griffith, 69.
Pass of Hajeguk,[6] lat. 34°, 40', long. 67° 55' ...	11,700	[6] E.I.C. Ms. Doc.
Tukatoo,[7] on the southern frontier, lat. 30° 20', long. 66° 50', estimated	11,500	[7] Havelock's War in Afg. i. 248.
Pass of Oonna,[8] lat. 34° 23', long. 68° 15' ...	11,320	[8] Griffith, 69.
Tukht-i-Suliman,[9] lat. 31° 38', long. 69° 55' ...	11,000	[9] Wood's Oxus, 89.
Kurzar,[1] near the source of the Helmund, lat. 34° 30', long. 67° 54'	10,939	[1] Griffith, 71.
Kaloo,[2] hamlet of, lat. 34° 30', long. 67° 56' ...	10,883	[2] Griffith, 69.

* Outram makes the height 20,000 (Rough Notes, 127). Neither Wood (Oxus, 202) nor Eyre (Milit. Op. in Afgh. 357), who passed along its base, gives any estimate of the height.—See *Koh-i-Baba.*

FEET.

[3] Hough's App. 71.	Youart, or Oord, [3] lat. 34° 22′, long. 68° 11′ ...	...	10,618
[4] E.I.C. Ms. Map; Wood.	Gooljatooc, [4] lat. 34° 31′, long. 68° 5′ ...	... ...	10,500
[5] Jour. As. Soc. 1841, p. 118; Co-	Shebbertoo, [5] lat. 34° 50′, long. 67° 20′ ...	... ...	10,500
nolly, E., Report on Khorasan.	Siah Sung, [6] lat. 34° 34′, long. 68° 8′ ...	... ...	10,488
[6] Griffith, 60. [7] Griffith, 71.	Gurdan Dewar, [7] lat. 34° 25′, long. 68° 8′	... ...	10,076
[8] Griffith, 69.	Soktah, [8] lat. 34° 40′, long. 67° 50′	... ...	9,839
[9] Conolly, ut supra, 118.	Source of Heri Rood, [9] lat. 34° 50′, long. 66° 20′	...	9,500
[1] Wood's Oxus, 416.	Khawak Fort, [1] lat. 35° 38′, long. 70° 5′	... ...	9,300
[2] Griffith, 70.	Topchee, [2] lat. 34° 45′, long. 67° 44′ ...	... ...	9,085
[3] Hough, 239.	Crest of Highland of Ghuznee, [3] lat. 33° 40′, long. 68° 20′, estimated	...	9,000
[4] Griffith, 64.	Chasgo or Shushgao, [4] lat. 33° 43′, long. 68° 22′	...	8,697
[5] E.I.C. Ms. Map; Wood;	Pass of Ispehawk, [5] lat. 34° 22′, long. 68° 40′ ...	...	8,670
Griffith, 68. [6] Griffith, 70.	Bamian, [6] lat. 34° 50′, long. 67° 45′	... ...	8,496
[7] Griffith, 64.	Huftasaya, [7] lat. 33° 49′, long. 68° 15′ ...	... ...	8,420
[8] E.I.C. Ms. Doc.	Sir-i-Chushma, [8] principal source of Kabool river, lat. 34° 21′, long. 68° 20′	...	8,400
[9] Hough's App.74.	Zohak's Fort, [9] lat. 34° 50′, long. 67° 55′	... ...	8,186
[1] Hough's App.74.	Tezeen Pass, [1] lat. 34° 23′, long. 69° 30′	... ...	8,173
[2] Griffith, 65.	Killa Sher Mahomed, [2] lat. 34° 16′, long. 68° 45′	...	8,051
[3] Griffith, 68.	Kot-i-Ashruf, [3] lat. 34° 28′, long. 68° 35′	... ...	7,749
[4] Hough's App.74.	Maidan, [4] lat. 34° 22′, long. 68° 43′	... ...	7,747
[5] Griffith, 62.	Ghuznee, [5] lat. 33° 34′, long. 68° 18′ ...	... ...	7,726
[6] Griffith, 64.	Hyderkhel, [6] lat. 33° 58′, long. 68° 37′ ...	... ...	7,637
[7] Griffith, 66.	Urghundec, [7] lat. 34° 30′, long. 68° 50′	... ...	7,628
[8] Griffith, 61.	Yerghuttoo, [8] lat. 33° 20′, long. 68° 10′	... ...	7,502
[9] Hough's App.74.	Khoord Kabool, [9] lat. 34° 21′, long. 69° 18′	... ...	7,466
[1] Griffith, 56.	Khojuk Pass summit, [1] lat. 30° 45′, long. 66° 30′	...	7,449
[2] Griffith, 60.	Mookur, [2] principal source of the river Turnak, lat. 32° 50′, long. 67° 37′	...	7,091
[3] Hough's App.74.	Punguk, [3] lat. 32° 36′, long. 67° 21′ ...	... ...	6,810
[4] Griffith, 50.	Shuftul, [4] lat. 32° 28′, long. 67° 12′ ...	... ...	6,514
[5] Griffith, 67.	Kabool (Baber's Tomb), [5] lat. 34° 28′, long. 69°	...	6,396

FEET.

Boothauk,[6] lat. 34° 30′, long. 69° 15′ … … …	6,247	[6] Griffith, 73.
Sir-i-Asp,[7] lat. 32° 15′, long. 66° 54′ … … …	5,973	[7] Griffith, 59.
Kelat-i-Gilji,[8] lat. 32° 8′, long. 66° 45′… … …	5,773	[8] Griffith, 58.
Julduk,[9] lat. 32°, long. 66° 28′ … … …	5,396	[9] Griffith, 58.
Jugduluk,[1] lat. 34° 25′, long. 69° 46′ … … …	5,375	[1] Griffith, 74.
Hydurzie,[2] lat. 30° 23′, long. 66° 51′ … … …	5,259	[2] Hough's App. 74.
Hykulzie,[3] lat. 30° 32′, long. 66° 50′ … … …	5,063	[3] Griffith, 55.
Teer Andaz,[4] lat. 31° 55′, long. 66° 17′ … …	4,829	[4] Griffith, 58.
Gundamuk,[5] lat. 34° 17′, long. 70° 5′ … … …	4,616	[5] Griffith, 74.
Kandahar,[6] lat. 32° 37′, long. 65° 28′ … … …	3,484	[6] Griffith, 57.
Crest of Khyber Pass,[7] lat. 34° 8′, long. 71° 15′ …	3,373	[7] Hough's App. 74.
Ali Musjid,[8] lat. 34° 3′, long. 71° 22′ … … …	2,433	[8] Griffith, 79.
Jelalabad,[9] lat. 34° 25′, long. 70° 28′ … … …	1,964	[9] Griffith, 76.
Peshawur,[1] lat. 34°, long. 71° 40′ … … …	1,068	[1] Hough's App.74.
Dera Ismael Khan,[2] lat. 31° 49′, long. 70° 58′ …	914	[2] Wood's Oxus, 89.
Mittun Kote,[3] lat. 28° 52′, long. 70° 26′ … …	220	[3] Burnes' Bokhara, iii. 208.

The principal rivers of Afghanistan[4] are the following. The
river of Kabool, which, taking its rise at the southern base of the
Pughman mountain, flows eastward, receiving from the south the
river of Logurh, the Soorkh Rood, the Kara Su, the Bara, and some
others of less importance—from the north the Punchshir, the Tagoa, the Alishang, the Kama or Kooner, and the Lundye—and after
a course of above 250 miles, falls into the Indus close to Attock. The
Toe river, flowing from the Kala mountains, also falls into the Indus,
and south of it the Kurum, taking its rise in the Suliman mountains, finds the same outlet. The Gomul, still farther south, rises
in the Suliman range, and has a course of considerable length,
generally eastward, but is ultimately absorbed by the arid soil.
The Zhobe river rises in the west of Sewestan, and, flowing to the
north-east, joins the Gomul. The Lora rises in Pisheen, and,
flowing to the south-west, is lost in the arid expanse of Shorawuk. The Doree river rises on the western slope of the
Amran mountains, and, flowing south-west, joins the Turnak a
little above its confluence with the Urghundab. The river of
Ghuznee discharges itself into the Ab-istada Lake. The Turnak
flows in a direction from north-east to south-west, and joins the

[4] E.I.C.Ms. Doc.; Eud. Map ; Masson's Bab. Afg. Panj. ii. 224-228, 264-267; Elph. Caubul, 655; Wood's Oxus,165; Burnes'Pers. Narr. 277.

Urghundab, having the same direction; the united stream falls into the Helmund, which, flowing farther to the west, discharges its waters into the swamp of Hamoon. Into this last receptacle are also discharged the Khash Rcod, the Ibrahim Jooee, the Furrah Rood, and the Adruscund, or river of Subzawur, all flowing southwards from the Huzareh mountains. The Hury or Heri Rood flows westward, the Moorgaub,[5] the river of Andkhoo, and the Bund-i-Burbur,[6] flow northward from the same range. The only lake of any importance is the Ab-istada, but there is a small piece of water [7] of this description four miles north of the city of Kabool.* The extensive lake, or swamp, of Hamoon, on the south-west frontier, can scarcely be considered to belong to Afghanistan. (See *Hamoon*.) Afghanistan, like the neighbouring countries of Beloochistan and Persia, is characterized by a great deficiency of water.

Our information respecting the geology of Afghanistan is very imperfect. The great core of the Hindoo Koosh[8] is, as might be expected, of primary formation, inclosed by alternating strata of more recent date; the Kurkutcha[9] range is also of primary formation—blue slate, capped with limestone, and in many places overlaid with sandstone, conglomerate, and other recent deposits. This primary formation may be traced through the Khyber range, whence it passes eastward into the Punjab.†

The mountains of Bamian are of recent formation [1]—sandstone and conglomerate, in some instances passing into clay, though granite occasionally crops out. The Kala,[2] or Salt range, is of recent formation, consisting of iron ore, aluminous clay, gypsum, bituminous shale,† spurious coal, sulphur, and rock salt, and yielding naphtha in many places. Little is known of the geological structure of the Suliman mountains. Where examined by Vigne[3] in the Gomul Pass, they were found to consist of secondary formation, sandstone and limestone, abounding in marine *exuviæ*. There are extensive indications of volcanic action along the southern base of the Hindoo Koosh, especially in the valleys of Ghorbund and Bamian;[4] and the great frequency of earthquakes in the valley of Kabool shews that these operations have not yet

Marginal notes:
[5] Fraser's Jour. Khorasan, 57; Burnes'Bokh.ii.34; Abbott's Heraut and Khiva, l. 30.
[6] Burnes' Bokhara, i. 102.
[7] E I.C. Ms. Map; Baber's Memoirs, 137; Jour. As. Soc. 1841, p. 817; Griffith's Rep. on subject con. with Afg.
[8] Koh-l-Damun, 49.
[9] Wood's Khyber Pass, 4; Jour. As. Soc. 1841, p. 803; Griffith on Afg.
[1] Jour. As. Soc. 1833, 7; Gerard's Route from Peshawur to Bokhara.
[2] Lord's Koh-i-Damun, 49; Wood's Oxus, 145; Jour. As. Soc. 1842, p. 1; Jameson on Salt Range.
[3] Ghuznee, 102.
[4] Koh-l-Damun, 53.

* Baber states it to lie southward of the town, but this is unquestionably a mistake, perhaps of the translator.

† Jameson is of opinion that no coal worth working exists in this range.

ceased there. In February, 1842,[5] an earthquake extensively demolished the defences of Jelalabad, and destroyed a third of the town; a hundred more shocks were felt in the course of a month.[6] There are also extensive traces of volcanic action north-west of Ghuznee, about the sources of the river of Logurh.

[5] Milit. Op. in Afg. 271.

[6] Masson's Bal. Afg. Panj. ii. 357.

Afghanistan for four-fifths of its extent is a region of rocks and mountains, interspersed occasionally with well-watered valleys of great fertility and picturesque beauty, and in many places containing elevated table-lands, cold, bleak, barren, and yielding a scanty pasture to hardy stock. With a surface as rugged as that of Switzerland, and summits of much greater height, it exceeds Spain in extent, and, having the latitude of Barbary, Egypt, and Syria, its climate in the lower parts brings to perfection many of the productions of the tropics,[7] whilst its lofty mountains produce the vegetation of the colder parts of the temperate zone. From its geographical position, being traversed by the routes from Western and Central Asia to India, it has frequently been overrun by invaders, who seem to have speedily relinquished it as a prey hard to be retained and of little intrinsic value. The weakness and fluctuating character of its government have prevented it from having any well-defined and permanent political divisions. The customary and popular denominations of the various parts are generally based on natural circumstances, and will here be very briefly enumerated, a fuller account being given of each under their respective names in the alphabetical arrangement. In the north-west is the Huzareh country, perhaps a fourth of all Afghanistan. It is for the most part very mountainous, cold, and barren, inhabited by a barbarous, yet, in general, peaceable Tartar race, bearing in the northern part the name of Huzareh, in the southern that of Eimauk. East of this is the small district of Bamian, still more elevated, few parts being less than 10,000 feet above the level of the sea. It derives importance from containing a system of passes between Kabool and Turkestan. Eastward of Bamian, is the elevated valley of Kabool, in every point of view the most important district in the country. It has on the south the fertile district of Logurh, extending up the northern slope of the highland of Ghuznee. On the north it has the Koh-i-Damun, greatly celebrated for its fertility, high cultivation, and beauty. To the north also lie the fertile vales of Ghorbund,

[7] Jour. As. Soc. 1841, p. 982-1006; Griffith, Rep. on subjects con. with Afg.

Punchshir, Nigrow, and Tagoa, and the plain of Begram. East is the district of Lughman, hilly, but in many places fertile. Eastward of this is the rich and beautiful vale of Jelalabad, and south of this last, the district called Nungnehar extends along the northern base of Sufeid Koh, rivalling the Koh-i-Damun in fertility, cultivation, and picturesque beauty. To the north-east of Jelalabad lie Bajour and the little-explored valleys drained by the Panjkora, the Suwat, and the Lundye rivers. This tract is generally known by the name of the Eusufzye country, being held by the powerful tribe so called. The lower parts are well watered and fertile, and have a fine climate, though rather warm; the higher parts are generally clothed by dense and lofty forests. Southward of this is the district of Peshawur, low, level, very fertile, and in climate and produce resembling Northern Hindostan. Further southward, the Salt range contains the rich and beautiful valleys of Murwut, Kohat, Banoo, Bungush, as well as some others. Still farther to the south, the Daman, or Derajat (for the names are almost synonymous), stretches nearly to the northern frontier of Sinde, which it resembles in climate, soil, and produce. Westward of this is Sewestan, hitherto unexplored, but ascertained to have a sultry climate, and in many places to be rich and abundant in some of the most valuable products of the earth, especially grain. Westward of Sewestan is the elevated plain or valley of Pisheen, possessing considerable fertility, and a climate cold in winter, but not to an extreme. North of Pisheen, and between it and Ghuznee, is the country overspread by the Toba, and some other less-known mountain ranges, and containing the basin of the Ab-istada Lake. It is generally rocky, rugged, barren, and in winter severely cold. The district of Ghuznee lies south of those of Logurh and Kabool, and is separated from them by a highland stretching nearly east and west, and having an elevation of nearly 9,000 feet above the sea. The valleys of the Turnak and Urghundab are subdivided into numerous small and politically un-important districts, which stretch south-west to the plain of Kandahar, and are amazingly productive in grain, particularly wheat. The plain of Kàndahar, where watered, is fertile, and having an elevation of from 3,000 to 4,000 feet above the sea, it in some degree resembles Northern Hindostan both in climate and in the nature of its produce. To the south it has the little-known district of Shorawuk ; to the south-west the sultry, level, and swampy tract

of Seistan, in many places overspread with shallow waters, replenished by the Helmund and other rivers flowing from the
north.

Most mineral productions are obtainable in Afghanistan, especially in the tracts of primary formation. Gold is procured from
the sands of the Kabool river and of the Indus;[6] it is also brought
down from Hindoo Koosh in the streams of Lughman, and
Drummond believes that it exists throughout that vast range.[9]
It is unnecessary, however, to add that a vague belief is not entitled to the respect due to even the slightest degree of evidence.
He considers the Huzareh mountains to be the richest in gold,
and mentions a number of accounts which he received corrobora-
tive of this opinion. A vein of silver ore was observed by Lord[1]
in the mica-slate of the Ghorbund valley, and he heard that a
very rich vein was formerly worked by the Jagatais, in the valley
of Punchshir. Drummond[2] was informed that there are three
silver mines at present not worked in the Huzareh mountains.
Cinnabar is reported to be found in the same group. Copper is met
with in many places in Afghanistan. Masson[3] found it more or
less abundant in the Kurkutcha range. Drummond[4] found the
vitreous and purple sulphurets, containing from sixty to eighty
per cent. of the metal, and is of opinion that abundance of
ores could be obtained, yielding from twenty to thirty per cent.
In the vicinity of Tezeen, according to Masson, large specimens of pure malleable copper have been obtained. It is to be
regretted that the specification of the localities by this last writer
is very confused, but we learn from him that in general the
richest deposits of copper ore are south-east of Kabool, and probably in Sufeid Koh. Copper ore is also met with in Bamian.[5]
There are very rich and extensive lodes of lead in the Ghorbund
valley, in the lower part of Hindoo Koosh, north-west of
Kabool. Antimony has also been discovered in the same vicinity.
This mineral is abundant in Afghanistan, being met with at
Bamian, and existing to such an extent in the Khyber range,
that the water is rendered deleterious by it.[6] Burnes[7] mentions
tin at Bamian, but so vaguely as to entitle the intimation to little
credit. Zinc occurs in the Ghorbund valley, as do sulphur, sal-
ammoniac, and nitre. "Iron ore (observes Lord)[8] occurs so abundantly through the entire range (Hindoo Kosh), that I have
thought it unnecessary to particularize its localities." At the Pass

[6] Burnes' Bokhara,
i. 80; Wood's
Oxus, 122; Jour.
As. Soc. 1842, p. 2;
Jameson's Letter
on Minerals of
Afg.

[9] Jour. As. Soc.
1841, p. 88, 89;
Drummond on
Mineral Resources
of Afg.

[1] Lord, Koh-i-Da-
mun, 47.

[2] Ut supra, 91.

[3] Bal. Afg. Panj.
iii. 177.

[4] Ut supra, 78.

[5] Burnes' Bokhara,
ii. 246; Lord, Koh-
i-Damun, 54.

[6] Reid, as quoted
by Hough, Narr.
315.

[7] Burnes' Bok-
hara, ii. 246.

[8] Ut supra, 55.

of Hajeguk, near Bamian, very rich black iron ore forms entire hills. Bajour, and other places in the north-east, about the upper part of the river Panjkora, contain inexhaustible deposits of ore of iron of the finest quality, but that portion only which is swept down by the torrents, in the form of sand, is at present used. It is smelted with charcoal,[9] and the metal obtained is of such superior quality, that it sells in India at three times the price of common iron. Coal is found (as has been already mentioned) in the Kala range ; also at Dobundee,[1] in the north of the plain of Peshawur, and in the Huzareh country, in the north-east of Afghanistan. The mountains and rocks, which so extensively overspread the middle and central parts of Afghanistan, appear to be in general of secondary formation, and they yield no metal, except, in some places, iron.[2]

There is much diversity of climate in Afghanistan, resulting less from difference of latitude (though this extends to above seven degrees) than to difference of elevation. The country is, however, in general, characterized by dryness and great extremes of temperature, according to the season of the year, the cold being usually severe in winter, even where the heat in summer is great. Thus at Ghuznee, where the snow lies for three months in winter and the thermometer sinks to from 10° to 15° below zero,[3] it during the summer months ranges from 90° to 94°,[4] a degree of heat scarcely ever known in Britain, even for a day. In Kabool snow lies for two or three months together, during which the people seldom leave their houses, sleep, like the Russians, close to stoves, and the thermometer falls to 5° or 6° below zero.[5] At Khoord Kabool,[6] 1,070 feet higher than Kabool, the cold on the 16th of October was intense, the thermometer being below zero all night, and the water in the water-bags frozen into solid ice. It is universally believed in the country that the entire population of Ghuznee[7] has been destroyed by snow-storms, and that this dreadful calamity has several times occurred. As there is great scarcity of fuel there,[8] it is by no means improbable that, in a very prolonged and severe winter, snow might interrupt communication and intense cold destroy the inhabitants. It may be concluded in general, on unquestionable grounds, that throughout Northern Afghanistan, with the exception of the plains of Jelalabad and Peshawur, the cold is intense in winter, varying, however, in degree according to the elevation of the

[9] Drummond, 83.

[1] D.ummond, 80.

[2] Jour. As. Soc. 1842, p. 2 ; Jameson on Mineralogy of Afg.

[3] Crawfurd, inApp. to Eyre's Milit. Op. at Caubul, 400.
[4] Hough's Narr. App. 65.

[5] Hough, 232.

[6] Hough, App. 68.

[7] Elphinstone's Caubul, 137.

[8] Hough, 226.

surface; and that, in a latitude lower than that of Spain or Italy, the severity of a Russian winter in most places is endured. In the Kurkutcha mountains, not more than from 1,000 to 2,000 feet above Kabool,[1] the frost is in winter so intense as to burst the rocks; at Jelalabad,[2] scarcely differing in latitude from Kabool, the winter is as mild as in Hindostan, and so sudden is the change of climate, that at Gundamuk, where the highland of Kabool sinks abruptly to the plain of Jelalabad, the traveller finds, at the same time, snow falling above and rain below the pass. This sudden change is noticed by Baber.[3] The elevation of Jelalabad is 1,964 feet, 4,000 less than that of Kabool; but the mean temperature of Jelalabad is greater than this fact will satisfactorily account for.[4] Wood attributes it to the reverberation of the sun's rays, and the radiation of heat from the surrounding hills. In Peshawur, though nearly 1,000 feet lower than Jelalabad, there are frosts, during the night, to the beginning of March.[5] In Daman, also, though 400 or 500 feet lower than Peshawur, there is generally frost during the nights in midwinter.[6] In the Huzareh country, in the north-western extremity of Afghanistan,[7] the cold is intense during the winter, the snow lying, without intermission, four or five months. Towards the southern frontier, where the table-land between the Hala and Amran mountains has an elevation exceeding 5,000 feet above the sea, the cold is likewise severe in winter, and Masson,[8] in some places, found the roads covered with ice. Kandahar has a mild climate in winter, snow is scarcely known, and water is for the most part but slightly frozen; circumstances which are the more remarkable, as its elevation is considerable, amounting to 3,484 feet.[9] The heat of summer is almost everywhere very great, except in the very elevated parts of Hindoo Koosh and other lofty mountains. In the lower parts of Sewestan the heat is proverbially compared to that of the infernal regions. In the Daman the summer heat exceeds that of Hindostan. In Peshawur it is also for some time very hot,[1] the thermometer reaching 110° and 112° in the shade, but falling on the setting in of breezes from the snowy mountains. In the confined plain of Jelalabad the heat is sometimes so intense as to produce simoom and destroy animal life. At Kandahar the thermometer, in summer, is frequently above 110° in the shade,[2] and the fatal simoom is felt. Even at Kabool, though having an elevation of

1 Wood's Khyber Pass, 4.

2 Wood's Khyber Pass, 7.

3 Memoirs, 41.

4 Wood's Khyber Pass, 6.

5 Elphinstone's Caubul, 133.

6 Id. 135.

7 Id. 482; Wood's Oxus, 108, 202; Baber, 200-211.

8 Bal. Afg. Panj. 320, 321, 329.

9 Hough's App. 74; Jour. As. Soc. 1842, p. 57; Grif, Bar. and Ther. Meas.

1 Elph. 132, 133.

2 Hough, App. 64.

above 6,000 feet, the thermometer ranges from 90° to 100° in

¹ Hough, App.66-7. summer.¹ The monsoon, which deluges Hindostan, has scarcely
² Elph. 129. any effect in Afghanistan farther west than the Suliman mountains;²
nor are the falls, either of rain or snow, heavy, during the cool
season, while, in the hot season, the rains are, for the most part,
slight and of rare occurrence. It may tend to give a vivid impression of the great aridity of Afghanistan to compare its means
for the transmission of water with those of France, a country of
inferior extent. Afghanistan, it may be said, has but one river—
that of Kabool—which sends its water to the ocean, the Toe and
the Kurum being very insignificant streams, while France, besides
the two great rivers—the Loire and the Rhone—has the Garonne,
the Seine, the Somme, and several others, exclusive of the large
feeders of the Rhine. With respect to the effect of the climate
on the human constitution, Elphinstone expresses himself as
³ Elph. 140. follows :³—" Judging from the size, strength, and activity of the
inhabitants, we should pronounce the climate favourable to the
human constitution, and many parts of the country are certainly
remarkable for their salubrity. But on an inspection of the facts, it
appears doubtful whether the diseases of Afghanistan are not more
fatal than those of India. Yet those diseases are not numerous,
and few of them are of those descriptions which make most havoc
in other countries. Fevers and agues are common in autumn,
and are also felt in spring. Colds are very troublesome, and
sometimes dangerous in winter. Opthalmia is common." These
and small-pox are the more common diseases in Afghanistan.

Notwithstanding that a large portion of the country is irreclaimable desert, that most is unenclosed, and that nearly everywhere difficult fastnesses abound, there is no great variety nor large
number of wild animals. Lions are said to haunt the Kohistan
⁴ Elph. 141. of Kabool, and other places at the base of Hindoo Koosh,⁴ but
to be neither so large nor so fierce as those of warmer regions ; their existence, however, seems doubtful. Leopards
⁵ Jour. As. Soc.
1839, p. 1007;
Irwin, Memoir of
Afg. Id. 1841, p.
978; Grif. Rep. on
Afg. are very common in the Kohistan, but they do not attack men.⁵
Tigers haunt the jungles of the Daman, and among the Suliman mountains, but both in strength and boldness they are
inferior to those of Hindostan Proper. Hyænas are numerous,
⁶ Elph. 141; Ba-
ber, 264.
⁷ Havelock, War
in Afg. II. 94. and attack sheep and large cattle. Wolves principally frequent
the cold country, and in winter collect in troops and destroy both
domestic animals and men.⁶ There are two kinds of bears⁷—the

black bear, common in many parts of India, and another of a dirty white, or rather yellow colour. Elephants are unknown in a wild state, and the few which are kept for the purposes of state have been brought from Hindostan. The rhinoceros, common in the time of Baber[3] in the Eusufzye country, does not [3] Mem. 253. now appear to be found there. Jackals and foxes are numerous, and in many places troublesome. Monkeys are found in the north-eastern part.[4] Wild sheep and goats are common [4] Elph. 142. in the mountain tracts in the north. Antelopes are rare, elks more common. The markhur, a powerful quadruped, in size and figure between the goat and elk, frequents the wilds of the Suliman and some other mountains. One measured by Vigne[5] was [5] Ghuznee, 86. five feet eight inches long, three feet three inches high, its horns each two feet seven inches long, the circumference of its fore hoof eleven inches, yet it was not considered a large one. Afghanistan also affords a home to the wild ass or gorkhar, the wild hog, the porcupine, various kinds of deer and goats, the wild dog, the mongoose, the ferret, and the hare.[6] The variety [6] Irwin, 1007; of cat called the Persian properly belongs to Kabool. Of domes- Grif. 977—982; tic animals, the dromedary, or one-humped camel, is the usual Elph. 141—145. beast of burthen throughout the plain country. The Bactrian, or two-humped variety, is of unfrequent occurrence. The horses of. Afghanistan are not much esteemed, but some of those bred about Herat are valuable. In the Huzareh country is an excellent hardy race of ponies called yaboos. Asses are much used for burthen, but they are not of a superior kind. Buffaloes are scarcely known, except in the Daman, in Peshawur, and Kandahar. The cow is kept in great numbers in the Daman, but elsewhere receives little attention. The species resembles that of India in having a hump, but is in most respects inferior. In the cooler tracts, where the pasture is good, a quantity of milk is obtained which would scarcely be credited by those acquainted only with the dairies of Europe. Oxen are generally kept for the plough, and amongst the pastoral tribes for carrying their tents. The great dependence of those tribes is on their sheep, which are of the broad-tailed kind called *doomba*.[7] [7] Griffith, 981. Their tails weigh ten or twelve pounds, and the fleece is large and fine. Goats are very numerous, and some are kept with each flock of sheep to lead them to pasture. Dogs are kept in great numbers, and in general of good breeds; the greyhounds espe-

cially are very fine and much valued, the people being greatly
addicted to the sports of the field. The birds are eagles,
hawks of several varieties (many of them excellent for fal-
conry), swans, wild geese and ducks, herons, cranes, storks, partridges, quails, and a variety of small birds. Parrots are found
in the warmer parts. The snakes are seldom poisonous. Scorpions are common at Peshawur, where their stings, though severe,
are not often fatal.

Our acquaintance with the vegetable productions of Afghanistan is not at all proportioned to the importance of the subject.
Many European trees are common there, and several of our finest
fruits grow wild.[8] The principal forest-trees are the *baloot*, a
species of oak growing on the mountains, from the elevation of
2,000 feet to 4,500 feet above the sea ; the *zaitoon*, or wild olive,
from that limit up to 6,500 feet, where the *deodar*, a large and
noble species of pine, begins to flourish and continues as far as
the limit of 10,000 feet. With these are intermixed, at various
heights, the cypress. walnut, birch, holly, pistachio mastrah, the
sinjit (eleagnus orientalis), the *pinus chilgozeh*, producing edible
seeds slightly flavoured with turpentine, the hazel, and the mulberry. On the plains are found tamarisks, willows, planes, poplars, and some others.

A large proportion of the population of Afghanistan is in the
pastoral state, partly in consequence of imperfect civilization and
hereditary habits, partly because a large part of the country is so
rugged, ill-watered, and barren, as to be unfit for cultivation,
yielding only a scanty pasturage for camels, sheep, and goats.
It is a proof of the barbarous nature of the government and of the
state of society, that in the Daman[9] and many other parts, large
tracts, which might be cultivated with the most successful result,
are for a great part of the year overrun by the rude mountain
tribes, who, during winter, seek there a milder temperature and
more abundant pasturage. The disturbed state in which the
country has continued, with little intermission, from time imme-
morial, may be regarded both as a cause and an effect of the prevalence of the pastoral life. Such a life affords readier means than
any other for eluding violence and oppression ; and it is notorious
that a nomadic population is everywhere prone to marauding
and plundering habits. Next to Peshawur and the Daman, the
most generally cultivated tracts are the valley of Kabool, with

[8] Jour. As. Soc. 1841, p. 797; Grif. Rep. on Subjects con. with Afg.

[9] Burnes's Trade of the Derajat, 98.

the lesser valleys which open into it, the country about Kandahar, and the valley of Boree in Sewestan.

There are two harvests in the year in most parts of Afghanistan :[9] the *rubbee*, or *behaureh*, sown in autumn and the beginning of winter and reaped late in spring or early in summer ; and the *khureef*, or *panizeh*, sown in the end of spring and reaped in autumn : the former consists of wheat, barley, *addus* (ervum lens), *nukhod* (cicer arietinum), beans and peas, rye and oats, the last two being cultivated for the straw for fodder. The khureef consists chiefly of rice, *arzun* (panicum Italicum), *gall* (panicum miliacum), *jowauree* (holcus sorghum), *bajreh* (holcus spicatum), maize. Wheat is the staple article of food for the Afghans, but rice is grown as high up as from 6,000 to 7,000 feet above the level of the sea. Maize is ground into flour, and is also, when unripe, roasted, and thus used as food. Cotton, sugar, safflower, madder,and tobacco, are grown in the warmer parts of the country. The description of cultivation called *paulacz* is very important ; it includes melons and various kinds of cucumbers, gourds, and pumpkins. Natural grasses are scarce, and hay is seldom made ; sometimes, however, the leaves and stems of thistles, docks, rhubarb, and other similar wild plants, are cut and dried for this purpose. Esculent vegetables are in general of inferior quality. Those cultivated are cabbages, cauliflowers, spinach, lettuce, onions, garlic, beet-root, egg-plant. The potato was introduced by Burnes, but became extinct. Kabool probably excels all other places in the variety, abundance, and excellence of its fruits, which are also surprisingly cheap. The principal are peaches, apricots, nectarines, grapes, pomegranates, figs, apples, pears, plums, quinces, cherries, mulberries, walnuts. Citrons and dates are produced at Jelalabad. Fruit, both fresh and preserved in various forms, constitutes a considerable article in the diet of the people.

Should Afghanistan advance in cultivation and commercial prosperity, its wool would unquestionably become its most important element of wealth, unless the mineral resources of its extensive mountain ranges should prove available in a higher degree than is at present anticipated. The fine wool of Afghanistan* is produced both from goats and sheep; that of goats is

[9] Elph. Caubul, 300 ; Jour.As. Soc. 1840, p. 39; Irwin, Memoir of Afg. ; Jour. As. Soc. 1841, p. 982; Grif. Rep. on Subjects con. with Afg.

---

* See a valuable paper, by Hutton, in "Transact. of As. Soc. of Bengal," 1840, vol. ix. 327, "On wool and woollen manufactures of Khorassan." The physiology of wool appears to be very little understood ; it is produced of

a fine and remarkably soft down, lying at the roots of the outer or
true hair. It is generally of a rich dark-brown hue, while the long
coarse hair is jet black: it is sometimes found of a white colour,
but not often. The breed of goats is short-legged and shaggy,
but symmetrically and beautifully formed. The fleeces are obtained at two seasons: the winter covering is shorn in spring,
and is cleared of the long hairs in a very tedious manner by
hand-picking;[1] the summer fleece, which is much finer, softer,
and more silky,[2] is obtained only from the skins of the slaughtered
animals. The skins are rubbed with lime and potash, which
loosens the long hair and renders it easy of removal from among
the more tenacious short hair, which is taken off separately afterwards. The fine wool is manufactured throughout Afghanistan, but
especially at Kabool, into shawls and other fine fabrics. The long
coarse hair is made into grain bags, tent cloths, ropes, and various
coarse fabrics. The fleeces of the sheep are also finer in summer
than in winter, and these animals are in like manner shorn in
spring, while in autumn the wool is obtained only from the
slaughtered sheep. The winter wool, as that of goats, is manufactured into coarse fabrics, the autumn into shawls or cloaks, or
sometimes it is prepared with the leather to form posteens or
warm upper garments, well calculated to fence off the intense
cold of the approaching season. The Huzareh territory in the
north-west of Afghanistan produces and maintains great numbers
of sheep, goats, and camels bearing the finest wool.[3] The principal places of woollen manufactures are Kabool and Kandahar,
those of the former being considered the finer. The process of
making a fine shawl is very tedious; half a dozen men are
generally employed on it at once,[4] with implements of the rudest
kinds, resembling those used in making hand-lace in Europe.
The price is consequently very high, amounting to 100l. sterling
and upwards; yet these shawls are considered inferior to those
of Kashmir, being stiff and harsh to the touch. The woollen fabrics
of Afghanistan are seldom exported, as from the scarcity of arti-
ficers, the want of machinery, and the great demand, there are not
enough produced to supply the home market. The rural popula-

[1] Burnes' Wool of Kabool, 105-107.
[2] Hutton, 327.

[3] Burnes' Wool of Kabool, 107.

[4] Kennedy, Sinde and Kabool, ii.101.

the finest quality, both in the sultry wilds of Kandahar and of Spain, and in
the table-land of Pamir, near the limits of perpetual congelation. A dry atmosphere and fine herbage appear the most indispensable requisites for its
perfection.

tion generally wear woollen cloths made at home by their own families. Felting, the earliest invented and most obvious method of forming cloths of wool, is conducted in a very simple manner.[3] A [3] Hutton, ut supra, 330. mat of rushes is laid open on the ground and the wool spread over it; the mat is then folded up and rolled backwards and forwards by men pressing on it, and the process is continued until a complete felt is formed. It is called vernacularly *nummud*, of which the finer and thinner kinds are used for clothing, the coarser and thicker for carpets and tent cloths. Vigne whimsically supposes, that the *Numidæ* and *Nomade* tribes in general received the names from using these nummuds. In a country where every one goes heavily armed the quantity of arms sold must be considerable :[4] [4] Nowrozjee Furdoonjee, 148. those of the finer and dearer kinds are of Russian manufacture, and a few of British, but the greater part of those in use are made at Kabool, especially the long and formidable jezail or rifle. The fire-arms, as well as all the cutlery and hardware made in the country, are of very coarse and clumsy fabrication. A little silk is made up for the home market as well as a few coarse cottons, but in general the Afghans are dependant for these articles on foreign supplies. Manufactures in leather, saddlery, trappings, and harness for horses, camels, and bullocks, are the only important branches of handicraft besides those already mentioned.

That Afghanistan should retain any foreign trade, in spite of the exorbitant exactions of the men in power and the rapacity of the wild tribes infesting the passes, may be regarded as an extraordinary illustration of the pervading force of mercantile enterprise and perseverance. Commerce flows chiefly in two directions—to the east with Hindostan, and thus circuitously with Great Britain, and to the north-west with central Asia and Russia. There is another course of less importance southwards, through Kelat to Sonmeanee, on the Indian Ocean. The three great eastern passes, the Khyber in the north, the Bolan in the south, and the Gomul between them, are capable of great improvement by the judicious application of labour and engineering skill; but the country has been so often invaded by armies forcing their way to India, that it has been the policy of the inhabitants rather to obstruct than to clear the channels of communication. From the want of more commodious roads, goods are transported on the backs of beasts of burthen, principally camels,

4 Irwin, ut supra, 1015. to the total neglect of the facilities afforded by wheel carriages.[4]
Yet, under all these discouraging circumstances, the amount of
5 App. 194. imported goods sold in Kabool annually is considerable.[5] Burnes,
in a report drawn up in 1838, states the amount of British cloths
sold there in one year at 478,000 rupees value; of Indian goods,
at 933,000 rupees. Those most in demand are broad cloths, velvets, shawls, carpets, muslins, chintzes of various colours and
patterns, long-cloth, loongees, or thick and costly stuffs of silk
and cotton for scarfs, handkerchiefs, and various fancy articles in
silk and cotton; total value, 141,100*l.* Indigo and other dye stuffs,
of which there is a large consumption, drugs, groceries, cutlery,
fire-arms, hardware in general, leather, paper, jewellery, trinkets,
porcelain, glass, and ivory, will probably raise the amount
to about 300,000*l.* annually. The quantity of goods taken by
Peshawur, Daman, Kandahar, and the wild tribes scattered over
6 Burnes, on Fair for the Indus, 121. the country, may make the whole amount taken from us 500,000*l.*[6]
The returns are principally made in madder and other dye-stuffs,
assafœtida and other drugs, dried and fresh fruits, raw silk,
tobacco, wool, lead, sulphur, alum, zinc, horses, ponies, and
camels. The communication with central Asia and Russia by the
north-western frontier is far more difficult than that with Hindostan. It is principally by the passes of Hindoo Koosh or by the Bamian route. Of the passes of Hindoo Koosh, the most frequented is
that of Koushan, over the north-eastern shoulder of the principal
summit, and at the most elevated part of the road estimated to
7 Koh-i-Daman, 52. be 15,000 feet high.[7] It is described by Lord as "narrow, rocky,
and uneven, with a fall of 200 feet a mile, so that it was impossible
that it should have ever contained any other waters than those of
a headlong rapid torrent." As this is the most frequented pass
through Hinuoo Koosh, it is probably the best; but it is scarcely
practicable for beasts of burthen at its upper part, where the transport of goods is effected on men's shoulders, and it is totally closed
by snow in winter. The Bamian route, the principal course across
the north-west frontier, lies for above 100 miles over a succession
of mountain ridges, varying in height from 8,000 to 13,000
8 Burnes' Bok. i. 178-200; Moorcr. Punj. Bokh. II.385. feet;[8] one of them, indeed, estimated by Outram to have
an elevation of 15,000 feet.[9] There is also a caravan route across
9 Rough Notes, 120. the Huzareh mountains from Herat, and this probably was
1 Arrian, iii. 28. taken by Alexander in his pursuit of Bessus.[1] The route south

of Herat from Yerd to Kandahar is scarcely used as a channel of commercial intercourse. Difficult as communication is, Kabool is supplied with manufactured goods in greater abundance from Russia than from either Great Britain or from India. The imports from Russia are gold and gold-dust, jewellery, copper, fire-arms, cutlery, hardware in general, gold, copper, and iron wire, trinkets, glass, porcelain, paper, leather, dye stuffs, drugs, tea, refined sugar, broad-cloth, velvet, satins, and other silks; chintzes, calicos, muslins, and handkerchiefs. No accurate information has been obtained how the returns arc made. It is obvious that the raw produce of Afghanistan is in general too bulky to bear profitable transport to Russia, and that the return in goods must be made to Bokhara, Kunduz, and Kokan. The rapacious invasions of neighbouring countries, especially Hindostan, by the Afghans, and the heavy tributes exacted by them, must have diverted a large quantity of the precious metals into their country; but the stock, it is to be believed, must now be nearly exhausted. In addition to the imports already enumerated, much raw silk[3] of fine [3 Nowrozjee Furdoonjee, 150.] quality is brought from Bokhara, and some tea and other goods from China, by way of Yarkund, Kokan, and Bokhara.

The denominations and value of the currency expressed in decimals of English currency are, respectively—

						s.	d.
Kowree ...	... shell	...	...	...	,,		·010
Kuseera ...	... copper	...	...	...	,,		·083
Ghaz ...	... do.	...	...	...	,,		·166
Pysa ...	... do.	...	...	...	,,		·333
Shahee ...	... silver	...	...	...	,,		1·666
Sunnar ...	... do.	...	...	...	,,		3·333
Abbasee	... do.	...	...	...	,,		6·666
Rupee ...	... do.	...	...	...	1		8·000
Tilla ...	... gold	...	...	...	11		9·027
Boodkee or ducat	do.	...	...	...	9		9·048

Silver is virtually the standard, the value of gold fluctuating according to its abundance or scarcity. Thus the gold mohur is sometimes worth 15 rupees, sometimes 18; its average value may be taken at 1l. 10s.[4] The toornoin is an imaginary money [4 Glossary to Sale, in voce.] of account, equal to 20 rupees, or 1l. 13s. 4d.

5 Nowrozjee Fur-doonjee, 148.
In the monetary transactions of this country,[5] the relative value of gold coin, or bullion, to silver is found to be much lower than in Europe, being generally 11, 12, or 13 to 1, instead of 14 or 15; but this anomaly (according to our notions) prevails through the greater part of Eastern Asia.

The principal commercial weights are the—

	lb.	oz.	gr.
Nukhoad	,,	,,	2·958
Miscal	,,	,,	71·000
Pow	,,	12·	428
Seer	12·	15·	,,
Khurwar	1038·	6·	,,

The principal measures of length are the—

	MILES.	FEET.	INCHES.
Khoord	,,	,,	0·632
Gheerah or Pow	,,	,,	2·531
Ghuz-i-Shah	,,	,,	40·500
Biswah	,,	4·	,,
Jurceb	,,	80.	,,
Kroe or koss	2·	,,	,,
Munzil	24·	,,	,,

The commerce and carrying trade of Afghanistan are, to a considerable extent, conducted by tribes who combine pastoral occupations with these pursuits.[6] The principal of them are the Lohanis, perhaps the most extensively and regularly migratory race in existence.[7] They amount to above 100,000 persons, and take with them 24,000 camels, of which 5,140 in one year were loaded with merchandize, and on that occasion they had, besides, with one of their companies, 60,000 sheep; so that the whole train of domestic animals must have amounted to some hundreds of thousands. They winter in the Daman, which produces abundant pasture at that time, and has besides a delightful climate. Here the families, cattle, and bulky property of the tribe, are left in charge of a force adequate for their management and protection, while the rest proceed to lay in merchandize at Dera Ismael Khan, Dera Ghazee Khan, or even at Bombay or Calcutta. When the return of spring opens the passes and brings forward the pastures throughout the higher parts of Afghanistan, they

6 Burnes' Trade of the Derajat, 99.

7 Burnes' Rep. 99; Mohan Lal. Baha-wulpur, 73.

rendézvous at the town of Drabund in the Derajat, and proceed with supplies suited to the markets of central Asia and Afghanistan. Their route is by the Gomul Pass, where they are obliged to fight their way through the Vaziris, the Sulernan Kal, and other predatory tribes.[8] This system is very ancient.[9] Sultan Baber relates that, in 1505, he robbed the Lohani merchants of articles of the same kind as they now carry. [8] Vigne's Guznee, 105. [9] Memoirs, 161.

There is considerable, though not complete, uniformity of religious belief in Afghanistan. The Afghans for the most part are Mahometan Soonnees,[1] acknowledging the three first Kaliphs, and rejecting the claim of Ali to the immediate succession to the prophet's powers; but the Huzarehs are Shias, a fact attested both by Wood[2] and Masson.[3] In Afghanistan, as elsewhere, there is the bitterest animosity between the votaries of the respective sects, insomuch that Persians in Kabool live in continual dread of massacre. More indulgence is shewn to Christians, and even to Hindoos, than to Shias. Both Elphinstone[4] and Masson[5] bear ample evidence of the toleration shewn to Christians; and it is not unworthy of remark, that in the late atrocious massacre of the Anglo-Indian troops, no exemption was made in favour of Mahometans. The Shias, Elphinstone[6] observes, are much more bigotted than the Soonnees. The moollahs or priests are very numerous.[7] Their character and name are conferred by an assem- bly of members of the order, on candidates who have undergone a regular course of study and examination, the essential ceremony consisting in placing on the new member the turban of a moollah, which is white, very large, and of a peculiar shape. Besides the turban, the moollahs wear a distinctive dress, consisting of a large loose gown of white or black cotton. Neither in Afghanistan, nor in any other Mahometan country, is the priesthood so distinct from the laity as in the chief Christian churches, whether Greek, Roman, or Protestant. They live in many respects as laymen, trading, farming, and lending money on usury. Some, indeed, are supported on pensions from the state; and those who discharge religious duties throughout the country receive a proportion of the rural produce. Legacies are frequently made to them. Some subsist by teaching and practising the law, others by preaching, and in consequence receiving remuneration from the congregations to whom their exhortations are addressed; some are mere amateur priests and students, who, as Elphin-

[1] Elph. 200.
[2] Route of Kab. and Toorkestan, 22.
[3] Bal. Afc. Panj. 290 to 301.
[4] 201-205.
[5] Passim.
[6] 200.
[7] Elph. 218.

[1] Elph. 218.

[2] 218.

[3] 220

[4] Elph. 557.

stone observes,[1] " live on their own means, and pursue their studies and amusements at leisure." The same eminent writer says,[2] " there are no corporate bodies of moollahs as there are of monks in Europe, nor is the whole order under the command of any chief, or subject to any particular discipline like the clergy in England. All except those who hold offices under the Crown are entirely independent, and the co-operation among them is only produced by a sense of common interest." There are sundry minor religious professors—Syuds, who are considered to be descended from Mahomet, Dervises, Fakeers, Calenders; but a discriminating account of them would occupy nearly as much space as a similar account of the monastic orders in Europe. Extraordinary reverence is paid to those who aim at acquiring the reputation of superior sanctity, either by real or pretended austerity,[3] and Elphinstone mentions some of these aspirants before whom the king did not venture to be seated until pressed. Tombs, and other localities, associated with the names of these deluding or deluded saints, are of frequent occurrence, and command the humble adoration of the people.

Of the history of Afghanistan little is known till comparatively modern times. Its condition from the period of its being peopled has perhaps never varied much from what it is now. It was probably at all times occupied by fierce and lawless tribes, among whom regular government was scarcely known, and who recognized no authority that was not enforced by the sword. Their country has shared the fate of the greater part of the East, in being repeatedly overrun by conquerors, but the traces of conquest have been generally evanescent. The Afghans in turn have carried their arms beyond their own frontier, into Persia to the west and India to the east, gaining, like their enslavers, temporary triumph and supremacy, but, like them, establishing no permanent dominion.

The dominant power in Afghanistan in later times has been exercised by the tribe of the Dooranees. Ahmed Shah, the founder of their government, after experiencing many vicissitudes in contests with the Persians and his own countrymen, procured himself to be crowned at Kandahar, in the year 1747. His reign, which continued twenty-six years, was occupied with wars, external and internal; but at his death the dominions which acknowledged his sovereignty extended from the west of Khorassan to Sirhind,[4] and from the Oxus to the sea. His son and successor, Timur, Shah, seems to have been a man of tamer character than his father, and to have had no desire as to empire beyond that of preserving the dominions which he inherited. He did not succeed even in this limited object of ambition, having suffered from the encroachments of the King of Bokhara, against whom he was ultimately induced to march with an immense army. This movement, however, produced nothing but many professions of respect from the King of Bokhara, and a peace, by which that prince was allowed to retain all the fruits of his aggressions. By Timur the chief seat of government was removed to Kabool.[5]   [5] Elph. 559—565.

The ordinary rules of succession have little force in oriental countries. Timur was succeeded by Zemaun Shah, a younger son of the deceased prince, to the exclusion of Hoomayon, to whom the throne belonged, if the right were to be adjudged according to primogeniture. Zemaun Shah repeatedly threatened India with invasion; the last time in the year 1800, when his design was arrested by apprehensions for the safety of his own dominions on the west. He was finally compelled to yield to his elder brother, Mahmood, by whom, in accordance with Asiatic precedent, he was imprisoned and deprived of sight. Zemaun Shah had inflicted the like penalties on his elder brother Hoomayon.[6]   Mahmood did [6] Elph. 579—599. not enjoy his success undisturbed. His possession of the throne was contested by another brother, named Shoojah-ool-Moolk, and after a severe struggle the latter became master of the prize in dispute, and of the person of his rival. On this occasion Shoojah-ool-Moolk exercised unusual clemency. He imprisoned his brother, but he spared his sight. This humanity was but ill rewarded. In the course of the intrigues and convulsions which marked the reign of Shoojah, in common with all eastern princes, Mahmood obtained his freedom, and reappeared in arms against his competitor. The result was disastrous to Shoojah, who fled to Lahore, where he was confined and plundered by Runjeet Singh. He ultimately escaped and found a retreat in the British territory.[7]   [7] Hough, 380—399.

Mahmood owed his success to the talents of his vizier, Futteh Khan; but Kamram the son of Mahmood, having taken an aversion to the minister, prevailed on his father to imprison him and put out his eyes. Eventually Futteh Khan was murdered with great cruelty. This treatment of the vizier laid the foundation of another revolution, in which the brothers of that person-age were the chief actors. Mahmood fled to Herat, where he died, and was succeeded in the portion of authority which he had been able to retain by his son Kamram. The rest of the country passed into the hands of the brothers of Futteh Singh, the most able and active of them being Dost Mohammed Khan. Shoojah made two attempts to recover his lost throne, but failed, and was compelled again to seek refuge beyond the limits of the dominions which he claimed.[7]

[7] Hough, 400—416.

About the year 1837, the conduct of certain agents of Russia in the countries lying to the westward of India, excited the ap-prehensions of the British government. It was consequently desired to establish an alliance with the ruling powers in Afghan-istan, and overtures were made to Dost Mahomed Khan. They failed: the attention of the British authorities was then turned to the exiled prince, Shah Shoojah, and an expedition from British India on a large scale was prepared for the purpose of restoring him to the throne from which he had been expelled. At this time Dost Mahomed held Kabool and a considerable portion of the Huzareh country, having a revenue of 260,000l. His regular army amounted to 14,000 men,[8] of whom 6,000 were cavalry, and his artillery consisted of 40 guns. The three brothers of Dost Mahomed, Kohen Dil Khan, Rehem Dil Khan, and Mehir Dil Khan, held Kandahar with the surrounding country, and an in-come of 80,000l. per annum.[9] They were supposed to have at the same time 3,000 cavalry, 1,000 infantry, and 15 pieces of cannon.[1] Herat, the fourth sub-division of Afghanistan, continued to be held by Kamram.

[8] Hough, 280.

[9] Hough, 140.

[1] Conolly, ii. 12.

The British force destined to act in Scinde and Afghanistan was furnished partly from Bengal, partly from Bombay, and con-sisted of 28,350 men.[2] These were to be aided by a Sikh force amounting to 6,000, and by a force nominally assigned to the Shazada (Shoojah's eldest son) of 4,000; while a Sikh army of observation, amounting to 15,000, was to assemble in Peshawur. The chief command was held by Sir John Keane, commander-in-chief of the army under the presidency of Bombay. The march of the invading force was attended by many difficulties and privations, but it was successfully pursued to Kandahar, where, on the 8th of May, 1839, Shah Shoojah was solemnly enthroned. On the 21st of the same month, the British army

[2] Hough, 5.

was before Ghuznee; on the 23rd, the gates of that place were blown in and the fortress successfully stormed. On the 7th of August, the victors entered the city of Kabool (Dost Mahomed having previously quitted it), and the war was regarded as at an end. A few months dispelled this illusion. The British troops, though engaged in maintaining the throne of the prince, who from the chief city of eastern Afghanistan claimed to exercise the power of a sovereign, found that they were virtually in an enemy's country. The wild tribes manifested the most inveterate hostility to the English, and the 2nd of November, 1841, was signalized by a fearful outbreak at Kabool, in which several distinguished British officers were massacred. Among them was Colonel Sir Alexander Burnes, whose authority is so frequently referred to in this work. From that time the situation of the British force at Kabool was one of continued danger and suffering. Akbar Khan, son of Dost Mahomed Khan, arrived to co-operate with the desperate bands previously engaged against them; and late in the month of December, Sir William Macnaghten, the British envoy in Afghanistan, unfortunately agreed to hold a conference with him. At this meeting, the British representative and several officers were treacherously murdered. A convention, under which the British were to evacuate Afghanistan, was subsequently concluded: in the belief that its terms would be observed, the remnant of the army began to move. They were attacked on the road, exposed to miserable hardships from cold, hunger, and fatigue, as well as from the annoyances of the enemy, into whose hands many fell, some as ordinary prisoners, others (including the high-minded Lady Sale and several of her countrywomen) by arrangement with Akbar Khan. The remainder pushed on for Jelalabad, which was held by Sir Robert Sale; but only one European* and four or five natives succeeded in reaching it. Such was the fate of a force which, about two months before, numbered 5,000 fighting men, with an array of camp followers more than three times as many. Other disasters followed, and Ghuznee, so recently and so brilliantly won, returned by surrender into the hands of the enemy. The course of events thus direful to the British army was not less so to the prince in whose behalf it was engaged. Shah Shoojah met the fate which had overtaken so many of his English supporters, and Public Official Papers, E.I.C. Ms. Doc. died by the hands of assassins.

* Dr. Bryden, a medical officer of the Bengal army.

Gloomy as were now the fortune and prospects of the British in Afghanistan, the darkness was relieved by many displays of brilliant and successful valour. General Nott at Kandahar, and Sir Robert Sale at Jelalabad, must be especially named as having nobly maintained the honour and interests of their country. Preparations were also in progress for vindicating them on a larger scale, before finally abandoning a spot where so much of treachery had been encountered, and so much of disaster incurred. A force of 12,000 men was assembled under General Pollock, and this army, having successfully advanced through the Khyber Pass, joined the force under Sir Robert Sale at Jelalabad. Gen. Pollock subsequently advanced towards Kabool; he was joined by the army under General Nott from Kandahar, and on the 15th September, 1842, the British national anthem pealed forth by the band of her Majesty's 9th foot, with three vociferous cheers from the soldiery, marked the elevation of the British colours upon the spot from which they had not long before been driven under circumstances of treachery and murderous cruelty. One of the most gratifying results of this success was the rescue of the European prisoners from the hands of Akbar Khan. It was not intended to retain possession of Kabool, and after destroying the fort, the magnificent bazaar, the principal mosque, and some other buildings, the British army withdrew, leaving Afghanistan to the anarchy which it seems destined long to endure. Dost Mahomed Khan had been taken in the course of the war, and it was apparently intended to keep him permanently under *surveillance* within the British dominions, but on the abandonment of Afghanistan he was set at liberty.[1]

[1] Public Official Papers, E.I.C. Ms. Doc.

Scarcely any country of the same extent has such a mixture of races constituting its population as is observable in Afghanistan. The two leading divisions set down by Elphinstone are Afghans, properly so called, and Taujiks, which last term, he observes,[2] is applied to all who, living where Pushtoo is most generally spoken, have Persian as their vernacular language. To these should be added Hindkees, or persons of Hindoo descent and Hindustani dialect, most numerous in the eastern part, and Huzareh, or those of Tartar descent, most numerous in the north-west. The Kuzzilbaushes,[3] a highly influential body, in proportion to their numbers, though often deemed Persians, are not actually of that stock, being members of that colony of

[2] 310.

[3] Burnes' Pers. Fac. in Kabool, 7.

Toorks* who now predominate in Persia. They were settled here under the governments of Nadir and of Ahmed Shah, and owe much of their influence to the diplomatic affairs [4] of Afghanistan being in a great measure in their hands. But so great is the variety of language and race [5] in this singular country, that besides Pushtoo, the great national tongue, no fewer than ten dialects are enumerated as spoken vernacularly, and this extent of variety often occurs in districts at no great distance from each other. In attempting to trace the origin and descent of the Afghans, we find that probably the first authentic notice of them is under Subuctageen [6] and his still more celebrated son, Mahmood of Ghuznee, who ascended the throne A.D. 998, and extended his empire from the Ganges to the Caspian. The Afghan historians, however, pertinaciously, and without much violation of consistency, maintain that numbers of the Jews brought away captives by the Babylonians were banished to the mountains of Ghore, between Herat and Kabool; that they there multiplied greatly, and as they had kept up correspondence with some of their race in Arabia, on the appearance of Mahomed [7] acknowledged the authenticity of his mission; that Keis, an Afghan chief of that time, accompanied by some others, joined the standard of Mahomed, and assisted in his attack on Mecca, and that from this Keis the noble families of Afghans are descended. This claim of descent is favourably entertained by Sir Wm. Jones,[8] who says, "the Pushtoo language, of which I have seen a dictionary, has a manifest resemblance to the Chaldaic;" but this last statement is very vehemently and coarsely denied by Klaproth,[9] who asserts that neither in words nor in grammatical structure, is there the slightest resemblance between Pushtoo and any Semitic language, and that unquestionably Pushtoo is a branch of the great Indo-Germanic division of languages. Leech [1] also states that it is decidedly of a Sanscrit complexion. Dorn [2] asserts that the "Pushtoo language bears not the slightest resemblance to the Hebrew or Chaldaic," and concludes by expressing his opinion that though the Afghans may

[4] Burnes on Persians in Kabool, 6.

[5] Elph. 309.

[6] Price, Mahomedan Hist. ii. 277.

[7] Malcolm, Hist. of Persia, i. 597.

[8] Asiatic Research. ii. 76.

[9] Asia Polyglotta, 44, 54, 56.

[1] Jour. As. Soc. Beng. 1839, p. 1; Grammar of the Pushtoo Language, by Lieut. Leech.

[2] Neamet Ullah, ii. 65, 72.

* The Kazal-bashi (red heads), under which denomination of military force these colonists were classed, are considered to be the descendants of the captives given to Shaikh Haidar by Tamerlane, and who wore red caps as a mark of distinction.—Shakespear in v. قزل باشي

belong to the great Indo-Teutonic family of nations, they are aborigines of the land they now inhabit. Very different is the

³ Baptist Missions, 27. opinion of the Scrampore missionaries,[3] to whom "the Pushtoo and Belochee languages appear to form the connecting link between those of Sungskrit and those of Hebrew origin." Ade-

⁴ Mithridates, i. 255. lung[4] considers Pushtoo a peculiar and original dialect, but acknowledges his acquaintance with it to be very slender. Elphin-

⁵ 190-191. stone,[5] too, is not fully satisfied of the parentage of Pushtoo, as he states that "its origin is not easily discovered," but he observes that of 218 Pushtoo words, not one had the smallest appearance of being deducible from any of the Semitic languages. He thinks that a resemblance can be traced between it and the

⁶ Klaproth, 75. Curdish, considered to be an Indo-Germanic[6] tongue. The Afghans use the Persian alphabet, and generally write in Nushk character.

It cannot be denied that there is something in the strongly-

⁷ Moorcroft, Punj. Bokh. ii. 253. marked resemblance[7] which they are observed to bear to the Jews, that affords countenance to the opinion which found support from Sir William Jones. "Their tall figures, dark black eyes, marked features, and western complexions indicate a race that may, without the least violation of probability, be referred to

⁸ Kennedy, Sinde and Kabool, ii. 94. a Jewish original."[8] And though there may not be any certain ground for admitting the Jewish descent of the Afghans, the whole system of society amongst them rests upon the supposition that they are sprung from one family. Elphinstone describes the population as divided into great tribes, and these into smaller sections, bearing the name of khail or clan, or one terminating with *Zai*, exactly corresponding with the *O'* of the Gaelic tribes,

⁹ Elph. 161. the *Mac* of the Erse.[9] Thus Eusufzais means the son or descendant of Eusuf, like O'Donnell or Macpherson.

Of the Afghan tribes, the Duranis are considered the greatest, both on account of the superior extent of the tract which they inhabit, and because the royal family and high ministers of state belong to it. They were called Abdalli until Ahmed Shah, the founder of the Durani dynasty, who, in consequence of the

¹ Malcolm, Hist. of Persia, ii. 599; Elph. 396. dream of a certain saint, assumed the title of Duri Duran,[1] which may be translated "age of fortune," and styled the tribe Durani. It is divided into two great branches, Zeeruk and Punjpaw, and these again as follow :—

Zeeruk.	*Punjpaw.*
Populzai,	Noorzai,
Allekkozai,	Alizai,
Baurikzai,	Iskhaukzai,
Atchikzai.	Khouganee,
	Maukoo.

Until late events, the Populzai was considered the royal stem, as the Suddozai, one of its families, gave a sovereign to the empire.[1] The Baurikzais latterly engrossed the office of vizir and some others of high importance. [1] Elph. 398.

The Berduranis[2] also received their name from Ahmed Shah; they inhabit the north-east quarter, and comprise the [2] Elph. 324.

Eusufzais,	Momunds and other tribes
Otmun Khail,	of Peshawur,
Turcoulaunees,	Bungush,
Khyberees,	Khuttuks.

The Ghiljies are, after the Duranis, the most eminent of the tribes, as, in the early part of the last century, the head of them possessed the sovereignty, not only in Afghanistan but in Persia, and routed the Turkish armies, until their power was broken by Nadir Shah. They are divided into the two families of Toraun and Boorhaun, of which the first is subdivided into two, the second into six clans.

The Cauker tribe, who hold the most southern part of the Khakas country, about the Toba and Khojch Amran mountains, were amongst the least known of the Afghan tribes, until in conjunction with the Atchikzai they became notorious by incessant attacks and depredations on the British troops in their marches and countermarches through the Bolan and Kojuk Passes. Our limits do not admit the enumeration of a great number of other less important tribes. The following table of population is given with much diffidence, though collected with great caution and care from the scanty data afforded by Elphinstone and others.

Duranis	...	...	...	...	800,000
Eusufzais	...	...	...	...	700,000
Ghiljies	...	...	...	...	600,000
Peshawur tribes	...	...	...	300,000
Daman tribes	...	...	...	200,000
Caukers	...	...	...	...	200,000

Khyberees ...	...	...	...	...	120,000
Khuttuks ...	...	...	...	...	100,000
Bungush, Banoo, and Murwut		...	...	100,000
Suliman tribes	...	...	...	...	100,000
Otmun Khail	...	...	...	...	60,000
Momunds ...	...	...	...	...	40,000
Nausseers and other wanderers		...	...	100,000
Huzareh and Eimauk	...	...	...	200,000
					3,620,000
Tajiks, Hindkees, Hindoos, Kuzzulbaushes, &c. ...:					1,500,000
Total					5,120,000

Being little more than at the rate of about twenty persons to the square mile. Elphinstone [2] makes the population greater, but when we consider that the country is, for the most part, rugged, barren, and ill-cultivated, that there are few towns of any importance, and that destructive wars are of frequent occurrence, or rather that they are incessant, the smaller number will appear more probable.

The resources of the governments, such as they are, may be judged from the following estimate, referring to a period subsequent to the expulsion of Shah Shooja. Kamram, who held Herat, drew a revenue, loosely stated [3] at about 100,000*l.* per annum, in money, and perhaps as much more in produce. Dost Mahomed Khan, who seized Kabool and its immediate dependencies, is thought to have annually squeezed from those territories 240,000*l.* [4] His brothers, who made themselves masters of Kandahar and the adjacent territory, drew therefrom an annual revenue, stated at 80,000*l.* [5] Burnes [6] estimated the army of Dost Mahomed at 13,000 horse and 2,500 infantry. The greatest force mustered by the Afghans during the late war, appears to have been about 16,000 men, brought against General Pollock at Tezeen. [7] The discipline of the Afghans is very imperfect, and they are embarrassed by the multitude of their arms. A military authority, [8] well acquainted with them, observes, " an Afghan horseman never thinks himself safe until he has a long heavy matchlock, with a bayonet, a sabre, a blunderbuss, three long pistols, a couteau-de-chasse, a dagger, and four or five knives,

[2] 84.

[3] Conolly, Journ. to India, ii. 12.

[4] Burnes' Personal Narr. App. iii. 370.
[5] Hough, 110.
[6] Personal Narr. 379.

[7] Mil. Op. in Afg. 396.

[8] Abbott, Herant and Khiva, ii. 196.

besides a shield and a complete rigging round his waist of powder flasks, powder measures, powder magazines, bullet pods, and fifty nameless articles."

The whole state of society in Afghanistan is a singular compound of the patriarchal and republican forms.[1] Each tribe [1.Elph. 159.] has, in general, its territory compact and confined to its own people. It is divided into *oloosses*, or divisions of population descended from some one ancestor, and each of these is sub-divided, until the lowest portion is reduced to a few families. The chief of an oolooss is called Khan, and is always chosen from the oldest family in the oolooss. In most cases the sovereign of the country is able to secure a khan or to remove him, appointing one of his relations in his stead. Sometimes the khans are chosen by the tribes-men. Nothing seems fixed or certain, though primogeniture, property, and character have influence ; and this unsettled state of succession prevailing throughout the political organization of the country, from the throne to the lowest office in the tribe, appears to be the fatal cause of the incessant and devastating anarchy which prevails. Where there is no great deviation from the usual constitution of these tribes, the principal duties and powers of .the khans are twofold—to command in war and to preside in the *jeergas* or assemblies, which the chieftains of the tribe hold for managing its concerns. The stringency of obligation is very different in different tribes, being in some, as the Eusufzais, very weak, and in the Duranis and others in the west, for the most part sufficient to restrain the tribes-men from mutual injury.[2] In general the [2 Elph. 163.] clannish attachment of individuals is rather to the tribe than to the chief, and throughout all stations there is such a laxity of political and civil organization as accounts for the sudden and capricious revolutions which take place with regard both to the sovereignty and the great offices of state. Elphinstone compares the state of this distracted nation to that of Scotland during the feudal ages.[3] Perhaps a closer parallel might be found in the [3 173.] ever-raging warfare and anarchy described by Bruce in Abyssinia. It is quite clear that at no time has there been in Afghanistan that reverential affection for the reigning family which has, through so many ages of decay, preserved the Ottoman empire from total dissolution. In the case of Ahmed Shah and of the Baurikzais, who lately seized the sovereignty, the object aimed at was attained by the sword, and the command of this was gained by talent and courage, aided indeed to a certain extent by hereditary influence, and in the instance of the first mentioned chief by the possession of treasure. The codes regulating the decisions in the tribes are the Mahomedan law, derived from the Koran and re-

4 Elph. 165.

ceived comments, or the *Pooshtoonwulle*,[4] or usage of the Afghans, and bearing some analogy to the common law of the Anglo-Saxons. This code, being throughout pervaded by a pernicious spirit favourable to retaliation and revenge, tends to stimulate the fierce tempers of the people, to perpetuate strife, and increase bloodshed.

The personal appearance of the Afghans differs in different parts of the country. In the east they are more swarthy; in the west they have olive complexions, and some are as fair as Europeans.

5 Elph. 245.

The men are of a robust make,[5] generally lean, bony, and muscular, with high noses, high cheek-bones, and long faces, bearing, as has been already mentioned, a strong resemblance to the Jews.

6 Burnes' Pers. Narr. 140.

The features of Dost Mahomed Khan[6] are described as having an exaggerated Jewish expression. The hair and beards of the Afghans are generally black, sometimes brown, rarely red, and always coarse and strong. They wear the hair in long, large locks, hanging down each side of the head, according to the

7 Bal. Afg. Panj. i. 14.

fashion of the Asiatic Jews, so that, observes Masson,[7] " one of the latter on seeing them, unhesitatingly pronounces them to be

8 Havelock, War in Afg. ii. 147.

of his stock." The language,[8] dress, and manners of the Persians prevail among the higher order, especially in the vicinity of that people. The original national dress, still retained among the lower classes, consists of a pair of loose trowsers of dark-coloured cotton, a large *camiss*, or shirt, worn over the trowsers, and reaching down to the knees, a low cap, with sides of black silk cloth and top of gold brocade, a pair of half-boots of brown leather, and in cold weather a *portin*, or large cloak, of well-tanned sheep-

9 Elph. 239.

skin thrown over all.[9] In the eastern part of the country, the dress bears considerable resemblance to that of Hindostan. The Afghan women are large, fair, and handsome; they wear loose camisses like those of the men, but longer, and made of fine and highly-ornamented stuffs, when they can afford it, and a small hood of bright-coloured silk. A large, long outer dress, in the

1 Elph. 240; Hough, 136.

form of a fine sheet[1] * (it might, perhaps, be called a shroud),

* Few of the women make their appearance abroad, and those who do so are completely enveloped in the long white veil called *boorku*. It has eyelet and breathing holes, but so entirely shrouds the person as to give the form

is thrown over the whole person when a stranger approaches. Their ornaments are in general cumbrous and inelegant chains of gold and of silver, or strings of coins of either of these metals; rings for the fingers and thumbs, bracelets, earrings, and pendants for the nose. Unmarried women are distinguished from those married by wearing their hair loose, and by their trowsers being white. Wives are purchased here, and, as a natural consequence, are considered property[1]—nay, currency;[2] for, in some cases of delinquency, the penalty is paid in a certain number of young women. Thus, for murder, twelve young women are paid; for cutting off a hand, knocking out a tooth, or destroying an eye, six are paid; for breaking a tooth, the fine is three girls. After all that has been stated as to the civilization of this singular people, such facts as these perhaps afford the best illustrations of its degree. The most usual age for marriage is about twenty in the man and fifteen or sixteen in the woman; but if the friends of the former bring forward the price, the marriage takes place much earlier. Sometimes the husband has numbered only fifteen or sixteen years, the wife not more than twelve. But on the other hand, where funds are scarce, the men often remain unmarried till forty, women till twenty-five, so that the preventive checks devised by Malthus appear to be in operation in a country where his name was never heard. According to the well-known tenet of Mahomedan law, those who can afford it espouse four wives, adding to the number several other females, whose claim to the title is not recognized by either legal or social authority. In general, the measure of indulgence which a man takes in this respect is limited solely by his means. Women enjoy more freedom in the country than in towns. Those in easy circumstances travel on horseback, wrapped in cumbrous upper dresses, or in *kajawars* or panniers, slung on each side of a camel. They have more influence than among the neighbouring nations, and "their condition,"[3] it is said, "is very far from being unhappy."

As both wine and gambling are forbidden, and the Afghans in general pay little regard to intellectual pursuits, they are often at a loss for the means of passing their time when confined at home

[1] Elph. 179.
[2] 163.

[3] Elph. 184.

moving under it the appearance of a walking mummy. Not a glimpse can be obtained of either the features or the shape."—Havelock, ii. 147.

by the weather. Smoking tobacco affords some resource ; another is furnished by bang, gunjah, or hemp, the smoke of which is inhaled, or the extract swallowed. The effect is the production of the most powerful and illusory form of intoxication* of which the human constitution seems capable.[4] Even wine is sometimes secretly indulged in by the wealthy. The use of snuff is a luxury well known. Music is discouraged by strict religionists, who do not scruple to break lutes[5] and other instruments when they fall in their way. Much time is spent in singing and in story-telling ; the latter faculty being exerted much in the manner common with children in Europe, the incidents being furnished by kings, viziers, genii, fairies, love, war, and exaggerated adventures. Their most usual repast is mutton, either roasted or boiled, and eaten with the broth ; their drink sour milk, sherbet, or tea,[6] but this last being expensive, is only within reach of the wealthy. The diet of the pastoral population consists largely of milk, *roghan*, or clarified butter, and *koroot*, or sour milk inspissated, and of this last food they seem never to tire.[7] The rich indulge in highly spiced pilaws, ragouts, and savoury stews. All classes are very fond of sweet-meats and fruits. The favourite amusement of the Afghans is hunting, which is managed like the *tinkal* of old in the Highlands of Scotland, the country to a great extent being inclosed by large parties of horsemen and footmen, who gradually contract their circuit, and collect the game into a valley, where they fall on it with dogs and guns. They ride down partridges, one horseman taking up the pursuit when the horse of another is tired, and those of the party who come up with the bird knock it down with sticks. Horse-races are conducted on a great scale, twenty or thirty horses starting and running from ten to twenty miles. Their national dance, the Attun, resembles the Albanian dance, as described by Hobhouse, and is very violent and exciting.[8] It is performed by thirty or forty men, who bound with the wildest gestures round one who stands playing or singing in the middle. Conolly[9] describes it in these words :—
" They stamped their feet in regular time, becoming more and more excited, and then with one accord they flung their hands loose, clapped their palms, and tossed their arms about, now making

Margin notes:
[4] Burnes' Pers. Narr. 236.
[5] Elph. 215.
[6] Burnes' Pers. Narr. 260.
[7] Conolly, Jour. to India, ii. 101.
[8] Elph. 238.
[9] Jour. to India, ii. 210.

* See an extraordinary account of its effects on the human constitution in " Journ. As. Soc. of Bengal," 1839, 732. It effectually calms the horrors of hydrophobia.

measured movements with their hands and feet, setting their teeth tight, frowning, rolling their eyes, and grunting, and then twisting their bodies round and round, like drunken men, winding into each others' places, and shrieking and whooping as Scotchmen do in a reel." The dance lasted until the performer sank down in exhaustion.

The Afghans[9] pride themselves on conventional hospitality, [9] Elph. 226. and in each oolooss or khail a certain fund is set aside for the entertainment of strangers, who are considered as public guests; and the instance of Masson,[1] who, without funds, traversed the [1] Bal. Afg. Punj. country through its whole extent, corroborates the statement [i. ch. iii.-xvi.] of Elphinstone, that " a man who travelled through the country without money would never be in want of a meal." It is also said that " a man's bitterest enemy is safe while he is under his roof." Such importance do the Afghans attach to the ostentation of hospitality, that a common method of obtaining or enforcing a request is for the suppliant to go to the house or tent of the person whose favour is sought, and refuse to sit on his carpet or partake of his hospitality until the boon be granted.* Compliance is rarely withheld from this mode of supplication, which is called *Nannawautee* in Pushtoo—" I have come in." Another custom indicates a desire to secure a character for chivalric gallantry not less than for hospitality. The protection of an Afghan is commanded even more forcibly than by an appeal to his household pride, when a woman sends him her veil and implores assistance. It may, however, be conjectured, from the relative position of the sexes in Afghanistan, that there is, in reality, not much of that refinement of feeling of which such a custom would seem to imply the existence; and it is certain that there is little of real benevolence[2] in the manifestations of hospi- [2] Elph. 227. tality and generosity previously noticed, since an Afghan will not hesitate to rob the man whom he has entertained as soon as he shall have left his residence. The sincerity of Afghan hospitality was strikingly exemplified at the commencement of the war with Persia, early in the last century. The first step of the Afghan leader[3] was to invite the Persian governor of Kan- [3] Malcolm, i. 607. dahar to his house and there massacre him with all his attendants. After Mahmood, the Afghan ruler, had taken

* This resembles the expedient of Themistocles, when he seated himself on the hearth of the King of the Molossians.

Ispahan, he sought to consolidate his power by similar acts of hospitality.[4] He invited 300 of the principal Persians to a feast and murdered every one. He provided a feast for his Persian guards, in number about 3,000, and, as soon as they were seated, caused them to be attacked and slain to a man. He then, in cool blood, put to death every Persian who had been in the service of the vanquished monarch, and reduced that wretched people to such prostration of spirit that it was common to see one Afghan lead to execution three or four Persians, who, though doomed unsparingly to death, made no resistance. Mahmood and two or three of his favourites, with their own sabres, massacred thirty-nine youths of the blood royal of Persia. Malcolm sums up the merits of the Afghan invader of Persia in a few words, which recent events prove to be entirely applicable to the nation at large at the present day.[5] " He appears to have combined in his character the most consummate deceit with the most ferocious barbarity." It is remarkable that the final consummation of the massacre of our brave but helpless troops, in the attempted retreat from Kabool at the commencement of 1842, was brought to pass by an exercise of Afghan hospitality. Six officers had made their way to within a few miles of Jelalabad, when, deceived by the friendly professions of some peasants, they stopped to satisfy their hunger with food brought them by the miscreants,[6] and, while partaking of the refreshment, were cut down by their villainous entertainers. This was the last specimen which the British allowed themselves to receive of the *Nung-du-pooshtauneh*, or "honour of the Afghan name."[7]

The rapacity of the Afghans is prominent among their many bad qualities, and seems universal, from Dost Mahomed Khan,[8] who plundered Honigberger, and Mahomed Shah Khan,[9] who robbed Lady Macnaghten of her clothes and jewels, to the Cauker wretch who stripped Masson,[1] leaving him nothing but his trowsers and shoes. They are formidable in war, being ruthless and bloodthirsty in the extreme—active and alert to take advantage of every opportunity; but they seem greatly deficient in intrepidity, and incapable of standing the charge of determined adversaries. This appears from their defeats by the Sikhs, and still more from their being unable on any occasion, with enormous superiority of numbers, to withstand the British troops, whose disasters were the result of the treachery of their adversaries, the

[4] Malcolm, ii. 8,9.

[5] Malcolm, ii. 10.

[6] Eyre, 251.

[7] Elph. 251.

[8] Trans. As. Soc. Beng. 1834, 246.
[9] Eyre, 289.

[1] Masson, i. 302.

severity of the season, and the unexampled strength of the
country. On the 29th of May, 1842, General Nott, at the
head of 1,200 men, defeated, in the space of an hour, 8,000
Afghans, driving them in the utmost confusion from a very
strong position close to Kandahar. The victor, with natural and
creditable exultation, observes,[2] "I would at any time lead 1,000
Bengal sepoys against 5,000 Afghans." On the 30th of September of the same year, General M'Caskill,[3] at the head of two
brigades of infantry about 2,000 strong, stormed the town of
Istalif, celebrated for its almost impregnable defences, and garrisoned by Afghans and Taujiks, in numbers five times those of
the assailants. It is worthy of note, that the Taujiks of Istalif
are considered the most ferocious and warlike of the inhabitants
of Afghanistan.[4] By some who seek in natural causes a solution
of every difficulty, the choleric and sanguinary disposition of
these Taujiks is attributed to the heating nature of their staple
article of food,[5] bread made of mulberries dried and ground to
meal. Elphinstone, who is in general favourable to the Afghan
character, draws a frightful picture when he particularizes the
state of society among them.[6] "Scarce a day passes without a
quarrel. If there is a dispute about water for cultivation on the
boundaries of a field, swords are drawn and wounds inflicted,
which leads to years of anxiety and danger and ends in assassination. Each injury produces fresh retaliation, and hence arise
ambuscades, attacks in the streets, murders of men in their
houses, and all kinds of suspicion, confusion, and strife. As
these feuds accumulate, there is scarce a man of any consequence
who is not upon the watch for his life. In every village are seen
men always in armour to secure them from the designs of their
secret enemies, and others surrounded by hired soldiers to the
number of ten, twelve, and sometimes of fifty or one hundred."
" Even within the clans there is nothing like peace or concord,
the slightest occasion gives rise to a dispute which soon turns
into an affray." " In most parts of the country the inhabitants live
in perpetual fear, like savages, and plough and sow with their
matchlocks and swords about their persons." No less conclusive
on this point is the evidence of Burnes.[7] " A week never passes
without strife or assassination ; and I have been assured, on the
best authority, that a man frequently remains immured in his
own *tower* for two or three years, for fear of his enemies, leaving

[2] Mil. Op. in Afg.
314.

[3] Mil. Op. in Afg.
412.

[4] Burnes' Pers.
Narr. 149.
Elph. 313.

[5] Burnes, Elph. ut
supra.

[6] Elph. 339.

[7] Pers. Narr. 149.

his wife to take charge of his property and discharge his duties ; nay, that in some instances, this durance has lasted for eight or ten years." The state of society here described is at Istalif, in the neighbourhood of Kabool. Such is the conduct of Afghan to Afghan. Elphinstone,[8] who regards the Afghan character with more complacency than most other observers, admits the existence of many of those detestable elements which enter into it, though he gives them credit for qualities which there is little evidence of their possessing. He says "their vices are revenge, envy, avarice, rapacity, and obstinacy. On the other hand, they are fond of liberty, faithful to their friends, kind to their dependants, hospitable, brave, hardy, laborious, and prudent; and they are less disposed than the nations in their neighbourhood to falsehood, intrigue, and deceit." This last position seems quite at variance with the testimony of historic fact.

Afghanistan, in its architecture and numismatic relics, presents an ample and interesting field of research to the antiquary, though written documents afford but a scanty light to his course. Still the labours of Wilson, Lassen, and Prinsep, employed upon materials furnished by the enterprise and industry of Masson and others, have succeeded to a surprising extent in illustrating the obscure and difficult subject to which they have been applied. The chief ruins now to be found in Afghanistan appear to belong to a period of very remote antiquity, and denote a people numerous and powerful, but not highly advanced in the arts, the slaves of superstition and of their rulers. Wood,[9] in describing Kafir Kote, on the border of the dreary valley of Largee, says, " Slavery would seem to have been prevalent in those days, for without such a supposition it is impossible to account for the remains of many similar structures in Afghanistan and the adjoining countries. Freemen would never have consented to the erection of such stupendous edifices on sites so arbitrarily chosen and so little calculated for the general good." This opinion, however, may be regarded by many as questionable. Wood considers those erections coeval in their origin with the pyramids of Egypt, the round towers of Ireland, and the sculptured caves and undeciphered antiquities of Hindostan, and that those who constructed them were by some political convulsion swept away before the time of the Macedonian irruption. Ritter,[1] on the contrary, assigns to their construction the prolonged period

[8] 253.

[9] Oxus, 94.

[1] Erdkunde von Asien, B. vii. 206, S.

commencing eight centuries before the Christian era and terminating eight centuries after it, during which, according to him,
Buddhism universally prevailed in Afghanistan and the adjacent
countries, until destroyed by the furious fanaticism of the Mahomedans. He consequently regards the Macedonian irruption as
having produced a very circumscribed effect on the opinions and
condition of the people at large.

Several great relics of remote periods in Afghanistan, the caves
and gigantic idols of Bamian,[2] the fortress of Kafir Kote, already
mentioned, Zohak Castle, in the vicinity of Bamian, the ruined
city of Ghulghuleh, in the same vicinity, and the fortress of Saiyadabad, also at no great distance, are described under their respective
names. The *topes* of the natives, the *stupas* of the Sanscrit authorities, are vast and solid masses of masonry of the shape of
short cylinders surmounted by hemispherical domes. They are of
most frequent occurrence in the plain of Peshawur and in the valleys of Jelalabad, of Kabool, and of Begram, north of the town of
Kabool. Similar remains are also found in the Punjab, especially in
the parts adjacent to the Indus. It is the most received opinion
that they are monuments peculiar to the faith of Buddhism, or
shrines inclosing some sacred relic—a hair, a tooth, a bone, a walk-
ing-stick, for instance, of some character deemed by the Buddhists
to have been eminent for sanctity;[3] though Court, Masson, and
some other authorities consider them to have been places of regal
sepulture. Prinsep[4] and Ritter are indeed inclined to consider
both opinions correct to a certain extent, and to regard these
monuments as at once places of burial for the great and depositories of superstitious relics. The size of any hitherto surveyed in Afghanistan is insignificant compared with some mentioned by Professor Wilson as having been constructed in Ceylon 400 feet high.[4]

The most interesting department of archæology connected
with Afghanistan is the numismatical. No country has produced
such vast quantities of antique coins as have been and are daily
collected by turning up its earth. Masson, during the researches
of several years, collected many thousands. Some account of
his success will be found under the head Begram.

It is remarkable that though numismatology displays to us
such numerous and important traces of the Greeks, there are no
architectural remains which can be attributed to them. The vast
ruined fortresses of Kafir Kote, Zohak, Saiyadabad, and Ghulghuleh are built generally in a massive style,[5] and exhibit great

[2] Burnes, i. 182;
Moore. Punj.Bok.
ii. 386; Masson,
Bal. Afg. Punj. ii.
ch. xv.; Elph.153;
Sale, Disasters in
Afg. 423; Eyre,
Mil. Op. at Cau-
bul, 361.

[3] Wilson, Ariana
Antiqua, 45; Rit-
ter, Erdkunde
von Asien, v. 208.
[4] Quoted in Ari-
ana Antiqua, 45.

[4] Ariana Antiq. 4.

[5] Wood, Oxus,
93.

architectural skill, but without any thing that appears indicative of Grecian art. In the case of the three latter, the material is kiln-burnt bricks, of such superior quality as to have in a wonderful degree resisted the assaults both of men and of the inclement climate.

The towns of Afghanistan are few in proportion to its extent: the principal are Kabool, Kandahar, Herat, Peshawur, Dera Ghazee Khan, Dera Ismael Khan, Ghuznee, Istalif, Charikar, Jelalabad, Kala Bagh, Kohat, Giriskh, Furrah, Subzawur, and Mittunkote. (See their respective names.)

E.I.C. Ms. Doc.

AGAUM, in Afghanistan, is a village in the district of Jelalabad. It is situated in a well-watered tract, abounding in gardens and rich cultivation, and studded with villages as far as the eye can reach. Lat. 34° 25', long. 70° 26'.

Pottinger, Beloochistan, 301; Jour. As. Soc. 1839, p. 103; Carloss, Acc. of Jour. to Beylah; Jour. As. Soc. 1840, p. 147-150; Hart, Acc. of Jour. from Kurrachee to Hinglaj.

AGHOR, or HINGOL RIVER, in Beloochistan, rises in the mountains in the north of Lus, and, taking a southerly course, falls into the Arabian Sea, in lat. 25° 19', long. 65° 26'. Its stream never intermits, as most of those in this arid region, and when inundated by the melting of the snows on the mountains, it acquires a considerable volume of water. Where surveyed by Hart, about six miles from its mouth, it was found to be sixty yards wide and one foot and a-half deep, in January, when its stream is not swelled by melted snow. Its water is regarded as unwholesome, in consequence of the sand suspended in it. Near its right bank is the cave of Hinglaj, a celebrated place of pilgrimage, and in the bed of the river is a deep abyss, regarded by the credulous natives as unfathomable. The Aghor, or the Hingol as it is called in the uppermost part of its course, forms the boundary between the dominions of the Jam, or ruler of Lus, and the Khan of Kelat.

E.I.C. Ms. Doc.

AGRA.—A small village in Sinde, lying on one of the routes from Sehwan to Larkhana, is situate fifty-five miles north of the former place and two miles from the west bank of the Indus. The surrounding country, part of the insulated district of Chandkoh, is fertile and well cultivated, Lat. 27° 8', long. 68° 2'.

AHMEDABAD.—A fortress in Sinde, called also DEEJY, which see.

E.I.C. Ms. Doc.

AHMED KHAN.—A village in Sinde, on the route from Kurrachee to Sehwan. Lat. 25° 29', long. 67° 53'.

Leech, Rep. on Sindh. Army, 89.

AHMED KHAN KA MAGHA.—A small town of Afghanistan, on the route from Shawl, or Quetta, to Ghuznee. Its posi-

tion is assigned, apparently from the report of natives, in lat. 31°
21', long. 67° 20'.

AHMED KHAN'S TANDA.—A large village of Sinde, in E.I.C. Ms. Doc.
the route from Sehwan to Kurrachee, sixty-eight miles north-east
of the latter place, about two miles south-west of Murraie Mukam, and lying above that place, on the river Murraie.   Lat. 25°
27', long. 67° 54'.

AHMEDPOOR.—A village in the Punjab.   Lat. 30° 34', E.I.C. Ms. Doc.
long. 71° 46'.

AHMEDPOOR.—A town in Bhawlpoor, sometimes called Leech, Sindh.
Barra, or " the great," to distinguish it from Ahmedpoor Chuta, Army, 81 ; Burnes'
Bokh. iii.221 ;
or " the little," in the same country.   It is situate seventeen Masson, Bal. Afg.
Panj. i. 22 ;
miles east of the Punjund river, on the route from the city of Hough, Narr.Exp.
Bhawlpoor to Khanpoor, and thirty miles south-west of the in Afg. 12 ; Havelock, War in Afg.
former place.   It was originally a military cantonment only, but i. 112; Atkinson,
Exp. into Afg. 74.
having been chosen as a residence of the Khans of Bhawlpoor,
in consequence of its vicinity to the fortress of Derawal in the
desert, it has become a place of considerable importance.   The
country around is saturated with moisture, so that water can
everywhere be obtained by sinking wells to a slight depth.   The
water thus abundantly available is raised by the Persian wheel,
and poured over the surface of the soil, which is divided into
small inclosures or beds of about twenty feet square.   Under this
management, the ground brings forth very luxuriant crops.
" The verdure of each bed," observes Atkinson, " was of the
brightest hue, the trees were numerous, roundly formed and full
of foliage, which gave a richly picturesque garden-look to the
whole view."   The heat in summer is intense, and, acting on
the moist soil, renders the air very unhealthy ; but the means
of subsistence being abundant, the country is populous.   The
Khan takes much interest in the improvement of the town, and
has lately built a sort of fort as a residence.   There is a large and
lofty mosque with four tall minarets, but the private houses are
in general meanly built of mud.   Ahmedpoor has manufactures of
matchlocks, gunpowder, cotton, silks, and loongees, or fabrics for
scarfs in which the two materials last mentioned are combined.
The population may probably be about 20,000.*   Lat. 29° 8',
long. 71° 15'.

* Hough (p. 12) states it at 30,000 ; Atkinson (p. 75) at between 9,000
and 10,000.

Leech, Sindh. **AHMEDPOOR CHUTA** (or "the little "), a town of Bhawl-
Army, 81; Masson Bal. Afg. Panj. pöor, so called to distinguish it from Ahmedpoor Barra, or "the
i. 21, 23. great," from which it is distant sixty-five miles south-west. Notwithstanding the appendage to its name, it is far from being an inconsiderable town. It is inclosed with mud walls, and has a few scattered works, built of burned bricks, intended as defences, though, from their very unskilful construction, very ill-adapted to answer the purpose. Before the annexation of Sub-zuleote to the Bhawlpoor territory, in February, 1843, Ahmedpoor was the frontier town toward Sinde, defended by six cannon and between 300 and 400 men. Lat. 28° 17', long. 69° 48'.

AIRUL.—See Arul.

E.I.C. Ms. Doc. AISABAD.—A village in Afghanistan, on the route from Herat to Kandahar. Lat. 33° 22', long. 62° 20'.

Hough, 355. AKALIGURH, in the Punjab; a large town a little south of the route from Ramnuggur to Lahore. Is so called from having been built and peopled by the Akalis (*immortals*) or fanatic Sikhs, who live here in a state of desperate independence of the Sikh government, but are tolerated on account of their ferocious valour in foreign wars. Lat. 32° 17', long. 73° 37'.

E.I.C. Ms. Doc. AKKEHU.—A village situate in the north of Afghanistan. Lat. 36° 50', long. 66° 7'.

E.I.C. Ms. Doc. AKMUK.—A village in Afghanistan, on the right bank of the Helmund. Lat. 31° 31', long. 64° 10'.

[1] Journ. As. Soc. of Bengal, 1841, 113; Von Hugel, i. 154. AKNUR,[1] in the Northern Punjab, is situate on the banks of the Chenaub, here a very large river. At the beginning of August, when largest, it was found by Broome and Cunningham to have seven channels, the broadest* 920 yards wide, some of the others breast deep, and all having very rapid streams. The Chenaub is navigable downwards, from a point a short distance [2] Vigne, Kashmir, i. 217; Macartney in Elph. 660. above Aknur to the sea.[2] The town, though mostly in ruins, has a very fine and picturesque appearance when viewed from without, the remains of the old palace being strikingly contrasted with the buildings of the new fort. Here is a ferry over the river. Aknur is situated at the base of the lowest or most southern range of the Himalaya, where it first rises above the plain of the Punjaub. Lat. 32° 42', long. 74° 41'.

---

* Vigne states the breadth of the river at Aknur, in the beginning of July, at 100 yards. (i. 221.)

AKORA, the chief town of a small district of the same name belonging to the Khuttuks, is situate on the south or right bank of the Kabool river, about ten miles above its confluence with the Indus at Attock. At the commencement of the present century, it was a considerable and prosperous town, with a neat mosque and a handsome bazaàr, built of stone ; but has been nearly laid in ruins by the Sikhs. Lat. 34° 3′, long. 72° 10′. *Elph. Acc. of Caubul, 72, 300 ; Moorcr. Panj. Bokh. ii. 333 ; Forster, Jour. Beng. Eng. ii. 51; Burnes' Bokh. i. 82; Hough, Narr. of Exp. to Afg. 333.*

AK SERAI.—A village in Afghanistan, twenty-two miles north of Kabool. Lat. 34° 45′, long. 69° 16′. *E.I.C. Ms. Doc.*

ALEE BOOLGHAN.—See ALI BOGHAN.

ALEM KHAN.—A village in Afghanistan, in the Daman, near the right bank of the Indus. Lat. 30° 23′, long. 70° 50′. *E.I.C. Ms. Doc.*

ALGHOEE.—A village in Afghanistan, nine miles north of Kabool. Lat. 34° 34′, long. 69° 1′. *E.I.C. Ms. Doc.*

ALIABAD.—A village in Western Afghanistan, on the Adruscund river. Lat. 33° 24′, long. 62° 18′. *E.I.C. Ms. Doc.*

ALIAR-KA-TANDA.—See ALLA-YAR-KA-TANDA.

ALI BAGH.—A village in Sinde, in the eastern desert. Lat. 27° 1′, long. 69° 43′. *E I.C. Ms. Doc.*

ALI BOGHAN,[1] called also Surkh Dewar,[2] in Afghanistan, is a small town giving name to a range of hills on the eastern boundary of the valley of Jelalabad, and situate about ten miles east of that town. Here, in October, 1842, the British army, under General Pollock, encamped on its march homewards, after destroying the fortifications of Jelalabad. Lat. 34° 20′, long. 70° 34′. Elevation above the sea 1,911 feet.[3] *[1] Milit. Op. in Afg. 424 ; Wood, Mass. Bal. Afg. Panj. iii. 334 ; Jour. As. Soc. 1842, p. 118 ; MacGregor, Geogr. Notice of Valley of Jullalabad ; E.I.C. Ms. Map. [2] Moorcr. Panj. Bokh. ii. 356. [3] Hough, Narr. of Exp. to Afg. 304.*

ALI BUNDER.—In Sinde, a small town on the Gonnee, one of the offsets of the Indus to the east. Here is a dam made in 1799 by Futteh Ali, one of the Ameers of Sinde. This, according to Pottinger,[1] was "the only work of public utility ever made by one of the reigning family," being intended to retain the water of the river for the purposes of irrigation, and to exclude the salt water, which, sent upwards by the tide, rendered sterile the surrounding country. This barrier had the natural consequence of causing in the channel of the Gonnee a deposit of alluvial matter, which is gradually filling it ; so that, though formerly navigable throughout the year, this branch of the Indus had in 1809 become so shallow, that boats could ply only during four months of the inundation between Ali Bunder and Hyderabad. The channel below Ali Bunder has also become nearly obliterated,[2] though *[1] Beloochis. 358. [2] Burnes' Bokh. iii. 239, 311, 312.*

formerly by far the greatest estuary of the Indus. The contiguous
part of Cutch also suffered the most disastrous consequences from
the water being cut off; the district of Sayra, formerly remarkable for fertility, ceasing to yield a blade of vegetation, and becoming part of the Runn, or Great Salt Desert, on which it bor-
dered. Ali Bunder is in lat. 24° 18′, long. 69° 14′.

ALI MUSJID, in Afghanistan, is a fort in the Khyber Pass,
about eight miles from its eastern entrance, and is so called from
a small ruined mosque in its neighbourhood.[1] The width of the
pass here is about 150 yards;[*2] the elevation above the sea is
2,433 feet. The fort is built on a peaked oblong rock,[3] about
600 feet high, nearly isolated, and with almost perpendicular
sides. It is commanded at a distance of 300 yards by two positions,[4] one to its south, the other to its west, from which it could
be breached and the garrison dislodged by shells; at its base[5]
flows the torrent which holds its way towards the eastern entrance of the pass. There is no water within the fort, but the
garrison might be supplied from a well to which (according to
Hough[6]) there is a covered way. The water, however, though
beautifully clear,[7] is very unwholesome, in consequence, it is said,
of being impregnated with antimony,[8] the spring rising from under
a rock composed of the sulphuret of that metal. It appears, indeed, that all the water in the neighbourhood is so impregnated.
From this or some other cause, the mortality by sickness of the
British troops posted here in 1839 was frightful; of 2,442 no less
than 243 died in fifty-seven days. The fort at the time of its
capture by the British army was 150 feet long,[9] and sixty wide;
it consisted of two small castles joined by a dilapidated wall; the
whole inclosed space was 300 feet by 200, and a garrison of
500 or 600 men might be contained within the walls. Leech[1]
remarks, " It is situated at too great a height to be of much service in stopping a force passing below, while at the same time
the steepness of the hill on which it is built would be a great
obstacle to the same force storming it, which would be absolutely
necessary to secure the passage of the main body or baggage in
safety;" and Hough adds, " The garrison could not hold out
against an enemy using shells; from the narrowness of the pass
and the height of the fort, there could not be a *plunging fire* from

* Moorcroft states that the defile here is in no place above twenty-five
paces broad, and in some not more than six or seven (ii. 349).

E.I.C. Ms. Map.

[1] Leech, Khyber Pass, 10 ; Wood, Khyber Pass, 3.
[2] Hough, Narr. of Exp. to Afg. 312.
[3] Moorcr. Punj. Bokh. ii. 340 ; Mil. Op. in Afg. 133.
[4] Hough, 235 ; Allen, March through Sinde and Afg. 355.
[5] Havelock, War in Afg. ii. 101.
[6] Narr. of Exp. to Afg. 313.
[7] Burnes' Pers. Narr. 131 ; Mass. Bal. Afg. Panj. i. 140.
[8] Reid, quoted in Hough, 315, n. 18.
[9] Hough, 312 ; Mil. Op. in Afg. 40, 133.
[1] Ut supra, 10.

above." In July, 1839, the British force under Lieutenant Macke-
son, investing the fort, took up a position[2] from which shells could [2] Hough, 233;
be thrown into it, and it was immediately evacuated by the Afghan Havelock. ii. 131.
garrison. In November, 1841, it was invested by a large force
of Afghan insurgents, whilst the garrison holding it for the British government consisted only of 150 of the Eusufzai[3] tribe, [3] Mil. Op. in Afg.
who remained faithful to their engagements and maintained their 39.
post until reinforced, though the enemy had succeeded in cutting
off the water,[4] blowing up some of the defences, and establishing [4] Id. 40.
a position from which they galled the defenders with their *jezails*
or long rifles. In the January following,[5] when a fruitless attempt [5] Id. 128.
was made by General Wild to force the Khyber Pass, the garrison
was reinforced by two regiments, who, a few days afterwards,
succeeded in evacuating the fort, with the loss,[6] however, of thirty- [6] Id. 132-134.
two men killed and 148 wounded. On the opening of the Khyber
Pass in the beginning of 1842, a garrison was again posted here
by General Pollock,[7] and on the final evacuation of the country [7] Id. 232, 233.
in November of the same year, it was entirely destroyed[8] by order [8] Id. 423.
of General Nott. Ali Musjid is in lat. 34° 3 , long. 71° 20'.

ALINGAR,[1] called also the Kow, a river of Afghanistan, [1] Mass. Bal. Afg.
rising in Hindoo Koosh, and running south-west a distance of about Panj. i.208, iii.288.
100 miles, until it joins the Alishang in the district of Lughman,
and in lat. 34° 50', long. 70° 8'. After a farther course of twenty-
five miles, the united stream falls into the river of Kabool on its
northern side, in lat. 34° 36', long. 70° 4'. It derives its appellation from the valley of Alingar[2] (part of the present district of [2] Baber, Mem.143.
Lughman), through which it flows. Elphinstone,[3] from native [3] Acc. of Caubul,
reports, describes this valley as very fertile, especially in grain. 98.

ALIPHUR, in the Punjab, a small town on the route from Hough, 360.
Surrukpoor to Ferozpoor. Here a road branches off on the north
to Lahore. Lat. 31° 18', long. 74° 10'.

ALIPOOR, a village in Sinde, on the left or eastern bank of Burnes' Bokh.
the Indus. It is the usual landing-place for communication with iii. 60.
Khyerpoor, by means of the river. Lat. 27° 40', long. 68° 36'.

ALIPOOR, a village in the Punjab, situate on the road from E.I.C. Ms. Doc.
Lahore to Ramnuggur, six miles from the latter place. Lat. 32°
18', long. 73° 39'.

ALISHANG,[1] or river of Nadjil, in Afghanistan, rises in [1] Masson, Bal.Afg.
the unexplored tract called Nadjil, on the southern slope of Panj. I. 207, 208,
Hindoo Koosh, and flows southwards for about ninety miles, until iii. 288.

E 2

it joins the Alingar, flowing from the north-east. The confluence
is at Tirgaree, in the province of Lughman, and in lat. 34° 50′,
long. 70° 8′. For the course of the united stream, see *Alingar.*

[2] Court, Conjec-
tures on the
March of Alexan-
der, in Jour. As.
Soc. 1836, p. 302;
Baber, Mem. 142;
Ayeen Akbery, ii.
181; Eph. 99.
E.I.C. Ms. Doc. There are also in the province of Lughman a valley and a town,
each called Alishang, but scarcely any thing is known of either
but the name.[2]

ALIZYE.—A village in Afghanistan, situate near the junction
of two roads, one from Kandahar, and the other from Babur-ka-
killa to Quetta, from which place it is distant about forty miles.
Lat. 30° 40′, long. 66° 50′.

Masson, Bal. Afg.
Panj. i. 19-21. ALLAHABAD.—A town of Bhawlpoor, twenty-five miles
south-west of Ahmedpoor. Lat. 28° 53′, long. 70° 58′.

Burnes, Rep. on
Com. of Hydera-
bad, 20; Bokhara,
iii. 227. ALLA-YAR-KA-TANDA.—A town in Sinde, twenty miles
east of Hyderabad. It is situate at the intersection of the two
great routes from Hyderabad eastward, and from Cutch to Upper
Sinde and the Punjab. It has some manufactures, principally
in cotton and in dyeing. Population 5,000. Lat. 25° 21′, long.
68° 40′.

E.I.C. Ms. Doc. ALLI JAH'S KILLA.—A village in Afghanistan, thirty-six
miles north-east of Ghuznee. Lat. 33° 41′, long. 68° 50′.

ALMA-DI-GOT.—See Amrajee Kote.

ALTUMGOT.—See Amrajee Kote.

E.I.C. Ms. Doc. ALTUMOOR.—A village in Afghanistan, s.   ⸱e in the
Sufeid Koh mountains. Lat. 33° 57′, long. 69° 35′.

Jour. As. Soc.
1840, p. 031; Co-
nolly (E.), Notes
on the Eusufzyes,
931; Burnes, Pol.
Pow. of Sikhs, 1. AM, in Afghanistan, is a stronghold on the right or north-
western bank of the Indus, and inclosed between that river and the
lofty and thickly-wooded range of the Mabeen Hills, an offset
of the Himalaya. The only access to it is from the south, by a
difficult path, cut in the face of the rock, which overhangs the
river. It is held by Paiendah-Khan, a Mussulman freebooter of
Mogul descent, who, though having no other possessions than
this, with the adjacent stronghold of Chutter-bai, and a few villages on the east bank of the Indus, has uniformly lived in open
defiance of the Sikh power, and with impunity plundered its
territory for the means of supporting his small armed force. Am
is about fifty miles north-east of Attock, and in lat. 34° 17′,
long. 72° 54′.

'E.I.C. Ms. Doc. AMAWANEE. — A village in the Punjab. Lat. 31° 20′,
long. 71° 45′.

Moorcroft, i. 119. AMB.—A small town in the Punjab, close to the southern

base of the Himalaya, and on the route from Lahore to Nadaun.
Lat. 31° 40′, long. 76° 10′.

AMBAR.—A village in Afghanistan, on the route from the E.I.C. Ms. Doc.
Derajat to Kandahar, by the Buzdar Pass. Lat. 29° 51′, long.
70° 12′.

AMDABAD.—A village in the Punjab, situate two miles E.I.C. Ms. Doc.
from the right bank of the Jailum river. Lat. 32° 33′, long.
72° 42′.

AMEENANA.—A town in Sinde, on the route from Lar- E.I.C. Ms. Doc.
khana to Sehwan, and twelve miles north of the latter place. It
is situate in the fertile island formed by the Narra and the Indus,
and two miles west of the latter river. It is a considerable place,
supplied with water from wells. Lat. 26° 31′, long. 67° 55′.

AMEEN-LA-KA-JO-GOTE.—A village in Sinde, two miles E.I.C. Ms. Doc.
from the left bank of the Indus. Lat. 25° 56′, long. 68° 23′.

AMEER ALTALTA.—A village in Sinde, situate on the
right bank of the Indus. Lat. 26° 40′, long. 67° 56′.

AMERKOTE.—See OMERCOTE.

AMIL GOT.—A village in Sinde, near a ferry over the E.I.C. Ms. Doc.;
Indus, on the route from Subzulcote to Shikarpoor, and about Havelock, War in
Afg. i. 116;
twenty miles east of the latter place. It is situate about a mile Hough, Narr. of
Exp. in Afg. 15.
from the right bank of the Indus, in a fine plain. Water for any
considerable number of persons must be brought from the river,
as the village has only a small well. At this ferry, the army of
Shah Shoojah, amounting to 6,000 men, passed in January,
1839. The passage occupied seven days. Lat. 27° 53′, long.
68° 58′.

AMOO MAHOMED.—A village in Afghanistan, twenty- E.I.C. Ms. Doc.
five miles south of Lake Ab-istada. Lat. 32° 8′, long. 67° 45′.

AMRAJEE KOTE.[1]—A small town in Sinde, situate on the [1] Rough Notes,
left or eastern bank of the Indus, sixteen miles above Tatta. It 28; Burnes (J.),
Mission to Sinde,
corresponds, according to the statement of Outram, with Alum- 38.
gote in the quartermaster-general's MS. map, and Altumgot in
that of Walker, to which they assign lat. 24° 51′, long. 68° 4′,
and seems to be the place mentioned by Masson[2] under the name [2] Bal. Afg. Panj. i.
of Alma-di-got. 467.

AMRAN MOUNTAINS,[1] in Afghanistan, are a range bound- [1] E.I.C. Ms. Doc.
ing the table-lands of Shawl and Pisheen on the west, as the
Hala range does to the east. The elevated tract thus bounded
connects the highlands of Tukatoo and the Toba mountains with

2 Hough's Narr.
of Exp. in Afg. 81;
Jour. As. Soc.
1842, p. 56; Grif.
Bar. and Ther.
Obs.; Conolly,
Jour. to India, ii.
125
3 Elph. Acc. of
Caubul, 105, 124.
4 In Map to Elph.
5 War in Afg. i.
253.
E.I.C. Ms. Doc.

those about Kelat. The Kojuk Pass traverses this range, and as the summit of the pass is 7,457 feet[2] above the sea, and the summits of the Amran mountains are about 1,200 feet higher, the total elevation of the highest part of the range can be little less than 9,000 feet. This is the range called by Elphinstone,[3] Macartney,[4] and Havelock,[5] Khojah-Amraun. Lat. 30° 50′, long. 66° 30′.

AMREE.—A village in Sinde, on the route from Kotree, near Hyderabad, to Sehwan, and twenty-four miles south-east of this latter place. Amree is situate on the right bank of the Indus; it is a small and apparently a poor village, but there is much green cultivation near it. There is a small hill, about fifty feet high, on its north side, from which a great extent of cultivation is discernible in the dry bed of an offset of the Indus, running a considerable distance to the north-west. The road here is in general good, though occasionally rendered rather difficult by deep sands and sand-hills. Lat. 26° 7′, long. 68° 2′.

E.I.C. Ms. Doc

AMREE NULLAH, in Sinde, a water-course crossing the route between Sehwan and Kurrachee, eight miles east of the latter place. It takes a direction from north to south of about ten miles, and falls into the Gisry in lat. 24° 52′, long. 67° 15′.

E.I.C. Ms. Doc.

AMRIE.—A small river in Beloochistan, rises in the Pubb mountains, near the frontier of Sinde, and after a southerly course of about twelve miles, joins the Vehrab river in lat. 25° 40′, long. 67° 10′.

AMRITSIR.—A city of the Punjab, is situate nearly half-way between the rivers Beas and Ravee. According to Baron Von Hügel,[1] it is a larger town than Lahore, and the wealthiest and most commercial place in Northern India. It owes its importance to a *Tulao* or reservoir, which Ram Das, the fourth *Guru*, or spiritual guide of the Sikhs, caused to be made here in 1581, and named Amrita Saras, or "fount of immortality." It thenceforward became a place of pilgrimage, and bore the names Amritsir and Ramdaspoor. Nearly two centuries after, Ahmed Shah, the founder of the Durani empire, alarmed and enraged at the progress of the Sikhs, blew up the shrine with gunpowder, filled up the holy *Tulao*, and causing kine to be slaughtered upon the site, thus desecrated the spot, which was drenched with their gore. On his return to Kabool, the Sikhs repaired the shrine and reservoir, and commenced the struggle

1 iii. 400; Burnes'
Bokhara, iii. 176;
Malcolm on the
Sikhs, 29; Wolff,
Jour in Afg. and
Punjaub, 351-353.

which terminated in the overthrow of Mahomedan sway in Hindostan. The *Tulao* is a square of 150 paces, containing a great body of water, pure as crystal, notwithstanding the multitudes that bathe in it, and supplied apparently by natural springs. In the middle, on a small island, is a temple of Hari or Vishnu ; and on the bank a diminutive structure, where the founder, Ram Das, is said to have spent his life in a sitting posture. The temple on the island is richly adorned with gold and other costly embellishments, and in it sits the sovereign *Guru* of the Sikhs, to receive the presents and homage of his followers.[2] There are five or six hundred Akalees or priests attached to the temple, who have erected for themselves good houses from the contributions of the visitors. [2 Asiatic Ann.Reg. ii. 430; Leech on Multan, 79.]

Amritsir is a very populous and extensive place. The streets are narrow, but the houses in general are tolerably lofty and built of burnt brick. The apartments, however, are small, but on the whole Amritsir may claim some little architectural superiority over the towns of Hindostan. It has spacious bazaars[3] furnished with the richest wares ; it has also considerable manufactures of coarse cloths and inferior silks, but especially of fine shawls, made in imitation of the Kashmir fabric, in which great quantities of goats' wool from Bokhara are consumed. There is besides a very extensive transit trade, as well as considerable monetary transactions with Hindostan and Central Asia, the prosperity of the place having, in these respects, resulted from the decay of Shikarpoor and Mooltan. Rock salt is brought on the backs of camels from a mine near Mundi,[4] about 120 miles to the northward of Lahore, a large and solid lump, resembling a block of unwrought marble, being slung on each side of the animal. [3 Moorcr. Punj. Bokhara, i. 114; Leech, viii.3, p.79; Burnes, Trade of the Derajat, 98-101.] [4 Moorcr. Punj. Bokhara, i. 159; Vigne, Kashmir, i. 101.]

Runject Singh constructed a canal from the Ravee, a distance of thirty-four miles, but it is a mean and inexpensive work. The most striking object in Amritsir is the huge fortress Govindghur, built by Runjeet Sing in 1809, ostensibly to protect the pilgrims, but in reality to overawe their vast and dangerous assemblage. Its great height and heavy batteries, rising one above the other, give it a very imposing appearance. It contained, at the time of Hügel's visit,[5] the treasure of Runject Singh, computed to amount to 30,000,000l. sterling, a sum which there is good reason to believe greatly exaggerated. [5 iii. 309.]

Here also is the mint of the Sikh government. According to
Hügel,[6] all the wealth of the Punjab is accumulated in Amritsir,
and as it is larger than Lahore, its population is probably about
120,000. Lat. 31° 42', long. 74° 47'.

6 S. 400.

AMURGURH.—A fortress in the north of the Punjab, situate
two or three miles to the right of the route from Lahore to Kashmir.
It belonged to Dyhan Singh, a powerful vassal of the Maharaja
of the Sikhs. The jealous aversion of the proprietor has prevented any European from closely surveying it, but Vigne, who
at a distance examined it by means of a telescope, states it to be
built on the precipitous bank of a ravine to the westward of it.
The outline is rectangular, and though built of stone and of
very solid masonry, it must fall before a regular attack, being
commanded from other eminences at no great distance. It is
supposed to contain a large treasure and a magazine of artillery, ammunition, and small-arms, surreptitiously taken by Dyhan
from Runjeet Singh. Lat. 32° 55', long. 74° 11'.

Kashmir, i. 245.

AMURNATH.—A cave amidst the mountains bounding
Kashmir on the north-east. It is a natural opening in a rock of
gypsum, and is, according to Vigne,[1] about thirty yards high and
twenty deep, but Moorcroft[2] states it to be 100 yards wide, thirty
high, and 500 deep. It is believed by the Hindoos to be the
residence of the deity Siva, and is hence visited by great crowds
of both sexes and all ages. A great number of doves inhabit the
cave, and these, being frightened by the shouts and tumultuous
supplications of the pilgrims, fly out, and are considered thus to be
evidence of a favourable answer to the prayers offered ; the deity
being supposed to come forth in the shape of one of these birds.
Amongst other fables, it is asserted that those who enter the
cave can hear the barking of the dogs in Thibet. It is mentioned
by Hügel[3] under the name of Oumrath. Lat. 34° 17', long.
75° 32'.

1 Kashmir, ii. 10.

2 Punj. Bokh. ii.
200.

3 P. Von Hugel,
Kashmir, ii. 190.

E.I.C. Ms. Doc.

ANARDURRA.—A village in Western Afghanistan, situate
on the Haroot or Subzawur river. Lat. 32° 46', long. 61° 50'.

E.I.C. Ms. Doc.

ANDAVRE.—A village in Afghanistan. Lat. 33° 45', long.
71° 59'.

Burnes on Herat,
48 ; Wils. in Pref.
Moorcr. Travels,
x. L. vii. ; Wood,
Oxus, 407.

ANDKHOO.—A town in Afghanistan, on the northern
slope of the Huzareh mountains. It is ruled by a petty chieftain,
generally dependent on Kabool, though occasionally assuming a
precarious independence. He has several Arabs in his service,

and can bring 500 horse into the field. The population, consisting of Soonnee Mahomedans, is considerable, and the situation advantageous, being on the route to Balkh, but the country suffers from the want of water, though the town itself is seated on a stream of some importance, which, flowing northwards from the Huzareh mountains, is lost in the lowlands of Bokhara, Here is grown a sort of wheat which produces its grain for three years. Andkhoo has a melancholy interest, as being the place of the death of Moorcroft, who came here to purchase horses. Lat. 36° 54′, long. 65° 23′.

ANGEERA.[1]—A halting-place in Beloochistan, on the route from Kelat to Sonmeance, and sixty miles south of the former place. It is situate in a plain and on a water-course, one of the sources of the Moola river, which flows down the Gundava Pass to Cutch Gundava. It was formerly inhabited by Beloochees of the Zechree tribe, but was found deserted at the end of 1839, when the British army, under General Willshire, after storming Kelat, passed it, marching to Sinde by the Gundava Pass. The road at Angeera divides; one branch proceeding southwards to Sonmeeanee, the other eastwards through the Moola or Gundava Pass. At a short distance to the south[2] are the remains of massive and extensive ramparts, skilfully constructed to secure the passes in that direction. Pottinger,[3] in the beginning of February, found the cold intense; the water in the water-bags being frozen into a solid mass. This fact is readily explainable by reference to the elevation of the plain above the level of the sea, which is 5,250 feet. Angeera is situate in lat. 28° 10′, long. 66° 12′.

[1] E.I.C. Ms. Doc.; Outram, Rough Notes, 255.

[2] Masson, Kal. 63.

[3] Beloochistan, 27.

ANGHORIAN.—A village in Afghanistan, eight miles south of Kandahar. Lat. 31° 31′, long. 65° 28′. E.I.C. Ms. Doc.

ANIAN.—A village in Afghanistan, situate on the right bank of the Indus. Lat. 34° 5′, long. 72° 24′. E.I.C. Ms. Doc.

ANJEERA.—See ANGEERA.

ANJYRUK.—A village in Afghanistan. Lat. 35° 35′, long. 64° 10′. E.I.C. Ms. Doc.

ANTRE ROUSTAM.—A village in Afghanistan. Lat. 34° 28′, long. 72° 12′. E.I.C. Ms. Doc.

AOWBUH.—A village in Afghanistan, situate on the Heri-Rood, or Hury river. Lat. 34° 19′, long. 63° 7′. E.I.C. Ms. Doc.

ARABUL, in Kashmir, a beautiful cataract on the Veshau, Vigne, i. 207.

one of the principal tributaries of the Bchut or Jailum. Lat.
33° 35′, long. 74° 40′.

ARAK.—See ERAK.

E.I.C. Ms. Doc.   AREDO.—A village in Afghanistan, situate on the Alishang
river. Lat. 35° 6′, long. 70° 8′.

E.I.C. Ms. Doc.   AREEJAW, in Sinde, a large village on the route from Sehwan to Larkhana, in the fertile island inclosed between the
Indus and its offset the Narra. It is situate eight miles a little
west of south from Larkhana, the same distance west of the
Indus, and one mile east of the Narra. Lat. 27° 22′, long. 68°
12′.

[1] Elph. Acc. of Caubul, 116;   ARGHASAN, or URGHESSANN.[1]—A river in Afghanistan,
Masson, Bal. Afg. rising in the western declivity of the Amran mountains, and
Panj. ii. 186.   flowing westward to its confluence with the Turnak, about lat.
31° 31′, long. 65° 30′. It is a rapid transient torrent, seldom
retaining any depth of water for more than two or three days, and
leaving its bed dry for the greater part of the year. It was
[2] Havelock, War in Afg. i. 330. found totally devoid of water[2] when the British army marched
across it in 1839.

E.I.C. Ms. Doc.   ARS BEGHEE, in Afghanistan, is a small walled town,
about sixty-two miles a little west of south from Ghuznee, and
about twelve miles north-west of Ab-istada lake. It is situate on
the great route from Ghuznee to Shawl, in a very fertile country.
Lat. 32° 48′, long. 67° 41′.

Outram, 47; Burnes' Pers. Narr. 41; Kennedy, i. 176.   ARUL, or AIRUL, in Sinde, is a water-course, or channel,
proceeding from the south-eastern part of Lake Manchur (an ex-
pansion of the Narra), and discharging its water into the Indus,
on the western side, about four miles below Sehwan, after a
course of about twelve miles. At Sehwan it is a deep, sluggish
stream 200 feet wide. The Narra, the lake, and the Arul form a
continuous channel communicating at both extremities with the
Indus, and running for above 200 miles nearly parallel to it on
the western side.* As the current is very moderate in this

* Outram, on the authority of Holland, states (p. 46) that the Arul is a
regurgitation from the main stream of the Indus in an opposite or northerly
direction, expanding into Lake Manchur, and in this he is followed by Pos-
Jour. As. Soc. tans; but Westmacott, who gives a minute, well-digested, and probably
1840, p. 1207, correct account of this body of water, notices distinctly (p. 1207) its
Acc. of Khyrpoor and Fortress of " emerging from the east side of Lake Munchur," and states that there is
Bukur.

channel during the inundation, it is then more frequented than the main stream.   Lat. 26° 25′, long. 67° 50′.

ASLOO.—A village in the Punjab, twenty miles south of Lahore.   Lat. 31° 20′, long. 74° 20′. *E.I.C. Ms. Doc.*

ASTOR, or HUSARA.—A large and turbulent river, flowing generally from south-east to north-west, and discharging itself into the Indus on the eastern side, at Acho.   It drains a valley called also Husara, which lies between lat. 35°—35° 25′, long. 74° 30′—75°, and is described by Vigne, perhaps the only European who has visited it, as " narrow, picturesque, and fertile," but in the southern part desolate, in consequence of the devastations of the Sikhs and of the neighbouring marauders of Dardu.   It is rich in botanical treasure, and produces a great variety of trees—the fir, pine, *jelgozu*, or pine bearing edible seeds, juniper, mulberry, walnut, wild peach, apricot, almond, berberry, gooseberry, currant, and vines.   The rajah of this valley, who has been generally dependent on that of Iskardho, resides at the fort of Astor, situate on an angle formed by the confluence of a tributary stream and the river Husara, and built of wood and stones, with ramparts surrounded by square towers, so strong as, if well defended, to be proof against any attack by means of small-arms.   The language of the people is Pushtoo.   The fort of Astor is in lat. 35° 16′, long. 74° 44′. *Vigne, Kashmir, ii. 296-300, 309, 310.*

ASTOLA.—An island situate eighteen miles off the southern coast of Beloochistan.   It is three miles in length from east to west, and of a moderate breadth.   On the north side are shoals and inlets abounding in turtle.   Between the island and the main land is a safe channel eight miles broad, with soundings from five to eight fathoms.   Lat. 25° 7′, long. 63° 40′. *Horsburgh, E.I. Dir. i. 494 ; E.I.C. Ms. Doc.*

ATGAH.—A village in Sinde, on the route from Omercote to Nuggur Parker, and sixteen miles south-cast of the former place. Lat. 25° 12′, long. 70° 2′. *E.I.C. Ms. Doc.*

ATLAH.—A village in Afghanistan, twenty-eight miles north-east of Ghuznee.   Lat. 33° 52′, long. 68° 33′. *E I.C. Ms. Doc.*

ATTAUREE.—A village in the Punjab, five miles from the right bank of the Sutluj.   Lat. 30° 37′, long. 73° 53′. *E.I.C. Ms. Doc.*

ATTOCK.[1]—A fort and small town in the Punjab, on the left through the weedy surface of the lake a channel fifty or sixty feet wide, in which the current sets to the eastward, towards the Indus, at about two miles an hour. *[1] E.I.C. Ms. Doc.; Hough's Narr. Exp. in Afg. 334 ; Atkinson's Exp. into Afg. 387 ; Allen, March through Sinde and Afg. 365.*

[2] Wood in Burnes' Pers. Narr. 305. or east bank of the Indus, 942 miles from the sea,[2] and elose below the place where it reeeives the water of the Kabool river, and first beeomes navigable. The name, signifying *obstacle*,* is supposed to have been given to it under the presumption that [3] Asiatic Researches, vi. 528, 533; Wilford, on Mount Caucasus. no serupulous Hindoo would proeeed westward of it;[3] but this striet principle, like many others of similar nature, is little acted on. Some state that the name was given by the Emperor Akbar,[4] [4] Leech on Attock, 15. beeause he here found much difficulty in crossing the river. The [5] Wood, Oxus, 121. river itself is at this place frequently by the natives called Attoek.[5] Here is a bridge, formed usually of from twenty to thirty boats [6] Leech, ut supra. [7] Burnes' Pers. Narr. 119. across the stream,[6] at a spot where it is 537 feet wide.[7] In summer, when the melting of the snows in the lofty mountains to the north raises the stream so that the bridge becomes endangered, it is withdrawn, and the communieation is then [8] Leech, ut supra; Burnes' Bokh. i. 79; Elph. Acc. of Caubul, 71*. effeeted by means of a ferry.[8] The banks of the river are very high, so that the enormous aecession which the volume of water reeeives during inundation scarcely affects the breadth, but merely increases the depth. The roek forming the banks is of [9] Moorer. Punj. Bokh. ii. 326; Lord, Koh-i-Damun; Elph. ut supra. dark-eoloured slate,[9] polished by the force of the stream, so as to shine like black marble. Between these "one elear blue [1] Wood in Burnes' Pers. Narr. 305. stream shot past."[1] The depth of the Indus here is thirty feet in the lowest state, and between sixty and seventy in the highest,[2] [2] Wood, Oxus, 121. and runs at the rate of six miles an hour. There is a ford at some distance above the eonfluenee of the river of Kabool; but the extreme coldness and rapidity of the water render it at all [3] Burnes' Bokh. i. 69; Leech on Fords of Indus, 18; Masson, Bal. Afg. Panj. i. 140; times very dangerous,[3] and, on the slightest inundation, quite impraeticable. The bridge is supported by an association of boatsmen, who reeeive the revenue of a village allotted for this purpose [4] Leech, Attock, 15. by the Emperor Akbar,[4] and seeured to them by the Sikh government at present holding the plaee. They also receive a small daily pay as long as the bridge stands, and levy a toll on all passengers. On the right bank, opposite Attoek, is Khyrabad, a [5] Leech, Attock, 15. fort, built according to some by the Emperor Akbar,[5] according [6] Elph. 71*. to others by Nadir Shah.[6] This loeality is, in a military and commereial point of view, of much importance, as the Indus is here erossed by the great route which, proceeding from Kabool eastward through the Khyber Pass into the Punjab, forms the main line of eommunieation between Afghanistan and Northern India. The river was here repeatedly erossed by the British

* Shakespear, in v. اَڻ.

armies during the late military operations in Afghanistan; and here, according to the general opinion, Alexander, subsequently Timur, the Jagatayan conqueror, and still later Nadir Shah,[7] crossed; but there is much uncertainty on these points. The fortress was erected by the Emperor Akbar[8] in 1581, to command the passage, but though strongly built of stone on the high and steep bank of the river, it could offer no effectual resistance to a regular attack,[9] being commanded by the neighbouring heights. Its form is that of a parallelogram; it is 800 yards long and 400 wide. The town, which is inclosed within the walls of the fort, was formerly considerable, but has now gone greatly to decay. The population is estimated by Burnes at 2,000.[1] Runjeet Singh obtained possession of Attock with his characteristic trickery, having by a bribe induced the Afghan commander to surrender it to him.[2] Lat. 33° 54', long. 72° 18'.

[7] Rennell, Memoirs of a Map of Indus, p. 85.

[8] Leech, Attock, 15.

[9] Elph. ut supra; Moorcr. Punj. Bokh. ii. 324; Hough, Narr. Exp. in Afg. 334.

[1] Bokh. i. 79.

[2] Masson, Bal. Afg. Punj. iii. 28.

ATUK, in Afghanistan, is a village in Jamrad, a well-watered district in the Durani country, about forty-five miles a little west of south of Ghuznee, and twenty-five miles north-west of Abistada lake. It lies on the great route from Ghuznee to Shawl. Lat. 33° 4', long. 68°. E.I.C. Ms. Doc.

ATUK.—A village in Bhawlpoor, situate on the left bank of the Ghara river, and twenty-five miles west of the town of Bhawlpoor. Lat. 29° 24', long. 71° 13'. E.I.C. Ms. Doc.

AUGOO.—A village in Afghanistan, eighteen miles south from Lake Ab-istada. Lat. 32° 17', long. 67° 48'. E.I.C. Ms. Doc.

AUGOOMANOO.—A village in Sinde, situate on the Poorana river and twenty-five miles south-west of Hyderabad. Lat. 25° 6', long. 68° 43'. Ms. Survey Map.

AUK TUPPA.—A village on the north-western frontier of Afghanistan, situate on the banks of the Kooshk river, about five miles south from its confluence with the river Moorghab. Lat. 36° 10', long. 62° 31'. E.I.C. Ms. Doc.

AWAN.—A village in the Punjab, ten miles north-east of Lahore. Lat. 31° 41', long. 74° 26'. E.I.C. Ms. Doc.

AWCHIRI RIVER.—A river in the north of Afghanistan, which takes its rise in the mountains north of the district of Panjkora, in lat. 35° 45', long. 72° 33, and, after a southwesterly course of about forty miles, joins the Lundye river, in lat. 35° 30', long. 72° 1'. E.I.C. Ms. Doc.

AZEEZPOOR,[1] a village in Sinde, lies on the route from

[1] E.I.C.Ms. Doc.; Atkinson's Exp. into Afg. 95.

Subzulcote to Shikarpoor, and eighteen miles a little south of west of the latter place. It is situate on the east bank of the Indus, over which is a ferry called Azeezpoor Patan. By

treaty of November,[2] 1842, it was ceded, together with Subzulcote and several other towns, to Mahomed Bhawlkhan, and in the following February it was transferred accordingly. Lat. 27° 52′, long. 69° 2′.

AZEREE CHUKEE, in Afghanistan, is a post and mill, on the route from Kandahar to Ghuznee. It is situate on the right or west bank of the Turnak river, twelve miles south-west of Kilat-i-Ghiljie, at a spot where a sort of pass is formed by the high ground on the west closing down on the river. A road running off to the east over a small stone bridge is the boundary between the Duranis and Ghiljies; and it is in consequence of this division, perhaps, that the country is peculiarly dangerous, from the marauding practices of the people. Lat. 30° 2′, long. 66° 33′.

AZIM KHAN.—A village in Afghanistan. Lat. 31° 59′, long. 66° 25′.

B.

BAB.—A village in Sinde, on the right bank of the ndus. Lat. 28° 10′, long. 69° 10′.

BABA HADJEE.—A village in Afghanistan, twelve miles south-west of Giriskh, and seven miles from the right bank of the Helmund. Lat. 31° 39′, long. 64° 13′.

BABA KARA.—A village in Northern Afghanistan, situate on a branch of the Lundye river. Lat. 35° 16′, long. 71° 29′.

BABA MOORGHAB.—A village in Western Afghanistan, on the right bank of the river Moorghab. Lat. 35° 40′, long. 63°.

BABER-KA-CHA, in South-western Afghanistan, is a collection of wells, said to have been made by Sultan Baber for the relief of the travellers on the dreary and little frequented route from Ghuznee to Shawl. It is about eighty miles a little west of south from Lake Ab-istada. Lat. 31° 23′, long. 67° 25′.

BABLA.—A village in Sinde, on the road from Garrah to E.I.C. Ms. Doc.
Tattah, and twenty-three miles south-west of the latter town.
Lat. 24° 42', long. 67° 40'.

BABOORA RIVER, in Beloochistan, a small stream cross- E.I.C. Ms. Doc.
ing the route from Kurrachee to Haja Jamote, in Lus. Lat. 25°
30', long. 67° 6'.

BABOOS.—A village in Afghanistan. Lat. 34° 4', long. Walker's Map of
68° 51'.								Afg.

BABOO SABOO.—A village in the Punjab, situate on the E.I.C. Ms. Doc.
left bank of the Ravee river, and five miles south-west of Lahore.
Lat. 31° 31', long. 74° 10'.

BABUR-KA-KILLA.—A village in Afghanistan, on the in- E.I.C. Ms. Doc.
tersection of the eastern route from Ghuznee to Shawl with that
from Dera Ismael Khan to Kandahar. Lat. 31° 34', long. 67° 56'.

BABUTU.—A village in Sinde, situated on the Kukiwaree E.I.C. Ms. Doc.
mouth of the Indus. Lat. 24° 2', long. 67° 35'.

BADABEER.—A village in Afghanistan, seven miles south- Walker's Map of
west from Peshawur. Lat. 33° 54', long. 71° 34'.		Afg.

BADDRA.—A village in Beloochistan, about twenty miles E.I.C. Ms. Doc.
north of Dadur, and close to the frontiers of Sewestan. It contains 500 inhabitants, who, though located in Beloochistan, are
Afghans, ruled by a Barukzye chief. Lat. 29° 44', long. 67° 50'.

BADOO RIVER.—See BADOOR.

BADOOR.—A river in Beloochistan. Pottinger, who crossed Beloochistan, 134,
it in lat. 28° 37', long. 64° 30', found its channel 500 yards wide, 303.
and covered with jungle, harbouring wild beasts, but, at that season, devoid of water. The course of this channel is south-west,
and Pottinger was informed that, about 150 miles below the point
where he saw it, a large body of water rises in the bed, and,
flowing south-west, passes by Kedge, where it is called the
Mooleeanee river. Below that town it is called Bhugwar, and
still farther down, the Dustee, falling into the Arabian Sea in lat.
24° 5', long. 61° 50'. It can be traced upwards to the Gurmsehl, or depressed tract, about the lower course of the Helmund, and Pottinger supposes the water of that river to have
been at a remote period discharged into the Arabic Sea by this
channel.

BAGAE GOTE.—A village in Sinde, on the route from E.I.C. Ms. Doc.
Sehwan to Larkhana, and thirteen miles south of the latter place.
It is situate in a very fertile country between the Indus and its

offset the Narra, seven miles from the former and a mile and a half from the latter. Lat. 27° 20′, long. 68° 12′.

BAGH.—See BHAG.

E.I.C. Ms. Doc.

BAGHAW, in Afghanistan, is a small town of Sewestan ; it is situate on the route from Dera Ghazee Khan to Kandahar, through the Sukkee Surwar Pass, and westward of the Suliman mountains. A small stream rises here. Population about 2,000. Lat. 30° 16′, long. 68° 34′.

E.I.C. Ms. Doc.

BAGH-I-ALUM.—A village in Afghanistan, situate in the plain of Begram, thirty-one miles north from Kabool. Lat. 34° 54′, long. 69° 20′.

BAGHWAN, BAGWANA, or BUNKAR, in Beloochistan, on the road from Khozdur to Kelat, and seventy miles south of the latter place, is a cluster of villages, situate in a fertile valley,

[1] Masson, Bal. Afg. Panj. ii. 45.

amidst gardens and orchards,[1] producing figs, apricots, pomegranates, grapes, apples, plums, and melons. There is also abundance

[2] Beloochistan, 37.

of grain and grass. The cold here is severe in winter. Pottinger[2] found the contents of the water-bags carried with his party frozen into solid ice in the beginning of February. Such a circumstance in so low a latitude proves the elevation above the sea to be very considerable, probably not less than 5,000 feet. For this reason the inhabitants emigrate to Gundava in winter. Lat. 27° 55′, long. 66° 18′.

Von Hugel, iii. 414.

BAGHWARRAH, in the Punjab, a considerable town near the western bank of the Sutluj, and on the route from Loodiana to Lahore. It is situate in a fertile region containing numerous gardens and orchards. The population is about 15,000. Lat. 31° 13′, long. 75° 47′.

E.I.C. Ms. Doc.

BAGOO.—A village in Afghanistan, situate on the right bank of the Indus, twelve miles north-east from Mittunkote. Lat. 29° 3′, long. 70° 31′.

E.I.C. Ms. Doc.; Atkinson's Exp. into Afg. 87.

BAGOODRA.—A village in Sinde, on the route from Subzuleote to Shikarpoor, and twenty-four miles south-west of the former place. It is situate ten miles from the left bank of the Indus, in a swampy tract liable to inundation, and close to a considerable nullah, over which passes the road, which in many places is very indifferent. There is an encamping-ground on the south of the village, supplied with five wells of good water. Lat. 28° 4′, long. 69° 10′.

E.I.C. Ms. Doc.

BAGURAMEE.—A village in Afghanistan, eight miles south-

cast of Kabool, on the left bank of the river Loguhr. Lat. 34°
27', long. 69° 11'.

BAGWANA.—See BAGHWAN.

BAHAWULPOOR.—See BHAWLPOOR.

BAHRAM.—A village in Sinde, on the route from Larkhana E.I.C. Ms. Doc.
to Gundava, and twenty-five miles north-west of the former place.
Lat. 27° 43', long. 67° 55'.

BAHREH RIVER.—See BARA.

BAHUR, in Beloochistan, a torrent, the bed of which for a Jour. As. Soc.
great part of the year is a ravine devoid of water. When the 1840, p. 135; Hart, Jour. from Kur-
stream flows, it falls, after a course of about eight miles, into the rachee to Hinglaj.
Bay of Sonmeanee. Lat. 25° 12', long. 66° 43'.

BAIDA.—See BODA.

BAIDYANATHPUR, in the Northern Punjab, a small town Moorcr. i. 150.
near the eastern bank of the Binoa river, which lower down falls
into the Beas. It is a very poor place, but contains a Hindoo
temple. The surrounding country is very fertile, yielding every
year two crops; the first principally of rice, considered the finest
among the hill states, the second of wheat. Lat. 32° 8', long.
76° 35'.

BAIRAN.—A village in Afghanistan, situate on the Tur- E.I.C. Ms. Doc.
nak river. Lat. 32° 28', long. 67° 12'.

BAJAR, in Sinde, a large village, about nine miles south- E.I.C. Ms. Doc.
west from Sehwan, on the route from that place to Kurrachee.
Lat. 26° 16', long. 67° 48'.

BAJOORAH, in Sinde, on the route from Hyderabad to E.I.C. Ms. Doc.
Sehwan, and twelve miles south of the latter place. It is
situate on the north-west bank of a dund, or extensive pool, left
by the inundation of the Indus. Lat. 26° 14', long. 68° 2'.

BAJOUR,[1] on the north-east of Afghanistan, is a territory [1] Acc. of Caubul,
containing a town of the same name. Though at no great dis- 351; Baber, Me-moirs, 247, 248;
tance from the Punjab and the plain of Peshawur,* scarcely any Ayeen Akbery, ii. 170-171.
thing is known concerning it beyond what was gleaned by the sa-
gacity and industry of Elphinstone from native information. It is
a plain, or rather a spacious valley, on the south side of the Hindoo
Koosh, from which a lofty ridge runs southwards, dividing Bajour
on the west from Kafiristan. On the north-east it opens to

* Conolly (Edward) had explored this territory to a considerable extent, Jour. As. Soc.
and was preparing to give his information to the public—a step frustrated by 1840, p. 924,
his lamented but honourable death. Notes on the Eusufzyes.

Panjkora, by a tract of no great elevation called Berawul. On the east it is bounded by the hills held by the Otmaunkhail; on the south it communicates with the Suwat and the Eusufzai country, by the valley, through which the Lundye river flows. It lies between lat. 34° 45'—35° 10', long. 71° 5' — 71° 35', and is about twenty-five miles long and fifteen broad. The mountains which inclose it are nearly inaccessible from their steepness, and the forests, principally of oak and cedar, which cover them, are so thick as to exclude the rays of the sun. These afford covert for numerous wild beasts. The plain of Bajour resembles that of Peshawur, and is very productive, especially in wheat. It is held by the Afghan tribe of Tureolaunce, who, unlike their neighbours, the Eusufzai, are ruled by a chief having considerable power, and bearing the title of *Bauz*. Their number is probably about 70,000 or 80,000; but as there are other inhabitants, descendants of Kafirs, Hindoos, Moguls, and others, the total number may be about 120,000. The chief is said to have an income of about a lac of rupees annually, and has usually, on emergencies, furnished a body of troops to the Afghan govern-

2. Mil. Op. in Afg. 209.

ment. In the battle of Jelalabad,[2] in April, 1842, he was among the discomfited parties. Bajour contains an inexhaustible supply of iron-ore of the finest quality.[3] It is found in the form of a black sand, washed down by the torrents from the deposits in the mountains, and from this source the greater part of Northern Afghanistan and the neighbouring states are supplied. The two chief towns, Bajour and Nawagye, have each about 5,000 inhabi-

3 Jour. As. Soc. 1840, p. 83; Drummond on the Min. Resources of Afg.

tants. Bajour is supposed to be the Bazira mentioned by the historians of Alexander.[4] Lat. 35° 2', long. 71° 23'.

4 Jour. As. Soc. 1836, p. 392; Court, Conject. on the March of Alexander. E.I.C. Ms. Doc.

BAKASIR.—A village in Sinde. Lat. 24° 46', long. 71° 11'.

Hough, 343.

BAKERALA, in the Punjab, a small town on the route from Attock to Rotas, is situate on the banks of the Kasee, which here winds its way through frightful defiles. Lat. 33° 5', long. 73° 20'.

BAKKAR.—See Buккur.

E.I.C. Ms. Map; Masson, Bal. Afg. Panj. i. 182, iii. 186-187; Moorcroft, Punj. Bokh. ii. 259; Forster, Jour. Beng. Eng. ii. 63.

BALA BAGH, in Afghanistan, a small walled town in the valley of Jelalabad, and about fifteen miles west of the town of that name, is situate on the left bank of a large stream falling into the Soorkh Rood. It is celebrated for its fruits, as well as for its sugar-cane, which is here extensively cultivated, more,

however, for a sweetmeat than for the manufacture of sugar.
The neighbourhood abounds in topes or monuments of an hemispherical form, usually standing on a cylindrical base, the date
and object of whose erection have been the subject of much
controversy. The best-founded opinion, however, appears to be
that they were places of burial of eminent followers of the Buddhist creed.* By some they are considered to have been merely
repositories of relics, to which veneration was attached by the
Buddhists. In a commercial point of view, the town is the most
important place in the valley of Jelalabad. Lat. 34° 22', long.
70° 14'.

BALADEH.—A village in Afghanistan, seven miles south E.I.C. Ms. Doc.
from Kandahar. Lat. 31° 32', long. 65° 30'.

BALE RIVER.—A small river in Beloochistan; takes its
rise in the Sarawanee mountains, and, flowing by the town of
Sarawan, disappears to the eastward of it, the water being
totally absorbed or evaporated. Where observed by Pottinger, Beloochistan, 128.
in lat. 29°, long. 64° 42', it was found to have a supply of
excellent water, represented by the natives as never failing, and
when swollen by rain, to become a large and rapid torrent.

BALLA ATTA KHAN.—A village in Afghanistan, situate E.I.C. Ms. Doc.
on the right bank of the Helmund river, six miles north-east
from Giriskh. Lat. 31° 50', long. 64° 26'.

BALLOO JIRDA REE KA KOOBEH.—A village in Sinde. E.I.C. Ms. Doc.
Lat. 26° 20', long. 68° 47'.

BALLYAREE.—A village in Sinde, situate about five miles E.I.C. Ms. Doc.
north from the Great Western Rin. Lat. 24° 11', long. 69° 37'.

BALTI, or BALTISTAN.—See BULTI.

BAMBOORA, in Sinde, near Garrah or Gharry-Kote, is a Outram, 6;
ruined city exhibiting marks of great antiquity, displaying the Burnes' Pers. Nar.
18; De la Hoste,
remains of ramparts, bastions, towers, and houses, and bearing Jour. As. Soc.
1840, p. 912;
evidence of former population and trade in the number of coins Wood, Oxus, 18;
Macmurdo, in
washed up in time of rain. Lat. 24° 40', long. 67° 41'. Jour. of As. Soc.

BAMBUT POORA.—A village in Sinde, on the route from of Great Brit. and
Irel. 1834, i. 25;
Shikarpoor to Larkhana, and sixteen miles north-east of the Pottinger, 346.
latter place. It contains 300 inhabitants, and is supplied with E.I.C. Ms. Doc.
water from a well. Lat. 27° 41', long. 68° 30'.

* Much profound learning has been displayed on this curious and recondite
subject by Professor Wilson (Ariana Antiqua, p. 62, et al.) and by Ritter
(Erdkunde von Asien, vii. 286—303).

E.I.C. Ms. Doc.   BAMEEKUTAIR.—A village in the Punjab, situate on the left bank of the Ravee river.—Lat. 30° 58′, long. 73° 26′.

[1] Wood, Route of Kabool and Turkestan, 21, 22.   BAMIAN,[1] in Afghanistan, a celebrated valley on the route from Kabool to Turkestan, is generally regarded as the boundary between the Hindoo Koosh on the east, and the Paropamisan or Huzareh group on the west. It is of very great importance, being the only known pass across the Himalaya, or the Hindoo Koosh, practicable for artillery or heavy carriages. It is also the great commercial route, for though there are several passes to the eastward, they are less frequented, on account of their diffi-

[2] Burnes' Bokh. i. 182, 183. Lord, Koh-i-Damun, 53 ; Jour. As. Soc. 1833, p. 7 ; Gerard, Route from Pesh. to Bokhara.   culty and the elevation of their higher parts. The valley [2] is about a mile broad, and very fertile, and is bounded on each side by nearly perpendicular steeps, generally of conglomerate. It is situate just within the frontier of Afghanistan, where it joins Kunduz. On the southern or Afghan side are four principal passes ; Oonna 11,320, Hajeguk 11,700, Kaloo 10,883, and Erak 12,909 feet above the level of the sea ; on the northern or Kunduz side, three ; Akrobat, Dundun Shikur, and Kara Kotul, each

[4] E.I.C. Ms. Map; Wood, Route of Cab. and Toork. 24, 25 ; Moorc. Punj. Bokh. ii. 384-305.   between 9,000 and 10,000 feet above the sea.[4] As far as our information extends, it appears that the routes, both north and south, are very complicated, but that all are at Bamian restricted to one line, which holds its course through the valley. The

[5] Journ. As. Soc. 1842, p. 70 ; Grif. Bar. and Ther. Obs. in Afgh.   elevation of Bamian is 8,496 feet,[5] so that it is considerably depressed below the passes north and south.

Bamian and its vicinity are remarkable for some of the most extraordinary relics of antiquity ; its colossal idols, the castle of Zohak, the fortress of Saiadabad, and the ruins of Ghulghuleh. Though we have published accounts of this wonderful place by several travellers of note, there is so great uncertainty concerning the details, that even the number of the idols is not agreed on.

[6] Jour. As. Soc. 1836, p. 708, Notes on Antiq. of Bamian, and Bal.Afg. Panj. iii. 383. [7] ii. 183.   Masson[6] states that there are three, and is supported by the Ayeen Akbery,[7] in which it is stated, " Here (at Bamian) are three astonishing idols, one representing a man eighty ells high, another a woman fifty, and a third, which is the figure of a child, measuring fifteen ells in height." Burnes,[8] Moorcroft,[9] Eyre,[1]

[8] Bokhara, i. 185. [9] Punj. Bokh. ii. 388. [1] Mil. Op. at Cabul, 361-364. [2] Ut supra. [3] Acc. of Caubul, 487.   and Gerard,[2] mention only two. Elphinstone,[3] adverting to the subject, observes, " I have heard two idols described, though it is sometimes said there are more ; of these, one represents a man and one a woman ; the former is twenty yards high, the latter twelve or fourteen." There is equal discrepancy as to the dimen-

~ions of the figures. Burnes states the height of the smaller image at 60 feet, that of the larger at 120; Moorcroft states the height of the smaller idol at 117 feet, and his evidence is corroborated by the near approach to agreement of that of Eyre, who took extraordinary pains to arrive at correctness, having ascended to the crown of the figure's head. According to him, the height is 120 feet. Moorcroft states the height of the greater figure to be about 180 feet, Eyre about 160; Wood,[3] whose accuracy is remarkable, singularly enough, makes no mention of the images. He perhaps considered that they had received sufficient attention from Burnes. The discrepancy in the statements of different travellers upon this point is the more extraordinary, as there are stairs excavated in the rock, by means of which access can be had to the top of the heads of the figures, from whence their height could readily be ascertained by a plumb-line. The images are rudely sculptured in bold relief in the cliff; they are represented standing in deep niches, and clothed in flowing drapery. The ceilings of the niches are covered with a profusion of paintings; some, according to Moorcroft,[4] " of very beautiful delineation, and painted with much delicacy of colouring " It is strange that this should have continued fresh, exposed to the air in such an Alpine climate. The greater figure is called Sang Sal, and is supposed to be intended to represent a male; the less, called Shah-Muma, is thought to represent a female. Both figures are much mutilated, the greater especially, whose legs and arms have been shattered by cannonshot; the violence being attributed by some accounts to the orders of Aurungzebe, by others to those of Nadir Shah. Vast caves are everywhere excavated in the face of the rock for a distance of eight miles, and in some of these, caravans are occasionally sheltered. In that below the large idol half a regiment could find quarters. Some of the cells exhibit internally considerable architectural decoration, with tasteful and well-finished paintings in fresco, and also sculptures.

There is much discordance in the opinions of those who have speculated on the views and motives of the framers of these gigantic images and innumerable caves. Burnes says[5]— " It is by no means improbable that we owe the idols of Bamecan to the caprice of some person of rank who resided in this cave-digging neighbourhood, and sought for an immortality in

[3] Oxus, 205.

[4] Punj. Bokh. ii. 390, 391.

[5] Bokh. i. 188.

the colossal images which we have now described." Masson [6] attributes these great works to the Hiatilla or White Huns, [7] who conquered Transoxiana and Khorasan about the fifth century of the Christian era, were subsequently subdued by the Turkish hordes, and finally exterminated by Zingis Khan. This opinion receives countenance from the well-ascertained fact that Zingis Khan destroyed Ghulghuleh, the extensive ruins of which are scattered over the valley of Bamian. Masson considers the caves to have been catacombs, and the gigantic images intended to represent illustrious persons deceased. Moorcroft, [8] familiar with the opinions, faith, pageantry, and buildings of the lamas of Thibet, is of opinion that Bamian was the residence of a great Lama, bearing the same relation to the Lamaism of the West that the Lama of Lhassa does now to that of the East; "that those excavations, which were connected by means of galleries and staircases, constituted the accommodations of the higher orders of the Lama clergy, and that the insulated cells and caves were the dwelling-places of the lower classes of the monastic society, as the gelums and anis, monks and nuns, and as serais or hostels for visitors. The laity inhabited the adjoining city." On the whole, it seems most probable that these relics are of Buddhist origin, and this belief is countenanced by their resemblance to the images of Buddha, in the island of Salsette. [9] In any conjectures to fix the date of the formation of the idols of Bamian, it should be borne in mind that they are nowhere described by the Greek historians, who, cursory as their notices on this country generally are, could scarcely have failed to mention such extraordinary objects, if existing during the Macedonian campaigns. Elphinstone, [1] whose opinion seems to be the best supported, attributes these idols and the contiguous caves to the Buddhist princes of Ghore, who ruled the country between Kabool and Persia [2] in the early centuries of the Christian era. They are noticed by Sherif-o-Deen in his account of Tamerlane's campaigns, and this is perhaps the earliest authentic evidence which we have respecting them. If we consider them coeval with the topes or mounds of Jelalabad and other eastern parts of Afghanistan, we must assign them an origin not earlier than the Christian era, as the topes when opened have been found to contain coins struck by some of the early emperors of Rome, [3] and by some of the Byzantine emperors as late as 474. As yet,

[6] Bal. Afg. Panj. ii. 388.
[7] Malcolm, Hist. of Persia, i. 126.
[8] Punj. Bokh. ii. 392.
[9] Masson, Bal. Afg. Panj. ii. 385.
[1] 153.
[2] Malcolm, i. 327.
[3] Masson, in Wilson's Ariana Antiqua, 110.

much obscurity envelopes this curious subject. It is remarkable
that Baber,[4] in recounting his march through Bamian, makes no
mention of those striking objects. ⁴ Memoir, 212.

The learned orientalist Hyde, though he never in person explored this region, gives a detailed and in general correct description of these colossal idols, but it will be observed that he con-
founds Balkh and Bamian. " The Chinese and Hindoos, besides
the huge images in their pagodas or temples, were accustomed
to carve great, sometimes entire, rocks into idols, especially if
they found any having naturally a pyramidal form. Such were
those near the city of Bamiyan, which was afterwards called
Balkh or Bactra. They were those immense and prodigious
figures, called in Persian *Surch-But* (red idol) and *Chingh-But*
(grey idol). They were two vast statues carved out of the rock, of
the height and size of towers, being hollow within, so that a person
entering at the sole of the foot could make his way through the
whole of the interior to the extremities of the fingers and toes. In
the book Pharh Gj., written in India, it is stated that these two
statues are fifty cubits high, and that in the time of ignorance,
the pagans used to congregate at them in a certain part of the
city of Bamiyan, from the territory of Cabul, on the frontier of
the country of Badacshan." "And at no great distance from these,
is said to be another idol of the same sort, in the form of an old
woman, called *Nesrem* or *Nesr.*" Hyde recounts an opinion entertained by some, that they were identical with idols mentioned
in the Khoran. This might give rise to some curious speculations
as to whether the idolatry of the Arabians, previously to the rise
of Mahomet, might not be connected with Hindoo superstitions,
and the black stone of the Kaaba be a *Lingam*.[5]

⁵ Hyde, De Reli-
gione Veterum
Persarum, 4to.
Oxon. 1760,* 129,
130.

* As the work is not of common occurrence, and the passage very curious,
it is given at length in the original : " Chinenses et Indi præter imagines in
pagodis, seu delubris, prægrandes, aliquando etiam integras rupes (præsertim
si naturâ in pyramidalem formam vergebant), in idola formare solebant. Talia
propè urbem Bamiyân (quæ posteà Balch, seu Bactra), erant immania et pro-
digiosa, illa Persicè dicta ﺑﺖ ﺳﺮخ Surc'h-Bùt, *i. e.* idolum rubrum, et
ﺑﺖ ﺟﻴﻨﮓ C'hingh-Bùt, *i. e.* idolum griseum seu cinereum. Hæc (ut in
Libro Masâlik Mamâlik Persicè describuntur), erant duæ prægrandes statuæ
ad altitudinem et magnitudinem turrium è rupibus excisæ, intus cavæ, ita ut
quis per plantam pedis subintrans, totam interiorem earundem partem usque
ad extremos manuum et pedum digitos permeare posset. In Libro Pharh. Gj.
in Indiâ conscripto, hæ duæ statuæ dicuntur quinquaginta cubitos altæ, ad

On the summits of many eminences in Bamian and its vicinity
are slender towers remarkably well built, which Masson supposes
were pyrethræ or fire-altars, perhaps similar in purport, as they
are in construction, to the celebrated round towers of Ireland.

[5] Jour. As. Soc. 1840, p. 68; Hay on Coins found at Bamian.
Great numbers of coins and rings are dug up in the vicinity ;[5]
they bear Cufic inscriptions, and are generally of later date than
the era of Mahomedanism. Some, however, belong to the age
of the Indo-Bactrian kings, and date previously to our era.
Burnes considers Bamian the site of Alexandria ad Caucasum,

[6] vii. 272.
[7] In Sainte Croix, Examen Critique des Historiens d'Alexandre, 827.
and his opinion is supported by that of Ritter,[6] Gosselin,[7] and
some others. The establishment of a city which might command the great communication between Transoxiana, Ara-
chosia, and India, would seem well suited to the comprehensive
and sagacious views of the great conqueror. The whole valley
of Bamian is strewed with the ruins of tombs, mosques, and
other edifices, in such numbers as prove the destroyed city of
Ghulghuleh to have been very extensive. Yet it must have
been extremely difficult to supply provisions to a numerous population in a district so barren. The ruins of the citadel are on a

[*] Ut supra, ii. 393.
detached hill in the middle of the valley. Masson[8] well describes
the emotions excited in the spectator of those scenes of departed
greatness, the origin and history of which are veiled in im-
penetrable darkness, though the extinction is known to be the
effect of the devastating fury of Zingis Khan, who, in 1221,
stormed the city and exterminated the inhabitants.* " The traveller surveying from the height of Ghulghuleh the vast and
mysterious idols, and the multitude of caves around him, will
scarcely fail to be absorbed in deep reflection and wonder, while

quas tempore ignorantiæ confluebant مشركان Pagani in aliquo loco urbis
Bamiyân ex territorio كابل Câbul, in limitibus regionis بدخشان Badach-
shân. Hinc veniunt Rubini Balascii. Hæc idola (inquit dictus autor) à qui-
busdam censentur esse ea quæ Arabibus dicta sunt يغوث Yagûth, et يعوق
Yâûk tempore Noæ : et ab aliis habentur pro مناءت Manât, et Lâtt. Et
haud procul ab istis, dicitur esse aliud ejusmodi idolum paulò minus, formâ
vetulæ, dictum نسرم Nésrem, seu نسر Nesr."

[9] Punj. Bokh. ii. 387-393.
[1] Mah. Hist. 410, 519, 533.
[2] Hist. of Persia, 418.
* Such is the statement of Moorcroft,[9] who does not give his authority,
and seems to follow " Mahomedan traditions." Price[1] and Malcolm[2] assign
the ravages of Zingis in Khorasan to A.D. 1221—1224. A well digested
article by Prinsep (H. T.), in Journal of As. Soc. Beng. 1842, p. 557, states
Zingis's march on Bamian, apparently on the authority of the Rozut-oos-
sufa.

their contemplation will call forth various and interesting associations in his mind. The desolate spot itself has a peculiar solemnity, not merely from its lonely and startling evidence of past grandeur, but because nature seems to have invested it with a character of mystery and awe. The very winds, as they whistle through its devoted pinnacles and towers, impart tones so shrill and lugubrious as to impress with emotions of surprise the most indifferent being. So surprising is their effect, that often while strolling near it the mournful melody irresistibly riveting my attention, would compel me involuntarily to direct my sight to the eminence and its ruined fanes, and frequently would I sit for a long time together expecting the occasional repetition of the singular cadence. The natives may be excused who consider these mournful and unearthly sounds as the music of departed spirits and invisible agents."

Eight miles to the east of Bamian, and on one of the routes between it and Kabool, are the ruins of the fort of Zohak,[3] so called [3] Wood, Oxus, 205. because its origin is attributed to the fabled demon-king of Persia of that name. It is built of fine burnt bricks, which in the construction of the towers, walls, and other buildings are arranged in a variety of quaint devices. These ruins, which, in consequence of the excellence of the material, are in a state of wonderful freshness and preservation, are supposed by Masson[4] to be [4] ii. 390. places of sepulchral and religious privacy, as he finds it difficult to suppose that a fortress should have been built in so unprofitable a locality. Yet the ramparts, which are between seventy and eighty feet high, indicate that defence was the object of their construction, and a purpose obviously sufficient is found in securing the command of the pass. Bamian is in lat. 34° 50', long. 67° 48'.

BAMINACOTE.—A village in Sinde, on the eastern side of the Hujamaree mouth of the Indus, near Vikkur.[1] Here, at the [1] Kennedy, Sinde and Kabool, i. 34. close of 1838, the Bombay army destined to act in Sinde and Afghanistan was landed and rendezvoused.[2] Lat. 24° 11', long. [2] Outram, Rough Notes, 9. 67° 34'.

BAMMOO CHAKUR.—A village in Sinde, on the route E.I.C. Ms. Doc. from Subzulcote to Shikarpoor, and eight miles south-west of the former place. It is situate ten miles from the left bank of the Indus, in a low alluvial country, rendered swampy by inundation, but at other times affording a good road. Lat. 28° 10' long. 69° 44'

E.I.C. Ms. Doc. BANAHOU.—A village in Sinde, on the route from Rorec to Jessulmair, and forty-five miles south-east of the former place. Lat. 27° 25′, long. 69° 30′.

BANAUL.—See BANIHAL.

E.I.C. Ms. Doc. BANDEE.—A village in Sinde, situate on the road from Bukkur to Hyderabad. Lat. 26° 36′, long. 68° 16′.

BANDER VIKKAR.—See VIKKUR.

E.I.C. Ms. Doc. BANGUDJEE.—A village in Sinde, on the route from Sukkur to Larkhana, ten miles north-west of the former place. It is situate on the right bank of the Indus ; has convenient encamping-ground and abundant supplies of forage. The road from Sukkur, though merely a footpath through the jungle, is not bad. Lat. 27° 42′, long. 68° 44′.

BANIHAL, in the Northern Punjab, is a pass over the mountains of the same name, bounding Kashmir on the south. The formation is a mygdoidal trap. The ascent is much more considerable on the southern than on the northern side, where it descends into Kashmir, which country has a greater elevation than that part of the Punjab lying to the south. Though by no means the highest, being but 8,500 feet above the sea, it is one of the most difficult passes into Kashmir, and is seldom attempted with horses, though Vigne[1] passed it in that way. Forster[2] entered Kashmir on foot through this pass. The pergunna, or district, also bears the name of Banihal. Lat. 33° 25′, long. 75° 10′.

[1] Vigne, Kashmir, i. 334; Von Hugel, Kaschmir, ii. 169, 172.
[2] Journey Beng. Eng. i. 318.

BANOO, or BUNNOA.—A fertile plain, south-west of the Kala, or Salt Range, in Eastern Afghanistan. It is well watered by the river Kurum, and produces abundant crops of wheat, rice, barley, maize, and other grain, sugar-cane, tobacco, and ginger. From these advantages it might be expected to be populous, were it not exposed to the incursions of the Sikhs and of the neighbouring mountaineers, whose attacks keep the inhabitants in continual alarm, so that every house is a small fortress, and sometimes the whole population is obliged to fly and seek safety in concealment. Lat. 33° 15′, long. 71° 10′.

Elph. Acc. of Caubul, 364; Burnes' Pol. Pow. of Sikhs, 4; Masson, Bal. Afg. Panj. i. 85; Moorcr. Punj. Bokh. ii. 241.

E.I.C. Ms. Doc ; Masson, Bal. Afg. Panj. 114. BAPAW.—A village in Beloochistan, in the Moola or Gundava Pass, from Kelat to Gundava, and forty-nine miles south of the former place. The road here runs along the bed of the Moola or Mulloh, which in some places is hidden in the sand ; in others, flows in a small stream a few inches deep. The mountains inclosing the pass are, in this part, of very great height. The clevation of Bapaw above the sea is 5,000 feet. Lat. 28° 16', long. 66° 20'.

BAPPOO.—A small village in Sinde, on the route from Seh- E.I.C. Ms. Doc. wan to Larkhana, and thirty-seven miles north of the former place. It is situate about a mile and a half from the landing-place at Rookun, on the Indus, from which place to Bappoo the road, which is close along the left bank, is bushy, but good. Lat. 26° 54', long. 67° 54'.

BARA.[1]—A small but highly important river of Afghanistan, in the province of Peshawur. It rises in Tirah, or the hilly tract lying between Sufeid Koh and the Salt Range. From the bene- fits which it confers on the country through which it flows, it has, in conformity with oriental feelings, become an object of vene- ration ; and Shekhan, the spot where the apportioning of the water takes place, is regarded as sacred. Here a certain quan- tity, reckoned by the number of mills which it can turn, is taken for the town of Peshawur. The remainder should be equally divided between the lower Momunds and the Khuleets of the plain, but the division is never effected without jealousy, discon- tent, and strife. The Afreedies, who possess the highlands through which the Bara flows, can stop its stream, and, since the occupation of Peshawur by the Sikhs, have caused the latter much vexation and injury, by frequently cutting off the supply. The Sikhs have lost many troops in conflicts with these mountaineers, originating in their attempts to restrict the flow of the river. On one occasion the Afreedies, by allowing the water to accumu- late and then cutting the mound, caused so great an inundation that Runjeet Sing's camp was nearly swept away, and those alert freebooters, who had watched the opportunity, secured great plunder. The length of the river is about sixty miles. Shekhan enters the plain of Peshawur in lat. 33° 53', long. 71° 32'. The rice grown in this plain is considered superior to any other, and so highly esteemed, that in the Tripartite treaty of 1838, Run- jeet Sing stipulated to supply a certain quantity of it yearly to Shah Shoojah.[2]

[1] Jour. As. Soc. 1830, p. 478, Court, Mem. of a Map of Peshawur, and 1830, p. 771, Irwin, Mem. of Afg.; Masson, Bal. Afg. Panj. i. 165, iii. 233.

[2] Correspondence on Sinde, 7.

BARADREE.[1]—A village in Beloochistan, on the route [1] E.I.C. Ms. Doc. from Kelat to Dadur, by the pass which enters that of Bolan from the west at Beebee Nanee. It is distant from Kelat sixty- eight miles north-east, and close to it is another village of the same size, called Jam. These villages are situate on a slightly elevated plateau, a little to the south of the road, in a very fertile valley, producing abundance of fine fruit and grain, especially rice. As the river watering this valley flows into the Bolan at Beebee Nanee, which is 1,695 feet above the sea,[2] the elevation of the ground about these villages must exceed that height. The inhabitants are Belooches of the tribe called Prij. They do not pay tribute to the Khan of Kelat, and, when circumstances call for it, are charged with the duty of guarding travellers through the Bolan Pass. Lat. 29° 39′, long. 67° 11′.

BARAK.—A village in Afghanistan, on the route, by the Sakhee Surwar Pass, from Dera Ghazee Khan to Kandahar, and eighty miles west of Dera Ghazee Khan. Lat. 30° 3′, long. 69° 35′.

BARAKAIL, in Afghanistan, is a collection of large open villages contiguous to each other, on the route from Ghuznee to Shawl, and about twelve miles south of Lake Ab-istada. The country is productive, and capable of yielding considerable supplies. It belongs to a Ghilji chief, who resides in a fort about ten miles from this place. Lat. 32° 22′, long. 67° 52′.

BARAKHAIL.—A village in Afghanistan, situate on the road from Barakail to Quetta. Lat. 32°, long. 67° 30′.

BARAKZYE.—A village in Afghanistan. Lat. 35°, long. 69° 36′.

BARAL.—A village in the Punjab, situate near the left bank of the river Jailum. Lat. 32° 32′, long. 72° 42′.

BARAMGULA.—See Barumgula.

BARAMULA, in Kashmir, is a gorge in the mountains forming the south-western boundary of the valley. Through this aperture the Jailum flows, draining the whole of this extensive basin. The Hindoos attribute its formation to Vishnu,[1] the Mussulmans to King Solomon ; some give the credit to a saint called Kasyapa[2] by the Hindoos, and Kashib by the Mahometans. This remarkable opening, according to Vigne[3] and Bermier,[4] has been caused by the gradual operation of the river Jailum wearing away the inclosing barrier, or by earthquake. The soil and hills in the immediate neighbourhood of Baramula are alluvial, but below the town the Jailum enters into a channel in the rock, the sides of which are from 500 to 1,000 feet high.[5] In one place this river passes through an opening only fifteen yards wide. The scenery[6] in the pass is described as singularly beautiful. The town is situate on the west or right bank of the river, here crossed by a bridge of eight piers. There

² Jour. As. Soc. 1842, p. 55 ; Grif. Bar. and Ther. Mea. in Afg.

E.I.C. Ms. Doc.

E.I.C. Ms. Doc.

E.I.C. Ms. Doc.

E.I.C. Ms. Doc.

E.I.C. Ms. Doc.

¹ Vigne, Kashmir, i. 377.
² Asiatic Res. xv. 9; Wilson, Hist. of Cashmir.
³ i. 297; Von Hugel, Kaschmir, i. 359; Moorcr. Punj. Bokh. ii. 280.
⁴ Voy. aux Indes Orientales, ii. 208.

⁵ Vigne, Kashmir, i. 278.
⁶ Vigne, i. 279.

are about 300 houses and a small fort, garrisoned by the Sikhs. This is the most practicable pass for an army invading Kashmir, and that by which the Sikhs themselves entered it, carrying a six-pounder, their only artillery, slung on a pole.[7] Near this place [7] Moorcr. ii. 316. the river ceases to be navigable, and does not again become so until it reaches Oin, in lat. 33° 40', long. 73° 50'. It holds a rapid course until it enters the plain of the Punjab, near the town of Jailum. Baramula is in lat. 34° 8', long. 74° 11'.

BARATA.—A village in North Afghanistan, thirty miles E.I.C. Ms. Doc. north-east of Peshawur. Lat. 34° 15', long. 72° 10 .

BARRA AHMEDPOOR.—See AHMEDPOOR.

BARSHOREE.—See BURSHOREE.

BARSNOW.—A village in Sinde, situate on the route from E.I.C. Ms. Doc. Jessulmair to Wadole. Lat. 25° 57', long. 69° 56'.

BARUK, a village in Afghanistan, on the right bank of the E.I.C. Ms. Doc. Punchshir river. Lat. 35° 18', long. 69° 30'.

BARUMGULA, a town in the north of the Punjab, and on Vigne, Kashmir, the southern slope of the Pir Panjal, which bounds Kashmir on the south, is situate in the Pir Panjal, or Nandan Sar Pass, from the Punjab into Kashmir. The situation is beautiful and picturesque, at the extremity of a dark and deep defile, through which the Punch river flows. Close to the town is a small fort, garrisoned by the Sikhs. There are probably 400 or 500 inhabitants, who are employed in weaving shawls. The height above the sea is 6,800 feet. Lat. 33° 30', long. 74° 18'.

BARUS KE GOT.—A village in Sinde, on the road from E.I.C. Ms. Doc. Tattah to Bander Vikkar. Lat. 24° 37', long. 67° 38'.

BASHKALA.—A village in North-eastern Afghanistan. E.I.C. Ms. Doc. Lat. 34° 22', long. 72° 9'.

BASHOREE.—See BURSHOREE.

BASSOWAL, in Afghanistan, a small walled town on the Hough, Nar. of route from the Khyber Pass to Kabool, thirteen miles from the Ex. to Afg. 305; Masson, Bal. Afg. western extremity of the pass. Lat. 34° 16', long. 70° 58' Panj. i. 167.

BASTER BUNDER.—A village in Sinde, situate on the E.I.C. Ms. Doc. right bank of the Koree estuary of the Indus, thirty miles from its mouth. Lat. 23° 49', long. 68° 41'.

BATCHAW, or BUTCHA.—A small village in Sinde, on E.I.C. Ms. Doc. the route from Hyderabad to Sehwan, and ten miles south-east of the latter place. It is situate on the west bank of a watercourse a mile from the right bank of the Indus. Lat. 26° 16', long 68°

E.I.C. Ms. Doc.   BAU SOOLTAN.—A village in the Punjab, two miles west of the river Chenaub. Lat. 30° 44', long. 71° 51'.

BAYLA.—See BELA.

E.I.C. Ms. Doc.   BAZAAR-AHMED-KHAN.—A village in Afghanistan. Lat. 32° 54', long. 70° 59'.

Walker's Map of Afg.   BAZARUK.—A village in Afghanistan, on the Punchshir river. Lat. 35° 16', long. 69° 20'.

BEAH RIVER.—See BEAS.

BEAS, one of the great rivers of the Punjab, rises on the southern verge of the Ritanka Pass, in Lahoul, a Himalayan region north-east of the Punjab, and at a point 13,200 feet above the sea, in lat. 32° 34', long. 77° 12'. This information [1] Punj. Bokh. i. 190.   is derived from the lamented Moorcroft,[1] who visited the spot, which is considered sacred by the Hindoos, like the other sources of their great rivers, and has its name from being consecrated to Beas or Vyasa, who is reputed to have compiled the Puranas, and arranged the Vedas of the Hindoos, about 5,000 years ago, and hence is called Beas *Rikhi*, or " the Sage." The river takes a southerly course of about 100 miles to Mundi, and being increased by the access of numerous streams, has there a considerable body of water, and a width of from 150 to 200 yards, with a depth of twelve feet. The depth, however, in the warm season constantly varies, beginning to swell in the evening, attaining its maximum by morning, and declining through the day, losing about one-third of its water. This periodical change results from the melting of the snow diurnally by the heat of the sun. From Mundi the Beas takes a course of fifty miles, chiefly westerly, to [2] Kashmir, i. 132.   Nadaun, where Vigne[2] found it, in the low season, 150 yards wide, twelve feet deep, and running at the rate of three miles and a half an hour. Within this distance from its source, it has been joined by numerous feeders, of which only two require notice. [3] Moorcr. i. 166.   They are both from the north : the more eastern, the Hulku,[3] having a course of about thirty miles, and joining the Beas a few miles east of Mundi ; the more western, the Binoa (which is the greater), having a course of about fifty miles, and joining the Beas [4] i. 260.   about twenty miles west of the same place. Forster,[4] who crossed the Beas a short distance below Nadaun, states that he found it to [5] i. 69.   have a rapid stream about 100 yards wide, but Moorcroft,[5] about a quarter of a mile above the town, found it only 100 feet wide, [6] Kaschmir, ii. 79.   and running at the rate of five miles an hour. B. Von Hügel [6] describes it here as an unfordable clear rapid stream, running between steep and lofty banks, access being obtained to the water by large and well-constructed stairs. From Nadaun it takes a wide sweep of about eighty miles to the north-west, and having entered the plain of the Punjab, it, about lat. 32° 5', long. 75° 20', turns southward, a course which it holds for about eighty miles further to its confluence with the Sutluj.[7] A short distance below Nadaun it receives the river of Kunyar, flowing from the south.[8] Macartney measured it at the ferry of Bhyrawul, about twenty miles above the confluence, and there found it 740 yards wide, and so rapid that, in crossing, the boats were driven ten or twelve miles down the stream. This was in August, at a season when the river is at its greatest height. In the low or cold season it is fordable in most places. By the competent observer last quoted, the Beas is regarded as larger than the Sutluj, though in length of course it is greatly inferior to that river. But Burnes states, that though they have the same breadth each, about 200 yards, the Sutluj has the greater volume of water.[9] The confluence of the Beas with the Sutluj takes place at Endreesa, near the village Hurekee, and in lat. 31° 12', long. 74° 56', after a course by the former river of from 210 to 220 miles. The Beas is considered to be identical with the Hyphasis of Arrian,[1] the Greek name being a corruption of *Beypasha*, given it by the natives. The united stream below the confluence bears the name of the Ghara until the confluence with the Chenaub.

BED TILLA.—A village in Afghanistan, situate on the road from Bamian to Giriskh. Lat. 33° 49', long. 67° 49'

BEEAH.—A large and fine village in Sinde, situate on the right bank of the Indus, amidst much cultivation and many trees. The road passes through the bazaar of the village, and about a furlong further reaches the river. It lies on the great route from Hyderabad to Sehwan, and twenty-five miles north of the former place. Lat. 25° 43', long. 68° 20'.

BEEBEE NANEE.—A halting-place in the Bolan Pass, in Beloochistan, situate twenty-six miles from the eastern entrance of the pass. Here a road strikes off from the main pass, and proceeds west to Rod Bahar and Kelat. Elevation above the sea 1,695 feet. Lat. 29° 39', long. 67° 28'.

BEEBEENAUNEE.—See BEEBEE NANEE.

BEEBOO TRIGGUR.—A village in the Punjab, situate on

[7] Elphinstone,662.

[8] F. Von Hugel, i. 77.

[9] Bokh. i. 7.

[1] L. vi. c.14; Renell, 82.

E.I.C. Ms. Doc.

E.I.C. Ms. Doc.

E.I.C. Ms. Doc.;
Jour. As. Soc.
1842, p. 54; Grif.
Bar. and Ther.
Meas. in Afg.;
Hough,Nar. Ex. in
Afg.56; Atkinson,
Ex. in Afg. 114;
Havelock, War in
Afg. i. 225; Kennedy, Sinde and
Kabool, i. 215;
Conolly, Jour. to
India, ii. 220.
E.I.C. Ms. Doc.

the right bank of the river Chenaub.   Lat. 30° 28', long.
71° 40'.

E.I.C. Ms. Doc.   BEELALPOOR.—A village in Sinde, about thirteen miles
north of Sehwan, on the road from thence to Larkhana.   The
surrounding country is level and, after rain, swampy.   It affords
ground for encampment.   Lat. 26° 30', long. 67° 53'.

E.I.C. Ms. Doc.   BEELUN.—A village in the Punjab, six miles north of Mooltan, on the left bank of the Chenaub river.   Lat. 30° 13', long.
71° 30'

Havelock, i. 159.   BEERALOO, in Sinde, is a small town near the left or
eastern bank of the Indus, and on the route from Khyerpoor to
Roree, from which last place it is distant about four miles south.
Lat. 27° 39', long. 68° 54'.

E.I C Ms. Doc.   BEETUN.—A village in Sinde, situate on the right bank of
the Narra river.   Lat. 26° 38', long. 67° 47'.

BEGHRAM, in Afghanistan, a plain, with a collection of
ruins bearing the same name, is situate twenty-five miles north
of Kabool.   It was formerly the site of a great city, the ruined
walls of which were found by Masson[1] to measure above sixty
feet in breadth, and to have been built of unburnt bricks of unusual size.   This locality has, however, principally attracted
attention from the enormous quantity of antique coins which
Masson and others have collected there.[2]   In the first year,
these numbered 1,865 of copper, with a few of silver, together
with many rings, signets, and other relics; in the next the
number was 1,900; in the next, 2,500; in the next, 13,474;
finally, in 1837, it was increased to 60,000; besides great
numbers of engraved seals.   These coins exhibited extraordinary diversity of origin: among them were Greek and Roman coins, Greco-Bactrian and Bactrian, Indo-Parthian and
Indo-Scythian, Sassanian, Hindoo, and Indo-Mahometan, besides a great variety of others.   In point of date, they extended from the third century before the Christian era to the
thirteenth century after that epoch.   They were submitted to the
examination and arrangement of the learned Professor Wilson,
who, in his erudite treatise on *Ariana Antiqua,* has made great
and successful use of them in throwing light on the history and
antiquities of Afghanistan, India, and Central Asia.   Masson attributes the vast number of coins and other relics found at Beghram
to its having been the site of an immense cemetery, in which

[1] Bal. Afg. and Panj. iii. 140.
Jour. As. Soc. 1836, p. 1-28;
Masson, Mem. on the Ancient Coins found in Beghram.
[2] Lord, Koh-i-Damun, 56.

they were deposited with the ashes of the dead, and regards the vast quantities of broken pottery mixed with the earth as the fragments of funeral vases. He considers the city of Beghram as having been the Alexandria ad Caucasum of the Greeks, and to have been destroyed by Zingis, since the historians of Timur make no mention of it in describing his march through the plain of Beghram, from which it may be inferred that it then no longer existed. This opinion as to the locality of Alexandria ad Caucasum receives some support from Professor Wilson ;[3] but on the other hand, it may be urged, that as Beghram is situate nearly opposite the mouth of the Koushan Pass,*[4] or Pass of Hindoo Koosh, which is only practicable in summer ; and as Arrian[5] relates that Alexander crossed the Caucasus in spring, he must have taken the route by Bamian, which is open all the year round ;[6] and as, according to the same authority, his march brought him to Alexandria ad Caucasum, we must assign Bamain as its locality. Accordingly we find Ritter,[7] Rennell, Vigne,[8] Gosselin,† and Burnes[9] of opinion that Bamian was the Alexandria ad Caucasum.‡ With reference to this controversy, it is not unworthy of remark, that no traces have been discovered of Grecian architecture in the mud-built ruins of Beghram. The structures of Ghulghuleh and Saiyadabad have at least been more lasting. Beghram is in lat. 34° 53′, long. 69° 19′.

BEHUT.—See JAILUM.

BELA, the capital of the province of Lus, in Beloochistan, is a town containing 800 houses, built of mud, and 5,000 inhabitants. It is the residence of the Jam, or chief of the province,

[3] Ariana Antiqua, 181.

[4] Lord, Rep. viii.

[5] L. iv. c. 12.

[6] Masson, in Jour. As. Soc. ut supra, 10.

[7] Erdkunde von Asien, v. 272.
[8] Ghuznee, 195, 199.
[9] i. 184.

E.I.C. Ms. Doc.; Pott. Belooch. 19; Masson, ii. 27 ; Jour. As. Soc. 1839, p. 190 ; Carloss, Jour. to Beylah ; Outram, Rough Notes, 187.

* At page 182 of his learned work, Professor Wilson says, " The road by the Khoshal Pass, or some others running perpendicularly across the mountains, are much more likely to have been followed by the Macedonian army ;" but he admits (p. ix.) that the Khoshal (the Koushan of Lord and Leech) is not open throughout the year.

† In Sainte Croix, " Examen Critique des Historiens d'Alexandre, p. 827."

‡ In an article by Prinsep (H. T.), " On Passes into Hindostan," in Jour. As. Soc. Beng.1842, in general exhibiting much learning, sagacity, and judgment, it is taken for granted that Beghram is Alexandria ad Caucasum, and in a letter published in Jour. of Geog. Soc. of London, 1842 (p. 113), " On Comparative Geography of Afghanistan," by Rawlinson, we are informed that " Beihram (Beghram) is certainly the Alexandria ad Caucasum ;" but in each case neither proof nor argument is given.

whose fortress, built of mud, and surrounded with high battle-mented ramparts, flanked with towers at the angles, forms a striking object. Within the inclosure of this fortress is a large mosque, covered with a dome. The town is partly surrounded by a mud wall. Its situation is close to the Poorally river, and in a hilly tract, but which is capable of cultivation in the watered valleys. It is supported partly by being the seat of government, and partly by the transit trade from Sonmeanee to Kelat and Khorasan, the road passing through it. The bazaar is small, but neat, and the streets, though narrow and humbly built, are said to possess the distinction, so unusual in an Oriental town, of being clean. Lat. 26° 9', long. 66° 24'.

Burnes' Pers.Narr. 96.

BELOAT.—A village in Afghanistan, situate on the right bank of the Indus. Lat. 32° 11', long. 71° 16'.

BELOOCHISTAN, an extensive country of Southern Asia, is bounded on the north by Afghanistan, on the east by Sinde, on the south by the Indian Ocean, and on the west by Persia. It lies between lat. 24° 50' and 30° 20', and long. 57° 40' and 69° 18'. Its greatest length is from east to west, and is about 700 miles; its greatest breadth, from north to south, is 380 miles; its area is 160,000 square miles. The outline of the sea-coast is in general remarkably regular, running nearly due east and west a little north of lat. 25°, from Cape Monze, on the border of Sinde,

[1] Horsbugh, i.407.

in long. 66° 35', to Cape Jask,[1] in long. 57° 48'. It is, for the most part, craggy, but not remarkably elevated, and has, in some places, for considerable distance, a low sandy shore, though almost everywhere the surface becomes much higher inland. The principal headlands, proceeding from east to west, are Cape Monze, or

[2] Id. l. 493.
[3] Id. 494.
[4] Id. 494.
[5] Id. 494.
[6] Id. 495.
[7] Id. 497.

Ras Moarree,[2] which is the eastern headland of Sonmeanee Bay; Goorab Sing,[3] Ras Arubah,[4] Ras Noo,[5] forming the western headland of Gwadel Bay; Ras Jewnee,[6] forming the eastern point of Gwettar Bay, and Cape Jask[7] at the western extremity. There is no good harbour along the coast, though extending about 600 miles; but there are several roadsteads, having good holding-ground, and sheltered on several points. Of these, the best are Sonmeanee Bay and Choubar Bay, at which last point is the only place on the coast deserving the name of a town, there being elsewhere nothing but small and wretched villages.

The most remarkable features of this country are its rugged and elevated surface, its barrenness, and deficiency of water. To the eastward, that lofty range of mountains, known by the name of the Hala range, and called the Brahooick mountains by Pottinger,[8] rises from the Indian Ocean at Cape Monze.* The breadth in the southern part is about thirty miles, but it increases to the northward, where the Lukkee mountains of Western Sinde shoot off to the east. To the west, the Brahooick or Hala range expands to a vast extent, forming either rugged table-lands or intricate mountain groups. To the north-west,[9] these mountains continually diminish in height until the ground sinks to the level of the desert, through which the lower part of the Helmund holds its course, and which is probably, on an average, between 2,000 and 3,000 feet above the level of the sea. In the north-east, the Hala or Brahooick mountains join the southern part of the Suliman range. In the north,[1] they join the Toba and the Khojeh Amran mountains, which attain a very considerable height, the peak of Tukkatoo[2] being considered to have an elevation of above 11,000 feet. Chehel Tan,[3] a mountain to the south-west of that last mentioned, has an equal, or perhaps greater, elevation, as its summit is covered with snow to the end of June or beginning of July, and some remains throughout the summer in the deep ravines. The whole of the country in this region has a great elevation, the bottom of the valley of Shawl being 5,637 feet,[4] and Dasht-i-bedowlut, another extensive depression, 5,793 feet above the sea. Pottinger[5] considers Kelat the highest part of Beloochistan ; but Chehel-Tan and Tukatoo are unquestionably much higher, and on reference to the table † it will be seen that the height of Kelat is only 6,000 feet. The valleys here are for the most part sandy and barren, and all, in consequence of the great general elevation, have a very rigorous climate, snow lying on the ground from November to February, and the crops being later than in Great Britain.[6] In brief, Beloochistan may be described as one maze of mountains, except on the north-west, in which direction the surface descends, as already observed, to the Great Desert on the south, where a low tract stretches along the sea-shore, exhibiting a dreary waste of inconsider-

[8] Beloochistan, 251.

[9] Pottinger, 252.

[1] Elph. 105.

[2] Havelock,i. 249 ; Conolly, ii. 125.
[3] Masson, ii. 82.

[4] Hough, 74; Masson, 318.

[5] 259.

[6] Pottinger, 258.

* According to Pottinger, "it springs abruptly to a conspicuous height and grandeur out of the sea." Horsburgh states it to be of "moderate height" (p. 493).

† Infra, 87.

G 2

able rocks, or dry and barren sands ;* and for a small extent
on the east, where the burning plain of Cutch Gundava extends along the eastern base of the Hala mountains. From this
plain to the elevated table-land lying to the west, the eastern
face of the mountain range is furrowed by two long and very deep

7 309. ravines, through which the Bolan (called by Pottinger[7] Koahee)
and Moola rivers hold their way. Along the courses of these
rivers lie the celebrated passes bearing their names, and affording
the means of communication between the valley of the Indus and
Beloochistan.

   In the northern part of Beloochistan, the only rivers of any
importance are the Bolan and the Moola, and these are little
more than prolonged torrents, being ultimately lost in the sands

8 259. of Cutch Gundava. Pottinger[8] observes that "there is not a
single body of running water in this part of the country worthy
of a higher appellation than that of a rivulet, unless when swollen
by partial floods to a tumultuous and unfordable torrent, nor one,
even of that description, that can be said to flow through a regular
and unbroken channel to the main." The southern part abounds
in torrents, which rise in the mountains, and cross the low sandy
tract lying between them and the ocean. Near the base of the
mountains, the channels are very small, and in the dry season
are filled with vegetation. Towards the coast, they are much
broader, and deeper. Of this description of water-course
is the Hub, rising in that part of the Hala mountains which

9 Hart, in Trans.
of the As. Soc. ix.
135. separates Beloochistan and Sinde. After heavy rains,[9] it rushes
down with a vast body of water ; but, on the setting in of dry weather, the flow ceases ; there is no longer any stream, the bed merely

1 Id. 141. containing a few pools. The Poorally,[1] another of these torrents,
further west, has generally a very inconsiderable stream, which,
in long-continued dry weather, totally ceases at Lyaree, about
twenty miles from its mouth. Below that town it becomes a

2 Pottinger,299 ;
Masson, Kalat, 25. creek of the sea,[2] navigable for small boats. The Aghor, farther
west, passes by Hinglaj, the celebrated place of Hindoo pilgrim-

   * At Bunpoor, in the Kohistan, in the extreme west, are two sandy deserts,
each about twenty-five miles square. Between them is an oasis, or fertile slip
of land, about six or seven miles broad and thirty long, well watered by numerous springs, and producing grain in such abundance as to supply most part
of the surrounding countries. (Grant's Journal of a Route through Makran,
in Transact. of Royal As. Soc. of Great Brit. and Irel. vol. v. 333.)

age. It is thought to have a longer course than most of the streams along this coast, and to rise amidst mountains frequently covered with snow,[1] as at the setting in of hot weather, like rivers having such a source, its water becomes higher. Proceeding westward from Hinglaj to the mouth of the Dustee, a distance of 250 miles, we find that only a few small rivulets occur. The Dustee, where Pottinger crossed it, was, within 100 yards of the beach, about twenty inches deep and twenty yards wide ; yet, if his opinion be correct, it has a course of nearly 1,000 miles, rising in the Gurmsehl,[2] near the southern course of the Helmund river.[3] The upper part, called the Boodoor, makes its way, in the wet season, through the loose and parched sands of the desert south of Seistan ; but, for the greater part of the year, its channel is a dry ravine. Pottinger makes a bold, yet perhaps not improbable conjecture, that this was formerly a channel through which the superfluous water of the valley of the Helmund was discharged into the ocean, but that now the whole is carried off by means either of absorption or of evaporation from the swamp of Hamoon. Westward of the Dustee, there are only a few small brooks, which discharge themselves into the sea, and, in fact, along the whole distance of 600 miles, through which the coast of Beloochistan extends, there is no stream which might not, in dry weather, be forded by a child.

The climate of Beloochistan presents extraordinary varieties. In most parts, on account of the great elevation of the surface, it is mild, and even cool, bringing to perfection only the productions of the more northern parts of the temperate zone, whilst a short journey will bring the traveller among the crops of the torrid zone. Thus, Pottinger, on the 31st of January, halted at a field of sugar-canes ; on the succeeding 7th of February, his water-skins[4] and their contents were frozen, and at Kelat,[5] on the 14th of the same month, he found the frost so intense that water froze instantly when thrown on the ground. Masson[6] also found the cold extreme, and the roads sheeted with ice, in the country west of Shawl. He adds, that snow lies on the ground for above two months in the fertile valley of Shawl.[7] In a descent of a few miles down the eastern face of the Hala mountains, the surface sinks from this elevated table-land to Cutch Gundava, the commencement of that vast extent of level country which stretches into Hindostan. At Dadur, lying at the foot of the range, the

[1] Hart, 147 ; Pottinger, 301.
[2] 135.
[3] 303.
[4] 29-37.
[5] 47.
[6] Bal. Afg. Panj. i. 317-321.
[7] Kalat, 313.

heat is overpowering, and the unburnt bricks, according to the report of the natives,[8] are made red by the scorching rays of the sun. Such is the result of the difference of elevation, the table-land being, on an average, between 5,000 and 6,000 feet above the level of the sea,[9] and Dadur only 742.

The climate along the low coast, which forms the southern boundary of Beloochistan, is in some degree tempered by the vicinity of the ocean;[1] but probably nowhere is the effect of a scorching sun more felt than in the Western Desert, south of Seistan. Here the sand, so fine as to be almost impalpable, is raised by the wind and held in suspension. The surface assumes the appearance of the waves of the ocean, gradually sloping on the windward side, but on the leeward displaying a front, steep and even perpendicular, resembling a wall rather than a loose and accidental aggregation of minute particles of sand. During the hottest part of the summer, the winds are so scorching[2] as utterly to destroy animal life, and consequently to render the tract at that period quite impassable.

Little is of course known respecting the geology of a country so extensive and so little explored. Masson[3] found the ranges about Kelat and Moostung generally to consist of a very compact secondary limestone, containing numerous ammonites, corallines, and other fossil remains, and he found that a similar formation extends southward to the sea.[4] It does not appear that primary formations have been observed *in situ* in any part of Beloochistan, though Hart found fragments of quartz in Lus. The Bolan Pass, which cuts and discloses the strata of the Hala mountains to a great depth, lies through recent formations—sandstone, puddingstone, and secondary limestone.[5] The low hills along the coast are of recent limestone, sandstone, conglomerate, and shells, as is the lower part of the Hala range, forming the line of separation between Beloochistan and Sinde.[6] The Kohistan,[7] or hill country in the north-western extremity, bears strong marks of existing volcanic action.*

The mineral wealth in a country so mountainous and extensive may be expected to be considerable. Pottinger[8] vaguely

8 Masson, Bal. Afg. Panj. i. 340.

9 Hough, App. 74.

1 Jour. As. Soc. 1842, p. 54; Grif. Bar. and Ther. Obs. in Afg.

2 Pottinger, 130, 137.

3 Bal. Afg. Pang. ii. 78, Kalat, 400.

4 Kalat, 30.

5 Hough, 53.

6 Jour. As. Soc. 1840, p. 142-148; Hart, Jour. from Kurrachee to Hinglaj.

7 Pottinger, 179.

8 322.

* In Lus is a singular volcano, or *geyser*, of liquid mud, ejected at intervals from four circular basins on the tops of the same number of hills grouped together. This singular phenomenon bears a close resemblance to the Malacuba, or mud volcano of Sicily. (Hart, 143.)

states that the precious metals have been discovered near the town of Nal, 150 miles south-west of Kelat. This statament, if taken in its full and literal meaning, is startling, as it is not easy to point out a locality where gold and silver are found together. Pottinger adds, that the ores are disposed of in the crude state to the Hindoos, who smuggle them to avoid duties; but it is clear that ores of silver, at least, do not admit of furtive transport for several hundred miles through a rugged country. He says, also, " Gold, silver, lead, iron, copper, tin, antimony, brimstone, alum, sal-ammoniac, and many kinds of mineral salts and salt-petre, are found in various parts of Beloochistan," but such vague and sweeping statements are of little value. It has, however, been ascertained by careful investigators, that in Lus, in the hills between Lyaree and Bela, copper is found in large quan-tities.[7] A Hindoo merchant, of Kurrachee, brought away twenty camel-loads of ore, which yielded about thirty per cent. of metal. " The whole country," observes Hart,[8] " is indeed rich in mineral productions, and well worthy the attention of an experienced geologist." Lead, according to Masson,[9] is abundant in the mountains of Beloochistan, and he mentions a hill at Kappar, about eighty miles south-west of Kelat, as appearing to be entirely composed of lead-ore,[1] which is very easily reduced. The lead is used for making balls for muskets and rifles, and, as it seems, for scarcely any other purpose. Antimony[2] abounds in the same range of hills. Iron-ore is of very general occurrence, but the want of skill in the natives prevents its being much worked. The principal deposits at present known are in the north of Lus.[3] The mines of sulphur at Sunnee, south of the Bolan Pass, are very rich in that mineral, and were extensively worked under the Durani sway. Alum is found in the same locality. Common salt is unfortunately too general, destroying vegetation and vitiating the streams and springs.

[7] Hart,154; Trans. of As. Soc. Beng. 1840, p. 30; De la Hoste on Copper in Luz.
[8] 154, ut supra.
[9] ii. 55.
[1] Kalat, 43.
[2] Masson, Kalat, 462.
[3] Id. 462; Pottinger, 323; Leech, Rep. on Sindh. Army, 66.

TABLE OF HEIGHTS.

	FEET.	
Kelat,[4] lat. 28° 53′, long. 66° 27′	6,000	[4] E.I.C. Ms. Doc.
Sohrab,[5] lat. 28° 22′, long. 66° 9′	5,800	[5] E.I.C. Ms. Doc.
Siriab,[6] in the table-land of Shawl, lat. 30° 3′, long. 66° 53′	5,793	[6] Jour. As. Soc. 1842, p. 55; Grif. Bar. and Ther. Heights in Afg.
Munzilgah,[7] near summit of Bolan Pass, lat. 29° 53′, long. 67°	5,793	[7] Hough, Narr. of Exp. in Afg. App. 74.

FEET.

[*] Griffith, 55.	Shawl,[8] or Quetta, lat. 30° 10′, long. 66° 57′	5,563
[9] E.I.C. Ms. Doc.	Angeera,[9] lat. 28° 10′, long. 66° 12′	5,250
[1] Ead.	Bapaw,[1] lat. 28° 16′, long. 66° 20′	5,000
[2] Ead.	Peesee-Bhent,[2] lat. 28° 10′, long. 66° 35′	4,600
[3] Hough's App. 74.	Siribolan,[3] lat. 29° 50′, long. 67° 14′	4,494
[4] E.I.C. Ms. Doc.	Putkee,[4] lat. 28° 5′, long. 66° 40′	4,250
[5] E.I.C. Ms. Doc.	Paeesht Khana,[5] lat. 27° 59′, long. 66° 47′	3,500
[6] Ead.	Nurd,[6] lat. 27° 52′, long. 66° 54′	2,850
[7] Griffith, 55.	Ab-i-goom,[7] lat. 29° 46′, long. 67° 23′	2,540
[8] E.I.C. Ms. Doc.	Jungikoosht,[8] lat. 27° 55′, long. 67° 2′	2,150
[9] Ead.	Bent-i-jah,[9] lat. 28° 4′, long. 67° 10′	1,850
[1] Hough's App. 74.	Beebee Nanee,[1] lat. 29° 39′, long. 67° 28′	1,695
[2] E.I.C. Ms. Doc.	Kohow,[2] lat. 28° 20′, long. 67° 12′	1,250
[3] Hough's App. 74.	Gurmab,[3] lat. 29° 36′, long. 67° 32′	1,081
[4] Id. 74.	Kundye, or Kohan Delan,[4] lat. 29° 22′, long. 67° 36′ ..	904
[5] E.I.C. Ms. Doc.	Kullar,[5] lat. 28° 18′, long. 67° 15′	750
[6] Griffith, 54.	Dadur,[6] lat. 29° 26′, long. 67° 41′	742
[7] E.I.C. Ms. Doc.	Kotree,[7] lat. 28° 25′, long. 67°, 26′	600

Little attention has been given to the investigation of the vegetable kingdom in this country, which is the more to be regretted, as the great varieties of soil and climate must necessarily make it very rich. The *appurs*,[8] a species of *Zizyphus jujuba*, clothes the loftier ranges, where the soil is sufficiently deep. It affords an excellent timber, greatly resembling teak. The tamarind-tree also attains a great size, and yields excellent timber : the babool, a species of mimosa, the lye, or tamarisk, and the mulberry-tree, in some places attain the size of timber-trees; the oriental plantain, the walnut, sycamore, mango, wild fig, willow, and wild olive, are found in various divisions of the country. Date-trees abound in the hot regions, and yield good fruit.

[8] Masson, Kalat, 450; Pottinger, 327.

The wild animals are lions, tigers,* leopards, hyenas, wolves, jackals, tiger-cats, wild dogs, foxes, various sorts of the lemur

* Pottinger enumerates lions and tigers, but Masson, who had traversed the country so often and in so many directions, does not mention them.

and monkey genera,[1] wild goats, wild sheep, wild asses, eagles, | Pottinger, 328 ; Masson, Kalat,
kites, vultures, magpies, crows, falcons of various kinds, wild 444.
geese and ducks, phenicopters, herons, bustards, parroquets,
and almost every class of small birds. The jungle-fowl, the original stock of our barn-door fowl, abounds in the thickets in the
hot districts. Neither reptiles nor insects are peculiarly abundant
or remarkable. The rivers are too shallow and intermittent to
contain fish, which, however, swarm on the coast ; and the people
there, like their ancestors the *Icthyophagi*, principally subsist on
this species of food.[2] Of domestic animals, camels are the most [2] Pottinger, 328.
universally valuable. The Bactrian variety, or that which has two
humps, is found only in the elevated tracts, where it is used only
for burthen, for which it is admirably suited, being strong, clumsy,
rough, and incredibly patient of hunger, thirst, fatigue, and extremes of temperature. It is of a black colour. The light-coloured,
tall, slender, one-humped species, called dromedaries, are peculiar
to the low and hot regions, where they are much used by the predatory tribes in their plundering expeditions, in consequence of
their superior speed.[3] The best horses are in the north and west, [3] Id. ibid.
where the breed is much improved by the admixture of Arabian
and Persian blood. The horses of Lus and Mekran are small,
weak, and spiritless. Those imported into India from this country
are generally from the south of Kelat and from the more elevated
part of Cutch Gundava. These are strong, well made, and large,
but excessively vicious.

In so barren and rude a country, the condition of most of the
inhabitants must be necessarily pastoral ; and as the pastures are
generally poor, sheep and goats are kept for milk in preference to
cows or buffaloes, which are both very rare. The milk is generally converted either into *mass* or curd, or else into *roghan* or
clarified butter, known in Hindostan by the name of *ghee*. The
process of clarification is performed simply by boiling in water,
and the quantity of ghee prepared both for home consumption and
sale is very great. *Shelanch*,[4] the *koroot* of the Afghans, and so [4] Masson, Kalat,
much relished both by them and by Belooches, is inspissated 435-437.
buttermilk. Camels' milk is little used, except in the hot region,
where it is considered superior to any other. The sheep, however, is the great support of the pastoral tribes, the milk and flesh
supplying food, and the skins and wool (which last is of superior
quality) furnishing clothing. They are generally of the species

called in Persia *dumba*, with large tails, weighing from 10lbs. to 15lbs., and consisting of a rich fat-like marrow. The skins of sheep and goats are also converted into bags for carrying water, milk, flour, grain, or other articles. The crops most cultivated in Beloochistan are wheat, barley, oil-seeds, millet, madder, various kinds of pulse, and, in the low and hot regions, rice, cotton, maize in small quantities, indigo, and tobacco.

The management of gardens and orchards receives great attention about Kelat, Moostung, and Shawl. Apricots, peaches, grapes, almonds, pistachio-nuts, apples, pears, plums, cherries, quinces, figs, pomegranates, mulberries, plantains, and small fruit of various kinds are produced in great abundance. Melons[4] are of very fine flavour and of so great a size that, it is said, a man can scarcely lift one of the largest kind. Apricots and some other fruits are dried, and in this state used in great quantities as food. Mulberries,[5] as in Afghanistan are dried, ground into meal, and made into bread, which has a peculiar honeyed flavour, not unlike that of gingerbread. The principal esculent vegetables are turnips, carrots, cabbages, lettuces, cauliflowers, peas, beans, radishes, onions, celery, parsley, egg-fruit, cucumbers. *Rhuwash*, or edible rhubarb, is consumed in great quantities in spring, but the great delicacy of the natives of this country, as of other adjacent countries, is *hing*, or assafœtida, so detestable to Europeans, both as to smell and flavour. Here it is called emphatically *khush korak*,[6] or "pleasant food."

This rude country can scarcely be considered to have any manufactures, certainly none destined for foreign markets. The skins of sheep, goats, and other quadrupeds undergo a coarse and imperfect tanning; wool[7] is felted by a process similar to that used in Afghanistan. It also, as well as the hair of goats and camels, is spun, made into ropes and strings, and woven into carpets and coarse cloths, for making grain-bags or covering tents. Sheep's-wool is spun and woven into cloths of finer fabric, which are dyed with madder or some other native product. The quality of the manufactured articles might be greatly improved by the introduction of better processes, as the wool is very fine and natural dyes are plentiful. The notice of a few matchlocks[8] and other arms made at Kelat may be considered nearly to complete the list of the manufactures of this barbarous people. The external trade of a country exercising little manufacturing industry and possess-

4 Pottinger, 324.

5 Masson, Kalat, 438.

6 Masson, Kalat, 438.

7 Masson, Kalat, 440.

8 Pottinger, 66.

ing no great abundance of raw material must necessarily be very small. Sonmeanee,[9] its only port, contains about 200 huts, constructed of wattle and mud, and roofed with mat; and, as vessels cannot reach the beach, horses, the principal article of export, are swum out to them in spring tides, when alone they can approach sufficiently near. The other exports are butter, hides, wool, a few coarse drugs, dried fruits, fish, a little grain, and vegetable oil. The imports consist of a small quantity of British and Indian manufactures, rice, spices, dye-stuffs, and slaves from Muscat.[1] In 1840 there were but six vessels of any size belonging to the port of Sonmeanee, five of which were the property of the Hindoos, who have most of the trade in their hands.[2] There were, besides, twenty coasting and fishing boats. The customs were farmed for 34,000 rupees annually, and were on the increase.[3]

[9] Jour. As. Soc. 1840, p. 138; Hart, Jour. from Kurrachee to Hinglaj; Horsburgh, i. 493.

[1] Pottinger, 294; Masson, Kalat, 409.

[2] Hart, 139.

[3] Id. 138.

Beloochistan is usually considered to contain six provinces: 1st, Sarawan; 2nd, Kelat; 3rd, Cutch Gundava; 4th, Jhalawan; 5th, Lus; 6th, Mekran. These are noticed separately in their alphabetical order; but, it is to be remembered that, under circumstances so fluctuating and precarious as those of Beloochistan, any political divisions must be regarded as arbitrary and uncertain. At present, the four first-mentioned provinces are considered subject to Mir Nasir Khan, chief of Kelat, son of Mehrab Khan, killed by the British troops when they stormed his capital in 1839.[4] Lus is in vassalage to the same prince, the immediate government being exercised by a petty chief, whose right is hereditary, and who is styled the Jam.[5] He is not considered actual ruler until recognized by the Khan of Kelat, but when fully established, he possesses sovereign power, merely furnishing a military contingent when required by his superior. Mekran, subjected in a certain sense by Nasir Khan, the great-grandfather of the present Khan of Kelat, was at no time reduced to farther vassalage than that implied by paying a trifling tribute, and lately this extensive district has thrown off even that badge of submission.[6] It now enjoys the independence of anarchy, under the sway of numerous wild chieftains. The Khan of Kelat is absolute, having no check to his acts excepting the ordinary check upon extreme tyranny, the dread of insurrection. This unlimited power over life, person, and property is also possessed by subordinate officers. Mustapha Khan, the governor of Cutch Gundava, exerted himself much, and to a certain extent success-

[4] Masson, Kalat, 383; Hough, App. 24; Outram, 164.

[5] Masson, Kalat, 301; Journ. As. Soc. Beng. 1839, p. 196, 197, Chrloss on Lus.

[6] Masson, Kalat, 362-364.

fully, to repress the predatory habits of the Belooche tribes. To exhibit the force of his authority, he caused rolls of cloth and other articles of value to be thrown on the roads. If they were removed, a rigorous search was instituted for the offenders, who, when discovered, were impaled.[7] It is said that by this terrific mode of proceeding, he so restrained the lawlessness of the natives, that if they saw a piece of cotton on the ground, they would run away in terror, leaving it untouched. Similar relations exist as to other countries while in a state of comparative barbarism, and all such statements must be received with allowance; but it is not to be doubted that the decisive proceedings of Mustapha Khan made him feared.

The amount of revenue [6] enjoyed by the Khan of Kelat is inconsiderable, as the ruling races, Belooche and Brahu, pay no direct taxes, and their poverty and simple habits prevent them from contributing much indirectly. His income is therefore derived from his resources as a proprietor of lands or towns: from a proportion of the produce paid in kind by the Afghan, Dehwar (Parsee), and Jet cultivators; from dues on direct and transit trade, and from arbitrary exactions, a never-failing mode with eastern potentates of recruiting an exhausted treasury. Pottinger [9] estimates the amount at 350,000 rupees. Masson,[1] who had ample means of acquiring information through colloquial channels, at 300,000; which of these statements makes the nearest approximation to correctness cannot be determined, but neither seems improbable. With such a revenue, it is obvious that no standing army can be maintained, and Masson,[2] certainly very competent to the task of acquiring information on this subject, states that Mehrab Khan, the late ruler, "nearly destitute of troops in his own pay, was compelled, on the slightest cause for alarm, to appeal to the tribes, who attended or otherwise as suited their whims or convenience." Pottinger [3] computes the numbers available for the service of the khan at 60,000 fighting men, but has not mentioned how so vast a host could, if collected, find food in this barren country. Mehrab Khan could, on no occasion, assemble more than 12,000, and in his final struggle for property, power, and life, the number of his troops did not amount to 3,000.[4] The Belooche soldier is heavily incumbered with arms, carrying a matchlock, a spear, a sword, a dagger, and a shield. Pottinger [5] considers them good marksmen, and states that in

[7] Masson, Kalat, 369.

[8] Masson, Kalat, 708.

[9] 294.

[1] Kalat, 408.

[2] Kalat, 407.

[3] 294.

[4] Willshire in Despatches, Hough's App. 27; Outram, 168; Jackson, 18.
[5] 65.

action they trust principally to their skill in this respect, avoiding close combat; but their readiness in general to close with the British troops shews that he is in this instance mistaken. They formed the strength of the armies of Sinde, but the late decisive conflict there shewed how little, with great superiority of numbers, they are able to withstand a disciplined force. The greater part serve on foot, but a number, not inconsiderable, have horses, and in their irregular forays, camels, which they often prefer, on account of their greater powers of endurance.

The inhabitants of Beloochistan are, with few exceptions, Mahometans of the Soonnee persuasion, maintaining the authority of the three first kaliphs, and are so bigoted, that, in the opinion of Pottinger,[5] a Shia or votary of Ali would encounter [5 61.] more enmity amongst them than would a Christian.[6] Even the [6 Id. 80.] Dehwars, speaking the Persian language, and considered to be of Persian descent, reject the Shia doctrine so generally received in the country from which they derive their vernacular tongue, and it is supposed their origin. Passing from religious distinctions to those of race and tribe, we find the majority of inhabitants of this extensive region who may be styled by a common name, Beloochee, to comprehend[7] five principal classes—Brahuis, Nha- [7 Masson, Kalat,] roes, Mughsees, Rinds, and Lumris. Of this widely dispersed [336.] and incongruous population, Masson, who has had more ample means of information than any other European, observes, " It is clear, that in this community are comprised many tribes of very different descent, inferring from the physiological distinctions which prevail amongst them, setting aside the variety of dialects spoken by them." Of the Brahuis, Pottinger[8] enumerates [8 73.] seventy-four tribes; of the others, who may be properly classed as Beloochees, according to him forty-eight; and he adds, no doubt with truth, that he might recount as many more. Masson[9] [9 Kalat, 338.] gives a list of thirty-five tribes, but to such minute enumerations, with regard to a country so imperfectly known as Beloochistan, a remark of Sir John Malcolm[1] may probably be [1 History of Persia, i. 125.] applied with much justice—" It is a common fault of historians to be desirous of giving a finished picture of the nations of whom they treat, but such descriptions must, in many cases, be like finished maps of unsurveyed regions, which are calculated only to mislead." The Brahuis, according to Pottinger[2] and [2 271.] Masson, are so called from the words bah-roh-i,[3] *on the waste,* [3 Kalat, 338.]

and are more erratic and more exclusively pastoral in their
habits and pursuits than the other Belooches. They spend [4]
their lives in roaming during the continuance of summer, in
winter seeking shelter under rude tents of felt or coarse cloths,
of goat or camel hair; and they subsist almost exclusively on
animal food. They are most numerous [5] in the northern and
western parts, but may be found in less or greater numbers
everywhere. They differ from the other Belooches in being of
much shorter and broader make, in having round faces and broad
flat features; their hair and beards are frequently brown, and
Pottinger [6] observes, that they bear no resemblance to any other
Asiatics that he had ever seen. Their dialect also varies considerably from that of the other classses of Belooches, though in
all can be traced a close affinity with the Teutonic languages,
apparently justifying the classification by Klaproth,* who places
Belooche in the great Indo-Germanic family of languages. A
few instances in illustration of this opinion may not be uninteresting:—

Brahooi.

Brahooi.	German.	Latin.	English.
I	Ich	Ego	I
Da	Das	,,	That
Ed	Es	Id	It
Der	Der	,,	Who
Are	,,	Eras (Imp.)	(Thou) art
Areri	,,	,,	(You) are

Belooch.

Belooch.			
Ma (I)	Mich (Acc.)	Me (Acc.)	Me
Mi	Mein	Mei	My
Thau	Du	Tu	Thou
Ki	,,	Qui	Who
Do	,,	Duo	Two
Shash	Sechs	Sex	Six
Hapt	,,	Septem	Seven
		(Greek Hepta) †	

* Zwischen dem Lande der Afg'anen und Persien wohnen längs dem
Meere die Belutzchen deren Sprache ebenfalls zum Indo-Germanischen
stamme gehört. (Asia Polyglotta, 74.)

† Further information on this very interesting subject, too extensive and
intricate to receive more than the most cursory notice here, may be found in
Leech's Brahoic and Belooche Grammars, Calcutta, being No. xii. (pp. 81—

[4] Pottinger, 71.
[5] Masson, Kalat, 340.
[6] 71.

The Rinds and Musghces[6] are more stationary than the other 6 Pottinger, 60;
Belooche tribes, and are settled for the most part in the eastern Masson, Kalat, 348.
tracts toward Sinde, and between it and Kelat. Hence they have
constituted the strength of the armies of the Ameers of Sinde.
They are considered to be less addicted to the predatory habits
which constitute a general characteristic of the Belooche tribes
than the people of the north and west. The Nharoes hold
the extreme west, and being most remote from Hindostan, the
great source of such civilization as is known in this part of
the world, are the rudest, most ferocious, and most predatory,
but at the same time the most active and stirring of the
Belooches.[7] Their great delight is in *chupaos*, or plundering 7 Pottinger, 59.
expeditions; during which, mounted on fleet camels, they will
sweep over an extensive tract of country at the rate of seventy or
eighty miles a day, burning, slaying, and pillaging wherever they
go, until, worn out by fatigue, or sated with blood and plunder,
or dreading the vengeance of those who have suffered from
their atrocities, they make homewards by a route different
from that by which they advanced.* The Lumris, sometimes called Numris, for the most part hold the maritime province of Lus. They are an active, hardy people, subsisting on
their herds of camels, buffaloes, kine,[8] and goats; dwelling 8 Masson, Kalat, 298.
under tents of felt or coarse cloth, obtaining such grain or
other articles as their necessities require, but which their own
avocation cannot furnish, by barter for wool, hides, butter, and
other similar produce. The other branches of the population
deserving of notice are few. The Dehwars,[9] inconsiderable in 9 Pottinger, 80.
number, are devoted to agricultural and other industrial pursuits.
They are inoffensive in their manners, and of decent morals. They
speak pure Persian, and, as already mentioned, are understood to
be of Persian descent. The Jets, of Indian origin, constitute a
large portion of the fixed population of Cutch Gundava; others
of them wander[1] over a great part of the rest of the country, 1 Masson, Kalat, 351.
leading lives similar to the gypsies of Europe. They speak a

115) of the geographical section of " Reports and Papers, &c.," printed by
order of government, fol. Calcutta, 1839.

   Adelung mentions the Belooches, but considers them merely an Afghan Mithridates, i.
tribe.   253.

   * The habits of these people seem not unlike those of the Pindarries, the
scourge of India, till put down by the Marquis of Hastings.

peculiar dialect, called Jetki, allied to Hindustani. Hindoos are everywhere sparingly scattered through the towns wherever there is a chance of gain. They manage exclusively the money trans-actions of the country (few and unimportant as indeed they must be among so indigent a people), and carry on most of the opera-tions of trade. In these pursuits, poor as is the country, they sometimes succeed in amassing considerable wealth. · They are treated with much indulgence by the Mahometans, and, on the other hand, they relax greatly from the strictness of the native superstitions as observed in their own country. At Hinglaj, in Lus, is a celebrated shrine or object of Hindoo pilgrimage,[2] " one of the fifty-one places or *pitas* celebrated as the spots on which the dissevered limbs of Sati or Doorga were scattered." Besides the people already mentioned, there are a few Afghans in the valley of Shawl and its vicinity, and some of that peculiar race known in Afghanistan under the name of Taujiks.

The only towns demanding attention are Kelat, the capital, in the province of the same name; Shawl, Nooshky, and Moostung, in the province of Sarawan; Khozdur and Zeehree, in the pro-vince of Jhalawan; Gundava, Bagh, and Dadur, in the province of Cutch Gundava; Bela and Sonmeanee, in the province of Lus. They are all noticed in their proper places. Their aggregate population does not amount to 50,000. The amount of the popu-lation of the entire country can only be vaguely guessed at; but when it is recollected that there are scarcely any towns, that the country generally is very barren, and the people for the most part pastoral, without resources from commerce, manufactures, or skilful agriculture, perhaps three to the square mile is as large a proportion as ought to be assigned, and this would give a sum of about 480,000.* Masson[3] estimates the number at 450,000. Though a small portion of the population live in mud huts, and a few in forts, their favourite mode of residence is in their *toomuns* or encampments, formed of tents of black felt, coarse blanket, or carpet, stretched over a rude framework of sticks.

The people of Beloochistan are considered to be hospitable; after the fashion of other barbarous tribes in this part of the world, they will protect and kindly entertain a stranger while

[2] Trans. of As. Soc. 1840, p. 154; Editor's note on Hart, Jour. from Kurrachee to Hinglaj.

[3] Kalat, 335.

* Elphinstone (Account of Caubul, 84) states the number of the Beloochas at 1,000,000, and adds that he considers such an estimate much too low. Such assumptions appear to require no comment.

their guest, but feel no scruple in robbing and murdering him as soon as he has left their precincts. They are indolent, and, unless excited by amusement or war, or compelled to action by some urgent motive, spend their time in the manner common to all savage people—in idleness, rude dissipation, and the enjoyment of such coarse luxuries as they can procure, in lounging, gambling, smoking tobacco or hemp, and chewing opium. The tenets of their religion, and still more, perhaps, their poverty, preserve them from the abuse of fermented liquors. Their principal articles of food are milk in all its forms, the flesh of domestic animals, not excepting that of the camel, and game, including wild asses, the flesh of which is considered a delicacy.[4] Their appetites, like those of most savages, are voracious ; they consume incredible quantities of flesh when it can be obtained, and prefer it in a half-cooked state. They also use grain, in the form of bread and of various preparations, but they enjoy most such articles of food or condiment as possess a strong and stimulating flavour, as capsicum, onions, garlic, and especially assafœtida.[5] Their indolence prompts them to keep as many slaves as they can obtain and support. Polygamy is universal, some of the lower order have as many as eight women, either as wives or mistresses, and the number is increased in proportion to the rank and means of the man. Wives are obtained by purchase ; payment being made in cattle or other articles of pastoral wealth. The ceremony of marriage is performed by the moollah or priest, and on this occasion, as well as on some others affecting females, practices[6] similar to those of the Levitical law are observed. For instance, in this country, as also among the Afghans,[7] a man is expected to marry the widow of a deceased brother. When a death takes place, the body is watched for three successive nights by assembled friends and neighbours, who spend their time in feasting, so that the ceremony seems intended rather to furnish enjoyment to the living than to render honour to the dead.

Among the amusements of the Belooches gambling of various kinds must be reckoned ; but there are others of less debasing and more manly character—field sports, cudgel playing, sword practice, throwing the spear, and tilting on horseback with a sharp lance against a stake stuck in the ground, the object being to force it out of the earth and bear it away on the point of the lance in mid career. The men wear a white or blue shirt, or loose tunic of cotton cloth,

[4] Pottinger, 71.

[5] Pottinger, 64.

[6] Pottinger, 69.

[7] Elph. 179; Burnes' Pers. Narr. 142.

not unlike the frocks worn by waggoners and other classes of
country people in England, but not so long. Beneath are worn
loose trowsers, puckered about the ancles, and a *loongee*, or scarf,
about the waist. The head is covered by a cap, fitting close to
the hair, which falls down below it in the large locks for which
the Belooches are remarkable. In winter, men of rank wear an
upper coat or tunic of quilted cotton, the lower orders a rough
capote[7] of felt or coarse cloth. The women, within doors, dress
much in the same way as the men, excepting that their trowsers are
wider; and as their cotton tunic, the only covering of the upper
part of their persons, is open in front below the bosom, their
persons are a good deal exposed. When they go abroad, they
muffle themselves from head to foot in the long shroud-like
drapery worn in Afghanistan. They are in general treated with
more indulgence than among other Mahometan nations.

    It seems probable that Beloochistan was among the one hun-
dred and twenty-seven provinces over which Ahasuerus ruled
" from India even unto Ethiopia."[8] The first distinct account which
we have of this country is from Arrian,[9] who, with his usual brevity
and severe veracity, narrates the march of Alexander through it,
which he calls the country of the Oritæ and Gadrosii. He gives a
very accurate and judicious geographical account of this forlorn
tract, its general aridity, and the necessity of obtaining water by
digging in the beds of torrents; the food of the inhabitants, dates
and fish; the occasional occurrence of fertile spots; the abundance
of aromatic and thorny shrubs, and fragrant plants, and the violence
of the monsoon in the western part of Mekran. He notices also
the impossibility of subsisting a large army, and the consequent
destruction of the greater part of the men and beasts which formed
the expedition. At the commencement of the eighth century,[1]
this country was traversed by an army of the Kaliphate. It
was subsequently exposed to the transient and devastating inroads
of the Moguls; it became partially and nominally a portion of the
empire of Akbar. Towards the middle of the eighteenth century, it was made tributary by Nadir Shah, who bestowed on
Nasir Khan, the great-grandfather of the present ruler, the rank
of begler beg, or commander-in-chief. In 1839,[2] when the British
army advanced through the Bolan Pass towards Afghanistan, the
conduct of Mehrab Khan, the ruler of Beloochistan, was considered so treacherous, hostile, and dangerous, as to require " the

[7] Pottinger, 65.

[8] Esther i. 1.

[9] L. vi. cc. xxi.-
xvi.

[1] Pottinger, 389.

[2] Official An-
nouncement of
Gov.-Gen. in
Hough's App. 24.

exaction of retribution from that chieftain " and " the execution of such arrangements as would establish future security in that quarter." Gen. Willshire was accordingly detached from the army of the Indus at Quetta to assault Kelat. A gate [3] was [3] Willshire in knocked in by the field-pieces, and the town and citadel stormed Desp., Hough's App. 24; Outram, in a few minutes. Above 400 Belooches were slain, and among 166. them Mehrab Khan himself: 2,000 prisoners were taken.[4] The [4] Hough, 30, 31. British force consisted of 1,049 men.[5] In the following year [5] Masson, 175-178, 384. Kelat changed hands, the governor established by the British, together with a feeble garrison, being overpowered. At the close of the same year, it was re-occupied by the British under Gen. Nott. In 1841, Nasir Khan, the youthful son of the slain Mehrab Khan, was recognized by the British, who soon after evacuated the country.

BELUR, in the Punjab, at a short distance east of the Burnes, i. 71. Indus, has a tope or antique structure similar to that of Manikyala, but of smaller dimensions, being only fifty feet high. The lower part is a truncated cone, the base of which is uppermost. At an elevation estimated at fifteen feet, the building is encircled by a row of pilasters about five feet high. The upper part is in the shape of a dome. Lat. 33° 50′, long. 72° 51′.

BEMANJOPORO.—A village in Sinde, situate on the road E.I.C. Ms. Doc. from Bander Vikkar to Tattah, and thirty miles south-west of the latter place. Lat. 24° 26′, long. 67° 40′.

BENEE BADAM.—See BHEENEE BADAM.

BENEER.—See BOONEERE.

BENT-I-JAH.—A village in Beloochistan, in the Moola or E.I.C. Ms. Doc. Gundava Pass, between Kelat and Gundava, and seventy miles south-east of the former town. The village is situate on the river Moola, and is capable of yielding a few supplies. Elevation above the level of the sea, 1,350 feet. Lat. 28° 4′, long. 67° 10′.

BERAWUL.—See BHYROWALAH.

BERENG.—See BURENG.

BERMUL.—A village in Afghanistan, a few miles west of the E.I.C. Ms. Doc. crest of the Suliman mountains. Lat. 32° 50′, long. 69° 45′. E.I.C.Ms. Doc.; Elph. Acc. of Cau-
BERRAVOL.—A town of Northern Afghanistan, in the dis- bul, 351; Jour. trict drained by the upper part of the river Lundye, and generally As. Soc. 1839, p. 306, 312; Court. known by the name of the Eusufzai country, being inhabited Alexander's Exp. principally by the tribe of that name. The town is situate near on the Western Bank of the Indus.

H 2

the right bank of a stream of the same name. Lat. 35° 32′, long. 71° 40′.

BERRAVOL.—A river, or rather stream, which, rising on the southern declivity of the range of Hindoo Koosh, takes a south-easterly course of about fifty miles, and falls into the Lundye river on the western side, in lat. 35° 13′, long. 71° 57′.

BERRAVOL.—A valley in Northern Afghanistan, in which the town of the same name is situate, and through which the river Berravol flows. It is long and narrow, and extends from the plain of Bajour up the slope of Hindoo Koosh. The lower part is fertile and well cultivated; the upper, overgrown with thick forests of oak, cedar, and pines, abounds in wild beasts. Berravol is a distinct state, governed by its own chief.

F..I.C. Ms. Doc.　BETA.—A village in the Punjab, situate about six miles east of the river Indus, in lat. 33° 20′, long. 72° 3′.

E.I.C. Ms. Doc.　BETSUL.—A village in Afghanistan, situate in the Gomul Pass, about a mile from the Gomul river. Lat. 32° 8′, long. 69° 10′.

E.I.C. Ms. Doc.　BEZAISE.—A village in Afghanistan, sixteen miles north-west of the city of Kabool. Lat. 34° 40′, long. 68° 56′.

E.I.C. Ms. Doc.;
Jour. As. Soc.
1842, p. 53; Grif.
Bar. and Ther.
Meas. in Afg.;
Leech, Sindhian
Army, 94; Hough,
Narr. Exp. in Afg.
41; Atkinson,
Exp. in Afg. 106;
Havelock, War
in Afg. i. 192;
Conolly, Jour. to
India, II. 216;
Masson, Bal. Afg.
Panj. i. 348.

BHAG, or BAGH, in Beloochistan, a considerable town in Cutch Gundava, on the route from Shikarpoor to Dadur, close to the entrance of the Bolan Pass, and thirty-seven miles south of Dadur. It is surrounded by a ruinous mud wall, has a large roofed bazaar well supplied with wares, and is estimated to contain 2,000 houses. These, however, are wretchedly built of mud. It is situate on the river Nari, the current of which is interrupted in dry weather, when the inhabitants suffer much from the want of water, that obtained from tanks and wells being brackish and unwholesome. Adjoining to the town is an extensive cemetery, containing some remarkable tombs, and near it a large mosque, surmounted by a white dome, and having numerous minarets, covered with glazed green tiles. The only manufacture of importance is that of gunpowder, the sulphur for which is obtained from the neighbouring mine of Sunnee. Bhag, in consequence of its position on the great route from Sinde to the Bolan Pass, has considerable transit trade. The neighbouring country is very fertile in grain, where irrigated; but, without moisture, it is a dreary, barren, treeless plain of hard-baked clay. The climate is remarkably sultry. Lat. 28° 56′, long. 67° 54′.

BHAGAH-KI-TANDA.—A village in Sinde, on the road E.I C. Ms. Doc.
from Hyderabad to Wanga bazaar, sixty miles south-east of the
former, and twenty miles north-west of the latter town. It is
situate about two miles from the left bank of the Goomee river,
eight miles from its confluence with the Goongroo. Lat. 24° 42′,
long. 68° 53′.

BHAHALL.—A village in the Punjab, situated on an offset E.I.C. Ms. Doc.
of the Indus, and two miles east of the main channel. It is
about eighteen miles south of the town of Bukkur, which is on
the same stream. The road from Dera Ismael Khan to Mooltan
crosses the Indus at the Kaheree ferry, nine miles south of this
place. Lat. 31° 25′, long. 71° 3′.

BHAT.—A village in the Punjab, situate on the left bank of E.I.C. Ms. Doc.
the Ravee river, on the route from Lahore to Mooltan, thirty-
three miles south-west of the former city. Lat. 31° 19′, long.
73° 49′.

BHAUDA.—A village in the Punjab, about fifteen miles E.I.C. Ms. Doc.
from the right bank. of the Ghara river, and forty north-east of
the city of Bhawlpoor. Lat. 29° 54′, long. 71° 5S

BHAWLPOOR,[1] a state of Western India, is bounded on [1] Leech,Sindh.
the north-west for a short distance by Sinde, and for the rest of Army, 80-82.
the long frontier in that direction by the territory of the Sikhs;
on the east, south-east, and part of the south, by the deserts
of Bhutneer, Beekanair, and Jessulmair; and on the remaining
part of south by Sinde. It is a long, narrow tract, of shape approaching to that of an elongated oval. It is three hundred and
ten miles in length from north-east to south-west; one hundred
and ten in breadth at the widest part, measured at right angles to
the line of its length; and 22,000 square miles in superficial extent, of which, however, only about a sixth part is capable of
cultivation, or of supporting any considerable population. This
fertile tract, extending along the river Ghara, and having a completely alluvial soil, bears a strong resemblance to Sinde, both in
climate and aspect. The remainder, though in many parts exhibiting signs of former cultivation and population, is now, from
want of water, irreclaimable desert, either of hard dry clay, or of
loose shifting sands. The north-western frontier is formed by
a river-line, consisting in its successive parts of the Ghara,
the Punjnud, and the Indus. The Ghara, constituting the

most northern portion, is the great stream of the united waters of the Sutluj and Beas, the confluence of which is at some distance above the northern extremity of this frontier. The Ghara flows in a direction from north-cast to south-west, a distance of 200 miles, to its confluence with the Chenaub, after which the united stream is called the Punjnud, which forms the frontier of Bhawlpoor until its confluence with the Indus at Mittunkote, a distance of fifty miles. The Indus is then the boundary for fifty miles, until it flows southward into Sinde. This perfects a continuous river-line of 300 miles in length, and, allowing for sinuosities, about 350.

Bhawlpoor is a remarkably level country, there being no considerable eminence within its limits, as the occasional sand-hills, seldom exceeding fifty or sixty feet in height, cannot be considered exceptions.[2] The cultivable part extends along the river-line for a distance of about ten miles in breadth, from the left or eastern bank. In the sandy parts of the desert beyond this strip of fertility, both men and beasts, leaving the beaten path, sink as if in loose snow. Here, too, the sand is raised into ever-changing hills by the force of the winds sweeping over it.[3] In those parts of the desert which have a hard level soil of clay, a few stunted mimosas, acacias, and other shrubs are produced, together with rue, various bitter and aromatic plants, and occasionally tufts of grass. The mirage or sirraub, that strange illusive vision of lakes or sheets of water, mocking the sufferings of the wretched traveller over the more parched and scorched portions of desert lands, is here of frequent occurrence, and the deceptive effect is rendered complete by the reflection of men and animals passing along the plain, as if from the surface of an unrippled pool. Much of the soil of the desert appears to be alluvial; there are numerous traces of streams having formerly passed over it,[4] and still, where irrigation is at all practicable, fertility in the clayey tracts follows; but the rains are scanty, the wells few, and generally 100 feet deep or more : that at Beekanair, in the desert eastward, is 300 feet.

The transition from the desert to the cultivated tract is very abrupt and striking.[5] In the course of half a mile, or less, the country changes from a howling wilderness to a scene where thick and verdant groves, green fields, and luxuriant crops de-

[2] Jour. As. Soc. 1837, p. 198; Mackeson, Jour. of Wade's Voyage down the Sutlaj.

[3] Elph. Introd. 16.

[4] Masson, Bal. Afg. Punj. i. 19.

[5] Mackeson, ut supra, 198; Conolly, Jour. to India, ii. 282.

light the eye, and offer supplies for all the wants of man. In this fine tract, if water cannot be distributed by means of canals, it is found everywhere at a little depth, and raised, in abundant quantities, by the Persian wheel. But by far the greater part of the water required for irrigation is obtained from the rivers, and conducted to the crops by innumerable artificial channels. In the season of inundation, the surface is, for a great extent, completely flooded, the banks being in general low. The Ghara[5] is a slug- [5] Lord, Medical gish, muddy stream, and, as the soil along its banks is a rich, Mem. on the Plains of the alluvial, and tenacious mud, the moisture of the inundation is Indus, 66. long retained. This circumstance, while conducing to the most luxuriant fertility, has a very unfavorable effect on the health of the inhabitants. The water also of the wells is impure and rather nauseous, having a taste as if decayed vegetable matter were steeped in it. From these causes result intermittents and disordered state of the bowels, producing inflammation, passing into induration of the abdominal viscera, and terminating in incurable dropsy. In the hot weather, catarrh or influenza is universal, no one escaping, at least, one attack. The chief crops are wheat, rice, and various other grains; indigo, sugar, cotton, opium; together with the finest fruits[6] (including dates and man- [6] Hough, Narr. of goes, oranges and apples) and a profusion of esculent vegeta- Exp. into Afg. 11-13. bles. Just before harvest, the country exhibits a surface of fine grain and esculents, broken only by groves of fruit-trees, and quickly after the crops have been removed, it is converted into a thick jungle, through which, in many places, roam numbers of wild hogs. This exuberant productiveness[7] results from the [7] Wood's Oxus, 63; heat, which is intense in summer, acting on the rich soil, satu- Burnes' Bokh. i. 97. rated with moisture.

The wild animals are tigers[8] (which, however, though nume- [8] Havelock, War in Afg. i. 110. rous,[9] are timid, seldom attacking man), wild hogs, various kinds [9] Mackeson, ut of deer, aquatic fowl, and winged game in great abundance. The supra, 180. domestic animals are camels, very numerous, and fine cows, buffaloes, broad-tailed sheep, and goats, besides vast quantities of the finest poultry. The milch cattle yield great quantities of ghee, or butter; that of the buffalo is most prized; that of the cow holds the next place; after which ranks the produce of the goat and sheep. The flesh of the buffalo is preferred to any other. Wild fowl are so abundant that a wild goose, it is said, may be purchased for the value of a halfpenny. In few coun-

⁹ Masson, Bal. Afg Punj. i. 21.

tries are provisions finer, more abundant, or cheaper,⁹ and great quantities are sent to the less productive tracts eastward

The principal exports are cotton, sugar, indigo, hides, ghee, and various sorts of provision; drugs, dye-stuffs, wool, and coarse cotton cloths; the imports are not considerable, as the country is rich in natural productions, the inhabitants simple in their habits, and having themselves some manufacturing ingenuity. The principal imports are the wares of Britain and Hindostan.

There are three principal routes through the state of Bhawl-poor : 1st, that from east to west, across the desert from Beeka-nair to the town of Bhawlpoor, and across the Indus, forming one of the chief lines of communication from Hindostan to Khorasan; 2nd, that proceeding north-west from Jessulmair to Khanpoor, where it intersects the next described line, and then crosses the Indus at Mittunkote, so passing westward into Afghanistan ; 3rd, that running in a north-easterly direction from Sinde to Bhawlpoor, through Khanpoor, and parallel to the river frontier.

The population of Bhawlpoor consists chiefly of Jets of Hin-doo descent, of Hindoos of more recent settlement in the country, of Beloochees, and Afghans. The large admixture of the blood of the hardy mountaineers of the west causes the people to differ widely in appearance and constitution from the more eastern

¹ Elph. Introd. 17.

Hindoos. They are bulky,[1] strong, dark-complexioned, and harsh-featured, with long hair and beards. The upper classes use the dress and language of Persia. The language of the bulk

² Leech, Gram. of Punjabee, 117; Mackeson, ut supra, 180.

of the people is a patois[2] of Hindostani, mixed with Pushtoo and Beelooche, and is rendered disagreeable to strangers by the nasal drawling tone in which it is uttered. The Khan and a great majority of the inhabitants are Mahomedans, but Hindoos are treated with much toleration. The dominant race are the Jets,

³ Leech, Report on Sindh Army, 80-82; Masson, i. 26.
Jour. As. Soc. 1838, p. 27;
Mohun Lal, Orig. of Daud Putrees.

generally known in the country by the name of Daudputrees,[3] or sons of David, having been first collected, as is supposed, by David, a chieftain of Shikarpoor, in Sinde,[4] who, being driven thence, found refuge in the present location of those who bear his name. Bhawl Khan, one of his descendants, founded the capital, and called it after himself, Bhawlpoor. The present khan is the lineal descendant of the founder of the race. The annual revenue is about a million and a half of rupees.

The rulers of Bhawlpoor were, during the flourishing state of the Durani monarchy, nawabs, or deputy-governors, for that power. On its dismemberment, consequent on the expulsion of Shah Shoojah, the nawab of that time, without a struggle, became independent, and assumed the title of khan. On the rise of Runjeet Sing, the present ruler, Mahomed Bhawl Khan, thought it prudent to acknowledge his supremacy, and paid him an annual tribute of 800,000 rupees, more than half of his revenue. What may be the results in this respect, of his having been taken under British protection, it is impossible to predict. The khan has invariably acted as the steady friend of the British, and the support given by him to their troops in the wars in Sinde and Afghanistan, was rewarded in February, 1843, by the annexation to his territories of a portion of the northern part of Sinde, including Subzulcote [5] and the fertile district of Bhoong Bara.

[5] Corresp. relative to Sinde, 507.

The regular troops consist of seven regiments of infantry, each containing 350 men, and having six field-pieces : the latter are worked by 400 artillery-men.[6] Besides this force, 1,000 Afghans and 3,000 irregular horsemen are retained, making a total of 6,850 men; but in a popular cause the ruler could draw out the whole of the armed men of the country, probably 20,000 ; the Jets alone are reputed to amount to 12,000. The total population of Bhawlpoor may, with probability, be rated at about 250,000. The principal towns are Bhawlpoor, the capital, Ahmedpoor, Ooch, and Khanpoor.

[6] Masson, Bal.Afg. Panj. i. 26.

BHAWLPOOR,[1] the capital of the state of the same name, is situate on a branch of the Ghara, about two miles from the main stream and thirty miles above its confluence with the Chenaub.[2] It is surrounded by a ruinous wall of mud, which is about four miles in circuit, but part of the inclosed space is occupied by groves of trees. The houses are built, some of burnt, some of sun-dried bricks, but they are in general mean. The residence of the khan, like the rest, is in a very plain style of architecture.[3] Bhawlpoor is celebrated for the manufacture of loongees, for scarfs and turbans, made by Hindoo weavers, who are numerous here. There are also manufactures of chintzes and other cottons, of the total annual value of 520,000 rupees. Its commerce is considerable, the town being situate on the junction of three routes, from the east, south-east, and south. The Hindoo merchants, who are very enterprising, send wares to Central

[1] Leech, Commercial Information on Bhawlpoor, 60.

[2] Elph. Acc. of Caubul, Introd. 20.

[3] Mohun Lal, Trade of Bhawlp. 71.

[4] Burnes' Bokh. iii 293 Masson, Bal Afg. Panj.

i. 21; Hough,
Narr. Exp. into
Afg. 12; Atkin-
son, Exp. into
Afg.; Havelock,
War in Afg. i. 106. Asia, and even as far as Astracan. The country about Bhawlpoor is remarkably fertile, producing in great abundance grain,
sugar, indigo, tobacco, and butter; and abundance of mangoes,
oranges, apples, and other fruits in perfection. Population about
20,000. Lat. 29° 26′, long. 71° 37′.·

E.I.C. Ms. Doc. BHEEM-KA-KUBBA.—A halting-place in Sinde, on the
route from Hyderabad to Jessulmair, and fifty miles south-west
of the latter town. It is a wretched place, devoid of water.
Lat. 26° 42′, long. 70° 22′.

E.I.C. Ms. Doc. BHEENEE BADAM, in Afghanistan, is an extensive fertile
and well-cultivated plain, thirty miles south-west of Kabool. It
contains several forts and is traversed by the great route from
Ghuznee and Kandahar to Kabool. Lat. 34° 18′, long. 68° 37′.

E.I.C. Ms. Doc. BHEKEE.—A village in the Punjab. Lat. 32° 32′, long.
73° 17′.

E.I.C. Ms. Doc. BHELAR.—A halting-place in Sinde, on the route from Subzulcote to Shikarpoor, thirty-eight miles south-west from the
former place. It is situate ten miles from the left bank of the
Indus, on a "dund" or stagnant piece of water, left by the inundation of the river. Lat. 27° 56′, long. 69° 12′.

E.I.C. Ms. Doc. BHERA.—A village in the Punjab, on the road from Lahore
to Attock, and seventy miles south-east of the latter place. Lat.
33° 18′, long. 73° 5′.

E.I.C. Ms. Doc. BHERANAH.- -A village in the Punjab, eighteen miles
south-east of Lahore. Lat. 31° 30′, long. 74° 29′.

E.I.C. Ms. Doc. BHETLEE.—A village in the Punjab, situate on the road
from Mooltan to Dera Ghazee Khan, and twenty miles south-west
of the former place. Lat. 30°, long. 71° 12′.

BHIMBUR.—See BIMBER.

E.I.C. Ms. Doc. BHIRA.—A village in the Punjab, thirty-five miles east of
Shahpoor. Lat. 32° 7′, long. 72° 52′.

E.I.C. Ms. Doc. BHIRHTEE.—A village in Sinde, on the route from Subzulcote to Shikarpoor, and twenty-five miles south-west of the former
place. It is situate ten miles from the left bank of the Indus,
in a low alluvial tract, covered with jungle. Lat. 28° 3′, long.
69° 20′.

BHOLAN PASS.—See BOLAN.

E.I.C. Ms. Doc. BHOODLUH.—A village in Bhawlpoor, about three miles
from the left bank of the river Ghara. Lat. 30° 27′, long. 73° 29′.

E.I.C. Ms. Doc. BHOOL, in Sinde, a halting-place at the eastern foot of a pass over the Bhool hills, on the route from Sehwan to Kurra-chee, and ninety-nine miles south of the former town. There is a good supply of water from a water-course, and abundance of forage, the neighbourhood being covered with grass and jungle. A little south-west of it two roads pass off eastward, one to Hyderabad, another to Jurruk. Lat. 25° 10′, long. 67° 38′.

BHOOLDRA.—A village of Beloochistan, situate on the road E.I.C. Ms. Doc. from Kedje to Punjgoor, about a mile and a half from the left bank of the Bhugwur, or, as it is called lower down, the Dustee river. Lat. 26° 36′, long. 62° 31′.

BHOONG BARA.—A pergunnah or district of Sinde, in Correspondence on Sinde, 255, the vicinity of Subzulcote. It contains fifteen villages, and, when 445, 501, 507. subject to the Talpoor Ameers of Khyerpoor, yielded an annual revenue of 60,000 rupees. This territory had been wrested by the Ameers from the Khan of Bhawlpoor, but in the beginning of 1843 the British authorities in Sinde transferred it to Mahomed Bhawl Khan, the ruler of Bhawlpoor, as a reward for his zealous and long-tried friendship. Lat. 28°, long. 69°.

BHOOR.—A village in Sinde, situate on the road from E.I.C. Ms. Doc. Hyderabad to Kotree, and eighty miles south of the former place. This route takes first a southerly direction, and about thirty miles from Hyderabad verges slightly to the south-east. It is in lat. 24° 11′, long. 68° 30′.

BHOORAIWALA.—A village in Bhawlpoor, twenty-six miles E.I.C. Ms. Doc. north-east of the town of Bhawlpoor, and four miles from the left bank of the Ghara river. Lat. 29° 30′, long. 72° 2′.

BHOORKA-MU.—A village in Bhawlpoor, situate on the E.I.C. Ms. Doc. road from Jessulmair to Mittunkote, and thirty-six miles from the left bank of the Indus. The surrounding country is in general sterile and uncultivated. Lat. 28° 31′, long. 70° 47′.

BHUGWUR RIVER.—See BADOOR and DUSTEE.

BHULLEE-DE-CHUK.—A village in the Punjab, situated Walker, Map of close to the left bank of the Chenaub river. Lat. 32° 4′, long. N.W. Frontier. 73° 19′.

BHUSOOL, a small river in Beloochistan, has a course of Pott. Belooch.302. forty miles, generally from north to south, and falls into the Arabian Sea in lat. 25° 18′, long. 64° 44′.

BHYRAWUL.—See BHYROWALAH. Macartney in App.

BHYROWALAH.—A village in the Punjab, at a ferry over to Elph. Account of Caubul, 662; the Beas river, here found to be 740 yards wide when crossed P. Von Hugel, Kaschmir, iii. B. 409, S.

by the British mission, under Elphinstone, in the end of July, at which season the water is highest. The current was so rapid on that occasion that several of the boats employed were swept ten miles down the stream. Though the river is so formidable, the boats are wretched craft, no better than small rafts, with a plank, one foot high, all round, and draw only six inches water. Lat. 31° 21', long. 75° 7'.

Moorer. Punj.
Bokh. ii. 240;
Von Hugel,
Kaschmir, i. B.
273, S.

BIJBAHAR, or VIGIPARA, in Kashmir, the largest town in the valley, after the capital, is situate on the banks of the Jailum, about twenty-five miles south-east of the city of Kashmir. Over the river here is one of those singular and simply-constructed timber bridges, which, notwithstanding the apparently frail nature of their fabric, have endured for centuries, in consequence of the exemption of the country from storms or inclement weather. There is nothing else worthy of notice except a considerable bazaar. Lat. 33° 47', long. 75° 4'.

BIJORE.—See BAJOUR.

E.I.C. Ms. Doc.

BILLUNDEE.—A village in Bhawlpoor, situate near the left bank of the Ghara river, and twenty miles north-east by east of the town of Bhawlpoor. Lat. 29° 30', long. 71° 55'.

Vigne, Kashmir, I.
239; F.Von Hugel,
Kaschmir, i. 35;
Bernier Voyage,
ii. 263.

BIMBER, in the Punjab, a town on the route from Lahore to Kashmir, through the Baramula Pass. It is situate on a small stream, which falls into the Chenaub,* from which river the town is distant about forty miles. The houses are low and flat-roofed. Their number is estimated at 1,000, and that of shops at 150. About thirty years ago, it was governed by an independent rajah, who had an annual income of 60,000 rupees. He was seized and blinded by the Sikhs, by whom the place is now held. Lat. 32° 51', long. 74° 8'.

E.I.C. Ms. Doc.;
Survey Map.

BINDEH.—A village in Sinde, situate on the road from Bukkur to Hyderabad (by way of Khyerpoor). It is about twenty miles from the west bank of the eastern Narra river, in lat. 26° 37', long. 68° 47'..

Moorer. Punj.
Bokh. i. 150.

BINOA, a river in the Northern Punjab, rises in the raj of Chumba, near the southern bank of the Ravee, and flowing south-east for about fifty miles, falls into the Beas, east of Tira, and opposite Kumla Gurh, in lat. 31° 45', long. 76° 36'. Like all the streams of the Himalaya, it varies greatly in volume,

* Moorcroft states that this stream falls into the Jailum (ii. 303).

according to the season, being fordable in cold weather, but in the hot season, in consequence of the melting of the snow, becoming a deep and rapid stream. Where crossed by Moorcroft on skins, at the Golden Ferry, it was sixty feet broad and eight feet deep.

BIRALEE.—A village in the Punjab, situated near the junc- E.I.C. Ms. Doc. tion of the Chenaub and Ravee rivers, on the route from Mooltan to Lahore, about thirty miles north-east of the former place. Lat. 30° 30′, long. 71° 48′.

BIROZABAD.—A village in Bhawlpoor, about seventy miles E.I.C. Ms. Doc. south-west trom the town of the same name, on the route from thence to Khanpoor, from which place it is distant about twelve miles. Lat. 28° 45′, long. 70° 49′

BISULI.—A town in the north-east of the Punjab and on one Kashmir, i. 171. of the southern ranges of the Himalaya, situate on the river Ravee, which is here about eighty yards wide. There is a large, irregularly-built bazaar, but the place is chiefly remarkable for the huge palace of the rajah, regarded by Vigne as the finest building of the kind in the East; "exhibiting in its square turrets, open and embattled parapets, projecting windows, Chinese-roofed balconies, and moat-like tank in front," a striking likeness to the great baronial mansions which in some parts of Europe remain as memorials of the feudal ages. Lat. 32° 25′, long. 75° 28′

BITNGEE.—A village in Afghanistan, situate about ten Walker's Map of miles east of the range of the Suliman mountains, on a route from Afg. Ghuznee to Kala Bagh. Lat. 33° 10′, long. 70° 21′.

BODA or BAIDA, in Sinde, a large village on the route E.I.C. Ms. Doc. from Hyderabad to Sehwan, and ten miles north-west of the former place. It is situate close to the right bank of the Indus, along which a good road runs, and near the village is ample space for an encampment. Lat. 25° 29′, long. 68° 18′.

BOKHAREE.—A village in the Punjab, about three miles E.I.C. Ms. Doc. from the left bank of the Chenaub river. Lat. 31° 41′, long. 72° 55′.

BOLAN PASS,[1] in Beloochistan, on the great route from [1] E.I.C. Ms. Doc. Northern Sinde, by Shikarpoor and Dadur, to Kandahar and Ghuznee. It is not so much a pass over a lofty range, as a continuous succession of ravines and gorges, commencing near Dadur and first winding among the subordinate ridges stretch-

ing eastward from the Hala chain of mountains, the brow of
which it finally cross-cuts, and thus gives access from the vast
plain of Hindostan to the elevated and uneven tract extending
from the Hindoo Koosh to the vicinity of the Indian Ocean. Its
commencement on the eastern side, from the plain of Cutch Gundava, is about five miles north-west of Dadur, and in lat. 29° 30',

<sup>2 Jour. As. Soc.
1842, p. 54 ; Grif.
Bar. and Ther.
Meas. in Afg.;
Hough, Narr. Exp.
in Afg. 49.</sup>
long. 67° 40'; the elevation of the entrance being about 800 feet
above the level of the sea.[2] The valley through which the road
runs is here about half a mile wide; the inclosing hills, 500 or
600 feet high, consist of coarse conglomerate.[3] The road ascends
<sup>3 Havelock, War
in Afg. i. 215;
Pottinger, Beloo-
chistan, 309.</sup>
along the course of a river, called among the mountains the Bolan,
or Kauhee. The river in this part of the pass varies in depth from
a few inches to about two feet, and in the first five miles of the road
<sup>4 Atkinson, Exp.
into Afg. 111;
Hough, 49.</sup>
is crossed eight times.[4] The bed of the stream, in many places
forming the road, is of round stones, affording unstable footing
to horses, but less inconvenient for camels, and presenting no serious obstacle to the passage of wheel-carriages, as the ascent is
gradual. At Drubbee, about two miles and a half from the
entrance, the pass expands into a small verdant valley, through
which the river flows, and in which a caravan of 1,500 persons
<sup>5 E.I.C. Ms. Doc.;
Conolly, Jour. to
India, ii. 223;
Hough, Narr. of
Exp. in Afg. 49;
Atkinson, 111.
6 Conolly, ii. 223.</sup>
might encamp. At Kundye,[5] or as it is sometimes called Kondilan,
six miles from the entrance, the pass again expands into a small
oval valley, 600 yards by 400, with a hard surface of large stones
and pebbles. This in time of heavy rains becomes a lake,[6] and
^{7 Rough Notes, 71.} then, as Outram[7] observes, the steepness of the inclosing hills
"would preclude the possibility of escape to an army caught in
the torrent." Up to Kundye the course of the pass for six miles
is south-west ; from this point, a route strikes off south-east to-
^{8 Conolly, ii. 224.} wards Bagh,[8] and affords means of entering the pass from the
vicinity of that town, without taking the usual route by Dadur.
The elevation of this expansion is 904 feet above the sea.
Immediately beyond it the road turns due north, the ascent becomes greater, amounting to one foot in 304, and the route more
<sup>9 E.I.C. Ms. Doc.;
Kennedy, Sinde
and Kabool, i. 215</sup>
difficult, still lying up the course of the river, which in ten miles[9]
and half as far as Kista, is crossed seventeen times. This point,
^{1 Grif. ut supra,54} about seventeen miles[1] from the entrance of the pass, is 1,081 feet
above the level of the sea. The breadth of the valley increases
considerably from this spot, being in some places three or four
miles : the direction also of the route turns north-west, and the
^{2 Hough, 51.} ascent becomes still steeper, being about one foot[2] in seventy-

seven as far as Beebee Nanee, twenty-six miles from the entrance, and having an elevation of 1,695 feet above the level of the sea. The surrounding mountains in some places in the lower part of the pass are described as consisting of " coral rock[3] of a grey- white colour, and a compact homogeneous substance, splintering with a smooth surface of fracture, precisely like the stone used in lithography." At Beebee Nanee a road strikes off due west[4] to Rod Bahar and Kelat, while the principal road continues its north-westerly course towards Shawl and Kandahar. Here the serious difficulties of the pass commence, from the increased roughness and acclivity of the ground, and from its being commanded from various parts of the impending cliffs. To these difficulties the want of water is soon added, the river disappearing, and pursuing its course for several miles below the shingly deposit which forms the bottom of the valley. The route proceeds ten miles up the bed of this concealed stream, as far as Ab-i-goom, or " the lost river," a post so called from the circumstance just mentioned. This point is 2,540 feet[5] above the level of the sea. From thence the route continues its north-westerly course up the stream, now no longer choked up, but generally from two to three feet deep, and, after an ascent of eight miles and a half, reaches Sir-i-Bolan,[6] where the river gushes out of an opening in the rock in a large clear spring. The elevation is 4,494 feet above the level of the sea, and the acclivity for the last eight miles one foot in twenty-five, being the greatest met with in any part of the pass. The distance from the eastern entrance is about forty-five miles, and so barren is the country, that only two green spots are observed in this interval.

From Sir-i-Bolan to the top of the pass, the route takes a westerly course, and for a distance of ten miles is totally without water. The last three miles of this distance is the most dangerous part of the pass,[7] " the road varying from forty to sixty feet, and flanked on each side by high perpendicular hills, which can only be ascended at either end." The elevation of the crest of the pass is 5,793 feet. There is no descent on the western side, as the route opens on the Dasht-i-Bedowlut, a plain as high as the top of the pass. The total length is between fifty-four and fifty-five miles ;[8] * the average ascent ninety feet in the mile.

[3] Kennedy, i. 211.

[4] E.I.C. Ms. Doc. ; Kennedy, i. 216 : Havelock, War in Afg. i. 226.

[5] Grif. ut supra, 54.

[6] E.I.C. Ms. Doc Hough, 54 ; Connolly, ii. 219 ; Atkinson, 117 ; Havelock, i. 231 ; Kennedy, i. 219 ; Masson, Bal. Afg. Panj. i. 334.

[7] Hough, 55.

[8] E.I.C. Ms. Doc. Hough, 56.

* Outram erroneously states the length at seventy-five miles.   Rough Notes, 75.

The Bengal column in 1839 spent six days in marching through the pass, entering it on the 16th and leaving it on the 21st of March.   Its artillery,[9] including eight-inch mortars, twenty-four-pounder howitzers, and eighteen-pounder guns, were conveyed without any serious difficulty.   The eminences bounding the pass have in general no great height above it, in most places not exceeding 500 feet; but at Beebee Nanee,[1] they are very lofty.   The air in the lower part of the pass is, in summer, oppressively hot, and excessively unhealthy, so that scarcely any persons then venture through it, except messengers on urgent business, whose poverty compels them to brave the danger, and these frequently perish.   Some British troops[2] who advanced through it at this season found the climate fatal.   The pass is infested by Belooches,[3] principally of the Maree and Khaka, or Cauker tribes, a lawless, treacherous, sanguinary race, living partly on the produce of their flocks of sheep, and partly by plunder, attacking indiscriminately all travellers who they think may be overpowered, murdering them, and carrying off the acquired booty to fastnesses among the adjacent hills.   In some instances whole caravans have been exterminated by them.   They are as cowardly as cruel, seldom attacking where effectual resistance can be made.   The Bolan Pass, though very important in a military point of view, as forming the great communication between Sinde and Khorasan, is inferior in a commercial interest to the Gomul,[4] farther north, through which the Lohani Afghans, in their annual migrations, conduct the main portion of the traffic between Hindostan on the one point, and Afghanistan and Central Asia on the other.   The western extremity and highest point of the Bolan Pass is in lat. 29° 52′, long. 67° 4′.

BOLAN,[1] a small river of Afghanistan, rises in the Bolan Pass, at Sir-i-Bolan, in lat. 29° 51′, long. 67° 8′, and at an elevation of 4,494 feet above the level of the sea.   The road through the pass generally follows the course of the river, except for about ten miles between Kirta and Beebee-Nanee, where the stream winds considerably to the north-east of it.   The declivity of its bed is very rapid, as in fifty miles, from Sir-i-Bolan to Dadur, it falls 3,751 feet.   After a course of about seventy miles remarkably sinuous, but generally in a south-easterly direction, it, in lat. 29° 24′, long. 67° 58′, forms a junction with the Nari, coming from the north, and loses its own appellation in that of the river with

Side notes:

9 Hough, App. 78.

1 Havelock, i. 228.

2 E.I.C. Ms. Doc.; Conolly, ii. 224.

3 Leech on Sindhian Army, 90; Atkinson, 113.

4 Burnes on the Trade of the Derajut, 99.

1 E.I.C. Ms. Doc., End. Map; Hough, Narr. Exp. in Afg. 48-54; Havelock, War in Afg. i. 196; Jour. As. Soc. 1842, p. 55; Grif. Bar. and Ther. Meas. in Afg.; Masson, Bal. Afg. Panj. i. 334; Pottinger, Buloochistan, 309; Kennedy, Sinde and Kabool, i. 212-224; Atkinson, Exp. into Afg. 111-120.

which it unites. The Bolan river is liable to sudden and great inundations, and as its bed, in some parts of the pass, occupies the whole breadth of the ravines through which it flows, and the cliffs on each side are, in many places, so steep as to be inaccessible, travellers are frequently overtaken and drowned by the furious torrent. By such a casualty, in 1841,[2] a detachment of the Bengal army lost its baggage and forty-five men. The Bolan river is also known among the natives by the name of Kauhee. [2 Allen, March through Sinde and Affghan, 104-114.]

BONAKOT, in the Punjab, is a valley, containing a village of the same name, on the northern frontier of Kashmir. Here is the residence of a Malek or chieftain, whose family was once of considerable importance, but is now much decayed. It is situated on the principal route from Kashmir to Iskardoh, in lat. 34° 25', long. 74° 32'. [Vigne, Kashmir, ii. 198.]

BONYR.—See BURRINDOO.

BOODOOKE.—A village in the Punjab, situate near the right bank of the Ghara river. Lat. 30° 46', long. 74° 13'. [E.I.C. Ms. Doc.]

BOODOOR RIVER.—See BADOOR.

BOOLOO.—A village of Afghanistan, in "the Desert" south of the Helmund. There is forage for camels, and sheep can be obtained from the pastoral population in the neighbourhood. Lat. 29° 34', long. 63° 40'. [Christie in App. to Pott. Belooch. 405.]

BOOM. — A village in Afghanistan, situate on the route from Giriskh to Bamian. Lat. 32° 8', long. 65°. [E.I.C. Ms. Doc.]

BOOMBULPOORA. — A village in Sinde, on the route from Larkhana to Shikarpoor, and sixteen miles north-east of the former place. It is supplied with water from a well, and has about 250 inhabitants. Lat. 27° 42', long. 68° 27' [E.I.C. Ms. Doc.]

BOONEERE, in Northern Afghanistan, is the tract lying north-west of the Indus, and north of the Kabool river, and bearing the general name of the Eusufzai country. It is inclosed by the Indus on the south-east, the Hindoo Koosh on the north; on other sides by mountains separating it from Suwat on the west, and on the south from the country held by the Khuttuk and Eusufzai tribes, on the lower course of the Kabool river. In its general character it is rugged, being composed of a number of small valleys, opening into one larger, through which flows the Burrindoo,* a stream falling into the Indus on the west side, [Vigne, Kashmir, ii. 304; Elph. Acc. of Caubul, 97, 329; Jour. As. Soc. 1836, p. 469-480; Map of Peshawur and Memoir on it by Court; Jour. As.Soc.1840, p. 924-932; Conolly, Notes on Eusofzye tribes.]

* The Burrindoo river of Elphinstone is the Bonyr (Booneere) river of Walker's map.

a little below Torbela, in lat. 34° 8′, long. 72° 37′. The most fertile parts lie along the course of this river, and are cultivated with much care, the soil on declivities being formed into terraces, rising one above the other. Some rice is produced, but the principal crop is millet. Booneere lies between lat. 34° 10′— 34° 40′, long. 72° 15′—73°.

Jour. As. Soc. 1837, p. 213; Wade, Voyage from Lodiana to Mithankot.

BOONGA.—A village in Bhawlpoor, situate about a mile from the left bank of the Ghara river. Lat. 30° 13′, long. 73° 19′.

E.I.C. Ms. Doc.

BOONGA. — A village in the Punjab, situate on the left bank of the Ravee river, on the route from Mooltan to Lahore, 100 miles from the former, 110 from the latter place. Lat. 30° 39′, long. 72° 44′.

Vigne, Kashmir, ii. 303.

BOONJ.—A narrow plain, stretching along the left bank of the Indus, from north to south, in long. 74° 28′, and between lat. 35° 20′—35° 35′, being bounded on the north and west by the Indus, south by the Husora river, east by the lofty mountains north of Kashmir. It is in general sandy and barren; in a few places it is fertile, but ill cultivated, in consequence of the incursions of the predatory tribes surrounding it.

E.I.C. Ms. Doc.

BOOQUIE.—A small village in Sinde, on the route from Sehwan to Larkhana, and three miles south of the latter place, to which there is a good road. Lat. 27° 28′, long. 68° 17′.

Hough, 337; Moorcr. ii. 321.

BOORHAN, in the Punjab, is a small town situate on the Hirroo river, twenty miles south-east of Attock, to which there is a good road. Lat. 33° 48′, long. 72° 35.

E.I.C. Ms. Doc.

BOORKHOE.—A village in Beloochistan, eighteen miles east of Sonmeanee, from which there is a good road. Lat. 25° 24′, long. 66° 50′.

[1] E.I.C. Ms. Doc; Eyre, Mil. Op. at Kabool, 10; Sale, Dis. in Afg. 232; Hough, Narr. of Exp. to Afg. 296; Havelock, War in Afg. ii. 175; Mil. Op. in Afg. 399, 400.
[2] Masson, Bal. Afg. Panj. iii. 175; Wolff, Jour. 335.

BOOTHAUK.—A fortified village, twelve miles east of Kabool, on the route to Jelalabad. According to some,[2] the name is properly But-Khak * (idol-dust), bestowed in consequence of Mahmood of Ghuznee having broken some idols here. This derivation, like many others of similar nature, rests on popular tradition. At this place commence the series of defiles which intervene between Kabool and Gundamuk. The pass of Boothauk is five miles long and, where narrowest, about fifty yards wide, hemmed in on each side by heights rising almost perpendicularly to the elevation of 500 or 600 feet. Close to it

* بت خاک Shakespear, in v۱.

on the eastward, the route to Jelalabad divides into two lines, that to the north proceeding through the Luttabund Pass, and that to the south by Khoord Kabool and the Taugee Turkai Pass. Near Boothauk the British troops, under command of General Elphinstone, attempting to make their way to Jelalabad, in 1842, first encountered that attack of the Afghans, which did not cease until the whole army was either butchered or captured, almost without exception. Lat. 34° 29', long. 69° 15'.

BOOTIA.—A village in Sinde, situate on the route from Hyderabad to Jodhpoor, by way of Omercote, from which last place it is distant eighteen miles east. It is in lat. 25° 22', long. 70° 6'. Ms. Survey Map.

BOOTLA.—A village in Bhawlpoor, situate on an offset of the Indus, about three miles from the left bank of the main stream, in lat. 28° 30', long. 69° 54'. E.I.C. Ms. Doc.

BOREE.—A large fortified town of the province of Sewestan, in Afghanistan, inhabited by Caukers. By it proceeds the route called the Boree Pass,[1] leading from Dera Ghazee Khan to Kandahar and Ghuznee. Baber led his army through it in 1505, and it is still used by caravans. The country[2] in which this town is situate is fertile, well cultivated, and has a dense population almost exclusively agricultural. It is irrigated by numerous *kareezes*, or subterraneous water-courses and brooks, which discharge themselves into a considerable stream, flowing southwest, and which is lost by absorption and evaporation, without reaching the sea. Lat. 30° 55', long. 68° 35'. [1] Leech, App. 40; Memoirs, 102; [2] Elph. Acc. of Caubul, 451.

BOWYNUH.—A village in Afghanistan, among the Huzareh mountains, on the route from Bamian to Sir-i-pool, from which latter place it is distant about thirty miles. Lat. 35° 50', long. 65° 57'. Walker's Map of Afg.

BRENG.—See BURENG.

BRIJKY.—A village in Afghanistan, on the road from Ghuznee to Dera Ismail Khan, on a route collateral with the Gomul Pass and north of it. It is seventy miles south-east of Ghuznee. Lat. 33°, long. 69° 14'. E.I.C. Ms. Doc.

BRYGY.—A village in Afghanistan, situate on the river Gomul, about sixty miles south-cast of Ghuznee. It is in lat. 32° 46', long. 68° 53'. E.I.C. Ms. Doc.

BUBUK.—A village in Sinde, situate on the north-east shore of Lake Manchur. Lat. 26° 26', long. 67° 52'. Ms. Map of Sinde.

BUCHOO.—A village in the Punjab, situate on the right bank of the Ravee river, forty miles south-west of Lahore. Lat. 31° 19′, long. 73° 48′.

BUCKRANEE.—A village in Sinde, on the route from Sehwan to Larkhana, and seven miles south of the latter place. It is situate in the extensive island contained between the Indus and its offset, the Narra; being distant eleven miles from the left bank of the former and about half a mile from a ferry over the latter, known as the ferry of Buckranee. From this ferry to the ford opposite Tonia Hassem, the distance is about a mile and a half. The neighbourhood is fertile and well cultivated. Lat. 27° 25′, long. 68° 17′.

BUDDEEABAD, in Afghanistan, in the province of Lughman, a large and strong fort, belonging to a Ghilji chief. It is a square, each side being eighty yards long, with a tower at each corner. The walls, twenty-five feet high, are strengthened by a fausse-braye and deep ditch. Here, the sixty-three British captives, spared from the massacre in the attempted retreat from Kabool in 1842, were imprisoned for a short time. Lat. 34° 55′, long. 70° 14′.

BUDEENA.—A village in Sinde, seventy miles south-east of Hyderabad, and seven miles west of the Goonee river, a great offset of the Indus. Lat. 24° 33′, long. 68° 52.

BUDRAWAR[1] ("the stronghold of Buddha").—A town in the Northern Punjab, on the southern slope of the Himalaya, near the left bank of the river Chenaub, and on one of its feeders. The neighbouring country is beautiful, picturesque, fertile, and well cultivated. It was formerly governed by an independent Rajpoot rajah, but is now subject to the Sikh chief of Chumba. There is a large and well-supplied bazaar. The population is probably about 2,000, of whom a considerable proportion are Kashmirian weavers of shawls, employing about 250 looms. There is a large square fort, built of stone. It is about 5,000 feet above the sea.[2] Lat. 32° 53′, long. 75° 28′.

BUDWAN, in Western Afghanistan, a village on the route from Kandahar to Herat, from the former of which places it is distant about fourteen miles south-west. The road here is good, and the place important, from having a plentiful supply of water. Lat. 31° 34′, long. 65° 16′.

BUGGAUR,[1] in Sinde, is the western branch of the Indus, diverging a little below Tatta, at the head of the Delta, the Sata being the eastern branch. In 1699, when visited by Hamilton,[2] it was a very great stream, navigable as high as Lahoree-bunder, twenty miles from the mouth, for vessels of 200 tons, but now, except during the inundation,[3] it has scarcely any stream, in consequence of a sandbank five or six feet above the level of the water stretching across the channel at the place of divarication. Where forded by the British army during the season of low water, in 1839, it was two feet and a half deep, and fifty yards wide; lower down, the channel was completely dry. When the stream was greater, it parted into four branches, entering the sea by the Pittee, the Pintianee, the Joah, and the Richel mouths. These have all become merely inlets of the sea, containing salt water, excepting during the inundation. The word Buggaur signifies *destroyer*, a name given in consequence of the effect of the river on the lands through which it flowed. Its main course is generally westerly, extending about eighty miles from the place of divergence, in lat. 24° 38', long. 68° 1', to the Pittee mouth, in lat. 24° 42', long. 67° 8'.

[2] New Acc. of the East Indies, 8vo. Edin. 1727, l. 114.

[3] Kennedy, Sinde and Kabool, i. 73.

BUGUT.—A village in Afghanistan, six miles west of the road from Ghuznee to Shawl. Lat. 31° 47', long. 67° 13'.

Walker, Map. of Afg.

BUKAPOOR, in Sinde, a large village on the route from Sehwan to Larkhana, and two miles south of the latter place, to which the road is good. There is an abundant supply of water from wells, and ground for encampment. Lat. 27° 29', long. 68° 11'.

E.I.C. Ms. Doc.

BUKÉRALA,—See BAKERALA.

BUKKUR, in Sinde, a celebrated fortress on an island in the Indus, between the towns of Roree on the eastern and Sukkur on the western bank.[1] The eastern channel, dividing it from Roree, on the left bank, is 400 yards wide and thirty feet deep in the middle, with a current of four miles an hour; the western, dividing it from Sukkur, on the right bank, is ninety-eight yards wide, and fifteen feet deep in the middle, with a current of three miles an hour. Such is the measurement when the river is lowest, and made in a right line across the island from the eastern to the western shore of the Indus; but at some distance to the north of this right line, a spit of land from the island of Bukkur projects westward into the river, leaving between its extremity and the western shore a channel only fifty yards wide, seven feet deep in the middle, and with a current of four miles an hour. In the

[1] Wood, in Rep. on the Indus, in App. to Burnes' Pers.Narr. 345; Burnes' Bokh. iii. 72, 270.

[2] Hough, 27; Havelock, War in Afg. i. 158. beginning of 1839,[2] the engineers of the Bengal army, marching to Afghanistan, threw here a bridge of boats over the Indus. The number of boats employed for this purpose was nineteen for the western or narrower channel, and fifty-five for the eastern, and on this the army, with its baggage and battering-train, passed [3] In Jour. As. Soc. 1834, p. 235. over.* Soon afterwards the bridge was swept away. Macmurdo[3] states that the water in the western channel disappears in the [4] Bokh. iii. 271. season when the river is lowest; and Burnes,[4] that the eastern is said to have been once forded in the same season. Wood, however, found the former seven feet deep, and the latter thirty, in the dry season.

The island of Bukkur is a rock of limestone, interspersed with flint, of an oval shape, 800 yards long, 300 wide, 1,875 in circuit, [5] Leech, Rep. on Sind. Armies, 66, 79; Hough, 21; Masson, Bal.Afg. Panj. i. 362; Wood's Oxus, 51; Conolly, Jour. to India, ii. 200; Westmacott, in Jour. As. Soc. 1841, p. 395; 1840, p. 1200. and about twenty-five feet high.[5] Almost the whole of it is covered by the fortress, the walls of which are double, from thirty to thirty-five feet high, built partly of burned, partly of unburned bricks, with sixty-one bastions, loop-holed, and having a weak parapet. There is a gateway facing Roree on the east, and another facing Sukkur on the west, and there are two wickets. Though apparently so strong, it could offer no effectual resistance to a regular and well-sustained attack, as it is commanded from the heights on both the east and west sides of the river, and might be successfully assaulted by escalade from a small island lying to the north, and separated from it by a narrow channel of easy passage. In 1839, the fortress was ceded by the Ameers of Khyerpoor to the British, to remain occupied by their garrison during the then existing war. To its ultimate destination it would be premature to advert. Lat. 27° 41', long. 68° 52'.

Leech, Leia, 93; Masson, Bal. Afg. Panj. i. 65. BUKKUR.—A commercial town in the Punjab, on a small offset of the Indus, and about three miles eastward of the main stream. It has a well-supplied and busy bazaar, and the neighbouring country is so well cultivated and productive, that provisions are probably as cheap as in any part of the world. It yields a revenue of about 10,000 rupees per annum. Population 5,000. Lat. 31° 39', long. 71° 7'.

BUKRALA.—See Bakerala.

Ms. Survey Map. BUKWA.—A village in the "Little Desert" of Sinde,

* So states Wood (347), who was on the spot; but Havelock, also present, states (i. 158), "The whole of our siege-train and park had been safely ferried across the Indus on rafts."

situate sixty-five miles south of Omercote, and twenty miles from the north boundary of the Great Western Runn. Lat. 24° 27′, long. 69° 45′.

BUKWA-A-KARAIZ.—A village in Afghanistan, situate on the road from Furrah to Giriskh, about fifty miles east of the former place, and ninety miles north-west of the latter, in lat. 32° 17′, long. 62° 56′. Walker's Map of Afg.

BULAMEEN.—A village in Afghanistan, situate on the route from Ghuznee to Kohat. Lat. 33° 30′, long. 70° 31′. E.I.C. Ms. Doc.

BULBUT.—A village in the Punjab, situate on the east bank of the river Chenaub, twelve miles south-west of Mooltan. Lat. 30° 3′, long. 71° 18′. E.I.C. Ms. Doc.

BULEAS.—A village in the Punjab, situate on the right bank of the Veyut or Jailum river, and on the route from Baramula to Mazufurabad, thirty-five miles west of the former, and eight miles east of the latter. Lat. 34° 10′, long. 73° 29′. Walker's Map of N. W. Frontier.

BULLOO.—A village in the Punjab, situate near the left bank of the Chenaub river, on the road from Mooltan to Ramnuggur, a hundred and ten miles north-east of the former, and a hundred and fifty south-west of the latter place. Lat. 31° 16′, long. 72° 30′. E.I.C. Ms. Doc.

BULRIA.—A small village in Sinde, a short distance to the left of the route from Sehwan to Larkhana, and nine miles north of the former place. It is situate in a populous and well-cultivated tract, close to an offset of the Indus, and a mile from the right bank of the main channel. Lat. 26° 30′, long. 67° 57′. E.I.C. Ms. Doc.

BULTI, or BULTISTAN. [1]—A small state north of Kashmir, and bearing also the name of Little Tibet, by which prefix it is distinguished from Middle Tibet or Ladakh, and Great Tibet or Southern Tartary. Bulti is also sometimes called Iskardoh, from the name of its capital. It is bounded on the north by Chinese Tartary, from which it is separated by the Mustag or Mooz-Taugh [2] (icy mountains), and the Karakorum mountains, prolongations of the Hindoo Koosh, to the eastward. On the east it has Ladakh or Middle Tibet, [3] on the south Deotsuh and other elevated and desert tracts, which separate it from Kashmir; on the west, Ghilgit, Yessen, and Astor, small independent states. Its limits have varied with circumstances, and at no time have they been well defined; but as the result of the safest estimate of them, Bulti may be stated to lie between lat. 34° 40′—35° 30′,

[1] Ritter, Erd-
kunde von Asien,
ii. 640.

[2] Elph. Acc. of
Caubul, 86; Jour.
As. Soc. 1835, p.
593; Wade, Notes
relative to Iskar-
doh; Burnes'Bokh.
ii. 210.
[3] Moorer. Punj.
Bokh. I. 258.

long. 74° 40'—76° 20'. Its greatest length, which is about 170 miles, is from south-east to north-west; its breadth not more ⁴ Vigne, Kashmir, than fifty or sixty. Its superficial extent is about 12,000 [4] square ii. 249. miles. It consists principally of a valley, having an average elevation of from 6,000 to 7,000 feet above the sea, and through the lowest part of which the Indus flows in a north-westerly direction. It is inclosed by enormous mountains, rugged, bare, and nearly inaccessible, which rise above it to the height of 6,000 or 8,000 feet, except where the Indus rushes with vast rapidity from the south-east, and makes its way to the north-west, previously to its turning towards the lower country, north of Attock. From the valley of the Indus numerous gorges and ravines furrow the inclosing mountains, serving as the channels of streams feeding the main river, and form passes, by which access is gained to the neighbouring countries. Geologically, the formation of the mountains is generally of gneiss, that of the low ground along the banks of the Indus of shingle and sand, mixed with a little alluvial mould, requiring frequent irrigation from the streams to render it

[5] Wade, 593; productive, as rain scarcely ever falls there, [5] and in consequence Vigne, ii. 266. the atmosphere is very clear and dry. But though rain is almost unknown, snow falls and lies to the depth of from one to two feet. The cold in the elevated parts is intense in winter; on the high

[6] Vigne, ii. 267. and unsheltered table-land of Deotsuh, it at that season [6] totally precludes the existence of animal life. The heat in the lower parts in summer is considerable, the thermometer ranging from 70° to 90° in the shade at noon.

Besides the principal valley of the Indus, there are two others; that of Shighur, down which the large river of that name flows from the north to join the Indus at Iskardoh, and that of Shyyok, the great river flowing down which has its confluence with the Indus a few miles farther to the east. (See Shighur and Shyyok.) Numerous mountain torrents fall into these main streams, both on the right and the left. At the confluence of

[7] Vigne, ii. 315. the Shyyok and Indus [7] the former is above a hundred and fifty yards wide; the latter is only eighty yards in width, but it is deeper and has a larger body of water than the Shyyok. The average breadth of the Indus, in its course through Little Tibet, is from one hundred to two hundred yards; near Iskardoh it is comparatively tranquil, but elsewhere it is a rapid torrent. There are five lakes known in this country: that of

Satpur-Tsuh, in the Satpur Pass, a few miles south of the town of Iskardoh; that of Juba-T'suh, in the valley of Shighur; the shallow lake of Ranga, near the Indus; and the two small lakes of Kutzura, near the western boundary.[8] Satpur-T'suh, the largest of all these, is only one mile long and three-quarters of a mile wide.

[8] Vigne, Kashmir, ii. 262; Erdkunde, Von Asien, iii. 657.

A careful search would probably be rewarded by the discovery of mines of gold in Bulti, as almost[9] every stream brings it down, but the quantities being small, the process of washing the sands is attended with little profit. Arsenic is met with in Bulti, and sulphur abounds. Little else is known respecting the minerals of this country. Thermal springs[1] are numerous, some so hot as to scald those who incautiously expose themselves to their operation.

[9] Vigne, ii. 245-287; Wade, 593; Ritter, 657.

[1] Vigne. ii. 273-285; Wade, 593.

Of beasts, the most worthy of notice is the " yak," or grunting ox, which attains the size of our large domestic ox. The hybrid between this animal and the common cow is called the " bzho," and is more useful as a beast of burthen than either of the pure races. There are various wild animals, of species allied to the sheep, goat, or deer; the " kuch-kar," a gigantic mouflon, or wild sheep; the " rass," supposed by Burnes[2] to be an enormous sort of goat, with horns so large that one man could not lift a pair of them; a species of ibex, larger than that of Europe, and with longer horns; the " markhur," a species of large goat; the " sha," a quadruped intermediate between the goat and the deer; the " sna," similar to the last, but smaller; the musk-deer, the marmot, the hare, the leopard, the bear, the wolf, and the fox. The eagle is frequently seen; more rarely, the " vulture on Imaus bred." The red-legged partridge is common, as is a gigantic species of the size of a common hen. The rivers abound with the Himalaya-trout, but have scarcely any other fish. Serpents are rare, and do not appear to be venomous.

[2] Bokh. ii. 208.

The country is not fertile, but the inhabitants are industrious and make the most of it, forming terraces on the sides of the mountains, and giving great attention to irrigation. By these means they raise crops of wheat, barley, millet, buck-wheat, turnips, and a little rice. The cockscomb[3] or crested amaranth (Celosia cristata), is cultivated for its seeds, which are ground into flour for making bread. There is a variety of excellent fruits:

[3] Vigne. ii. 263, 272; Falconer.

apricots so abound that the Kashmirians call the country Suri-
³ Vigne, ii. 248. Butan,³ or Apricot Tibet.   The other fruits are peaches, apples,
pears, grapes, mulberries, walnuts, melons.

⁴ Vigne, ii. 271;
Wade, 597. The inhabitants⁴ are of the variety of the human race called
by physiologists Mongolian, bearing a strong resemblance to
their Tartar neighbours on the north, but shewing an admixture of Hindu and Persian blood. They are usually sallow,
thin, and care-worn, from their laborious habits and scanty
fare, and are seldom long-lived. They are considered to be
phlegmatic, but peaceable and well-intentioned. The food of
the majority of the population is grain, prepared in various
ways, and dried fruits; the higher classes alone being enabled
to eat flesh. Tea, though very expensive, is much used, being
the great luxury of all who can at all command the means of its
purchase. It is prepared by boiling the leaf with soda, and adding salt-butter and cream to the decoction, in which mode it is
said to be both palatable and nutritious.   The people have
a singular amusement—the "Chaughan," which may be described
as cricket played on horseback with long sticks, having at the end
large wooden knobs. They shew great eagerness, activity, and
dexterity in this exercise. As to religion, they are Mahometans,
of the Shia persuasion, or such as reject the succession of the
three first kaliphs; but many adhere to a portion of Hindu
⁵ Vigne, ii. 267. usages. Their language is Tibetian,⁵ with a slight admixture of
Arabic and Persian. Their dress, a long full tunic and cap, is
generally made of the wool of their sheep and goats, but sometimes, though more rarely, of cotton. The government, until the
late Sikh conquest, was vested in a hereditary rajah, who, under the
native title of Gylfo, exercised an unlimited but mild sway. The
military force was a rude militia, in which almost all free men
capable of bearing arms were bound to serve in consideration of
the lands allotted to them. The amount of population has sometimes been preposterously exaggerated, being stated at 300,000
⁶ Wade, 597. families,⁶ or (if five persons be allowed to each family) at 1,500,000
souls; a twentieth part of this amount, or 75,000, would proba-
bly be not remote from the truth. Such a supposition would rate
the density of the population at a little more than six to the square
mile. The principal place is Iskardoh, a straggling collection
of houses, situate at the base of a lofty isolated rock, on which
is a fort, the residence of the gylfo. (See ISKARDOH.) The

only other places requiring notice in Bulti are Parkuta, Khopalu, Kcris, Katakchund, and Tolti. (See the respective names.) The principal routes into or through Bulti are—first,[7] one, very difficult, from the north-west, following the course of the Indus upwards to Iskardoh; second,[8] one joining the last on the east side, and affording a communication with the Eusufzai country; third,[9] from Kashmir to Iskardoh, by the Gurys valley, and across the table-land of Deotsuh; fourth,[1] another route from Kashmir, by the Bultul Pass, down the course of the Duras or Dras river, to its confluence with the Indus; fifth,[2] that proceeding in a south-eastern direction up the course of the Indus to Ladakh. There is a path from Iskardoh to Yarkund over the Mustag, but now scarcely ever frequented,[3] from dread of freebooters or of perishing in the snow. Some have idly supposed that the people of Bulti[4] are descended from some settlers of the army of Alexander, and that Iskardoh is a corruption of Iskanderia, or Alexandria, but they might as plausibly assign such a descent to the Esquimaux. Their physical, moral, and intellectual qualities, as well as language, prove them related to the inhabitants of Great or Eastern Tibet, and conseqently members of the great Mongolian family of Central Asia. The ancestors of Ahmed Shah, the present gylfo, are said to have ruled here uninterruptedly for fourteen generations;[5] but, two or three years ago,[6] Iskardoh and the other strongholds of Bulti were seized by Gholab Singh, the cruel and rapacious Sikh ruler of Jamu.

[7] Vigne, ii. 304.
[8] Id. ii. 294;
[9] Wade, 505. Vigne, Kashmir, ii. 203, 216.
[1] Moorer. Punj. Bokh. ii. 1-44, 83-94; Vigne, ii. 380-396.
[2] Moorer. Punj. Bokh. ii. 3-8; Vigne, Kashmir, ii. 315, 331.
[3] Vigne, ii. 263.
[4] Wade, 592; Vigne, ii. 240.
[5] Wade, 599.
[6] Vigne, ii. 374.

BUL-TUL, or KANTAL,[1] in Kashmir, a pass over the range of mountains inclosing that valley on the north-east. It forms the water-summit between Kashmir and Little Thibet, as from its northern declivity the Duras river flows northward to the Indus, and from its southern flows southward a feeder of the small river Sinde, a tributary of the Jailum. Its elevation above the level of the sea is 10,500 feet. It is also called the Shur-ji-La, generally pronounced Zoj-i-La;[2] and in old maps this summit bears the name Kantal, signifying "lofty-hill." Lat. 34° 10′, long. 75° 15′.

[1] Vigne, Kashmir, ii. 395; Quarterly Oriental Mag. 1825, p. 104; Izzet Ullah, Travels beyond the Himalaya.
[2] Moorer. Punj. Bokh. ii. 95.

BUMBEYA, in Sinde, on the route from Sehwan to Larkhana, and nineteen miles north of the former place. It is situate close to a channel through which the waters of the Indus find their way in time of inundation, and a mile from the right bank of the main channel. Lat. 26° 38′, long. 67° 55′.

E.I.C. Ms. Doc.

E.I.C. Ms. Doc.   BUMBRA.—A village in Sinde, on the route from Hyderabad to Sehwan, and twenty miles south-east of the latter place,
is situated near the right bank of the Indus. Lat. 26° 3′, long.
68° 6′.

BUMBUTPOORA.—See BOOMBULPOORA.

E.I.C. Ms. Doc.   BUND.—A small village in Sinde, on the route from Larkhana to Bagh, and twenty-two miles north of the former place.
It is situate on the border of the Runn or Desert of Shikarpoor.
It has no claim to notice beyond that of possessing a supply
of water from a well. Lat. 27° 50′, long. 68° 8′.

E.I.C. Ms. Doc.   BUNDA.—A village in the Punjab, situate on the road from
Julalpoor to Attock, forty-five miles north of the former. Lat.
33° 23′, long. 73° 3′.

E.I.C. Ms. Doc.   BUNDEE BOREE.—A village in Afghanistan, on the left
bank of the Urghundab river, thirty miles south-west of Kelat-i-
Ghilji, and sixty miles north-east of Kandahar. Lat. 32° 6′,
long. 66° 15′.

BUNDER GURREE.—See GHURRY.

[1] Burnes' Bokh. ii.   BUND-I-BURBUR,[1] near the north-western frontier of Af-
162; Jour. As.
Soc. 1841, p. 118; ghanistan, twenty miles west of Bamian, is a celebrated dam or
Conolly, Report mound, the origin of which is ascribed to a miracle,* but which
on Khorasan.
appears to be in reality nothing more than a vast mass of earth
that has fallen into a ravine from an adjacent height. Near it,
in lat. 34° 40′, long. 67° 18′, is the source of the stream generally called the Bund-i-Burbur river, and sometimes the Durya,
which flows from a large lake, the result of the accumulation
[2] Moorcroft, Punj. of water caused by the dam.[2] It is in the mountains a clear
Bokh. ii. 393.
rapid stream, which has a course of about 250 miles, generally
northward, to the vicinity of Balkh, where it is divided into
eighteen canals, and totally expended in irrigation. Its praises
[3] Lalla Rookh, 63. have been celebrated by Thomas Moore,[3] under the name of the
Bendemeer.

Vigne, Kashmir,   BUNDIPUR, or BUNDURPUR, in Kashmir, a village at
ii. 198.
the commencement of the route to Iskardoh over the range
bounding the valley of Kashmir on the north. Close to it, two
considerable streams flow into the Wulur Lake from the north.
The water of the lake formerly reached to the village, but at
present is a mile distant, in consequence of its outlet, the river

232.   * In Burnes' Personal Narrative a curious account is given of this tradition, but it is too long for insertion here.

Jailum, continually deepening its bed. Bundurpur is in lat. 34° 23', long. 74° 31'.

BUNGALA.—A village in the Punjab, six miles from the right bank of the Sutluj, and ten miles north of the town of Ferozpoor. Lat. 31° 5', long. 74° 29'. *Map of N. W. Frontier.*

BUNGOOL DEHRA, in Sinde, a village on the route from Shikarpoor to Larkhana, and twenty-two miles north of the latter place. It has about 250 inhabitants, and is supplied with water from a well. Lat. 27° 43', long. 68° 27'. *E.I.C. Ms. Doc.*

BUNGUSH, in Afghanistan. A valley extending across the Suliman range, in lat. 33° 20', long. 70° 30', and expanding into a plain about twelve miles in diameter.[1] The valley is called Upper and the plain Lower Bungush. The plain is fertile, and well watered by a stream, which flows south-east, and is probably the same which, near the Indus, is called the Kurum river. The uncultivated parts are covered with dwarf palms, but there are few other trees. Upper Bungush is well watered, productive in the bottoms, and considerably wooded[2] in the mountainous part, which is covered with snow as late as March, though there is seldom any below. It is subject to the chief of Kohat,[3] who has an income of 80,000 rupees per annum. Through it lies one of the routes from Hindostan to Khorasan, now much frequented in consequence of the depredations committed at the Khyber Pass.[4] *[1] Elph. Acc. of Caubul, 362.* *[2] Masson, Bal. Afg. Panj. i. 115.* *[3] Wood's Oxus, 151.* *[4] Burnes' Trade of the Derajat, Map; Id. on Fair for the Indus.*

BUNIAH WALLEE, in Sinde, a halting-place on the route from Sukkur to Jessulmair by way of Khyerpoor, and seventy-seven miles east of the last-named place. There is here a pool filled with rain-water during part of the year, but dry in the hot season. Coarse grass is plentiful. Lat. 27° 23', long. 69° 54'. *E.I.C. Ms. Doc.*

BUNKA.—A village in the Punjab, on the route from Ferozpoor by way of Hureeke to Lahore, and thirty miles south-west of the latter place. Lat. 31° 23', long. 74° 39'. *E.I.C. Ms. Doc.*

BUNKAR.—See BAGHWAN.

BUNNA, in Sinde, is a town on the route from Cutch to Hyderabad, and on the east or left bank of the Indus, which at this place is nearly a mile wide, and even in its low state filling the channel from bank to bank. Here the Pinyaree, a great branch, diverges from the main stream, and, flowing southwards, is discharged into the sea by the Sir mouth. Bunna is in lat. 25° 4', long. 68° 18'. *Burnes' (James) Mission to Sinde, 40.*

BUNNOO.—See BANOO.

BUNPOOR, in Beloochistan, in the district of Mukran. It consists of a fertile tract, thirty miles long and five broad, stretching from east to west, and having a sandy desert of about twenty-five miles broad on each side of it. On the south it is bounded by the Mukran mountains, on the north by a range parallel to them. Grant[1] describes it as well irrigated, and in consequence producing grain in abundance; yet Pottinger[2] states it as devoid of rivers, having merely a brook, which, as early as April, gave indications of speedily becoming dry. It is at present held by a Beloochc race, called Narrois, who seized it about fifty years ago, and whose exact origin it is vain to seek in this barbarous and extensive tract. Their force amounts to about 300 cavalry and 2,500 infantry, and these support themselves by predatory inroads on the neighbouring countries, especially Persia. Among their multifarious booty the wretched inhabitants are considered an important part, being sold as slaves to traders coming from the north. The chief resides in the fort of Bunpoor, built on a mound of earth, visible from a distance of twenty-five miles, and said by the natives to have been made by order of a Gucbre chieftain, who commanded his innumerable cavalry to fill the nose-bags of their horses with earth and empty them here. The mound is described by Pottinger[3] to be 100 yards high and 800 in circuit. It is ascended by means of flights of stairs practised in the body of the mound. Half-way up is a very deep well of fine water. Though rudely built of mud, the fort would probably, from the strength of its site, be impregnable against any force which the Persians could bring against it. In addition to the results of his forays, the chief has a fixed revenue, stated by Pottinger at 26,000 rupees, 140 camels, 140 matchlocks, 140 sheep or goats, 140 measures of wheat, and the same of dates, each measure being 106 lbs. Lat. 27° 20′, long. 60° 45′.

BURA.—A village in the Punjab, situate on the right bank of the river Ravee, eighty-five miles south-west of Lahore. Lat. 30° 58′, long. 73° 11′.

BURAKHAIL.—A village in Afghanistan, on the route from Ghuznee to Kohat, forty miles west of Kohat and sixty miles south-west of Peshawur. Lat. 33° 30′, long. 70° 48′.

BURANGHUR.—A village. in North-western Afghanistan, forty-five miles south-west of Sir-i-Pool. Lat. 35° 54′, long. 64° 58′.

[1] Jour. As. Soc. 1839, p. 333; Grant, Jour. of a Tour through the Western parts of Makran.
[2] Belooch. 312.
[3] Ut supra, 177.

E.I.C. Ms. Doc.

E.I.C. Ms. Doc.

E.I.C. Ms. Doc.

BUREEN CHENON.—See BUREEN CHINAR.

BUREEN CHINAR.—A village in Beloochistan, on the route E.I.C. Ms. Doc. from Shawl to Kelat, and sixty miles south-west of the former place. It is supplied with water from an aqueduct, and there is much cultivation around it. The road here is excellent. Lat. 29° 26′, long. 66° 27′.

BURENG, BERENG, or BRENG.—A valley of Kashmir, Moorcr. Punj. Bokh. ii. 247; extending in a direction from south-east to north-west, between F. Von Hugel, lat. 33° 20′—33° 30′, long. 75° 10′—75° 26′. Its upper ex- Kashmir, i. 330. tremity reaches nearly to the summit of the Snowy Panjal mountain, bounding Kashmir on the east, and the route by the Mirbul Pass, over that ridge, proceeds up the valley, which is drained by the river of Bureng. The whole of the valley appears (as Vigne expresses it) honeycombed by caves and sub-terraneous water-channels, and in consequence abounds in springs of great volume and force. Of these the principal are the in-termitting fountain of Sondibreri, and the vast spring of Echi-bul, which last is supposed to be the efflux of the engulfed water of the Bureng river. (See BURENG RIVER, ECHIBUL, and SONDIBRERI.)

BURENG RIVER, in Kashmir,[1] flowing through a valley of [1] Vigne, i. 337. the same name, is formed by the junction of two streams, one having its source in a large spring near the summit of the Wurd-wun Pass, and flowing southwards, the other rising on the western declivity of the Snowy Panjal, and flowing north-west. After their junction[2] a great part of the water sinks suddenly by an [2] Moorcr. Punj. opening in the rocky bed of the stream, the rest is saved by Hugel, Kaschmir, means of a canal, and conveyed north-westward toward Islamabad, ii. 190. beyond which, in lat. 33° 42′, long. 75° 2′, it joins the Lidur river, forming one of the principal feeders of the Jailum. The length of the course of the Bureng is about forty miles.

BURG.—A village in Beloochistan, on the route over the E.I.C. Ms. Doc. elevated country between Shawl and Kelat, and distant fifteen miles west of the former place. The road here (which is excel-lent) passes through a well-watered valley, about eight miles wide. Lat. 30° 6′, long. 66° 45′.

BURGUNA.—A village in Afghanistan, situate on the road E.I.C. Ms. Doc. from Kandahar to Quetta, and thirty-two miles south-east of the former place. This route takes a south-easterly direction from Kandahar to Pisheen valley, when it runs due south to Quetta, where it branches off, one route to the south of Beloochistan, through Kelat and Bela, the other westward, through the Bolan Pass. It is in lat. 31° 22', long. 65° 57'.

Vigne, Kashmir, l. 164.   BURMAWUR, a small town in the north-east of the Punjab, among the southern ranges of the Himalaya, is situate on the river Ravee, and on the route from Chumba to Lahoul. Lat. 32° 30', long. 76° 30'.

E.I.C. Ms. Doc.   BUROBERA.—A considerable village in Sinde, on the route from Hyderabad to Sehwan, and thirty-two miles south-east of the latter place. It is situate a mile from the right bank of the Indus, amidst considerable cultivation. Lat. 25° 58', long. 68° 12'.

E.I.C. Ms. Doc.   BURRA CHICHER.—In Sinde, a thriving village on the route from Hyderabad to Sehwan, and sixty-two miles north-west of the former place. It has a large mosque, in front of which are numerous tombs. The road is good; there is space for encampment, and an abundant supply of water. The village is situate in a well-cultivated country, on a small water-course, discharging itself into the Indus a mile to the east. Lat. 26° 13', long. 68°.

Jour. As. Soc. 1840, p. 910; De La Hoste, Rep. on Western Sinde; E.I.C. Ms. Doc.   BURRAN.—A river in Sinde, which takes its rise in the Keertar mountains, in lat. 25° 54', long. 67° 45', and, after a south-easterly course of sixty-five miles, falls into the Indus. Lat. 25° 14', long. 68° 17'. In the upper part of its course it is called the Dhurwal. For a mile before its confluence with the Indus it has a large body of water.

Elph. 329.   BURRINDOO, or BONYR.*—In Northern Afghanistan; a small river, which, rising in the ridge dividing Booneere or Bonyr from Suwat, takes a course in a south-easterly direction of about forty miles, and discharges itself into the Indus on the west side, in lat. 34° 12', long. 72° 36'. It drains the fertile valley of Boonere.

E.I.C. Ms. Doc.   BURROOKULLAN.—A village in Afghanistan, situate on the road from Peshawur to Kabool, about a mile south of the Kabool river, and eighteen or twenty west of the western extremity of the Khyber Pass. Lat. 34° 16', long. 70° 43'.

E.I.C. Ms. Doc.; Hough's Narr. of Exp. in Afg. 40.   BURSHOREE.—A halting-place near two walled villages in Beloochistan, on the route from Shikarpoor to Gundava, and thirty-five miles east of the latter town. It is situate on the

* Called by the latter name in Walker's Map.

border of the Runn or Desert of Shikarpoor, and is supplied with water of indifferent quality from wells. In the vicinity is a little cultivation, and some scanty supplies may be obtained. Lat. 28° 27′, long. 68° 6′.

BURT.—A village in Sinde, near the right bank of the In- Ms. Survey Map. dus, forty-four miles north-east of Sukkur, in lat. 28° 15′, long. 69° 18′.

BURUKHANU.—A village in Afghanistan, eleven miles Walker's Map of south-west of the Koh-i-Baba mountains, and fifty-four miles Afg. south-west of the town of Bamian. Lat. 34° 18′, long. 67° 6′.

BUSSEEN.—A village in the Punjab, on the route from E.I.C. Ms. Doc. Amritsir to Lahore, and midway, or twenty miles, from either town. Lat. 31° 40′, long. 74° 37′.

BUSSEERAH.—A village in the Punjab, situate about ten E.I.C. Ms. Doc. miles east of the river Indus, and twenty-two miles south-west by east of Mooltan. Lat. 30° 6′, long. 71° 5′.

BUSSOOR KHAIL, in Afghanistan, is a village having E.I.C. Ms. Doc. several others in its immediate vicinity, lying on the route from Ghuznee to Shawl, from which latter place it is distant about a hundred and thirty miles north. Lat. 31° 54′, long. 67° 23′.

BUSSOUL.—See Bassowal.

BUTCHA.—See Batchau.

BUTCHEAL LUGAREE.—A village in Sinde, situate on the Ms. Survey Map. right bank of the Western Narra river, on the road from Schwan to Larkhana; fifty miles north-west of the former, and forty miles south-west of the latter. Lat. 27° 5′, long. 67° 47′.

BUTCHRAL.—A village in Sinde, situate on the road from Ms. Survey Map. Bukkur, by way of Khyerpoor, to Hyderabad. Lat. 27° 11′, long. 68° 54′.

BUTORA, in Sinde, is a small village or station on the route Burnes' (J.), Mission to Sinde, 38. from Cutch to Hyderabad. Lat. 24° 25′, long. 68° 30′.

BUTTE KOTE.—A village and desert of the same name, at Wood, Khyber the eastern extremity of the district of Jelalabad, lying between Pass, 6; Burnes' Bohk. i. 120; the Khyber and Ali Boghan mountains. Here, the heat of sum- Moorcr. Punj. Bokh. ii. 330; mer acting on the bare stony surface of the ground, and the air Jour. As. Soc. confined by the adjacent mountains, produces a dreadful simoom 1836, p. 477; Court, Memoir on or pestilential wind, which scorches like the blast from a furnace. a Map of Pesha- wer, also 1842, The bodies of those attacked by it are covered with blue spots, 118; Macgregor, and death and putrefaction immediately follow. Lat. 34° 16′, Geo. Notice of Jallalabad; Hough, long. 70° 51′. Narr. of Exp. to Afg. 305.

BUZDAR PASS.—See Sangad Pass.

E.I.C. Ms. Doc.   BYABANCK, in Western Afghanistan, is a village on the route from Herat to Kandahar. It has a supply of fresh water from a *kareez* or subterraneous aqueduct, which renders it of importance in this country, where there is a general dearth of that indispensable necessary of life. Lat. 32° 14', long. 64°.

E.I.C. Ms. Doc.   BYE DERA.—A village in the Punjab, situate on the river Ravee, on the route from Mooltan to Lahore, by the left banks of the Chenaub and Ravee rivers, sixty miles south-west of Lahore. Lat. 31° 2', long. 73° 26'.

Walker's Map of N.W. Frontier.   BYE DERU.—A village in the Punjab, about four miles from the left bank of the Ravee river, forty-four miles south-west of Lahore. Lat. 31° 12', long. 73° 40'.

C.

CABOOL, or CABUL.—See Kabool.

Burnes (James), Mission to Sinde, 38.   CABULPOOR, in Sinde, a town on the left or eastern bank of the Indus, and on the route from Cutch to Hyderabad. Lat. 24° 45', long. 68° 28'.

CAFERISTAN.—See Kafiristan.

CANDAHAR.—See Kandahar.

Leech, Khyber Pass, 11; Elph. Acc. of Caubul, 354.   CAROPPA, or KADAPA, PASS.—This pass lies across the mountains between the plain of Peshawur and that of Jelalabad. The route by it is very circuitous, proceeding northward from Peshawur, crossing the Kabool and Lundye rivers to Husht-nuggur, then again crossing the Lundye river and proceeding westward to Lalpoor, where it again proceeds southwards across the Kabool river, and joins the main route to Jelalabad. It is a tolerably good road and considerably frequented, not being infested by the Khyberees. Lat. 34° 20', long. 71° 30'.

E.I.C. Ms. Doc.; Jour. As. Soc. 1841, p. 330; Conolly (E.), Jour. of Travels in Seistan.   CARWAN CAZEE, in Western Afghanistan, a halting-place on the route from Kandahar to Herat, considered to be about half-way between those two places, or about a hundred and eighty-five miles from each. It is important merely on account of its having a supply of water. Lat. 32° 31', long. 62° 58'.

CASHMERE, or CASHMIR.—See Kashmir.

CATARH.—A village in Sinde, ten miles east of Omercote, Ms. Survey Map. on the road from thence to Balmair. Lat. 25° 22′, long. 69° 57′.

CAUBOOL, or CAUBUL.—See Kabool.

CHACHER.—A village in Sinde, situate on the right bank E.I.C. Ms. Doc. of the Indus, forty-five miles north of Bukkur, and ninety south-west of Mittunkote, from which place there is a road. Lat. 28° 12′, long. 69° 16′.

CHACHERA.—A village situate in the Little Desert of E.I.C. Ms. Doc. Sinde, thirty-five miles south-east from Omercote, on the road to Nuggur Parker. Lat. 25° 7′, long. 70° 20′.

CHADOOH.—A village in Sinde, twelve miles south-east of Ms. Survey Map. Khyerpoor, on one of the routes from Bukkur to Hyderabad. Lat. 27° 24′, long. 68° 51′.

CHAGAI, in Beloochistan, a village on the route from Masson, Bal. Afg. Sonmeanee to Kelat, and five miles north of the former place. Panj. ii. 105. Close to it, the route westward to the celebrated shrine of Hinglaj branches off. Chagai is in lat. 25° 28′, long. 66° 23′.

CHAGA SERAI.—A village of Chitral, in Northern E.I.C. Ms. Doc Afghanistan, situate on the river Kooner, about forty miles north of the town of Bajour. Lat. 35° 37′, long. 71° 14′.

CHA GOOROO.—A village in the province of Sarawan, in E.I.C. Ms. Doc. Beloochistan, situate on the road from Shawl to Kelat, forty miles south of the former place. The road near this place is level, and there is a supply of water from a well. Lat. 29° 36′, long. 66° 46′.

CHAH-I-JEHAN, in Afghanistan, a halting-place on the E.I.C. Ms. Doc. route from Kandahar to Herat, about ninety-five miles from the latter place. It has a supply of water, but the surrounding country, though capable of yielding forage in abundance, is uncultivated and nearly desert. Lat. 33° 20′, long. 62° 22′.

CHAH-I-MEERZA.—A village in Western Afghanistan, E.I.C. Ms. Doc. situate twenty-six miles south of Khash. It is about eighty miles south-east of Furrah. Lat. 31° 25′, long. 62° 45′.

CHAH-I-MOOSUK.—A village in Afghanistan, on the road E.I.C. Ms. Doc. from Giriskh to the province of Seistan, eighty-five miles east of Giriskh, and twenty miles from the town of Khash, through which this route passes. Lat. 31° 41′, long. 63°.

CHAIKAL.—A considerable village of the Koh-i-Damun, in Masson, Bal. Afg. Afghanistan, on the route from Istalif to Charikar, and fifteen Panj. iii. 124.

miles north of the former place. The vicinity is fertile, beautiful, and well cultivated, like the other parts of the Koh-i-Damun. Lat. 35°, long. 69° 2'.

Ms. Survey Map. CHAIN.—A village in the Punjab, situated about a mile and a half from the right bank of the river Ravee, and sixty miles south-west of the city of Lahore. Lat. 31° 7', long. 73° 26'.

As. Res. viii. 279;
Gerard, Obs. on
Spiti Valley;
Trebeck, in
Moorcr. ii. 51.

CHAMORERIL.—A lake in Ladakh, in the elevated table-land of Rupshu, situate between the valley of the Sutluj and that of the Indus, called by Trebeck, Tsummureri. It is 15,000 feet above the level of the sea, and is surrounded by mountains which rise in some places 5,000 feet above the surface of the water. The general breadth is about a mile and half; the length, which is in a direction from north to south, is between twenty and twenty-five miles; the circumference about fifty. The water is brackish, of a blue colour, and Trebeck conjectures it deep. He also states, but apparently rather rashly, that it contains no fish. Though far above the limit laid down by theorists for perpetual congelation in this latitude, it remains unfrozen during the summer months, according to the testimony of Gerard, who explored it in the end of September. Though receiving several considerable streams, it has no efflux, the water being carried off by evaporation, a process which is here found in operation more actively than in the most burning tropical regions. Lat. 32° 45', long. 78° 20'.

Map of the N.W.
Frontier.

CHANDEE.—A village of Bhawlpoor, situate on an offset of the river Indus, and on the route from Roree to Mittunkote. Lat. 28° 24', long. 69° 50'.

E.I.C. Ms. Doc. CHANDEE-JA-GOTE.—A village in Sinde, situate about eight miles from the east bank of the river Indus, on the route from Bukkur, by way of Nowsharra, to Hyderabad, and fifty-three miles north of the last-named place. Lat. 26° 7', long. 68° 12'.

E.I.C. Ms. Map. CHANDIA.—A village in Sinde, on the route from Sehwan to Lárkhana, and thirty-eight miles north of the former town. There is some cultivation in the neighbourhood. Lat. 26° 56', long. 67° 55'.

CHANDIA.—See DEHREE KOTE.

E.I.C. Ms. Doc. CHANDKHOTE.—A village of Sinde, situate on the right bank of the river Indus, ten miles south-east of Lárkhana. Lat. 27° 22', long. 68° 15'.

CHANDKOH,[1] in Sinde, a district stretching along the right bank of the Indus, between lat. 26° 40'—27° 20', and long. 67° 45'—68° 10'. It is intersected by the Narra, the great western offset of the Indus, and several other water-courses; it is level, and extensively flooded during the season of inundation. From the latter circumstance and the nature of the soil (a rich mud deposited by the river), it has a fertility scarcely anywhere exceeded. Under the Talpoor dynasty, it belonged to the Hyderabad Ameers, and yielded a considerable proportion of their revenue. It is called Chandkoh from being principally held by the Belooche tribe of that name. Pottinger,[2] who mentions it under the name of Chandookee, estimates the revenue derived from it by the Ameers at 100,000l. per annum, but there can be little doubt that this is an exaggeration. [1] Burnes, Bokh. ill. 270; Correspondence on Sinde, 488. [2] Belooch. 357.

CHANDOO, or CHANDRA.—A village in Beloochistan, situate on the high road from Kelat to Bela, about twelve miles north of the latter place, and near the left bank of the river Poorally. Lat. 26° 19', long. 66° 23'. E.I.C. Ms. Doc.; Outram, Rough Notes, 280.

CHANDOOKEE.—See CHANDKOH.

CHANDRA, in Beloochistan.—See CHANDOO.

CHANDRA, the principal feeder of the Chenaub. After receiving the water of the Surajbhaga, it bears the name of Chandrabhaga. (See Chenaub.) Moorcr. Punj. Bokh. i. 191-195.

CHANDRABHAGA.—The Chenaub bears this name in the upper part of its course after it has received the water of the Surajbhaga. (See Chenaub.) Id. i. 195.

CHANG.—A village in Sinde, on the road from Bukkur to Hyderabad, by way of Khyerpoor Lat. 26° 57', long. 68° 46'. Ms. Map of Sinde.

CHANNI-KHAN-DIGOT.—A small but thriving town of Bhawlpoor, on the route from the city of that name to Khanpoor, and eighteen miles north-east of the latter place. The surrounding country is generally dry, sandy, and overspread with tamarisk jungle. Lat. 28° 50', long. 70° 54'. Masson, Bal. Afg. Panj. i. 391.

CHAOGAONWA.—A village in the Punjab, situate on the road from Amritsir to Vazeerabad, about fifteen miles north-west of the former place, and twenty-three miles north-east of Lahore. Lat. 31° 45', long. 74° 35'. E.I.C. Ms. Doc.

CHAPPAR, in Beloochistan, an elevated table-land, a short distance west of the town of Kelat. It is at present thinly inhabited. Fragments of pottery, which occur in vast quantities, Masson, Kalat, 320.

and similar traces of human habitation, indicate it to have been formerly the seat of a dense population. It is well watered by streams, and produces abundance of melons and similar esculents for the Kelat market. Lat. 28° 50', long. 66° 22'.

Ms. Survey Map.   CHARAN.—A village in Sinde, situate on the Narra river, on the route from Larkhana to Sehwan, forty-five miles north of the latter place. Lat. 26° 56', long. 67° 49'.

CHARATTA.—See CHARRATTA.

E.I.C. Ms. Doc.   CHARBAGH.—A village in Afghanistan, situate on 'the route from Herat to Bamian, twenty-eight miles north-east of the former place. Lat. 34° 31', long. 62° 38'.

Walker's Map of Afg.   CHAR BOORJUK.—A village in Afghanistan, on the road from Kandahar to Herat, a hundred and thirty miles south of the latter place. Lat. 32° 36', long. 62° 30'.

E.I.C. Ms. Doc.; Leech, Hindoo Koosh, 33.   CHARDAR PASS.—A pass from Afghanistan to Kunduz over the Hindoo Koosh. Lat. 34° 55'—35° 15', long. 68° 35'.

E.I.C. Ms. Doc.   CHARDEH, in Afghanistan, a fort on the route from Kandahar to Ghuznee, about thirty miles south-west of the latter town. The surrounding district, called Karabagh, is very fertile, being in harvest time one large field of wheat as far as the eye can reach. Lat. 33° 13', long. 68°.

E.I.C. Ms. Doc.   CHARDEH.—A village in Afghanistan, situate in the valley of Ghorbund, twenty-eight miles west of Charikar. Lat. 34° 55', long. 68° 37'.

E.I.C. Ms. Doc.; Hough, Narr. of Exp. in Afg. 304; Mass. Bal. Afg. Panj. i. 168; Jour. As. Soc. 1842, p. 77; Grif, Bar. and Ther. Meas. in Afg.   CHARDEH.—A village of Afghanistan, in the valley of Jelalabad, is situate on the right bank of the Kabool river, at the confluence of a small stream from the Sufeid Koh. The neighbouring country is in general very sandy and barren, and in summer is sometimes swept over by the pestilential *simoom*, or scorching blast, fatal to animal life whenever exposed to its influence. The elevation of Chardeh above the sea is 1,822 feet. Lat. 34° 20', long. 70° 50'.

E.I.C. Ms. Doc.   CHAREE CHUCKOO.—A village in the Punjab, situate on the road from Ramnuggur to Attock, ten miles north of the former place. Lat. 32° 29', long. 73° 36'.

¹ Burnes, Pers. Narr. 151; Wood, Oxus, 187; Lord, Koh-i-Damun, 47; Masson, Bal. Afg. Panj. iii. 125.   CHARIKAR.[1]—A town in the Kohistan of Kabool, and close to the entrance of the Ghorbund valley, in Hindoo Koosh. It is the residence of the governor of the Kohistan, and has considerable transit trade to Turkestan and Central Asia, through the several passes which cross the Hindoo Koosh from the Ghorbund

valley, so that the duties, it is said, exceed 10,000 rupees per annum. It has also a direct trade in the coarse cotton cloths manufactured throughout this district. The most remarkable object in the town is a large castle, the residence of one of the great chiefs of the country. Charikar is the most flourishing, as well as one of the largest towns in the Kohistan, having a population of 5,000.

In 1839,[2] when the British took military possession of the greater part of Afghanistan, Charikar was garrisoned by a regiment raised from the native population, but towards the close of 1841, this was replaced by a Goorkha regiment in the service of Shah Shoojah, and under the command of Captain Codrington. On the outbreak of the insurrection in the Kohistan soon after, the garrison was attacked by an overwhelming force, and their commander slain. The position being completely commanded, and the supply of water cut off, an attempt was made to retreat on Kabool, but the result was disastrous, the whole force, after a most determined resistance, being destroyed, with the exception of Major Pottinger, Mr. Haughton, and a Goorkha sepoy. Lat. 35° 2', long. 69° 3'. [2 Eyre, Mil. Op. at Kabool, 90-103]

CHARNA.—See CHILNEY.

CHARRATTA, in Afghanistan, a small town in the Derajat, [E.I.C. Ms. Doc.] about twelve miles west of the Indus, and nine miles west of Dera Ghazee Khan. It lies in a low country intersected by canals from the Indus, and has two wells for the supply of water when other sources fail. Population about 1,000. Lat. 30° 3', long. 70° 42'.

CHARSIA.—A village in Afghanistan, ten miles south of [E.I.C. Ms. Doc.] Kabool, and situate on the route from thence to the Pisheen valley. Lat. 34° 23', long. 69° 4'.

CHASGO, or SHUSHGAO, in Afghanistan, a cluster of villages with a mud fort, situate in a fertile spot thirteen miles north of Ghuznee, and on the route from that place to Kabool. It is 971 feet above Ghuznee, or 8,697 above the sea. Between this place and Ghuznee, and about eight miles from the latter, the road passes over a rising ground, and is there estimated to have an elevation of 9,000 feet. This is regarded as the highest part of the route from Kabool to Ghuznee. The country between Chasgo and Ghuznee has some very strong and defensible positions, but it is in general barren. In consequence of the great elevation, the air here was found sharp and bracing when [E.I.C. Ms. Doc.; Hough, Narr. of Exp. to Afg, 239; Havelock, War in Afg. ii. 98; Jour. As. Soc. 1842, p. 65; Grif. Bar. and Ther. Meas. in Afg.]

the British army marched by, notwithstanding the march was performed in the month of July. Lat. 33° 43', long. 68° 22'.

E.I.C. Ms. Doc.   CHATCHUR.—A village in Bhawlpoor, situate on the east bank of the river Indus, opposite to Mittunkote. Lat. 28° 53', long. 70° 30'.

E.I.C. Ms. Doc.   CHECHENEH.—A village of Afghanistan, in Lughman, situate at the confluence of the Punchshir with the Kabool river. Lat. 34° 36', long. 69° 50'.

Walker's Map.   CHECHOKE.—A village in Bhawlpoor, situate near the left bank of the river Ghara. Lat. 30° 8', long. 73° 10'.

E.I.C. Ms. Doc.;
Conolly, Jour. to
India, ii. 68.   CHECKAU, or CHECKAUB, in Western Afghanistan, a fort, having a good supply of fine water from a spring, situate on the route from Kandahar to Herat, from which latter place it is distant 160 miles south. Though the neighbouring country is hilly, there is considerable cultivation, and good crops of wheat and barley are obtained. The roads are good. Lat. 32° 34', long. 62° 53'.

Correspondence
on Sinde, 498.   CHEEAPUT, in Sinde, a small town, between Hyderabad and Khyerpoor, and fifty miles south of the latter place. It is important as forming, with the contiguous town of Dingee, a commanding post in the communication of Khyerpoor and Emaum-Ghur with the part of the desert adjoining this last fort. Cheeaput is in lat. 26° 52', long. 68° 34'.

Masson, i. 455.   CHEECHAWUTNEE.—A village in the Punjab, situate on the left bank of the Ravee river, across which, at this place, is a much-frequented and important ferry. Lat. 30° 29', long. 72° 38'.

E.I.C. Ms. Doc.   CHEELA, a large water-course in Sinde, is a branch of the Narra, the great offset of the Indus to the west. It flows by several villages, of which the two more important are Kulorah and Dera. Lat. 27° 20', long. 68° 6'.

E.I.C. Ms. Doc.   CHÉENDEE.—A village in the Punjab, on the road from Ramnuggur to Attock: It is situate on a small branch of the Swan river. Lat. 33° 23', long. 73° 14'.

E.I.C. Ms. Doc.   CHEGHA.—A village in Sinde, situate in the " Little Desert," forty-two miles south-east of Omercote. Lat. 25° 5', long. 70° 24'.

E.I.C. Ms. Doc.;
Moorer. Punj.
Bokh. ii. 359;
Masson, Bal. Afg.
Punj. i. 181.   CHEHAR BAGH.—A village in Afghanistan, five miles west of Jelalabad, on the road from thence to Kabool. Here are the ruins of a royal garden, said to have been made by Sultan Baber.

and restored by Shah Zeman, of Kabool. It is merely an inclosure of about 200 yards square, with a few small buildings, all now in ruins. Lat. 34° 23', long. 70° 21'.

CHEHEL TAN.*—A lofty mountain of Beloochistan,[1] overhanging the town of Moostung, lying to the south. Its elevation probably exceeds 11,000 feet, as snow remains on its summit as late as the beginning of July, and is found throughout the whole summer in the indentations of the upper part. On the summit is a ziarat, or place of pilgrimage, much frequented by the Mahometans, in consequence of its being the locality of a superstitious tradition related differently by different persons. Pottinger,[2] who calls the mountain Kohechihultun (the mountain of forty bodies), states the tradition of the natives to be, that Mahomet paid them a visit one night mounted on a dove, and left several *peers*, or saints, among them for their spiritual guidance, whose remains are buried on this mountain. Masson's account is, that forty children born at one birth were exposed here, and being miraculously rescued from death, still in their infantine forms haunt the mountain. Lat. 29° 40', long. 66° 55'.

right margin: [1] Masson, Bal.Afg. Panj. ii. 82. [2] Belooch. 272.

CHEHL BUCHA GUM ("the forty lost children"), in Afghanistan, a place of pilgrimage, regarded as the burial-place of forty children, concerning whom there is a superstitious tradition. It is six miles south-west of Ghuznee, on the route from that place to Kandahar. Lat. 33° 32', long. 68° 13'.

right margin: E.I.C. Ms. Doc.

CHEHL DOCHTUR,[1] Shrine of, on the north-west frontier of Afghanistan, situate on the left bank of the river Kooshk, a tributary of the Moorghaub. The tradition connected with this shrine is thus related by Abbott,[2] probably the only European who has visited the place:—" A couple of mud huts near the left border of the valley were shewn me as the residence of forty Oosbeg virgins; and a little rude altar, or tomb, under the hills, as the place of worship to which they had resorted when surprised by a force of some neighbouring tribes. In this extremity the virgins prayed for death, and were instantly translated, but whether by men or spirits does not appear." "The place is called Chehl-Dochtur, or the forty virgins. The tradition, as well as the name, is obviously Persian." Lat. 35° 7', long. 62° 9'.

right margin: [1] E.I.C. Ms. Doc. [2] Heraut and Khiva, I. 14.

CHEIRJAGARAIN.—A halting-place in Afghanistan, on the

right margin: E.I.C. Ms. Doc.

* This is the mountain called Chiltern by Griffith,[1] and Chiltun by Allen.[2]

right margin: [1] Jour. As. Soc. 1841, p. 803. [2] March through Sinde and Afg.133.

route by the Gomul Pass from Ghuznee to Dera Ismael Khan, and sixty miles west of the latter town. There is abundance of good water, but the road in the vicinity is very bad. Lat. 31° 59', long. 70° 4'.

CHENAUB.—A river in the Punjab, and generally considered the largest of the five by which that country is traversed. Moorcroft,[1] who ascended, as he conjectured, to within thirty miles of its source, supposes it to rise about lat. 32° 30', long. 77° 40', in Lahoul, south of Ladakh or Middle Tibet. The source must be very elevated, as the river holds its course through the Ritanka Pass, which is 13,000 feet high. The spot from which it proceeds is, according to Vigne,[2] a small lake called Chandra-Bhaga, or the Garden of the Moon, and in the upper part of its course the river is called the Chandra. At Tandi, lat. 32° 40', long. 73° 55', it is joined by the Surajbhagha, a stream of about equal magnitude, running from the north, and thenceforward the river is known by the name of the Chenaub or Chinab, and sometimes of Chandra-Bhaga. The length of each of the streams contributing to its formation may be about fifty miles. After their confluence, Moorcroft[3] found the stream about two hundred feet broad, with a full steady current. It takes a north-west course of about a hundred and thirty miles to Kishtawar, in lat. 33° 15', long. 75° 43', and there receives the Muruwurdwun, a considerable tributary from the north. Vigne[4] calculates the height of Kishtawar at 5,000 feet, and consequently, the Chenaub must have descended 8,000 feet in less than two hundred miles, or at the rate of above forty feet in the mile. At Kishtawar, Vigne[5] found the Chenaub flowing in a deep rocky channel twenty-five yards wide. The river thence proceeds south-west by a very tortuous course, through a rugged country, to Rihursi, a distance of about ninety miles, where it leaves the mountains, and flows into the lower ground of the Punjab. It is here about two hundred yards wide, deep and tranquil, yet rapid. At Aknur,[6] about fifty miles lower down, it becomes navigable, at least for timber-rafts, which are despatched from it down the Punjab. It continues a south-westerly course to Vazeerabad, about seventy miles lower down, in lat. 32° 30', long. 74°, where Von Hügel[7] found the stream unfordable and half a mile wide.* Macartney[8] measured it there in the month of July,

Marginal notes:
[1] Punj. Bokh. i. 100.
[2] Kashmir, i. 164.
[3] i. 195.
[4] i. 203.
[5] i. 208.
[6] Id. i. 217.
[7] Kashmir, iii. 147.
[8] Elph. Acc. of Caubul, 660.

* Vigne (i. 238), in his cursory style, says between 200 and 300 yards.

when nearly at the fullest, and found it one mile three furlongs and · twenty perches wide, with a depth of fourteen feet, and a current running five miles an hour. From this point it holds a south-west course for about thirty miles, to Ramnegurh,[9] where, in the middle of February, and consequently the low season, it was found three hundred yards wide, and with a depth of nine feet where greatest, the current running a mile and a half an hour. Hough[1] states that it is fordable near this place in the season, but there is much reason to question this statement. It thence pursues a south-west course for about 150 miles, to its confluence with the Jailum, a little above the ferry of Trimo, in lat. 31° 10', long. 72° 9'. Arrian,[2] in the spirit of exaggeration, with which, according to ancient testimony,* the Greeks were not unfamiliar, describes the turbulence of the confluence as terrific; but Burnes,[3] who visited it at midsummer, when the streams are usually highest, found it free from violence or danger. The total length of the course of the river to this point is about five hundred and forty miles. Below the confluence with the Jailum, the Chenaub flows south-west for about fifty miles, to its confluence with the Ravee, a much smaller river,[4] which joins it in lat. 30° 33', long. 71° 46', through three mouths close to each other. The Chenaub was here, at the end of June, the season of the greatest height of water, three-quarters of a mile wide, and above twelve feet deep. From this place, it continues its course south-west for a hundred and ten miles, to the confluence of the Ghara, in lat. 29° 21', long. 71° 6'. At the intervening ferry opposite Mooltan, Burnes found it a thousand yards wide at midsummer, the season of greatest inundation. The meeting of the Chenaub and Ghara[5] is very tranquil; the water of the former is red, that of the latter pale, and these respective colours may be distinguished for some miles downwards in the united stream, the red on the right or western, the pale on the left or eastern side. The total length of course from the source to this confluence is about seven hundred miles. There the united stream is called Punjnud (five rivers), a name which it bears to its fall into the Indus. The ancient name of the Chenaub[6] is admitted unquestionably to have been Acesines.

[9] Burnes' Bok. i. 40.

[1] Narr. Exp. in Afg. 352.

[2] Exp. Alex. L. vi. c. 4, 5.

[3] iii. 127.

[4] Burnes, iii. 125.

[5] Id. iii. 98.

[6] Rennell, 82.

* " Quidquid Græcia mendax
Audet in historiâ."—Juv. x. 174.

E.I.C. Ms. Doc.   CHEPKEDAR.—A village in North-eastern Afghanistan, situate near the right bank of the river Lundye. Lat. 34° 19', long. 71° 38'.

E.I.C. Ms. Doc.   CHERAN, CHERAT, or SHAH NURUD DYN.—A village in Kashmir, fifteen miles south-west of Sirinagur. Lat. 33° 52', long. 74° 37'.

E.I.C. Ms. Doc.   CHERRA.—A village in Western Afghanistan, on the route from Kandahar to Herat, and a hundred and eighty-six miles north-west of the former town. It has a small fort with a good supply of water. Lat. 32° 31', long. 63° 9'.

E.I.C. Ms. Doc.   CHERRA.—A small river of Western Afghanistan, rises in the mountains south of Ghore, and takes a south-westerly course, probably joining the Furrah Rood. It is crossed by the route from Kandahar to Herat, in lat. 32° 35', long. 63°.

CHESGOW.—See CHASGO.

Kennedy, Sinde   CHEYCHUN, in Sinde, a flourishing town on the Indus, be-
and Kabool, ii. 207. tween Hyderabad and Sehwan. Lat. 26° 5', long. 68° 6'.

Ms. Map of Sinde.   CHEYLAR.—A village of Sinde, lying on the route from Omercote to Deyphlah, in the Little Desert. Lat. 24° 53', long. 69° 58'.

Ms. Map of Sinde.   CHEYLEE.—A village in Sinde, situate on the road from Hyderabad to Omercote, about thirty-two miles west of the latter place, and sixty from the former. This route from Hyderabad runs due west. Lat. 25° 24', long. 69° 18'.

Walker, Map of   CHIAGUZ.—A village in Afghanistan, on the road from
Afg.   Furrah to Kandahar, thirty-six miles east of the former place. Lat. 32° 17', long. 62° 45'.

E.I.C. Ms. Doc.   CHIARBAG.—A village in North Afghanistan, about three miles from the left bank of the Suwat, and twenty miles south from the range of Laram mountains. Lat. 35° 3', long. 72° 36'.

E.I.C. Ms. Doc.   CHIARBAGH.—A village of Afghanistan, in the district of Lughman, situate on the Kabool river, near the junction of the Alishang river. Lat. 34° 34', long. 70° 9'.

E.I.C. Ms. Doc.   CHIBREE.—A village in Beloochistan, situate on the route from Dadur to Bagh, about fifteen miles south-west of the former place, and thirty north-west of the latter. Lat. 29° 17', long. 67° 40'.

Walker's Map.   CHICHUNDEE.—A village in Afghanistan, on the road from Babur-ka-killa to Dera Ismael Khan, a few miles west of the

Suliman mountains, over which this route passes. Lat. 31° 42', long. 69° 49'.

CHIGANUK.—A village in Afghanistan, near the source of E.I.C. Ms. Doc. the Moorghab river. Lat. 34° 56', long. 65° 58'.

CHIKON.—See CHECKAU.

CHILIYA.—A halting-place in Sinde, on the right of the E.I.C. Ms. Doc. route from Tattah to Hyderabad, and seven miles north-east of the former town. It is a wretched place, not affording even water. Lat. 24° 51', long. 68° 8'.

CHILNEY, or CHURNA, a small island at the western Horsburgh, i. 403; extremity of the coast of Sinde, is four miles north-west of Jour. As. Soc. Cape Monze, or Ras Mooarree. The intervening channel has, 1840, p. 910; De La Hoste, Rep. on for about a quarter of a mile, a depth of six or seven fathoms. Country between This island is of a white colour, rocky, completely barren, desti- Kurrachee and Sehwan. tute of water, and uninhabited. Lat. 24° 51', long. 66° 34'.

CHINAB.—See CHENAUB.

CHINEE.—A large village in Sinde, on the route by the E.I.C. Ms. Doc. Arul river from Sehwan to Larkhana, and thirty miles north-west Map of Sinde. of the former town. Supplies and forage are good and abundant, but the people have the character of being dishonest. The road in its vicinity is good. Lat. 26° 40', long. 67° 46'.

CHININI, in the Northern Punjab, on the southern slope of Vigne, Kashmir, the Himalaya. It is situate on the Taui river, which, about fifty i. 192; Forster. Jour. Beng. i. 344. miles lower down, falls into the Chenaub. Chinini is a place of considerable size, is neatly built, and has a palace still belonging to the deposed rajah of the town and district, though his possessions have been seized by Gholab Sing, the usurping Sikh chief of Jamu. As its elevation is considerable, it commands a noble view south-wards over several mountain ranges, and beyond them across the vast plain of the Punjab. Chinini is in lat. 32° 55', long. 75° 8'.

CHINJAN.—A village in Afghanistan, on the road from E.I.C. Ms. Doc. Cutch Toba to Dera Ghazee Khan. Lat. 30° 52', long. 68° 50'.

CHIOUKIATAN.—A village in the Bajour country, in the E.I.C. Ms. Doc. north-east of Afghanistan, situate about a mile from the west bank of the Lundye river, and a few miles south of the Laspissor range. Lat. 35° 36', long. 72°.

CHIR.—A village in Sinde, situate on the route from Hyde- Ms. Map. rabad to Bukkur, sixty miles north-east of the former place. Lat. 26° 9', long. 68° 46'.

CHIRNAT.—A village in Sinde, situate on the road from E.I.C. Ms. Doc.

Sehwan to Larkhana, two miles and a half west of the river Indus. Lat. 26° 38′, long. 67° 53′.

Vigne, Kashmir, ii. 310; Masson, Bal. Afg. Panj. i. 198; Burnes' Bok. ii. 209; Wood, Oxus, 282; Moorcr. Punj. Bokhara, ii. 269, 270.

CHITRAL.—A secluded country on the southern slope of the Hindoo Koosh. It consists of a long valley extending in a direction from south-west to north-east for about a hundred miles, with a breadth of from fifteen to twenty miles. Along the middle flows the Kooner river, which falls into the Kabool river near Jelalabad. Chitral is also called Kashgar-i-Khurd, or Little Kashgar, and sometimes Katawar. It is bounded on the north by the summit ridge of Hindoo Koosh, east by Panjkora and some other petty independent states, south by Afghanistan Proper, west by Kafiristan. Access is generally had to it by ascending along the bank of the Kama or Kooner river. The inhabitants are for the most part idolaters, but Mahometanism is represented as making progress among them. The valley of Chitral lies between lat. 35° 45′—36° 25′, long. 71° 20′—73° 10′.

Moorcr. ii. 269.

CHITRAL, the capital (or the Mastuch, as it is called by the natives) of the country bearing the same name, is little known. It has been ascertained, however, to have a bazaar and between three and four thousand inhabitants, principally Shia Mahometans, mixed with a few Hindoo traders. It is situate in lat. 36° 11′, long. 71° 59′.

E.I.C. Ms. Doc.

CHITTROOREE.—A village in Sinde, situate fifty-five miles north-east of Hyderabad, on the road from that city to Bukkur. Lat. 25° 58′, long. 68° 32′.

Walker's Map of Afg.

CHOAKEE.—A village in North Afghanistan, situate on the right bank of the Kooner river, forty miles north of Jelalabad. Lat. 34° 53′, long. 70° 50′.

Ms. Map of Sinde.

CHOATILLOH.—A village in Sinde, on the road from Jessulmair to Halla, fourteen miles east of the Narra river. Lat. 26° 16, long. 69° 18′.

E.I.C. Ms. Doc.

CHOBARA, in Afghanistan, is a considerable village of Sewestan, on the road from Raknee to Kandahar. It is supplied with water both from a rivulet and from tanks. Lat. 30° 6′, long. 69° 58′.

E.I.C. Ms. Doc.

CHOHO.—A village in Sinde, situate on the road from Hyderabad to Nuggur Parker. Lat. 24°·21′, long. 69° 54′.

Ms. Map.

CHOKUNDEE.—A village in Sinde, situate about two miles from the left bank of the Mulleeree river, twenty miles east of Kurrachee. Lat. 24° 53′, long. 67° 18′.

CHOLALAJ PASS leads from Afghanistan to Kunduz, over the Hindoo Koosh. Lat. 34° 54′—35° 10′, long. 68° 32′. Leech, Hind. Koosh, 33.

CHOLL.—A cluster of villages in Sinde, on the route from Sehwan to Larkhana, and forty-two miles north-west of the former place. It is situate on a branch of the Western Narra, amidst much cultivation. Supplies and forage are good and abundant. The road from Chinee, distant twelve miles south-east, is a good one. Lat. 26° 55′, long. 67° 49′. E.I.C. Ms. Doc.

CHOOASHAHGUNEE.—A village in the Punjab, thirty miles north-west of Julalpoor. Lat. 32° 51′, long. 72° 49′. E.I.C. Ms. Doc.

CHOONEE.—A village in that part of Afghanistan called Daman, five miles west of the river Indus. Lat. 31° 17′, long. 70° 49′. E.I.C. Ms. Doc.

CHOONGA.[1]—A village in Sinde, on the route from Subzulcote to Shikarpoor, and forty miles east of the latter place. It is situate on the east bank of a deep and extensive *dund* or pool of water, replenished by the inundations of the Indus. The road in this part of the route is free from jungle, and there is a good encamping-ground. Choonga,[2] by the treaty of November, 1842, was, with several other towns, ceded to Mahomed Bhawl Khan, and accordingly transferred in the following February. Lat. 27° 56′, long. 69° 4′. [1] E.I.C. Ms. Doc. [2] Correspondence on Sinde, 443-507.

CHOONKA, in Sinde, a halting-place on the route from Khyerpoor to Emaum Ghur, in the Thurr or Great Eastern Desert. It is forty miles south-east from Khyerpoor. There is abundance of water, but other supplies are so scanty, that the British force proceeding in the beginning of 1843 to the destruction of Emaum Ghur found difficulty in obtaining forage for fifty horse. Choonka is in lat. 27° 2′, long. 69° 3′. Id. 495.

CHORE.—A village in Sinde, situate on the route from Omercote to Jessulmair, eight miles north-east of the former place. Lat. 25° 25′, long. 69° 51′. Ms. Map.

CHORLA.—A small river of Sinde, rises in the Keertar range of mountains, about lat. 25° 50′, long. 67° 50′. It has a course generally northerly, of about thirty-five miles, and is lost in the arid tract west of Sehwan, in lat. 26° 20′, long. 67° 45′. In the upper part of its course it is called the Mulleeree, lower down, the Joorunb, and, finally, the Chorla. It is dry for the greater part of the year, but water may be always obtained by digging in the bed. E.I.C. Ms. Doc.; Ead. Map; Jour. As. Soc. 1840, p. 910; De la Hoste, Rep. on the Country between Kurrachee and Sehwan.

E.I.C. Ms. Doc.   CHORLA MUKAM. — A halting-place in Sinde, on the route from Sehwan to Kurrachee, and twenty-four miles south-west of the former place. There are here some ancient tombs and several pools of water. Lat. 26° 8′, long. 67° 50′.

E.I.C. Ms. Doc.   CHOTA, or NAWA SUN. — A small village in Sinde, on the route by the right bank of the Indus from Hyderabad to Sehwan, and fifty-five miles north-west of Hyderabad. Lat. 26° 8′, long. 68° 2′.

E.I.C. Ms. Doc.   CHOTTA CHURNAUT. — A village in Sinde, on the route from Sehwan to Larkhana, and seventeen miles north of the former place. It is situate on the bank marking the limit of the inundation of the Indus, and a mile and a quarter from the permanent channel. Lat. 26° 35′, long. 67° 58′.

E.I.C. Ms. Doc.   CHOTTA GULLOO. — A village in Sinde, a little to the right of the road from Sehwan to Larkhana, and forty-five miles north of the former place. It is situate four miles from the right bank of the Indus, on the west shore of a small lake or *dund,* deriving its supply of water from the inundations of the river. The country around is flat, but in some places is rendered difficult for travellers by being overgrown with thickets and intersected by numerous water-courses. Lat. 27°, long. 67° 56′.

E.I.C. Ms. Doc.   CHOTTA LASSAREE. — A village in Sinde, on the route from Sehwan to Larkhana, and thirty-three miles north of the former place. Though situate in a flat alluvial tract, only two miles from the west bank of the Indus, there is a scarcity of water in its immediate vicinity. Lat. 26° 50′, long. 67° 55′.

E.I.C. Ms. Doc.   CHOTTA SEETA. — A village in Sinde, on the route from Sehwan to Larkhana, and forty-six miles north of the former place. It is situate on the right bank of the Indus, in a flat country interspersed with bushes, but traversed by a practicable road. Lat. 27° 2′, long. 67° 58′.

E.I.C. Ms. Doc.; Elph. Acc. of Caubul, 450.   CHOTYAALI, in Afghanistan, a village of Sewestan, on the road from Dera Gházee Khan to Kandahar. It is situate in a valley of the same name, which is continuous with the valley of Tull. There are some discrepancies of statement in the accounts furnished of the adjacent country, but the balance of testimony inclines to the conclusion that it is neither productive nor well supplied with water.* Of that article, so indispensable to the

---

* Baber states that he could not get forage even for his own horse. (Memoirs, 164.)

health and comfort of the Eastern traveller, the quality is represented as being indifferent, as well as the quantity scanty. Lat. 30° 3′, long. 69° 18′.

CHOUCHUCK.—A town in the Punjab, situate on the left E.I.C. Ms. Doc. bank of the river Ravee, on the route from Mooltan to Lahore. Lat. 31°, long. 73° 22′.

CHOUKOOLI.—A village in the Bajour territory, north-east E.I.C. Ms. Doc. of Afghanistan, situate about a mile from the west bank of the Lundye river. Lat. 35° 5′, long. 71° 51′.

CHOUTRA.—A village in the Punjab, situate on the right E.I.C. Ms. Doc. bank of the Ravee river, fifty-five miles north-east of Mooltan. Lat. 30° 34′, long. 72° 16′.

CHUCH, an extensive plain to the east of Attock, and, from its proximity to that place, sometimes called the Plain of Attock. Its extent from east to west is, according to Vigne,[1] twenty miles,* [1] ii. 189. and from north to south about fifteen miles. Burnes[2] observes," a [2] Bokhara, i. 75. horde as numerous as that of Xerxes or Timour might encamp on this spacious plain, which is an entire sheet of cultivation." Vigne,[3] [3] Kashmir, ii. on the contrary, describes it as " covered with long grass and low 189. jungle." Everywhere occur rounded boulders of granite, borne to their present places by the furious inundations of the Indus. Here the Afghans, under Vizier Futteh Khan, were defeated by the Sikh general Mokham Shand, and finally driven over the Indus. This plain[4] is remarkable for a numerous breed of goats [4] Von Hügel, larger than common-sized asses. Lat. 33° 50′, long. 72° 20′. Kaschmir, iii. 93.

CHUCK.—A village in Sinde, situate on the left bank of the Map of Sinde. river Indus. Lat. 28° 16′, long. 69° 31′.

CHUCKERALA.—A village in the Punjab, situate about E.I.C. Ms. Doc. eighteen miles east of the river Indus, on the route from Kala Bagh to Baral. Lat. 32° 52′, long. 72°.

CHUCKREALEE.—A village in the Punjab, situate on the E.I.C. Ms. Doc. road, by way of Vazeerabad, from Amritsir to Julalpoor, twenty miles east of the latter place. Lat. 32° 38′, long. 73° 30′.

CHUCKREE.—A village in Afghanistan, twenty-four miles E.I.C. Ms. Doc. south-east by south of Kabool. Lat. 34° 14′, long. 69° 20′.

CHUCKWUNDEE. —A village in the Punjab, situate on the Walker's Map of N.W. Frontier.

* Vigne states that " its extent from Attok to the *west* is about twenty miles ;" but it seems that he must have meant to the *east*, as the Indus flows on the west, and the country beyond the river is hilly.

left bank of the river Ravee, on the route from Mooltan to Lahore. Lat. 30° 35', long. 72° 39".

E.I.C. Ms. Doc.   CHUHKOWAL.—A village in the Punjab, situate forty-two miles from the left bank of the Indus. Lat. 33° 1', long. 72° 33'.

E.I.C. Ms. Doc.   CHUKKORA-NULLA, in Sinde, a halting-place on the route from Kurrachee to Hoja Jamote, and twenty miles north of the former place. There is no village, nor is any article of refreshment procurable excepting water, and that is brackish. Lat. 25° 9', long. 67°.

E.I.C. Ms. Doc.   CHUKRA.—A village in Sinde, on the route from Sehwan to Larkhana, and thirty-one miles south of the latter place. It is situate two miles from the right bank of the Indus. It has a good supply of water, and an open ground for encamping. Lat. 27° 15', long. 68° 14'.

E.I.C. Ms. Doc.   CHULLUK.—A village in Afghanistan, on the road from Ghuznee to Dera Ismael Khan, and thirty-two miles south-east of the former place. Lat. 33° 18', long. 68° 42'.

[1] Vigne, Kashmir, i. 153.   CHUMBA,[1] in the north-east of the Punjab, among the southern mountains of the Himalaya, is situate on the river Ravee, at the foot of a lofty peak covered with snow.* Its situation is very picturesque and beautiful. The number of houses is estimated at a thousand. They are built of wood, and ranged about a rectangular open space, five hundred yards long and eighty broad. Chumba is the residence of the rajah of the neighbouring country. The population is probably about 5,000. It appears to have decayed since the time of Forster, who calls it Jumbo, and describes [2] i. 282.   it as " a mart of the first note in this part of the country."[2] Lat. 32° 22', long. 75° 56'.

E.I.C. Ms. Doc.   CHUMBA.—A village in the Punjab, situate on the road from Attock to Torbela, about thirty miles in a north-easterly direction from the former place. Lat. 34° 4', long. 72° 43'.

CHUMMUN.—See Chumun Chokee.

CHUMOREREEL.—See Chamoreril.

Hough, Narr. of Exp. to Afg.; E.I.C. Ms. Doc.; Havelock, War in Afg. i. 301; Kennedy, Sinde and Kabool, i. 235; Jour. As. Soc. 1842, p. 56; Grif. Bar. and Ther. Meas. in Afg.   CHUMUN CHOKEE.—A watch-tower and halting-post at the western or Kandahar side of the Khojuk Pass. It is 5,677 feet above the sea. There are some springs here, but the supply of water would be found very insufficient to meet the wants of any large number of travellers. Lat. 30° 50', long. 66° 25'.

* Vigne congratulates himself on being the first European that visited this place; but Forster had anticipated him.

CHUND.—A village in the Punjab, situate about thirty miles E.I.C. Ms. Doc. from the left bank of the Indus. Lat. 31° 57', long. 71° 39'.

CHUNDERWON.—A village in Sinde, eighteen miles south Ms. Survey Map. from Omercote. Lat. 25° 6', long. 69° 43'.

CHUNDHA, in Sinde, a village and halting-place on the E.I.C. Ms. Doc.; route from Khyerpoor to Hyderabad, and thirty-five miles south Correspondence on Sinde, 481. of the former town. It is situated twelve miles west of the Narra river, and at the western base of the low range of limestone hills which stretch in a south-eastern direction from Roree. Lat. 27° 6', long. 68° 42'.

CHUNDIA.— A village in Sinde, on the route from Larkhana E I.C. Ms. Doc. to Bhag, and situate twenty miles north of the former place, near the borders of the desert. It has four wells, and is capable of furnishing abundant supplies. The road is good and level. Lat. 27° 50', long. 68° 8'.

CHUNDIA.—A village in Sinde, situate on the route from E I.C. Ms. Doc. Vikkur to Tatta, and eighteen miles south-west of the latter place. Lat. 24° 36', long. 67° 47'.

CHUNDRANEE.—A village of Bhawlpoor, situate about E.I.C. Ms. Doc. three miles from the left bank of the river Ghara. Lat. 29° 55', long. 72° 42'.

CHUNDUN.—A village in Sinde, on the route from E.I.C. Ms. Map. Hyderabad to Lukput, and seventy-five miles south of the former place. Lat. 24° 21', long. 68° 28'.

CHUNGAL.—A village in Sinde, on the road from Hyderabad E.I.C. Ms. Map. to Omercote, twenty-two miles west of the latter place, and eighty from the former. Lat. 25° 24', long. 69° 28'.

CHUNGOND.—A village in the north-east of the Punjab, Walker's Map of N.W. Frontier. situate on the Duras river, in lat. 34° 31', long. 76°.

CHUNGUR.—A cluster of villages in Sinde, twelve miles E.I.C. Ms. Doc. north-west of Sehwan, on the route from that place to Lar-khana by way of the Arul river, a branch of which flows to them. The road is good here, and supplies and forage are plentiful. Lat. 26° 29', long. 67° 47'.

CHUNNA.—A village in Sinde, on the route from Sehwan E.I.C. Ms. Doc. to Larkhana, and sixty-seven miles north of the former place. It is situate on the right bank of a large water-course, which, parting from the Indus on the west side, insulates a tract about seven miles long. Lat. 27° 14', long. 68° 12'.

CHUPPER MOUNT.—See Fort Chapper.

E.I.C. Ms. Doc.   CHURCHA.—A village in Cutch Gundava, in Beloochistan, situate on the route from Bhag to Hurroond, and twenty-four miles east of the former place. Lat. 29°, long. 68° 16'.

CHURNA.—See Chilney.

CHURRA FORT.—See Cherra.

E.I.C. Ms. Doc.;   CHUSMA I JADEE, in Afghanistan, a halting-place on the
Hough, Narr. of
Exp. to Afg. 153; route from Kandahar to Ghuznee, from which last place it is
Outram, Rough
Notes, 102; Jour. distant seventy-five miles south-west.   It is situate about a mile
As. Soc. 1842, p. from the right or western bank of the Turnak river, and con-
59; Grif. Bar.
and Ther. Meas. tains several springs of fine water.   The surrounding country is
in Afg.   crowded with forts of the Ghiljies.   The road in the vicinity is
good and passable for wheel-carriages.   The elevation is 6,668
feet.   Lat. 32° 33', long. 67° 15'.

E.I.C. Ms. Doc.;   CHUSMA PUNGUK, in Afghanistan, a halting-place on
Hough, Narr. of
Exp. to Afg. 153; the route from Kandahar to Ghuznee, from which last place it
Outram, Rough is seventy miles distant south-west.   It is situate two miles
Notes, 102; Jour.
As. Soc. 1842, p. from the right or west bank of the river Turnak, in a fertile and
59; Grif. Bar. and well-cultivated valley, and contains several fine springs.   The
Ther. Meas. in
Afg.   adjacent hills contain numerous forts of the Ghilji tribe.   The
road in the neighbourhood is in general good, and available for
all purposes of military as well as commercial communication.
The elevation of this place is 6,810 feet.   Lat. 32° 36', long.
67° 20'.

CHUTA AHMEDPOOR.—See Ahmedpoor.

Ms. Survey Map.   CHUTKA.—A village in Sinde, situate on the western side
of the Narra river, on the road from Sehwan to Larkhana.   Lat.
27° 23', long. 68° 6'.

E.I.C. Ms. Doc.   CHUTTAI KA GOTE.—A halting-place in Sinde, about four
miles and three-quarters north-east of Tattah, lying to the left of
the route which leads from that town to Kotree, near Hyderabad.
It is a wretched place, and destitute even of water.   Lat. 24° 50',
long. 68° 2'.

Jour. As. Soc.   CHUTTERBAI, in Afghanistan, a stronghold in the Eusuf-
1840, p. 931; Co-
nolly (E.), Notes zai country, on the right bank of the Indus, in a position which
on the Eusofzye renders it almost inaccessible.   It belongs to Poindu Khan, a chief
Tribes of Afg.;
Id. 1839, p. 313; of Mogul lineage, who, possessed only of this and of Am, a
Court, Alexander's
Exploits on the similar post, a few miles further down the river, with about two
West Bank of the hundred and forty square miles of territory, is completely inde-

pendent. He supports his small armed force by plundering the Sikhs. Lat. 34° 20′, long. 72° 58′. *Indus; Burnes' Pol. Pow. of Sikhs, 1.*

CHUWARI.—A small town of the Punjab, on the route from Nurpur to Chumba, and ten miles south-west of the latter place. It is situate on a feeder of the river Ravee, and at the south-western base of a mountain above 8,000 feet high, over which the road to Chumba passes. Lat. 32° 17′, long. 75° 45′. *Vigne, Kashmir, I. 150.*

COHAN.—See KAHUN.

COHAST GURMODE, in Beloochistan, a considerable village, about twenty miles north of the Bolan. It is inhabited by about a thousand freebooters, who bear the name of Dhumad Khakas, and appear to be an offset of the Afghan tribe of Khakas or Kakurs, that so severely annoyed the British troops in their marches between Sinde and Afghanistan. Lat. 29° 56′, long. 67° 30′. *E.I.C. Ms. Doc.*

COLEEW.—A village of Sinde, situate three miles north-west of Munoora Fort, on the same promontory. Lat. 24° 50′, long. 66° 58′. *E.I.C. Ms. Doc.*

COL-NARAWA.—A pass into Kashmir. It is more generally called Kuligum, which see.

COLUL.—A village in Afghanistan, on the route, by the Gomul Pass, from Ghuznee to Dera Ismael Khan, and one hundred miles south-east of the former place. It is situate near the left bank of the Gomul river, in lat. 32° 19′, long. 69° 5′. *E.I.C. Ms. Doc.*

COONDOR.—A village in Afghanistan, on the road from Babur-ka-Killa to Dera Ismael Khan. Lat. 31° 36′, long. 68° 44′. *Map of Afg.*

CORACHIE.—See KURRACHEE.

CUCHEE.—A large village in Sinde, on the right of the route from Sehwan to Kurrachee, and nine miles south-west of the former place. Lat. 26° 18′, long. 67° 50′. *E.I.C. Ms. Doc.*

CUCHEE.—A doab or narrow peninsula east of the Indus, and between it and the Punjnud. It is embodied with Dera Ghazee Khan, and with it forms one of the districts of the Sikh government, yielding it nine lacs of rupees annually. It is everywhere permeated by water-courses from the Indus, and is remarkably well cultivated and productive. Lat. 29° 20′—30°, long. 70° 40′—71° 10′. *Burnes, Pol. Pow. of Sikhs, 6; Id. Trade of the Do-rajat, 98.*

CUDDAN.—See KUDUN.

Horsburgh, Ind.
Dir. i. 494.
CUDJERAH, or KUTCHERIE, in Beloochistan, a small headland, forty-two miles west of Sonmeanee. It is low, but terminates precipitously at the water's edge, projecting there into the Arabian Sea. The adjacent land is low near the sea, but high and craggy further inland. The ground all along the coast is bold and safe to approach, there being a depth of twenty-five to thirty fathoms to a distance of about ten miles from land, and there the bottom shelves suddenly, so as to afford no soundings. A little to the westward, the rocks forming the site of the celebrated shrine of Hinglaj are visible. Cudjerah is in lat. 25° 20′, long. 65° 50′.

CUNDYE.—See KUNDYE.

[1] E.I.C. Ms. Doc.
CUTCH GUNDAVA.[1]—A district of Beloochistan, bounded on the north-east by Afghanistan, south-east by Sinde, and west by the Belooche districts of Jhalawan and Sarawan. Its shape is an irregular triangle, the vertex of which is directed towards the east, and the base forms the western frontier. It is situate between lat. 27° 40′ and 29° 50′, and long. 67° 20′ and 69° 17′ ; is a hundred and sixty miles in length from north to south, a hundred and thirty miles in breadth from east to west, and con-
[2] Masson, Bal. Afg.
Panj. i. 339; Pott.
Belooch. 255-257;
Havelock, War in
Afg. i. 197.
tains ten thousand square miles of surface.[2] The Hala range of mountains extends along its western frontier, and forms the eastern wall or face of the elevated table-land of Central Beloochistan. Through this range are two great passes ; the celebrated Bolan Pass in the north, leading in a north-wes-
[3] Masson, Bal. Afg.
Panj. i. 338.
terly direction, and the Moola,[3] or Gundava Pass, which, more to the south, takes an extensive circuit, the two extremes pointing towards the north, and the convex and middle part towards the south. (See BOLAN and MOOLA.) Cutch Gundava lies rather low, few parts having an elevation of 500 feet above the sea ; and this circumstance, combined with the general want of water and of forests, and the remoteness of the country from the ocean,
[4] E.I.C. Ms. Doc.;
Masson, Kelat,
333; Pott. 322.
[5] Hough, Narr. of
Exp. in Afg. App.
61.
causes the climate to be intensely hot.[4] The temperature in summer exceeds that of Sinde, lying further south: even in February[5] the thermometer reached 98°. The simoom or scorching wind is very frequent and fatal. In consequence of the mildness of the winter, the inhabitants of the elevated and cold region
[6] E.I.C. Ms. Doc.;
Pott. 310, 321.
of Kelat emigrate hither extensively during that season.[6] In the north-east is a hilly tract of considerable extent, being a pro-

longation of the mountains of Hurroond and Dajel,[7] in Southern Afghanistan. The climate there is very pleasant, being alike exempt from the extremes of heat in summer and of cold in winter. The great disadvantage of Cutch Gundava is want of water. The Nari, the Kauhce, and other streams of less importance, descend from the mountains, but are all lost by evaporation or absorption.[8] (See NARI and KAUHEE.)

The soil is in general a hard-baked clay, probably deposited by the numerous torrents holding their transitory and violent course over the surface. The aspect of the district is dreary and repulsive, especially in the south-eastern part, where the *Put Runn*, or Desert of Shikarpoor, stretches for a distance of forty miles. Kennedy[9] describes it as "a boundless level plain of indurated clay, of a dull, dry, earthy colour, and shewing signs of being sometimes under water. At first a few bushes were apparent here and there, growing gradually more and more distant, until at last not a sign of vegetable life was to be recognized." The only vegetation to be met with in these horrid wastes consists of a few *Euphorbia salina* plants and stunted bushes. The scene is often rendered still more dismal by the tantalizing *mirage*, or by a thick haze[1] everywhere overspreading it. In such tracts, when the rains and torrents fail, water can only be obtained from wells, which are generally dug in the beds of the channels. As in other places, the water yielded is brackish. Yet this apparently stubborn soil becomes highly productive under a careful course of irrigation and tillage, yielding annually two successive crops of pulse[2] and grain, principally millet, besides cotton, sugar-cane, madder, and similar products of a warm climate. Dates, oranges, limes, pomegranates, and mangoes are also grown in perfection. Cutch Gundava, indeed, could not fail to be a prosperous as well as a populous country under the dominion of a just and vigorous government, able and willing to protect the inhabitants in their labours, to aid the objects of the husbandman by saving and properly distributing the water of the various streams for the purposes of irrigation, and to secure to those who till the soil the enjoyment of the fruits of their industry.

The existing state of things is widely different from this; the cultivators, generally Jets of Hindoo descent,[3] and of indus- trious and peaccable habits, are miserably harassed and plundered by the Belooches of the neighbouring mountains. " It was

[7] Pott. 311.

[8] Conolly, Jour. to India, ii. 225; Masson, Bul. Afg. Punj. i. 348.

[9] Sind.and Kabool, 196.

[1] Atkinson, Exp. into Afg. 103-108.

[2] Masson, Kalat, 332.

[3] Id. 332.

4 Bal. Afg. Panj.
i. 350. wonderful," observes Masson,[4] " to see the immense fields of
Bajara (*Holcus spicatus*) in the most thriving state, and apparently mature for the sickle, but not a soul to reap them or even
to claim them. The cultivators had fled before the hill marauders
who had scoured the country." Notwithstanding this unhappy
condition, Cutch Gundava is the most populous part of Beloo-
5 Masson, Kalat,
335. chistan, the number of its inhabitants being estimated at 100,000,[5]
and that of the whole country at 450,000. The population, besides the Jet cultivators, comprises a considerable number of Rind
6 Id. 337; Pott.
Belooch, 310. Belooches [6] and Brahuis, both of which tribes have settled in the
country at a comparatively recent period. All these classes are
Mahometans, generally of the Sunni persuasion. There are also
a few Hindoos, who live in the towns, and principally conduct the
commercial affairs of the country. Cutch Gundava constitutes the
7 Pott. Belooch.
310. most valuable part of the dominions of the Khan of Kelat,[7] who,
during winter, resides at the chief town, Gundava, to avoid the
inclemency of the climate of Kelat. The other towns of any note are
Dadur, Bhag, Lehree, and Kotree ; of which some notice will be
found under their respective names. Cutch Gundava possesses
some commercial importance, in consequence of being traversed
by the two routes, one through the Bolan, the other through the
Moola Pass, connecting Sinde with Khorasan.

E.I.C. Ms. Doc.   CUTCH TOBA, in Afghanistan, a halting-station on the route
from Ghuznee to Shawl, and at the northern base of the Toba
mountains. It is held by the tribe of Khakas or Kakurs, who
have numerous hamlets in the neighbouring hills. Lat. 31°, long.
67° 28'.

D.

E.I.C. Ms. Doc.   DAAMRAH.—A small village in Sinde, on the route from
Larkhana to Kyra-ka-Gurree, and twenty miles north of the
former town. The road here is good, and water may be obtained
from two wells, but other supplies are scanty. Lat. 27° 46', long.
68° 12'.

E.I.C. Ms. Doc.   DABHU.—An estuary of the Indus, branching off from the
Buggaur or great western branch, in lat. 24° 34', long. 67° 20'.

After a course of about fourteen miles due west, it opens into the Arabian Sea or Northern Indian Ocean.

DADARAH.—A large village in Sinde, situate two miles É.I.C. Ms. Doc. from the right bank of the Indus, on the route from Larkhana to Sehwan, and thirty-two miles south-west from the former place. A little northward, the road to Peer Punja takes a direction due north, separating from the main route lying north-east, through a well-cultivated tract. Dadarah is in lat. 27° 3′, long. 68°.

DADOOLA.[1]—A village in Sinde, on the route from Shikar- [1] E.I.C. Ms. Doc.; Atkinson, Exp. poor to Subzulcote, and forty miles south-west from the latter into Afg. 95. town. It is situate four miles from the left bank of the Indus, in a populous and well-cultivated country, and is supplied with water from three wells. It was ceded, with a few other villages and the districts of Bhoong Bara and Subzulcote, to Mahomed Bhawl Khan, of Bhawlpoor, by treaty dated in November, 1842,[2] [2] Corresp. on Sinde, 419, 443, and transferred to him by the British authorities in the February 507. following. Lat. 28° 2′, long. 69° 8′.

DADUN KHAN PIND.—See PIND DADUN KHAN.

DADUR,[1] in Beloochistan, a town of Cutch Gundava. It is [1] E.I.C. Ms. Doc.; Hough's Narr. situate near the base of the Hala range, and five miles east of the Exp. in Afg. 48, entrance of the Bolan Pass. Though the Kauhee or Bolan river, [427]; Atkinson, Exp. in Afg. 109, on the banks of which it is built, sometimes rushes down with a 110. large volume of water,[2] the channel, for a great part of the year, [2] Pott. Belooch. 309; Conolly, is quite dry,[3] and the town is then supplied by means of tanks[4] Jour. to India, II. or wells dug in the bed ; but the water thus obtained is brackish[5] 323-325; Kennedy, Sinde and Kabool, and unwholesome. Dadur is described by Masson as a place of I. 206. [3] Masson, Kalat, considerable size, containing many well-built houses, and inclosed 331. by a wall. The population is probably about 3,000. The heat [4] Havelock, War in Afg. ii. 198. is intense; in evidence of which, the inhabitants point to the red [5] Masson, Bal.Afg. colour of the unburned bricks, asserting that it has been produced Panj. i. 341. by their torrefaction in the rays of the sun. Its heat probably exceeds that of any other place on earth in the same parallel of latitude. The Rev. J. N. Allen,[6] who resided there in February, [6] March through Sinde and Afg. 93. thus describes its state in this respect at that early season, when even the warmth of spring could not have been attained : " It is indeed a dreadful place, and seems from its situation formed to be, as it really is, one of the hottest places in the world. It receives the reflected heat of the sun from the towering bank of bare rocky mountains under which it lies, and which, surrounding it on three sides, casts down the rays upon it as upon the focus of a reflecting

mirror." Its state at a more advanced period of the year, when
the influence of the sun is greater, is thus noticed by the same
author, together with the feelings of those compelled to endure its
torments : " The descriptions given by those who have passed a
hot season there are most painful. Men by no means given to exaggeration assured me that they envied the dead, and that they
would rather die than pass another season there; that the thermometer in tents was at 130°, with an entire stagnation of air."
Describing the state of weather early in March, Mr. Allen adds,
" But Sunday, the 6th, exceeded all. There was a hot wind
whirling clouds of dust into my tent, and the plague of flics was
most intolerable. The heat in the house was such that I fairly
staggered, and the mountains for the last two days, though close
at hand, had been but dimly outlined through a flickering mist,
like that over a furnace."

Here, in November, 1840, a British force was attacked by
Nusseer, the son of Mehrab Khan, who had fallen in the storm
of his capital, Kelat. Nusseer's army, amounting to 4,000 Belooches, was quickly routed, and in the pursuit, the headless body
of Lieut. Loveday,[7] who had been located at Kelat as political
agent to the British government, was found chained in a *kajawa*,
or seat, fastened on a camel. Dadur is in lat. 29° 26', long. 67° 41'.

Ms. Survey Map. DAEBRAZ, in Sinde, a village on one of the routes from
Bukkur to Southern Sinde, fourteen miles from the left bank of
the Indus. Lat. 27° 8', long. 68° 26'.

E.I.C. Ms. Doc. DAHO.—A village in Afghanistan, among the Marree mountains, on the south-eastern frontier. It is situate on the route
from Bhag to Kahun, and twenty miles north-west of the last-
named place. Lat. 29° 26', long. 68° 58'.

Burnes' Trade of the Derajat, 100; Pol. Pow. of Sikhs, 4; Masson, Kal. 335; Pott. Belooch. 311. DAJEL.—A fort, town, and district on the route from Dera
Ghazee Khan to Bhag, situate among the mountains of Dajel
and Hurroond. The town is a small but rather flourishing
place, and important as commanding the communication through
the Derajat to Cutch Gundava and Beloochistan by the Bolan
Pass. It was seized by Runjeet Singh, and is still held by the
Sikhs. Lat. 29° 37', long. 70° 28'.

Walker's Map of Afg. DAKA.—A village in the Punjab, situate in the Doab of the
Punjnud and Indus, and twelve miles north-east of their confluence. Lat. 29° 5', long. 70° 40'.

E.I.C. Ms. Doc. DALANA.—A village in Afghanistan, situate on the route from Ghuznee to Shawl, by Ab-istada lake, and thirty-six miles south-west of Ghuznee. Lat. 33° 1′, long. 67° 58′.

DAMAJEE.—See DUMAJEE.

DAMA-KA-KOT, in Sinde, a small place on the route Burnes' Mission to from Cutch to Hyderabad. Lat. 24° 36′, long. 68° 28′. Sinde, 38.

DAMAN,[1] or THE BORDER, so called because it stretches [1] Burnes' Pol. between the Suliman mountains and the Indus. Where not 5, 6; Id. on the under the influence of irrigation,[2] it in general presents the Trade of the Derajat, 98; Elph. appearance of a plain of smooth, hard clay, bare of grass, but Acc. of Caubul, sprinkled with dwarfish bushes, tamarisks, and occasionally trees [2] Elph. 306. of larger size, but seldom exceeding the height of twenty feet, the soil or climate being unfavourable to their further growth. In place of the clay, the surface in some places consists of a loose and irreclaimable sand. The clay appears to be deposited by the waters either of the Indus or of the numerous small rivers which, during the season of the melting of the snow, stream down from the mountains, and add to the inundation. Where duly irrigated, the clay is very productive, and few countries are more fertile than the Derajat, or that part of the plain which extends along the western bank of the Indus. The Derajat, so called from the three towns, Dera Ismael Khan, Dera Fati Khan, and Dera Ghazee Khan, abounds in towns and good villages. In summer, the heat in the Daman is intense, and the productions in a great measure resemble those of India. The Sikhs hold military occupation of this province, and levy on it an annual tribute of about fifteen lacs of rupees, or 150,000*l.* sterling.

The Daman is two hundred and twenty miles long, from the Kala or Salt range on the north, to the confines of Sinde on the south, and has an average breadth of about sixty miles. Lat. 30°—33°, long. 70°—71°.

DAMUNKOH.—A village in Western Afghanistan, twenty- E.I.C. Ms. Doc. four miles north of the town of Furrah, and forty-four miles south of Subzawur, is situate about ten miles to the right of the road between these two towns. Lat. 32° 44′, long. 62° 10′.

DAN, in Beloochistan, a village on the route from Kelat to Sonmeanee, and forty miles south-west of the former place. As it is 5,800 feet[1] above the level of the sea, the climate is tempe- [1] E.I.C. Ms. Doc. rate in summer, and very cold in winter ; but the soil is fruitful, and being well irrigated[2] by means of canal cultivation, is very [2] Masson, Bal. Afg. productive. Lat. 28° 20′, long. 66° 10′. Panj. ii, 47.

DANEH CHEKOW.—A town in North-eastern Afghanistan, thirty miles south of the town of Bajour. Lat. 34° 37', long. 71° 25'.

DAR.—A village in. the Punjab, on the road from Jamu to Chumba, and eight miles north-west of the latter place. Lat. 32° 24', long. 75° 49'.

DARA.—A village in the Punjab, eighteen miles from the left bank of the Indus, and fifteen miles south-east of the town of Bukkur. Lat. 31° 31', long. 71° 20'.

DARAH.—A village in the Punjab, situate in the Doab between the Indus and the Chenaub, twenty miles from the left bank of the former, and thirty from the right bank of the latter. Lat. 30° 42', long. 71° 20'.

DARAJEE, in the Delta of Sinde, a small town on the Buggaur, or great western branch of the Indus. When, about two hundred years ago, this branch was navigable from the sea to the main channel of the river, Darajee and Lahorybunder, about two miles lower down, were the principal ports of Sinde, being accessible for vessels of 200 tons burthen.[1] The Buggaur,[2] however, has now, for many years, ceased to be navigable during the season of low water in the Indus, and goods landed at Darajee are,[3] by means of camels, conveyed to Tatta overland, a distance of thirty miles. Though, during the season of low water, the Buggaur is unnavigable above Darajee, it has, at all times, a depth of at least twelve feet[4] from that place downwards as far as the Pittee mouth of the Indus, a distance of twenty-eight miles. This easy access from the sea renders Darajee the port of Tatta and the greater part of the Delta, as Kurrachee is the general haven for the upper part of Sinde. The closure of the port of Vikkur, in consequence of the great alteration which took place in the Hujamaree mouth,[5] in 1839, will probably cause an increased resort to Darajee. Burnes estimates the population of Darajee at 2,000. Lat. 24° 30', long. 67° 23'.

DARAPOOR,[1] in the Punjab, a small village, about a mile from the right or west bank of the Jailum. Close to it are extensive ruins, called Oodenuggur, which Burnes supposes to be those of Nicæa,[2] built by Alexander, to commemorate his victory on this spot over Porus. Lat. 32° 49', long. 73° 26'.

DARAZOO-KA-KOT, in Afghanistan, a small town of the Derajat, on the route from Dera Ghazee Khan to Kandahar, being sixty-five miles west of the former place. It has a good supply of water from a stream called Han, and sheep and grain of various kinds are abundant. Population about 3,000. Lat. 30° 3', long. 69° 45'.

DARBARRA, in Afghanistan, a large fortress of the Daman. It is situate twelve miles north-west of Tak, and at the mouth of a pass into the Suliman mountains. Its walls are very lofty, but it does not appear to be otherwise of importance, and it is situate in a very barren and secluded country. Lat. 32° 18', long. 70° 35'. Masson, Bal. Afg. Panj. i. 52.

DARRAGOTE.—A small village in Sinde, on the route from Sehwan to Larkhana, and seventeen miles south of the latter place. It is situate in the extensive and fertile island inclosed between the.Indus and its great offset the Narra, and is seven miles from the right bank of the former and three miles from the left bank of the latter. The road lies through a thin jungle. Lat. 27° 17', long. 68° 15'. E I.C. Ms. Doc.

DARUNTA,[1] in Afghanistan, a small district in the valley of Jelalabad, and lying west of the town of that name. It is a gorge or valley in the Siah Koh or Black Mountains, where the river of Kabool makes its way eastward through that range. It contains eleven topes or mounds, similar to that of Manikyala, in the Punjab, but of smaller size. These topes have been opened by Masson, Honiberger, and Pigou, and found to contain coins (mostly of the Greco-Bactrian princes), jewellery, and bones. They are generally situate on artificial eminences of earth, are of cylindrical form below, and above are surmounted by a hemisphere or dome. Much of our information on the antiquities of this country we owe to Mr. Masson, an inquirer whose singular aptitude for a pursuit very dissimilar from that to which his earlier attention was devoted has frequently called forth surprise and praise. Lassen[2] says, "Mr. Masson, I believe, first served in the artillery, and he knows, certainly, much better how to deal with numismatic inquiries than most numismatists would know how to serve a gun." Darunta is in lat. 34° 36', long. 70° 19'. [1] Masson, in Wilson Ariana Antiq. 62; Pigou, Jour. As. Soc. 1841, p. 381; Ritter, Erdkunde von Asien, v. 296. [2] On Indo-Bactrian Coins, Jour. As. Soc. Beng. ix. 258.

DASHT-I-BEDAULAT[1] (the wretched plain), in Beloochistan, between the summit of the Bolan Pass and Shawl. It is described by Masson as "a good march in breadth, nor (he adds) is its length less considerable." The British force which invaded Af- [1] E.I.C. Ms. Doc.; Jour. As. Soc.; Grif. Bar. and Ther. Meas. in Afg.; Hough, Narr. Exp. in Afg.; Atkinson,

Exp. into Afg. 123; Conolly, Jour. to India, II. 218; Havelock, War in Afg. i. 236; Kennedy, Sind. and Kabool, i. 224; Allen, March through Sinde and Afg. 116; Elph. Acc. of Caubul, 124. [2] Kelat, 318.

ghanistan found it about eighteen miles across, destitute of water, and covered with wild thyme and southernwood, the food of a scanty stock of goats and camels belonging to the wild tribes holding the surrounding mountains. During spring, crocuses, tulips, and various other wild flowers render the scene " unprofitably gay." Such was the appearance which it presented in the prime of that beautiful season when our troops marched over it. Masson,[2] departing from his usual accuracy, describes it, from hearsay accounts, to be at that season a pastoral paradise, and he even provides it with harvests. The elevation exceeds 5,000 feet above the level of the sea. Lat. 30°, long. 67°.

E.I.C. Ms. Doc.

DAVOUCH.—A village in Sinde, on the route from Sehwan to Larkhana, and thirty miles north of the former town. It is situate two miles from the right bank of the Indus, in a well-cultivated country. The road in the neighbourhood is not very good, being broken up by water-courses and ditches. Lat. 26° 48', long. 67° 52'.

E.I.C. Ms. Doc.

DAWUN.—A village in Sinde, situate ten miles east of the river Indus, on a cross road between two of the high roads from Bukkur to Hyderabad. Lat. 27° 6', long. 68° 19'.

DEBALPOOR.—See DEPAULPOOR.

Walker's Map.

DEEDLED.—A village of Afghanistan, in the Daman. It is situate near the right bank of the Indus, and twenty miles south of Dera Ghazee Khan. Lat. 29° 50', long. 70° 54'.

Walker's Map of N.W. Frontier.

DEEDWAL.—A village in the Punjab. Lat. 32° 57', long. 72° 43'.

Leech, on Sindh Army, 66, 79; Burnes' Pers. Narr. 49; Westmacott, Acc. of Khyrpoor, in Jour. As. Soc. 1840, p. 1196; Correspondence on Sinde, 494.

DEEJY.—A fort in Sinde, which belonged to the Ameer of Khyerpoor, from which town it is distant ten miles south. It is built on a range of low limestone hills, proceeding in a direction from south-east to north-west, and reaching the Indus at Roree. It consists of a number of fortifications crowning several eminences, and connected by a single mud wall pierced with loop-holes. Here, in January, 1843, the British army was encamped during the advance of Sir Charles Napier to destroy Emaum Ghur. Though stronger than most of the fortresses of Sinde, Deejy is open to capture by escalade. There is a large tower, which was intended to contain the treasure of the Ameer, and which is covered by an irregular outwork in a singular style. On the south side of the fort is a magazine and manufactory of powder. This fort is called also Ahmedabad. Lat. 27° 24', long. 68° 58'.

DEELA.[1]—A village in Afghanistan, situate on the river of [1] E.I.C. Ms. Doc.
Ghuznee, three or four miles above its efflux into Lake Ab-istada.
Outram[2] found the banks of the river hereabouts covered with [2] Rough Notes,149.
vast quantities of dead fish. Deela is in lat. 32° 43', long. 68° 3'.

DEEMBRA.—A village in Sinde, on the route from Bhawlpoor E.I.C. Ms. Survey.
to Roree, and forty-six miles north-east of the latter town. It is
situate twelve miles from the left bank of the Indus, in an alluvial tract, in many places subject to inundation. Lat. 27° 56',
long. 69° 11'.

DEENARH.—A village in Sinde, situate on the road from E.I.C. Ms. Doc.
Omercote to Joudpoor, and twenty-five miles east of the former
place. Lat. 25° 23', long. 70° 14'.

DEENGAH.—A village of Beloochistan, in the province of E.I.C. Ms. Doc.
Sarawan, on the western route from Quetta to Kelat, and twenty-
five miles south-west of the former place. Lat. 29° 52', long.
66° 43'.

DEENGANA.—See Dincana.

DEENGURH.—A village in Bhawlpoor, thirty miles south E.I.C. Ms. Doc.
of the town of that name. Lat. 28° 56', long. 71° 48'.

DEERAH JALLAH.—A village in the Punjab, situate ten E.I.C. Ms. Doc.
miles from the left bank of the river Jailum. Lat. 31° 48', long.
72° 14'.

DEESHOO.—A village in Western Afghanistan, situate on Jour. As. Soc.
the river Helmund. Lat. 30° 33', long. 62° 52'. 1840, p. 724; Conolly (E.), Map of

DEEWALIK, in Afghanistan, is a ruined fort, formerly of Seistan.
great importance, on the eastern route from Kandahar to Ghuz- E.I.C. Ms. Doc.
nee, from the former of which places it is distant about ninety-five
miles north-east. The country in the vicinity is tolerably cultivated, and is crowded with the forts of the Ghiljies, who hold it.
Lat. 32° 9', long. 67°.

DEH HINDOO.—A village of Northern Afghanistan, in the E.I.C. Ms. Doc.
district of Lughman, situate on the river Alingar. Lat. 34° 56',
long. 70° 16'.

DEH-I-HAJEE, in Afghanistan, is a walled town, on the E.I.C. Ms. Doc.;
route from the Khojuk Pass to Kandahar, and twenty miles south- Campbell; Havelock, War in Afg.
east of this last place. The houses, which are from twenty to li. 328; Kennedy,
Sinde and Kabool,
thirty feet high, are built of sun-dried bricks, with dome-shaped i. 245; Hough,
roofs constructed of the same material, which is so hardened by Narr. of Exp. to
Afg. 93.
the heat of the sun as to form a good protection against all
weather. There is a good stream of water, and the surrounding

country is very productive. Population about 2,000. Lat. 31°
23′, long. 65° 44′.

E.I.C. Ms. Doc.;
Mass. Bal. Afg.
Panj. III. 110.
DEH-I-KEPUK.—A village of Afghanistan, in the Koh-i-
Damun, close to the western extremity of the lake of Kabool, and
five miles north-west of that city. Like most places in the Koh-i-
Damun, it is rudely fortified, being surrounded by a wall of
little strength. The population is about 500. Lat. 69° 1′, long.
34° 32′.

E.I.C. Ms. Doc.
DEH-I-NOU.—A village in Afghanistan, on the road from
Kandahar to Quetta, and twenty-five miles south-east of the
former place. Lat. 31° 28′, long. 65° 50′.

E.I.C. Ms. Doc.
DEH-I-SUBZ.—A village in Afghanistan, situate twelve
miles north-east of Kabool, and on a feeder of the Punchshir
river. Lat. 34° 36′, long. 69° 14′.

E.I.C. Ms. Doc.
DEH KOONDEE.—A village in Afghanistan, situate on the
river Helmund, one hundred miles north of Kandahar. Lat. 32°
59′, long. 65° 49′.

E.I.C. Ms. Doc.
DEH LAHOUR.—A village in Afghanistan, thirty-two
miles north of Kandahar. Lat. 32° 4′, long. 65° 42′.

DEHR, in the Punjab, on the right or north-western bank of
the Sutluj, where there is a ferry, generally crossed on inflated
I. 40; Vigne, i. 78. hides of buffaloes or bullocks. Moorcroft here forded the river at
the beginning of March, when it is nearly at the lowest. It was
then a hundred and fifty feet broad, and running at the rate of
five miles an hour. Lat. 31° 42′, long. 77° 38′.

E.I.C. Ms. Doc.
DEHRA.—A village in Sinde, situate on the route from Jes-
sulmair to Halla, twenty-five miles north-east of the latter place.
Lat. 25° 57′, long. 68° 46′.

Burnes' Rep. 2.
DEHRA-JAM-KA, or AURUNGA BUNDER, in Sinde, was,
at the commencement of the eighteenth century, the seat of an
English factory, the first founded in this country. At that time,
a branch of the Indus, the Mugrah, now dried up, ran by the
town. When the channel became deserted by the stream, the
factory was removed to Shahbunder, twenty miles west, and the
town fell to decay. Lat. 24° 10′, long. 68° 2′.

E.I.C. Ms. Doc.
DEHRA KHAN GANCHA.—A large village in Sinde, on
the route from Hyderabad to Sehwan, and thirty miles south-
east of the latter place. It is situate close to the right bank of
the Indus, amidst much cultivation. Lat. 26° 5′, long. 68° 5′.

E.I.C. Ms. Doc.;
Corresp. on Sinde,
DEHREE KOTE, or DERA GHABI (the station of Ghabi), so

called because built by Ghabi, a chieftain of the Chandi tribe of 487-493; Masson,
Belooches. It is a small town of Cutch Gundava, consisting 129.
only of huts and mud houses, the best of which belong to Hindoo traders. The Chandi tribe have been the most formidable supporters of the Talpoor dynasty of Sinde, of whose armies they formed the principal part during the late conflict with the British, and Dehree Kote appears to be at present the place of refuge for the refractory members of the late ruling family. Wali Mahomed, the present chief of the Chandi tribe, is said to be able to raise 12,000 men. Dehree Kote lies at the base of the Hala range, in a level country, well cultivated, and especially productive of millet. Lat. 27° 38', long. 67° 34'.

DEH ZIRGARAN.—A village of Afghanistan, in the Koh-i- Masson, Bal. Afg.
Damun, twenty miles north-west of the town of Kabool. It is Panj. iii. 117.
situate on an eminence near the south bank of the river of Furza, a small feeder of the Punchshir river. It commands a fine view over the adjacent country, which is populous, fertile, and singularly picturesque. A deep artificial cave leads into the interior of the eminence on which the village stands, where there are spacious ruins. Lat. 34° 42', long. 68° 50'.

DEO CHUNDAISUR MAHADEO.—A village situate in the Ms. Maps.
Great Desert of Sinde. Lat. 26° 17', long. 69° 56'.

DEOGONDA.—A village in the Punjab, on the route from E.I.C. Ms. Doc.
Lahore to Kashmir, by the Banihal Pass. It is situate near the right bank of the Chenaub river, a hundred and twenty miles north-east of Lahore. Lat. 33°, long. 75° 6'.

DEOTSUH, in Bultistan or Little Thibet, is an elevated table-land, south of the valley of Iskardo. It is a dreary tract about thirty miles long, with a breadth of about half as much, uninhabitable in winter from excessive cold, having a rocky surface of granite and gneiss, and though 12,000 feet above the sea, sur- Vigne, Kashmir, i. 219; Moorcr.
rounded by mountains which tower to a still greater elevation. Punj. Bokh. ii. 263.
Numerous small streams rise in this tract, those on the south flowing into the Jailum, and those on the north into the Indus. Lat. 34° 30', long. 75° 20'.

DEPAULPOOR.—A town in the Punjab, situate in the E.I.C. Ms. Doc.;
Ayeen Akbery,
Doab, between the Ghara and the Ravee, twenty-five miles from ii. 295.
the right bank of the former, thirty from the left of the latter. In the time of the Emperor Acbar it was the chief town of a district, which yielded an income of 3,233,353 rupees, a much

larger sum than could at present be levied on it. Lat. 30° 40′, long. 73° 27′.

Ms. Survey Map.   DERA.—A village in Sinde, situate on the Narra river, fifteen miles south from Larkhana, from which there is a good road. Lat. 27° 20′, long. 68° 6′.

DERABUND.—See DRABUND.

E.I.C. Ms. Doc.;   DERA DEEN PUNAH.—A town of Afghanistan, in the Dera-
Wood, Oxus, 88.   jat, on the right or west bank of the Indus. It was nearly de-
stroyed by the great earthquake of 1819 and the overwhelming floods which at the same time descended from the Suliman mountains. Lat. 30° 40′, long. 70° 51′.

[1] E.I.C. Ms. Doc.   DERA DEEN PUNAH.[1]—A town in the Punjab, situate near the left bank of the Indus, on the route from Mooltan to Leia, and forty miles north-west of the former place. Attached to it
[2] Acc. of Caubul, is a small but fertile district, which, at the time of Elphinstone's[2]
504.   visit, yielded 150,000 rupees to the Afghan chief, who held it in jaghire. Lat. 30° 34′, long. 71°.

Masson, Bal. Afg.   DERA FATI KHAN.—A town in the Derajat, is situate
Panj. i. 38.   in a very fertile country, on a small western branch of the Indus, and at no great distance from the main stream. The crops in the vicinity are principally cotton, grain of various kinds, indigo, and some sugar and opium. The bazaars of Dera Fati Khan are good, and well supplied with wares; and the town is altogether in rather a thriving state, though under the Sikh sway, which is much disliked by the Mahometans, who form the bulk of the inhabitants. It is retained in subjection by the fortress of Gerong, about four miles west of the town, where is maintained a garrison of 300 men. The population of Dera Fati Khan may be estimated at 5,000. It was, about three hundred years ago, a dera, or camp, of Fati Khan, an adventurer in this region, and hence its name. Lat. 31° 7′, long. 70° 52′.

[1] Burnes' Pol.   DERA GHAZEE KHAN.[1]—The most southern and also the
Pow. of Sikhs, 6;
Id. on the Trade most important of the three towns which contribute to give to
of the Derajat,100; the Derajat its name. It is a large, populous, and commercial
Id. Bokh. iii. 282;
Id. Pers. Narr. 82; place, situate in a low alluvial tract, four miles from the right
Wood, Oxus, 80.   or west bank of the Indus, and contains numerous ruins of
[2] Masson, Bal. Afg. mosques,[2] and of the extensive and well-constructed residences of
Panj. i. 31.   the former Durani governors and officers. It has in many respects decayed since it passed under the sway of the Sikhs, but has notwithstanding retained considerable transit trade.

The retention of this advantage is attributable to its being situate at the point where one of the great routes from Eastern India and the Punjab into Beloochistan and Khorasan intersects the great route from north to south into Sinde. The bazaar contains sixteen hundred shops, the inmates of five hundred and thirty of which are engaged in weaving and selling cloth. It is in other respects well supplied with goods, but ill-built and dirty. Some manufactures are carried on here in silk, cotton, and mixed fabrics of silk and cotton, called loongees, intended for scarfs and waistbands. Coarse cutlery is also manufactured to a considerable extent. The entire value of the various manufactures is estimated to be 200,000 rupees per annum.

The surrounding country is very unhealthy during the hot season, but remarkably fertile, being well irrigated, and producing grain, fruits in abundance and of fine quality, sugar, cotton, and much indigo, in which a considerable traffic is driven. Both the transit and the direct carrying trade are conducted almost exclusively by the Lohani Afghans, who are at once a pastoral and a mercantile tribe.

Dera Ghazee Khan, in consequence of its advantageous position, has been recommended by Burnes and others as the best site for a great annual fair, to be held under the protection of the British government, commanding, as it does, such important routes and the navigation of the Indus north and south. The population is about 25,000, of which nearly one-half are Hindoos, the rest Mahometans. It was a dera, post, or camp of Ghazee Khan, who, about three centuries ago, figured as an adventurer here. Lat. 30° 5', long. 70° 52'.

DERA ISMAEL KHAN,[1] in Afghanistan, a considerable town of the Derajat, built a short distance from the right or west bank of the Indus, to replace the former town, which, having been situate only a hundred yards from the river,[2] was, a few years ago, swept away by it so completely that not a vestige was left. The town is well laid out, but is ill built of unburnt brick, and in general has an air of desolation, though in spring there is much business, it being then crowded by the Afghans of the Lohani tribe, who purchase great quantities of goods to transport by their caravans for the supply of Afghanistan and Central Asia. The most important article of commerce is white cotton cloth, of which two millions of yards are

[1] E.I.C. Ms. Doc.; Pers. Narr. 91; Pol. Pow. of Sikhs, 4; Trade of the Derajat, 102; Burnes.
[2] Elph. Acc. of Caubul, 28; Mas. Bal. Afg. Panj. i. 39; Wood, Oxus, 90.

yearly sold here, and eighteen millions of yards taken through,[3] in transit from Hindostan to the north and west of this place. There is also a considerable trade, by way of the Indus, southward, in grain and salt, from Kala Bagh. The position of Dera Ismael Khan is important, being situate on one of the great routes from the north to Sinde and the Southern Punjab, and also in the vicinity of the ferry at Kaheree, one of the most frequented over the Indus. There is another ferry over that river [4] three miles to the eastward of the town. About three centuries ago, there was here a dera, post, or encampment of Ismael Khan, an adventurer in this country, and hence the name which the town bears. It was wrested from the Durani empire by the Sikhs. Its population is stated to be 8,000.[5]   Lat. 31° 50′, long. 70° 58′.

Marginal notes:
[3] Burnes' Trade of Derajat, 103.
[4] Burnes' Pers. Narr. 91.
[5] Burnes' Trade of the Derajat, 102.
[1] Burnes' Trade of the Derajat, 98; Id. Pol. Pow. of Sikhs, 6.
[2] Masson, Bal. Afg. Panj. i. 40, 41.
[1] E.I.C. Ms. Doc.; F. Von Hugel, iii.

DERAJAT,[1] in Afghanistan, a fertile, populous, and well-cultivated tract, extending along the western bank of the Indus, about three hundred miles, from the Kala or Salt range of mountains to the northern frontier of Sinde. Its situation is low; its fertility owing to irrigation from the Indus. It is of small breadth, being hemmed in by the Suliman range of mountains and the desert stretching along its eastern base. The name is derived from the three towns of Dera Ghazee Khan, Dera Fati Khan, and Dera Ismael Khan, which were originally the three deras,[2] posts, or encampments of the three chiefs whose names they respectively bear. The revenue exacted by the Sikh government amounts to 1,400,000 rupees annually, and would be cheerfully paid by the inhabitants for the protection afforded them against the predatory hordes of the Suliman mountains, were not their opinions and feelings grievously outraged by their conquerors, who desecrate their mosques and prohibit the public exercise of the Mahometan religion. The Derajat, in addition to its intrinsic resources, is very important, as the Kaheree and some of the other chief ferries over the Indus, and several of the chief routes from India to Khorasan, are in this territory. The inhabitants, according to Masson, are favourably distinguished from the neighbouring Afghans and Belooches, being peaceable, kind, industrious, and unostentatiously hospitable. The Derajat forms the eastern or more fertile portion of Daman, or " the border," an extensive tract so called, because it borders on the Suliman mountains.

DERBEND.[1]—A military post of the Sikhs, on the north-west

frontier of the Punjab It is situate on the left bank of the Indus, 28; Burnes' Pol. Pow. of the Sikhs, 1. where the stream, previously straitened in its passage through the mountains, expands on entering into the plain, and hence probably the name of Derbend, which signifies the place of a dam or strait.[2] In its neighbourhood, in 1827, Sheer Singh, the Sikh 2 Vigne, Kashmir, ii. 184, 188. commander, defeated Saiyid Ahmed, the fanatic Afghan, who had excited a religious war against the Sikhs. Lat. 34° 30′, long. 73° 5′.

DERISTAN.—A village in Afghanistan, about six miles from Walker's Map of Afg. the left bank of the Urghundab, and eight miles from the right bank of the Turnak river. Lat. 32° 26′, long. 66° 58′.

DERRA GUZ.—A village in Afghanistan, on the northern E.I.C. Ms. Doc. declivity of the Huzareh mountains. It is situate on the Durya-i or Bund-i-Burbun river, thirty miles south of Balkh. Lat. 36° 19′, long. 66° 57′.

DERWAZEH.—A village in Afghanistan, eighteen miles Walker's Map of Afg. from the right bank of the Helmund river. Lat. 30° 59′, long. 63° 2′.

DEWALAN.—A village in Western Afghanistan, on the road E.I.C. Ms. Doc. from Kandahar to the province of Scistan, a hundred miles west of Kandahar, and forty miles south-west of the town of Giriskh. It is situate fourteen miles from the right bank of the Helmund, and a small branch of that river crosses the road at this spot. Lat. 31° 29′, long. 63° 47′.

DEWALIK.—See DEEWALIK.

DEYHIFAIZ.—A village in Afghanistan, on the circuitous Walker's Map. route from Bamian to Mymunuh, and fifty miles south-east of the latter place. It is situate on a small feeder of the river of Andkhoo, and deeply embosomed among the Huzareh mountains. Lat. 35° 35′, long. 65° 14′.

DEYPLAH.—A halting-place in Sinde, on the route from E.I.C. Ms. Doc. Hyderabad to Bhooj, in Cutch, and a hundred miles south-east of the former town. It is situate in the Thurr, or desert, a few miles north of the boundary of the Great Western Runn. Lat. 24° 20′, long. 69° 29′.

DEYRAH.—A post and defile in South-eastern Afghanistan, E.I.C. Ms. Doc.; among the Murree mountains. It is on the difficult and perilous route from Northern Sinde to Kahun, and thirty miles south-east of this latter place. Lat. 29° 1′, long. 69° 33′.

DHAK.—A village in the Punjab, situate four miles from the E.I.C. Ms. Doc. right bank of the river Jailum, in lat. 32° 20′, long. 72° 20′.

E.I.C. Ms. Doc.   DHEENG.—A small river or rather torrent of Sinde, rises in the Lukkee mountains, about lat. 26° 10′, long. 67° 50′. After a north-westerly course, estimated at twenty miles, it is lost in the barren country west of Sehwan.

Hough, 352.   DHEENGEE, in the Punjab, a town on the route between the towns of Jailum and Ramnuggur, and about twenty miles from the right bank of the Chenaub. It contains a considerable number of well-built houses. Lat. 32° 42′, long. 73° 38′.

E.I.C. Ms. Doc.   DHER.—A village in the Punjab, situate on the left bank of the Indus, a little north of the mouth of the Hirroo river, and about eight miles south of Attoek. Lat. 33° 48′, long. 72° 20

E.I.C. Ms. Doc.   DHERIA GOTE, SOE, or SOVEE, in Sinde, a village on the route from Sehwan to Larkhana, and sixty-three miles north of the former place. It is situate on the right bank of an offset of the Indus, in a low, alluvial country, having considerable cultivation. Lat. 27° 13′, long. 68° 5′.

E.I.C. Ms. Doc.   DHEYRIALEE.—A village in Sinde, on the south-east frontier of that country. Lat. 24° 43′, long. 71° 8′.

E.I.C. Ms. Doc.   DHODA.—A village in Afghanistan, situate eight miles south of Kohat, and forty of Peshawur. Lat. 33° 27′, long. 71° 29′.

Ms. Survey Map.   DHO DAEE.—A village in Sinde, on the route from Larkhana to Shikarpoor, and four miles north-east of the former place. It is situate near the left bank of an intermitting stream, or rather torrent, which, descending from the Hala mountains in the season of inundation, flows by Larkhana, and discharges itself into the Indus. Dho Daee is in lat. 27° 36′, long. 68° 16′.

E.I.C. Ms. Doc.   DHOWLER.—A village in the Punjab, situate in the Doab or tract between the Ravee and the Ghara rivers. It is twenty-four miles from the left bank of the former, and eighteen from the right bank of the latter. Lat. 30° 33′, long. 73° 17′.

E.I.C. Ms. Doc.   DHUNNEEAL.—A village in the Punjab, on the route from Attoek to Pind-Dadun-Khan, and fifty miles south-east of the former place. It is situate on the left bank of the Swan river, among the hills connecting the Salt range with the southern Himalaya. Lat. 33° 12′, long. 72° 31′.

DHURWAL.—See Burran.

[1] Vigne,Kashmir. II. 311.   DHYR.[1]—A town of Afghanistan, in the Kohistan or highland north of Bajour, is situate on a feeder of the Lundye river.

[2] Elph. Acc. of Caubul, 343; Jour. As. Soc. 1840, p.   Its chieftain[2] is the most powerful of the Eusufzais, having, by a long course of daring and decisive policy, rendered himself abso-

lute. Very little is known of the town or surrounding country, and the prospect of obtaining authentic information on the subject was destroyed by the death of Captain Edward Conolly, who, in 1840, after his journey in the district, was killed in action in the Kohistan[3] of Kabool. About three miles to the west of the town of Dhyr is a large collection of ruins, attributed by the natives to the Kafirs or heathens of remote times, and considered by Court[4] to be the remains of Dirta, mentioned by the historians of the exploits of Alexander. Dhyr is in lat. 35° 50', long. 72°. 930; Conolly (E.), Notes on the Eu- sofzye Tribes.
[3] E.I.C. Ms. Doc.
[4] Exploits of Alex- ander; Jour. As. Soc. 1839, p. 309.

DIARMUL, or NANGA PURBUT.—A lofty mountain on the northern boundary of the Punjab, is covered with perpetual snow, and estimated by Vigne to be 19,000 feet above the sea. Its summit is finely peaked, with very steep sides. Lat. 35° 10', long. 74° 20'. Von Hugel, i. 349; Vigne, ii. 204.

DIE.—A village on the southern frontier of Afghanistan. It is situate among the Murree mountains, on the route from Bagh to Kahun, and forty miles west of the latter place. Lat. 29° 23', long. 68° 40'. Ms. Survey Map.

DILARAM, in Western Afghanistan, is a ruined fort and halting-place on the southern road from Kandahar to Herat, and about a hundred and forty-five miles a little north of west from the former place. Hence the southern route between the towns of Furrah and Giriskh is called the Dilaram road, in contradistinction to that which runs ten or twelve miles north of it, and nearly parallel to it. This ruin is situate near a rivulet, on the margin of which are a few trees, almost the only ones found in this barren and uninhabited country. Lat. 32° 11', long. 63° 20'. E.I.C. Ms. Doc.; Forster, Jour. Beng. Eng. ii. 124.

DILAWUR.—See DIRAWUL.

DILAZAK.—A village in Afghanistan, in the plain of Pesha- wur, and twelve miles south-east from the city of that name. Lat. 33° 53', long. 71° 49'. Ms. Survey Map.

DILIAR.—A halting-place in Sinde, on the route from Bukkur to the fortress of Omercote, and twenty miles north-west of the latter place. It is situate close to the channel of the Eastern Narra, which is sometimes dry, but during extensive inundations bears along a vast volume of water from the Indus to the Koree estuary. Lat. 25° 36', long. 69° 39'. Walker's Map of Afg.

DINGANA, or DEENGANA.—A village in the Punjab, E.I.C. Ms. Doc.

situate near the right bank of the river Jailum. There is a
road from this place to Bukkur, distant sixty miles north-west.
Lat. 31° 18′, long. 72° 3′.

Walker's Map of DINGANA.—A village in Sinde, on the route from Bukkur
Afg.
to Hydcrabad, and fifty miles north of the latter place. Lat. 26°
10′, long. 68° 30′.

Corresp. on Sinde, DINGEE, in Sinde, a fort between Khyerpoor and Hyderabad,
483-498.
and fifty miles south of the former town. It is surrounded by
walls fifteen feet high, and has an abundant supply of water from
wells. Here, in the beginning of 1843, the Ameers of Sinde collected an army, preparatory to their final struggle with the British.
Lat. 26° 52′, long. 68° 40′.

[1] Leech, Rep. on DIRAWUL or DILAWUR[1] (the l and r being interchange-
Sindh. Army, 81;
Burnes' Bokhara, able).—A fortress of Bhawlpoor, situate in the desert, forty miles
iii. 291; Masson, from the left bank of the Punjnud. It is strongly fortified ac-
Bal. Afg. Panj. i.
25.   cording to the notions of native powers, and with reference to
their practical skill in the arts of defence; but its safety principally lies in the difficulty of access to it, the road lying through
a parched desert totally devoid of water, so that a besieging army
must draw its supply from a distance of fifteen miles. It contains
[2] Atkinson, Exp. the treasure of Bhawl Khan, vaguely estimated at 700,000l.[2]
into Afg. 76.
Here also is his zenana, and thither he retires for relaxation from
the fatigues of business (as far as he ever endures them), or for
security when threatened with invasion. There is here a manufactory of gunpowder for artillery, but the produce is of very indifferent quality. Lat. 28° 44′, long. 71° 17′.

E.I.C. Ms. Doc. DOBRE.—A village in Afghanistan, situate in lat. 31° 57′,
long. 71° 1′.

[1] Macartney, in DOBUNDEE, in Afghanistan,[1] a village on the right bank
Elph. App. 656.
of the Kabool river, just below where three channels unite. The
river here is about three hundred yards wide, and navigable for
large boats, and so far appears to be the greatest length of navigation from the sea by the channel of the Indus and its great
[2] Wood, Oxus, 165; tributary, the Kabool. Higher, the navigation can be safely
Burnes' Pers.
Narr. 277; Jour. effected only by means of muchuks or inflated hides.[3] Coal strata
As. Soc. 1841, p.
811; Griffith, Rep. crop out here,[3] but as yet only thin seams have been discovered,
on Afg.
[3] End. 1841, p.89; and these yield merely pulverulent specimens, resembling rather
Drummond on   coal-dust than any thing of superior quality and value. Lat. 34°
Min. Resources
of Afg.   14′, long. 71° 44′.
Vigne, 1. 201.   DODA.—A town in the Northern Punjab, amidst the moun-

tains south of Kashmir, situate on the right or north-west bank of the Chenaub, nearly opposite its confluence with the river of Budrawar. The Chenaub, here sixty yards broad, is crossed by a *jhoola* or bridge, formed by a cable stretched from bank to bank, and traversed by a suspended seat, drawn backwards and forwards by means of a rope. Doda is a neat, well-built town, with a good bazaar, and a square fort having a tower at each angle. The fort is garrisoned by the Sikhs, which power is in possession of the adjacent country. Lat. 33° 2′, long. 75° 18′.

DO DUNDAN (two teeth) is a lofty mountain in Beloochis- Masson, Bal. Afg. tan, with two peaks towering over the Gundava or Moola Pass, Panj. ii. 117. from Kelat to Gundava. Lat. 27°, 50′ long. 66° 50′.

DOLA.—A village in the Punjab, situate on the right bank of Walker's Map of N.W. Frontier. the Ravee river, in lat. 31°, long. 73° 16′.

DOOBAH.—A small river of Sinde, rises in the southern E.I.C. Ms. Doc.; part of the Keertar mountains, about lat. 25° 54′, long. 67° 45′. Jour. As. Soc. 1840, p. 910; De After a course which may be estimated at forty-five miles, ge- La Hoste, Rep. on Country between nerally in a south-easterly direction, it forms a junction with Kurrachee and the Damajee river, coming from the south-west, and below the Sehwan. confluence the name is changed for that of Dhurwal. In the commencement of its course it bears the name of the Pokrun river, and lower down, that of the Kajoor. It is dry for the greater part of the year, but water may always be obtained by digging in its bed.

DOOBAH.—A halting-place in Sinde, on the river Doobah, E.I.C. Ms. Doc. and on the route from Kurrachee to Sehwan, sixty-six miles south of the latter town. Forage may be obtained, though in no great quantity. The road in the vicinity is tolerably good, though in some places impeded by water-courses. Lat. 25° 34′, long. 67° 58′.

DOOB GAU.—A village in Kashmir, situate on the river E.I.C. Ms. Doc. Jailum or Veyut, eight miles north from Baramula. Lat. 34° 12′, long. 74° 18′.

DOOBOORJIE.—A village in the Punjab, on the road from E.I.C. Ms. Doc. Ferozpoor to Mooltan, and eighteen miles west of the former town. It is situate three miles from the right bank of the Ghara river. Lat. 30° 54′, long. 74° 15′.

DOODEE GHAT.[1]—A village in the Punjab, situate on the [1] E.I.C. Ms. Doc. right bank of the river Chenaub, and five miles north-west of Mooltan, from which there is a good road. It is mentioned by

Elphinstone[2] under the name of Oodoo-ka-Gote. Here is a much-frequented ferry, by which the great route lies from Mooltan to Dera Ghazee Khan. Lat. 30° 11′, long. 71° 22′.

DOO KOOEE.—A village in Afghanistan, situate forty miles south of Ghuznee, and in the elevated and mountainous tract lying between that place and Lake Ab-istada. Lat. 32°.57′, long. 68° 2

DOONAH.—A village of Afghanistan, in the Daman,·distant eight miles from the right bank of the Indus. Lat. 30° 50′, long. 70° 48′.

DOONDEY.—A village in Sinde, on the road from Hyderabad to Lucput Bunder, and thirty miles south of the former town. It is situate close to the left bank of the Indus, in the low alluvial tract insulated by that river and its offsets the Fulailee and Piniaree. Lat. 24° 59′, long. 68° 17′.

DOORA.—A village of Beloochistan, situate in the district of Lus, and twenty miles north-east from Sonmeanee. Lat. 25° 38′, long. 66° 41′.

DOOSHAK.—See JELALABAD.

DOOSHAUK, in Western Afghanistan, is a village, surrounded by a mud wall, surmounted by towers, on the route from Herat to Kandahar, and a hundred and ten miles a little north of west from the place last named. It is situate at the eastern base of some hills, over which the road passes at the height of about nine hundred feet. The road is hard, but uneven, near this town. Water and forage may be obtained here   Lat. 32° 11′, long. 64° 5′.

DOR, a small river of the Punjab, rises in the mountains west of Mazufurabad, which divide the valley of the Indus from that of the Jailum. It holds a westerly course of about fifty miles, and, uniting with the Sarn, falls into the Indus on the eastern side, near Torbela, in lat. 34° 12′, long. 72° 39′.

DORAHA.—A village in Afghanistan, situate in the mountainous tract north-east of the town of Furrah, from which it is distant thirty miles east. Lat. 32° 22′, long. 62° 40′.

DOREE RIVER, in Afghanistan, takes its rise near the Kojuk Pass, on the western side of the Khojeh Amram mountains. It holds a westerly course of about ninety miles, and falls into the river Turnak a little above its confluence with the Urghundab, and in lat. 31° 24′, long. 65° 18′. The water, though very brackish, was drunk most greedily by the soldiers of the British army in their dreadful extremity during the advance on Kandahar in April, 1839. Where crossed by the route from Shawl to Kandahar, thirty miles south-east from the last place, the river is four or five yards wide and eighteen inches deep.

DOSHAK.—See Doosnauk.

DOST MAHOMED'S FORT, in the district of Mekran, in E.I.C. Ms. Doc. Beloochistan. It is situate on the route from Belah to Kedje, and a hundred and fifty miles west of the former place. Lat. 26° 22', long. 64° 1'.

DOULUTPOOR.[1]—A village in Sinde, situate near the left [1] Walker's Map of bank of the Indus. It forms part of the district of Bhoonj N.W. Frontier. Bhara,[2] and was comprised in the transfer of territory made by [2] Correspondence the British, in 1843, from the Ameers of Khyerpoor to Mahomed on Sinde, 255, 507. Bhawl Khan, in reward of his steady friendship. Lat. 28° 21', long. 69° 41'.

DOUR.—A village of Afghanistan, situate in the Daman, on Walker's Map of the road from Ghuznee to Kala Bagh, and sixty miles west of the Afg. latter place. Lat. 33° 6', long. 70° 35'.

DOWD KHAIL.—A village in the Punjab, situate on the E.I.C. Ms. Doc. left bank of the Indus. It is about eight miles lower down the river than Kala Bagh, and on the opposite side. Lat. 32° 52', long. 71° 33'.

DOWLATABAD, in Western Afghanistan, is a ruined fort E.I.C. Ms. Doc.; on the route from Kandahar to Herat, from which last place it Conolly, Jour. to India, ii. 63. is distant ninety-five miles. It is situate on the bank of the Furrah-Rood, in a fertile valley, yielding abundant supplies, especially southwards, towards the town of Furrah. Lat. 32° 36', long. 62° 27'.

DOWLUTDYAR.—A village in Afghanistan, lying among E.I.C. Ms. Doc. the Huzareh mountains. It is situate on the Sir-i-Jungle, near its confluence with the Heri-Rood. Lat. 34° 15', long. 65°.

DOWLUTPOOR.—A village in Sinde, situate two miles Ms. Survey Map. from the left bank of the river Indus, on a road leading from Bukkur to the south of Sinde. Lat. 26° 37', long. 68° 1'.

DOWULUTPOOR.—A village in Sinde, situate on the left bank of the Indus, ten miles north-east of Schwan, in lat. 26° 27', long. 63°.

DOZAN.—A village in Sinde, on the route from Sehwan to E.I.C. Ms. Doc. Kurrachee, and twelve miles north-east of the latter town. It is situate on the bank of the Amree, which, though dry during the greater part of the year, in the season of rain becomes a torrent, discharging itself into the Gisry river, about eight miles to the south of Dozan. This village lies in lat. 24° 54′, long. 67° 15′.

E.I.C. Ms. Doc.

DRABOGAM.—A village in Kashmir, situate on the road from Shahbad to Baramula, and seventy miles north-west of the former place. Lat. 33° 48′, long. 74° 40′.

E.I.C. Ms. Doc.;
Elph. Acc. of Cau-
bul, 31 ; Leech,
App. 43;' Burnes,
Trade of the De-
rajat, 98; Masson,
Bal. Afg. Panj. i.
72; Vigne, Ghuz-
nee, 57.

DRABUND, or DERABUND, in Afghanistan, a small town in the Derajat, about thirty miles south-west of Dera Ismael Khan. It is the place of rendezvous of the Lohani and other caravans, which every spring depart westward with the annual supply of British and Indian wares for Central Asia. These Lohanis descend, with their camels and other cattle, to spend the winter in the mild climate and luxuriant pastures stretching along the western bank of the Indus, and at the same time to furnish themselves with articles suitable for supplying their customers in Afghanistan and the countries north and west of it ; and they assemble at Drabund to muster their strength for resisting the predatory tribe infesting the roads through which they have to pass. In one year they have taken with them above five thousand camels laden with merchandize, twenty-four thousand camels attending them for other purposes, and above a hundred thousand sheep, besides other animals. The town of Drabund is a small ill-built place, but bearing evidence of having been more prosperous, until ruined by the predatory attacks of the Vaziris and other marauders from the west. The permanent population is scarcely 1,000. Lat. 31° 45′, long. 70° 32′.

DRAS.—A river falling into the Indus. (See DURAS and INDUS.)

E.I.C. Ms. Doc.

DREY.—A village near the south-east frontier of Sinde, on the route from Omercote to Nuggur Parker, and six miles north-west of the latter place. Lat. 24° 25′, long. 70° 40′.

DRIBBAR.—A village in Southern Sinde, situate on a road twenty miles from the north bank of the Great Western Rin. Lat. 24° 25′, long. 69° 39′.

E.I.C. Ms. Doc.

DROUBUND.—A village in Afghanistan, situate about three miles from the right bank of the Indus, and ten miles south of Dera Ismael Khan, on the route from thence to Mooltan. Lat. 31° 42′, long. 70° 56′.

Hough, Narr. of
Exp. to Afg. 40;

DRUBBEE, in Beloochistan, a part of the Bolan Pass, where

the inclosing hills receding, leave room for a small valley, covered with green sward, and having space for an encampment of 1,500 men. There is a plentiful supply of excellent water from the Bolan river, which flows through the valley. Lat. 29° 27′, long. 67° 32′. Havelock, War in Afg. i. 215.

DRUMTOOR.—See DUMTAUR.

DUB, in the Punjab, a pass over a mountain on the route from Attock to Kashmir, by the Baramula road. It was at a recent period infested by freebooters, who held possession of the fort of Futighur and spread terror over the whole vicinity. Hari Singh, the intrepid and energetic Sikh chieftain, attacked them, drove them out of a jungle where they took refuge, by firing it, and put the whole body to the sword. The Dub Pass is situate on the water-line dividing the feeders of the Kishengunga, and consequently of the Jailum, on the east side, from those of the Indus on the west. Lat. 34° 17′, long. 73° 21′. P. Von Hugel, iii. 34.

DUBAR, in Sinde, a village on the route from Roree to Sub-zulcote, and twelve miles north-east of the former place. It is situate near the left bank of the Indus and close to a water-course. Lat. 27° 50′, long. 69° 4′. Masson, Bal. Afg. Panj. i. 308.

DUBLEE, in Sinde, a village on the route from Sehwan to Larkhana, and eighteen miles south of the latter town. It is situate in a level alluvial country, and close to a water-course communicating with the Indus. The road in the vicinity is narrow, and cut through the jungle, here overrunning the country. Lat. 27° 15′, long. 68° 15′. E.I.C. Ms. Doc.

DUCHIN.—A village in the Northern Punjab, situate on the Muru Wurdwun river, a short distance above its confluence with the Chenaub. Lat. 33° 25′, long. 75° 45′. E I.C. Ms. Doc.

DUFEHR.—A village in Sinde, on the Western Narra, a great offset of the Indus; it is situate on the western road from Sehwan to Larkhana, and thirty-five miles south of the latter place. Lat. 27° 5′, long. 67° 52′. E.I.C. Ms. Doc.

DUKA, or DAKA,[1] in Afghanistan. There are two villages of this name, one at the western extremity of the Khyber Pass, called Duka " Kula," or " the great;" the other, about two miles to the east of the other, called Duka " Khurd," or " the little." The latter is on the road by which the two northern passes, the Abkhana and the Tatara, debouch westward. Both villages [1] Leech, Khyber Pass, 11; Masson, Bal. Afg. Panj. i. 101; Hough's Narr. Exp. to Afg. 306; Burnes' Bokh. i. 116; Id. Pers. Narr. 130; Wood, Oxus, 162; Havelock, War in Afg. ii. 187.

are situate on the south or right bank of the Kabool river, and are surrounded by walls. The ground is saturated with soda, and, in consequence of this and the contiguity of the river, is very damp. The immediate vicinity is barren, but as the plain of Bassowal, at a short distance to the west, is fertile and well cultivated, considerable supplies can be obtained here. Duka was a place of importance in 1842, during the time that the British force, under Sir Robert Sale, was cooped up in Jelalabad, as it commanded the Tatara and Abkhana passes,[2] by which communication with the garrison was frequently effected, whilst the Khyber Pass was completely closed. On the evacuation of the country, towards the close of 1842, a portion of the British army encamped here,[3] previously to making its way through the Khyber Pass. The elevation of Duka above the sea[4] is 1,404 feet. Lat. 34° 15′, long. 71° 12′.

2 Mil. Op. in Afg. 42, 63.

3 Id. 427.

4 Hough, Narr. of Exp. in Afg. 300.

DUKKEE.—See DURKHEE.

Walker's Map of Afg.

DULHUK.—A village in Afghanistan, on the road from Furrah to Girişkh, and thirty-seven miles north-west of the last-named place. Lat. 32° 4′, long. 63° 48′.

E.I.C. Ms. Doc.

DULLAH.—A village in Afghanistan, situate on the right bank of the Indus, twenty-two miles north of Dera Ismael Khan. Lat. 32° 6′, long. 71° 10′.

E.I.C. Ms. Doc.

DUMAJEE.—A village in Sinde, on the route from Sehwan to Kurrachee, and sixty miles north-east of the latter town. The road near Dumajee is represented as indifferently good, and forage can be obtained to a considerable extent. The supply of water is rather scanty : there are two wells which afford it, but they are liable to fail in the dry season. After rainy weather, a torrent, called the Dumajee river, flows by the village and falls into the Dhurwal river, about twelve miles to the north-east. Dumajee is in lat. 25° 21′, long. 67° 52′.

E.I.C. Ms. Doc. Jour. As. Soc. 1840, p. 910; De La Hoste, Rep. on Country between Sehwan and Kurrachee.

DUMBA, a small river in Sinde, rises in the southern part of the Keertar range of mountains, about twenty miles north-east of Kurrachee, in lat. 25° 4′, long. 67° 18′, and, after a southerly course, estimated at eighteen miles, falls into the river Mularee, in lat. 24° 48′, long. 67° 15′. About ten miles above its mouth it is crossed by the route from Kurrachee to Sehwan, and is at that point, during the rainy season, a small stream. In the dry season, the channel has no stream, though water may be obtained by digging in the bed. The place where it is crossed by the road as above mentioned is called the Dumba Camp. The road there is generally good, and forage may be obtained in considerable quantities.

DUMDUM.[1]—A valley in Kashmir, and also a river, along the course of which lies a pass over the mountains which inclose Kashmir to the south. This pass, situate between the mountains Futi Panjal and Pir Panjal, is generally called the Pir Panjal Pass, but sometimes the Nandan Sar Pass. It is 11,800 feet above the sea, and through it lies the route into Kashmir from the Punjab, by Rajawur. The river rises about the summit of the pass, and, flowing north-east, falls into the Vehut or Jailum, which drains the whole of Kashmir. It is called the Huripur river by Vigne.[2] Lat. 33° 40′, long. 74° 40′. [1] Von Hugel, i. 204.
[2] i. 254.

DUMTAUR, or DHARUM TAWUR, in the Punjab, a valley extending nearly in a direction from east to west, in lat. 34° 5′—34° 10′, and long. 72° 45′—73° 15′. It is described by Baron Hügel, who explored it, as giving the impression of having been once the bed of a vast torrent. It is still furrowed by numerous water-courses, discharging themselves into the river Dor, which flows with a scanty stream in a stony channel half a mile wide. Here the traveller, descending from the elevated country lying to the north, finds the vegetation assuming the character of that which prevails in Hindostan. The sugar-cane especially is grown in such abundance, that it forms a principal article of fodder for cattle. The mountains which inclose the valley on the north-west are clothed with dense and luxuriant forests of oak, pine, walnut, wild olive, and plane trees. The valley is populous, and abounds in villages, each defended by a small fort. `Dumtaur, which gives name to the valley and district, is a small and poor place. The inhabitants are Eusufzai Afghans, who yield a very reluctant obedience to the Sikh government. Elph. Acc. of Caubul, 329, 531; P. Von Hugel, Kaschmir, iii. 63-65.

DUMTAUR, in the Punjab, a small town, a few miles east of the Indus, lying on the route into Kashmir by the Dub Pass. It is situate in a beautiful, well-watered, and productive valley, crowded with small forts, erected and maintained on account of the dangerous proximity of the Eusufzais. Lat. 34° 5′, long. 73° 6′. Von Hugel, iii. 64,

DUND, in Afghanistan, is a village on the route from Dera Ismael Khan to Ghuznee, from which last place it is distant twenty-seven miles south-east. The road here is good, and the E.I.C. Ms. Doc.

supply of water abundant from the river of Ghuznee. Lat. 33 °1′. long. 68° 16′.

E.I.C. Ms. Doc. DUNDAL.—A village north-east of Kashmir, and situate in the valley of Duras, on the river of the same name. Lat. 34° 21′, long. 75° 42′.

E.I.C. Ms. Doc. DUNDEE.—A village in the Punjab, situate on the east bank of the river Indus, twenty-four miles south-west of Attock. Lat. 33° 36′, long. 72° 4′.

E.I.C. Ms. Doc.; Hough, Narr. Exp. in Afg, 84; Havelock, War in Afg. 320; Kennedy, Sinde and Kabool, i. 242. DUNDI GOOLAI, in Afghanistan, is a halting-place, with a reservoir of water, on the route from the Kojuck Pass to Kandahar, from which town it is distant seventy miles south-east. The reservoir is supplied with water by means of a canal from the mountains to the north-east, so that the supply may be cut off, by damming up the channel. This was done when the British army was encamped there, in April, 1839, and dreadful suffering thereby caused. The reservoir is 4,036 feet above the sea. Lat. 30° 56′, long. 66° 16′.

E.I.C. Ms. Doc. DUNDYA.—A village in Beloochistan, in the province of Lus. It is situate near the road from Belah to Sonmeanee, about seven miles south-east from the former place. Lat. 26° 6′, long. 66° 30′.

E.I.C. Ms. Doc. DUNWULLEE, in Sinde, a small village on the route from Sehwan to Larkhana, and twelve miles south of the latter place. It is situate in the fertile island inclosed between the Indus and its offset the Western Narra, being distant eight miles from the right bank of the former, and two from the left bank of the latter. The country around is level and fertile, occasionally overspread with jungle, and the road near Dunwullee is said to be good. Lat. 27° 20′, long. 68° 15′.

DURAJEE.—See DARAJEE.

Moorcroft, ii. 36-44; Vigne, ii. 393. DURAS, or DRAS, in Ladakh, at a short distance north of the northern frontier of Kashmir, is a collection of villages in a valley of the same name, through which lies the route from Le to Kashmir by the Bultul Pass. Through the middle of the valley flows the river of Dras, which, rising in the Bultul or Kantal Pass, a little to the south, flows northward to the Indus, which it joins opposite the village of Morul, in lat. 34° 44′, long. 67° 9′. Dras is 9,000 feet above the sea, and in lat 34° 22′, long. 75° 30′

Walker's Map of N.W. Frontier. DURASIND.—A village in Sinde, on the right bank of the

Fulailee or Goongroo, a great branch of the Indus. It is situate on the route from Hyderabad to Lucput, and fifty-two miles south-east of the former place. Lat. 24° 41', long. 68° 37'.

DURAWAT.—A village in Afghanistan, fifty-five miles north Walker's Map of from Kandahar. Lat. 32° 22', long. 65° 40'. Afg.

DURAZ, in Sinde, is a small town about twenty miles south Westmacott, Acc. of Khyerpoor, and on the great route from that place to Hyder- of Khyrpoor, Jour. of As. Soc. 1840, abad. The population is entirely employed in the manufacture of p. 1189. loongees and cotton cloths. Lat. 27° 8', long. 68° 28'.

DURBAN.—A village in Northern Afghanistan, a short dis- Map of Afg. tance south of the Hindoo Koosh, and near the source of the Tagoo river. Lat. 35° 46', long. 70° 30'.

DUREE.—A village in Sinde, a few miles from the west E.I.C. Ms. Doc. bank of the river Indus. Lat. 28° 8', long. 69° 4'.

DURIA KHAN.—A village in the Punjab, situate on an off- E.I.C. Ms. Doc. set of the Indus, about three miles from the main channel, and fourteen miles north of Bukkur. Lat. 31° 50', long. 71° 9'.

DURKKEE, in Afghanistan, is a large village of Sewestan, E.I.C. Ms. Doc. on the route from Dera Ghazee Khan to Kandahar, by the Sakhee Sarwar Pass. The surrounding country is very pro- ductive in grain, but the supply of water is uncertain, so that at times it must be procured from Baghaw, ten miles to the north- west. Lat. 30° 9', long. 68° 47'.

DURMAGEE.—A village in Afghanistan, situate on the Walker's Map. river Adruscund, or Haroot, ten miles south of the town of Sub- zawur. Lat. 33° 12', long. 62° 10'

DURNAMEH.—A village of Afghanistan, in the Kohistan of Mass. Bal. Afg. Kabool, and thirty miles north-east of the city of that name. Panj. iii. 152. This village has an infamous reputation, from the character of its inhabitants, who are desperate robbers, infesting the more peace- able districts lying farther south; and it affords a place of refuge to outlaws compelled to fly from better regulated communities on account of their crimes. Lat. 35°, long. 69° 25'.

DURRAHA.—A village in Sinde, on the route from Shikar- E.I.C. Ms. Doc. poor to Sukkur, and seven miles north-west of the latter town. It is situate four miles from the right bank of the Indus, in a well- cultivated country abounding in trees. The road near it may in general be described as pretty good; but water-courses intersect- ing it are of frequent occurrence. Lat. 27° 49', long. 68° 52'.

DURRUK RIVER.—See Nal River.

Walker's Map of   DURWAZA PASS, in Afghanistan, situate on the road
Afg.   from Giriskh to Furrah, in lat. 32° 6', long. 63° 45'.

DURYA.—See BUND-I-BURBUR.

DUSHT-I-BEDOWLUT.—See DASHT-I-BEDAULAT.

Ms. Survey Map.   DUSTALEE.—A village in Sinde, situate on the road from
Gundava to Larkhana, and twenty-five miles north-west of the
last-mentioned place. Lat. 27° 38', long. 67° 58'.

DUSTEE.—A river of Beloochistan, discharging itself into
Beloochistan, 302. the Arabian Sea, in lat. 25° 3', long. 61° 50'. Pottinger states
that at low water the depth within a hundred yards of the beach
is about twenty inches, and the breadth from ten to thirty yards.
The tide flows up a mile or two, and those who then see it might
suppose that they were viewing the estuary of a large river. The
author just quoted, who has furnished all the information at present to be had on the subject, conjectures that, though so diminutive, it has a course of nearly a thousand miles, and considers it
identical with the Badoor, or Bhugwur, a stream which he crossed
about four hundred miles from the mouth of the Dustee, and
supposed to have been at one time a branch of the Helmund.

E.I.C. Ms. Doc.   DUTURNA.—A village in Sinde, situate near the right bank
of the Indus, on the road from Larkhana to Sukkur; twenty-
seven miles north-east of the former, and eighteen miles west of
the latter place. Lat. 27° 43', long. 68° 36'.

E.

1 Vigne, Kashmir,   ECHIBUL,[1] in Kashmir, a fine fountain, discharging a vast
i. 348, 349.   quantity of the most beautifully limpid water. It is situate in
the eastern part of the district of Bureng, and has four or five
orifices, from the principal of which the spring rises with such
force as to form what may be termed a mound of water, a foot
and half high, and twelve feet in diameter. Vigne, with much
probability, supposes it to be the efflux of that portion of the
water of the river Bureng which sinks into the ground about ten
miles to the south-east. If, however, this opinion be correct,
the sunken stream must receive large additions from springs in its
subterraneous course, as the volume of water discharged at

Echibul far exceeds that which disappears in the bed of the Bureng. (See Bureng.) According to Vigne, the water is not very
good for drinking. Bernier,[2] on the contrary, who describes this ² Voyages, ii. 205.
vast fountain under the name of Achiavel, states the water to
be excellent (*admirablement bonne*) ; he adds, that it is so cold
as to be almost insupportable to the touch. At the time of his
visit (1665), it was surrounded by a superb pleasure-ground, belonging to Aurungzebe, having been made by order of his grandfather, Jehangir ; but all is now in utter ruin. Lat. 23° 39′,
long. 75° 12′.

EEJMUT, in Sinde, a small town, on the route from Sub- E.I.C. Ms. Doc.
zulcote to Shikarpoor by the Amil *Got*, or ferry over the Indus,
from the right bank of which river it is about a mile and half
distant. The water in the neighbourhood is obtained from wells,
and is but of indifferent quality. Lat. 27° 55′, long. 68° 56′.

EEKUNG-CHOO,[1] or RIVER OF GHERTOPE, in South- ¹ Moorcr. in As.
ern Tibet, is by some [2] considered a branch of the Indus, by Res. xii. 440, 450,
others,[3] the main stream of that great river, in the upper part of ² Gerard, Koona-
its course. Moorcroft crossed it at a place which he considered ³ Ritter, Erd-
near the source, and, in lat. 31° 25′, long. 80° 30,′ found it two kunde von Asien,
and a half feet deep, eighty yards wide, and very rapid. After a iii. 504, 606.
course of between forty and fifty miles in a north-westerly direction, it joins another river,* flowing from the south-east, and the
united stream thenceforward bears the name of the Sinh-kha-bab,
and, lower down, of Sindh or Indus. (See Indus.)

EESA KHAN.—A village in Western Afghanistan, twelve Walker's Map of
miles from the right bank of the Haroot or Subzawur river. N.W. Frontier.
Lat. 32° 33′, long. 61° 30′.

ELEEGILL.—A village in the Punjab, situate on the road E.I.C. Ms. Doc.
from Attock to Ferozpoor, forty miles north-west of the latter
place, and twenty miles south-west of Lahore. Lat. 31° 21′,
long. 74° 9′.

EMAUM GHUR, in Sinde, was lately a strong fortress Correspondence
in the Thur or Great Sandy Desert, separating that country on Sinde, 483, 484,
from Jessulmair. As scarcely a drop of fresh water can be had 500, 501.
on the route from Sinde after leaving Choonkee, distant about
fifty miles from Emaum Ghur, this fortress was generally con-

* The existence of this river and confluence is alleged, on the credit of the
map accompanying Moorcroft's travels, and stated to have been compiled
from his notes and field-books.

N 2

sidered by the Ameers as an inexpugnable place of refuge.   On this account, when the disputes between them and the British came to extremity, Sir Charles Napier determined at all risks to attempt its seizure.   Setting out with fifty cavalry, two twenty-four-pound howitzers, drawn by camels, and three hundred and fifty European infantry, mounted on animals of the same descrip-. tion—two on each, he, after a very trying march of three days, over a succession of steep sandhills, reached the fort, which was immediately surrendered.   The captor describes it as " exceedingly strong against any force without artillery.   The walls are forty feet high, one tower is fifty feet high, and built of burned bricks.   It is square, with eight round towers, surrounded by an exterior wall of fifteen feet high, lately built.   There are some bomb-proof chambers."   Twenty thousand pounds of powder were found in various places built up for concealment.   These were employed in springing thirty-four mines, which reduced the fort to a mass of ruins, shapeless and irretrievable.   The grain found in store had been previously distributed in rations.   The British force marched back to the interior of Sinde without any loss.   Emaum Ghur is in lat. 26° 31′, long. 69° 31′.

E.I.C. Ms. Doc.

EMENABAD.—A village in the Punjab, on the great route from Amritsir to Vajeerabad, thirty miles south from the last-named place.   At Emenabad, a road branches off southwards to Lahore, about seventy miles distant in that direction. Lat. 32° 7′, long. 74° 11′.

Burnes' Bokh. III. 7.

ENDREESA, in the Punjab, a village situate in the bifurcation where the Beah and Sutluj rivers unite.   Burnes sought here in vain for the altars dedicated by Alexander to commemorate his conquests.   He found nothing but a brick ruin, unquestionably of Mahometan origin.   Were this even the actual locality of those altars which have given rise to so much controversy, the probability of their still existing is perhaps not great; it being unlikely that the natives would allow the trophies of the invader's triumph to remain after his disappearance.   Endreesa is in lat. 31° 11′, long. 75°.

Jour. As. Soc. 1841, p. 801, Grif. Rep. on Subjects connected with Afg., also, 1842, p. 49; Id. Tables of Bar. and Ther. Obs.

ERAK, in Afghanistan, is a pass on the most north-easterly of the four routes which, diverging from the valley of Siah-Sung, debouch in that of Bamian.   These passes are the lines of communication between the valley of Kabool and Kunduz, and lie over that range which connects the south-western extremity of

Hindoo Koosh with the Koh-i-Baba mountain farther south. It is the highest of the four passes, and has an altitude above the sea of 12,909 feet. Lat. 34° 40', long. 68° 5'.

EREE.—A village of Cutch Gundava, in Beloochistan, about fifteen miles south-east of Dadur. It is situate on the Nari, a violent and rapid torrent, but intermitting for a great part of the year, so that the channel at such times becomes quite dry. Lat. 29° 25', long. 68°. *E.I.C. Ms. Map; Pott. Belooch. 309; Masson, Kalat, 332.*

ESOTT.—A village in Afghanistan, forty miles south of Lake Ab-istada. It is situate on the eastern route from Ghuznee to Shawl, and one hundred and ten miles south of the former place. Lat. 32°, long. 68° 6'. *Walker's Map of Afg.*

ESSUN DE WUSTEE.—A village of Afghanistan, in the Daman. It is situate about eight miles from the west bank of the Indus, and eleven miles south of Dera Ghazee Khan. Lat. 29° 56', long. 70° 49'. *E.I.C. Ms. Doc.*

EYZULAT KHAN.—A village in Afghanistan, situate about two miles from the left bank of the Turnak river, near the route from Kandahar to Ghuznee, and distant sixty miles north-east of the former town. Lat. 31° 54', long. 66° 25'. *E.I.C. Ms. Doc.*

F.

FAKIR MAHOMED KA KOTE, in Sinde, a halting-place on the route from Hyderabad to Sehwan, and forty-seven miles north of the former place. It is situate two miles from the right bank of the Indus, in a level fertile country, intersected by numerous water-courses, and bounded by the river on the east, and the rugged Lukkee mountains on the west. Lat. 25° 56', long. 68° 15'. *E.I.C. Ms. Doc.*

FALOUR.—See Filor.

FAPREE.—A village in Daman, Afghanistan, situate three miles from the right bank of the river Indus. Lat. 30° 19', long. 70° 50'. *Walker's Map of Afg.*

FARAJGHAN.—A village in Kafiristan, on the southern declivity of Hindoo Koosh, near the source of the Tagoo river. It is a mart for the trade between the Afghans and Kafirs, who *E.I.C. Ms. Doc.; Leech, Hindoo Koosh, 37.*

bring for barter slaves and the rude produce of their country; and the village therefore is, in the case of war, considered a neutral place. Lat. 35° 42′, long. 70° 22′.

Ms. Survey Map. FATTA DUR.—A village of Sinde, in the Great Thur, or Sandy Desert. It is situate on one of the routes from Hyderabad to Jessulmair, and is sixty miles south-west of the latter place. Lat. 26° 16′, long. 70° 19′.

Masson, Bal.·Afg. Panj. i. 25, 382. FAZILPOOR, in Bhawlpoor, on the east bank of the Indus, is a small town, defended by a fort of kiln-burnt bricks, now greatly decayed. The adjacent country is very fertile, but low and swampy, being laid extensively under water in the season of the inundation of the river. The numerous ruins scattered over the neighbourhood shew the district to have formerly been much more densely peopled and prosperous than at present. Lat. 28° 30′, long. 69° 50′.

Masson, Bal. Afg. Panj. ii. 333. FERAI KHOLM, in Afghanistan, an elevated district, inclosed between the river Helmund on the east and south-east, and the Koh-i-Baba range on the west and north-west. Though situate amidst rugged hills, it is fertile, populous, and well cultivated. It contains numerous castles and small forts built by the Huzarehs for their defence. Lat. 34° 20′, long. 67° 54′.

Id. ii. 70; Id. Kalat, 314, 315. FERINGABAD.—A village in Beloochistan, on the route from Moostung to the Bolan Pass, and six miles north-east of Moostung. It is advantageously situated at the foot of the range of hills over which the road passes from Moostung to Shawl, and on the right of that route. The climate is delightful, and the vicinity fertile and pleasant, abounding in orchards and gardens. The population is about 800. Lat. 29° 50′, long. 66° 50′.

E.I.C. Ms. Doc.; Masson, Bal. Afg. Panj. iii. 118. FERZAH, in Afghanistan, a village in the Koh-i-Damun, thirty miles north-west of Kabool. It is situate at the eastern base of the Pughman mountain, on a small stream called the river of Ferzah, discharging itself into the Punchshir. The scenery is very beautiful, the country highly cultivated and very productive, especially in fruit, which is of fine quality. The small district of Ferzah contains twelve villages and four forts, and an aggregate population of about 4,000, partly Afghans, and partly Tajiks In the north-western and highest part of the valley is a delightful garden, formerly held and enjoyed by some ruler of Kabool, but at present quite in ruins. Its great natural beauty

is heightened by a small but picturesque cascade. Lat. 34° 45',
long. 68° 56'.

FERENGAL.[1]—A lead mine in the valley of Ghorbund, in
Northern Afghanistan, worked at a period so remote that its
existence was unknown to the neighbouring inhabitants until
rediscovered by Dr. Lord. The ore is very abundant and valuable, being a rich sulphuret of lead. Lord[2] observes that the shaft
descended a hundred feet perpendicular before it reached the ore,
and that " the galleries have been run and the shafts sunk with a
degree of skill that does no little credit to the engineering knowledge of the age." He farther remarks that the *dialling* (as a
Cornish man would call it) " shewed an acquaintance with the lie
of the mineral and the level at which they had arrived, that could
scarcely be exceeded in the present day." So extensive were the
workings, that Lord employed three hours in exploring them, yet
without ascertaining their full extent. The mine of Ferengal is
distant eighteen miles south-west from the village of Ghorbund. A pass little frequented proceeds from the mine northward over Hindoo Koosh into Kunduz. Lat. 34° 55', long.
68° 33'

FEZAN KHYLE.—A village in Afghanistan, on the road
from Kala-Bagh to Dera Ismael Khan, and twenty-six miles south-
west of the former place. It is situate in the dreary Largee
valley, near the left bank of the river Kurum, and three miles
from its confluence with the Indus. Lat. 32° 37', long. 71° 22'.

FILOR, or FALOUR.—A town in the Punjab, on the route
from Amritsir to Loodiana, and about six miles north-west of the
latter place. It is situate on the right bank of the Sutluj, and is
defended by a fort built on the high steep rising from the river.
The fort, which was constructed by order of Runjeet Singh in
1809, is small, affording accommodation for a garrison of only
a hundred and fifty men, but it is rendered conspicuous by its
large barbican. Here is the ferry over the Sutluj, for the communication of Loodiana and its neighbourhood with Amritsir and
Lahore. The Sutluj, in inundation, forms extensive sheets of
water round the town, and these remain after the river has shrunk
to the confines of its usual channel. Lat. 31° 2', long 75° 49'.

FOOTAKEA.—A village in the Punjab, situate on the road
from Julalpoor to Attock, and twenty-five miles north of the
former place. Lat. 33° 3', long. 73° 7'.

[1] E.I.C. Ms. Map; Leech, Hindoo Koosh, 33; Lord, Koh-i-Damun, 54; Burnes' Pers. Narr. 153.
[2] Report, 54.

E.I.C. Ms. Doc.

F. Von Hugel, iii. 414, 415.

Walker's Map of N.W. Frontier.

E.I.C. Ms. Doc.   FOR CHAPPER.—In Afghanistan, a mountain on the route from Dera Ghazee Khan to Kandahar, by the Sakhee Sarwar Pass. The road along its base is nearly level, with a slight and gradual ascent, and close to it is a supply of water from a rivulet. The country is uninhabited. Lat. 30° 23', long. 68°.

FRINJAL PASS.—See FERENGAL.

[1] Burnes' Bokh. iii. 201; Pott. Belooch. 358; Wood in Rep. by Carless, 17.   FULAILEE,[1] in Sinde, is a branch of the Indus, leaving the main channel about twelve miles above Hyderabad, and in lat. 25° 31', long. 68° 24.' It flows southward, after proceeding a short distance to the east of Hyderabad, which it insulates by sending off to the westward a branch which rejoins the main river about fifteen miles below the town. Below this last divarication it bears the name of the Goonee, takes a south-easterly course, and again divides, discharging part of its water eastward into the Purana, or Phurraun, and ultimately into the sea by the Koree mouth, and part westward into the Pinyaree, or Goongroo, disemboguing itself by the Sir mouth. On the Pinyaree, or Goongroo, a bund, or dam has been thrown up below the town of Maghribee, by which the water above is retained, and the sea prevented from flowing up the estuary. The formation of this

[2] Bokh. iii. 311.   dam is attributed by Burnes [2] to a malignant intention in the native Sindhian government to deprive the western part of Cutch

[3] Pottinger, Belooch. 358; Pott. (W.), on the present state of the Indus, in Jour. As. Soc. 1834, p. 200; Carless, 17.   of the supply of water necessary to its fertility; but others,[3] perhaps with more probability, maintain that it was made to secure a supply of water for the purposes of irrigation, and to exclude the sea from overspreading the cultivated lands, and rendering them barren. Below the bund this branch is navigable to the Sir mouth, a distance of about fifty miles.

Ms. Survey Map.   FUQUEERKA KOOH.—A village in Sinde, on the eastern route from Bukkur to Hyderabad, and sixty-five miles north-east of the latter place. It is situate on the border of the Thurr, or Great Sandy Desert, and ten miles from the right bank of the Eastern Narra. Lat. 26° 13', long. 68° 51'.

Walker's Map of N.W. Frontier.   FUREEDABAD.—A village in the Punjab, situate on the right bank of the river Ravee. Lat. 31° 2', long. 73° 20'.

[1] E.I.C. Ms. Doc.; Conolly (A.), Jour. to India, ii. 07.   FURRAH,[1] in Western Afghanistan, formerly a considerable town, is situate a hundred and forty miles south of Herat, in a fertile, though in some places swampy, valley, watered by a fine

[2] In App. to Pott. Belooch. 411.   stream called the Furrah-Rood, or River of Furrah. Christie [2] describes it to have been at the time of his visit, in 1810, a large

walled town, with a good bazaar, and it seems probable that then the population was about 10,000 ; but when Conolly visited it, in 1839, it had been reduced to ruins in the course of hostilities [3 Jour. As. Soc. 1841, p. 325;] between the chieftains of Herat and Kandahar, so that no part [Conolly (E.),] was inhabited but the fort, which was fortified by walls of consi- [Jour. in Seistan; Fraser, Khorasan,] derable thickness, and contained about twenty houses[3] built of mud, [App. 29, 120 ;] with domed roofs of the same material. Lat. 32° 24', long. 62° 7'. [Elph. Acc. of Caubul, 123.]

FURRAH-ROOD, or RIVER of FURRAH, in Western [E.I.C. Ms. Doc.; Conolly,] Afghanistan, rises among the mountains in the unexplored coun- [Jour. to India, ii.] try of the Tymunees, north-east of Toot-i-Gusseerman. It has [108; Christie, Journal in App.] been traced as far up as Dowlatabad, on the route from Kandahar [to Pott. 411;] to Herat, and in lat. 32° 36', long. 62° 27'. Here it was found, [Fraser, Jour. to Khorasan, App.29.] in the middle of July, thirty-five yards wide, from two to three feet deep, with an uneven bed, and a current of a mile and a half an hour, the water being remarkably fine and clear. In spring, when swollen, it becomes a large, rapid, and unfordable stream, so that caravans are sometimes detained for weeks in consequence of its being impracticable to cross it.* At a short distance below Dowlatabad it turns to the south-west, and runs about ninety miles to the point where it falls into the Lake of Hamoon, about twenty miles below Laush and in lat. 31° 45', long. 61° 40'.

FURZA RIVER.—See FERZAH.

FUTEH JUNG.—A village in the Punjab, thirty miles [E.I.C. Ms. Doc.] south-east of Attock, and the same distance east of the left bank of the Indus. Lat. 33° 31', long. 72° 39'.

FUTEHPOOR.—A village in the Punjab, near the right [E.I.C. Ms. Doc.] bank of the Ghara river, thirty miles north-east of the town of Bhawlpoor. Lat. 29° 39', long. 72° 2'.

FUTIGHUR.—A ruined fortress in the north of the Punjab, [E.I.C. Ms. Doc.; F. Von Hugel,] on the route from Attock to Kashmir, by the Dub Pass. It is [Kaschmir, iii. 36; Vigne, Kashmir,] situate on a steep and lofty mountain, an offset from the Hima- [ii. 185.] laya, and close to a torrent which a few miles lower down falls into the Jailum. Formerly it was held by a band of freebooters, who kept the adjacent country in alarm. Being attacked by Hari Singh, the Sikh chieftain, they took refuge in a neighbour-

* Conolly (Edward), " Sketch of the Physical Geography of Seistan," Journ. As. Soc. Beng., 1840, p. 712, states that it is nearly dry during the greater part of the year, though water may be always found by digging in its bed.

ing jungle. This was fired by their enemics, by whom they were intercepted and cut to pieces in attempting to escape. Lat. 34° 17′, long. 73° 20′.

FUTI PANJAL.—A mountain in Kashmir, is one of that range which bounds the valley to the southward. According to the estimate of Vigne, its height must exceed 12,000 feet, as its summit rises above the lake Hosah Nag, which has that elevation. Its name signifies the mountain of victory. Its culminating ridge in some measure resembles the arc of a circle, the extremities of which are east and west, and the northern or concave part, directed towards Kashmir. Its total length is about forty miles. Lat. 33° 20′, long. 74° 30′.

Burnes' Pol. Pow. of Sikhs, 3; Hough, Narr. of Exp. in Afg. 229; Mil. Op. in Afg. 43. FUTTEGHUR.—A fort built by the Sikhs, to command the eastern end of the Khyber Pass. It is situate a mile north-east from Jamrood, and being close to the entrance of the pass, has great command over it. The defences consist of a square of three hundred yards, protecting an octagonal fort, in the centre of which is a lofty mass of buildings commanding the surrounding country. The supply of water from the mountain-streams is liable to be cut off by the hostile Khyberees of the adjacent hills. In the hope of providing a remedy for this inconvenience, the Sikhs have sunk a well two hundred feet deep, but without reaching water. Lat. 33° 58′, long. 71° 30′.

Jour. As. Soc. 1837, p. 190; Wade, Jour. of a Voyage down the Sutluj. FUTTEGURH.—A town in the north-eastern extremity of Bhawlpoor, about a mile from the left bank of the Ghara river. Lat. 30° 26′, long. 73° 54′. The surrounding country forms a district bearing the same name.

¹ Mil. Op. in Afg. 379. FUTTEHABAD.¹—A small town in the plain of Jelalabad, occupied by the British troops, under Sir Robert Sale, during the advance on Kabool in 1842. The elevation above the sea is ² Hough, 302. 3,098 feet. ² Lat. 34° 21′, long. 70° 13′.

E.I.C. Ms. Doc. FUTTEHPOOR, in Beloochistan, a village in the province of Cutch Gundava, situate on the road from Gundava to Larkhana, five miles south of the former place. Lat. 28° 25′, long. 67° 35′.

E.I.C. Ms. Doc. FUTTEHPOOR.—A town in Sinde, on the great route from Hyderabad to Bukkur, and forty miles south-west of the latter place. It is situate at the northern extremity of an extensive plain, stretching above a hundred miles in a southerly direction, and at the distance of eight or ten miles from the left bank of the Indus. This plain having an elevation of from thirty to sixty feet above the river, and consisting of a hard tenacious marl, generally free from saline efflorescence, is considered by Lord[2] the most salubrious part of Sinde, and consequently the best locality for the cantonment of troops, Futtehpoor is in Lat. 26° 20′ long. 68° 10′. [2] Medical Mem. 67.

FUTTEHPOOR, in the Punjab, a village situate on the left bank of the Indus, thirty-eight miles above the confluence of the Punjnud. Lat. 29° 24′, long. 70° 49′. E.I.C. Ms. Doc.

FUTTEHPORE, in Afghanistan, a halting-place on the route from Kandahar to Ghuznee, and thirty-seven miles south-west of this last place. The country is open, well watered, and fertile, but intersected by numerous water-courses. It is in an elevated tract 7,426 feet above the level of the sea. Lat. 33° 2′, long. 67° 44′. E.I.C. Ms. Doc.; Jour. As. Soc. 1842, p. 60: Grif. Bar. and Ther. Obs. in Afg.

FUTTEYULI JULLAILEE.—A village in Sinde, situate on the right bank of the Poorana, a great offset of the Indus. Lat. 24° 52′, long. 68° 56′. Ms. Survey Map.

FUTTIHPOOR.—A town in the Punjab, on the route from Lahore to Mooltan, and a hundred miles south-west of the former place. It is situate in a fertile and well-cultivated country, on the left bank of the river Ravee. Lat. 30° 50′, long. 73° 2′. E.I.C. Ms. Doc.; Burnes' Bokh. iii. 141.

FUTTIPOOR.—A large village in Sinde, on the right of the route from Sehwan to Larkhana, and seventy miles north of the former place. It is situate on an offset of the Indus, and three miles from the right bank of the main stream of that river, in a level and fertile country. Lat. 27° 16′, long. 68° 15′. E.I.C. Ms. Doc.

FUTTOOLAH KILLA, or PUTTOOLA KILLA, in Afghanistan, is a village with a fort, on the route from the Kojuk Pass to Kandahar, from which town it is distant fifty miles south-east. It is dependent for water upon a canal, by which that important agent to the maintenance of existence and comfort is brought from some hills lying about fifty miles to the north; so that the supply can be easily intercepted. From this cause the British army was subjected to severe suffering when encamped here in April, 1839. The elevation of this place above the sea is 3,918 feet. Lat. 31° 7′, long. 66° 4′. E.I.C. Ms. Doc.; Hough, Narr. of Exp. to Afg. 90; Conolly, Jour. to India, ii. 115.

FUTTY KHAN.—A village in Daman, Afghanistan, situate on an offset of the river Indus, four miles west of the main Walker's Map of Afg.

stream, fifty miles south of Dera Ismael Khan, and seventy miles
north of Dera Ghazee Khan. Lat. 31° 5′, long. 70° 49′.

Walker's Map of   FYZABAD.—A village in Western Afghanistan, situate on
Afg.   the river Hury or Heri Rood, thirty-two miles east of the town of
Herat. Lat. 34° 22′, long. 62° 44′.

G

E.I.C. Ms. Doc.   GAD or GHAR, in Afghanistan, is a fort on the right bank
of the river Turnak, and on the route from Kandahar to Ghuznee,
from which last place it is distant seventy-five miles south-west.
When Kandahar and Kabool were under separate and independent
governments, this place belonged to the former, being just within
the frontier-line dividing the two states. Lat. 32° 40′, long.
67° 34′.

E.I.C. Ms. Map.   GAHAYJA, in Sinde, a village on the route from Shikarpoor
to Larkhana, and fourteen miles south-west of the former town.
It is rather a thriving place, having about five hundred inhabitants.
There is a supply of water from wells. Lat. 27° 47′, long.
68° 30′.

GAHRAH.—See GARRAH.

E.I.C. Ms. Doc.;   GAJEN.—A village of Cutch Gundava, in Beloochistan, is
Masson, Kalat,   situate about eight miles north-west of the town of Gundava.
331.
Lat. 28° 33′, long. 67° 28′.

GAJIN.—See GAZIN.

E.I.C. Ms. Doc.   GANCHA, in Sinde, a village on the route from Kotree to
Schwan, and thirty-nine miles south-east of the latter place. It
is situate a mile from the right bank of the Indus, in a fertile and
well-cultivated tract. Lat. 26° 4′, long. 68° 4′.

Map of N.W.   GANGA.—A village of the Punjab, situate on the right bank
Frontier.   of the Chenaub river, forty miles south-west of Mooltan. Lat·
29° 38′, long. 71° 11′.

E.I.C. Ms. Doc.   GANGREH GOTE, in Sinde, a village on the route from
Kotree to Sehwan. It is situate on the right bank of the Indus,
in a fertile and well-cultivated tract. The road near this place,

though not altogether free from impediments, is in general good. Lat. 25° 44', long. 68° 20'.

GANSYH BUL.—See GUNYSH BUL.

GARDOU.[1]—A halting-place in Afghanistan, situate on the [1] Ms. Survey Map. route from Kandahar, by Babur-ka-Killa, to Dera Ismael Khan, and one hundred miles west of the latter place. This route lies between the Gomul route on the north and the Boree on the south. It has been very little explored, but seems, westward of the Suliman mountains, to join that described by Leech,[2] under the [2] App. 40. name of the Hyob, or Wahwa Pass, from Dera Deen Puna to Kandahar. Lat. 31° 40', long. 69° 29'.

GARRAH.—A village in Sinde, on the north-western border Outram, Rough of the Delta of the Indus, and twenty-five miles from its western Notes, 6. bank. Lat. 24° 44', long. 67° 36'.

GARRAH.—A small stream in Sinde, flowing by the village Pott. Belooch. 345; of the same name, and falling into a long creek opening into Horsburgh, E.I. Dir. I. 492; Mass. the Indian Ocean ten miles east of Kurrachee. The mouth of the Bal. Afg. Panj. I. 469 ; Kennedy, Garrah creek is in lat. 24° 45', long. 67° 10'. As the country Sinde and Kabool, on each side of Garrah is low, both westward, to the mouth of this ii. 214. creek, and also eastward, and the stream communicates with the Indus, it seems probable that a ship-canal might be formed, to connect Kurrachee with the deep and wide part of the Indus, near Tatta. The country between the Garrah river and the port of Kurrachee, it is to be observed, is also low and suitable for the purpose.

GARTOPE, GARDOKH, or GARO.—A village, or rather As. Research. xii. 440-450; Moorcr. pastoral station, in Southern Tibet, close to the border of Ladakh. Jour. to Lake Moorcroft (who, with his companions, are the only Europeans Manasa-rovara; Id. Punj. Bokh. I. known to have visited it) describes the village as consisting of 363, 364. little more than a number of felt tents, with a few houses of un-burnt brick. It is, however, a place of some trade in summer, when the productions of Tibet and China are exchanged for those of Kashmir and Hindostan. Amongst these articles of commerce, tea and shawl-wool are the most important. The place is almost deserted in winter; the elevation, which exceeds 16,000 feet, then rendering the climate too severe for animal life. Its vicinity is the natural and favourite *habitat* of the shawl-goat, and besides, it in summer feeds numerous herds of yaks and kine, and flocks of the hardy Himalayan sheep. Moorcroft states those that he saw here to be not fewer than 40,000, though vast numbers had just perished by an epidemic. The stream which flows by Gartope, and which is called the Eekung Choo, is supposed by Moorcroft to be the principal stream of the nascent Indus, though the truth of this position may be doubted. Gold abounds remarkably in this region, being principally found in a red auriferous earth, but the quantity extracted is inconsiderable. This is owing partly to the scantiness, weakness, and ignorance of the population, and partly to the operation being discouraged by the Chinese authorities, who entertain a dread that the knowledge of such natural wealth would incite foreign aggression. Lat. 31° 40', long. 80° 24'.

[1] E.I.C. Ms. Doc.   GAZAH,[1] in Beloochistan, a halting-place, with a collection of springs from subterraneous aqueducts, on the route from Munzilgah, at the western entrance of the Bolan Pass, to Kelat, and forty miles north of the latter place. The elevation must be very

[2] Jour. As. Soc. 1842, p. 55 ; Grif. Bar. and Ther. Obs. in Afg.
[3] E.I.C. Ms. Doc.

great, as Munzilgah[2] is 5,793 feet above the level of the sea, and Kelat[3] 6,000, and the road between them level. Hence the cold is so severe, that the population, generally of a migratory and pastoral character, descends every autumn, to spend the winter in the level warm plains of Cutch Gundava. Gazah is in lat. 29° 24', long. 66° 35'.

E.I.C. Ms. Doc.   GAZIN.—A village of the province of Jalawan, in Beloochistan, about forty-two miles south of Kelat, and near the western extremity of the Gundava or Moola Pass. Its elevation above the sea is about 5,000 feet, yet neighbouring mountains rise to a great height above it in many directions. Lat. 28° 18', long. 66° 29'.

Jour. As. Soc. 1841, p. 807 ; Grif. Rep. on Subjects connected with Afg.; Hough, Nar. of Exp. to Afg. 333 ; Lord, Koh-i-Damun, 45.

GEEDUR GULLEE.—In Afghanistan, in the province of Peshawur, is a pass between Peshawur and Attock, and has received its name, *the Jackal's Pass*, or *Neck*, from its being so extremely narrow, that the natives, in exaggeration, say that a jackal only can make its way through it. The defile is not more than ten or twelve feet wide, and is bounded on each side by rather high and rugged hills. Though much frequented, it does not appear to be regarded as important in a military point of view, probably from the facility with which it can be turned. It is five miles west of Attock. Lat. 33° 56', long. 72° 10'.

E.I.C. Ms. Doc.   GERAEE REMAN, in Afghanistan, is a village of the Derajat, on the Gomul route from Ghuznee to Dera Ismael Khan, and about eighteen miles westward of the latter place. The road is in this part good, and there is a copious supply of water from a kareez, or subterranean aqueduct. Lat. 31° 48′, long. 70° 34′.

GERAMNEE.—A village in the south-west of Sinde, four or five miles north of the border of the Great Western Rin. Lat. 24° 28′, long. 70° 36′. _{E.I.C. Ms. Survey Map.}

GHAH KIRBEH.—A village in Afghanistan, situate on the road between Kandahar and the province of Seistan, seventy-five miles west of the town of Giriskh. Lat. 31° 42′, long. 63° 6′. _{Walker's Map of Afg.}

GHAIN-I-BALA.—A village in Kafiristan, situate on the Tagoo river, seventy miles north-east of Kabool. Lat. 35° 15′, long. 69° 54′. _{Walker's Map of Afg.}

GHAR.—See Gad.

GHARA, the name by which the united streams of the Beas and Sutluj are known, from their confluence at Endreesa to the confluence with the Chenaub, in lat. 29° 20′, long. 71° 5′. The length of course between these points is about three hundred miles. After the confluence last mentioned, the united streams are called the Punjnud. At the ferry of Hurekee, a short distance below the confluence of the Beas and Sutluj,[1] Burnes found " the Ghara a beautiful stream, never fordable," two hundred and seventy-five yards wide at the lowest season, and twelve feet deep, running at the rate of two miles and a quarter an hour. In the same locality Vigne found it two hundred yards wide.[2] It is remarkably direct in its general course, which is south-west, but tortuous at short intervals. In the lower part of its course, where it forms the boundary, it is a slow muddy stream,[3] with low banks of soft alluvial earth, overflowed to the extent of several miles on occasion of the slightest swell. The confluence with the Chenaub takes place without any turbulence, in a low, marshy track, in which the channels of the rivers are continually changing.[4] Each river is about five hundred yards wide, and the united stream about eight hundred yards. The water of the Chenaub is reddish, that of the Ghara pale, and for several miles downwards the difference of hue may be observed, the right side of the stream being of a red, and the left of a pale hue.

[1] Bokh. i. 5.
[2] Ghuznee, 10.
[3] Lord, Med. Rep. on Indus, 66; Elph. 20.
[4] Burnes, iii. 98, 237.

GHAZEE-ABAD.—A village in Northern Afghanistan, situate on the left bank of the Alishang river. Lat. 35° 18′, long. 70° 19′. _{Walker's Map of Afg.}

GHIZNI.—See Ghuznee.

E.I.C. Ms. Doc.; **GHOJAN,** in Afghanistan, a fort and district on an elevated
Outram, Rough
Notes, 102; part of the valley of the Turnak river, from the right bank of
Hough, Nar. of which the fort is distant about four miles. This valley is watered
Ex. to Afg. 164.
by several clear streams, and is fertile and well cultivated. The
elevation above the sea is 7,068 feet. It is on the route from
Kandahar to Ghuznee; from which last place it is distant eighty
miles south-west. Lat. 32° 42′, long. 67° 23′.

Outram, Rough **GHOLAM-SHAH-KA-KOTE,** in Sinde, a small but thriving
Notes, 17; Ken-
nedy, Sinde and town in the delta, is situate on the right or western bank of the
Kabool, i. 75. Buggaur, or western branch of the Indus, and on the route from
the sea-port of Vikkur to Tatta. The surrounding country is
well cultivated and productive, especially f sugar-cane. Lat. 24°
39′, long. 67° 41′.

Walker's Map of **GHOLAM SHAH.**—A village in Afghanistan, now in ruins.
N.W. Frontier.
Lat. 29° 35′, long. 64° 23′.

E.I.C. Ms. Doc.; **GHONDAN,** in Afghanistan, is a mountain, giving name to
Kennedy, Sinde
and Kabool, ii.135. a district on the route from Shawl to Ghuznee, and about a hundred and twenty miles south of this last place. The country here
is very rugged, and the road presents difficulties which render it
nearly impassable for wheel-carriages. There is a good supply of
water brought to the foot of the mountain by a small canal. Lat.
32°, long. 67° 33′.

E.I.C. Ms. Doc. **GHONDEE JOOMA.**—A village in Afghanistan, on the road
from Ghuznee to Kandahar, about one hundred miles south-west
of the former place, and one hundred and twenty miles north-east,
of the latter. Lat. 32° 22′, long. 67° 13′.

Walker's Map of **GHOORKA.**—A village in the Punjab, forty-five miles south-
N.W. Frontier.
east of Lahore, on the road from Attock to Ferozpoor. Lat. 31°
16′, long. 74° 58′.

GHORABAREE, in Sinde.—See VIKKUR.

¹ E.I.C. Ms. Doc. **GHORA TRUP.**[1]—A village in Afghanistan, situate on the
right bank of the river Indus, eleven miles south-west of Attock,
and thirty south-east of Peshawur. The river here has a very
dangerous rapid, with a sudden fall of a foot and a half, resulting
from the lateral contraction of the high and rocky banks inclosing
² Oxus, 125. it, as the depth is no less than a hundred and eighty-six feet. Wood[2]
describes the passage as very dangerous. "Though the fall was
shot with startling rapidity, the boat, when over, seemed spell-
bound to the spot, and hung for some time under the watery wall
in spite of the most strenuous efforts of her crew. At last she

moved, the men cheered, and out she darted into the fair channel." The breadth of the Indus here, is only two hundred and fifty feet, and through this narrow gut the whole of its immense volume of water rushes at the rate of from nine to ten miles an hour, and with the noise of thunder. Ghora Trup is about six miles below Nilab, and the whole of this distance may be described as one immense and irresistible rapid. Lat. 33° 46', long. 72° 9'.

GHORBUND.[1]—A village in Northern Afghanistan, in a gorge on the southern slope of the Hindoo Koosh. It gives name to the valley of Ghorbund, in which it is situated, and also to the river, which flowing down the valley, falls into the river of Punchshir, on the western side. The valley of Ghorbund is fertile, and extends about fifty miles in a direction from south-west to north-east, between cliffs of slate and quartz, occasionally interrupted by basaltic rocks, amygdaloid, volcanic ashes, sulphate of lime, and other indications of igneous action. It abounds in minerals, and at Ferengal, a mine of very rich lead ore has been worked to a great extent and with remarkable skill. (See FERENGAL.) There are also deposits of lapis-lazuli and veins of silver, of antimony, and especially of iron in the valley of Ghorbund. [2]This valley is mentioned in the Ayeen Akbery, as having an inconceivable variety of fragrant shrubs and flowers, there being thirty sorts of tulips. Mention is also made of mines of silver and lapis-lazuli. The village of Ghorbund, which is surrounded by fine and productive gardens and orchards, is in lat. 35° 4', long. 68° 47'.

The Ghorbund Pass proceeds from Charikar, in the Kohistan, up this valley and debouches into the Pass of Hageguk. About ten miles from its entrance, the Koushan Pass diverges to the north and crosses the Hindoo Koosh into Kunduz.

GHORE,[1] in Western Afghanistan, is a ruinous, ill-peopled town, the capital of a petty province, professedly dependant on Herat, from which last city it is distant a hundred and twenty miles south-east. It is, however, actually independent; the weak governor who represents the Shah of Herat being unable to levy any taxes on the chieftains and people who inhabit forts scattered over the surrounding country, or lie encamped in the neighbourhood of those strong holds. Though now so insignificant, Ghore was at one time the capital of sovereigns whose power extended over Khorasan, Afghanistan, Sinde, and Lahore. In the year 1010,[2] it was subdued by the celebrated Mahmood of Ghuznee, but forty-

[1] Lord, Koh-i-Damun, 53; Baber, Mem. 445; Wood, Oxus, 186-187; Burnes' Pers. Narr. 153.

[2] ii. 183.

[1] E.I.C. Ms. Doc.; Conolly, Jour. to India, ii. 70.

[2] Price, Mahometan Hist. ii. 286, 309-316, 453-456;

Malcolm, Hist. of one years afterwards the Prince of Ghore revolted, and, taking
Persia, I. 344-346. Ghuznee, carried the principal inhabitants to Ghore, where he
caused their throats to be cut, and used their blood in the preparation of mortar for repairing the fortifications. In 1186 Mahmood, sultan of Ghore, made himself master of Lahore. He left
no successor, and his dominions were seized by his slaves. The
Ghorian sovereignty then disappears from history, and the relics
of its dominion were finally swept away by the Tartar hordes of
³ Acc. of Caubul, Zingis Khan and his successors. Elphinstone³ supposes Ghore
152, 153. to have been one of the earliest seats of the Afghan race, and to
have been, in the ninth century, subject to an Arabian sovereign.
Ghore is situate in lat. 32° 58′, long. 63° 21′.

E.I.C. Ms. Doc.   GHORO TROP.—See GHORA TRUP.

GHOSGURH, or ROOKHUNPOOR, in Bhawlpoor, is situate
in the Great Desert, on the road from the city of Bhawlpoor to
Jessulmair. It is eighty-four miles south of Bhawlpoor. Lat.
28° 24′, long. 72° 4′.

Map of N.W.   GHOSPOOR.—A village in Bhawlpoor, eight miles south-
Frontier. east from the river Indus, and eighteen miles north from Khanpoor, from whence there is a road. Lat. 28° 51′, long. 70° 36′.

GHULGHULEH.—See GULGULA.

Walker's Map of   GHUNYMUT HUZARUH.—A village in Afghanistan, two
Afg. miles north of the Moorghab river. Lat. 34° 59′, long. 65° 12′.

Ms. Survey Map.   GHURRUK.—A village of the province of Kelat, in Beloochistan, on the road from the town of Kelat to Nooshky, and
eighteen miles distant from the former place. Lat. 29° 6′, long.
66° 21′.

E.I.C. Ms. Doc.   GHURRY, in Sinde, a village on the route from Roree to
Jessulmair, and sixteen miles south-east of the former place.
It is situate on the northern boundary of the Thurr or Great Sandy
Desert, and about three miles east of the left bank of the Eastern
Narra, a great offset of the Indus. This stream in time of inundation is here fifty yards wide and twenty feet deep, but it becomes
nearly dry at other times. Ghurry is a considerable village with
about a dozen shops, and is capable of furnishing supplies in
moderate quantity. Lat. 27° 31′, long. 69° 7′

E.I.C. Ms. Doc.   GHUZAMURIDEE.—A village in Afghanistan, situate on
the road from Ghuznee to Dera Ismael Khan, about two miles
from the right bank of the Gomul river. Lat. 32° 22′, long.
68° 58′.

GHUZNEE.[1]—An ancient and celebrated town and fortress of Afghanistan, situate on the western extremity[2] of a range of hills running east and west and rising a moderate height above the plain.[3] As the plain itself lies very high, the site has an elevation of 7,726 feet above the sea.[4] The shape of the whole inclosed fortress is nearly an irregular square, the angles of which stand in the direction of the four cardinal points,[5] and the total circuit is about a mile and a quarter. The face of the rock on which the walls are built is about thirty-five feet high, and scarped nearly perpendicularly; the walls themselves are about the same height, so that the parapet is seventy feet above the ditch.[6] This wall is flanked by numerous towers, and surrounded by a *fausse braye.* A wet ditch runs along the bottom of the steep on which the wall is built, but for about a furlong on the north-eastern side from the northern angle this defence is wanting. The ditch is supplied with water from the river of Ghuznee, which flows round the western angle, and is crossed by two bridges. The citadel, in the north of the town, is an irregular square, having a magazine in the west quarter and a granary in the east. Under the rule of Dost Mahomed Khan, it was occupied as the palace of the governor, one of his sons. Though much higher than the town, and from this cause presenting a formidable appearance, it is commanded by neighbouring hills, from which shot and shells could be showered down on it with great effect.[7] There are three gates the Khenak, at the bridge-head over the river, at the western angle; the Kandahar gate in the south-eastern side; the Kabool in the north-eastern. The two former had been walled up previously to the arrival of the British army; the Kabool gate was left unobstructed, in the expectation of reinforcements from that quarter. The river was at one time dammed up by a mound eighty feet high and six hundred feet long, made by the Gaznevide Sultans, to collect water for irrigation and other purposes; but when Allahudeen, the Prince of Ghore, stormed and destroyed Ghuznee, he also destroyed this useful work.[8]

The present population of Ghuznee has been variously estimated. By some it has been computed at not more than 3,000,[9] exclusive of the garrison. By others it has been thought probable that in ordinary times the population amounts to 10,000.[1] The bazaars are extensive, and the town is repre-

[1] E.I.C. Ms. Doc.;
Ead. Ms. Map.
[2] Hough, Jour.
Exp. to Afg. 227.
[3] Forster, Jour.
Beng. Eng. ii. 110.
[4] Jour. As. Soc.
1842, p. 62; Grif.
Bar. and Ther.
Obs. in Afgh.
[5] Plan of Fortress
in Outram, Rough
Notes, 113.

[6] Lord Keane, in
Despatch in App.
to Kennedy, Sinde
and Kabool, ii.
249; Thomson
and Peat, ibid.
266.

[7] Havelock, War
in Afg. ii. 70;
Allen, March
through Sinde and
Afg. 266; Mil.
Op. in Afg. 392.

[8] Baber, Mem.
149; Elph. Acc.
of Caubul, 433.

[9] Hough, ut supra, 227.

[1] E.I.C. Ms. Doc.

o 2

sented as an *entrepôt* for merchandize between the Punjab, the
Indus, and Kabool. There are many villages and much cultivation in the neighbourhood. Ghuznee was one of the stages of
the Dawk, or mounted post, during the reign of the Mogul kings.
It is thirteen miles and a quarter from the ruined Chupar-
kana of the Dawk, near Ranee ; the road from thence is for the
first six miles moderately good. In that distance it crosses one or
two dry nullahs and five running streams. Afterwards it becomes
sandy, and a broad river-bed is crossed. At seven miles and a
quarter from Ranee, a deep narrow water-course is passed, and
thenceforward the road to Ghuznee is good.

In consequence of the elevation of the site, the cold is intense in
winter, causing the mercury to fall from 10° to 20° below zero, and
freezing the streams and pools to the depth of several feet.[2] There
are accounts of the population having been several times destroyed
by snow-storms.[3] Three miles to the north-east of Ghuznee are
the ruins of the old city, destroyed in the middle of the twelfth
century by the Prince of Ghore.[4] Amidst the destruction which
overtook nearly all beside, the conqueror spared the tomb of the
renowned Mahmood of Ghuznee, the ruler of Persia, Turkestan,
Afghanistan, and a considerable part of India. The tomb is a
rude and humble structure, consisting of an oblong chamber,
thirty-six feet long and eighteen wide, with a mud cupola. The
grave-stone is of marble, covered with inscriptions and highly
polished, the result of being handled by numerous visitors during
several centuries. The interior is hung with ostrich eggs, pea-
cock feathers, and other trumpery. The apartment in which repose
the relics of the " mighty victor, mighty lord," was, previously
to the British invasion, closed by the gates which it is believed he
triumphantly removed from the temple of Somnauth, in Guzerat.
These gates, to which a rather disproportionate importance has
been attributed by Christian, Hindoo, and Mussulman, are of
sandal-wood, eighteen feet high, each five feet broad and three
inches thick, very beautifully carved in tasteful arabesques As
Mahmood is said to have removed these gates in 1024, they
must, in this view, be above eight hundred years old, yet
they are still in perfect preservation. In 1842, when the
British, under General Nott, dismantled Ghuznee,* they car-

[2] Crawford in App.
to Eyre, Mil. Op.
at Kabool, 400.

[3] Elph. Acc. of
Caubul, 137.

[4] D'Herbelot,
Bibl. Orientale,
iii. 216 ; Price,
Mahom. Hist. ii.
312 ; Feruhta, l.
167 ; Malcolm,
Hist. of Pers. i.
345.

---

* It has been doubted whether these gates were those of the Temple of Somnath at Pattan, in Guzerat, and the doubt has probably arisen from the absence

ried off these gates, with the view of restoring them to their original place in the temple at Pattan, in Guzerat. The mace,[5] asserted to be that of "the destroyer," the name under which Mahmood is familiarly designated in Oriental history and tra-

[5] Atkinson. Exp. to Afg. 222; Masson, Bal. Afg. Panj. ii. 220.

of any mention of the circumstance in Ferishta,[1] in the Rozet as Sefa,[2] and in several other works. These authorities, while they recount the well-known story of the idol which Mahmood broke with his mace, and which, thereupon (according to the current tradition), was found to contain vast treasure, make no reference to the gates. In this silence they are followed by the Ayeen Akbery,[3] D'Herbelot,[4] Price,[5] Malcolm,[6] Gibbon,[7] and Wilson.[8] There is certainly a deficiency of written evidence on the side of those who maintain that these gates were once those of the Temple of Somnath; but, on the other hand, the voice of tradition is very loud and general in their favour. Elphin-stone,[9] who has drawn so large an amount of information from oral state-ments of the natives, having described the tomb of Mahmood, adds,—"The doors, which are very large, are of sandal-wood, and are said to have been brought by the sultaun as a trophy from the famous Temple of Somnaut, in Guzerat, which he sacked in his last expedition to India." To the same effect are the statements of Wood,[1] Hough,[2] Havelock,[3] Kennedy,[4] Atkinson,[5] and Masson.[6] The Governor-General, Lord Ellenborough, who, it is to be presumed, would be careful to proceed upon accurate information in a matter concerning which the government was about to be committed, writes thus to General Nott: "You will bring away from the tomb of Mahmood of Ghuznee his club, which hangs over it, and you will bring away the gates of his tomb, which are the gates of the Temple of Somnaut."[7] Allen,[8] mentioning their removal, gives the following vivid description of the affliction and humiliation of the Afghans at their loss: "This morning the sandal-wood gates were taken from the tomb of Mahmood of Ghuznee and brought into camp, previous to their being removed to Hindostan. Upon the possession of these gates the people greatly prided themselves, and the numerous fakeers attending at the tomb wept at their removal, as they accounted them their most valuable trea-sure." Burnes,[9] writing in 1832, several years before any intention of in-vading Afghanistan was entertained, thus refers to the position ascribed to these gates by the prevailing belief: "It is worthy of remark, that the ruler of the Punjab, in a negotiation which he lately carried on with the ex-king of Cabool, Shooja-ool-Moolk, stipulated as one of the conditions of his restora-tion to the throne of his ancestors, that he should deliver up the sandal-wood gates at the shrine of the Emperor Mahmood, being the same which were brought from Somnath, in India, when that destroyer smote the idol, and the precious stones fell from his body. Upwards of eight hundred years have elapsed since the spoliation, but the Hindoo still remembers it, though these doors have so long adorned the tomb of the Sultan Mahmood."

With reference to the controversy that has arisen, as well as for the pur-pose of presenting a minute description of the gates in their present state, the subjoined report of a committee of engineer and artillery officers, assembled by order of General Nott, may possess some interest. It also affords informa-tion, completing the account given in the text of Mahmood's tomb.

[1] Ferishta, i. 73.
[2] As quoted by Kittoe, in Note, Jour. As. Soc. 1838, p. 883.
[3] ii. 88.
[4] Bibl. Orientale, iii. 520.
[5] Mahommedan Hist. ii. 290.
[6] Hist. of Pers. i. 334, 335.
[7] Decline and Fall.
[8] On Religious Sects of the Hin-doos, As. Re-searches, xvii.195.
[9] Acc. of Caubul, 432.
[1] Oxus, 5.
[2] Narr. of Exp. in Afg. 228.
[3] War in Afg. ii. 94.
[4] Sinde and Ka-bool, ii. 61.
[5] Exp. into Afg. ii. 220.
[6] Bal. Afg. Panj.
[7] Letter of Gov.-Gen. in Mil. Op. in Afg. 328.
[8] Ut supra, 277.
[9] Bokhara, i. 175.

dition, has been usually exhibited by the priest who officiates at his tomb, and it is, as might be expected of one assigned to the use of so mighty a hero, too ponderous to be wielded by

"Camp, near Peshawur, 8th November, 1842.

" Considering the great age of these gates, the probable injury sustained by them in their displacement from the temple of Somnath and transport to Ghuznee, the circumstance of their having been taken down and buried during the invasion of Afghanistan by Chenghiz Khan, to preserve them from destruction by the troops of that conqueror, and their subsequent disinterment and re-erection, they must be deemed in good preservation. Great care has been observed in their packing and carriage since their removal from the tomb of Mahmood at Ghuznee, and they do not appear to have sustained any material damage from their transport thus far on their return to India.

" The tomb of Mahmood of Ghuznee has been for ages a place of pilgrimage, almost of adoration, to Mahomedans, and the gates objects of especial attention ; it is not, therefore, matter of surprise that the lower portions of the gates, within the reach of a man's hand, have suffered greatly ; the carved work has in some places disappeared, small portions having, probably, from time to time, been abstracted as relics. Here and there, pieces of carved wood, perhaps of the same antiquity as the gates brought with them from Somnath, dissimilar in pattern, have been used to replace the original carving, and in other places inferior material and workmanship have been employed to repair the fabric. But the upper portions of the gates still retain much of the original carving, which is in high relief, of beautiful execution, and in a wonderful state of preservation.

" The gates appear to have been formerly decorated with plates of some precious metal, fixed to the wood-work round the carved compartments by small slips of iron. Many of these slips still remain, in regular patterns, over the top of the gates ; lower down they have altogether disappeared.

" The frames of the gates are in double folds, hinged in the centre ; their height is eleven feet, and their aggregate width nine and a half feet.

" The gates are surrounded by a framing, composed of small pieces of carved wood, united by numerous joints in regular pattern. This portion of the work, though of great age, seems of more modern and slighter manufacture than the gates themselves. The exterior dimensions of their framing (now in four separate portions) are sixteen and a half feet in height, and thirteen and a half in width. The framing is in very fair preservation, excepting near the ground, where seats seem to have existed on either side the gateway, and the portions of the framing in this position, to the height of a man's shoulders, have been fairly rubbed away. The construction of either framing, and the numerous joints of the work, render it peculiarly liable to damage from travelling over rough roads, or from frequent removal.

" We are of opinion that it will not be difficult to restore all essential portions of the gates that are now wanting, and to fix them in serviceable condition in any building destined to their reception ; but some judgment would be required to make any repair or restoration harmonize with the air of extreme antiquity possessed by the original portions of the gates.

any of the present race of men. Previously to the capture of the place by the British, it had been removed, that it might not fall into their hands. The building is environed with luxuriant gar-

" In consonance with the Major-General's request, we have the honour to forward herewith sketches of the gates, with the dimensions accurately entered on the face of the drawing.

" The Major-General having desired the committee to state their opinion as to the expediency of conveying the gates in a frame adapted to elephant-carriage, we beg to state our apprehension that such a mode of conveyance might be productive of serious injury to them. The wood is extremely dry and brittle, and the greatest care is requisite to guard against the more delicate portions of the work being even touched. The gates are not heavy—they do not probably exceed 500 lbs. in weight—and we estimate the entire weight of the gates and framing at less than half a ton ; but their surface is great compared with the scantling of the frame-work ; and the swaying motion of the elephant, and the necessity that would exist for daily loading and unloading the animal, could scarcely fail to open the joints and dislodge the frailer portions of the work, however carefully secured.

" We would, therefore, respectfully suggest that a car, with a double framing, between which the gates should be placed, and to which they should be secured by wedges well padded, measures being taken to prevent the entire weight of the gates falling on any portion of their own frame-work, might be expediently prepared at Ferozepore to receive them, such car being adapted to elephant-draft. But the gates alone should, we think, be thus carried, the framing being transported to its destination, packed as (with the gates) it is at present, in felts and tarpaulins. In any case, we would recommend that, on their arrival at Ferozepore, both gates and framing should be carefully examined, and some strengthening, by ties and braces, given to the slighter portions, to guard, as far as possible, against the chance of small pieces becoming dislodged, and perhaps lost on the road.

" In examining, on this occasion, the framing surrounding the gates, the committee observed a Cufic inscription carved in the wood, with a copy and translation of which, appended to our report, we have been furnished by Major Rawlinson. We think that it will give an interest to this document if we attach to it a translation of the inscription on Mahmood's tomb, with which we have been favoured by the same distinguished Orientalist. Lieut. Studdart has also enabled us to annex a drawing of the sarcophagus, with an exact copy of the Cufic inscription thereon."

(Signed)   Edw. Sanders, Major, Eng., and President.
C. Blood, Capt., Bombay Art., and Member.
John Studdart, Lieut., Bombay Eng., and Member.
C. F. North, Lieut., Bombay Eng., and Member.

Translation of an Arabic Inscription on the Gates of Somnath.

" In the name of the most merciful God ! (May there be) forgiveness from God for the most noble Ameer, the great King, (he who was) born to become the lord of the state and the lord of religion, Abul Kasim Mahmúd, the son

dens and orchards, watered by an aqueduct discharging an abundant supply of fine water; and this delightful suburb is hence denominated Roza, or the garden.

The ruins of the old city consist of a vast extent of shapeless mounds. The only remains of its former splendour are two minarets, four hundred yards apart, which are said to mark the limits. of the bazaar of the ancient city. They are of brick, above a

of Subaktagin! May the mercy of God be upon him! [the remaining phrase illegible.]"

Translation of the Inscription in Cufic Characters on the Sarcophagus of the Tomb of the Sultan Mahmúd at Ghuznee.

" May there be forgiveness from God upon him, who is the great lord, the noble Nizam-ud-din Abul Kasim Mahmúd, the son of Subaktagin! May God have mercy upon him!"

Mem.—On the reverse of the sarcophagus there is an inscription, in the Neskh character, recording the date of the decease of Sultan Mahmúd as Thursday, the 7th remaining day (*i. e.* the 22nd or 23rd) of the month of Rabi Akhir, A. H. 421.

Translation of the Cufic Inscription, in the Suls character, on the Minaret nearest the village of Rozah.

" In the name of God the most merciful!

"The high and mighty Sultan, the melic of Islam, the right arm of the state, trustee of the faith, the victory-crowned, the patron of Moslems, the aid of the destitute, the munificence-endowed Mahmúd (may God glorify his testimony!), son of Subaktagin, the champion of champions, the emir of Moslems, ordered the construction of this lofty of loftiest of monuments: and of a certainty it has been happily and prosperously completed."

Translation of the Cufic Inscription, in the Suls character, on the Minaret nearest the town of Ghuznee.

" In the name of God the most merciful!

" (Erected.) By order of the mighty Sultan, the melic of Islam, the standard of dominion and wealth, the august Maso'od, son of the supporter of the state, Mahmúd, father of Ibraheem, defender of the faith, emir of Moslems, the right arm of dominion, the trustee of the faith, the master of the necks of the nations, the noble and imperial Sultan, lord of the countries of Arabia and Persia. May the great God perpetuate his throne and kingdom! Commemorated be his beneficence! May God forgive the sins of himself, his parents, and of all Moslems!"

Somnath, or *Somanath*,[1] was a name of Siva. The temple is still in such a state of preservation as to shew that it was skilfully constructed in a massive and imposing style of architecture, but it is utterly neglected and filthy. Full and excellent accounts of its present condition are given by Postans,[2] Kittoe,[2] and Burnes.[3]

[1] Wilson, in As. Researches, xvii. 195.
[2] Jour. As. Soc. 1838, p. 805, 888, Notes on a Jour. to Glrnar.
[3] Jour. of As. Soc. 1838, p. 104, 107, Acc. of the Temple at Pattan Somnath.

hundred feet high and twelve in diameter; and their proportions and style of architecture give them an interest for the eye equal to that afforded by their antiquity and historical associations to the imagination. One of them has a winding staircase within, and inclines considerably over its base. That buildings so easily demolished should have been spared in the destruction of the old city by the Prince of Ghore, may perhaps have resulted from some religious feeling with which they were associated.

Probably the earliest authentic notice which history affords of Ghuznee is of the date 976, when it was made the seat of government by Abustakeen, an adventurer of Bokhara. He was, after a short interval, succeeded by Subuctageen, the father of the renowned Mahmood the *destroyer*. Few pursued the career of conquest with more perseverance or success than Mahmood, whose empire extended from the Tigris to the Ganges, and from the Indian Ocean to the Oxus. It fell to pieces on his death; and in 1151, his capital, Ghuznee, was stormed by Allahudeen, Prince of Ghour, who massacred the inhabitants on the spot, with the exception of those of rank, whom he conveyed to Ghore, and there butchered them, using their blood to moisten the mortar with which he constructed fortifications. From that period Ghuznee ceased to be independent, and at the time of the British invasion, was held by a garrison of 3,000 men, under the command of Mahomed Hyder Khan, son of Dost Mahomed Khan. On the 23rd of July, 1839, it was stormed by the British army, commanded by Sir John Keane, amounting to 4,863 men; 514 of the garrison were killed, 1,500 prisoners taken, with a loss on the part of the captors of only seventeen killed. In place of the tedious process of breaching, for which the assailants were but ill-prepared, Captain Thomson, of the Bengal Engineers, undertook to blow in one of the gates with gunpowder. This was effected in a most masterly and effective manner, and an opening thus made for the entrance of the storming party, who, after a severe struggle within the town, succeeded in planting the British colours on the citadel. In 1842, Ghuznee was surrendered by the British garrison to the Afghans; and shortly after, in the same year, retaken by the army under General Nott, by whom it was dismantled, and immediately evacuated. Lat. 33° 34′, long. 68° 18′.

GHUZNEE, River of, in Afghanistan, rises in the Huzareh

E.I.C. Ms. Doc.; End. Map; Outram, Rough Notes, 149.

mountains about lat. 33° 50′, long. 68° 20′. It takes a course, generally southerly, to the town of Ghuznee, and flows along the western base of its rampart. Thence it continues a generally southerly course, as far as lat. 33°, from which the direction changes to south-west, and, after running in its entire length about sixty miles, the river falls into Lake Ab-Istada at its northern extremity, in lat. 32° 42′, long. 68° 3′.

E.I.C. Ms. Doc.

GIDRAWALA.—A village in Bhawlpoor, on the route from Khanpoor to Subzulcote, and twelve miles north-east of the latter place. It is situate fourteen miles from the left bank of the Indus, in an alluvial tract extensively flooded during inundation. Lat. 28° 17′, long. 69° 52′.

Walker's Map of N.W. Frontier.

GIDURI KE PATUN.—A village in the Punjab, situate on the River Ravee, forty miles north-east of Amritsir. Lat. 32° 10′, long. 75° 8′.

Vigne, Kashmir, ii. 292-310; Jour. As. Soc. 1839, p. 313; Court, Expl. of Alexander; Burnes' Bokh. ii. 210.

GILGHIT.—A small unexplored and independent country on the southern declivity of Hindoo Koosh; lying between Bultistan, or Little Tibet, on the east, and Chitral on the west. It consists principally of one large valley, down which the stream called the river of Gilghit flows, and falls into the Indus on the right or north-western bank in lat. 35° 28′, long. 74° 28′. The inhabitants of this country appear to be Mahometans of the Shia persuasion, recently converted from idolatry of the same kind as that followed by their neighbours of Kafiristan, whom they still resemble in their social habits, and more especially in their great fondness for potent home-made wine. Their country is very rugged. The mountainous parts are barren; the lower, though sandy, are rendered productive by irrigation and industrious culture. There is also a village of the same name on the right bank of the stream, in lat. 35° 35′, long. 74° 15′.

E.I.C. Ms. Doc.

GIRDEE.—A village in Afghanistan, situate on the Kabool river, three miles south-west from Lalpoor, and near the entrance to the Khyber Pass, on the route from Peshawur to Kabool. Lat. 34° 15′, long. 71° 5′.

E.I.C. Ms. Doc.; Forster, Jour. Beng. Eng. ii. 121; Conolly, (A.), Jour. to India, ii. 87; Hough, Narr. Exp. to Afg. 107, 119; Elph. Acc. of Caubul, 393; Journ. As. Soc. 1840, p. 712:

GIRISHK.—A fort and village in Western Afghanistan, on the high road from Kandahar to Herat, nearly twenty-four miles from Khak-i-Chapan, the road from which is generally good. The march from that place, however, is inconveniently long, and might be shortened by resting at a halting-place about half-way, were there a certainty of procuring water. But this is not to be depended on, as, though there is a well, the supply is scanty. A garden with an artificial water-course lies a little beyond this spot, but the whole is in a state of decay. It is said that it would not be a work of much labour to re-open the water-course, and thus secure that which alone is wanting to render practicable the division of the march. When a British force passed by this route in 1839, a line of a hundred laden camels performed the march in nine hours. Conolly, (E.), Sketch of the Physical Geography of Seistan.

Girishk is situate on the Helmund, here a deep and rapid river in the spring, and when at the highest, a thousand yards wide; but in autumn, when lowest, easily fordable, and not more than three hundred and fifty yards wide. The British detachment, which occupied it in 1839, passed the river on rafts made of empty casks. The country immediately adjacent to the river is very fertile, but its productive resources are to a great extent unimproved, in consequence of the oppression of the government. At a short distance from the river cultivation entirely ceases, and a harsh gravelly bank, with an almost desert plain above, extends several miles to the northward. Forage, however, is procurable, both for camels and horses, excellent in quality, and abundant in quantity, but the place was found so unhealthy by the British, that its early evacuation became necessary. The fort, which is not of great strength, is built upon a mound about two miles from the right bank of the river. The village is wretched, consisting only of a few mud huts. Lat. 31° 46′, long. 64° 18′.

GIRONEE, in Beloochistan. A collection of villages on the route from Moostung to Kelat, and twelve miles north of the latter place. It is situate in a pleasant but very elevated plain, The water is remarkably fine and abundant, and the road is good. The population consists of about two hundred Brehooes, but these, for the most part, emigrate in winter to Cutch Gundava. Lat. 29° 5′, long. 66° 25′. E.I.C. Ms. Doc.; Masson, Kelat, 319.

GISRY, in Sinde, is a creek of the sea, receiving a small torrent flowing from the southern part of that mountain range called, farther north, the Keertar and Lukkee hills. It falls into the sea by three channels, between the Garrah creek and Kurrachee harbour, and four miles east of the entrance of this last. An army not possessed of Kurrachee would find this the best position for landing a force in Sinde. Lat. 24° 48′, long. 67° 8′. Burnes' Bokh. iii. 240.

GOBERUNCE.—A village in Afghanistan, situate on a Walker's Map of N.W. Frontier.

stream tributary to the Helmund river, forty miles north of Giriskh. Lat. 32° 21', long. 64° 16'.

Walker's Map of Afg. **GODA.**—A village in Afghanistan, fifty miles south-west of Kabool. Lat. 34° 5', long. 68° 18'.

E.I.C. Ms. Doc. **GOHAR TULAO,** in Sinde; a tank on the summit of a strong pass on the route from Kurrachee to Sehwan, and thirty-four miles north-east of the former place. The importance of the place results merely from its having a supply of water. In other respects it offers nothing to the traveller, the country around having a rugged surface of bare rock, and yielding neither forage nor provisions. Lat. 25° 5', long. 67° 30'.

E.I.C. Ms. Doc. **GOINDWAL.**—A village in the Punjab, situate on the road from Lahore to Loodiana, on the right bank of the Beas river, fifty-two miles south-east of Lahore. Lat. 31° 21', long. 75° 4'.

E.I.C. Ms. Doc. **GOL.**—A village in Bulti, or Bultistan, eighteen miles east of the town of Iskardoh. Lat. 35° 10', long. 75° 46'.

E.I.C. Ms. Doc. **GOLAKEE.**—A village in South-eastern Afghanistan, on the road from Dadur, by way of Tull, to Dera Ghazee Khan, and twenty-eight miles south-west of Tull. Lat. 29° 54', long. 68° 42'.

E.I.C. Ms. Doc. **GOMA GHONDU.**—A village in the Shighur Valley of Little Tibet. Lat. 35° 30', long. 75° 24'.

E.I.C. Ms. Doc.;
Leech, App. 42;
Vigne, Ghuznee, **GOMUL.**—A river or rather a prolonged torrent, rising in the eastern part of Afghanistan, and making its way through the
88; Elph. Acc. of Suliman range of mountains towards the Indus. After a course
Caubul, 115. of about a hundred and sixty miles, it is lost in the sands to the east of the Suliman range. Its bed for a great distance forms the Goolairee Pass, or great middle route from Hindostan to Khorasan, by Dera Ismael Khan and Ghuznee, the northern being through the Khyber Pass, and the southern through the Bolan. It crosses the Suliman range about lat. 32°.

E.I.C. Ms. Doc. **GOMUL.**—A village in Afghanistan, on the road from Ghuznee to Dera Ismael Khan, and forty miles west of the latter place. It is situate near the eastern entrance of the pass of Gomul, and on the river or torrent of the same name. Lat. 31° 59', long. 70° 12'.

GOMUL PASS.—See Goolairee.

GONNE, or **GOONEE RIVER.**—See Fulailee River.

Ms. Map of Sinde. **GOOBLA.**—A village in Sinde, situate on an offset of the Indus, and two miles from the right bank of the main channel. Lat. 28° 17', long. 69° 22'.

GOODAKE.—A village in the Punjab, on the right bank of the Ghara river. Lat. 30° 21', long. 73° 29'. Walker's Map of N.W. Frontier.

GOODEOOBUSHD.—A village in Afghanistan, situate on the northern route from Ghuznee to Dera Ismael Khan, sixty-eight miles south-east of the former place. Lat. 32° 57', long. 69° 10'. E.I.C. Ms. Doc.

GOOGOO.—A village in the province of Cutch Gundava, in Beloochistan, situate on the route from Shahpoor to Lehree, and eight miles north-west of the latter place. Lat. 28° 47', long. 68° 34'. Ms. Survey Map.

GOOGROE BHEERUN LUK, in Beloochistan, an inlet on the sea-coast of the province of Lus. It was visited by Hart in his journey from Kurrachee to Hinglaj, and is mentioned by him under the name of Ghooroo Bherund. Lat. 25° 24', long. 65° 56'. E.I.C. Ms. Doc. Journ. As, Soc. 1840, p. 143.

GOOJAH,[1] in Sinde, a town on the route from Kurrachee. to Tatta, and ten miles west of the latter town. Masson[2] describes it as " a small bazaar town, with pools or deposits of rain-water." It is situate close to the head of the Kulairee, which communicates with the Indus above Tatta. Situate only eight miles east of Garrah, and on a navigable creek debouching into the Indian Ocean close to Kurrachee, it is believed that an inland navigation might easily and advantageously be effected here between that sea-port and the main channel of the Indus, the intervening ground being low and level. Lat. 24° 45', long. 67° 48'. [1] Pott. 246.

[2] Bal. Afg. Panj. i. 400; De La Hoste, in Jour. As. Soc. 1841, p. 908.

GOOJERANWALA.—See GUJURU WALLA.

GOOJERAT.—See GUJERAT.

GOOLAB SEAH, in Sinde, a small village on the route from Larkhana to Kyra ka Ghurree, and twenty-seven miles north of the former place. It is situate on the southern boundary of the Pat or desert of Shikarpoor, a waste producing only a few stunted bushes. It is a wretched village, scantily supplied with brackish water. Lat. 27° 54', long. 68° 8'. E.I.C. Ms. Doc.

GOOLAIREE.[1]—An important pass across the Suliman range, from the Derajat into Kabool. It holds its course along the channel of the Gomul river, or (in the words of Burnes) " leads by broken rugged roads, or rather the water-courses of the Gomul, through the wild and mountainous country of the Muzarees." It is a pass of great importance, being the [1] Burnes, Trade of the Derajat, 98 ; Leech, App. 42 ; Vigne, Ghuznee, 88.

middle route from Hindostan to Afghanistan, as the Khyber is
the northern, and the Bolan the southern. Immense caravans,
consisting principally of Lohani Afghans,[2] every spring traverse it
westward from the Indus and the adjacent countries, and, returning
in autumn, winter in the Derajat. The Goolairee Pass enters the
Suliman mountains at their eastern base in lat. 32°, long. 70° 30'.
Its course is very winding : for about twenty miles from its entrance into the mountains the direction of the road is north-west ;
then for about eighty miles it proceeds in a south-west direction,
though with numerous deviations at short intervals : it then turns
to the north-west, in which direction generally it holds a sinuous
course to Ghuznee. It is much infested by freebooters of the
Vaziri Afghan tribe, and the caravans have often to fight their
way with much loss of life and property.

GOOLAM ALI.—A village in Sinde, situate on the Poorana
river, a great offset of the Indus, and forty-two miles south-east
of Hyderabad. Lat. 24° 56', long. 68° 50'.

GOOLAM HOOSEINGOLA.—A village in the Punjab, on
the route from Mooltan to Roree, situate on the left bank of the
river Chenaub, a few miles from its confluence with the Ghara
river. Lat. 29° 26', long. 71° 7'.

GOOLAM HUSSAIN SEIR KA GOTE.—A small village
of Sinde, on the route from Tatta to Kotree, and five miles north
of the former place. It is a wretched place, said to be deficient
of water, and incapable of yielding even the slightest and most
ordinary supplies. Lat. 24° 48', long. 68° 2'.

GOOLAM JA GOTE.—A village in Sinde, on the route
from Bukkur to the south-eastern frontier, and thirteen miles
north-west of Omercote. Lat. 25° 26', long. 69° 37'.

GOOLAUB SHEE.—See Goolab Seah.

GOOLISTAN.—A village in Afghanistan, twenty-two miles
south-west of Ghuznee. Lat. 33° 20', long. 67° 56'.

GOOLJATOOE, in Afghanistan, a village on the route from
Kabool to Bamian, and seventy miles west of the former place.
It is situate on a feeder of the Helmund, and near the eastern
base of the Hajejuk ridge. Elevation above the sea 10,500 feet.
Lat. 34° 31', long. 68° 5'.

GOOLKOO, in Afghanistan, a range of mountains thirty
miles south-west of Ghuznee, and bounding on the west the basin
drained by the river of Ghuznee. These mountains are covered

Marginal notes (left column):

[2] Jour. As. Soc. 1834, p. 175-178, Honiberger, Jour. of Route from Dera Ghazi Khan to Kabool.

Ms. Survey Map.

E.I.C. Ms. Doc.

E.I.C. Ms. Doc.

E.I.C. Ms. Doc.

Walker's Map of Afg.

E.I.C. Ms. Doc.; Wood, Oxus, 202.

E.I.C. Ms. Doc.; Outram, Rough Notes, 104.

with snow throughout the year, and their altitude above the sea was estimated by the British engineers to exceed 13,000 feet. Lat. 33° 22′, long. 67° 50′.

GOOLKUTS.—A village in Afghanistan, situate on the Walker's Map of Gomul river and in the Gomul Pass. Lat. 31° 58′, long. 69° 22′. Afg.

GOOL MAHON.—A village in Sinde, situate about eight Ms. Survey Map. miles from the left bank of the river Indus, eight miles west of the river Goonee, and thirteen miles south of Hyderabad. Lat. 25° 12′, long. 68° 25′.

GOOMERAN.—A village in Afghanistan, situate on the E.I.C. Ms. Doc. river of Logurh, and nineteen miles south of the town of Kabool. Lat. 34° 15′, long. 69° 4′.

GOONDEE AZIM KHAN, in Afghanistan, a town of the E.I.C. Ms. Doc. Derajat, on the route from Ghuznee to Dera Ismael Khan, from which last place it is distant, west, about twelve miles. The road in this part is good, and there is water obtained from a kareez, or subterraneous aqueduct. Lat. 31° 50′, long. 70° 44′.

GOONEE RIVER.—See FULAILEE.

GOONGREE.—A village in the south-cast of Sinde. Lat. Walker's Map of 24° 44′, long. 71° 4′. N.W., Frontier.

GOONGROO RIVER.—See PINYAREE.

GOORAB SING is a rock about half a mile from the coast, E.I.C. Ms. Doc. in Beloochistan, in lat. 25° 14′, long. 65° 36′.

GOORBAN, in Sinde, a village on the route from Sehwan to E.I.C. Ms. Doc. Kurrachee, and thirty miles north-east of the latter place. It is situate on the river of the same name, where it receives a small torrent called the Kuttagee. Water consequently may readily be obtained, and even when the rivers have ceased to run it may be had from pools or wells dug in their beds. The country hereabouts is very rocky and barren, and supplies are scanty. Lat. 25° 5′, long, 67° 28′.

GOORBAN.—A river in Sinde, so called from a village of E.I.C. Ms. Doc.; that name on its bank. It rises in the mountainous tract between 1840, p. 910; Kurrachee and Sehwan, about lat. 25° 20′, long. 67° 38′, and, De la Hoste, Rep. after a south-westerly course of about sixty miles, falls into the between Kur-Bay of Kurrachee by the Gisry creek, in lat. 24° 48′, long. 67° 6′. wan. Like most of the streams in this part of Sinde, it is known by different names in different parts of its course, being called Vuddia near its source, Goorban in the middle, and Mulleeree lower down. Though occasionally flooded, and having then a considerable body of water, it is dry for the greater part of the year; but water, as stated in the preceding article, may at all times be obtained by digging in its bed. It is crossed by the route from Kurrachee to Sehwan, at the village of Goorban.

E.I.C. Ms. Doc.   GOORDOO BAGH.—A village in Afghanistan, five miles south of Herat, situate on the Hury river, and on the road from Herat to Subzawur, in lat. 34° 20′, long. 62° 11′.

Masson, i. 34; Jour. As. Soc. 1837, p. 190; Mackeson, Jour. of Wade's Voy. down the Sutluj.   GOORJEANUH.—A town of Bhawlpoor, near the northern frontier, and about two miles south of the river Ghara. It has a good bazaar, and some trade. A regiment with six pieces of cannon are usually stationed here by the khan. Lat. 30° 17′, long. 73° 35′.

Ms. Map.   GOOROO.—A village of the province of Jhalawan, in Beloochistan, situate on the road from Gundava to Khozdur, fifteen miles from the latter place. Lat. 27° 50′, long. 66° 40′.

Walker's Map of Afg.   GOOROO KILLA.—A village in Afghanistan, eighteen miles south-east of Kilat-i-Ghilji. Lat. 32° 4′, long. 67° 2′.

Walker's Map of Beloochistan.   GOORUH.—A village in Beloochistan, situate near the coast. Lat. 25° 14′, long. 63° 10′.

Walker's Map of Afg.   GOORZÝWAN.—A village in the district of Mymunuh, in North Afghanistan. Lat. 35° 45′, long. 64° 58′.

E.I.C. Ms. Doc.   GOOSTANG.—A village in Beloochistan, situate on the route from Kedje to Belah, about thirty-five miles east of the former place. Lat. 26° 22′, long. 62° 50′.

Walker's Map of Afg.   GOOTIE.—A village in Afghanistan, about ten miles west of the Khyber Pass, and sixty miles west of the town of Peshawur. Lat. 34° 11′, long. 70° 53′.

E.I.C. Ms. Doc.   GOOZARAT.—A village in the Punjab, situate on an offset of the Indus, about three miles from the main stream, and thirty miles north-west of Mooltan. Lat. 30° 11′, long. 71°.

Jour. As. Soc. 1840, p. 724; Conolly (E.), Sketch of Geog. of Seistan. Map.   GOOZUR-I-KHASHI.—A village in Western Afghanistan, twenty miles south-west of the town of Khash, on the road from Giriskh to the province of Seistan. Lat. 31° 29′, long. 62° 26′.

Walker's Map.   GOOZURISTAN.—A village in Afghanistan, situate a mile from the left bank of the river Helmund. Lat. 33° 35′, long. 67° 14′.

E.I.C. Ms. Doc.   GOPANG, in the Punjab.—A village situate about eight miles north-east of the junction of the united streams of the rivers Chenaub and Ghara with the Indus. Lat. 29° 1′, long. 70° 36′.

E.I.C. Ms. Doc.   GOPANG, in Sinde, a village on the route from Kotrec to Schwan, and fifty-six miles south-east of the latter place. It is situate on the right bank of the Indus, in a fertile and well-cultivated tract. Lat. 25ᶜ 50', long. 68° 18'.

GORAZAN.—A village in Afghanistan, on the road from E.I.C. Ms. Doc.
Kandahar to Herat, forty-eight miles north-west of the town of
Giriskh. Lat. 32° 16', long. 63° 45'.

GOREE.—See MUNNEJAH and KOOKEWAREE.

GOREEWALA, in Afghanistan, a village on the right Walker's Map of
bank of the river Kurum and fifteen miles west of the town of Afg.
Kala Bagh. Lat. 33° 1', long. 71° 12'.

GORIAN.—A village in the Great Desert of Sinde, sixty- Ms. Survey Map.
five miles south-east of Omercote. Lat. 24° 45', long. 70° 35'.

GOTKEE, in Sinde, a small town on the route from Subzul- E.I.C. Ms. Doc.;
cote to Shikarpoor, and twenty-seven miles west of the former Atkinson's Exp.
place. It is situate six miles from the left bank of the Indus, in into Afg. 87-95.
a low, level, alluvial country, much overspread with jungle.
Though the houses are meanly built of mud, there is a showy
bazaar, with numerous verandahs, decorated with various fantastic
devices. The town also possesses a mosque of considerable size,
surmounted by a cupola covered with glazed tiles. The vicinity
is infamous on account of the predatory and sanguinary character
of its inhabitants. Lat. 28° 10', long. 69° 17'.

GOTTARAO, in Sinde, a fort on the route from Roree to E.I.C. Ms. Doc.;
Jessulmair, and fifty miles north-west of the latter place. It is Ead. Map.
situate near the eastern frontier, in the Thur or Sandy Desert, the
surface of which undulates in a succession of sandhills, not totally
barren, as they produce a spare vegetation of stunted bushes and
tufted grass. Water in this district is scarcely to be had except
during rains, and even then in small pools barely capable of supplying a hundred men. The fort of Gottarao is built of brick,
and forms a square of about two hundred yards. The wall is
from twenty to twenty-five feet high, and a keep in the interior
is about ten feet higher. On the east and the greater part of the
north side is an outer wall of about ten feet high. There are
about a dozen round bastions in various parts of the walls. The
fort is supplied with water from a depth of a hundred and fifty
feet by five wells. Two of these are within the walls ; the remaining three without, but close to them. During the sway
of the Talpoor dynasty this place belonged to the Ameers of
Khyerpoor, and was defended by two guns and a garrison of a
hundred and fifty matchlock-men. An inconsiderable village is

attached to the fort. It is frequently called Sirdar Ghur (the Sudur Ghur of Walker's map). Lat. 27° 13′, long, 70° 15′.

GOURJEANUH.—See Goorjeanuh.

E.I.C. Ms. Doc. GUDDRA.—A village near the south-eastern frontier of Sinde, two miles from the border of the Great Western Rin, and twenty miles north-east of Nuggur Parker. Lat. 24° 35′, long. 70° 57′.

E.I.C. Ms. Doc. GUDDRA.—A village in Sinde, on the route from Omercote to Balmair, fifteen miles from the eastern frontier of Sinde. Lat. 25° 37′, long. 70° 37′.

GUGAH.—See Goojah.

Ms. Survey Map. GUGGEIRA.—A village in Sinde, situated about two miles from the right bank of the Narra river, on the route from Bukkur to the south-east frontier of Sinde. Lat. 27° 19′, long. 69° 2′.

E.I.C. Ms. Doc. GUGGUR.—A village in Sinde, situated on a small stream falling into the Garrah creek, thirteen miles north-west of the town of Garrah, and twenty-eight miles east of Kurrachee. Lat. 24° 51′, long. 67° 26′.

F. Von Hugel, iii. 147. GUJERAT.—A considerable walled town of the Punjab, about ten miles from the right bank of the Chenaub, and on the great route from Attock to Lahore. It was invested by Maha Singh, who sickened and died in the course of the siege. It subsequently fell into the hands of his more fortunate son, Runjeet Singh, early in the course of his career. It is situated in lat. 32° 38′, long. 73° 14′.

F. Von Hugel, Kaschmir, iii. 154; Vigne, Kashmir, l. 235; Atkinson, Exp. into Afg. 403. GUJURU-WALLA, in the Punjab, a town on the route from Amritsir to Vazeerabad, and twenty-two miles south of the former place. Here is a large square fort with mud walls, surrounded by a ditch. It was the original residence of the family of Runjeet Singh, whose grandfather, born at this place, was a common soldier. The ashes of Runjeet Singh's father and mother are deposited here in tombs of plain appearance. It a few years ago was the residence of the celebrated Hari Singh, the most dauntless of all the Sikh chieftains. The interior of the fort is very highly decorated, and the garden is described by Baron Von Hugel as one of the finest he saw in India. It abounds in fine fruit-trees, especially orange-trees, covered with fruit, superior to that of China. The fragrance from the superb collection of trees, shrubs, and flowers, is described as almost overpowering.

Numerous ornamental buildings appropriately embellished, and a fountain always playing so as to send forth a broad sheet of limpid water, complete the attractions of the scene. Gujuru Walla is in lat. 32° 36′, long. 73° 57′.

GULAMURG, in Kashmir, a mountain at the north-west- Vigne, Kashmir, ern extremity of the Pir Panjal range. At its south-eastern ii. 147. base is the Pass of Gulamurg, which is not passable for horses, but is practicable on foot from the middle of April to the end of November. Lat. 34° 2′, long. 74° 12′.

GULBAHAR.—A village in Northern Afghanistan, twenty- Walker's Map. two miles south of the Hindoo Koosh. Lat. 35° 13′, long. of Sinde. 69° 13′.

GULGULA,[1] in Afghanistan, a ruined city of great extent, [1] E.I.C. Ms. Map. in the valley of Bamian. It is situate on the south side of the valley, and on the right bank of the river of Kunduz, here a very small stream. Nearly opposite are seen the fort of the governor of the district, the vast idols of Bamian, and the adjacent cliffs, excavated for miles into innumerable caves. The ruins are scattered over and about a conical hill,[2] and are so extensive as to [2] Moorcr. Punj. prove that the population must have been formerly very con- Bokh. ii. 387; siderable. As the neighbourhood in every direction is remarkably Panj. ii. 390; deficient in provisions and even fuel, the means of subsistence i. 183. must have been brought from afar ; but the instances of Tyre, Ormuz, and many other places, prove that motives of policy, religion, or military expediency have often led to the establishment and maintenance of large cities in the most barren and repulsive spots. The awe-inspiring local superstitions, and the command of Bamian, the principal pass from Turkestan to Afghanistan and India, may have determined the site of Gulgula. On the summit is a ruined citadel of great height, considerable size, and skilful construction. The ramparts have loopholes, apparently for the discharge of arrows. The material is unburnt brick, which must have singular tenacity, as the ruins are in good preservation.[3] Numerous excavations everywhere penetrate [3] Eyre, Mil. Op. the hill, and some contain the remains of reservoirs, which con- at Kabool, 360. tained water for the garrison. Moorcroft states that, according to Mahometan traditions, the city was built by Jelul-ud-din, King of Khwarism, but he adds with justice that it is of much earlier date. It was in fact destroyed in the reign of that prince by Zingis

P 2

Khan, probably in the celebrated campaign of 1221-1222,⁴ in which he sacked Herat and drove Jelul-ud-din over the Indus. Wilford,⁵ without stating his authorities, relates the horrible event in the following words :—" There were even kings of Bamiyan, but this dynasty lasted but a few years, and ended in 1215. The kings and governors resided at Ghulghuleh, called at that time the fort or palace of Bamiyan. It was destroyed by Genghiz-Khan in the year 1221, and because the inhabitants had presumed to resist him, he ordered them to be butchered, without distinction either of age or sex ; in his rage he spared neither animals nor even trees. He ordered it to be called, in his own language, Mau-balig, or the city of grief and sorrow ; but the inhabitants of that country called it, in their own dialect, Ghul-ghuleh, which word, used also in Persian, signifies the cries of woe. To have rebuilt it would have been ominous : for this reason, they erected a fort on a hill to the north of Bamiyan, which is called to this day the imperial fort. This fort also was destroyed by Zingis the Usbeck, in the year 1628, and has not been rebuilt since." Gulgula is in lat. 34° 49', long. 67° 46'.

GULISTAN KAREZ.—A village in Afghanistan, situate on the river Lora, in the valley of Pisheen, ninety miles south-east of Kandahar. Lat. 30° 36', long. 66° 32'.

GULLAH, in the Punjab, a small town about seven miles from the right bank of the Ghara. Lat. 31° 5', long. 74° 30'.

GULLAH, in the Punjab, seven miles west of the ferry over the Sutluj, near Ferozpoor. Lat. 30° 50', long. 74°.

GULLEAN KA GOTE.—A village in Sinde, situate near the left bank of the river Indus, about three miles from the place where the Fulailce branch diverges from the main stream. Lat. 25° 30', long. 68° 21'.

GULLOO GOTE, in Sinde, a village on the route from Schwan to Larkhana, and forty-five miles north of the former place. It is situate a mile and a half from the right bank of the Indus, in a fertile country, in many places well cultivated, but in others overrun with bushes. The road northwards to Larkhana is made with considerable care. Lat. 26° 57', long. 68°.

GUMBUT, in Sinde, a town about twelve miles south of Khyerpoor, and ten miles east of the Indus. Though one of the principal places in the country for the manufacture of cotton goods, the process is very rude, and the quantity produced does not exceed 5,000 pieces in the year. The population is about 3,000. Lat. 27° 24′, long. 68° 23′.

GUMHA.—A small town in the north-east of the Punjab, Moorcr. i. 158. and on the southern slope of the Himalaya. The houses are built of stones, cemented with mud, and strengthened with timbers of fir laid horizontally. The roofs are of fir spars covered with slates, but as these are laid loose, they form a very imperfect protection against the weather. There is here a mine of rock-salt, which is worked to considerable extent, but in a very rude manner. The salt is of a reddish colour, and is very compact and heavy. The Rajah of Mundi clears 16,000 rupees a year by its sale. Lat. 31° 56′, long. 76° 38′.

GUNAIDIO.—A village in Eastern Sinde, on the route from E.I.C. Ms. Doc. Jessulmair to Halla, and ninety miles south-west of the former place. It is situate on the bank of a small lake, the water of which is saturated with natron. Lat. 26° 22′, long. 69° 48′.

GUNDAMUK.—A walled village, on the eastern brow of the Wood, Khyber Kurkutcha range, on the road from Jelalabad to Kabool, twenty- Pass, i. 3, 6; Burnes' Bokh. i. eight miles west of the former place. As it is 4,616 feet above 124; Mil. Op. in Afg. 14; Eyre, the sea, the climate is mild in summer but severe in winter, and Mil. Op. at Ka- there is so marked a difference between the temperature of the bool, 250; Sale, Dis. in Afg. 277; high table-land to the west and the lower plain of Jelalabad, that Hough, Nar. of Exp. to Afg. 300; it is said that when it rains on the eastern side of Gundamuk it Havelock, War in snows on the western. Here, during the disastrous attempt to Afg. ii. 180; Forster, Jour. retreat from Kabool made by the British army at the beginning Beng. Eng. 68. of 1842, the last surviving force, amounting to about 100 soldiers and 300 camp-followers, were finally overpowered, only one man making his escape. Lat. 34° 17′, long. 70° 5′.

GUNDAVA PASS.—See Moola.

GUNDAVA, a town in Beloochistan, the capital of the pro- E.I.C. Ms. Doc.; vince of Cutch Gundava, is situate on the Baddra, a small torrent 309; Masson, Ka- which flows down from the Hala Mountains, and is lost in the lat. 330. desert farther east. It is a small place, surrounded by a high mud wall, and has little trade, the slight importance which it possesses resulting from its being the winter residence of the Khan of Kelat, who, before the inclement season, leaves his elevated capital, and with his family, officers, and principal subjects, descends to the warm lowland of Gundava. Pottinger describes it as smaller than Kelat, but built with more regularity. The inhabitants are for the most part Jets, a race of Hindoo descent, but converts to Mahometanism, and are little better than serfs to the Belooches, who own the greater part of the lands. There are a few Hindoos, of more recent introduction into the country, who carry on trade by barter, in this way collecting grain and other raw produce, which they subsequently export. Lat. 28° 29', long. 67° 32'.

Ms. Survey Map. GUNDERRA.—A village in Sinde, situate on the Western Narra river, thirty-two miles north of Sehwan. Lat. 26° 49', long. 67° 50'.

E.I.C. Ms. Doc. GUNDUTSAN, in Afghanistan, a small stream or rather water-course, on the route from Kandahar to Herat, and eighty-six miles south-east of the latter town. It is important in a military view, as water can be obtained in pools in the bed of the channel even when the stream ceases to flow. The place where it crosses the route is in lat. 33° 10', long. 63° 20'.

GUNEEMURAH.—See GUNNEEMURGH.

Vigne, i. 153. GUNGA BAL.—A small lake in Kashmir, on the Haramuk mountain, on the north-eastern boundary of the valley. It is a mile and a half long, and two or three hundred yards wide. Its appearance presents nothing remarkable, and its dimensions, it has been seen, are inconsiderable, but it is regarded with a superstitious veneration of the deepest kind by the Hindoos. Pilgrims flock to its banks, and into its waters are thrown such fragments of bone as remain undestroyed by the fires lighted by Hindoo feeling to consume the fleshly habitations from which the spirit has departed. Lat. 34° 25', long. 74° 39'.

E.I.C. Ms. Doc. GUNGATEE.—A village in the Punjab, eighteen miles south of Lahore. Lat. 31° 22', long. 74° 12'.

E.I.C. Ms. Doc. GUNGUNI.—A village in the north-east of the Punjab, situate on the right bank of the river Duras, and on the route from Bultistan to Kashmir by the Bultul Pass. Lat. 34° 36', long. 76° 2'.

Hough, 350. GUNJATEE, in the Punjab, a small town about ten miles from the east bank of the Ravee, and on the route from Surrukpoor to Ferozpoor. Lat. 31° 17', long. 73° 58'.

E.I.C. Ms. Doc. GUNNEEMURGH, in Western Afghanistan, is a small valley on the route from Kandahar to Herat, and about half-way between those places. It is watered by a fine stream, and is surrounded by both garden and field cultivation. Lat. 32° 26', long. 63° 14'.

GUNYSH BUL, in Kashmir, a place of Hindoo devotion, at the eastern extremity of the valley, on the route to the celebrated cave of Amur Nath. According to Vigne, the name signifies " the place of Gunysh" or Ganesa, the only son of Siva. The object of superstition is a large fragment of rock lying in the Lidur river, and worn by the current into what the Hindoos fancy a representation of an elephant's head, to which a trunk, ears, and eyes have been added by human art. The superstitious feeling caused by this object results from the belief that Ganesa has the head of an elephant. Here, the pilgrims proceeding to Amur Nath make their preparatory ablutions and prostrations. Gunysh Bul is in lat. 34°, long. 75° 12'. *Kashmir, ii. 6.*

GURANEE.—A village in Afghanistan, situate on the Furrah river, twenty-four miles north-east of the town of the same name. Lat. 32° 37', long. 62° 25'. *Walker's Map of Afg.*

GURDAIZ.—A village in Afghanistan, on the route from Ghuznee to Kohat, fifty-five miles east of the former town. Lat. 33° 32', long. 69° 12'. *E.I.C. Ms. Doc.*

GURDAN DEWAR,[1] in Afghanistan, a village in a small valley where the river Helmund, a few miles from its source, crosses the route from Kabool to Bamian. It is situate between the pass of Oonna, on the south-east, and Koh-i-Baba mountain, on the north-west. The Helmund is here knee-deep, and about ten yards wide.[2] The elevation of Gurdan Dewar is 10,076 feet. Lat. 34° 25', long. 68° 8'. *[1] E.I.C. Ms. Doc.; [2]Moorcroft, Punj. Bokh. ii. 383.; Jour. As. Soc. 1842, p. 69; Grif. Bar. and*

GURIBAI PASS.—In Afghanistan, on the eastern route from Ghuznee to Shawl, and a hundred and twenty miles south of the former place. It is situate where the rough country between Lake Ab-istada and Toba mountains slopes down eastward to Sewestan. Lat. 31° 54', long. 68° 8'. *Ther. Obs. in Afg. E.I.C. Ms. Doc.*

GURILLA, in Sinde, a large village on the route from Sehwan to Larkhana by the Arul river, and nine miles south of Larkhana. It is situate on the Cheela, a water-course connected with the Western Narra. The road in this part of the route is good, and supplies are attainable in moderate quantities. Lat. 27° 24', long. 68° 8'. *E.I.C. Ms. Doc.*

GURMAB.—A village in Afghanistan, on the route from *Walker's Map of Afg.*

Giriskh to Furrah, by the Dilaram road, and twenty-eight miles east of Furrah. It is situate among the mountains rising north of Seistan, and stretching into the Huzareh country. Lat. 32° 24', long. 62° 37'.

Walker's Map of Afg.
GURMAB.—A village in Afghanistan, eighteen miles east of Giriskh. Lat. 31° 50', long. 64° 36'.

¹ E.I.C. Ms. Doc.; Masson, Bal. Afg. Panj. i. 325; Hough, Narr. of Exp. in Afg. 50; Allen, March through Sinde and Afg. 106.
GURMAB,[1] in Beloochistan, a halting-place in the Bolan Pass, about half a mile south of the village of Kirta,·and seventeen miles from the eastern entrance of the pass. Here is a rather copious spring, the water of which flows into the Bolan river, or torrent. The name, signifying "hot water," seems to indicate that it is a thermal spring; but there does not appear to be any satisfactory evidence that such is the fact.* The elevation of this place above the sea is 1,081 feet.[2] Lat. 29° 36', long. 67° 32'.

² Jour. As. Soc. 1842, p. 54; Grif. Bar. and Ther. Obs. in Afg.

GURMSEHL (warm place), in Afghanistan, a narrow depressed tract, extending along the lower course of the Helmund.

¹ Jour. As. Soc. 1840, p. 712; Sketch of the Phys. Geogr. of Seistan.
According to Conolly,[1] the current of the river holds its course with much force and rapidity along the left bank, and, deserting the right, leaves between the water's edge and the line of cliffs which formerly bounded it on that side, a low and very fertile

² Acc. of Kabool, 137, 392; Kinneir, Geogr. Mem. Persia, 215.
strip, of the average breadth of two miles. Elphinstone[2] calls it Gurmseer (warm region). It is laid down in the map accompanying his work, and attributed to Macartney, as extending between lat. 30° 50'—31° 50', long. 63°—65°, and is thus assigned an extent probably too great. There is no mention made of it in the map given by Conolly, though the course of the Helmund is laid down in that part where he in his sketch describes it as flowing through the Gurmsehl. This omission is the more remarkable, as the map is crowded with details of inferior importance. Pot-

³ Beloochistan, 316.
tinger[3] describes this tract as exceedingly productive of wheat, rice, and other grains, in consequence of great natural fertility and the copious and.well-diffused irrigation from the river Helmund, which, in this part of its course, has at all times a large body of water, and in the season of inundation is a vast, deep, and rapid stream. The inhabitants are notorious robbers, being outcasts from the neighbouring people. At the beginning of the present century it paid a revenue of 4,000 rupees to the

War in Afg. i. 224.
* Havelock, indeed, states cursorily, that "near Kirtah, a tepid spring is found in the mountain-side," but the other authorities make no mention of a point so remarkable.

Shah of Kabool, but latterly it appears to have attained a sort of vague and preearious independenee, under a native ehief, pro- teeted by the Shah of Herat.[4] [4] Leech, Seisthan, 150.

GURNAGH.—A village in the Punjab, situate on the road E.I.C. Ms. Doc. from Mooltan to Ferozpoor, and ten miles north of the Ghara river. Lat. 30° 14', long. 72° 59'.

GURNEE.—A village in Afghanistan, eighteen miles north- Map of Afg. east of Kandahar. Lat. 31° 45', long. 64° 45'.

GURREE.—See GHURRY.

GURSEAH.—A village in Sinde, about thirteen miles from Ms. Survey Map. the eastern frontier. Lat. 26° 57', long. 70° 8'.

GURUK TEELAH.—A village in the Punjab, situate on the E.I.C. Ms. Doc. Salt Range, about seven miles north-west of Julalpoor, and five miles from the right bank of the river Jailum. Lat. 32° 43', long. 73° 10'.

GURUNEE.—See GIRONEE.

GURYS, in Bultistan or Little Thibet, is situate elose to the Vigne, Kashmir, northern boundary of Kashmir : it is an elevated valley five miles ii. 207. long and one mile wide. The upper part of the Kishengunga flows in a direetion from east to west along the bottom of the valley, whieh, though 7,200 feet above the sea, is surrounded by lofty and very abrupt peaks, chiefly limestone. Lat. 34° 33', long. 74° 36'.

GUSWAP, in Afghanistan, a halting-plaee at a piece of stand- E.I.C. Ms. Doc. ing water on the route from Kanhahar to Herat, and a hundred and thirty miles north-west of the former plaee. It is situate on a road a little south of the main route, collateral to it, and in some degree preferable, on aeeount of the more abundant supply of water. Lat. 32° 12', long. 63° 54'.

GUZ.—A village of the provinee of Jhalawan, in Belooehistan, E.I.C. Ms. Doc. situate a few miles west of the Gundava, or Moola Pass, on the road from Gundava to Khozdur, and twenty-two miles east of the latter plaee. Lat. 27° 50', long. 66° 47'.

GWADEL, a bay on the eoast of Belooehistan, is formed by Horsburgh's Ind. Cape Gwadel, or Rass Noo, on the east, and Ras Pishk on the Dir. i. 495. west. It is three leagues from east to west at the entranee, and about as mueh from north to south, with regular soundings of eight and seven fathoms at the entranee, and six, five, and four fathoms inside. The bottom is entirely mud, and there is good shelter from all winds, excepting those which blow between east and south-south-west. The coast is of moderate height, but the country inland is lofty and rugged. At some distance inland, and directly north of the bay, is a remarkable cleft in the mountain, serving as a landmark. Eastward of Cape Gwadel is another inlet, sometimes called Gwadel Bay, but not so well sheltered as that just described, yet having a good bottom of sand, with soundings at the entrance of ten or twelve fathoms, decreasing inside with considerable regularity to six, five, and four fathoms, and sheltered from south-west, west, and north winds. The eastern bay lies in lat. 25° 5'—25° 10', long. 62° 12'—62° 20'; the western in long. 61° 57'—62° 10', and same lat. as the eastern.

Horsburgh, Ind. Dir. i. 495.

GWADEL CAPE, or RAS NOO, in Beloochistan, projects southward from the coast into the Arabian Sea, between the eastern and western bays of Gwadel. It is a peninsula of moderate height, six miles in length, and joined to the mainland by an isthmus not half a mile over. There are remains of a wall with towers on this isthmus, constructed for the defence of a town which formerly stood on the cape, and the site of which is still marked by the ruins of houses and wells. The few inhabitants now reside three or four miles north of this, in wretched hovels of mats. The water of the wells is brackish, so that supplies of this article for shipping must be obtained from the interior. A few goats, sheep, and fowls may be purchased. Lat. 25° 5', long. 62° 10'.

E.I.C. Ms. Map; Leech, Hind. Koosh.

GWALIAN PASS.—A pass in Afghanistan over the Hindoo Koosh mountains, on the route from Kabool to Kunduz. The route proceeds from the Koh-i-Damun, and, entering the valley of Ghorbund, takes a south-westerly direction for about twenty miles to the point where the Gwalian Pass turns off northward, and holds its way in that direction about thirty miles to the summit of the range of Hindoo Koosh, which it crosses ten miles east of the great peak of that name. Though easier than the Koushan Pass farther east, it is less frequented, through dread of the predatory tribes which infest it. The summit of the pass is in lat. 35° 25', long. 68° 42'.

E.I.C. Ms. Map; Leech, Hind. Koosh, 32.

GWAZGAR PASS, in Afghanistan, over the Hindoo Koosh mountain from Afghanistan to Kunduz. The route by this pass first proceeds up the valley of Ghorbund, and at the ruined town of the same name turns off in a direction nearly due north.

It is scarcely frequented by travellers, in consequence of the predatory character of the Huzareh tribes who hold it. Lat. 35° 15′, long. 68° 38′.

GWETTER, in Beloochistan, an inlet of the Arabian Sea, is Horsburgh, Ind. five leagues wide at the entrance, and runs three leagues up the Dir. i. 495. country. The depth of water at the entrance is about six fathoms, shoaling farther in to four, three, and two, close to shore. Ras Jewnee headland forms the east side of the bay; on the west side the land is low, so that it cannot be seen at a short distance, with the exception of two hummocks, which appear like islands. The land at the northern side or head of the bay is so low as to be scarcely discernible until approached very closely, and then it becomes visible principally by means of the bushes growing on it. A village, called Gwetter, is situate on the north-west side of the bay, and another, called Jewnee, lies close to the point forming the eastern limit of the entrance. Gwetter Bay is between lat. 25° 2′—25° 12′, long. 61° 18′— 61° 40′.

GYDUR KHYLE.—A village in Afghanistan, situate in Walker's Map of lat. 33° 40′, long. 71° 32′. Afg.

H.

HAGAH, in Afghanistan, a village in the district of Nungna- E.I.C. Ms. Map; har, at the foot of the Sufeid Koh mountain. It is situate on the Wood, Khyber Pass, 5; Burnes' southern road between the Khyber Pass and Kabool, and seventy- Pers. Narr. 133. five miles south-east of the latter place. This road, though more direct than that lying farther to the north through Jelalabad, is less frequented, in consequence of the sanguinary and rapacious character of the people and the number of difficult passes. The adjacent country is watered by numerous streams descending from Sufeid Koh, and is remarkable for picturesque beauty. It abounds in fertile valleys, thickly peopled and well cultivated. Hagah is in lat. 34° 14′, long. 70° 20′

HAGEGUK.—A mountain in the north-west of Afghanistan, Wood, Route of Kab. and Toor- extending from north to south transversely from Koh-i-baba to kistan, 24; Id.

Oxus, 204;
Burnes' Bokh. i.
181; ii. 240;
Sale, Dis. in Afg.
419; Jour. As.
Soc. 1842, p. 69;
Grif. Bar. and
Ther. Obs. in Afg.;
Hindoo Koosh. Its summit is 11,700 feet above the sea.* It is traversed by two passes, that of Hageguk near the southern extremity, and that of Erak near the northern. By both of these passes, roads proceed from Kabool to Bamian, and thence to Kunduz. Lat. 34° 30′—40′, long. 67° 55′.

Outram, Rough
Notes, 126.
E.I.C. Ms. Doc.;
Leech, Khyber
Pass, 12.
HAIDAREE, in Afghanistan, a village of the Khyberees, situate about a mile south of the Khyber Pass, and four miles from its eastern entrance. Lat. 33° 58′, long. 71° 22′.

HAJAMAREE.—See Hujamree.

Walker's Map of
N.W. Frontier.
HAJEECHURM.—A village in the Punjab, situate on the road from Mooltan to Ferozpoor, about forty miles south-west of the latter place. Lat. 30° 41′, long. 73° 56′.

E.I.C. Ms. Doc.
HAJEEKA.—A village in Beloochistan, situate a short distance to the right of the road from Kelat to Sonmeanee, thirty-five miles in a direction nearly south from the former. Lat. 28° 26′, long. 66° 12′.

Ms. Survey Map.
HAJEEKAJOKE.—A village of Cutch Gundava, in Beloochistan, situate on the road from Bagh to Larkhana, eighteen miles south of Bagh, and thirty-two miles north-east of Gundava. Lat. 28° 43′, long. 67° 56′.

E.I.C. Ms. Doc.
HAJEE KURREEMDAD.—A village in Afghanistan, situate about ten miles from the right bank of the river Urgundab, forty-five miles north-east of Kandahar, and the same distance west of Kelat-i-Ghilji. Lat. 32° 8′, long. 65° 59′.

E.I.C. Ms. Doc.
HAJEEPOOR, in the Punjab, a village situate on the left bank of the river Chenaub, eighteen miles from its confluence with the Ghara river, and forty-two miles south-west of Mooltan. Lat. 29° 36′, long. 71° 12′.

HAJEGUK.—See Hageguk.

Vigne, Kashmir, i.
277.
HAKRIT SAR (or Lake of Weeds), an extensive but shallow lake, nearly in the middle of the valley of Kashmir, and on the south side of the river Jailum, from which it is separated by an embankment. Lat. 34° 6′, long. 74° 30′.

E.I.C. Ms. Doc.
HALACHEE, in Beloochistan, a village in the Moola or Gundava Pass. It is situate near the left bank of the Moola river, in a vicinity which, though mountainous, is capable of yielding a moderate portion of supplies. Lat. 28° 2′, long. 67° 9′

1 E.I.C. Ms. Doc.
HALA MOUNTAINS,[1] in Beloochistan, an extensive and

---

* This is the height given by Wood in Map E. I. C. MS. Burnes (ii. 240) gives 12,400; Griffiths, as quoted above, 12,190.

lofty range, stretching from north to south, generally between the meridians 67°—68°. They are connected with the elevated region of Afghanistan by the Toba mountains, of which they may be considered a prolongation, and which rise in the two summits of Tukatoo, in lat. 30° 18′, long. 67°, to a height estimated at be-- tween 11,000 and 12,000 feet.[2] If we consider this mountain as the northern limit of the Hala range, it will be found to ex- tend, from north to south, a distance of about four hundred miles, and to terminate at Cape Monze,[3] projecting into the Arabian Sea in lat. 24° 48′.   About lat. 29° 30′, a large offset extends east- ward, forming the mountains held by the Murree tribe of Kahun, and joining the Suliman range about Hurrund and Dajel. South- ward of this, the Hala range becomes rapidly depressed to- wards the east; descending with considerable steepness in that direction to the low level tract of Cutch Gundava; viewed from which, these mountains present the appearance of a triple range,[4] each rising in succession as they recede west- ward.   The elevation above the sea of the plain of Cutch Gundava at Dadur, close to the mouth of the Bolan Pass, is 742 feet.[5] The height of the mountains in that part has not been ascertained; viewed from the British encampment in the plain, they gave the impression of great elevation.   According to the graphic account of an intelligent observer,[6] " the Bolan (Hala) range of mountains was the great attraction throughout the march.   It would be little to say that they towered towards the clouds; for the clouds were rolling along their breasts, and their peaks rose high above them.   Ridge appeared above ridge, and the effect of light and shade from passing clouds, now throw- ing prominently forward, and now obscuring, their inequalities and chasms, was so varied and sublime, that the eye was never wearied with watching it.   Though at the distance of at least fifty miles, they were so vast that their bases appeared within a moderate morning's canter."   Viewed from the west, they appear of far less elevation, as the table-land stretching from their bases in that direction has a height in few places less than 5,000 feet; thus the valley of Shawl is 5,500 feet high,[7] the table-land of Kelat 6,000.[8] The Hala forms the great eastern wall or buttress of the highlands of Kelat, marking their descent to the vast plain of Western Hindostan.   This huge mountain brow is furrowed by two main passes—the Bolan and Moola, each the channel of a considerable

[2] Havelock, War in Afg. i. 248; Elph. Acc. of Caubul, 105.

[3] Pottinger, Belooch. 251.

[4] Havelock, ii. 303.

[5] Jour. As. Soc. 1842, p. 54; Grif. Bar. and Ther. Obs. in Afg.

[6] Allen, March through Sinde and Afg. 88.

[7] Jour. As. Soc. 1842, p. 55; Grif. Bar. and Ther. Obs. in Afg.

[8] E.I.C. Ms. Doc.

torrent, and each 'affording a tedious but not very difficult access from the plains on the east to the western highlands. Thus the Bolan Pass is a little more than fifty miles in length, in which distance the ascent is 5,000 feet, or something less than a hundred fcet in a milc. The length of the Moola Pass is about one hundred miles, and the ascent in that distance about 4,500 feet,[9] or forty-five fcet in a mile. (See BOLAN and MOOLA PASSES.) Such an angle of inclination admits the transport of artillery and heavy goods, and altogether the communication between the table-land and the plain is probably as easy as between any places having, at the same distance, as great difference of level. About one hundred miles south of the Moola Pass, and in lat. 26° 30′, the Hala range stretches with diminished elevation to the south-east, forming the mountains of Jutteel, Keertar, Lukkee, and others of less note, which constitute the dreary and sterile tract occupying the greater part of Western Sinde.[1] A little farther south, the range becomes much lower and narrower, not exceeding thirty miles in breadth, being defined on the east by the low alluvial tract of Sinde, on the west by that of Lus. In the most southern part it is called the Pubb mountains, and, as already mentioned, terminates at Cape Monze. Pottinger[2] calls the Hala the Brahooic range, to which he assigns very extensive limits, comprehending under the name the table-land rising between the plains of Sinde and of Kandahar, and the extensive and intricate highlands stretching far to the west into Mekran, and ultimately joining the mountains of Persia. The greatest height ascertained of any point in this mountain system is that of Kelat, amounting to 6,000 feet,[3] but other parts rise much above this ; Cheheltan, for instance, north of Moostung, is, with probability, estimated by Masson[4] to have a height of above 11,000 feet, as, though its summit is divested of snow in summer, some is always found in the deep ravines, a circumstance indicating a very great height in this latitude. In a country so barbarous and so little explored, our information on the geology of this vast range is necessarily scanty in the extreme. Masson[5] tells us that the huge Cheheltan is of secondary limestone, abounding in marine *exuviæ*. Similar formations are observable in the Bolan Pass,[6] where the strata are cross-cut by that great ravine. Overlying were observed vast deposits of more recent and diluvial formation—conglomerate and pebbly mud—to the depth of a thousand feet and upwards. There

[9] E.I.C. Ms. Doc.

[1] Jour. As. Soc. 1840, p. 911 ; De La Hoste, on Country between Tatta and Schwan.

[2] Belooch. 252.

[3] E.I.C. Ms. Doc.

[4] Bal. Afg. Panj. ii. 82.

[5] Id. ii. 78.

[6] Kennedy, Sinde and Kabool, i. 214; Haveluck, War in Afg. i..223.

is scarcely any evidence of the existence of primary formation in this range, except the well-ascertained fact that the Pubb mountain contains a rich deposit of copper,[7] perhaps nowhere found *in situ* in recent formations.

7 E.I.C. Ms. Doc.; Jour. As. Soc. 1840, p. 30; De La Hoste, on the Existence of Copper near Bela. E.I.C. Ms. Doc.

HALAN SYUDS, in Sinde, a village on the route from Hyderabad to Schwan by way of Kotree, and forty miles north of the last-mentioned place. It is situate about a mile and a half from the right bank of the Indus, and close to a *shikargah* or hunting preserve, formerly belonging to one of the Ameers of Hyderabad. Lat. 25° 52', long. 68° 18'.

HALIPOOTRA, in Sinde, a village on the route from Sehwan to Larkhana, and four miles north of the former place. It is embosomed in high trees, and is situate two miles from the right bank of the Indus, in a tract overrun with jungle and interspersed with pools and water-courses supplied from the river. Lat. 26° 23', long. 67° 54'.

E.I.C. Ms. Doc.

HALLA, in Sinde, near the left or eastern bank of the Indus, is situate in a tract of no great fertility, the soil being impregnated with salt. The new town is larger and more wealthy than the old one, which is contiguous to it. There is here a much-frequented shrine of a reputed Mahometan saint. The bazaar, which is partially roofed over, is well supplied, and considerable business is transacted there. Sindian caps, the general head-dress of all in the country except the Hindoos, are made here in great numbers, and of excellent quality. Halla new town is celebrated for its earthenware, the coarser kinds of which are manufactured from clay taken from the bed of the Indus. In the finer kinds this material is mixed, in a large proportion, with ground flints: the decorations are very showy, and sometimes tasteful; the colours, which are obtained from the oxides of copper, lead, or iron, being remarkable for brilliancy and richness. A sort of unctuous earth, called "*chunniah*," is obtained from lakes near the town, and is eaten in considerable quantities, especially by the women. Estimates of the population differ widely, and Burnes upon this point is not consistent with himself. In one place (vol. iii. 264), he states it at 2,000, and in the same volume (p. 227) at 10,000. The latter seems the more probable amount. Lat. 25° 45', long. 68° 28'.

Wood, Oxus, 36-38.

HAMOON, on the south-western frontier of Afghanistan, is

a shallow lake, or rather a very extensive reedy morass, of Seistan.
The word Hamoon is a generic term, signifying, in Persian, a plain
level ground ;* it is applied by the inhabitants of Seistan to any

¹ Jour. As. Soc.
1840, p. 715 ;
Conolly, Sketch
of the Physical
Geogr. of Seistan.
shallow lake or morass,¹ of which great numbers are formed in
time of inundation, by the Helmund and other rivers pouring
their waters over that level region.　The name, however, is
peculiarly and emphatically applied to the principal and permanent
watery expanse, which is of an irregular elongated form, about
seventy miles in length from north-east to south-west, and from
fifteen to twenty miles in breadth.　At the north-east side is an
opening about five miles wide, communicating with the Duk-
i-Teer, an expanse similar to the great Hamoon, and about a third
of its extent.　This smaller morass was formerly a separate
Hamoon or swamp, but about fifteen years ago, the Helmund,
which had previously discharged itself into the great Hamoon on
its eastern side, poured a vast volume of water into the Duk-i-Teer,
which in consequence was so swollen as to sweep away the dividing bank, and become permanently united with the larger swamp
or lake.　At the same time, the channels, by which hitherto the
water of the Helmund flowed eastward into the Hamoon, became
nearly deserted and obliterated, and the vast volume of that
great river is now principally discharged into the Duk-i-Teer,
from which it expands over the surface of both swamps.　" The

² Ut supra, 716.
more fitting appellation of the Hamoon," observes Conolly,² " is the
classical one of Ari-a-Palus, for it is in reality almost everywhere
a mere marsh.　It has rarely a depth of more than from three to
four feet, and is almost entirely covered with reeds and rushes."
Insulated in the Hamoon, and above a mile from its eastern bank,
is a hill, called Koh-i-Zor, or Roostum by some, Koh-i-Khwajeh
by others.　It has a fort accessible only by means of a channel
cut through the reeds, which are so close and strong as to preclude the passage of either man or beast unless thus cleared
away.　By means of this channel, which has a breadth of
about three feet, and is filled with water having an average
depth of about the same number of feet, very salt, thick with
mud, black and putrid, horses, cows, and even men wade
to the island.　Some of the richer and more fastidious inhabitants are conveyed on rafts formed of reeds and pushed

*حامون

forward by men wading in the mud. The view from this fortress is very extraordinary. Conolly[3] thus describes it: " Immediately [3] Ut supra, 717. beneath me lay a yellow plain, as level as a calm sea, formed by the tops of reeds, and extending north and south far beyond the reach of vision. On the east it was bounded by a paler yellow, marking the borders of the lake, where the less thickly growing reeds are annually burned down, and a few poor Kheels clear away the ground for the cultivation of water-melons. Beyond, again, in this direction, appeared the dark-green tamarisks, whole forests of which fringe the lake. Here and there, as we looked around on every side, were seen patches of blue water, and on the west, a large clear lake stretched away until out of sight." The latter part of this quotation is at variance with the author's previous statement that the Hamoon " is almost entirely covered with reeds," and should probably be qualified, by assuming that he means that the water of this vast swamp is, to a great extent, free from reeds to the west of the island. The saltness of the water varies in different parts, according to the depth, nature of the soil on which it rests, and proximity to the mouths of the rivers. Though so brackish at the Koh-i-Khwajeh that the horses of the travellers refused it, the people drank no other, and boasted that it was the best in the world, causing appetite, promoting digestion, and conducing to general health. The surface of the Hamoon is considered to be on the increase, probably in consequence of the quantity of water brought down by the rivers being constant, and the depth being continually diminished by the alluvial deposit. There is no vent whatever for the water, the increase of quantity being checked merely by evaporation. Innumerable wild hogs harbour in the reeds and commit great havoc on the cultivated grounds. They congregate in herds of thirty or forty, and when hunted, often kill the huntsmen or dogs, though the latter are very powerful as well as courageous. To the people of many countries these animals would be acceptable on account of the value of their flesh as an article of subsistence, but the natives, being Mahometans, use it only as food for their dogs. The reeds form an excellent pasture for cows, which animals eat them with greediness and soon fatten on them. Geese, ducks, and some other water-fowl are, as might be expected, very numerous. The pelican is common, and is believed by the natives to carry water far into the desert, and there barter it with other birds for food ; a process, the authentication of which would shake the definition given by some philosophers of man—that he is an animal that contracts or makes a bargain. Fish does not appear to be abundant. The Hamoon, in addition to the Helmund, receives the Adruscund, the Furrah Rood, and some other rivers of less importance.   Some geographers [4] have confounded the Hamoon with the Lake of Zirreh, a little further south, which is nearly if not entirely dried up.[5] Elphinstone [6] gives a general and brief, but accurate, description of the Hamoon, and adds judiciously, " I suspect it has no name at all in the neighbourhood, but is merely called the lake, or the sea." In both the maps, however, accompanying his work, it is laid down erroneously, and equally so in that of Pottinger, who gives a short and rather inaccurate description of it.[7] In the hypso-metrical map accompanying the *Asie Centrale* of Humboldt it is also erroneously laid down as to shape, and placed a degree more to the west and likewise to the north than it ought to be. Hamoon, in its average extent, is in lat. 30° 42'—31° 54', long. 61° 8'—62° 10'.

HANGU, or HANGOO.—A small town at the southern base of the Salt range or Kala Bagh mountains, fifteen miles west of Kohat, and on the route from India to Khorasan, through Bungush.   It is situate in a pleasant and fruitful country, well watered by numerous fine springs. There is a small bazaar and a stone-built fort. The inhabitants are Afghans, ruled by their own chiefs, but the Sikhs make continual incursions, and levy contributions. Population about 1,500. Lat. 33° 31', long. 71° 15'.

HARAMUK. — A lofty summit in the range bounding Kashmir on the north. Vigne states, that " Haramuk signifies all mouths or faces, and that the application of the word in this case is either derived from the square-sided, rick-shaped figure of its summit, or from its being visible from all sides by reason of its insulated situation and superior height." Its mass appears to consist principally of basaltic amygdaloid, though granite has been observed on it, but not *in situ*. In a depression on the northern declivity is a small lake, called Gunga Bul, " the place of the Ganges," which, like many other reservoirs of water, is

[1] Kinneir, Geogr. of Persia, 100.

[5] Conolly, ut supra, 716.

[6] 492.

[7] Belooch. 316.

Masson, Bal. Afg. Panj. i. 107.

Vigne, Kashmir, ii. 151.

held in high veneration by the Hindoos. The elevation of Haramuk above the level of the sea is estimated by Vigne at 13,000
feet. Lat. 34° 26′, long. 74° 43′.

HARAPA.[1]—A village of the Punjab, close to the left bank of [1] Masson, Bal.Afg.
the Ravee, and seated amid very extensive ruins, the most striking Panj. i. 453;
being the relics of a large brick fortress. This is considered by Mas- Burnes' Bokh. iii. 137.
son to be the site of the Sangala of Arrian, where the Indians made
such an obstinate defence against Alexander; but this opinion
is regarded by eminent authority as open to question. Professor
Wilson observes,[2] "Whether they (the Macedonians) followed the [2] Ariana Antiq.
course of the Iravati (Ravee) to Harapa, may be reasonably 198.
doubted." Harapa is in lat. 30° 37′, long. 72° 43′.

HARAWUG.—A castle in the north of the Punjab, on the Vigne, Kashmir,
route from Lahore to Kashmir, by the Banihal Pass, and twenty- i. 420.
eight miles south of the last-mentioned place. It is built of
wood, in a ravine on the right bank of a stream which, at a short
distance below, falls into the Chenaub. From the hill above
is a noble view up that river, which here flows for fifteen or
twenty miles in a straight line. The coldness of the water of
the Chenaub causes its course in hot weather to be marked by
dense vapour, which floats over it. Harawug is in lat. 33° 1′, long.
75° 7′.

HARIPOOR, in Kashmir, a small town situate in the Punch F.Von Hugel, i.
Pass from the Punjab into that valley, and near the spot where 199.
the pass opens into the low ground of Kashmir. It is close to
the right bank of the Rembeara, a considerable feeder of the
Veyut, or Jailum. Hence the Rembeara is sometimes called the
River of Haripoor. The town is small and mean, remarkable
only for its picturesque site beneath the Pir Panjal mountain,
which on the south rears its towering summit, covered with
snow during the greater part of the year. Lat. 33° 37′, long.
74° 37′.

HARIPOOR, in the north-east of the Punjab, among the F. Von Hugel,
lower mountains of the Himalaya, is a fort, surrounded by a small i. 100.
town, which contains a good and well-supplied bazaar. The name
signifies the town of Hari, one of the incarnations of Vishnu, and
Hindoo superstition here flourishes in the highest degree of
vigour. The town and its vicinity are crowded with apes and
pea-fowl, considered to be under the protection of the deity, and
enjoying in consequence such a measure of respect as secures

them from all molestation. Haripoor is in lat. 31° 54', long.
75° 53'.

F. Von Hugel,
iii. 67.

HARIPOOR, in the Punjab, a town on the great route by the
Dub Pass into Kashmir, is a populous and thriving place, with a
handsome and well-supplied bazaar. Von Hügel considers it one
of the wealthiest places in the Punjab, the streets being thronged
with a busy and cheerful crowd, exhibiting evident indications of
prosperity, and the shops supplied with all that can contribute to
the gratification of Indian taste. It is situate on the river Dor,
which, about ten miles westward, falls into the Indus near Torbela.
Lat. 34° 4', long. 72° 53'.

Leech, App. 30.

HARNAVEE.—A pass little frequented, leading across the
mountains from Tull to Dadur. It is very difficult, and scarcely
practicable for horses. Lat. 29° 27', long. 68°.

HAROOT.—See SUBZAWUR and ADRUSCUND RIVER.

Moorer. Punj.
Bokh. ii. 321;
Hough, Narr. Exp.
in Afg. 337;
Wood, Oxus, 123.

HARU.—A small river of the Punjab, rises at the base of the
Himalaya, and receiving the Nilab from the north-east, and several
smaller streams, flows into the Indus on the eastern side, a few
miles below Attock, after a course of about sixty miles. This confluence is in lat. 33° 49', long. 72° 16'.

E.I.C. Ms. Doc.

HASHIM CHICHER, in Sinde, a village on the route from
Hyderabad to Schwan, by Kotree, and fifty-five miles north of the
last-mentioned place. It is situate in the narrow alluvial tract between the Lukkee mountains and the Indus, and a mile from
the right bank of the main channel. The road, for some miles
north and south of the village, is good, but water is scarce except when obtained from the Indus. Lat. 25° 58', long. 68°
14'.

E.I.C. Ms. Doc.

HASSAN KHAN.—A village in Afghanistan, on the route
from Ghuznee to Shawl, and fifty miles north of the latter place.
It is situate on the right bank of the river Lora, and on the descent
from the Toba mountain to the valley of Pisheen. Some supplies are obtainable here, but they are not abundant. Lat. 30° 45',
long. 67° 20'.

E.I.C. Ms. Doc.

HATTYAREE, in Beloochistan, a village in Cutch Gundava,
is situate on the Moola river, twenty miles south-east of the town
of Gundava. Lat. 28° 14', long. 67° 43'.

Walker's Map of
N.W. Frontier.

HAVALEE, in the Punjab, a village on the route from Mooltan to Ferozpoor, and seventy-five miles south-west of the latter
place. Lat. 30° 28', long. 73° 31'.

HAZARJOOFT.—A village in Afghanistan, situate on the left bank of the Helmund river. Lat. 31°, long. 63° 45'.

HEDDEEALEE, in the Punjab, a village situate about six miles from the right bank of the river Jailum. Lat. 32° 3', long. 72° 2'.

HELAI.—See HILIYA (in Sinde).

HELMUND,[1] a river in Western Afghanistan, has its remote source on the eastern declivity of the ridge of Hageguk, which connects transversely Hindoo Koosh with Koh-i-baba. This ridge divides the waters flowing southward and eastward into the Helmund, from those flowing northward and westward, into the Oxus or Central Asia. The spot where it rises is well ascertained, as it is three or four miles on the right of the route from Kabool to Bamian. A little below this point the elevation of the bed of the stream above the level of the sea is 11,500 feet,[2] and this may be taken as the height of the source of the Helmund, which is in lat. 34° 40', long. 68° 2'. Its fall in the early part of its course is very rapid, as at Gurdan Dewar, at the western end of the Oonna Pass, and about fifteen miles further down the stream, the elevation is 10,076 feet. According to Elphinstone, who, however, writes on report, the Helmund holds its course for two hundred miles through the Huzareh mountains, and leaves them to enter the Durani possessions, through which it pursues a south-westerly course to Giriskh, situated about three hundred and fifty miles from its source. The same authority[3] states that it is in this part breast-high at the fords during the season when lowest; and Griffith intimates that it is navigable[4] downwards, though upwards, navigation is impracticable, in consequence of the rapidity of the current. At Giriskh, where it has been surveyed by Europeans, the banks are about a thousand yards apart; in spring, at which season it is fullest, in consequence of the melting of the snow, it spreads beyond these limits, and has a depth of ten or twelve feet, with a very powerful and rapid current. At this time it is said to be a favourite trial of skill in archery to attempt to shoot an arrow across, though it does not appear that the object is ever effected. As summer advances, however, the water becomes much lower as well as narrower,[5] and is in many places fordable. Conolly, who crossed it at the lowest season, near Girishk, found it stirrup-deep, with a clear, smooth, rapid current, and three hundred and fifty yards wide.

E.I.C. Ms. Doc.

Walker's Map of N.W. Frontier.

[1] E.I.C. Ms.Doc. Map, from Gooljatooe to Bamian; Wood, Oxus, 204; Baber, Mem. 146; Masson, Bal. Afg. Panj. ii. 333; Jour. As. Soc. 1833, p. 6; Gerard, Route from Peshawur to Bokhara.

[2] Jour. As. Soc. 1841, p. 814, Grif. Rep. on Subjects connected with Afg.; Id. 1842, p. 69, Grif. Bar. and Ther. Obs.; Outram, Rough Notes, 138; Hough, Narr. Exp. in Afg. App. 74; Wood, Route of Kab. and Toorkestan, 24. [3] Elph. Acc. of Cabul, 115.

[4] Jour. As. Soc. Grif. Rep. on Subjects connected with Afg.

[5] Conolly (A.), Jour. to India, ii.

7 Journ. Beng.
Eng. ii. 121.

Forster,[7] who crossed it at Girishk, in November, describes it as " a small stream of good water." The immediate banks are very fertile, but at a short distance from the river the country on each side is an arid, barren desert, nearly uninhabited. At about twenty-five miles below Girishk, it receives the Urgundab, flowing from the east; a hundred and twenty miles lower down, it takes a westerly direction, and, after a further course of thirty miles, turns at Pullaluk north-west. At Pullaluk it was crossed by

8 In App. to
Pott. Belooch.
400.

Christie,[8] who found it, at the end of March, four hundred yards wide, and very deep; but by proceeding some distance down the stream, he succeeded in fording it. In this part of its course it flows through the valley of Gurmsehl, two or three miles in width, and luxuriantly fertile, being formed, apparently, by the violence of the broad and rapid river in time of inundation. Everywhere traces of former cultivation, wealth, and civilization are visible, in the ruins of buildings and contrivances for irrigation; but the country is at present occupied by a few barbarous Afghans and Belooches, both nomadic and predatory. Here, however, as in an earlier part of the course of the Helmund, the country, a few miles from the river, is a desert of the most forbidding aspect. Holding a north-westerly course of about a hundred miles, the

9 Jour. As. Soc.
1840, p. 711-719;
Conolly (E.),
Sketch of the
Phys. Geogr. of
Seistan; Pott.
Belooch. 316.

river pours its water over a country perfectly level,[9] and divides into numerous channels, forming various marshes and pools, and, about lat. 31° 30′, long. 62°, discharges itself partly into the extensive lake of Hamoon, and partly into the smaller lake of Duk-i-Teer, situate at a short distance to the east of the former, and communicating with it. Both have brackish water, are very

1 Belooch. 303.

shallow, and are overgrown with reeds. Pottinger[1] supposes, with some probability, that it formerly held a southerly course across the desert of Beloochistan to the Indian Ocean, and debouched by the estuary of the Dustee, a scanty, shallow stream, but the channel of which can be traced nearly to the most southern flexure of the Helmund. The total course of the Helmund at present is above six hundred and fifty miles.

1 E.I.C. Ms.Doc.;
Conolly(A,), Jour.
to India, ii. 2;
Frazer, Jour.to
Khorasan, App.
29, 30.

HERAT,[1] in Afghanistan, is a city near the western frontier, the capital of a state formed in 1818 by Shah Mahmood, on the dismemberment of the Durani monarchy. It is situate three miles north of the Heri Rood or Hury river; from which it is supplied with water by means of aqueducts. The valley in which it is

2 Christie, in App.
Pott. Belooch. 411;

seated is very fertile and well watered,[2] but was left in a state of utter desolation by the Persians, on their retreat, when baffled in their attempt to take Herat in 1838. The city is of an oblong shape, one thousand six hundred yards in length and one thousand four hundred broad. It is entirely inclosed by an artificial mound of earth, varying from forty to sixty feet in height, surmounted by a wall rising from twenty-five to thirty feet above the mound. There are about thirty round bastions on each face, those at the angles being much larger and higher than the rest. The bastions, as well as the wall, are built of unburned brick. The mound of earth slopes down from the base of the rampart to the ditch, at an angle of from thirty-five to forty-five degrees; its breadth at the base is from ninety to a hundred feet. On this exterior slope, a trench, about seven feet deep, runs all round, parallel to the rampart, from which it is distant about thirty feet; and at the same distance outside this and parallel to it, there is a similar trench. These communicate with each other and with the town by subterraneous passages. At the bottom of the mound,[3] a deep wet ditch, thirty feet wide, runs entirely round the town. There are five gates, each defended by a small outwork. At the northern end of the town is a citadel, flanked with large massive towers of burned brick, sixty or seventy feet high, surrounded by a deep wet ditch, twelve yards wide, and accessible only by a bridge, which might be destroyed in a few minutes. The citadel is so strong, that it might probably be held for a considerable time after the fall of the town. On the northern face of the town is an outwork, which covers the citadel and one of the gates. On the same side, and about five hundred yards from the walls, is an immense mound, raised by Nadir Shah[4] when he besieged the town. From the extent of the place, it has been calculated that from 25,000 to 30,000 men would be required to invest it, and that at least 10,000 would be required to adequately garrison it. Its great strength would render its capture under any circumstances a work of extraordinary difficulty. Water is abundant, there being several springs in the ditch, and numerous wells, not more than twelve or fourteen feet deep, in the town; besides which, the water brought from the Heri Rood by means of aqueducts is stored in numerous extensive reservoirs of masonry covered over.

The city is divided into quarters by four long bazaars, covered with arches of brick, and meeting in the centre in a small

Forster, Journ. Beng. Eng. ii.129; Jour. As. Soc. 1334, p. 10; Mohun Lal, Brief Descrip. of Herat; Elph. Acc. of Caubul, 488.

[3] Burnes on Herat, 38.

[4] Malcolm, Hist. Persia, ii. 51.

quadrangle, surmounted by a dome. The houses are generally two stories high, and have very small doors. Herat is one of the dirtiest places in the world.[4] Many of the small streets branching from the main ones are built over, and form dark, low tunnels, loaded with revolting filth. There are no channels for drainage, and the waste water is allowed to collect and stagnate in pools. The streets, the receptacles of every sort of refuse, are filled with heaps of dung, and are often encumbered with the putrifying carcases of animals. So gross a disregard of cleanliness is necessarily productive of infectious disease, but, independently of this source of sickness, the climate is in general considered healthy. The residence of the Shah is a mean building. The Musjid-i-Juma, or principal mosque, once a very grand one, is going fast to decay. It was erected in the thirteenth century, to replace a similar fabric destroyed by Zingis Khan. When perfect, it was four hundred and sixty-five feet long,[5] and two hundred and seventy-five feet wide; it had four hundred and eight cupolas, a hundred and thirty windows, four hundred and forty-four pillars, six entrances, and was adorned in the most magnificent manner with gilding, carving, mosaic, precious stones, and other elaborate and costly embellishments. About a mile to the north of the city are the magnificent ruins of a Moosullah or place of worship, dedicated to the memory of the Imaum Reza, and still exhibiting the remains of a vast series of beautiful and costly buildings. Behind a lofty front is a court of a hundred yards square, the cloistered sides of which are embellished with beautiful designs of flowers and other light and fanciful objects, executed in highly-finished mosaic. Opening into this is a large circular hall, covered by a dome, and communicating with other fine apartments. There are the remains of twenty minarets, among many buildings at once chaste and costly. "We ascended," observes Conolly,[6] " by one hundred and forty steps, to the top of the highest minaret, and thence looked down upon the city, and the rich gardens and vineyards round and beyond it—a scene so varied and beautiful, that I can imagine nothing like it, except perhaps in Italy." There are numerous fanes, public buildings, and gardens, scattered over the neighbourhood, affording evidence of the former splendour of the city, which, if native contemporary writers may be credited, was, in the fifteenth and sixteenth centuries, one of the finest in the world.

[4] Conolly, ut supra, ii. 3.

[5] Price, Mahom. Hist. iii. 644.

[6] ii. 20.

Baber[7] observes, " that in the whole habitable world there was [7] Mem. 204.
not such another city." But all this glory has departed, under
a course of oppression and misrule, and amidst the long-continued and devastating wars of the Persians and Afghans. Conolly,[8] who visited the city in 1830 (eight years before the last [8] ii. 3.
ruinous siege by the Persians), computed that there were 4,000
dwelling-houses and 1,200 shops, with a population of 45,000.
Christie,[9] above twenty years before, stated, " No city has less [9] App. to Pott.
ground unoccupied, and none of its extent can boast of a greater
population," which he computed at 100,000.

Herat is still of importance, from its position in a very fertile
country. The valley in which it is situate is thirty miles long
and fifteen broad. " The space between the hills," observes Co-
nolly,[1] " is one beautiful extent of little fortified villages, gardens, [1] ii 4.
vineyards, and corn-fields; and this rich scene is lightened by
many small streams of shining water." The fruits are remarkably fine, and the bread is proverbially good. The elevation of
the city above the sea is probably very great. The height of the
source of the Heri Rood is 9,500 feet,[2] and if we assign to it a [2] Jour. As. Soc. 1841, p. 118;
fall of twenty feet in the mile, which would make it a very rapid Extracts from
torrent, its descent to Herat would be 7,000 feet, and conse- Deni-Official Rep., Conolly (E.)
quently the height of this city 2,500 feet.* In consequence of this
elevation, the winters are cool, and snow lies for several days,
though the latitude is below that of any part of Europe. The
heat[3] is excessive for about two months in summer. [3] Conolly (A.), Jour. to India,

The position of Herat is also important in both a military and ii. 5; Jour. As.
commercial view, as commanding the most frequented route from Conolly (E.),
Persia to Afghanistan. In settled times, perhaps no inland place Sketch of Phys.
in Asia has so brisk or lucrative a trade, and hence it has received Geog. of Seistan.
the name of *Bunder*, or port. From Hindostan and Eastern
Afghanistan it receives shawls, indigo, sugar, spices, muslins,
chintzes, brocades, (' loongees" or rich scarfs, peltry, dressed leather, and hides ; from Persia, Turkey, Russia, and Central Asia,
bullion, tea, fine sugar, porcelain, glass, silk, and fine fabrics of
cotton, broad-cloth, coarse woollens, felts, carpets, shawls, metals,
and hardware. Silk is produced in the neighbourhood, but not

---

* Humboldt, in the hypsometrial map accompanying *Asie Centrale*, states
the elevation of Herat at four hundred and thirty-eight toises, or two thousand seven hundred and fifty-nine feet, but does not give any authorities for
this estimate.

to an extent adequate to the demand. Lamb-skins and sheep-skins are made up into cloaks and caps in great quantities. The carpets of Herat have been long much esteemed for their softness and the brilliancy and permanency of their colours ; these are fully equal to those of Turkey. The price varies from one to a hundred pounds, but the manufacture is considered to be decaying. The native articles of commerce are not numerous nor important ; the principal are saffron and assafœtida. Conolly[4] states the annual revenue of Herat at 89,248*l*. Burnes[5] thinks that " it is doubtful if the revenue amounts to thirteen lacs of rupees" (about 130,000*l*.). The chief of Herat is Kamran, the son of Mahmood Shah of Kabool, and nephew of Shah Shoojah. His dominion extends but a few miles northward of the city ; on the east it reaches to the Khaush Rood (river), half-way to Kandahar ; on the south it includes Seistan. It is closely pressed on the west by Persia, by which country, a few years ago, the important province of Ghorian was seized. The population both of the city and territory is of a mixed character—Persian, Afghan, Taujik, Belooche, Mogul, Hindoo, and a few Jews. Commerce, capital, and the monetary transactions are for the most part in the hands of the Hindoos. The Persians are generally Shias, the other Mahometans Sunnis. Herat is in lat. 34° 22', long. 62° 9'.

HERI ROOD, or HURY RIVER,[1] in Afghanistan, is a considerable stream rising in the Huzareh country, on the western declivity of Koh-i-Baba, and about lat. 34° 50', long. 66° 20'. Its source is described by Conolly[2] as "a pool of gently bubbling springs, where the boiling point shewed an elevation of 9,500 feet." It hence holds a course generally westerly for about three hundred and fifty miles, to the vicinity of Herat, running about three miles south of that city, at a place where the great route from Kandahar to Herat crosses it. The passage over the river here was formerly[3] made by means of a bridge four hundred yards in length,[4] built of brick, of thirty-three arches,* but about ten years ago three of them were swept away, and, in consequence, the communication is intercepted in time of inundation, when the river is often deep and very rapid. When low, it is here divided into several channels, the

* Abbott occupies ten closely printed pages in relating a tradition respecting this bridge. It is an extravagant, idle, whimsical story, whimsically told. (Heraut and Khiva, 1. 239—249.)

widest of which has a breadth of about forty yards, and a depth of
about eighteen inches.[5] At that time the diminution of its water is   [5] Christie, App. to Pott. Belooch.414.
produced in no small degree by the large quantity drawn off for
irrigation. It is remarkable for the great purity of its water.
The bridge bears the name of Pal-i-Malan, by which appellation
the river is also commonly known.[6] From Herat it takes a north-   [6] Elph. Acc. of Caubul, 117, 665.
westerly course of about two hundred and fifty miles, to its
junction with the Moorghab,[7] and the united stream is subsequently   [7] Fraser, Journ. in Khorasan, App. 57.
lost in the desert of Khorasan.

HIDDA.[1]—A village in Afghanistan, five miles south of the   [1] E.I.C. Ms. Doc.
city of Jelalabad. It is remarkable for several topes, mounds, and
caves, the relics of a people of whom no other memorial exists.
The topes may be described as structures of rude masonry,
having generally a cylindrical base, surmounted by a hemisphe-
rical dome. They are solid,[2] as the fact that they have been   [2] Wilson, Ariana Antiqua, 39.
found in most instances to contain small cases, the depositories
of relics, cannot be considered to negative this position. There
are thirteen or fourteen topes at Hidda. Those which have been
opened have been ascertained to contain ashes, bones, and other
decayed animal matter, metallic and earthen vessels, gold and
silver ornaments, and many gems and coins; to quote the words
of Masson, " the major part silver Sassanian, but also seven gold
ones, of which, singular to relate, are five of Roman emperors—
two of Theodosius, two of Leo, and one of Marcianus."[3] As those   [3] Jour. As. Soc. 1835, p. 234.
emperors reigned between A.D. 408 and 474, there is thus con-   Acc. of Masson's Oper. and Disco-
clusive evidence that the structures in which these coins have   veries.
been found must have belonged to an era not earlier than the
fifth century; and as they are by the best judges regarded as unquestionably Buddhist monuments, they cannot be referred to a
later period than the eighth century, at which period Mahometanism became predominant in Afghanistan. The conclusion
of Professor Wilson[4] on this subject is as follows : " It seems   [4] Ariana Antiqua, 44.
likely that the interval between the beginning of the Chris-
tian era and the sixth century was the period when the
chief topes of this part of India were built, and the most
perfect of them in the present day may be dated about the
fourth and fifth centuries." According to the same high
authority, the topes were erected as depositories of Buddhist
relics. Others regard them as places of sepulture for eminent

[5] Prinsep, quoted in W ilson45. persons deceased. Others,[5] again, consider them as devoted to both purposes. Hidda is in lat. 34° 19′, long. 70° 25′.

E.I.C. Ms. Doc. HIDDAWGOTE.—A village of Sinde, on the route from Sehwan to Larkhana, and twelve miles north of the former place. The road north and south is rendered inconvenient by numerous water-courses, which aid the cultivation of this fertile and populous tract. The village is situate about a mile from the right bank of the Indus. Lat. 26° 32′, long. 67° 53′.

HILIYA.—See HILLAYA.

HILIYA.—See CHILIYA.

E.I.C. Ms. Doc. Wood's Oxus, 24; Burnes' Pers Narr. 10; Lord, Med. Mem. on the Plain of the Indus, 50. HILLAYA, in Sinde, a small town on the route from Tatta to Hyderabad, by Kotree, and thirty-two miles south of the last-mentioned place. It is situate near the eastern extremity of the Kunjur Dund, a considerable expanse of brackish water, abounding in fish, and surrounded by low sandstone hills. Close *Shikarghas*, or " hunting-preserves," intervene between the town and the right bank of the Indus, distant about a mile and a half to the east. Plenty of forage may be obtained, and water is supplied from a small pond near the town. Lat. 24° 55′, long. 68° 8′.

Burnos (James), Mission to Sinde, 33. HIMIUT, in Sinde, a small village, having a scanty supply of brackish water, on the route from Cutch to Hyderabad. Lat. 24° 8′, long. 68° 40′.

E.I.C. Ms. Doc. HINDAN, in Afghanistan, a village on the route, by the Gomul Pass, from Ghuznee to Dera Ismael Khan, and twenty miles west of the latter place. Lat. 31° 49′, long. 70° 39′.

[1] E.I.C. Ms. Map. HINDOO KOOSH.[1]—A vast and lofty mountain between Afghanistan and Turkestan. It is also frequently called the [2] As. Researches, vi. 461, on Mount Caucasus. Hindoo Koh (Hindoo mountain), but this, Wilford[2] states to be a distortion by Persian authors and travellers; and he intimates that the correct name is Hindoo Koosh, and that it must have originated with the Tartars, amongst some nations of whom [3] Id. 458. *Chasu*[3] signifies snow, from which the derivation of the name is natural and obvious, the range being remarkable for the number of its snowy summits. The natives, according to Wilford, believe " that this name, Hindoo Koosh, was given to the mountains from a certain giant, who used to lie there in wait to catch (*cash*) or to kill (*kesh*) all the Hindoos who passed that way." [4] Asie Centrale, i. 147, N. [5] Erdkunde von Asien, vii. 199. Not less trivial is the etymology of Ibn Batuta (which, however, has been thought worthy of notice by Humboldt[4] and Ritter[5]),

that the mountain was so called from being, in consequence of the cold, the destroyer or killer * (*keesh*) of the Hindoo slaves whom the slave-dealers attempted to transport into Tartary.† But, however the appellation may have originated, it is at present that most usually given to the mountain. It has often been observed, the Koh Kosh, or mountain of Kosh, offers a plausible etymology for the Caucasus of the classical writers. It is supposed by Ritter[6] and Wilford[7] to be that mentioned by Pliny under the name of *Graucasus*, but slightly deviating from the Sanscrit *Grava-kasas*[8] (shining rock). Humboldt regards it as a part of a vast range to which, from Chinese authorities, he gives the name of Kouenlun, and represents as the " most striking geological phenomenon amongst all the mountain-ranges of the old world."[9] He considers that the range may be traced from Taurus, in Asia Minor, across Persia, then, in the maze of the Huzareh mountains, to Hindoo Koosh, and subsequently, in the Kouenlun, to the frontier of China Proper, from the thirtieth to the ninety-fifth meridian east, and between the parallels 34°—37° lat. north. He regards this prolonged range as altogether distinct from that of the Himalaya, farther south, and the distinction as not verbal merely, but substantial, having reference to the origin of the two ranges. Both, according to his theory, have arisen from the disruption and upheaving of the crust of the globe by the expansive force of the igneous interior, the Kouenlun in a direction nearly due east and west, the Himalaya, inclined to this direction, and a few degrees farther to the south. Whatever may be thought of the theory, it is certain that the two ranges are physically discriminated by the vast depression down which the Indus flows in a north-westerly direction, which, with its numerous rocky irregularities, it is not easy to believe could have been hollowed out by the waters even of that great river.

It is obvious that there must always be something arbitrary in defining and marking out a portion of a vast range to be designated by a particular name. Humboldt places the eastern limit

[6] Id.

[7] As. Researches, ut supra.

[8] Humboldt, i. 109.

[9] Asie Centrale, i. xxii. 106, 130; ii. 11, 12.

* Shakespeare, in v. ‮كش‬

† The words of Ibn Batuta are—" After this I proceeded to the city of Barwan, in the road to which is a high mountain covered with snow, and exceedingly cold ; they call it Hindu Koush, *i. e.* Hindoo slayer, because most of the slaves brought thither from India die on account of the intenseness of the cold." Pp. 97, 98.

1 Asie Centrale, ii. 373.
2 Elph. 87.
3 Bokh. ii. 238.

4 85.

5 Jour. As. Soc. 1841, p. 801, Rep. on Subjects connected with Afg.
6 Asie Centrale, i. xxii—xxvii, 25. 30,

7 Royle. Introd. to Botany of the Himalaya Mountains, xi. xxiii.

8 Koonawur, 141.

9 Elph. 86.
1 Punj. Bokh. i. 426-450.
2 Royle, ut supra, xxiv.

of Hindoo Koosh at Thsoungling,[1] where the great range of the Bolor, or Beloot Taugh,[2] passes off to the north at right angles. Burnes[3] places the eastern limit at the place where the range " crosses the Indus," or, as he explains it, takes a course due west. From this expression, he seems to place the eastern limit about long. 73°. Elphinstone[4] fixes the eastern limit about the meridian of the centre of Kashmir, or 74° 30', observing, " from Kashmir to Hindoo Koosh the whole range is known by the name of that peak." Griffith narrows its limits, placing the eastern extremity at Olipore,[5] in lat. 34° 54', long. 70° 12'. Humboldt[6] and others, who have attempted to draw information from Chinese sources, praise strongly the accuracy and copiousness of the writers of that nation on topography ; yet accurate information with regard to this part of Asia is limited to those portions from which the jealous and vigilant government of China has not been able to exclude Europeans. Thus in proceeding westward, our knowledge commences with the elevated region of Tibet, north of Lake Manasa Soravara, which was first made known to us by Moorcroft and Gerard. Here the Kailas mountain rises to a height perhaps not less than 30,000 feet above the sea.[7] One of the surveyors (probably the late Captain Gerard, who has been already mentioned), states that from the crest of the Hungarung Pass, he saw, in front, a granite range, upon which the snow found a resting-place only at 19,000 feet : beyond it, through a break, were discernible snowy mountains, appearing to rise out of the table-land on the banks of the Indus, " pale with distance, and like the memory of something that we have seen." From the angles of altitude observed, the pale outline of the mountains and the broad margin of the snow, the surveyor estimated that they could not be less than 29,000 feet in elevation. Gerard,[8] also, elsewhere estimates the height of this part of Kouenlun at 30,000 feet; and this is probably the most elevated part, not only of the range, but of the surface of the globe. Westward of the Kailas summit, and commencing about long. 79°, the Kouenlun range is generally known by the name of Mooz Taugh (ice-hill), and sometimes by that of Karakorum.[9] It has been, to a certain extent, explored by Moorcroft[1] and Trebeck, who travelled a considerable distance along its south-western base, and by Falconer,[2] who ascended to the limit of cultivation, where he was informed that a region of ice

extended in the direction of Tartary for a considerable distance.
Mir Izzet Ullah, an agent despatched by Moorcroft, crossed the
Mooz Taugh from Leh to Yarkund, by the pass of Karakorum,
in lat. 35° 30′, long. 77° 40′. This person found the ground
sheeted with ice, and experienced much sickness and difficulty
of breathing, from the height above the sea ; but notwithstanding, the range here must be considerably depressed, as it
permitted of his passage at the end of October.[2] This view [2] Travels beyond
of the subject is confirmed by Vigne, who ascended the Mooz the Himalaya,
Taugh for a short distance, and expresses his opinion " that terly Orient. Mag.
its elevation was not so great as that of many other passes in 1825.
Tibet." He adds, " putting together all I heard on the subject, I should say that it will be found somewhat under 15,000
feet."[3] Between Yarkund and Karakorum lies a waste, nearly [3] Kashmir, ii. 304.
three hundred miles across, which, like the table-land of Pamir,
farther west, is too elevated to admit of being permanently inhabited ; and should winter here overtake the traveller, he must
of necessity perish of cold or hunger. Westward of the Kara-
korum Pass, the Kouenlun becomes still more elevated, as Vigne [4] [4] Ut supra, ii. 358.
states that " the snowy Sierra of the Muztuk, extending from
Hunzeh to Nubra, arose with conspicuous and most majestic
grandeur."

About a degree farther west, Vigne explored this great range,
called variously the Kouenlun, Mooz Taugh, or Hindoo Koosh,
and still found it a series of summits covered with perpetual snow,
and having in the valleys vast and to the eye interminable gla-
ciers. Describing the valley of Tsutron, he states : " Enormous
mountains of gneiss rose on either side of it. Those over the
farther end were very elevated, and covered with eternal snow."[5] [5] Kashmir, ii. 270.
To the north of this part of the range is the elevated region extending south of Yarkund, comprising the Bolor mountains, and
extending east of them. This tract of frightful desolation appears
to have been brought to notice in recent times by the inquiries
of Vigne, and the journey of Mir Izzet Ullah. In the middle of
the thirteenth century it was referred to by the celebrated Marco
Polo.[6] Having mentioned the journey across Pamir, he adds : [6] Travels, transla-
"After having performed a journey of twelve days, you have still ted by Marsden,
forty days to travel in the same direction, over mountains and 142.
through valleys in perpetual succession, passing many rivers and

desert tracts, without seeing any habitation or the appearance of verdure. Every article of provision must therefore be carried along with you. This region is called Beloro."*

Here, about long. 74°, lat. 36°, Humboldt, in his map, lays down Thsoungling, the place of junction of the great mountain-range of Bolor, running from north to south, with that of Kouenlun, or Hindoo Koosh, running nearly east and west, or rather inclining towards a direction from north-west to south-east. This view corresponds with that of Waddington, in his excellent map and memoir [7] prefixed to Baber's Memoirs. This supposed junction of the two great ranges is, however, matter of conjecture, as it does not appear to have been ever explored. Arrowsmith, in his elaborate map accompanying Moorcroft's Travels, embellishes it with a goodly peak. Walker,[8] with his usual admirable accuracy, leaves it a complete blank. Humboldt, indeed, here in his map lays down the peak of Tutuean Mutcani as having an elevation of 3,000 toises, or 18,900 feet, but appears to give no authority, except a reference to Elphinstone which is erroneous. The silence of native report with regard to this part of the range appears to indicate its moderate height, as very lofty mountains have a prominent notice in popular accounts, in consequence of the awe and admiration which they cause. North and north-west of the place which Humboldt assigns to Thsoungling, is the elevated region of Pamir, giving rise, among other great rivers, to the Oxus, which flows from Lake Sir-i-Kol, at an elevation of 15,600 feet. Hindoo Koosh, or Kouenlun, he found here to be 19,000 feet above the sea. " The elevated expanse of Pameer," observes the intrepid and judicious traveller just quoted, " is not only a radiating point in the hydrographical system of Central Asia, but is the focus from which originate its principal mountain-chains," being " common to India, China, and Turkistan; and from it, as from a central point, their several streams diverge."[9] The line of perpetual congelation is at the height of 17,000 feet, in lat. 37°; and the ice is melted on the lake; by the end of June it becomes covered with water-fowl, and the surrounding plain, for a short time, yields

* Humboldt, with his usual acuteness and diligence, points out several passages in Marco Polo, which prove that his work was not a personal narrative, but an admirable compilation.

luxuriant pasture. In winter, it is an awful waste, utterly deserted by every form of animal life. That the range of Kouenlun,
or Hindoo Koosh, is considerably depressed at Thsoungling, or
about lat. 36°, long. 75°, is attested by Wood, who observes,[1] [1] Oxus, 36.
" from Pamir, the ground sinks in every direction, except to the
south-east, where similar plateaux extend along the northern face
of the Himalaya into Tibet. An individual who had seen the region between Wakhan and Kashmir, informed me that the Kuner
river had its principal source in a lake resembling that in which
the Oxus has its rise, and that the whole of this country, comprehending the districts of Gilgit, Gunjet, and Chitral, is a series
of mountain defiles that act as water-courses to drain Pamir."
It should be borne in mind that the Kuner falls into the river of
Kabool. While the Hindoo Koosh to the north has the elevated
table-land of Pamir, from its southern side stretch numerous
ridges in a south or south-west direction, inclosing the valleys
of Suwat, Panjkora, Chitral, Kafiristan, and some others further
west. These subordinate ridges pass off nearly south in a direction
inclined to the culminating ridge of Hindoo Koosh, which runs a
little south of west for about three hundred miles, from Thsoungling, the locality of which has been already stated, to the peak of
Hindoo Koosh Proper, rising, in lat. 35° 40', long. 68° 50', with
pre-eminent height and grandeur. From this culminating ridge,
the ground has a general slope to the banks of the Kabool river
and the Indus, in some places from an elevation of 20,000 feet,
in others of little more than one thousand. As the ridges which
inclose the valleys just described are usually very lofty, their extremities, seen obliquely from the valley of the Kabool river, present the appearance of a range : accordingly, Wood styles this
series of elevations the Himalaya, both in his map and text,
and in this he is followed by Humboldt in laying down his map.
The former states that the Himalaya, " as is well known,
bounds Hindustan on the north, and after crossing the river
Indus, extends westward to the valley of Punchshir and the meridian of Kabool."[2]   But there is surely very great laxity both of [2] Oxus, 367.
language and thought, in designating as a continuous range a series
of extremities of distinct ranges, separated in several instances by
spacious valleys and considerable rivers. Indeed, Wood[3] sub- [3] Id.
sequently observes, " the Himalaya is pierced by both the
Kuner and Indus rivers." He might have added, by the Suwat,

the Lundye, the Alingar, the Alishang, and the Tagow rivers.
Elphinstone[3] describes the mountains south of the culminating
range of the Hindoo Koosh as forming three several ranges,
rising in succession as they recede from the plain of Peshawur,
but certainly giving no appearance of a great continuation of the
Himalaya, or of Southern Hindoo Koosh, as Humboldt lays it
down in his map, slightly inclined to the great or northern range.
With respect to the height of the culminating ridge of Hindoo
Koosh, nothing, perhaps, can be regarded well ascertained, but
the measurement by Macartney[4] of a point, probably about
the meridian of Peshawur, or 71° 40', and in lat. 35° 30', which
was found to have an altitude of 20,493 feet; and again, the
measurement by Wood[5] of summits from the valley of Jelalabad, and about long. 70° 30', which were found to have a mean
elevation of 20,248 feet.   Between the part on which this last
measurement bears and the Khawak Pass, situate some distance
to the west, we know little of the culminating ridge.   It appears,
however, that Timur, the Jagatain conqueror, crossed it some-
where from Inderab to Kafiristan, but his army was obliged to
leave their horses behind, and slide down the mountain on the
ice.[6]   Kafiristan has hitherto been unexplored, but must in many
parts be considerably depressed, as the climate is so warm as to
allow the growth of the vine in great excellence, and from its
abundance the Kafirs have become notorious for their wine-bibbing
propensities.—See Kafiristan.

At the western extremity of their country our intimate knowledge of Hindoo Koosh commences with the Khawak Pass, explored and surveyed by Wood.   It lies in lat. 35° 38', long. 70°,
and from it the river of Inderab[7] flows to the north to join the
Oxus, and the Punchshir to the south to join the river of Kabool,
and ultimately the Indus.   The ascent of the pass on the north side
is an inclined plane, as Wood expresses it, "remarkably uniform, not a ridge occurring in the whole ascent to vary the same-
ness of its surface."   Its highest point is 13,200 feet above the sea.
It is probably the most practicable of the passes for an army, and
was that taken by Tamerlane[8] in his invasion of India, on which
occasion he rebuilt the fort of Khawak, visited by Wood, and
situated ten miles on the Kabool side of the summit.   Westward
of the Khawak Pass, the culminating ridge takes a direction, for
about fifty miles, nearly due west, as far as the summit of

3 204.

4 Elph. 95.

5 Khyber Pass, 2.

6 Price, Mahom.
Hist. iii. 222.

7 Wood's Oxus,
413.

8 Price, Chronol.
Retrospect, iii.220.

Hindoo Koosh Proper, or that great collection of peaks which gives name to the entire range. The surface to the north of the part of the ridge just described sinks very suddenly, so that the town of Kunduz, only eighty miles distant, is less than five hundred feet above the level of the sea,[9] or nearly 20,000 feet below the average height of that part of the range. This circumstance forms a remarkable contrast with the state of the surface on the south side of the range, as there the highlands of Kabool, Ghuznee, and Beloochistan extend, with an elevation averaging from 5,000 to 8,000 feet, to within [1] forty or fifty miles of the Indian Ocean. Consequent on this arrangement of surface are some remarkable peculiarities of climate observable in this vast mass of mountains. On Pamir, where there is a very great extent of surface having an average elevation nearly equal to that of the summit of Mont Blanc, the limit of perpetual congelation is probably, if compared with the latitude (37° 38′), much more elevated than in any other part of the world, being at the height of 17,000 feet,[2] while farther west, where the surface declines rapidly to Kunduz, the climate is much more severe, and the line of perpetual congelation proportionably descends.[3] Even on the southern face of the Himalaya, snow lies lower down than on the northern, to an extent corresponding with 4,000 feet perpendicular descent. On this Lord observes, " But the Himalaya and Hindoo Koosh have the same aspect, the same general direction, lie nearly in the same latitude, and in fact are little more than integral parts of the same chain. The local circumstances, however, connected with each are precisely reversed. The Himalaya has to the north the elevated steppes of Central Asia, and to the south the long low plains of Hindostan. Hindoo Koosh, on the other hand, has to the south the elevated plains of Kabool and Koh-i-Damun, between five and six thousand feet above the level of the sea, while to the north, stretch away the depressed, sunken, and swampy flats of Turkestan." Perhaps nowhere does the determination of the limit of perpetual congelation appear subject to greater anomalies than in this vast mountain system ; but with little exception, it seems to be more elevated than abstract reasoning would lead us to expect. Nowhere are more strikingly manifested the intricacy, variableness, and uncertainty of the data for ascertaining the position of the isothermal lines. An illustrious writer, though foremost amongst those who

[9] Lord, Koh-i-Damun, 49 ; Wood, Khyber Pass, 2.

[1] Pott. 32-47.

[2] Wood's Oxus, 364.

[3] Lord, ut supra, 48.

have attempted to reduce to system the speculations and facts
connected with this subject, has shewn that the task involves
the consideration of so great a variety of points as tó render
it one of the most difficult and hazardous within the range
of physical inquiry. He[4] observes, that it is " a problem
much more complicated than it was at first considered. In
proportion as greater number of elements are offered to our
discussion, we have found that the limit of perpetual congelation
is not exclusively a function of the latitude, and that it is not at
the equator that this limit attains the greatest elevation above the
level of the sea. It is, in the first place, requisite to ascertain the
facts and arrange them suitably. The variation of temperature in
different seasons; the dryness of the air; the thickness of the mass
of the clouds ; the proportion of the limit to the total height of the
summit; the proximity of neighbouring summits equally covered
with snow; the steepness of the slopes ; the extent, the position,
and the height of the plains; the radiation from those plains, according as they may be wooded, clothed in grass, or overspread
with arid sands; the direction of the prevailing winds, and their
contact with the sea ; such are the causes, acting simultaneously,
and one of which only—the variation of the temperature—depends
mainly on the latitude. This last cause is undoubtedly the most
energetic." From such considerations, he concludes[5] " that the
prodigious elevation of the snows on the Tibetan slope of the
Himalaya, between the rivers Gundhuk and Sutledge, admitted
of a satisfactory solution by means of the radiation of heat from
the adjacent table-land, as well as from the serenity of the sky
and the scanty snows which fall in an air intensely cold and extremely dry." Thus he, in the main, coincides with the opinion of
Lord, that the anomalous height of the limit of perpetual congelation on the southern slope of Hindoo Koosh results from the great
extent and elevation of the country stretching southwards of it.

The great summit of Hindoo Koosh Proper, remarkable for its
vast mass and elevation, as well as for giving name to the whole
range, is situate at an angle where the culminating ridge, previously
running east and west, turns to the south-west, or rather in a direction still more inclined to south. It is in lat. 35° 40′, long. 68° 50,′
and at Kabool, distant above eighty miles to the south, is distinctly visible, overtopping the lofty eminences intérvening,[6] and
entirely enveloped in snow. Viewed from Kaita Sang, in the

[4] Humboldt, Asie Centrale, iii. 247.

[5] iii. 244.

[6] Burnes' Bokh. ii. 247.

Koushan Pass, and distant ten miles south, its appearance is very sublime. The outline is serrated, it being crowned by a succession of lofty peaks, with sides often perpendicular, and it is wrapped in a perpetual covering of snow [7] in all parts not too steep [7 E.I.C. Ms.Doc.] to admit its lying. This vast summit is visible from Kunduz, a hundred and fifty miles north.[8] Though the engineers belonging [8 Burnes, Bokh. ii. 287.] to the British force stationed at Kabool were for two years in sight of Hindoo Koosh, it does not appear that any measurement has been made of its height. Lord and Leech, who ascended the Koushan Pass, which traverses the eastern shoulder of the summit, conjectured the crest of the pass to be fifteen thousand feet above the sea,[9] and as the highest peaks towered far above them, the ele- [9 Lord, Koh-i-Damun, 48.] vation of the culminating point may, with much probability, be conjectured to exceed twenty thousand feet. East and west of this great summit, numerous subordinate ridges stretch from the culminating range in a direction nearly due south, and parallel to each other, inclosing between them a succession of gorges or narrow valleys, up which various passes run, and afford communication between Afghanistan and Turkestan. Above twenty of these valleys have been ascertained to exist in a distance of about a hundred and fifty miles, between the Khawak Pass and Bamian, where the range of Hindoo Koosh may be considered to terminate to the west. Of these passes, the most important, the Khawak, the Shutul, the Sir Ulung, the Purwan, the Koushan, the Gwalian, and a few others, are described under their titles in the alphabetical arrangement. The total length of Hindoo Koosh, or that part of Kouenlun extending from Karakorum to Bamian, is about eight hundred and fifty miles. At the south-western extremity the range becomes considerably depressed, so as generally to be no longer regarded as part of Hindoo Koosh, but deemed merely a connecting elevation between that range and the Koh-i-Baba, running east and west, a little to the south. Yet so high is that tract,.though depressed as compared with Hindoo Koosh, that the crests of the passes which traverse it have elevations which in other regions would be thought extreme: Kaloo, 10,883 ; Oonna, 11,320 ; Hajeguk, 11,700 ; Erak, 12,909 feet.* To the west of Bamian we may, in the Huzareh mountains, trace the continuation of the great chain, called by Humboldt the Kouenlun,

* See BAMIAN, and the table of heights in Afghanistan, and the authorities there quoted.

and more generally Hindoo Koosh (see HUZAREH MOUNTAINS);
and still farther west, in that table-land which, with an elevation
of from three thousand to four thousand feet, extends across

¹ Fraser, Khora-
san, 244; Hum-
boldt, Asie Cen-
trale, i. 106.
Persia,¹ and is connected both with the Caucasus, properly so
called, and with the Taurus of Asia Minor. This has been shewn
² Id. l. xxii. xxiii.
139.
by Humboldt² not to have escaped the comprehensive views and
research of the Greek geographers. Of the passes over Hindoo
³ Wood's Oxus,
413, 417.
Koosh, that of Khawak, though probably the easiest,³ as already
mentioned, is little frequented, partly because the country
lying immediately north of it is less important, in a political,
commercial, and military point of view, than those farther west;
partly on account of dangers apprehended from the Kafirs who
infest it. The Koushan Pass has of late years been much fre-
⁴ Hind. Koosh,
29.
quented, as Leech⁴ observes, " not so much from its being less
free of material difficulties, as from its being less infested by robbers than others." The route by Bamian appears to be the only
one ascertained to be practicable for artillery, which has been con-
⁵ Wood, Route of
Kabool and Tur-
kestan, 24.
veyed over both the Hajeguk and the Erak passes.⁵ Though the
elevation of the ground to the north of Bamian in general dimi-
nishes as the road proceeds northwards, the height in many
places is considerable. The heights of the passes, traversed on the
⁶ Id. ut supra,
305.
road northwards, in Kunduz, are as follow—that of Akrobat,⁶
(lat. 34° 56′, long. 67° 40′) 10,200 feet; Kara Kotul (lat. 35° 26′,
long. 67° 53′), 10,500; of Dundun Shikun (lat. 35° 12′, long.
67° 42′), 9,000; the fort of Kamurd, four miles north of the last-
mentioned place, 5,600.

The passes, already described as traversing the range in a direction north and south, cross-cut the strata, and afford a remarkable
insight into the geological structure of the mountain in the vicinity
of the summit of Hindoo Koosh Proper. In the Koushan Pass, it
⁷ Lord, Koh-i-
Damun, 49, 50.
was found to consist of a core⁷ of granite of beautiful appearance,
the felspar being purely white, and the hornblende glossy, black,
and collected into large spheroidal concretions, varying in size
from two or three inches to upwards of a foot in diameter.
This granite has been ascertained to form the interior part of the
⁸ Burnes, ii. 246.
range to a great extent, being seen, both by Lord and Burnes,⁸ at
the western extremity of Hindoo Koosh, north of Bamian, and
there assuming an appearance resembling basalt. On each side
of the granite are huge strata of slate, gneiss, chlorite, carbonate
of lime, quartz, and, exterior to these, secondary limestone and

fossiliferous sandstones. The slate formation is much thicker on the south than on the north side of Hindoo Koosh ; in the former position it is between twenty and thirty miles thick,[9] in the latter, [9] Lord, p. 50. only four or five miles. The strata run due east and west, and have an angle of seventy-five degrees with the horizon. There are strong indications of volcanic action in the valley of Ghorbund,[1] at the base of Hindoo Koosh, and these are continued [1] Id. 53, 56. westward beyond Bamian, being traced for one hundred miles in that direction. It may be presumed that the earthquakes frequent at Kabool and in the valley of Jelalabad originate from this cause. The principal minerals are silver,[2] lead, iron, zinc, and [2] Id. 55. antimony. Gold[3] is obtained, according to Burnes, at Fouladut, [3] Burnes, ii. 246. in the vicinity of Bamian, as well as copper and tin ; but the last is of such rare occurrence, that his cursory and unsupported mention cannot be received as sufficient evidence of its existence. Lord states that copper is not to be found in the parts of Hindoo Koosh lying north of Kabool, but that it is met with at Bajour, farther east, where also iron-ore of the finest quality abounds. Lead-ore of the richest quality is abundant from Hindoo Koosh Proper to Bamian, and is extensively worked, but not so much so as formerly, as appears from the vast and skilful excavations of the Moguls still visible in the neglected mine of Ferengal, at the base of Hindoo Koosh Proper. The black iron-ore of Hajeguk, near Bamian, is in such quantities as to form great hills, and is of very rich quality.

Hindoo Koosh is in general characterized by barrenness, and in a remarkable degree by want of timber. Wood[4] observes, [4] Oxus, 365. that what most forcibly strikes a traveller in these regions is the nakedness of the country. " There are," he says, " no timber-yielding trees indigenous to the Hindoo Koosh, in which appellation I include the range from its first rise in Pamir to its termination at Koh-i-Baba, a remarkable mountain to the north-west of Kabool." There are, however, dwarf firs,[5] willows, [5] Moorcr. i. 306. poplars, and birches, besides a few others introduced by man, and numerous fruit-trees, also owing their existence to his fostering care. The general fuel is a scrubby sort of furze-bush, affording a very scanty and insufficient resource in this bitter climate. Some indigenous vegetables are highly useful. The prangos, according to Moorcroft, is the most valuable fodder in the world.[6] [6] Punj. Bokh. i. 288. It varies in size, according to its age, from a single leaf, not covering more than an inch in surface, to a cluster of leaves and flowers, spreading to a circumference of twelve or eighteen feet. The leaves are long and feathering. When full-grown, they attain a length of two feet. The flowers arc yellow, and produced in tufts at the tops of stalks five or six feet high. The plant is perennial, but does not attain perfection until three years old, after which it sows itself, and, as the natives assert, never dies. The leaves, flowers, stems, and seeds are made into hay, which is said to be so nutritious as to fatten sheep in twenty days. Growing in the bleakest and most sterile spots, and requiring no culture, Moorcroft observes, " that it might be introduced with national advantage into many parts of Britain, and would convert her heaths, and downs, and highlands, into storehouses for the supply of innumerable flocks." The seeds which that public-spirited man sent home had lost their vegetating quality. It is classed by botanists among *Umbelliferæ*, and supposed to be identical with the *silphium* mentioned by Arrian.[7] Rhubarb[8] grows wild in vast quantities, and the castern part of Hindoo Koosh may, perhaps, be regarded as its most favourite locality. The quality has been found equal to that produced in any other region.

The zoology of Hindoo Koosh is varied and interesting. The *kiang*,[9] an equine quadruped, roams in large herds over the table-lands, valleys, and less rugged mountains. Its height is that of a small horse. In shape it resembles the horse in some degree, but partakes also of the peculiarities of the ass, so that it might be considered a quagga, but that it is without the stripes which distinguish that beast, whose haunts, moreover, in the burning deserts of Africa, are much at variance with those of the kiang. Its fleetness enables it easily to distance pursuers; but it may sometimes be surprised in rugged places. The *yak*, or grunting ox, is also wild in these mountains, which seem to be its native soil, and where it most appears to thrive.[2] It requires no care, and is of great use for the saddle, for burthens, and for yielding milk. This animal seems most at ease when the temperature[3] is below zero. The *zho*, a mule between this creature and the cow, is a very valuable animal. The other animals most requiring notice are the *kutchkar*, or wild sheep, of the size of a small horse, and bearing huge curling horns; the *rass*, apparently a large species of antelope, considered by Vigne[4] to be identical with the mar-khur, or gigantic goat;

[7] iii. c. 28.
[8] Moorcr. I. 302.

[9] Trebeck, in Moorcr. i. 442.

[2] Moorcr. i. 309; Vigne, ii. 277.

[3] Wood's Oxus, 321.

[4] ii. 279.

the musk deer, the ibex, the horn of which is generally above four feet in length; the goat-deer, the bear, the wolf-leopard, a nondescript animal, having some resemblance to a tiger; the lynx, fox, ounce, marmot, hare, eagle, vulture, raven, and various kinds of partridges.

Besides the heights set down above, as ascertained in the vicinity of Bamian and in Kunduz, the elevation of the following points has been stated (9—10) in the article on Afghanistan. Summit north of Peshawur; summit north of Jelalabad; summit of Koushan, Khawak Pass, Khawak Fort. According to the limits assigned to Hindoo Koosh in the present article, it extends between lat. 34° 30′—37°, long. 68°—78°.

HINGLAJ, in Beloochistan, on the Aghor river, about twenty miles from its embouchure in the Indian Ocean. It is a celebrated place of pilgrimage for Hindoos, in consequence of being one of the fifty-one[1] *pitas* or spots on which the dissevered limbs of *Sati* or *Doorga* were scattered. Pottinger[2] states that it is dedicated to *Kalee*, or the goddess of fate, who in Hindoo mythology is identical with Doorga.[3] He informs us[4] that, close to the temple, is a well, into which several hundred fathoms of rope have been let down without reaching the bottom. The pagoda is a low mud edifice, containing a shapeless stone, the object of idolatrous adoration. Lat. 25° 33′, long. 65° 30′.

[1] Jour. As. Soc. 1840, p. 154.
[2] 207.
[3] As. Research. xvii.; Wilson, Sketch of Religious Sects of Hindus, 221.
[4] 302.

HINGOL.—See AGHOR RIVER.

HIRROO RIVER.—See HARU.

HISARUK.—See HISSARUCK.

HISSARUCK, in Afghanistan, in the valley of Jelalabad, and fifteen miles south-east of the town bearing that name, is a village on a small river also called Hissaruck, which, rising in the Sufeid Koh, flows northerly, and falls into the river of Kabool. The village is situate in lat. 34° 13′, long. 70° 35′.

E.I.C. Ms. Doc.; Jour. As. Soc. 1842, p. 120, MacGregor, Geog. Notice of Jullalabad.

HISSARUCK.—A valley in Afghanistan, about thirty miles west of the village of the same name above described. It is situate on the Kurkutcha Pass, which is south of the main route from Kabool to Jelalabad. The road is very difficult at this place, and impassable for wheel-carriages. The neighbourhood abounds in gardens, famous for their fine pomegranates, which have no seeds. Lat. 34° 14′, long. 69° 53′.

E.I.C. Ms. Doc.; Wood, Khyber Pass, 3; Id. Oxus, 169.

HOHLAL, in Sinde, a village on the route from Bukkur to Hyderabad, and a hundred miles north of the latter place. It

E.I.C. Ms. Doc.

is situate in a jungly tract, eighteen miles from the left bank of the Indus. Lat. 26° 41′, long. 68° 14′.

E.I.C. Ms. Doc.; Jour. As. Soc. 1840, p. 31; Do La Hoste, Mem. on Copper in tho Territ. of Lus.
HOJA JAMOTE KA GOTE, in Beloochistan, near the northern frontier of Lus, a village, or rather encampment, belonging to Hoja Jamote, a chieftain of the Jamote tribe. It consists of about forty huts, made of mats, and is capable of sending into the field about a hundred men armed with matchlocks. The heat here is so excessive in summer, that the people are then obliged to take refuge from it in the mountains to the north-east. Though an inconsiderable place, it has of late attracted attention, in consequence of its being ascertained that rich lodes of copper have been discovered in its vicinity. The ore which has been extracted and smelted in small quantities, afforded a large per-centage of metal, but further operations have been stopped by the Jam or ruler of Lus, who threatened the Hindoo adventurers that they should be buried alive if the works were renewed. The ores of antimony, lead, and silver are also reported to be abundant in the same vicinity. Hoja Jamote is in lat. 26° 13′, long. 66° 55′.

E.I.C. Ms. Doc.
HONSHAIRA.—A village in Afghanistan, twenty-two miles north of Mittunkote. It is situate on an offset of the river Indus, and a mile from the main channel. Lat. 29° 11′, long. 70° 38′.

Masson, Kalat, 307.
HOORMARA, in Beloochistan, a small town and port on the shore of the Arabian Sea. It formerly belonged to the province of Mekran, but has lately placed itself under the protection of the Jam of Lus, to avoid being reduced to subjection by the Imam of Muscat. The port has a few small vessels, which trade to the shores of Arabia, Persia, Sinde, and Cutch. The Jam of Lus appoints the governor, and receives a revenue annually of 1,000 rupees. The surrounding country for several days' journey is of the most barren description and dreary aspect. The population of the town is about 2,000. Lat. 25° 18′, long. 65° 6′.

Hough, Narr. Exp. in Afg. 340.
HOORMUK.—A small town in the Punjab, on the road made by the Mogul emperors from Rotas to Attock. It is situate in a very difficult country, abounding in intricate, deep, and narrow defiles. Lat. 33° 45′, long. 72° 51′.

E.I.C. Ms. Doc.
HOOSENEE, in Afghanistan, a village on the route from Kandahar to Furrah, and ninety miles east of the latter place. Lat. 32° 8′, long. 63° 38′.

HOOSHIARPOOR.—See HOSHYARPUR.

HOOSSEIN BELA, in Sinde, a village on the route from E.I.C. Ms. Doc.
Subzulcote to Shikarpoor, and fifteen miles cast of the latter place.
It is situate on the left bank of the Indus, here crossed by a
much-frequented ferry, generally called the ferry of Azeezpoor,
which place, however, is above a mile north-cast. The Indus is
here divided into two branches : the eastern, called the Dund, is
about a hundred and fifty feet broad and twenty-four feet deep ;
the western branch is very wide, between thirty and forty feet
deep, and is separated from the eastern by an island a mile and a
half in breadth. At a short distance higher up there is a good ferry
over the undivided stream of the river, and that would be a preferable place for the passage of any considerable number of persons,
but the boatmen prefer the lower ferry, as nearer their village.
This latter ferry is sometimes called Amil Got, from the village of
Amil on the western side. (See AMIL GOT.) Hoossein Bela is
in lat. 27° 52′, long. 69°.

HOSHYARPUR, in the Punjab, a small town near the Moorcr. I. 119.
southern base of the Himalaya mountains, and on the route from
Lahore to Nadaun. Lat. 31° 36′, long. 75° 56′.

HOUZI AHMED KHAN, in Afghanistan, a village on the E.I.C. Ms. Doc.
route from Kandahar to Shawl, forty-five miles south-east of the
former place. Lat. 31° 6′, long. 65° 56′.

HOUZI-MEER DAOUD, in Western Afghanistan, a halting- E.I.C. Ms. Doc.
place, important on account of a reservoir of water. It is on the
route from Herat to Kandahar, and fourteen miles south of the
former city. . Lat. 34° 10′, long. 62° 10′.

HOUZ-I-MUDDUD KHAN, in Western Afghanistan, is a E.I.C. Ms. Doc.
halting-place and reservoir for water, on the route from Kandahar
to Herat, and twenty-six miles nearly in a westerly direction from
the former place. It is situate about four miles north of the right
or northern bank of the Urghundab river, on an excellent road,
and is important on account of the abundant supply of water from
a canal which runs parallel to the road for several miles. The
country in the immediate vicinity is rather barren, and yields
little forage, except Juwassi, or camel-thorn. There is, however,
at intervals the appearance of considerable cultivation, and large
flocks of sheep and goats are to be seen. Lat. 31° 31′, long.
65° 5′.

HUBB.—A small river in Beloochistan, rises in the hilly Jour. As. Soc.
1839, p. 197; Car-
country north-east of Bela, in the province of Lus. It takes a less, Mem. on
Lus.

south-westerly course, and four miles north-east of the town of
Lyaree falls into the Poorally river, in lat. 25° 40', long. 66° 26'.

HUBB.[1]—A river forming for a considerable distance the western frontier of Sinde, and dividing it from Beloochistan. It has been
traced downwards from Hoja Jamote,[2] on the northern boundary
of Lus, in lat. 26° 12', long. 66° 55', and is supposed to rise near
that place. For about twenty-five miles in the upper part of its
course it flows south-easterly, and then turning due south, holds
its way for about fifty miles in that direction. It then turns to the
south-west, and, after a total length of a hundred miles, falls into
the Arabian Sea, on the north-west side of Cape Monze, in lat.

24° 50', long. 66° 36'. De la Hoste[3] states, that for a distance of
fourteen miles from the mouth, water was in the end of summer
found to the depth of eight inches, and that in some places deep
pools exist, abounding in fish and alligators. He adds, that the

river is said never to fail in the driest seasons. Masson[4] however
states, that it is only on extraordinary occasions that the water of

the Hubb reaches the sea, and in this he is supported by Hart,[5] who
crossed it about fifteen miles above the mouth, where the channel
was a hundred yards wide. Though, in consequence of heavy
rains, there was then a large body of running water, he found but
a small stream on his return a short time after, and was informed
it would soon cease to flow, and that water would then be found
only in detached pools. The whole course is described as a succession of rocky or gravelly gorges in the rugged and barren
Pubb mountains.

HUDEAH KHAD, in Afghanistan, a village on the route
from the Khyber Pass to Kabool. It is distant ninety miles east
of the latter place, twelve miles south of Jelalabad, and eighty
miles north-west of Peshawur. It is situate on the southern route,
which passes through Nungnehar and along the base of Sufeid
Koh, and which, though more direct than the northern by Jelalabad, is less frequented, on account of the great number of passes
and the turbulent and predatory character of the tribes in its
neighbourhood. The village is in lat. 34° 16', long. 70° 24'.

HUFT ASYA, or HUFTASAYA, in Afghanistan, is a village
with a fort, on the route from Ghuznee to Kabool, and distant
twenty-three miles north-east from the former place. There are
numerous streams and a fine tank of water. The country is well
cultivated, the soil being formed into terraces carefully constructed

on the slopes of the hills. The road near it is in general good, though rather sandy. It is 8,420 feet above the sea. Lat. 33° 49′, long. 68° 15′.

HUFT KOTUL,[1] in Afghanistan, is on the route from Jela- [1] E.I.C. Ms. Doc; Hough's Narr. of Exp. in Afg. 245; Sale, Dis. in Afg. 258; Eyre, Milit. Op. at Kabool, 230; Moorcr. Punj. Bokh. ii. 273. labad to Kabool, and about thirty-two miles east of this latter place. The name signifies " seven passes," though Hough reckoned eight, and remarks, " an enemy might dreadfully annoy a column moving down this last descent, as they would have a flanking fire on it ;" and in fact, in this defile, about three miles long, was consummated the massacre of the British force in the disastrous attempt to retreat from Kabool at the commencement of 1842. Here also,[2] in the September of the same year, the [2] Mil. Op. in Afg. 390-400. Afghans, after their defeat at Tezeen, attempting to make a stand, were again utterly routed with great slaughter by the British army under General Pollock. Lat. 34° 21′, long. 69° 27′.

HUJAMREE,[1] in Sinde, is an offset of the Sata, or great [1] Carless, Official Survey of the Indus, 4; Burnes, iii. 30, 37, 235; Id. Pers. Narr. 7. eastern channel of the Indus, and is called in the upper part of its course the Seeahn. The Hujamree mouth is wide, but rapidly narrows inland to about five hundred yards ; at Vikkur, twenty miles from the sea, it is only about a hundred and seventy yards wide ; and still higher up, near its junction with the Sata, its breadth is found not to exceed fifty yards. In 1831 it was navigable for boats from the sea to the entrance into the Sata, as the small flotilla which conveyed Captain Burnes and his party in that year passed this way. According to the statement of that officer,[2] there were then fifteen [2] iii. 236. feet of water on the bar at high tide, and a depth of four fathoms all the way to Vikkur. He observes, however, adverting to the changing character of the river, " the next season perhaps Vikkur will be deserted." The anticipated change occurred, though not so early as suggested. In 1839 the British troops, marching from Bombay to Afghanistan, ascended the Hujamree and landed at Vikkur ; and in the course of the same year this branch[3] was closed by a change in its channel, caused by the [3] Kennedy, ii. 221. violence of the current. The Hujamree mouth is in lat. 24° 10′, long. 67° 28′.

HULEEJEE, in Sinde, a village on the route from Kurrachee E.I.C. Ms. Doc. to Jurruk, and fifty miles east of the former place. It is situate among the low hills north-west of Tatta, and near the western shore of a considerable *dund* or piece of water communicating with the Indus by the Kulleree water-course. Lat. 24° 50′, long. 67° 46′.

E.I.C. Ms. Doc. HUMBOOWA, in Sinde, a village on the route from Shikarpoor to Larkhana, and eighteen miles south-west of the former place. It is situate twelve miles from the right bank of the Indus, and in that scantily cultivated tract where the fertile alluvial soil adjoining the river degenerates into the *Pat* or desert of Shikarpoor. Lat. 27° 48′, long. 68° 37′.

HUNGOO.—See Hangu.

E.I.C. Ms. Doc. HUNJUNBY, in the Punjab, a village.on the left bank of the Chenaub river, nineteen miles south from its confluence with the river Ravee. Lat. 30° 20′, long. 71° 37′.

Walker's Map of N.W. Frontier. HURDEH, in the Punjab, a village on the route from Attock to Ferozpoor, seventy miles north-west of the latter place. Lat. 31° 49′, long. 73° 54′.

[1] E.I.C. Ms. Doc. HUREEKE,[1] in the Punjab, a village situate on the right bank of the Ghara river, three miles below the confluence of the Sutluj and Beas. The name Ghara is in this instance given to the river with some latitude, as it is not usually so called above a spot

[2] Jour. As. Soc. 1837, p. 179; Wade's Voyage down the Sutluj, by Mackeson; Atkinson, Exp. into Afg. 62. twelve miles below Hureeke.[2] The site of the village is on the high bank of the river, and, when the water is low, distant a mile and a half from the ferry. Though a small place, the trade is very important, as nearly the whole traffic with Hindostan, from

[3] Wade, ut supra. Afghanistan, Kashmir, and the Punjab, passes through it.[3] There is besides great local traffic between the districts in its immediate vicinity on both sides of the river. During some days that Wade remained there, thirty-two boats, with three men to each, were incessantly employed, from morning till night, in transporting loaded carriages and beasts of burthen from one side to the other. No diminution of activity was observable during the period, but there was throughout a uniform scene of bustle and business. A body of 400 or 500 horse is stationed here by the government of the Punjab, to prevent its fanatic Sikh subjects

[4] Burnes' Bokh. i. 8. from crossing to devastate the British territories.[4] Hureeke is in lat. 31° 10′, long. 74° 53′.

HURIPUR FORT.—See Haripoor Fort.

HURJPUR.—See Haripoor.

[1] E.I.C. Ms. Doc. HURREAH, in the Punjab,[1] a village on the route from Ramnuggur to Pind Dadun Khan, and twenty miles east of the latter place. It is situate near the left bank of the river Jailum,

in a country described by Burnes[2] as a sterile waste of underwood. [2] Bokh. i. 49.
Lat. 32° 38', long. 73° 8'.

HURROO.—See HARU.

HURRUND, or HURROOND.—A small and hilly district, Leech, Rep. on with a town of the same name, in the south-eastern angle of Sindh. Army, 93; Burnes, Pol. Pow. Afghanistan, westward of the Derajat. The town of Hurrund is of Sikhs, 6; Masson, Kalat, 335; situated on the route from Dera Ghazee Khan to Cutch Gundava. Pott. Belooch. It has been lately taken by the Sikhs. It has a fort and a con- 311. siderable number of houses. Lat. 29° 25', long. 70° 12'.

HURVOOB.—A village in Afghanistan, one hundred miles Walker, Map of east of Ghuznee, and seventy miles south-east of Kabool, in lat. Afg. 33° 43', long. 69° 52'.

HURY RIVER.—See HERI ROOD.

HURYH.—A village of Kashmir, at the south-eastern base Vigne, Kashmir, of Seta Sar, a lofty and picturesque mountain bounding the ii. 161. valley on the west. On the mountain side above the village is a spring hemmed in with masonry, and adjoining a forest, called by the natives Dunduk Wun, signifying " the wood of abduction," in consequence of a tradition of Hindoo mythology. Lat. 34° 29', long. 74° 3'.

HUSARA.—See ASTOR.

HUSHTMY, in Afghanistan, a village situate on the Dura-i- E.I.C. Ms. Doc. Sarwan, a stream tributary to the Moorghab river. Lat. 35° 14', long. 64° 48'.

HUSHTNUGGUR (or "the eight towns ").—A town and Burnes' Pol. Pow. fortress of the province of Peshawur, situate north of the Kabool of Sikhs, 2; Masson, Bal. Afg. river, and twenty miles north of the city of Peshawur. The sur- Panj. i. 122; rounding country is very fertile, beautiful, and well watered, but 1836, p. 479, much exposed to the attacks of the restless and fierce tribes to Court, Mem. of a Map of Peshawur. the northward. Lat. 34° 16', long. 71° 45'.

HUSSAINWAH.—A village of Sinde, on the route from E.I.C. Ms. Doc. Sehwan to Larkhana, and sixteen miles south of the latter place. It is situate on the western bank of a *dund* or stagnant piece of water, in a country rendered rough by jungle and water-courses. Lat. 27° 16', long. 68° 12'.

HUSSEE.—A village in the Punjab, about eight miles south E.I.C. Ms. Doc. of the left bank of the river Chenaub, and sixteen miles cast of its junction with the river Jailum. Lat. 31° 6', long. 72° 22'.

HUSSUN ABDUL,[1] in the Punjab, near the east bank of [1] Moorcroft, Punj. the Indus, is so called from containing the tomb of a reputed Bokh. ii. 317; Burnes, Bokh. i. 73.

Mahometan saint of that name. It is situate in a delightful
valley,[2] watered by numerous springs, which gush from among
the rocks.* Here are the ruins of a pleasure-ground and small
palace, tastefully formed by the Mogul Emperor Akbar, and
though much decayed, displaying yet an exquisite combination of
elegance and refined luxury. Lat. 33° 54′, long. 72° 42′.

HUTIAL.—A village in the Punjab, situate on the route
from Chumba to Doda, fifty-two miles north-west of the former
place and thirty-five south of the latter. Lat. 32° 32′, long. 75° 8′.

HUWELEE.—A village in the Punjab, situate near the left
bank of the Chenaub, about eight miles south of the confluence
of the Jailum with that river. Lat. 31° 3′, long. 72° 7′.

HUZARA, or HUZROO, in the Punjab, a commercial town
situate on the route from Lahore to Attock, and twenty-seven
miles east of the latter place. The inhabitants are Afghans, and
speak the Pushtoo language. Lat. 33° 50′, long. 72° 45′.

HUZAREH COUNTRY,[1] in Afghanistan, an extensive mountainous region, so called because inhabited by a numerous Tartar
race of that name. It is by some geographers considered to be
the Paropamisus of the Greeks, and, viewed as coextensive with
that maze of mountains, is described by Elphinstone.[2] as extending " between Caubul and Herat, having the Uzbeks on the north,
and the Dooranees and Ghiljies on the south;" he states the
length to exceed three hundred miles, and the breadth to be
about two hundred. The shape is compact, and the surface is
about eighty thousand square miles. The population generally
of this extensive tract, considered in a physical point of view,
have the Mongolian or Tartar physiognomy, and are divided by
Elphinstone into two great classes; the Eimauks, for the most
part, holding the southern, the Huzareh Proper, the northern
part.

Probably the following are the safest limits to assign to

* Burnes states, " some hundred springs;" Von Hügel, three
(iii. 97). This last writer (iii. 71) denies that the place is a valley; he
also reproves Moore and Hamilton for giving too flattering a description of
it ; but it is not to be forgotten that the gorgeous Akbar expressed the feelings excited in his mind on the view of the spot, by exclaiming *Wah !* the
usual interjection of admiration, and hence the ruined garden is still so
named. Elphinstone styles it a valley, and the authorities to which we have
referred, and even the baron himself subsequently (98, 99), are warm in their
praises of the beauties of the place.

Margin notes:
[2] Elph. Acc. of Caubul, 73.
E.I.C. Ms. Doc.
E.I.C. Ms. Doc.
Burnes, Bokh. i. 73.
[1] Fraser, Jour. in Khorasan, 243.
[2] Acc. of Caubul, 478.

this region : on the north, Turkestan ; east, the river of Kunduz, the Pughman range, and Koh-i-Baba ; south-east, the valley
of the Urghundab ; south, the mountain-ranges rising to the north
of the plain country, about the lower part of the Helmund ;
west, the Khooshk, or Khaskh river, and that of Subzawur.
Though very little explored, we know the general surface to be
lofty, as considerable streams flow from it in every direction ; to
the north, the Kooshk,[3] Moorghab,[4] the river of Andkhoo, the
Bund-i-Burbur ;[5] to the north-east, the river of Kunduz ; to the
south-east, the river of Ghuznee ;[6] south-west, the Urghundab[7]
and Helmund ;[8] to the south, the Khash Rood, the Furrah Rood,
the Adruscund ; to the west, the Heri Rood. This would indicate
a considerable general elevation, yet not so great as to reach that
lofty region of the atmosphere where the highly rarefied air is
unable to hold much moisture in suspension ; it being known that
the air on very lofty mountains is characterized by a want of
moisture[9] quite unknown near the level of the sea. Besides the
elevation of the Koh-i-Baba, and of the passes connected with
Bamian, which have heights varying from 9,000 to 16,000 feet,
others very considerable have been ascertained in the Huzareh country. The Goolkoo range,[1] west of Ghuznee, is 13,000
feet high ; some mountains on the southern border of the Huzareh
have heights varying from 10,000 to 13,000 feet ;[1] the elevations
of various summits of a range about eighty or a hundred miles
east of Herat are computed at from 12,000 to 14,000 feet.[1]

The country of the Eimauks, or that more to the south and
west, according to Elphinstone,[2] who wrote from the reports of the
natives, " is reckoned less mountainous than that of the Huzareh ;
but even there the hills present a steep and lofty face towards Herat, the roads wind through valleys and over lofty ridges, and some
of the forts are inaccessible, so that all visitors are obliged to
be drawn up with ropes by the garrison. Still the valleys are
cultivated, and produce wheat, barley, and millet." Conolly[3]
considers the difficulty of the country to be greatly overrated, and
states that the extensive route which he pursued nearly from east
to west shewed it to be by no means so difficult as generally
represented. The climate in the northern, or Huzareh part, is
dreadfully severe, snow[4] lying for six months continuously.
The distress thence resulting is increased by the want of fuel,
as, from some unexplained cause, neither the hills nor vales

[3] Abbot, Heraut and Khiva, i. 13.
[4] Id. i. 30 ; Jour. As. Soc. 1841, p. 116. Conolly, Rep.
on Khorasan ; Fraser, Jour. in Khorasan, 245, App. 57.
[5] Conolly, ut supra, 118 ; Burnes, Bokh. ii. ii. 162.
[6] E.I.C. Ms. Doc.
[7] Elph. 116.
[8] E I.C. Ms. Doc.; Elph. 115 ; Masson, Bal. Afg.
Panj. li. 333 ; Jour. As. Soc. 1842, p. 69 ; Grif. Bar. and Ther.
Obs. in Afg. ; Wood's Oxus, 197.
[9] As. Researches, xviii. 259, Gerard, on Valley of Spiti.
[1] E.I.C. Ms. Doc.
[2] 479.
[3] Ut supra, 117.
[4] Burnes' Bokh. i. 177.

of this country produce trees, and the inhabitants are consequently reduced to the necessity of burning brushwood and cow-dung. The principal bush used for this purpose is a sort of furze; and so laborious is its collection, that the population employ all the time that can be spared from agriculture in cutting and conveying it home.[5] It its obvious that such physical circumstances must ever preclude any great advance in civilization. Still something might be done by a consolidated government of a mild, firm, enlightened character. At present the people are deplorably poor, in consequence of the oppressions of their numerous barbarous chieftains, their incessant intestine wars, and the attacks of the neighbouring powers, who enslave the population, and carry off the cattle, the only wealth of the country. Money is not current, its place, as with the primitive Latins, is supplied by sheep,[6] which constitute the medium of exchange where mere barter cannot be effected. Traders from Herat, Kandahar, and Kabool bring checked turbans, coarse cotton cloths, and chintzes, tobacco, dyes for felts, and carpets; those from Turkestan bring rice, cotton, and salt. The Eimauks and Huzarehs give in return for these, slaves, kine, sheep, butter, as well as strong woollens, felts, grain, sacks, carpets, made from the wool of their own flocks: they export no raw wool.[7] In addition to the articles above mentioned, they bring to market lead and sulphur, and, with much probability, state that their mountains contain mines of copper and silver, but these they do not work, perhaps from the knowledge that to render these sources of wealth productive would only be to make them the prey of rapacious rulers and invaders.[8] The trade of the country is altogether very small, in consequence of its general poverty, which is so severe that salt is but rarely tasted by a large portion of the population.

Subject to the most cruel treatment from all around them, the Huzarehs are cowardly rather than desperate men; their spirit being broken by their misfortunes, they seem in general incapable of making a vigorous and combined effort to assert their rights. An exception to this, however, occurred some years ago, when Mir Yezdanbaksh, one of their chiefs, contrived to acquire the command over a great number of his countrymen, and gave great alarm to Dost Mahomed Khan. The simplicity, however, which characterizes the Huzareh was his ruin, as he was cir-

[5] Wood, Oxus, 202.

[6] Conolly, ut supra, 117; Burnes' Bokh. i.177.

[7] Conolly, ut supra, 117.

[8] Id.

cumvented by the most detestable treachery, and cruelly put to death by Haji Khan Khaka,[8] the infamous and notorious Machia- 8 Masson, ii. 431. vel of Afghan politics. So great is the simplicity of the Huzarehs, according to Elphinstone,[9] that they believe the ruler of Kabool 9 48. to be as high as the tower of a castle. Like other rude people, they are much addicted to falsehood and theft. Their patient, laborious, and humble dispositions render them useful to the proud and impetuous Afghans, and hence considerable numbers find a livelihood in Kabool as scavengers, and in the exercise of similar employments of drudgery.[1] Wood, describing their 1 Wood, Oxus,
108, 109. appearance, states that " they are quite a Tartar race, and even more marked with the features of that nomade people than the Uzbeks in the valley of the Oxus. They strongly re- semble the Kirghiz of Pamir."[2] According to Elphinstone, 2 Id. 199. the regiments of the great Tartar conquerors were called *Hazaurehs*, and he conjectures that some of those bodies, ori- ginally left to occupy the conquered country, may have given rise to this people.[3] That their settlement in this region cannot 3 Elph. 482;
Burnes' Pers.
Narr. 231. be of very remote date, is clear from the fact, that it was the original seat of the Afghans of Ghore, who destroyed the empire of the Sultans of Ghuznee, and founded the Patan dynasty of Hindostan.[4] The sweeping change of the population probably 4 Price, Mahome-
dan Hist. ii. 316;
Ferishta, i. 170. took place about 1220-1225, when Zingis Khan, destroying Herat, Gulgula, and several other cities of Afghanistan, conquered the country as far as the Indus.[5] * It is singular that their lan- 5 Price, ii. 410-
412; D'Herbelot,
Bibl. Orien. ii. guage is Persian. The Huzarehs are Shia Mahometans; the Eimauks, Sunnis. Elphinstone[6] estimates the number of the 83, 84, 96, 97.
6 486. Huzarehs at from 300,000 to 350,000 persons; Burnes,[7] at about 7 Pers. Narr. 230. the same amount; Wood,[8] at 150,000, which last seems alto- 8 Oxus, 200. gether too small a number for a country more extensive than England, and does not allow three to the square mile of a population, agricultural as well as pastoral. On the west, these tribes are subject generally to the Shah of Herat; on the north, to the rulers of Bokhara and Kunduz; on the east, to Kabool; but nothing can be more precarious than the authority of these powers, as the tribute must usually be levied by an armed

* In the Ayeen Akbery, this event is stated to have taken place in the time of Halaku, the son of Zingis :—" The tribe of Hezareh are the remains of the Chaghtai army which Mangu Khan sent into those parts to the assist- ance of Halaku Khan."

force. In the whole country, there are no places which can properly be called towns, Ghore, Meimuna, Siripool, Andkhoo, and some others, generally so denominated, being little more than fortified villages. The Huzareh and Eimauk country, with the limits which are above assigned to it, lies between lat. 31° 30' —37°, long. 62°—68°.

E.I.C. Ms. Doc.
    HUZRELWALA.—A village in the ·Punjab, twenty-three miles north-east of Mooltan, on the road from thence to Ferozpoor, and twelve miles from the left bank of the river Indus. Lat. 30° 16', long. 71° 49'.

    HUZROO.—See Huzara.

    HYDASPES RIVER.—See Jailum.

[1] Pott. 361, 369;
Burnes, iii. 60;
Lord, Med. Mem.
of the Plain of
the Indus, 79;
Leech, on the
Army of Sinde,
79; Macmurdo,
Acc. of Sinde, in
Jour. Royal As.
Soc. 1834, p.234;
Masson, i. 462;
Outram, 31;
Burnes' (James)
Mission to Sinde.

    HYDERABAD,[1] in Sinde, is generally considered the chief town of that country, in consequence of its having been selected as the residence of the chief Ameers, or those ruling the southern and principal part of the country. It is situate four miles east of the eastern bank of the Indus, on an eminence of the low rocky range called the Gunjah hills, and in an island inclosed between the Indus and the Fulailee, a branch which, leaving the main stream about twelve miles above the town, communicates with it about fifteen miles below. The Fulailee flows about a thousand yards east of the town, the base of the rampart being washed by a creek from it in the season of inundation, though the whole branch is dry when the river is low. This fortress, which is esteemed very strong by the Sindians, and would no doubt prove so in their mode of warfare, was built nearly on the site of the ancient Nerunkot, by Futteh Ali, the first Ameer. The outline is irregular, corresponding with the winding shape of the hill's brow, on the very edge of which the walls, for the greater part of their extent, rise to the height of from fifteen to thirty feet. They are built of burnt bricks, and are thick and solid at the base, but taper so much, and are so greatly weakened by embrasures and loop-holes with which they are pierced, that a few well-directed shot would demolish any part, and expose the defenders to the fire of the assailants. The ramparts are flanked by round towers or lofty bastions, at intervals of three or four hundred paces, which, combined with the height of the hill, give the place an imposing appearance. Where the walls do not rise immediately from the edge of the declivity, the defence is strengthened by a ditch of ten feet wide and eight deep. The rock is too soft to admit of being scarped, and slopes so gently, that if the wall were breached, the rubbish would rest on the face of the hill, and afford footing for a storming party. The plateau [2] of the hill on which Hyderabad is [2] Wood, Oxus, 30. built is a mile and a half long and seven hundred yards broad; the height is about eighty feet, and on the southern part are the fortress and the suburbs or Pettah. There are about five thousand houses, meanly const cted of mud, one half of that number being within the fortress, the rest in the Pettah. The fortress contains the residence of the Ameers, and a massive tower, built as the repository of their treasures. The bazaar is extensive, forming one street the entire length of the town, and it displays considerable bustle and appearance of business. The most important manufacture of Hyderabad is that of arms of various kinds, matchlocks, swords, spears, and shields, and the skill of the workmen is said to be scarcely inferior to that attained in Europe. There is also a considerable manufacture of ornamental silks and cottons. A cemetery,[3] which overspreads the northern part of the eminence, [3] Id. 31. contains the tombs of the deceased members of the Talpoor dynasty, and of the preceding one of the Kaloras. That of Gholam Shah Kalora is a beautiful quadrangular building, with a handsome central dome. It is lined with fine marble, is highly ornamented with mosaic, and inscribed with sentences from the Koran. The tomb of the late Ameer Kurum Ali is also a handsome quadrangular building, surmounted by a dome and having a turret on each corner. When the Belooches, under the conduct of Futteh Ali, of the Talpoor tribe, overthrew the Kalora dynasty, that successful chieftain gave to one branch of his relatives Khyerpoor, with a considerable district attached; to another, Meerpoor, and allowed his three brothers to share with himself the government of Hyderabad and its dependent territory, comprehending the greater part of the country. Some light might be thrown on the relative power and resources of these divisions of Sinde by the statements furnished of their respective revenues. The Hyderabad family is said to have had an annual revenue equal to 150,000l. sterling,[4] that of Khyerpoor, [4] Burnes, Bokh. a revenue of 100,00l., and that of Meerpoor, of 50,000l. The iii. 213. treasure accumulated by those chiefs is estimated by Burnes[5] [5] Ibid. to have amounted to 20,000,000l., but the whole appears to be conjectural, and such vague and baseless statements can command little confidence. As the Talpoor dynasty did not last quite a century, it is obviously impossible that the members of it could have accumulated so vast a treasure from a revenue so moderate. Hyderabad is supposed to have a population of 20,000. Lat. 25° 22′, long. 68° 22′.

E.I.C. Ms. Doc;
Jour. As. Soc.
1842, p. 64, Grif.
Bar. and Ther.
Obs. in Afg.;
Hough, Narr. of
Exp. in Afg. 241;
Atkinson, Exp.
into Afg. 248;
Havelock, War in
Afg. ii. 99.

HYDERKHAIL, or HYDERKHEL, in Afghanistan, is a village in a pleasant valley, watered by a feeder of the river of Logurh, very well cultivated, and highly productive. The village lies on the route from Kabool to Ghuznee from which last place it is distant thirty-five miles north-east. It is 7,637 feet above the level of the sea. Lat. 33° 58′, long. 68° 37′.

E.I.C. Ms. Doc;
Masson, Bal.Afg.
Panj. iii. 237.

HYDER KHAN, in Afghanistan, a village on the route from Peshawur to Jelalabad, by the Abkhana Pass. It is situate in the hills which rise on the north-east, above the Kabool river. The population, about eight hundred, is supported by ferrying travellers over the river on jalawans, or inflated hides, a vocation in which they exhibit wonderful intrepidity, activity, and address. Hyder Khan is in lat. 34° 13′, long. 71° 28′.

HYDRABAD.—See HYDERABAD.

E.I.C. Ms. Doc.;
Conolly, Jour. to
India, ll. 127;
Hough, Narr. Exp.
in Afg. 76; Jour.
As. Soc. 1842, p.
55, Grif. Bar. and
Ther.Meas. inAfg.;
Atkinson, Exp.into
Afg. 138; Out-
ram, Rough Notes,
60; Havelock,
War in Afg. l.825.

HYDURZIE, or HYDURZYE, in Afghanistan, a village in the valley of Pisheen, on the route from Kandahar to Shawl, and twenty-five miles north of the latter place. It is situate on the banks of a good stream, which appears to have no other name than Lora (the Pushtoo word for river), and is inhabited by Syuds, or alleged descendants of Mahomet, who are considered by the Afghans to be endowed with high and miraculous powers. The country is fertile, well cultivated, and rather populous. The elevation is 5,259 feet above the level of the sea. Lat. 30° 23′, long. 66° 51′.

¹E.I.C. Ms. Doc.;
Jour. As. Soc.
1842, p. 55, Grif.
Bar. and Ther.
Meas.; Mil.Op.
in Afg. 221;
Hough, Narr.
Exp. in Afg. 77;
Havelock, War in
Afg. i. 288.

HYKULZYE,[1] in Afghanistan, is a large walled village on the route from Kandahar to Shawl, and thirty-five miles north of the latter place. It is situate about two miles south of the river Lora, in a fertile and well-cultivated country, and has a copious supply of water from a canal. The inhabitants are principally Syuds, or reputed descendants from Mahomet, much venerated by the superstitious Afghans. Here, on the 28th of March, 1842, a British army, under General England, met with a severe repulse in attempting to force its way to Kandahar. Here, too, on the 28th of the next month, the same commander, with his army reinforced, totally routed the enemy, and marched through the pass. The number of the Afghans, on this last occasion, was estimated at fifteen hundred; of whom about thirty were killed. The village was then reduced to ashes. The bodies of eighteen British soldiers who had fallen in the former action were found, after having been subjected to all the indignities suggested by feelings of barbarous triumph, and buried with due obsequies. The clergyman,[2] who officiated on that occasion, makes the following reflection : " But little more than a month before, I had seen them in all the vigour of life ; many of them so young that they seemed like blooming boys; and then to look at the blackened, sun-dried, and half-devoured skeletons before me—could they be the same !" Elevation above the sea, 5,063 feet. Lat. 30° 32', long. 66° 50'.

2 Allen, March through Sinde and Afg. 147.

HYPHASIS.—See BEAS.

I.

IBRAHIM BANNAS.—A fort on the route from Kedje to Belah, in Beloochistan, one hundred miles east of the former town. Lat. 26° 26', long. 63° 47'.

E.I.C. Ms. Doc.

IBRAHIM JOEE RIVER,[1] in Western Afghanistan, rises in the Tymuni country, near Ghore, and, flowing southward, crosses the route from Herat to Kandahar, in lat. 32° 22', long. 63° 20', and one hundred and seventy miles north-west of the latter place. Its banks are high, irregular, stony, and a considerable distance apart. In time of flood, it is a large, rapid, unfordable stream, sometimes precluding the advance of caravans for several days together. When surveyed by a British emissary, in July, it was found to be thirty-seven yards wide, eighteen inches deep, and to have a velocity of about a mile and a half an hour. Conolly,[2] who crossed it in October, describes it as " having a little water in a broad bed, which is filled in spring ;" and Forster,[3] by whom it was crossed at Dilaram, calls it a rivulet. Below this, its direction is south-westerly, and after a total course of, probably, a hundred miles, it is lost in the marsh of Ashkinuk, in lat. 32°, long. 62° 50'.

E.I.C. Ms. Doc.

2 Jour. to India, ii. 77, Conolly (A.) 3 Jour. Beng. Eng. ii. 124.
3 Jour. As. Soc. 1840, p. 714, Conolly (E.), Physical Geogr. of Seistan.

ILLIASSEE, a river, or rather torrent, in Afghanistan, rises in the mountains held by the Murree tribe, between Kahun and

E.I.C. Ms. Doc.

Hurrund, and in lat. 29° 18′, long. 69° 44′. After a course of ninety miles, generally in a westerly direction, it is lost in the sultry plain of Cutch Gundava, near Lehree, about lat. 29° 10′, long. 68° 20′.

INDUS, a great river of Asia, is the boundary of India on the west. Among the various tribes and people through whose territories it flows, it bears different names; but that by which it is most generally known and most highly celebrated, is *Indus*, derived from the Sanscrit *Sindhu*,[1]* which word, changed by the Greeks into *Sinthus*, and by the Latins into *Sindus*,† ultimately passed into the name now in ordinary use. Though the vigilant jealousy of the Chinese, who rule Tibet, has excluded Europeans from that country, the inquiries of Moorcroft,[2] Trebeck, and Gerard have established, beyond any reasonable ground of doubt, that the source of the longest and principal stream of the Indus is at the north of the Kailas mountain,‡ regarded in Hindoo mythology as the mansion of the gods,[3] and Siva's paradise, and which is probably the highest mountain in the world, being estimated by Gerard[4] to have a height of 30,000 feet, and described by Moorcroft,[5] who viewed it from a table-land between 17,000 and 18,000 feet high, as a stupendous mountain, whose sides, as well as craggy summits, are apparently thickly covered with snow. The exact locality of the source may be stated with much probability to be in lat. 31° 20′, long. 81° 15′.§ Near its source it bears the name of *Sinh-kha-bab*, or "lion's mouth,"[6] from a superstitious belief that it flows from one. It first takes a north-westerly direction to Tuzheegung, about a hundred and twenty miles from the place of its reputed source. It is there

[1] Wilford, in As. Res. iii. 348, 368; viii. 318, 331, 335; xlv. 408; Ritter, Erdkunde von Asien, ii. 11; v. 451, 495; Rennell, v., Indus in Index and Postscript, 285.
[2] Moorcr. i. 262, 363; Gerard (J. G.), Koonawur, 134.
[3] Wilford, in As. Res. iii. 401; Id. vi. 506; Id. viii. 315, 353.
[4] Koonawur, 141.
[5] As. Res. xii. 421.

[6] Moorcr. Travels, I. 261.

* وسند *Sind* or *Sindhu*, "the sea." Shakespear in v.

† Pliny observes, "Indus incolis Sindus appellatus."

‡ Ritter (Erdkunde von Asien, i. 13) derives the name Kailas, or Kailasa, from *kil*, "to be cold." Ideler, in the index to that work, translates it *hoch gipfel*, "high summit." Hodgson states "that Cylas is a general appellation for high ranges always covered with snow." (As. Res. xiv. 92.) Humboldt states that kylas signifies "cold mountain" (*montagne froid*), and Kailassa any "very elevated summit." (Asie Centrale, i. 112.)

§ This is the opinion of Gerard, probably the highest authority on the subject. Moorcroft, in the map accompanying his Memoir in vol. xii. of As. Res., considers the source of the Eekung Choo as actually that of the Indus. The same opinion is given in his Travels (i. 363), and repeated by Burnes (Bokhara, ii. 223). See EEKUNG CHOO, in the alphabetical arrangement.

joined on its left,[7] or south-western side, by the Eekung Choo, or "river of Gartope," which rises on the western base of the Kailas mountain. Moorcroft[8] found the "river of Gartope," at about forty miles from its supposed source, "a clear, broad, and rapid, but not deep, river." Within eight or ten miles of its source, in lat. 31° 24', long. 80° 34', it was found at the end of July to be two and a half feet deep, and eighty yards wide. The country through which these streams flow varies in elevation from 15,000 to 18,000 feet. It is one of the most dreary regions in existence, the surface being for the most part formed by the disintegration of the granite of the adjacent mountains. It is swept over by the most furious winds, generally blowing from the north. These are at once piercingly cold and parchingly dry, and no vegetation is visible but a few stunted shrubs and some scanty and frost-withered herbage. It is, however, the proper soil for the production of shawl-wool, which is obtained from the yak,[9] * the goat, the sheep, certain animals of the deer kind, and even, it is said, from the horse and the dog.

The united stream bears the name of the northern confluent, Sinh-kha-bab; and, near the La Ganskiel Pass, about thirty miles below the junction, the river leaves the table-land through which it had previously flowed, and enters the deep gorges of the great depression dividing the Kouenlun or Mooz Taugh from the Himalaya. To this point, five miles from the Chinese frontier,[1] and having an elevation of 14,000 or 15,000 feet, its course has been explored by Trebeck, the companion of Moorcroft. It is situate in lat. 32° 56', long. 79° 25', on the border of a sandy plain, or rather wide valley, studded with small lakes, having their edges incrusted with soda.† The river was here found to be about sixty yards wide, apparently deep, and in the middle of November frozen over in most parts. It is, however, fordable occasionally in this neighbourhood, becoming in summer shallower during the

Side notes:
[7] Gerard, Koonawur, 134.
[8] As. Res. xii. 440-450; Id. 454.
[9] Moorcr. in As. Res. xii. 457; Gerard (J. G.), on the Spiti Valley, As. Res. xviii. 245; Vigne, Kashmir, ii. 124.
[1] Trebeck, in Moorcr. i. 440.

---

* Gerard, just quoted, observes (245), "the silky softness of the goat's fleece, and even its existence, depends on the arid air and vegetation," as the coldest tracts of the Himalaya, where not characterized by dryness, fail to support this state of animal life in perfection. This view of the subject is supported by the observations of Conolly on the Angora goat. (Journal of Roy. As. Soc. 1840, p. 159.)

† This appears to be the farthest point to which the Sinh-kha-bab has been ascended by any European, though, as has been seen, its feeder, the "river of Gartope," was crossed and surveyed by Moorcroft much higher.

2 Moorcr. l. 285. progress of night,[2] and deeper as the day advances, in consequence of the melting of the snows on the adjacent summits, through the sun's heat. A few miles below this, the river turns nearly due west for a short distance, and then takes the direction of north-west. At Uk-shi, which is about three hundred miles from the source, it was surveyed by Moorcroft,[3] and found to be about fifty yards wide. Close to Le, the capital of Ladakh, and thirty miles below Uk-shi, the elevation of its bed is not less than 10,000 feet ; and if that of its source be assumed at 18,000, and its length, so far, at three hundred and twenty miles, its fall * will be found to be twenty-five feet per mile ; above seventy times greater than (according to Rennell[4]) the fall of the Ganges through the plain of Bengal. Yet the descent of the bed of the Sinh-kha-bab is far less rapid than that of the Sutluj,[5] which in thirty miles descends 2,300 feet, or about seventy-six feet in the mile. Holding its course in a direction approaching to north-west, the Sinh-kha-bab, about fifteen miles below Le, is joined, opposite to Niemo, by the river of Zanskar, flowing from the district of the same name, and in a direction from south-west to north-east. The Zanskar[6] is a very rapid, turbid river ; the Sinh-kha-bab, a clear and placid stream. About twenty-five miles below this, and 360 from its supposed source, Vigne[7] found the river, at Kulutzi, crossed by a wooden bridge, and only twenty-five yards wide. The small size of the river, after a course of nearly four hundred miles, can only be accounted for by the excessive aridity[8] of the elevated tract through which it has held its way. Moorcroft[9] estimates the breadth of the river at this place at only twenty yards, but he found that it rose nearly forty feet during the season of inundation. Having flowed between seventy and eighty miles below this place, in a north-west direction, it receives from the south the river of Dras, which, rising in the mountains forming the north-eastern frontier of Kashmir, holds a north-easterly course of about ninety miles, and, receiving several streams both from the east and west,

3 Moorcr. Punj.
Bokhara, i. 230.

4 Ut supra, 260.

5 Gerard (A.),
Map of Koona-
wur ; see also
Gerard (J. G.),
Koonawur, 132,
and Colebrook
(H. T.), on the
Sutluj, Jour.
As. Soc. i. 302.
6 Moorcr. i. 263,
417.

7 ii. 384.

8 Vigne, ii. 266 ;
Moorcr. i. 209 ;
Gerard (J. G.),
on the Spiti Val-
ley, As. Res.
xviii. 258, 262.
9 ii. 10.

* Vigne (Kashmir, ii. 341) states the elevation of Le at about 10,000 feet, according to which, the bed of the Indus there must be below that height. Moorcroft states the elevation of Le to be above 11,000 feet, and that of the confluence of the Zanskar river and Sinh-kha-bab, about twenty miles farther down the stream, and consequently less elevated, at nearly 12,000 feet.

i. 417 ; ii. 259.

discharges a considerable volume[1] of water at its confluence. From this confluence the Sinh-kha-bab takes a more northerly direction, for about forty miles, to the fort of Keris, in lat. 35° 8′, long. 75° 50′, where[2] it receives, from the north, the water of the Shy-yok, by far its most important tributary above the river of Kabool. The Shy-yok, though not explored to its source by any European, is considered, from the concurring testimony of the natives, to have its origin at the southern end of an extensive glacier, or frozen lake, embosomed in a gorge on the southern side of the Karakorum or Mooz Taugh mountains, and in lat. 35° 20′, long. 77° 35′. It holds a generally southerly course for about eighty miles, and then turns, first to the north-west, and afterwards to the west, for about one hundred and forty miles farther, to its junction with the Sinh-kha-bab.

The accumulation of ice in the great glacier from which this river proceeds, its subsequent dislodgement, and the obstruction thereby caused in the channel of the Shy-yok, have from time to time caused the water to make violent irruptions through its ordinary barriers, leading to dreadful inundations. The great and sudden flood of the Indus, which, in the summer of 1841, was felt as far as Attock, and even beyond it, has been generally attributed to such a cause.[3] At the confluence of the two rivers, the Shy-yok is about one hundred and fifty yards broad, the Sinh-kha-bab not more than eighty ; but the latter is the deeper, and has a greater body of water. Below the confluence, the river is known by the name Aba Sind[4] (Indus Proper). About twenty-five miles below the point of junction, and westward of it, the Indus, opposite Iskardoh, receives from the north the river of Shyghur. No European appears to have examined the downward course of the Indus between Iskardoh and Makpon-i-Shagaron, in which interval it runs a distance of about seventy miles in a direction west-north-west.[5] At Makpon-i-Shagaron, in lat. 35° 34′, long. 74° 26′, according to Vigne, who viewed the place at the distance of eighteen miles, the river emerges from the mountainous region, and, turning nearly due south, a course which it thenceforth continues to keep generally to the sea, takes its way through the unexplored country north of Attock. Vigne caused the part intervening between Iskardo and Makpon-i-Shagran to be explored by his native servants, who found it to flow through a succession of rocky gorges and deep and narrow

[1] Vigne, ii. 329; Moorcr. i. 264.

[2] Falconer on Cataclysm of the Indus, Jour. As. Soc. 1841, p. 617; Vigne, ii. 315; Moorcr. i. 263.

[3] Journ. As. Soc. 1841, p. 616, Falconer. Cataclysm of the Indus.

[4] Moorcr. Punj. Bokh. i. 263.

[5] Vigne, Kashmir, ii. 302.

valleys, rugged and difficult, but presenting nothing else remarkable. About twelve miles south of Makpon-i-Shagaron it receives,
from the north-west, a considerable stream, called the river of

⁶ Id. 303. Gilghit.⁶ Vigne, who viewed the Indus at Acho, about ten miles
below this confluence, describes it there as a vast torrent rushing
through a valley six or seven miles wide, and holding a south-
westerly course, which might be traced downwards for at least
forty miles. This *autopsy* of the course of the Indus would extend to a point about eighty miles north-east of Derbend. For
these intervening eighty miles its course is through countries inhabited by barbarous, sanguinary, and fanatical tribes of Mussulmans, and which does not appear to have been ever explored by

⁷ Burnes, Pers.
Narr. 119. Europeans.⁷ At Derbend, at the north-western angle of the
Sikh territory, it was, in 1837, surveyed by Lieutenant Leech,
of the Bengal Engineers, and there, in the middle of August,
about which time it is fullest, he found it a hundred yards wide.
From this place, about six hundred and fifty miles from its supposed source, and in lat. 34° 30′, long. 73° 5′, he descended the

⁸ Leech, on the
Fords of the In-
dus, 19; Burnes,
Pers. Narr. 110;
Id. Bokh. l. 77. river on a raft to Attock, a distance of about sixty miles.⁸ In
this interval, the river, flowing through a plain, has a broad
channel of no great depth, containing many islands, and is
fordable in five places.

The fords are only available in winter, when the river is lowest,
and even then, the attempt is perilous, from the rapidity of the
current and the benumbing coldness of the water. If the account

⁹ l. 140. given by Masson⁹ be correct, 1,200 horsemen were swept away
and drowned on one occasion when the Indus was crossed by

¹ 334. Runjeet Singh at one of these fords. Hough¹ states the number
² Elph. Acc. of
Caubul, 114. lost at 7,000. Shah Shooja forded the Indus in 1809² above Attock, but his success was considered to be almost a miracle.

³ Jour. ii. 52. Where crossed by Forster,³ about twenty miles above Attock, in
the middle of July, and consequently when fullest, it was three-
quarters of a mile or a mile in breadth, with a rough and rapid
current, endangering the ferry-boat, though large enough to contain seventy persons, together with much merchandize and some
horses. Close above Attock, the Indus receives, on the western
side, the great river of Kabool, which drains the extensive basin of
Kabool, the northern declivity of Sufeid Koh, the southern declivity of Hindoo Koosh and Chitral, and the other extensive valleys
which furrow this last great range on the south. Both rivers have

large volumes of water and are very rapid,[4] and as they meet [4] Burnes, Bokh.
i. 79; Elph. 71*
Hough, 334.
amidst numerous rocks, the confluence is turbulent and attended
with great noise. The Kabool river appears to have nearly as
much water as the Indus, and in one respect has an advantage
over it, being navigable for forty miles above the confluence,[5] [5] Macartney, in
Elph. 656;
while the upward navigation of the Indus is rendered impracti- Burnes, Pers.
cable by a very violent rapid, immediately above the junction. Narr. 112-120.
Both rivers have gold in their sands, in the vicinity of Attock ;[6] [6] Burnes' Bokh. i
80 ; Wood, Oxus,
it is obtained in various places along the upper course of the 122.
Indus, or its tributaries ; as at Gartope,[7] in Undes, and also near [7] Moorer.
Jour. to Mana-
the confluence of the Shy-yok, and near Iskardo.   Attock, just Sarovara, As.
below the confluence of the Kabool river, about seven hundred Res. xii. 440 ;
Vigne, ii. 245,
miles from the supposed source of the Indus, and in lat. 33° 54', 287.
long. 72° 18', is remarkable, as being the limit of the upward navigation of the latter river, and the place most frequented for passage
over it from Hindostan to Afghanistan.   The passage is,[8] for the [8] Burnes, Bokh.
i. 79; iii. 284;
greater part of the year, made by bridges of boats, of which there Pers. Narr. 119;
are two; one is above the fort of Attock, where the river is eight Wood, in same
work, 346, and
hundred feet wide; the other, below, where it is above five hun- Oxus, 121; Leech,
dred and forty feet wide. Wood found the depth at Attock, in Passage of the
Indus at Attock,
August, to be sixty feet ; the rate of the current six miles an 16.
hour ; the breadth, where he measured it above the place of the
bridge, eight hundred and fifty-eight feet. The inundation affects
the depth and speed of the current, rather than the breadth, at
Attock. This remarkable point is about 1,000 feet above the
sea, and consequently about 17,000 feet below the source of the
Indus,* which falls, therefore, to that extent in seven hundred
miles. This is at the rate of about twenty-four feet per mile.
The length of its channel from Attock to the sea is nine hun-
dred and forty-two miles,[9] and consequently, in that lower [9] Wood, in
Burnes' Pers.
part of its course, it falls little more than a foot per mile. Narr. 305.
At Attock, the river, flowing generally south-south-west, as it
does below Derbend, enters a deep rocky channel in the Salt
range, or secondary mountains, which connect the eastern ex-

* Burnes (Personal Narrative, 112-120) reached Peshawur by water, a
distance of about fifty miles from Attock, and, consequently, the Kabool river
and its tributary, by ascending which this was effected, cannot have a fall
much exceeding a foot per mile.   Griffith (Append. to Hough, 74) ascertained the height of Peshawur to be 1,068 feet. It may, therefore, be safely
concluded that the height of Attock above the sea is about 1,000 feet.

tremity of Sufeid Koh with the base of the Himalaya, in the
Punjab. In this part of its course, the river, as well as the fort
on its left or eastern bank, is known by the name of Attock, in
consequence, as is generally supposed, of the prohibition under
which the Hindoos originally lay of passing it westward.[9]* (See
Аттоск.) For about ten miles below Attock, the river, though
in general rolling between high cliffs of slate-rock, has a
calm, deep, and rapid current ; but for above a hundred
miles farther down, to Kala Bagh, it becomes an enormous
torrent, whirling and rolling among huge boulders and
ledges of rock, and between precipices[1] rising nearly perpendicularly several hundred feet from the water's edge. The
water here is a dark lead-colour, and hence the name *Nilab*,[2]
or " blue river," given as well to the Indus as to a town on
its banks, about twelve miles below Attock. At Ghora Trup,
about twenty miles below Attock, the immense body of water
passes through a channel only two hundred and fifty feet
wide, but having a depth of one hundred and eighty feet, the
velocity being about ten miles an hour.

　　Wood, describing the course of the river from Attock to Kala-
Bagh, says,[3] " it here rushes down a valley varying from one
hundred to four hundred yards wide, between precipitous banks
from seventy to seven hundred feet high." During inundation,
the river rises in this part about fifty feet. It is obvious, that at
the season when this occurs, extending from the end of May to
September, the upward voyage is impracticable. The downward
voyage may at all times be performed, though attended with considerable danger during inundation. It has been suggested, that
there are several places along this rock-bound channel where it
would be practicable to construct an iron bridge across the river,
the breadth at various points not exceeding three hundred feet
(sometimes falling short of this), and the banks being solid limestone.[4] The natives frequently venture down this vast torrent floating on a *mussuk*, or inflated hide.[5] The boats employed here are
called *duggahs*,[6] and are heavier and more strongly built than the

[9] Wood, Oxus, 122.

[1] Id. 112.

[2] Wilford, in As. Res. vi. 530.

[3] 127.

[4] Id. 124.

[5] Id. 110.

[6] Id. 108; Burnes, Pers. Narr. 91.

　　* According to Wilford (As. Res. vi. 529), *Attaca*, or " the forbidden."
The prohibition of crossing seems, however, pretty generally set at nought,
as was seen in the case of the Hindoos in the British armies invading Afghanistan. Hough (334) derives the name from *Atuk*, or *Utuk*, " prevention,"
or " obstacle."

dundis, or boats used in the lower part of the river. The upward voyáge, when practicable, is effected by means of tracking,—sails resorted to previously, being either useless, from the prevalence of dead calm, or dangerous in consequence of the varying and violent squalls produced in the current of air by the effect of the lofty and irregular banks. As the river approaches the plain coun-try below Kala-Bagh, the channel expands nearly to the breadth of five hundred yards; just above that town the width is four hundred and eighty-one yards.[7] Below Kala-Bagh, in lat. 32° 57', long. 71° 36', and about eight hundred miles from the mouth, the river enters the plain, the east or left bank here becoming low, while on the right the Khussoree hills rise abruptly from the water, having, as Burnes[8] observes, "the appearance of a vast fortress, formed by nature, with the Indus as its ditch." Along the base of these hills, which stretch south-south-west for about seventy miles, the channel is deep, generally having soundings about sixty feet.[9] On entering the plain, the water loses its clearness, and becomes loaded with mud. In inundation, the depth of the stream is not so much affected in this part of its course as are the breadth and velocity; and here, as well as in the Delta, the river, when swollen, overflows the adjacent country to a great extent.[1] From Kala-Bagh, southwards to Mittunkote, distant about three hundred and fifty miles, the banks, either right or left, or both, are in several places so low, that the first rise of the river covers the country around with water, extending, as the inun-dation advances, as far as the eye can reach. On this portion of the river's course Wood[2] says—"So diffused was the stream, that from a boat in its centre no land could be discovered, save the islands upon its surface, and the mountains on its western shore. From Dera Ismael Khan to Kala-Bagh, a distance of above a hun-dred miles, the eastern bank cannot once be seen from the opposite side of the river, being either obscured by distance or hidden by interjacent islands." These islands, when the river is low, are gentle elevations of the mainland, much frequented on account of the luxuriant pasture; but during the season of inundation, they, as well as the immediate banks, are deserted, in consequence of the danger resulting from the sudden, irregular, and irresistible irruptions of the current. "In this month" (July), observes Wood,[3] "the islands are abandoned, and as the boat swiftly glides amidst the mazy channels that intersect them, no village cheers

[7] Wood, Oxus, 100.

[8] Pers. Narr. 97.

[9] Wood, in App. to Burnes, Pers. Narr. 365.

[1] Lord, Med. Mem. of the Plain of the Indus, 64; Elph. Acc. of Caubul, 27.

[2] Oxus, 99.

[3] Oxus, 100

the sight, no human voice is heard ; and, out of sight of land, the voyager may for hours be floating amidst a wilderness of green island fields." The habitations are generally placed at a considerable distance from the banks. If this precaution be disregarded, they are exposed to the fate of Dera Ismael Khan,[4] a large town, which, with its flourishing palm-groves, was totally swept away in 1829. Sometimes the Indus suffers very sudden and extraordinary changes. For instance, on one occasion, at the setting in of night, Wood found it to have an unbroken expanse of 2,274 yards in breadth,[5] and next morning its bed was a confused mass of sand-banks, in which the main channel was only two hundred and fifty-nine yards wide ; this extraordinary change having occurred in consequence of a great body of the water of the river having made its escape into a low tract in the vicinity of its course. As the inundation originates in the melting of the snows in the Hindoo Koosh and the Himalaya, it commences with spring, and retrogrades as autumn advances ; and so regular is this process, that, according to Wood,[6] it begins to rise on the 23rd of March and to subside on the 23rd of September, its maximum being about the 6th or 7th of August. The average rise of the inundation between Kala-Bagh and Mittunkote is eight feet and a half ;[7] the declivity of the water's edge is eight inches per mile. In this part of its course the Indus receives scarcely any accession to its water. Higher up it has a few tributaries, though of no great importance. Thus, on the right, or west bank, in lat. 33° 22', long. 71° 52', the Toe, described by Elphinstone[8] as a deep and clear stream, falls into it ; and lower down, on the same side, in lat. 32° 37', long. 71° 24', the Kurum, a broad stream, but so shallow, that where Elphinstone[9] crossed it was only a foot deep. On the left, or east side, in lat. 33° 49', long. 72° 16', the Indus receives the Hurroo,[1] a small stream, and on the same side, lower down, in lat. 33° 1', long. 71° 46', the Swan,[2] also an inconsiderable stream. The Indus, between Kala-Bagh and Mittun, in consequence of the great breadth of its channel, is scarcely affected by rain ; but in the narrow part, above Kala-Bagh, it sometimes rises eight or nine feet in a short time from this cause. In many places, where the river flows through the plain, there is an inner and an outer bank. The outer banks[3] run at a great distance from each other, and between them, during inundation, the vast body of water rolls often in several channels, separated by shifting

[4] Id. 90.

[5] Id. 84.

[6] In Carless, Offic. Survey, 20.

[7] Wood, in App. to Burnes' Pers. Narr. 307.

[8] 39 ; Wood, Oxus, 126.

[9] 35, 114 ; Macartney, App. to Elph. 657 ; Wood, Oxus, 99.

[1] Wood, Oxus, 120-123 ; Hough, 337, 433.

[2] Macartney, in Elph. 657 ; Hough, 340, 433 ; Wood, 108, 115.

[3] Wood, in App. to Burnes' Pers. Narr. 340, 341 ; Lord, Med. Mem. on the Plain of the Indus, 64.

islands; when the river is low, this great course becomes a shallow valley of very irregular breadth, and the shrunken river meanders along its bottom. If the outer banks were continuous, the river would roll along in a stream varying in breadth according to the greater or less degree of inundation; but at all times, even when fullest, in a defined channel of moderate breadth, though varying greatly in different parts. In many places, however, the outer bank is wanting, and, during inundation, the river expands over the country, converting it into an extensive lake. Between Mittunkote and Bukkur, the inundation extends sometimes twenty miles from the western side of the river, in its low state, and ten or twelve from the eastern side.[4] Wood[5] gives the width of the shrunken river as varying from four hundred and eighty to one thousand six hundred yards, and the average width at about six hundred and eighty yards; its usual maxima of depth at nine, twelve, or fifteen feet; but its bed is so irregular, and so liable to be obstructed by shifting shoals, that though it cannot be regularly and safely forded in any part, except that intervening between Torbela and Attock,[6] its navigation, even below the confluence of the Kabool, cannot be effected at all times, and continuously throughout its whole course, by boats drawing more than thirty inches water. The general velocity of the stream in its shrunken state is estimated by Wood at three miles an hour; but he observes,[7] " it is scarcely necessary to remark, that the three last items (breadth, depth, velocity) are very inconstant. At no two places are the measurements exactly alike, nor do they continue the same at one place for a single week." In fact, the breadth, during inundation, is only two hundred and fifty feet at Ghora Trup;[8] and below Mittunkote,[9] it in one place amounts to thirty miles; the depth at the same time and place is a hundred and eighty-six feet, and in other places only twelve feet : the velocity at Ghora Trup, during the inundation, is ten miles an hour; at other places, not half that, and when the river is low, often not more than two miles an hour.

The general course of the river is a little west of south from Attock to the confluence of the Punjnud, the channel which conveys the collected streams of the Punjab. This confluence is on the left or eastern side of the Indus, two or three miles below Mittunkote, in lat. 28° 55', long. 70° 28', and about four hundred and seventy miles from the sea. Above the confluence, the

[4] Wood, in Burnes' Pers. Narr. 341.
[5] Id. 305.

[6] Leech, Rep. on Fords of the Indus, 18; Wood, in Burnes, 330, 342.

[7] InApp. to Burnes' Pers. Narr. 306.

[8] Wood, Oxus, 125.
[9] In Burnes' Pers. Narr. 341.

breadth of the Indus is less than that of the other river, but, in consequence of the greater depth and velocity, the former has the greater volume of water. Wood[7] found the Indus having a breadth of six hundred and eight yards, a velocity of about five miles an hour, a depth of twelve or fifteen feet, and discharging 91,719 cubic feet per second. The Punjnud had a breadth of one thousand seven hundred and sixty-six yards, a velocity of about two miles an hour, a depth of twelve or fifteen feet, and discharged 68,955 cubic feet per second. Below the confluence, the Indus is in its lowest state two thousand yards wide. Its aspect in this part is well described by Boileau.[8] " At the place where we crossed the Indus, almost immediately below its junction with the Punjnud, its stream is two thousand and forty-one yards, or nearly a mile and a quarter, in breadth, at a place where its width was unbroken either by islands or sand-banks. The banks are very low and the water very muddy, having just begun to rise, from the melting of the snows at its sources; nor is the stream of very great depth, except in the main channel; but with all these drawbacks, it is a magnificent sheet of water—a very prince of rivers." For a considerable distance above and below Mittunkote, the country is low,* and the inundation extensive, reaching to Shikarpoor, and even to some places distant from the river twenty miles to the west, and extending eight or ten miles to the east. Lower down, at Roree, the stream makes its way through a low ridge of limestone and flint, which stretches from the mountains of Cutch Gundava,[9] eastward, to Jessulmair. There are strong indications that the stream, in remote ages, swept far eastward along their northern base, and irrigated the level tract at present desert, but exhibiting numerous proofs that it once was traversed by large streams,[1] and was both fertile and populous. At present, this ridge is cut, not only by the Indus, but, a few miles farther east, by the Eastern Narra, which diverges from the main stream, on the eastern side, a short distance above Roree, and takes a south-easterly course through the desert, in which it is usually lost, though in violent inundations it rolls onward to the sea in a great volume of

7 In Burnes' Pers. Narr. 354.

8 Ragwarn and Buhawulpoor, 57.

9 Havelock, i. 118; Lord, Med. Mem. on Plain of Indus, 60; Westmacott on Roree, in Jour. As. Soc. 1841, p. 394; Kennedy, ii. 169; Burnes' Bokh. iii. 73, 272; Wood, in App. to Burnes' Pers. Narr. 349; Oxus, 51; Hough, 20; Leech, on Sind. Army, 79.

1 Masson, i. 19; Macmurdo on the Indus, Jour. As. Soc. 1834, p. 41; Vigne, Kashmir, ii. 408.

* Such is the statement of Wood (in Burnes' Personal Narr. 341); Lord, on the contrary (Medical Mem. 64), states that the banks below Mittunkote are not much inundated; but Wood's industrious research and general accuracy are well known.

water, discharging itself through the Koree, or most eastern mouth, which is in general quite deserted by the fresh water. At Roree there are four rocky islets, the largest of which, that of Bukkur, contains an extensive fort, and divides the river into two channels. A few miles below this place, the Western Narra, a great and permanent branch, divaricates from the Indus on the western side, and, after a tortuous course of nearly two hundred miles, rejoins the main stream about four miles south-east of Sehwan. A little above that town, the Narra has a large but shallow expansion, called Lake Manchur, varying in circuit from thirty to fifty miles, according to the greater or less degree of inundation. This great water-course, in the part intervening between Lake Manchur and the Indus, has a name distinct from that of the Narra, being called the Arul. From Sehwan, downwards, to the efflux of the Fulailee, a distance of about eighty miles, the bed of the river is much depressed below the level of the adjacent country, and the banks are elevated from sixteen to twenty feet[2] above the surface in the low season; in this part of the course, inundations rarely overspread the country, and irrigation is effected by raising the water with the Persian wheel. The Fulailee, a large branch, though yearly diminishing, leaves the Indus, on the eastern side, about twelve miles north of Hyderabad, and, flowing south-east, insulates the Gunjah hills, on which that town is built, as, about fifteen miles below it,[3] an offset running westward rejoins the main stream. At Triecal, where is the point of re-union, in lat. 25° 9', long. 68° 21', the Delta commences; all below it, and contained between the Fulailee on the east and the extreme western branch of the Indus, being, with little exception, alluvial, and obviously deposited by the river. The Fulailee holds a south-easterly course, in the lower part of which it bears the name of the Gonnee, and about fifty miles below Hyderabad divides into two channels, one of which continues to hold a south-easterly course, communicating, during high inundations, with the Phurraun, by which it is discharged into the sea through the Koree mouth; the other flows south-west, and joins the Pinyaree, which diverges from the Indus at Bunna,[4] about forty miles below Hyderabad. The Koree mouth may more properly be termed an arm of the sea, as the water is salt, and it receives a current from the Indus only during inundations of unusual height. Burnes[5] found it

[2] Wood, in Burnes' Pers. Narr. 341, 342; Lord, Med. Mem. on the Plain of the Indus, 63.

[3] Wood, in Burnes' Pers. Narr. 342; Id. in Carless, Official Survey, 17; Burnes, iii. 261; Pott. 358.

[4] Burnes (J.), Mission to Sinde, 40.

[5] iii. 239.

seven miles wide and twenty feet deep at Cotasir, about twenty miles from the open sea. Some suppose it to have once been the principal mouth of the Indus, constantly discharging the water of the Narra, which they consider to have been the chief branch. It is at present the most eastern of the estuaries connected with the Indus. The Pinyaree, a wide branch, is navigable, downwards, to within fifty miles of the sea; at that distance the navigation is closed by a bund[5] or dam, thrown across it at Maghribee; but as the water makes its way through small creeks in time of inundation, the navigation recommences below the bund and continues to the sea. The Pinyaree discharges itself through the Sir estuary,[6] two miles wide at its mouth, with a depth on the bar of one fathom, and of from four to six inside: it is next, westward, to the Koree mouth. At about six miles above Tatta, the Kulairee, a small branch, leaves the Indus on the right or western side, and may be considered to mark the commencement of the Delta on that side. Were not its water lost by absorption and evaporation, it would generally insulate Tatta,[7] as it now does occasionally. At about five miles below Tatta,[8] and fifty miles from the sea, the Indus was formerly divided into two great branches, the Buggaur, which flowed westward, and the Sata, which maintains the previous course of the Indus southward, and is in strictness the continuation of that river. But the Buggaur has no current during the season when the Indus is low, there being a sand-bank at the entrance five or six feet above the surface of the water at that time. The Sata, below the division, is about a thousand yards wide. The Mull[9] and the Moutne formerly great branches leaving the left or eastern side of the Sata, are now so diminished in the season of low-water as to be almost dry. The estuaries,[1] however, remain: that of the Mull is navigable for boats of twenty-five tons as far as Shahbunder, about eighteen miles from the sea; it is the mouth next westward of the Sir mouth, and next westward of this is the Kaheer, or estuary of the Moutnee, at present unnavigable.[2] Two branches, the Kedywaree and Hujamaree, formerly left the right side of the Sata, and fell into estuaries of the same name.

The main stream of the Sata, known near the sea by the names Munnejah and Wanyanee, pursues a course a little to the west of south, and falls into the Indian Ocean by the Kookewarree mouth,

[5] Burnes (A.), Bokh. 238, 239.

[6] Burnes, iii. 238.

[7] Burnes, Pers. Narr. 18.
[8] Id. 229; Carless, Official Survey, 1; Kennedy, I. 73.

[9] Carless, 1.

[1] Burnes, iii. 337.

[2] Id. 237.

forming in 1837, when Carless published his account, "the
grand embouchure of the Indus."[3]   This principal mouth is in [3 Carless, 2.]
lat. 24° 2′, long. 67° 32′. It is the next mouth to the westward
of the Kaheer, and is 1,100 yards wide.[4] The mouth is rendered [4 Id. 9.]
difficult of navigation by a great bank stretching across it, and extending five miles out to sea. There are two channels across this,
and through them the current of the Indus rushes with a great
noise, forming vast cascades when the tide is out. There is
another channel, communicating with the Kedywaree mouth,
more northerly than these, as well as more accessible, less intricate,
and deeper, having nine feet at low-water where shallowest; and
this, when Carless wrote, appeared to have been the only entrance, affording at all seasons a communication between the sea
and the main channel of the upper part of the river. Even this
becomes dangerous after the setting in of the westerly winds in
February, as the sea then breaks violently across it. Under favourable circumstances, it may be safely entered by vessels not
drawing more than seven feet water, which, consequently, are the
largest capable of passing from sea into the main channel of the
river during the season of low-water. The Kedywaree is the
next mouth, proceeding westward, and is merely a small creek
affording a vent to the northern channel of the Munnejah, just
mentioned, and also to the Kedywaree branch, which, as already
observed, left the Sata on the right side,[5] but which is now shallow [5 Burnes, iii. 236.]
and little frequented. The Hujamaree estuary, next to the west-
ward, was, until lately, the most important mouth of the Indus,
because, though not affording a navigable communication with the
main river during the season of low-water,[6] it was the most easily [6 Carless, 4;
Burnes, iii. 36,]
accessible of all the mouths, admitting vessels not drawing more [37, 235; Pers.]
than seven feet and a half of water as high as Vikkur, twenty [Narr.7; Kennedy,]
miles from the mouth. In 1838, the English force advancing on [i. 57.]
Afghanistan was landed here, but soon afterwards, according to
the account given by Kennedy,[7] this branch was closed by a [7 ii. 221.]
change made in its channel. The Richel mouth, next in succession in the same direction, is now nearly filled up, though at a
former period one of the most frequented. The Joa, next westward,
is also nearly obliterated. Both these last appear to have at one
time communicated with the Sata. The Pinteeanee is next to the
west, and once communicated with the Buggaur branch, which,
being now deserted by the stream during the season of low-water,

8 Burnes, iii. 235. the Pintecanee mouth is of course deserted also.[8] Its entrance is rendered intricate and dangerous by sand-banks, but there are fifteen feet of wat~r at low tide, and boats of thirty tons can ascend it above thirty miles. Next and last, is the Pittee mouth, the most important at the commencement of the eighteenth cen- 9 Hamilton, New Acc. of the East-Indies, i. 114. tury, when the branch to which it gave exit[9] was accessible as far as Lahoree-bunder, twenty miles from the sea, for vessels of two hundred tons burthen. It was the principal outlet of the Buggaur branch, and as that has been deserted by fresh water, when the river is low, the estuary is in the like condition. It has nine feet of water at low tide, and eighteen at high-water, spring-tides, and it is navigable for thirty miles for vessels of twenty-five tons burthen. The width is five hundred yards at the mouth, and in general, for three hundred yards higher up. The Garrah creek, an estuary of an obliterated branch of the Indus, enters the sea still farther westward, and, according to Burnes 1 On the Navig. of the Indus, 4; Carless, Official Rep. of the Indus, 6. and Carless,[1] has an inland communication with the harbour of Kurrachee, though this seems very doubtful.[2] The distance from the Koree estuary, in the south-east, to the mouth of Garrah creek, 2 Kennedy, ii. 216. in the north-west, is about a hundred and thirty miles, and such is, consequently, the length of the sea-coast of the Delta. There are several mouths of less importance, and the enumeration of which is unnecessary. There are also numerous intricate cross-channels, allowing an inland navigation for small vessels between the various creeks and branches. To sum up briefly this involved subject—during the season of low-water, the Indus falls into the sea by only one channel of any importance : this, called the Sata, Munnejah, or Wanyanee, has its efflux by the Kookewarree mouth, the entrance of which is in general very unsafe, in consequence of shoals, and the great violence of the current : it is navigable with safety only in one narrow gut, and that but for vessels drawing not more than seven feet water. The other mouths are, in the season of low-water, little more than creeks silted up, and closed at various distances from the sea. The number of these creeks, or estuaries, at present at all worth noticing, is eleven, occurring in the following order in proceeding from south-east to north-west : the Koree, Seer, Mull, Kaheer, Kookewarree, Kedywaree, Hujamaree, Richel, Joa, Pintceanec, Pittee.

3 Wood, in Burnes' Pers. Narr. 308. The tide influences the Indus nearly up to Tatta,[3] a distance of about seventy miles. The spring-tide rises nine feet.

The description above given of the mouths and lower branches of the Indus is mainly applicable to their state when the river is lowest. When the river is at its height, as Burnes[4] observes, [4 iii. 240.] " the great branches of this river are of themselves so numerous, and throw off such an incredible number of arms, that the inundation is general, and in those places which are denied this advantage by fortuitous circumstances, artificial drains, about four feet wide and three deep, conduct the water through the fields." For about twenty miles from the sea, the whole country is nearly submerged. At this season, the water of the sea is fresh for some distance from the land, and discoloured for a still greater.*[5] [5 Id. iii. 9.] The quantity of water discharged by the Indus is by no means proportionate to the enormous supplies derived from its numerous tributaries ; the larger portion seems lost by evaporation, absorption, and employment for irrigation in a sultry climate where rain seldom falls. Wood and Lord[6] state the *maximum* [6 In Burnes' Pers. Narr. 306 ; Lord, Med. Mem. on Plain of Indus, 65.] discharge in August, at 446,080 cubic feet per second, and in December, at 40,857 cubic feet per second, and the total annual discharge, at 150,212,079,642 tons avoirdupois. The water, in the early part of the season of inundation, is very unwholesome, in consequence of the great quantity of decayed vegetable and animal matter held in suspension by it. Lord,[7] who made ex- [7 Ibid.] periments by desiccating the water and weighing the residuum, computes that the quantity of silt annually discharged by the river, during the seven months of inundation, would suffice to form an island or bank forty-two miles long, twenty-seven miles broad, and forty feet deep ; but it is clear, that this computation must be received with great allowances, as, according to it, the land of Sinde must have been much farther advanced into the Indian Ocean than it is found to be. After the early part of the season of inundation, if this water be kept until the earthy admixture has subsided, it is both palatable and wholesome.

The Indus is infested by alligators ;[8] they are of the *guryial* [8 Wood, Oxus, 25.] or long-snouted kind, the common kind being unknown in the river, though numerous in lagoons near Kurrachee. The *bolun*,[9] [9 Burnes, Pers. Narr. 9.] a cetaceous animal, the size of a porpoise, is common. Nowhere

* The junction of the fresh and salt water, according to Burnes, is " without violence, and might be now and then discovered by a small streak of foam and a gentle ripple." Pottinger states, that it causes " a very confused rippling." (p. 9.)

are fish finer or more abundant, and they form a large portion of the sustenance of the population of the adjacent country. West-

[1] Acc. of Khyr-poor, in Jour. As. Soc. 1193.

mocott[1] enumerates sixteen kinds, some as long as six or seven feet. The *pulla*, a species of carp, is a rich and delicious fish, though bony to a degree dangerous to an incautious eater. It is

[2] Leech, on the Commerce of Cutch, 51.

largely consumed on the spot and also dried for exportation,[2] forming an important article in the scanty trade of Sinde. The fisherman of the pulla floats, with his breast downwards, on an oblong earthen vessel, closed in all parts except an orifice, which he covers by applying his stomach to it. In this position, he passes along, taking the fish with a net at the end of a long bamboo, and depositing it in the vessel.

[3] Oxus, 104.

Wood[3] observes, that "the population of the banks of the Indus are almost amphibious. The boatmen of Lower Sinde, for example, live, like the Chinese, in their boats. If a native of the Lower Indus has occasion to cross the stream, a pulla-jar wafts him to the opposite shore. At Bukkur, the *mussuk* (inflated hide) supersedes the pulla-jar, and from Mittunkote upwards, every man living near the river has one. Kossids (couriers) so mounted make surprising journeys, and the soldier, with sword and match-lock secured across his shoulders, thus avoids the fatigue of a long march." The leisure time of every description of persons is spent in the water, or floating on it. Such familiarity with the water naturally inclines the population to regard it as the

[4] New Acc. of the East Indies, I. 114-116.

great medium of commercial intercourse, and Hamilton,[4] who visited Sinde at the close of the seventeenth century, found the traffic considerable. Of late years, the trade of the Indus has been obstructed, and in many places destroyed, by the oppression and vexatious rapacity of the various petty powers and tribes claim-ing sovereignty over divers parts of its course. The success of the British arms may be expected to lead to the restoration of a better state of things. Latterly, the commerce of the Indus has in a great measure been limited to the transport of grain from

[5] Wood, in Burnes' Pers. Narr. 314.
[6] Id. 320.

the upper to the lower part of the river.[5] The *doondah*,[6] or boat generally used in Lower Sinde, is a clumsy vehicle, flat-bottomed, of capacity varying from thirty to fifty tons, with bow and stern, each forming a broad inclined plane, having, the former, an angle with the surface of the water of about twenty, the latter of about forty degrees. The *jumptees*, or state barges of the Ameers, were of considerable dimensions. Wood measured one a hundred and

twenty feet long, eighteen and a half broad, and drawing two feet
six inches water. In the upper part of the Indus, the boat chiefly
used is the *zohruk*, in most respects resembling the doondah, except that it is smaller, lighter, and more manageable. The *duggah*,
used only in the boisterous part of the current above Kala-Bagh,
is very strongly built, with stern and bow greatly projecting, to
keep away the hull from the bank in case of collision with it.
It is so heavy and unmanageable, that if brought far down the
river, it is usually disposed of there, to save the labour and expense of tracking it back.[7] In proceeding up the stream when the
wind is unfavourable, as is generally the case during the half-year
between the autumnal and vernal equinoxes, way must be made exclusively by tracking. During the other half-year[8] southerly winds
prevail, and the boats run up under sail before it, except where the
use of sails becomes dangerous from peculiar circumstances. It
may be expected that steam, under judicious management, will
be found highly efficient in navigating the Indus. Wood[1] sug-
gests that steamers for this service should have a draft of two
feet six inches, no keel, great breadth in proportion to their
length, and high steam power in proportion to their tonnage ; and
Carless[2] recommends them to be one hundred and forty feet long
and twenty-five broad. The principal obstacle to the employment of steam is the dearness and inferior quality of the firewood
on Sinde, which renders it doubtful whether it might not be more
economical, as it certainly would be more efficient, to use coal
imported from England. Coal[3] has been discovered near the
banks of the Indus, both in the Punjab and on the Afghan side,
but further investigation is required as to its quality and quantity.
In estimating the advantages to be drawn from the navigation
of the Indus, reference should be had not so much to the petty
demand from Sinde, as to that of the countries on the upper part of
the river, through which Afghanistan, Khorasan, and Central Asia
are largely supplied; and the best means of advancing this most
important branch of trade seem to be the establishment of great
periodical fairs, at suitable points on the banks of the Indus, and
the affording facilities of communication and protection to the commercial classes. Burnes[4] and Wood[5] regard Dera Ghazee Khan,
in the Derajat, as the best site for this purpose.
Both the prosperity of Sinde and the commerce of the Indus

[7] Wood, in Burnes' Pers. Narr. 324.

[8] Wood, ut supra, 317.

[1] In Burnes' Pers. Narr. 330.

[2] In Postans, Observations on the Increase of Commerce of the Indus.

[3] Wood, in Burnes, 337; Id. Rep. on Localities of Coal, 80; Burnes, Rep. on Coal, 78 ; Pers. Nar. 113; Jour. As. Soc. 1842, p. 1, James on Min. Rep.

[4] On the establishment of a Fair for the Indus Trade, 111.

[5] Oxus, 80.

have much decayed since the commencement of the eighteenth century. Tatta, at the time of Hamilton's visit,[7] is said to have contained above 150,000 inhabitants ; and the Indus and its tributaries
then formed a much-frequented channel of communication with
Lahore* and other remote parts of the Punjab. At that time,
the whole of the navigable course of the Indus was through the
dominions of the Great Mogul ; now, the fluctuating imposts and
extortionate demands of several petty powers holding different
parts of it have operated so as to obstruct almost entirely intercourse by means of the river. In these mischievous proceedings,
the Ameers of Sinde have been foremost, partly from ignorance
and short-sighted rapacity, partly (it is generally supposed) from
a jealous anxiety to exclude from their dominions foreigners, and
especially the English.

Although some of the particulars following have been already
noticed, it may be convenient, in conclusion, to bring them into
one view. The length of the navigable part of the river from
the sea to Attock has been ascertained,[8] by measurement, to be
nine hundred and forty-two miles ; that of the upper part is about
seven hundred miles ; making a total length, in round numbers,
of one thousand six hundred and fifty miles. The average declivity of the water-course from the supposed locality of the source
to Attock is, per mile, twenty-four feet ; from Attock downwards
to Kala-Bagh, a distance of about a hundred and ten miles, it is
twenty inches ; from this last place to Mittunkote, a distance of
about three hundred and fifty miles, it is eight inches ; and
thence to the sea, six inches. The Indus is probably destined
to be an important channel of political and commercial communication ; but those speculating on the advantages to be derived
from its navigation should bear in mind the weighty remark of
Wood,[9] " that there is no known river in either hemisphere, discharging even half the quantity of water that the Indus does,
which is not superior, for navigable purposes, to this far-famed
stream."

* Hamilton states (i. 123), that it required six or seven weeks to reach
Lahore from the sea by the upward navigation of the Indus, and that the
return occupied sometimes eighteen, but at other times not more than twelve,
days. The leisurely voyage of Burnes occupied above three months. (Bokhara, iii. 39—147.)

[7] New Acc. of the East-Indies, i. 114.

[8] Wood, in Burnes' Pers. Narr. 305.

[9] Oxus, 75.

INLKAWN.—A village in Sinde, on the route from Omer- E.I.C. Ms. Map. cote to Joudpoor, and fifty miles north-east of the former place. It is situate north of the Little Desert, about twenty miles from the eastern frontier. Lat. 25° 34', long. 70° 32'.

IRAK MUKAM, in Sinde, a halting-place on the route from E.I.C. Ms. Doc. Kurrachee to Sehwan, and fifty-five miles north-east of the former place. It is situate on the Irak river, or rather torrent, and at the eastern base of the Bhool hills. Water can at all times be obtained in the channel of the river, and there is an abundant supply of forage. The road in this part of the route is good, but generally passes through jungle. Lat. 25° 11', long. 67° 47'.

IRAK RIVER, in Sinde, rises at the base of the Bhool hills, E.I.C. Ms. Doc. in the mountainous tract between Kurrachee and Sehwan, and in about lat. 25° 20', long. 67° 45'. It holds a course of about forty miles in a south-easterly direction, and empties itself in lat. 24° 53', long. 68° 6', into the dund, or lake, of Kunjur, a considerable body of brackish water, abounding in fish. Though the stream fails in time of drought, water may always be obtained by digging in the bed.

ISHIKAGHASY.—A village in Afghanistan, on the north- Walker's Map of ern slope of the Huzareh mountains, where they decline to the Afg. low country of Bokhara. It is situate on a feeder of the river of Andkhoo. Lat. 36° 6', long. 64° 48'.

ISHPAN, in Afghanistan, a small town near the right or E.I.C. Ms. Doc.; eastern bank of the Soork Rood, in the district of Jelalabad. MacGregor, Jour. As. Soc. Here, in 1801, Shah Shooja received a severe defeat from Shah 1842, p. 126; Mahmood, and was obliged to fly from the kingdom. Lat. 34° Elph. Acc. of Caubul, 581; 47', long. 70°. Hough, Narr. Exp. in Afg. 300.

ISHPEE.—A village in Kafiristan, on the river Tagao, ninety E.I.C. Ms. Doc. miles north-east of Kabool. Lat. 35° 26', long. 70° 3'.

ISKARDOH,[1] the capital of Bultistan, is situate in an elevated [1] Burnes' Bohk. ii. 210. plain, forming the bottom of a valley embosomed in stupendous ranges of mountains. The plain or valley of Iskardoh is nineteen miles long and seven broad.[2] Its soil is formed of the detritus [2] Vigne, Kashmir, ii. 246. brought down and deposited by the Indus, and by its great tributary the Shighur river; the confluence being at the northern base of the rock on which the fort is built. The killah, or rock, the site of the fort, is on the left bank of the Indus,[3] here a deep [3] Moorcr. Punj. Bokh. ii. 262.

and rapid torrent, above a hundred and fifty yards wide.* It is two miles long, and at the eastern end, where it is highest, rises nearly perpendicularly eight hundred feet above the river, from a buttress of sand, loose stones, and broken rocks. The killah has this mural face on every side, except the west, where it slopes steeply to the plain. Vigne considers that it could be rendered as strong as Gibraltar, to which, in appearance, it bears much resemblance. The castle of the *Gylfo*, or sovereign of Bultistan, stands on a small natural platform about three hundred feet above the bed of the river, and is built of stone, with a framework of timber, and numerous strong defences against musketry. It is approached by a steep zig-zag path, traversed by gateways and wooden defences, several of which are also disposed in such parts of the sides of the rock as require to be strengthened. There is a look-out house on a peak, a little above the castle, and another on the summit above that. Every thing in the interior of this stronghold is constructed for defence rather than comfort, the place " being a confusion of break-neck stairs, low doors, and dark passages." There is a splendid view of the valley and the river from the windows. The highest summit of the rock is a small level space of a triangular shape, and here are piled stones, ready to be rolled down for the destruction of assailants. It is scarcely accessible, except on the western side, and there, at a height of about two hundred feet, the acclivity is strongly fortified by walls and square towers. The formation of the rock is gneiss. There is no water in the upper part of the killah, but below the castle is a fine spring. The residence of the population attached to the seat of government of this petty state is on the plain at the base

4 ii. 249.

of the rock, and can, according to Vigne,[4] "hardly be called a town, being a straggling collection of houses." The number

5 ii. 262.

of these houses is estimated by Moorcroft [5] at one hundred and fifty. Vigne displays the enthusiasm of an ardent admirer of the picturesque in describing the appearance of this singular and secluded place, as viewed by him on his first visit to it from the direction of Kashmir. "I, the first European who had ever beheld them (so I believe), gazed downwards from a height of six or seven thousand feet upon the sandy plains and green

---

* According to Vigne (ii. 245), Moorcroft states it to be three hundred yards wide. (ii. 262.)

orchards of the valley of the Indus at Iskardo." "The rock of the same name itself with the rajah's stronghold on the east end of it, was a very conspicuous object. The stream from the valley of Shighur, which joins the Indus, as it washes its foot, was visible from the spot where I stood, but the latter river was hidden by the height of its left bank, whilst on the north, and wherever the eye could rove, arose with surpassing grandeur a vast assemblage of the enormous summits that compose the Tibetian Himalaya." [5]   [5] ii. 238, 239.

Respecting the origin of Iskardoh, Wade[6] mentions an absurd tradi- tion which at least has the interest of novelty for those whose know- ledge of the exploits of " the great Emathian conqueror" is derived from classical sources. It is, " that Alexander the Great came here on an expedition towards Khata, or Scythia (modern China), and that the Koteh Mustak, or the Mustak mountains, which lie between Yargand and Khata, being at that time impassable on account of the depth and severity of the snow, the Macedonian halted on the present site of the capital until a road could be cleared for his passage; when, leaving every part of his super-fluous baggage, together with the sick, old, and infirm of his troops, behind in a fort which he erected while there, he advanced against Khata. These relics of the army founded a city, which they named Iskandaria, or Alexandria, now pronounced Iskardoh." The tradition received no countenance from Ahmed Shah, the intelligent gylfo, or sovereign, of the country, to whom Moorcroft[7] applied for information on this curious subject. Neither the gylfo, nor any other inquirer, has been able to find any trace of Greek colonists. (See BULTISTAN.) Vigne,[8] who at one time maintained the fabulous Greek origin of Iskardoh, in retractation states, that " Iskardo, Skardo, or Kardo, as it is sometimes called, is obviously only an abbreviation of Sagara Do, the two floods or rivers." He then mentions, that the people of Ladakh call it Sagar Khood, and adds, " Sagara is an old Sanscrit word for the ocean ; and in this case Sagar Khood may signify the valley of the great flood or river : do signifying two in Persian ; and its cog-nate is added to the name Sagar, because the open space is formed by the junction of two streams, the Indus and the Shighur river." The plain or bottom of the valley of Iskardoh is 6,300[9] feet above the sea, and the summit of the rock is 7,100 above the same level   Ahmed Shah, the native sovereign, has ruled the country with a moderation and paternal regard for his people little

[6] Jour. As. Soc. 1835, p. 82.

[7] Punj. Bokh. ii. 262.

[8] Kashmir, ii. 249.

[9] Vigne, ii. 260.

known among Asiatic despots. He made some unsuccessful efforts to become a protected vassal of our Indian government, as he justly dreaded the power, rapacity, and cruelty of the Sikhs. His fears have proved true, as, a short time since, Iskardoh, notwithstanding its great natural strength, was seized by Gulab Singh,[1] the cruel and grasping Sikh chieftain of Jamu. Iskardoh is in lat. 35° 10′, long. 75° 27′.

[1] Vigne, ii. 374.

Moorcr. ii. 248; Forster, ii. 6; Vigne, ii. 39; Von Hugel, i. 278. ISLAMABAD, in Kashmir, a town situate on the north side of the Behut, or Jailum, here navigable, and running with a gentle current. The river is about eighty yards wide, and is crossed by a wooden bridge. Islamabad is built at the extremity of a long, low eminence extending from the mountains eastward. At the foot of this eminence is a spacious reservoir, of a triangular shape, supplied by a copious spring of clear water, slightly sulphureous, and from which gas is continually evolved. This spring, called Anat Nag, is supposed to have been produced by Vishnu. The gas does not prevent the water from swarming with fish, which are considered sacred. There are about three hundred shops of shawl-weavers at Islamabad, and a considerable quantity of chintzes, coarse cottons, and woollens are also manufactured here. It is a very filthy place, crowded with mendicants and unemployed and starving artisans, the victims of Sikh misrule. Its name was originally Anat Nag, which, in the 15th century, was changed to that which it now bears. Lat. 33° 43′, long. 75° 5′.

Leech, Rep. on Sindh. Army, 77. ISLAMCOTE.—A fort and village of Sinde, in the Eastern Desert, near the frontier of Cutch. The fort, three hundred and fifty yards from the village, is seventy yards square, with walls of burnt brick thirty feet high, having a tower at each angle. There is but one gateway, which is on the eastern side. Lat. 24° 32′, long. 70° 10′.

E.I.C. Ms. Doc.; Bolleau, Beeka-neer, Jesulmeer, and Jodhpoor, 50. ISLAMGURH, or NOHUR.—A fort of Bhawlpoor, on the route from Khanpoor to Jessulmair, and sixty-eight miles north of the latter place. It is a recent acquisition of the Khan of Bhawlpoor, who has made himself master of it at the expense of Jessulmair. The fort is a very ancient structure of small bricks, and has an area of about eighty yards square, with very lofty ramparts, varying in height from thirty to fifty feet. At the north-east angle is a high gateway, covered by an outwork. There are numerous bastions on the north and east faces, but few on the others. There is no ditch, and the situation is unfavourable for defence, as it is commanded on every side by sand-hills eighty feet high, and less than a quarter of a mile distant. There are a few buildings in the interior, and some straggling houses outside. Water is supplied from two wells. Islam-gurh is in lat. 27° 52', long. 70° 55'.

ISLAM KILLA, in Afghanistan, a halting-place on the E.I.C. Ms. Doc. route from Ghuznee to Shawl, and distant from the former place nearly sixty miles south-west. The road is good, sloping gently to the south. Forage and supplies are abundant. Lat. 32° 51', long. 67° 40'.

ISLAMKOTE.—See Islamcote.

ISMAIL PUTTAN, in Sinde, a village on the route from E.I.C. Ms. Doc. Hyderabad to Sehwan, by Kotree, and four miles west of the first-mentioned place. Here is a fine grove of trees and a garden, which formerly belonged to one of the Ameers of Hyderabad. It is situate about half a mile from the right bank of the Indus. Lat. 25° 22', long. 68° 17'.

ISPHAWK, in Afghanistan, the lowest and most eastern of E.I.C. Ms. Map; the passes between Kabool and the valley of Bamian. It com- Wood, Route of Kabool and Toor-mences sixteen miles south-west of the city of Kabool, and winds kestan, 2. round the south-eastern corner of the Pughman range. Though the inclosing cliffs are steep, the road is so good and the acclivities so gradual, that, according to Wood, a mail-coach might be driven through it. Lat. 34° 22', long. 68° 40'.

ISPINGLEE.—A considerable village of Beloochistan, on E.I.C. Ms. Map. the route from Kelat to Beebce Nanee, in the Bolan Pass, and sixty-five miles north-east of the first-mentioned place. The road in this part of the route is level and good, and there is an abun-dant supply of water from wells. The population, amounting to about 2,000, consists of Belooches. Lat. 29° 42', long. 66° 56'.

ISPUNGLEE,[1] in Beloochistan, a village on the route from [1] Map of N. W. Quetta to Kelat, by way of Moostung, and four miles west of the Frontier; Masson, Kalat, 313. first-mentioned place. The route from Quetta to Kelat, by Ispunglee, is more circuitous than that farther east, but better suited for military purposes, as it is practicable for artillery, which cannot pass by the other. The road is excellent,[2] and well suited [2] Outram, Rough for the passage of a large army. Lat. 30° 9', long. 66° 54'. Notes, 158.

ISTALIF,[1] a town in the Koh-i-Damun of Kabool, is twenty- [1] Wood's Oxus, two miles north-west of that city. Its situation is very pic- 177; Lord, Koh-i-Damun, 47 ;

Baber, Mem. 147;
Masson, Bal. Afg.
Panj. iii. 120. turesque, in an elevated country, at the base of the Hindoo Koosh, here rising to an elevation of from 15,000 to 20,000 fect. The town is embosomed in beautiful groves, gardens, and orchards, the latter loaded, in their season, with the most delicious fruits. Each orchard has a tower, to which, during the fruit season, the proprietor repairs, with his family, and lives in a round of festivity. The streets, being built on the acclivity of a steep hill, rise above each other; and though the houses are but mean, their arrangement presents a very striking appearance when viewed from the neighbourhood. The inhabitants are Taujiks, considered to be a mixed race, Arab and Persian, the descendants of the Mahometan conquerors under the Kaliphate. A considerable proportion of the population is engaged in manufactures, especially the spinning, weaving, and dyeing of cottons. The lower orders subsist, in a great measure, on bread made of mulberries, dried in the sun, and ground. This diet is considered very heating and exciting, and to this cause, it is said, the inhabitants themselves attribute the irascible and violent character ² Burnes' Pers.
Narr. 150.
³ Mil. Op. in Afg.
412. for which they are remarkable.[2] On the re-occupation of Kabool by the British troops, in September, 1842, a detachment,[3] under General McCaskill, pushed on to Istalif, defeated a greatly superior force of Afghans, stormed, and partly destroyed the town. The population, previously to this event, was estimated at 15,000. Lat. 34° 46′, long. 68° 58′.

Lord, Koh-i-
Damun, 45;
Masson, Bal. Afg.
Panj. iii. 124;
Baber, Mem. 146. ISTURGATEH, or ISTURGETEH.—A town in the Koh-i-Damun of Kabool, remarkable for its picturesque beauty and fine orchards and gardens. It is situate twenty-six miles north-west of Kabool. Lat. 34° 52′, long. 68° 58′.

J.

Walker's Map of
N.W. Frontier. JACKREE.—A village in the Punjab, situate on the left bank of the Jailum, or Hydaspes river, in lat. 32° 21′, long. 72° 28′.

E.I.C. Ms. Doc.;
Jour. As. Soc.
1842, p. 58; Grif. JADAK (Khand of), in Afghanistan, is a halting-place, with a village, on the route from Kandahar to Ghuznee, and seventy

miles north-west of the former place. It is situate near the right Bar. and Ther.
bank of the Turnak river, in a spot exhibiting considerable culti- Obs.; Atkinson, Exp. into Afg.
vation, and marked by ruins indicating former importance. Its 186.
elevation above the sea is 5,396 feet. It is generally called Julduk
in the maps. Lat. 32°, long. 66° 28'.

JAFFRABAD, in Sinde, a village on the route from Shikar- E.I.C. Ms. Doc.
poor to Sukkur, and five miles north of the latter place. The
country is fertile and well cultivated, and the road in this part of
the route in general good, except where cut up by water-courses
from the Indus. Lat. 27° 46', long. 68° 50'.

JAFUR, in the Punjab, a village in the tract between the Walker's Map of N.W. Frontier.
river Swan and the Indus, fourteen miles from the right bank of
the former, and twenty from the left bank of the latter. Lat. 33°
20', long. 72° 19'.

JAGAN.—A small town, with a fort, in the Northern Punjab, Vigne, Kashmir,
near the left bank of the Tohi, is neatly built on the summit of i. 190.
an eminence. It is held by the Sikhs, who some years ago expelled the Rajah. Lat. 32° 43', long. 75° 5'.

JAGHAN, or JAGHUN, a place in Sinde, twelve miles north- E.I.C. Ms. Doc.
west of Shikarpoor. It consists of a fort and village with some
lofty square fortified buildings outside. It has a small, but rather
well-furnished bazaar. Supplies may be procured in moderate
quantities, and forage, both for camels and horses, is plentiful.
Jaghan is eleven miles and a half from Janehdurra, from which
place the road lies over a level country with much wood. There
is an encamping ground on the south-east of the village. Lat.
28° 4', long. 68° 39'.

JAILPOOR.—A village in the Punjab, sixty-six miles south- E.I.C. Ms. Doc.
west of Lahore, and twenty miles from the right bank of the
Ghara river. Lat. 30° 45', long. 73° 46'.

JAILUM, or JELUM.[1]—A town of the Punjab, on the right [1] Von Hugel, iii.
bank of the river of the same name. Jailum is a town of consider- 143.
able extent, and, though the streets are narrow and intricate, it is
a clean place.[2] It is, however, rendered unhealthy by the inun- [2] Moorer. ii. 308.
dation, which extends widely over the eastern bank of the river.
The principal crops in the vicinity are wheat, barley, and cotton.
During the season when the river is lowest, there is a ford
nearly a mile above the town. The passable part of the bed
describes two sides of a triangle, the vertex of which is down the
river.[3] By this ford the British army crossed in the middle of [3] Hough, Narr. of Exp. in Afg. 345.

December, 1839, in its return from Afghanistan, and though this is the low season, several were swept down the stream, and eleven persons, including an officer, drowned. Hough, who was present on the occasion, states, " the ford extended over a line of about five hundred yards, and had more than three feet water and a strong current near the south bank." It is obvious that, for the greater part of the year, the ford must be totally impassable. The elevation of Jailum above the sea is estimated at 1,620 feet. It is in lat. 33° 2′, long. 73° 36′.

JAILUM, JELUM, JILUM, VESHAU, VEYUT, or BEHUT.
—A river of the Punjab; the most western, and probably the principal, of the five great rivers, which intersect that region east of the Indus. It rises in Kashmir, the whole valley of which it drains, making its way to the Punjab, through the Pass of Baramula,[1] in the lofty range of Pir Panjal. Its most remote source is the head of what is regarded by some as its principal feeder, the Lidur,[2] which rises in the mountain range, bounding the valley on the north-east, and in lat. 34° 21′, long. 75° 33′; and having drained the small mountain lake called Shesha Nag, takes a south-westerly course of about fifty miles to its confluence with the Breng, flowing from the south-east, with nearly an equal length of course.—(See BRENG.) About ten miles to the north-west, this united stream forms a junction with a large feeder flowing from the south, and itself formed by the junction of the Sandren, the Veshau, the Huripur, and some other streams of less importance, none having a length of course exceeding forty miles. Of these, the Veshau is the principal, and, according to Vigne, so far exceeds in size the other upper feeders of the Jailum, that its fountain-head should be regarded as properly the source of that great river. The Veshau flows by a subterraneous passage from Kosah Nag, a small but deep lake, situate near the top of the Pir Panjal mountain, and at an elevation of about 12,000 feet above the level of the sea. Here, Vigne[3] states, " its full strong torrent is suddenly seen gushing out from the foot of the last and lofty eminence that forms the dam on the western end of the lake, whose waters thus find an outlet, not over, but through, the rocky barrier with which it is surrounded." This remarkable spot is in lat. 33° 25′, long. 74° 45′. The stream thus produced and reinforced, subsequently receives numerous small feeders; passes through the City Lake, the

[1] Vigne, I.277-385; Moorcr. ii. 252.

[2] P. Von Hugel, Kaschmir, iv. 144.

[3] Ut supra, i. 292.

Manasa Lake, and the Wulur or Great Lake, and sweeps
through the country, confined by embankments, which prevent
it from overflowing the lower part of the valley. Previously
to entering the Wulur, it receives a considerable tributary
named the Sinde, which rises in the lofty range bounding the
valley on the north. The whole course of the Jailum through the
valley, before it finds an outlet through the Pass of Baramula into
the lower ground of the Punjab, is about a hundred and twenty
miles,[4] for seventy of which it is navigable. It is the opinion of [4] Von Hugel, ii.
191.
Vigne,[5] that the river made its way gradually through this pass [5] i. 287.
and thus drained the lake, which, according to tradition,[6] formerly [6] Rennell, 107.
occupied the site of the valley. At Baramula,[7] where the stream [7] Von Hugel, ii.
198.
is four hundred and twenty feet broad, is a bridge of seven
arches. At Mazufurabad, about a hundred and fifty miles from
its source, it is joined by the Kishengunga, a stream of nearly
equal volume, which rises in Little Tibet, receives a considerable
tributary from the valley of Gurys, and subsequently makes its
way through the mountains stretching from Kashmir to the vicinity of Attock. The united stream takes a course nearly due
south, from Mazufurabad, and about two hundred and twenty
miles from its source, leaves the mountains, and enters on the
plain of the Punjab. It is here a very great stream, though
considered by Burnes [8] less than the Chenaub. Von Hügel,[9] [8] i. 48.
[9] iii. 143.
at the commencement of January, when the rivers of the Punjab
are lowest, crossed, at the town of Jailum, on a bridge of
twenty large boats, and estimated it to have a greater volume of
water than the Indus at Attock. Moorcroft,[1] at the same place, [1] ii. 304.
found it, in the middle of October, a hundred and fifty yards wide,
and from twelve to sixteen feet deep ; but six hundred yards wide
at a short distance both above and below that point, and flowing
at the rate of about a mile an hour. At this place the direction
of the Jailum changes from southerly to south-westerly. The river,
on emerging from the mountains, is first navigable at Oin, about
a hundred and ten miles above the town of Jailum, and continues
so to the Indus.[2] At Julalpoor, from which point Burnes [3] de- [2] Moorcr. ii. 304.
scended by boat to Pind Dadun Khan, the stream was muddy [3] i. 48.
but rapid, with a current of three or four miles an hour. Elphinstone [4] crossed the river at Julalpoor in July, when he found it [4] Macartney, in
one mile, one furlong, and thirty-five perches wide, with a depth Elph. 659.

u 2

of from nine to fourteen feet, and a current running four miles an hour. It abounds in fish, and is infested by great numbers of crocodiles. Below Julalpoor, it takes a direction nearly southerly, and joins the Chenaub a little above the ferry of Trimo, in lat. 31° 10′, long. 72° 9′, after a course of about four hundred and fifty miles. The Jailum was, at the confluence, when observed by Burnes at the end of June, about five hundred yards wide.[5] After the union, the channel of the united waters was a mile broad and twelve feet deep.*

⁵ Burnes, 128.

The Jailum was unquestionably the Hydaspes of the Greeks. It is still known to the Hindoos of the vicinity by the name of Betusta,[6] corrupted by the Greeks according to their usage with respect to foreign names. The scene of the battle between Porus and Alexander is generally placed at Julalpoor.

⁶ Vigne, ii. 181; Burnes, iii. 228; Elph. 80; Rennell, 82.

Leech, Rep. on Sindh. Army, 93.

JAINPOOR, in Afghanistan, a small town on the route from Dera Ghazee Khan to Dadur, through the Hurrund Pass. Lat. 29° 32′, long. 70° 35′.

Map of the N.W. Frontier.

JAIRULA.—A village in the Punjab, situate about twelve miles from the right bank of the Ravee river. Lat. 30° 39 long. 72° 7′.

E.I.C. Ms. Doc.

JAITANU, in the Punjab, a village situate on the road from Julalpoor to Pind Dadun Khan, fifteen miles from the former place, and six miles north of the Jailum or Hydaspes river. Lat. 32° 42′, long. 73°.

JALENDHER.—See JULINDER.

Map of Afg.; Pott. Belooch. 138.

JALK.—A town in Afghanistan, situate a little north of the route from Nooshky to Bunpoor, and near the southern border of the Sandy Desert. Lat. 28° 20′, long. 62° 1′.

JALLINDER.—See JULINDER.

E.I.C. Ms. Doc.

JAM, in Beloochistan, a village situate to the left of the Bholan Pass, on the route to Kelat, from which place it is distant about seventy miles. Lat. 29° 39′, long. 67° 13′.

E.I.C. Ms. Doc.

JAMHALLAKA TANDA, in Sinde, a village on the route from Hyderabad to Allah Yar Ka Tanda, and nine miles east of the former place. Lat. 25° 21′, long. 68° 30′.

JAMOTE HOJA.—See HOJA JAMOTE.

---

* Burnes, who visited the confluence when the rivers were fullest, expresses his wonder that it should be so tranquil, contrary to the description of Arrian. (L. v. c. xx.)

JAMPOOR.—A village of Afghanistan, in the Daman, fifteen E.I.C. Ms. Doc.
miles west of the Indus, and forty miles south-west of Dera
Ghazee Khan. Lat. 29° 33′, long. 70° 38′.

JAMPOOR, in Bhawlpoor, a village on the route from the E.I.C. Ms. Doc.;
town of Bhawlpoor to Khanpoor, and thirty-six miles north-east Boileau, Bekaneer, Jesulmeer, and
of the latter place. Lat. 29° 2′, long. 71° 6′. Jodhpoor, Map.

JAMROOD.[1]—A small town in the province of Peshawur, [1] Burnes' Pol.
ten miles west of the city of that name, and at the eastern en- Pow. Sikhs; Id. Pers. Narr.
trance into the Khyber Pass. It was seized by the Sikhs in 1837, 126; Leech, Khyber Pass, 9, 10.
and an attempt of the Afghans to retake it led to a battle, in
which the Sikhs were defeated, and their general, Hari Singh, an
officer of high reputation, slain. The Sikhs have strengthened
their position here by building the fort of Futighur, on the west [2] Hough, Narr.
side of Jamrood. The town[2] is 1,670 feet above the sea. Jam- Exp. in Afg. 319;
rood is described by Forster under the name of Timrood.[3] Lat. Wood, Oxus, 156; Mil. Op. in Afg.
33° 59′, long. 71° 32′. 199.
[3] Jour. Beng.
JAMU.[1]—A considerable town in the north of the Punjab, Eng. ii. 62.
and among the mountains forming the southern range of the [1] Von Hugel, i. 143.
Himalaya, is situate on a small river, which, rising about forty
miles to the north, takes its course below the town for about
twenty miles, in a south-westerly direction, and falls into the
Chenaub. The town and palace are built on the right or western
bank of the river; on the east is the fort, elevated about a hundred and fifty feet above the stream, which is here fordable when
lowest. The place, with the lofty and whitened palace and fort,
has a striking and pleasing appearance when viewed from without. The bazaar is large, well built, and well supplied; the
streets are extensive, and the population considerable, amounting,
according to Vigne,[2] to about 8,000. The palace is a spacious [2] i. 183.
and handsome building. The fort, built with great cost and
labour, is untenable against a regular attack, being commanded
by an adjacent height of easy access. There is an extensive and
beautiful pleasure-ground, belonging to the rajah. About the
town are numerous ruins of great size, the evidence of its prosperity under its hereditary rajahs before the expulsion of their
family by the Sikhs, who at present rule it with great rapacity
and cruelty. After the Maha Rajah, the ruler of Jamu, Golab
Singh is the most powerful of the Sikhs. Jamu is in lat. 32°
33′, long. 74° 56′.

JAMUT THURA, in the Punjab, a village on the right bank Walker's Map of N.W. Frontier.

of the Ravee river, and forty-two miles north-east of Mooltan.
Lat. 30° 32′, long. 72°.

E.I.C. Ms. Doc.   JANA.—A village in Afghanistan, on the road from Dera
Ismael Khan to Ghuznee, thirty miles west of the former place.
Lat. 31° 50′, long. 70° 24′.

Hough, Narr.   JANEE KA SUNG.—A small town or village of the Punjab,
Exp. in Afg. 338.   on the route from Attock to Rotas. Lat. 33° 45′, long. 72° 48′.

E.I.C. Ms. Doc. ;   JANEHDURRA, in Sinde, a village on the route from Shi-
Hough, Narr.
Exp. in Afg. 38 ;   karpoor to Bagh, and twenty miles north-west of the former town.
Havelock, War in   It is situate near the border of the *Pat,* or desert of Shikarpoor,
Afg. i. 176; At-
kinson, Exp. into   yet the immediate vicinity is fertile, and was at one time well
Afg. 103.   cultivated; but it has suffered much from the devastations of the
marauding Belooches, who lately laid the village in ruins.
There is a fort of considerable size, containing a good well.
There are three other wells outside the fort. Lat. 28° 10′,
long. 68° 36′.

E.I.C. Ms. Doc.   JANGUR.—A village in Sinde, situate ten miles south from
Lake Manchur, and the same distance south-west from Sehwan.
Lat. 26° 16′, long. 67° 46′.

JANNOO KAREEZ.—See Junnoo Kareez.

Ms. Map of Sinde.   JANPOOR.—A village in Sinde, situate on the left bank of
the Indus. Lat. 28° 13′, long. 69° 25′.

E.I.C. Ms. Doc.   JANSER, in Sinde, a village on the direct route from Kurrachee to Sehwan, and seventy miles south of the latter town.
It is situate at the western base of a low range of hills in a
wretched country destitute of supplies. Lat. 25° 28′, long.
67° 54′.

Map of Sinde.   JAREJA.—A village in Sinde, five miles from the left bank
of the Indus. Lat. 28° 2′, long. 69° 7′.

JAYA.—See Adruscund and Jeja.

E.I.C. Ms. Doc.   JEHANGROO.—A village in the south-eastern frontier of
Sinde, eight miles from the northern boundary of the Great
Western Rinn. Lat. 24° 27′, long. 70° 29′.

Jour. As. Soc.   JEJA, or JAYA.—A town of Seistan, on the route from
1840, p. 713,   Herat to Furrah, and forty miles north-west of the latter
Conolly (E.), Phy-
sical Geog. of   place. It is situate in a narrow valley of the same name
Seistan.   and on the left bank of the river Adruscund, which, in this part
Id. 1841, p. 322,
Id. Jour. of   of its course, is in consequence generally called the river of Jaya.
Travelling in
Seistan.   Lat. 32° 53′, long. 61° 55′.

E.I.C. Ms. Doc.;   JELADABAD —A province of Afghanistan, so called from
Mil. Op. in Afg.

the name of the principal town. It is a valley forming a natural subdivision of the great valley of Kabool, being enclosed on the north by the Siah Koh and the mountains of Lughman, on the east by the Ali Boghan hills and the Khyber range, on the south by the Highlands of Nungnehar, on the west by the Kurkutcha range. •It is in its greatest extent about sixty miles in length from east to west, and thirty miles in breadth from north to south, and lies between lat. 34° 10'—34° 40', long. 70°—71°. Jelalabad is very well watered by the Kabool river flowing nearly through the middle from west to east, as well as by the Soorkh Rood and numerous other streams falling into that river from the south, and the Alishang and river of Kama or Kooner from the north. It is a beautiful district, and in general fertile, yielding all the vegetable productions of the finest part of the temperate zone. As its elevation above the sea in few parts exceeds two thousand five hundred feet, the climate, though not disagreeable in winter, is in summer so warm that the more wealthy inhabitants retire to the higher grounds adjacent. The mean temperature is altogether warmer than would result from the latitude and elevation above the sea; and the circumstance is to be accounted for by the radiation and reflection of heat from the high surrounding mountains. So high, indeed, is the mean temperature, that the sugar-cane, first planted by Sultan Baber, is produced in abundance and perfection. In the desert tract of Butte Kot, at the eastern extremity of the valley, the heat sometimes produces a violent and fatal simoom. Men or beasts exposed to its influence are struck dead, and their frames so disorganized, that the limbs can with little effort be torn from the body. The valley is not only productive and well cultivated, but densely peopled and crowded with villages and castles—the latter rendered necessary by the turbulent and rapacious habits of the Afghans. In regard to natural advantages, it is altogether a delightful tract, the beauty of the vale being contrasted with the sublime appearance of the stupendous snow-clad mountains which surround it. Masson, an eyewitness, observes, "Few countries can possess more attractive scenery, or can exhibit so many grand features in its surrounding landscape." The revenue is now calculated to amount to Rs. 300,000. It is stated by Moorcroft to have been at one time 652,000, but under so unsettled a

207; Jour. As. Soc. 1842, p. 117; Macgregor, Geo. Notice of Jullalabad; Wood, Khyber Pass, 1, 2; Oxus, 165; Masson, Bal. Afg. Panj. i. 177; Moorcr. Punj. Bokh. ii. 356; Burnes, Bokh. i. 122; Bab. Mem. 141; Jour. As. Soc. 1836, p. 477, Court, Mem. on a Map of Peshawur.

government as that of Afghanistan, such estimates must be liable to great inaccuracy.

JELALABAD, the capital of the province of the same name, is situated nearly a mile from the south bank of the river of Kabool, and five miles below the confluence of the Soorkh Rood. It is stated to have been founded by the Emperor Akbar, called also Jelal-ad-din. Two other towns of greater extent formerly stood near the site of the present, and their ruined defences can still be traced. Jelalabad is wretchedly built of unburnt bricks, and has little either of manufactures or trade, though advantageously situated on the main road from the Punjab to Kabool. The amount of population is doubtful, but probably does not exceed 3,000, though Havelock[1] estimates it at 10,000. A considerable portion of the number are Hindoos, here, as in other places, the monopolizers of trade. This place owes its importance to the fact of its being the residence of the governor of the fertile province of which it is the chief town. It will be ever celebrated in history, in consequence of the heroic and successful defence made during the winter of 1841-42 by a handful of British troops, under Sir Robert Sale, against a numerous and infuriate army of Afghans. The fortifications were destroyed in October, 1842, by order of General Pollock on his final evacuation of Afghanistan.[2] Elevation 1,964 feet above the sea. Lat. 34° 25', long. 70° 28'.

JELALABAD, called formerly Dooshak, is an ancient city of Seistan, situate four or five miles from the right bank of the Helmund. The extent of the ruins in and about the town prove that it once was large and flourishing. Christie[1] considers that it could not have been inferior in size to Isfahan. It was built of sun-dried bricks, the houses being two stories high, with vaulted roofs. The present town is neat, and in a state of improvement; it has a tolerable bazaar. It belongs to a chieftain who has an annual income of about Rs. 30,000, and appears to acknowledge the supremacy of the Shah of Herat. The population is about 10,000. The name of Jelalabad is recent, having been given to Dooshak in the beginning of the present century in honour of Jelal-ad-din,[2] the son of its chief, Behcram Khan. Lat. 31° 10', long. 61° 40'.

JELALPOOR.—See JULALPOOR.

[1] War in Afg. II.

[2] Mil. Op. in Afg. 424.

[1] In App. to Pott. 408; Malcolm, Hist. of Persia, l. 262; li. 238; Elph. Acc. of Caubul, 494; Jour. As. Soc. 1840, p. 724; Conolly (E.), Map of Seistun.

[2] Pott. Belooch. 315.

JELLOOGHEER, in Afghanistan, a narrow pass in a dis- E.I.C. Ms. Doc.;
trict of the same name, on the route from Kandahar to Ghuznee, Hough, Narr. of Exp. into Afg.
and fifty-two miles north-east from the former place.   Near it 147.
the cliffs abut so closely on the river Turnak that it was necessary to hew a road for the British army on its advance to
Ghuznee in 1839.   Lat. 31° 55′, long. 66° 17′.

JELUM.—See JAILUM.

JEMEL KHANS KOOA, in the Punjab, a village on the E.I.C. Ms. Doc.
route from Mooltan to Bhawlpoor, twelve miles north of the
latter, and forty miles south of the former place.   Lat. 29° 35′,
long. 71° 35′.

JENDIALEH.—See JINDIALEH.

JENDOUL, near the north-eastern frontier of Afghanistan, a E.I.C. Ms. Doc.;
town of the Bajour territory, situate on a feeder of the Lundye Jour. As. Soc. 1839, p. 312,
river, and twenty miles north-east of the town of Bajour.   Lat. Court, Alexander's Exploits on
35° 11′, long. 71° 41′.   the Western Bank
                                                                      of Indus. Map.
JESOOL,[1] in the Punjab, a small town on the route from [1] E I.C. Ms. Doc.
Mooltan to Leia, and ten miles south of the latter place.   It is
situate near the left bank of the Indus, the water of which of late
years has in this part of the course been directed to the right or west
side, so that the former bank on the east side now bears the appearance of a low brow or continuous eminence, running in some degree
parallel to the main channel, and seven or eight miles distant
from it.   Elphinstone [2] well describes this part of the country— [2] Acc. of Caubul, 26.
" It is a narrow tract, contested between the river and the desert.
If in hunting we were led many miles to the west of the road,
we got into branches of the river and troublesome quicksands
among thickets of tamarisk or of reeds ; and if we went as far to
the right, the appearance of sand, and even in some places of
sandhills, admonished us of the neighbourhood of the desert.
The fertile patches of ground, which are of frequent occurrence,
are remarkably well cultivated, and produce grain, cotton, tobacco,
and other less important crops."   The intelligent traveller just
quoted remarks how much he and his party were struck by the
contrast afforded by the style of farming, and of agricultural
structures and arrangements here, to that prevailing in eastern
India.   " Some of the houses near the river," he says, " attracted
our attention, being raised on platforms, supported by strong posts,
twelve or fifteen feet high.   We were told they were meant to
take refuge in during the inundation, when the country, for

twenty miles from the banks, was under water." The people, he adds, were remarkably civil and well-behaved, personable, well clad, and altogether of thriving appearance. Jesool is in lat. 30° 51′, long. 71°.

Von Hugel, Kaschmir, i. 130. JESROD, or JESROUTE, a small raj and town in the north-east of the Punjab, among the mountains of the southern range of the Himalaya. The residence of the rajah (the last occupant of which fell a victim to the rapacity of Runjeet Singh) is a stately mansion, with four towers. The town has a bazaar of small size and inconsiderable business. Lat. 32° 30′, long. 75° 10′.

Outram, Rough Notes, 256. JEWA, or JEWAH, a fertile valley of Beloochistan, is traversed by the route from Kelat to Sonmeanee, and is situate seventy-five miles south-west of the former place. Though bounded by rocky hills, which render it rather difficult of access from the north, the road through it is good, and supplies of forage and water are abundant. Cultivation and population are more considerable than in most parts of this barbarous country. Lat. 27° 58′, long. 65° 50′.

JEWALA MUKI, in the north-east of the Punjab, a celebrated Hindoo place of pilgrimage, ten miles north-west of Nadaun, situate in an elevated nook, immediately under the mountains of Changa, is frequented by votaries from all parts of Hindostan, anxious to worship the mythological personage called Devi, wife of Mahadeo, her presence being indicated, as they believe, by some inflammable gases which issue from fissures in the rock. The name Jewala Muki is composed of two Sanscrit words, *Jewala*, flame, and *Muki*, mouth. The flame, according to the legend, proceeds from the fire which Sati, the bride of Siva, ¹ Wilson, in Moorcr. i. 70. created, and in which she burned herself. Siva,[1] finding that this flame was about to consume the world, buried it in the hollow of the mountain. The temple is about twenty feet square, and the ² Von Hugel, i. 85. principal place of flame is a shallow trough,[2] excavated in the floor, where it blazes without intermission. There are several jets of less importance. The gas also lies on the surface of some small reservoirs of water, and, when ignited, continues to burn for a short time. The roof of the temple is richly gilt, but the interior is blackened by the smoke of burned butter, sugar, and other gross offerings. In 1839, Runjeet Singh, when ill, made an offering of butter, to the amount of £1,500, hoping the renovation of his health from the favour of the deity. The weight of

the offering was probably about sixty or seventy tons; and Vigne,[3] [3 i. 135.]
who was at the place while the burning was going forward, found
" the stench similar to that of a candle-maker's shop." Near the
principal temple is one smaller, called Gogranath, and hence concluded by Von Hügel[4] to be of Buddhist origin. The ground [4 i. 87.]
adjoining to the group of sacred buildings is crowded with cows,
Brahmins, pilgrims, and mendicants, and loaded with filth. The
pilgrims, most of whom are paupers, are supported for one
day from the funds of the temple. The town is dirty and
neglected, but has an extensive bazaar,[5] containing great quan- [5 Id. i. 83.]
tities of idols, votive garlands, rosaries, and other trumpery of the
like description. The population is about 3,000. Near the town
is a mineral spring, the water of which is found to be singularly
efficacious in discussing bronchocele. Moorcroft was unable to
analyze this water, but it probably contains some form of iodine,
now known to possess much efficacy in resolving glandular tu-
mours. The offerings are, in a great measure, appropriated by the
rajah, who derives from them an annual revenue of Rs. 30,000.[6] [6 Gerard, Koona-]
Lat. 31° 46', long. 76° 10'. [wur, 130.]

JEYKEIR, in Sinde, a village on the route, by the Narra [E.I.C. Ms. Doc.]
river, from Sehwan to Larkhana, and twenty miles south of the
latter place. It is situate on the right bank of that great offset
of the Indus, and in a low, alluvial, fertile tract. Lat. 27° 16',
long. 68° 4'.

JHALAWAN.—A province of Beloochistan, bounded on the
north by Sarawan and Kelat; on the east by Cutch Gundava and
Sinde; on the south by Lus and Mekran, and on the west by
Mekran and Sarawan. It lies between lat. 26° and 29°, and
long. 65° and 67° 30'. It is two hundred miles in length from
north to south, one hundred and fifty miles in breadth from east
to west, and has an area of about twenty thousand square miles.
It is extremely mountainous and uneven, containing only three
level spots of any extent—the valleys or plains of Wudd, of
Sohrab, and of Khozdar.[1] The climate is temperate; rain falls [1 Pott. 262;]
frequently, and there are several streams, the principal of which [Masson, Kalat,]
are, the Moolah, the Oornach, the Nal or Durruk, and the head- [325.]
water of the Poorally river. The Moolah is remarkable as forming by its channel the Moolah, or Gundava Pass, one of the great
lines of communication between the valley of the Indus and the
countries westward. Jhalawan is very barren and thinly peopled;

Outram ² traversed sixty miles, in two successive marches on horseback, across the country, without meeting a sign of human habitation ; and Masson ³ estimates the whole population at 30,000 ; about three persons to every two square miles. This, indeed, seems incredibly small, even for a pastoral population, of which description is that by which this country is generally held. The principal places are Nal, Khozdar, and Zehree.

JHOW, in Beloochistan, the chief place of a petty district of the same name, in the eastern extremity of Mekran. Ancient artificial mounds, of frequent occurrence, prove that this country was formerly less desolate than at present, a conclusion confirmed by the existence of extensive ruins, where coins, arms, trinkets, and other relics are frequently found. Lat. 26° 11′, long. 65° 35′.

JHUBBHER.—A village in the Punjab, forty-two miles north-west of the city of Lahore. Lat. 31° 55′, long. 73° 39′.

JHUNG.—See Jung.

JILUM.—See Jailum.

JIMPOOR, in Sinde, a village near the route from Kurrachee to Hyderabad, and forty miles south-west of the latter place. It is situate in the Doab, or tract between the Irak and Rodh rivers, and five miles north-west of the *Dund*, or small lake of Kunjur, into which they discharge themselves. Lat. 24° 59′, long. 68° 2′.

JINDALA.—A village in the Punjab, forty-five miles north-west of the city of Lahore. Lat. 31° 51′, long. 73° 32′.

JINDIALEH, in the Punjab, a town on the route from Loodianah to Amritsir, and ten miles south-east of the latter place. Lat. 31° 36′, long. 74° 56′.

JOA, in the Punjab, a large and flourishing town in the Salt range, about fifty miles east of the Indus. Here are said to be satisfactory indications of the existence of good coal. Lat. 32° 50′, long. 72° 30′.

JOA, in Sinde, is a mouth of the Indus, by which, in time of inundation, the water of the Buggaur, or great western branch of that river, is discharged. In the season when the water is low, Joa is merely a salt-water creek. Lat. 24° 15′, long. 67° 19′.

JOAGEH WALLA, in the Punjab, a village situate on an offset of the river Indus, and two miles from the left bank of the main channel. Lat. 29° 26′, long. 70° 53′.

JOALI, in the north-east of the Punjab, at the base of the Von Hugel, i. 111.
Mori mountains (one of the southern ranges of the Himalaya), and
on the route from Nadaun to Nurpur. It is a small town having
seven or eight hundred inhabitants. Lat. 32°, long. 75° 38'.

JODHAKE, in Bhawlpoor, a village between Gourjeanah and E.I.C. Ms. Doc.;
the town of Bhawlpoor, and eighty miles north-east of the latter Jour. As. Soc. 1837, Wade, Voy.
place. It is situate on the left bank of the Ghara river, in lat. down the Sutlaj.
29° 59', long. 72° 44'.

JOGA SYN, in Sinde, a village on the road from Kurrachee Ms. Survey Map.
to Jurruk, and fifty miles east of the former place. Lat. 24° 55',
long. 67° 46'.

JOHAN, in Beloochistan, a halting-place on the route from E.I.C. Ms. Doc.
Kelat to Beebee Nanee, in the Bolan Pass, and thirty miles north-
east of Kelat. It is supplied with water from a stream. The inhabitants are Belooches, of the Johanni tribe. Lat. 29° 10', long.
66° 51'.

JOK,[1] in Sinde, a village on the route from Hyderabad to [1] E.I.C. Ms. Doc.
Meerpoor, and thirty-eight miles south of the former town. It
is situate in the fertile alluvial tract insulated by the Indus and
its great offsets the Fulailee and Pinyaree. The adjacent country
is described by Pottinger[2] as very fine, and capable of producing [2] Belooch. 375.
rich crops, but in general waste, from the oppression of the
Ameers. Lat. 24° 52', long. 68° 19'.

JOKE, in Afghanistan, a village of the Daman, situate on the E.I.C. Ms. Doc.
right bank of the Indus. Lat. 31° 8', long. 70° 50'.

JOKHAY, in Sinde, a village in the barren and rugged tract Ms. Survey Map.
between the Pubb and Lukkee mountains. It is situate twenty-
eight miles north of Kurrachee. Lat. 25° 13', long. 67° 11'.

JOKHE, in Sinde, a village on the Pubb river, here forming E.I.C. Ms. Doc.
the boundary between Sinde and Lus. It is situate sixteen miles
north-west of Kurrachee, in a rugged, barren, and desolate tract.
Lat. 25° 7', long. 66° 59'.

JOLUNEE, in the Punjab, a village situate on the right E.I.C. Ms. Doc.
bank of the Ghara river, seven miles north of Ferozpoor, in lat.
31° 2', long. 74° 30'.

JOOA.—See JOA.

JOOEE CIRCAR, in Afghanistan, a village situate on the Walker's Map of Afg.
left bank of the Helmund river, and ten miles south of the fort of
Giriskh. Lat. 31° 38', long. 64° 15'.

JOOGEWALLAH.—See JOAGEH WALLA.

E.I.C. Ms. Doc.   JOORG, in Afghanistan, a small town of Seistan, near the left bank of the Adruscund, here generally called the river of Subzawur. It is thirty miles south-east of Furrah, and twenty-five miles north of Hamoon lake. Lat. 32° 9′, long. 61° 42′.

E.I.C. Ms. Doc.   JOORGEE, in Beloochistan, a village and halting-place on the direct route from Kelat to Pandura, in the Moola Pass, and eighteen miles south-east of Kelat. The road by Joorgee, though shortening the route through the Moola Pass above twenty miles, is not available for purposes requiring the use of wheel-carriages, being impracticable for them. Joorgee is in lat. 28° 42′, long. 66° 39′.

E.I.C. Ms. Doc.   JOREEND, in Sinde, a village on the route from Bukkur to Hyderabad, and seventy miles north of the latter place. Lat. 26° 20′, long. 68° 22′.

Walker's Map of N.W. Frontier.   JOSA, in the Punjab, a village situate on the right bank of the Ravee river. Lat. 30° 30′, long. 72° 7′.

E.I.C. Ms. Doc.   JOUREY, in the Punjab, a village eight miles from the right bank of the Jailum river. Lat. 31° 47′, long. 71° 55′.

E.I.C. Ms. Doc.   JUBBRA, in Afghanistan, a village on the route from Kandahar to Kabool, and one hundred and eighty miles north-east of the former place. Lat. 33° 5′, long. 67° 58′.

Walker's Map of N.W. Frontier.   JUGBARAH, in Bhawlpoor, a village on the left bank of the Ghara river. Lat. 30° 20′, long. 73° 40′.

E.I.C. Ms. Doc.   JUGDEE KHAEE.—A village in the Punjab, situate on the right bank of the river Ravee, forty-two miles south-west of Lahore. Lat. 31° 16′, long. 73° 40′.

JUGDULUK.—A village between Jelalabad and Kabool, at the point where the road to the latter place separates into three branches. It was one of the principal scenes[1] of the atrocious massacre of the British troops in their attempted retreat from Kabool in the commencement of 1842. Here also, the British[2] under General Pollock, in their advance on Kabool, in August in the same year, totally defeated a large army of Afghans. Jugduluk may be considered the commencement, in the direction from east to west, of the series of defiles between Jelalabad and Kabool. Hough[3] observes, " From the entrance to the Khoord Cabool Pass to Jugdulluk, a distance of forty-two miles, there is a succession of passes and defiles more difficult than any road we had yet seen. They beggar description." Its elevation above the sea is 5,375 feet. Lat. 34° 25′, long. 69° 46′.

[2] Mil. Op. in Afg. 385.
[3] Hough, Narr. of Exp. in Afg. 298 ; Have-lock, War in Afg. ii. 178 ; Wood, Khyber Pass, 6.

JUJJA, in Bhawlpoor, a town on the route from Khanpoor to E.I.C. Ms. Doc.; Mittunkote, and ten miles north-west of the former place. It Boileau, Rajwara and Buhawulpoor, is situate about fourteen miles from the left bank of the Indus, 56. in the alluvial tract extensively laid under water during the inundation of that river. It contains forty shops, a number which, according to the proportion usually found in such Indian towns, would indicate a population of about 600. Lat. 28° 46', long. 70° 39'.

JULALPOOR, a town in the Punjab, on the right or western bank of the Jailum, situate in a narrow valley of great fertility, extending between the river and the eastern extremity of the Kala, or Salt range. According to Elphinstone, [1] this was the 1 80. scene of Alexander's battle with Porus, but Burnes[2] thinks it 2 i. 57. must have been at Jailum, higher up, where the river, according to him, is fordable at all times except in the monsoon; but where Hügel[3] found it, at the beginning of January, when lowest, a 3 iii. 143. great stream, larger than the Indus at Attock, and bridged with twenty large boats. It is therefore unquestionable that the river could not at that point be forded at the season of inundation (when, as Arrian* informs us, it was crossed by Alexander); and where, indeed, the British army lost eleven men in fording it in December, which is the low season.[4] Julalpoor is 4 Hough, Narr. Exp. in Afg. 345. one of the great passages over the Jailum, on the route from Hindostan to Afghanistan. Lat. 32° 42', long. 73° 15'.

JULALPOOR. —A village in the Punjab, situate near the E.I.C. Ms. Doc. left bank of the Chenaub or Acesines river, sixty miles south-west of Vazeerabad, and fifty-two miles south of the town of the same name. Lat. 31° 58', long. 73° 15'.

JULDUK.—See JADAK.

JULINDER, in the Punjab, a considerable town near the Von Hugel, iii. 415. western bank of the Sutluj, was once the residence of the Lodi-Afghan dynasty. It is situate in a tract of great fertility, amidst flourishing orchards of mangoes and other trees. The vast number of large and finely-built mausoleums which are around, bear evidence of its former greatness. It has still a population of about 40,000. Lat. 31° 19', long. 75° 36'.

JULL, a town of Cutch Gundava, in Beloochistan, seventy- Masson, Bal. Afg. Panj. ii. 124; Kelat, 331; Ms. Survey Map.

* 'Εν μὲν τῷ τότε οἱ ποταμοὶ πάντες οἱ Ἰνδοὶ πολλᾶ τε ὕδατος καὶ 3ολερᾶ ἔῤῥεον καὶ ὀξέος τᾶ ῥεύματος. L. v. ix.

two miles south of the town of Gundava, on the road from thence to Larkhana. Lat. 28° 10′, long. 67° 33′.

JULLAL KAET.—See Jullalkote.

Kennedy, i. 69; Ms. Survey Map.
JULLALKOTE, in the delta of Sinde, a small town on the route from Vikkur to Tatta, thirty-five miles south-west of the latter place. Lat. 24° 22′, long. 67° 39′.

E.I.C. Ms. Doc.
JULLAL KHAN, in Afghanistan, a village on the route from Kandahar to Kabool, and a hundred and eighty miles north-east of the former town. Lat. 33° 6′, long. 67° 54′.

E.I.C. Ms. Doc.
JULLAREE, in the Punjab, a village on the route from Mooltan to Lahore, and forty miles north-east of the former place. It is situate on the left bank of the river Ravee. Lat. 30° 30′, long. 71° 58′.

E.I.C. Ms. Doc.
JULLAWGOTE, in Sinde, a village on the route from Sehwan to Larkhana, and seventeen miles north of the former town. It is situate on the right bank of a great water-course, filled by the inundation of the Indus, and a mile and a quarter from the main channel. Lat. 26° 37′, long. 67° 54′.

E.I.C. Ms. Doc.
JULLOO KOTUL, in Afghanistan, a pass on the route from Ghuznee to Shawl, and on the southern slope of the height bounding the basin of the Ab-istada lake on the south. The road here is very difficult, and scarcely practicable for wheel-carriages. Lat. 32° 4′, long. 67° 33′.

Sale, Dis. in Afg. 417; Jour. As. Soc. 1842, p. 71, Grif. Bar. and Ther. Obs.
JULRAIZ, in Afghanistan, a town on the route from Kabool to Bamian. It is situate in a beautiful, fertile, and well-cultivated valley, watered by the Kabool river. Numerous forts surround the town, which is rather large. Its elevation is 8,082 feet above the sea. Lat. 34° 23′, long. 68° 29′.

E.I.C. Ms. Doc.
JUMA, in the Punjab, a village situate about eighty-six miles south-west of Lahore, near the right bank of the Ravee river. Lat. 30° 54′, long. 73° 4′.

[1] E.I.C. Ms. Doc.
JUMA JAMOTE, in Beloochistan, a halting-place in Lus, on the Vinder torrent, which, rising in the hills in the south of Jhalawan, flows south, and is lost in the arid region of Lus. This desolate and repulsive country has lately attracted attention, in consequence of the rich lodes of copper which have been discovered there.[2] Juma Jamote is in lat. 25° 56′, long. 66° 56′.

[2] Jour. As. Soc. 1840, p. 30, De La Hoste, on Copper in Lus.

Walker's Map of N.W. Frontier.
JUMBURUM, a village in Afghanistan, situate on the road from Giriskh to Herat, sixty-six miles south of the latter place,

and ten miles north-east of the town of Subzawur. Lat. 33° 27', long. 62° 20'.

JUMEDARAH, in Sinde, a village situate near the left bank Ms. Map of Sinde. of the Indus. Lat. 26° 50', long. 67° 58'.

JUMEEAT, in Afghanistan, a small village, affording a halt-ing-place on the route from Ghuznee to Shawl, a hundred miles a little west of south from the former place, and twenty miles south of Lake Ab-istada. The neighbourhood abounds in villages, and the road is in general good. Lat. 32° 18', long. 67° 40'.

JUMLAIRA.—A village in the south of the Punjab, situate Walker's Map of on the right bank of the Ghara river. Lat. 30° 1 , long. N.W. Frontier. 72° 44'.

JUMRAJEE WUSSEE.—A town in Sinde, near the left or Burnes' (J.), Mis-east bank of the Indus, and on the route from Cutch to Hydera- sion to Sinde, 38. bad. Lat. 24° 54', long. 68° 30'.

JUNDRA, in Sinde, a village on the route from Rorce to Ms. Survey Map. Khyerpoor, and five miles south-west of the former place. Lat. 27° 39', long. 68° 51'.

JUNG, in the Punjab, an important manufacturing town two Burnes, on the or three miles from the left or eastern bank of the Chenaub. Trade of the Derajat, 103. Here, and at Meengana, and some other places in the same tract, are manufactured great quantities of white cotton cloth, princi-pally for the Afghan market. Lat. 31° 14', long. 72° 21'.

JUNGALEE, in the Punjab,[1] a village on the route from [1] E.I.C. Ms. Doc. Lahore to Ramnuggur, and fifty miles north-west of the former, place. The adjacent country is described by Burnes[2] as sandy, [2] Bokhara, i. 43. yet rather productive, being irrigated from innumerable wells, which yield water at a depth seldom exceeding twenty-two feet. Lat. 32° 5', long. 73° 45'.

JUNNOO KAREEZ, in Afghanistan, is a stream flowing E.I.C. Ms. Doc. from a subterranean aqueduct on the route from Kandahar to Ghuznee, and distant from the former place about eighteen miles north-west. The neighbourhood is well cultivated and produc-tive. Lat. 31° 41', long. 65° 45'.

JUNRUCK, in the Punjab, a village on the route from Lahore E.I.C. Ms. Doc. to Mooltan, and eighty miles south-west of the former place. It is situate on the left bank of the river Ravee. Lat. 30° 57', long. 73° 12'.

JUPP, in Sinde, a village between Bukkur and Hyderabad, Ms. Map.

and a hundred and five **miles north** of the latter place. It is forty miles distant from the **left bank** of the Indus, and lies in the tract where the rich alluvial country begins to assume the character of the desert to the east. Lat. 26° 50′, long. 68° 32′.

E.I.C. Ms. Doc.   JURROOP, in Sinde, a village on the route from Hyderabad to Omereote, and fifty miles east of the former place. Lat. 25° 24′, long. 69° 9′.

[1] Kennedy, Sinde and Kabool, i.118; Wood, Oxus, 20; Burnes' Pers. Narr. 22; E.I.C. Ms. Doc.   JURRUK,[1] a town of Sinde, is situate on an eminence of small elevation, which forms a headland projecting into the Indus on the western side, and rising about thirty feet above the water. The site is beautiful and advantageous, commanding the navigation of the river in both a military and commercial point of view. Here the rude tribes of the neighbouring part of Beloochistan come to supply themselves with manufactured wares. The advantageous position and salubrious air of Jurruk caused it to be recommended by Burnes as the best location for a British settlement in this part of Sinde. The principal manufacture is turnery of a very tasteful and highly-finished kind. Its

[2] Burnes' Bokh. 256.   population is probably about 1,500 or 2,000.[2] Lat. 25° 3′, long. 68° 15′.

E.I.C. Ms. Doc.   JUSSA, in the Punjab, a village situate thirteen miles north-east of Bhawlpoor, on the right bank of the Ghara river. Lat. 29° 32′, long. 71° 49′.

E.I.C. Ms. Doc.   JUTTA KA GOTE, in Sinde, a village on the **route from** Tatta to Hyderabad, by way of Kotree, and **twenty-two miles** north-east of Tatta. It is situate a mile **and a half from the** right bank of the Indus, and half-way between that river **and the** brackish *Dund*, or lake of Kunjur. The adjacent country is plain, and occupied principally by a Shikargah, or hunting-ground, lately belonging to one of the Ameers of Hyderabad. Lat. 24° 55′, long. 68° 8′.

E.I.C. Ms. Doc. ; Jour. As. Soc. 1840, p. 911; De La Hoste, Rep. on the Country between Kurrachee and Sehwan.   JUTTEEL MOUNTAINS, in Sinde, form a portion of that mountain system, which, stretching eastward from the great Hala range, terminates abruptly on the right bank of the Indus near Sehwan. The Jutteel Mountains run south-west from Sehwan to Dooba, a distance of between sixty and seventy miles. They are steep and of considerable height, probably in few places less than two thousand feet. The direct road from Sehwan to Kurrachee lies between them and the Keertar range, which is equally high, and holds a parallel course, but more to the west. The Jutteel range extends between lat. 25° 25'—26° 20', and long. 67° 45'—67° 55'.

JUTTOO, in the Punjab, a village on the route from Mooltan E.I.C. Ms. Doc. to Dera Ismael Khan, and eighteen miles north-west of the former town. It is situate ten miles from the right bank of the Chenaub river, in what Elphinstone calls the Little Desert, extending between the Chenaub and the Indus, and which he describes as having a length of two hundred and fifty miles from north to south, and, in the latitude of Juttoo, a breadth of two days' march, or about forty miles. It is a dreary tract, ill supplied with brackish water, and overspread with sandhills of a grey colour, among which the only vegetation is a scanty growth of stunted bushes. Lat. 30° 20', long. 71° 19'.

JYM KILA.—A village in North-Western Afghanistan, Walker's Map of situate on a branch of the Moorghab river, in lat. 35° 48', long. N.W. Frontier. 62° 47'.

K.

KABOOL,[1] a city of Afghanistan, is the capital of the [1] E.I.C. Ms. Doc.; province of Kabool, and before the dismemberment of the Durani Caubul, 434; empire was the seat of its government. It is seated on the Baber, Mem. 136. Kabool river, immediately above its confluence with that of Logurh. The immediate vicinity of the town is highly pictu- resque, well watered, and fertile. It is especially productive of the finest fruits; and the beautiful gardens, orchards, and groves are a source of great delight to the citizens during the fine season. Masson,[2] who had often joined their festive parties, thus describes [2] Bal Afg. Panj. the environs of the beautiful site of the tomb enclosing the remains i. 240. of the illustrious emperor Baber :—" Baber Badshah, so the interesting spot is called, is distinguished by the abundance, variety, and beauty of its trees and shrubs. Besides the imposing masses of plane-trees, its lines of tall, tapering, and sombre cypresses and its multitudes of mulberry-trees, there are wilder- nesses of white and yellow rosebushes, of jasmines, and other fragrant shrubs." " The place is peculiarly fitted for social enjoyment, and nothing can surpass the beauty of the landscape,

x 2

and the purity of the atmosphere." The river of Kabool, though giving name to the great body of water which is poured into the Indus at Attock, adds nothing to the charms of the landscape, at least below the city, being there a small and filthy stream. The city is situated at the western extremity of a plain of considerable extent, and in a recess formed by the junction 'of two ranges of hills. One of these ranges is on the south, the other on the north-west.[3] On the north-east is another eminence, much smaller than those just mentioned.[4] Baber's tomb is on one of the eminences to the south. The Bala Hissar, at once the citadel and the residence of the sovereign, is on the south-east side of the city, and is built on the acclivity of a hill. It joins the city, the street and lanes of which run up to the counterscarp of the western ditch. It is about half a mile long, and a quarter of a mile broad, the length being from east to west. The walls are of stone, lofty, and strengthened at intervals by towers. A broad stagnant moat defended by a *fausse braye* surrounds the whole. Within this extensive circuit is a small town, of which the population is estimated at 5,000, the rest of the space being occupied by the royal palaces and gardens, and various government offices. The whole is commanded by the upper fort within the same enclosure, and one hundred and fifty feet above the city. Both this upper citadel, and the more extensive enclosure surrounding, are commanded by a steep eminence, which rises above them to the south, but it would be difficult to form batteries on ground so elevated and hard of access. The whole city and its defences are also completely commanded from the eminences on the north-west. The city, about three miles in circuit, is not surrounded by a wall, being merely defended by a line of weak ramparts, running on the western side from one hill to another, and of course, if turned, affording no defence. Its greatest length, in a direction generally east and west, is two miles and one furlong ; its breadth at the widest part, which is at the west end, is one thousand two hundred yards, and it narrows to a few yards at the east end, where it joins the Bala Hissar. The entrance near the eastern extremity of the north side is called the Lahore gate ; here in former times commenced a wall constructed partly of burnt, partly of sun-dried, bricks, but which has completely fallen to decay. There are two other entrances on the north side, one

3 Burnes' Bokh. i. 142; Masson. Bal. Afg. ii. 248; Hough, Narr. Exp. in Afg. 284; Forster, Jour. Beng. Eng. ii. 70, 83; Atkinson, Exp. into Afg. 270; Havelock, War in Afg. ii. 136; Eyre, Mil. Op. at Cabul, 30; Allen, March through Sinde and Afg. 301; Kennedy, Sinde and Kabool, ii. 96; Jackson, Views in Afg. 1.
4 Eyre, Mil. Op. in Cabul (Plan).

towards the east, another towards the west, but none from the south, probably because the ground is precipitous and clevated in that dircction. At the western extremity of the city is a gate admitting the Kandahar road. There are two principal bazaars, running in some degree parallel to each other. The Shor bazaar, the most southern, runs west from the Bala Hissar, a distance of three-quarters of a mile : the other, more north, terminates in the Chahur Chatta, once the finest of the bazaars of Kabool. This consisted of four covered arcades, exhibiting considerable architectural beauty, each of equal dimensions, being one hundred and fifty feet long, thirty high, fifty wide, each separated from the rest by square open areas, containing wells and fountains. Such a construction is judicious in a sultry climate, as is that of Kabool during summer, the shelter above excluding the scorching rays of the sun, while the intervening spaces allowed a free circulation of air. These successive bazaars, with the intervening uncovered spaces, formed a continuous commercial street, which, during the prosperous period of Kabool, had a very fine appearance. Gerard, whose visit was in 1832, describes them as displaying " a scene which, for luxury and real comfort, activity of business, variety of objects, and foreign physiognomy, has no living model in India. The fruits which we had seen out of season at Peshawur loaded every shop. The masses of snow for sale threw out a refreshing chill, and sparkled by the sun's heat. The many strange faces and strange figures, each speaking in the dialect of his nation, made a confusion more confounded than that of any Babel, but with this difference, that here the mass of human beings were intelligible to each other, and the work of communication and commerce went on. The covered part of the bazaar, which is entered by lofty portals, dazzled my sight even quite as much as the snow of the Himalayan peaks when reflected against the setting sun. In these stately corridors the shops rise in benches above each other ; the various articles, with their buyers and sellers, regularly arranged in tiers, represent so many living strata. The effect of the whole was highly imposing, and I feel at a loss adequately to describe the scene presented to our eyes." [5] But this magnificent bazaar was demolished by the British on their recapture of Kabool, in revenge of the murderous treachery of the inhabitants a short time previously.

The bazaars during the peaceful occupation of the town by

[5] Jour. As. Soc. 1833, p. 3, Route of Burnes and Gerard.

the British used to be greatly crowded. Before the shops were counters, on which sat, with heaps of coin before them, the money-changers, and close to these their various wares disclosed to view, goldsmiths, jewellers, silk-mercers, tailors, cap-makers, shoemakers, saddlers, braziers, ironmongers, armourers, book-binders, furriers, and various other tradesmen. Cook-shops abounded, in which, together with more substantial indulgencies, ice and sherbet were to be obtained, and all at very moderate rates. In addition to native wares, the bazaars contained in abundance those of Great Britain, Russia, and India. Of these Russia supplied the largest proportion.

The gold which Kabool receives from Russia is in the form of venetians or ducats, called here *boodkees*, on account of the figure stamped on them. About the value of 20,000*l* is annually imported in this form, and sent forward to Hindostan; their value at Kabool varies from ten to fourteen shillings. The business done in them is contraband, to avoid the duty of one per cent. on the import, and of one and three-quarters on the export. Gold is also imported from Turkestan, in the form of tillas, of good standard, though not equal to the venetians. Their value is fourteen or fifteen shillings each, according to the demand. Silver is obtained from Russia in the form of *soours*, or roubles, which bear a disproportionate value to gold, being rated in currency of that metal at five shillings. Silver is also brought from China in *yamoos*, small ingots in the form of boats. They have a Chinese stamp in the middle, and are very pure, having only ·01 part of alloy. They are not always of the same weight, but the standard ingot ought to contain four pounds and a half. Gold-dust is brought from Turkestan, where it is obtained from the sands of the Oxus. Some gold-dust is also brought from Russia. The total value imported is about 10,000*l*. or 12,000*l*. This is all sent to Hindostan. Fire-arms are imported in considerable quantities from Russia; but those from England are greatly preferred, being lighter, neater, and more to be depended on. Russian cutlery and locks, needles, pins and trinkets, glass and porcelain, are also of common occur-rence. The only paper to be obtained is Russian, and the quality is inferior. The tea brought from Russia is highly prized, and sold at a dear rate, about fourteen shillings per pound; an inferior sort is brought from China, by way of Yarkund, which is cheaper, and a small quantity is brought from India, through the Punjab. Russia likewise sends cottons, especially chintzes, broadcloths, velvets, dye-stuffs, particularly *kirmiz*, producing a brilliant crimson, and by some erroneously confounded with cochineal, iron wares, such as trays, cooking utensils, and similar domestic articles, gold, brass, and iron wire. Raw silk, of excellent quality, is brought from Turkestan, to the amount of about two hundred camel-loads, of four hundred-weight each; the total value being estimated at from 40,000*l.* to 50,000*l.* per annum. It is, for the most part, sent to India.[6]

The manufacture and sale of spirits is confined to the Armenians, who obtain them of great strength from grapes. Abundance of fine white sugar is received from Persia, and of opium from Turkey and India. The tobacco is in general of home growth. The fruit market displays a greater profusion and luxuriance of fruits and flowers than is probably anywhere else to be met with; and the consumption of all kinds, especially melons, is very great. Besides these markets, there are a cattle market, one for wood and charcoal, and two for grain. Provisions are very fine, and, in general, cheap, with the exception of grain, of which there seems scarcely enough for the supply of the population; the consequences are, occasional scarcity, high prices, and even famine, especially in winter, when communication with the country is difficult, from the roads being blocked up with snow.

The city is divided into districts, and these are subdivided into sections, each well enclosed, and accessible only by small gates, which are walled up in time of siege or intestine war, and thus each section becomes a fortress. This arrangement has in general produced a narrow and intricate style of building. The dimensions of the streets are in many cases so contracted as to render it impracticable for two horsemen to pass each other. They are paved with stone, but the pavement is in very bad repair, and in some places broken into deep holes. By the termination of winter, the streets become difficult of passage, in consequence of the accumulation of snow thrown off the roofs of the houses, and never cleared away from the ground. The houses are in general two or three stories high, built of sun-dried bricks, with a large admixture of wood, as a security against earthquakes, which are here not of unfrequent occurrence. The roofs, generally made of wood coated with mud, are flat, and surrounded by a coarse frame-

[6] Bazaar of Kabool, 118, 119; Nowrozjee Furdoonjee, Bazaar of Kabool, 147, 154.

work of wood, and here, in warm weather, the inmates sleep.
So little attention is paid to comfort, that, notwithstanding
the severity of the winters, the windows are not glazed, being
closed only by lattices or shutters. The houses of the great
have extensive courts and gardens, ornamented with fountains.
The mosques and other public buildings have nothing to recommend them in an architectural point of view. There is but one
madressa, or college, and this has been allowed to fall into decay.
The serais, or public buildings for lodging and entertaining
strangers, are about fifteen in number, and are remarkable neither
for elegance nor convenience. There are several humaums, or public baths, repulsive alike from want of cleanliness and from an offensive smell, originating in the disgusting nature of the fuel used
for heating them. Water is sufficiently supplied, both for the irrigation of the adjacent country and for domestic purposes, by the
Kabool river. The river is crossed by three bridges. One, the
Pul Kuhti, is in the middle of the city, and is substantially built
of brick and stone ; another, the Pul Noe, is a frail fabric of wood,
trembling under the weight of foot-passengers, who alone can
cross it ; a third, to the west of the town, is a fortified bridge,
crossing the river, where it passes through the gorge between the
hills which enclose the city on that side, and by this means the
lines are continued across the stream.

In the south-west quarter of the town is a strongly fortified
district, called Chandol, inhabited by the Kuzzilbashes, or Persians,
descendants of those settled here by Nadir Shah, and who have
continued a distinct and important class, though exposed to the
jealousy and ill-will of the Afghans. For the existence of these
feelings there are two causes. The Kuzzilbashes are regarded
both as foreigners and heretics. Both Kuzzilbashes and Afghans
are indeed Mahometans, but the former are Shias, or votaries of
Ali, while the Afghans are furious Sonnees. In spite of these
circumstances, however, the Kuzzilbashes contrive to maintain
their position and exercise considerable influence. Their number
is estimated at between 10,000 and 12,000.* They have sometimes supplied a body-guard to the sovereign, and they exclusively

* 12,000 *familien*, according to Ritter, (Erdkunde von Asien, v. 317);
but this, allowing five to each family, would make the number of Kuzzilbashes amount to 60,000, equal to the whole amount of the population.
The account here given is carefully collected from the report of Burnes.

manage diplomatic affairs, every Afghan of importance having a
Kuzzilbash secretary.[7] They appear to be decidedly superior to
the Afghans, both in talent and civilization, but are reproached
with being inferior to them in personal bravery. The Afghans do
not in any respect appear to regard them in the light of inferiors,
and freely intermarry with them. The mother of Dost Mohamed
Khan was of this stock. The people of Kabool, according to
Kennedy, who, as a medical man, may be supposed to have particularly directed his attention to their *physique*, present the
Jewish type in " their tall figures, dark black eyes, marked features, and western complexion." In fine weather the men live
much abroad, so that then the streets are greatly crowded. Women, to whose humanizing influence Christians owe much of their
superiority to the rest of the world, here seldom appear out of
doors, and when visible they are enveloped from head to foot in
the *boorku*, a covering which has a net-work over the eyes and an
opening for breathing, but which so completely enwraps the
figure, that not a glimpse either of the features or the shape
can be obtained. The women of Kabool, however, enjoy the
reputation of possessing both beauty of face and elegance of
form.

As the elevation of Kabool is 6,396 feet,[8] the winters are very
severe, setting in at the beginning of October and continuing to
the end of March. During this season the more opulent inhabitants rarely stir out of doors, spending their time in such seden-
tary indulgencies as they can command. They lounge through
the day at the *sandali*, which is a table placed over a cavity in the
ground or some other receptacle for fire, and covered with a number of thick and large cloths drawn over the lap and lower part of
the body; and at night, when settling for sleep, they merely lie
back and draw the coverings of the sandali over them. The fuel
used is charcoal, and the occasional explosion of an ill-prepared piece sometimes causes severe burns. The fumes of the
charcoal are never known to produce death, the reason being that
the rooms in Kabool are not sufficiently secured from the access
of the external air to admit of such a result. Such a mode
of life is necessarily unhealthy, and the limbs become so
benumbed and cramped as to require much care and skilful treatment to revive their vigour and flexibility on the
return of the fine season. The opening of spring is a time of

[7] Burnes, Persians in Kabool, 7-13.

[8] Jour. As. Soc. 1842, p. 68, Grif. Bar. and Ther. Obs. in Afg.

high enjoyment. The inhabitants then form parties to roam through the country and enjoy the fine seenery, the genial weather, and the expanding beauties of nature; and Elphinstone expresses his surprise at the enthusiasm which these half-civilized people exhibit on these subjects, a taste for which is so intimately connected with refinement. The summer is rather hot, the thermomcter in the shade at noon being found to range, on different days in the month of August, from 91° to 75°   Its height generally exceeded 80°, though on one day (13th) it was only 63°.[9]

[9] Grif. ibid.

The higher orders in Kabool speak Persian with flueney and purity, Pushtoo, the vernaeular dialect, being for the most part spoken only by the lower classes. From the absence of any police arrangements or any regular administration of the laws, and from the unprincipled character of the people, there is little security either for life or property, and when the British were cantoned near it, in 1839-41, the banditti of the town committed with impunity continual acts of rapine, breaking into houses, murdering the inmates, and carrying off every valuable moveable. Their conduct towards the British during the disastrous events of which their town was the scene, at the commencement of 1842 was eharacterized not only by the most atrocious cruelty, but by the most abandoned falsehood and treachery.[1]

[1] Sale, Dis. in Afg., passim; Eyre, Mil. Op. in Cabul, passim.

Though the great proportion of the population is Afghan (with the Persian colony already mentioned), there is the usual admixture of Taijiks, Hindoos, Huzarehs, Armenian Christians, Jews, and others. The manufactures of Kabool are few and rude. They consist principally of leather and iron, with the weaving of cotton and of shawls, in imitation of Kashmir. It is supported by the transit trade, which it commands by its position on the great routes from north to south and from east to west. It is further the great mart for the extensive valley of Kabool, and since ehosen as the eapital by Timur Shah, has continued the seat of such government as existed in this part of Afghanistan.

Kabool, though displaying no important relies of antiquity, is known in history at least from A.D. 977, when Subuctageen, the grandfather of Mahomed of Ghuznee, and the founder of the Gaznevide dynasty, made himself master of it. At the close of the fourteenth eentury it fell before the arms of Tamerlane; and, above a century later, his great-grandson, the illustrious Baber, made it the seat of his government, as it is the resting-place of his mortal remains. In 1738 it was taken by Nadir Shah, after a brief attempt at resistance; and towards the close of the eighteenth century was made the capital of the short-lived Durani empire, by Timur Shah, the son of Ahmed, the founder of the dynasty. The tomb of Timur, though considered one of the ornaments of Kabool, has no pretensions to magnificence or beauty. It is an octagon of brick, surmounted by a cupola, shattered by cannon-shot, aimed at it wantonly by one of the descendants and kinsmen of him who sleeps within. In 1809 the empire was dismembered, and the sovereign, Shah Shooja, expelled by a knot of powerful chiefs. It is unnecessary here to pursue the subsequent history of the country with minuteness. It is enough to state that Herat, Kandahar, and Peshawur, being severed from Kabool, the latter came ultimately into the hands of a chief of some talent and great ambition, named Dost Mahomed Khan, who for some time maintained an unquiet and precarious rule. In 1839 a British army marched into Afghanistan, to restore to the throne Shah Shooja, who took possession of the city of Kabool, and retained it until the commencement of 1842, when a dreadful outbreak of native fury and perfidy deprived them of it. The chief civil officer, Sir William Macnaghten, was basely assassinated, the troops cut off from their magazines and stores, and compelled to attempt a retreat under circumstances which rendered its successful accomplishment hopeless. Of 3,849 soldiers, and about 12,000 camp-followers, only one man, severely wounded, escaped. In the same year a British army took the town, recovered some prisoners, including the heroic Lady Sale, wife of Sir Robert Sale, and having destroyed the principal bazaar and some other public buildings, returned, leaving the place to its fate. The population of Kabool is about 60,000. Lat. 34° 30′, long. 69° 6′.

KABOOL, a province of Afghanistan,[1] of which the city of Kabool is the chief town, once the centre of an extensive but short-lived monarchy. This ephemeral empire was founded by Ahmed Abdalli (subsequently Durani), an Afghan, after the assassination of Nadir Shah,[2] in 1747. It comprised, at the death of its founder, Afghanistan, Beloochistan, Khorasan, Turkestan, Sinde, and the Punjab. After his deccase it rapidly

[1] App. iil. to Burnes' Pers. Narr.

[2] Malcolm, ii. 100; Elph. 540-500.

declined, and, in 1809, on the expulsion of the sovereign, Shah Shooja, by his insurgent chieftains, it fell totally to pieces. Herat was erected into a separate state under Shah Mahmood, brother of Shah Shoojah; Peshawur and the Damaun were overrun by the Sikhs; Kandahar became independent under the Sirdars; the brother of Dost Mahomed Khan, and the last-named personage, seized the province of Kabool. This province extends from Hindoo Koosh, on the north, to some distance south of Ghuznee; and from Bamian in the west, to the Khyber mountains in the east. Its length is about two hundred miles from east to west; its breadth one hundred and fifty from north to south; its superficial extent probably about ten thousand square miles. The principal towns are Kabool, the capital, Istalif, Ghuznee, and Jelalabad. Dost Mahomed is reputed to have drawn from it a revenue of twenty-four lacs of rupees, or 240,000*l.* per annum;[3] but Masson[4] states the amount at only fifteen lacs, or 150,000*l.* per annum. The military force of Dost Mahomed Khan amounted to 2,500 heavy infantry, armed with the formidable jezails or long muskets, fired with a rest, and 12,000 or 13,000 horse, about 1,000 of whom were Kuzzilbashes, or descendants from the colonists planted here by Nadir Shah. About 9,000 of these were considered highly effective, and 3,000 received regular pay. The late violent and well-known revolutions and struggles, and the utter confusion which yet prevails, render it as impracticable to give any account of the present condition of this immature and feeble state, as to indulge in any rational speculation as to its future destiny. The information existing respecting the country over which it extended will be found under the head AFGHANISTAN.

KABOOL RIVER,[1] or JUI SHIR,[2] the only great tributary of the Indus from the west, drains the district of Logurh; the valley of Kabool, the Sufeid Koh, and the southern slope of the Hindoo Koosh.· The Kabool river is generally supposed to rise at Sir-i-Chushmuh, where, in lat. 34° 21', long. 68° 20',[3] at a height 8,400 feet above the sea, a very copious spring bursts out of the ground, and forms the chief source of the principal stream. But the extreme head is about twelve miles farther west, on the eastern declivity of the Oonna ridge.[4] In its course it is joined by many tributaries from much higher regions. It is at first an inconsiderable stream, everywhere fordable for

[3] Burnes, ut supra, 370.
[4] i. 407.

[1] E.I.C. Ms. Doc.; Wood, Khyber Pass, i. 7; Lord, Koh-i-Damun, 45.
[2] Moorcroft, Punj. Bokh. ii. 382.
[3] Burnes, Bukh. l. 174; Wood's Oxus, 196; Jour. As. Soc. 1841, p. 815, Orif. Rep. on Subjects connected with Afg.; Id. 1842,. Bar. and Ther. Meas. 68; Sale, Dis. in Afg. 417; Eyre, Mil. Op. at Cabul, 355.
[4] Outram, Rough Notes, 188.

sixty miles, as far as Kabool; at a short distance beyond which place it receives the river of Logurh from the south, and thenceforward is a rapid river, with a great body of water.[5] About forty miles below Kabool it receives from the north the Punchshir river, which has a course of a hundred and twenty miles, and brings a large accession of water, draining the Kohistan of Kabool and the adjacent part of Hindoo Koosh. About fifteen miles below this it receives the Tagoa river, also from the Hindoo Koosh, and having a course of about eighty miles from the north. The united streams of the Alishang[6] and Alingar, also flowing from the Hindoo Koosh, join the Kabool river about twenty miles farther down, after a course each of about a hundred and twenty miles. At the distance of about twenty miles more, the Soorkh Rood, or Red river, so called from the colour which its water derives from the earth suspended in it, falls into the Kabool river from the south, after a north-easterly course of seventy miles. As it drains the northern slope of the lofty Sufeid Koh, or snowy mountain, it shoots along with great velocity, and discharges a considerable body of water. Twenty miles farther east, the Kabool river receives from the north the river Kama, called also the river of Kooner, which rising in Chitral on the southern slope of the Hindoo Koosh, flows south-west through Kafiristan. Though the course of this last river is above two hundred and twenty miles, it, according to Moorcroft,[7] has no great body of water. After all these accessions, the Kabool river becomes a large stream, sweeping with prodigious rapidity and violence along the northern base of the Khyber mountains, and, in consequence of its boiling eddies[8] and furious surges, not navigable, except on rafts of hides. Eastward of these hills it divides into three branches, which, at Dobundee, twelve miles lower down, reunite, and thence[9] the river is navigable for boats of forty or fifty tons to Attock, near which it joins the Indus. Just below Dobundee it is joined from the north by the Lundye, or river of Panjkora, which, rising[1] in that unexplored region of the Hindoo Koosh lying east of Chitral, passes south-west by Panjkora, receives the river of Sewat from the north-east, and some tributaries of less importance from the west, and has a total course of above two hundred miles. After this confluence, the Kabool river continues to flow eastward for forty miles, and falls into the Indus on the western side, nearly opposite Attock,

[5] Masson, Bal. Afg. Punj. ii. 266.

[6] Id. 177-208.

[7] Punj. Bokh. ii. 357.

[8] Masson, Bal Afg. iii. 238; Panj. Jour. As. Soc. 1841, p. 817; Grif. Rep. on Subjects connected with Afg.; Burnes' Pers. Narr. 277.

[9] Macartney, in Elph. 656; Wood's Oxus, 16.

[1] Jour. As. Soc. 1839, p. 307; Court, on Alexander's Exploits on the Western Banks of the Indus.

having a total course of about three hundred and twenty miles
As both the rivers are very rapid, and have great bodies of water,
the confluence produces turbulent eddies and violent surges.[2]

[2] Elph. Acc. of Caubul, 71*.

E.I.C. Ms. Doc. KACHEE, in Sinde, a town on the route from Hyderabad
to Sehwan, by the way of Kotree, and thirty miles north of
Hyderabad. It is situate on the right bank of a large offset of
the Indus, and three miles from the main channel of the river.
Lat. 25° 54', long. 68° 18'.

Ms. Survey Map. KADIRPOOR.—A village in Sinde, between Subzulcote
and Shikarpoor, and twenty-four miles west of the former place.
It is situate near the left bank of the Indus, in a level country,
in some places overrun with jungle, but capable of successful
cultivation, in consequence of the facility of irrigation by means
of water-courses from the river. Lat. 28° 10', long. 69° 20'.

Masson, Bal. Afg. Panj. iii. 110;
Burnes' Pers. Narr. 146; Lord, Koh-I-Damun, 47. KADURRA.—A town of Afghanistan in the Koh-i-Damun of
Kabool, and seventeen miles north-west of the city of that name.
Lat. 34° 44', long. 68° 56'.

E.I.C. Ms. Doc. KAEE, in Sinde, a village on the route from Subzulcote to
Shikarpoor, and twelve miles east of the latter town. The road
in this part of the route is practicable for wheel carriages, but
travellers by it suffer from the quality of the water, which is
drawn from wells, and is very indifferent. Kaee is in lat. 27° 50',
long. 68° 52'.

E.I.C. Ms. Doc. KAFFIR KA BUND, in Sinde, a village on the route
from Kurrachee to Hyderabad, and sixty miles south-west of the
last-mentioned place. Lat. 24° 58', long. 67° 37'.

KAFIRISTAN.—A country adjoining the north-eastern
boundary of Afghanistan, and remarkable because, though surrounded by powerful and implacable enemies, it is not known to
have ever been conquered. The name Kafiristan, signifying
" land of infidelity " * has been given to the country by the
neighbouring Mussulmans, in consequence of the rejection of
Mahometanism by the inhabitants. These are called Siyah
Posh †, or " black-clad," from wearing black goat-skin dresses.[1]
According to Elphinstone, " The people have no general name
for their nation. Each tribe has a peculiar name, for they are all
divided into tribes, though not according to genealogies, but geo-

[1] Burnes' Bokh. ii. 210; Elph. Acc. of Caubul, App. 619; Jour. As. Soc. 1834, p. 76, 78, Mohun Lal, Information respecting the Siah Posh Tribe; Masson, Bal. Afg. Panj. i. 212.

* كفرستان [Shakespear in v.]

† سياه پوش [Shakespear in v.]

graphical position, each valley being held by a separate tribe.'' Burnes, however, states, " in speaking of their nation, the Kafirs designate themselves, as the Mahomedans do, Kafirs, with which they do not couple any opprobrious meaning." Kafiristan is bounded on the north by Badakshan, on the west and south by Afghanistan ; the exact boundary on the east does not appear to have been ascertained, as in that direction lies the unexplored country of Chitral. Masson considers the Kama river the eastern boundary. Defined by these limits, this country, which from the undaunted courage and singular character of its inhabitants has excited so much interest and curiosity, is but of moderate dimensions, being a hundred and twenty miles in length from north-east to south-west, sixty miles in breadth from south-east to north-west, and having a superficial extent of seven thousand square miles. It lies between lat. 35° and 36°, and long. 69° 20′—71° 20′. Elphinstone, from the report of an intelligent emissary whom he despatched from Peshawur, thus describes this region : " The whole of this alpine country is composed of snowy mountains, deep pine forests, and small but fertile valleys, which produce large quantities of grapes, wild and cultivated, and feed flocks of sheep and herds of cattle, while the hills are covered with goats. Grain is inferior both in importance and abundance. The common kinds are wheat and millet. The roads are only fit for men on foot, and are often crossed by rivers and torrents, which are passed by means of wooden bridges, or of swinging bridges made of ropes of withy or some other pliant tree."

It is drained by four considerable rivers, the Kama, the Alingar, the Alishang, and the Tagoa, which are reported to rise on the southern declivity of Hindoo Koosh, and which, holding a course generally to the south-west, pass into Afghanistan, and fall into the river of Kabool.[2] Each river flows down a great [2] Mass. Bal. Afg. valley enclosed on each side, south-east and north-west, by lofty Panj. i. 207. mountains, having in various places summits covered with perpetual snow, and furrowed by numerous valleys of inferior size to that through which the river takes its course. The Siyah Posh hold the ravines in the culminating ridge of Hindoo Koosh, and part of its northern slope towards Badakshan, with which last territory they maintain commercial intercourse.[3] [3] Burnes' Bokh. So steep are the slopes of the mountains, that in the villages, ii. 210; Wood, which are always built on the declivities, probably from re- Oxus, 287

gard to purposes of defence, the houses are reared several
stories high, with their backs against the precipice behind, in
such a manner that the roofs of one row form the street for the
one immediately above it.[4] The more southern part, contiguous
to the Afghan district of Lughman, appears to be the most level,
and from the Koh Karing, a mountain on that frontier, an extensive view can be had of Kafiristan; which there, according to
Masson,[5] consists of low rounded hills, with few prominent
ranges, or particular mountains of great elevation. The country is everywhere traversed by innumerable torrents and rivers,
but these fail to render it productive in consequence of the
deficiency of cultivable soil; though no spot admitting of
tillage is neglected, and terraces are formed on the sides of
the hills to obtain space for the growth of crops.[6] Baber
mentions that rice was largely cultivated; at present the
principal crop of grain is either wheat, maize, or millet;[7] but as
the cultivated spots are altogether too limited to yield subsistence
to the population, they live principally on flesh, cheese, milk,
curds, and fruits both fresh and dried. Burnes [8] seems scanda-
lized at their indiscriminate diet, and observes, "the Kafirs
appear to be a most barbarous people, eaters of bears and
monkeys;" yet these animals are eaten without scruple by civil-
ized Christians in Europe and America. They detest fish, but
do not reject any other animal food.[9] They are noted for being
addicted to wine. Baber,[1] who made this oppressed people the
victims of his remorseless butcheries, mentions that they drank
wine instead of water, and "that every Kafer had a *khig* or
leathern bottle of wine about his neck." Their wine is prepared
by boiling: probably the climate is too cool to produce a must
sufficiently strong to yield a generous wine without such management. Besides grapes, there are walnuts, apples, almonds, apricots,
and mulberries. Honey is also produced in abundance.

In person, the Siyah Posh are strongly-marked specimens of
what is called the Caucasian variety of the human race; and in
their fine figures, fair complexions, and regular features, bear a
strong resemblance to the Circassians. Burnes, who had many
opportunities of marking the physical peculiarities of the Siyah
Posh, thus notices them : "He (Deenbur, a Siyah Posh captive)
is a remarkably handsome young man, tall, with regular Grecian
features, blue eyes, and fair complexion, and is now a slave of the

[4] Elph. 619;
Masson, Bal. Afg.
Panj. i. 228.

[5] Ut supra, 210.

[6] Masson, ut supra, 211.

[7] Elph. 619;
Mass. ut supra.

[8] Bokh. ii. 211.

[9] Elph. 623.

[1] Memoirs, 144.

Ameer. Two other Kafir boys, who came along with him, had ruddy complexions, hazel eyes, and auburn hair; they also had less beauty and high cheek bones, but they were still handsome, and remarkably intelligent. None of these Kafirs, or two others which I saw, had any resemblance to the Afghans, or even Cashmerians. They looked a distinct race, as the most superficial observer would have remarked on seeing them.[2]" Wood[3] describes a Siyah Posh with whom he was acquainted, as an uncommonly handsome man, with an open forehead, blue eyes, and bushy arched eye-brows; his hair and whiskers black, and his figure well set and active. He invited Wood to visit Kafiristan, promising him " plenty of honey and oceans of wine." Atkinson[4] thus describes a Siyah Posh woman whom he saw : " She had, as is usual among her tribe, blue eyes and brown hair, but her complexion was dark, though the general tincture of the skin in Kafiristan is comparatively fair." The neighbouring Mahometans give them credit for superior intelligence, comparing them, in this respect, to the Europeans, or, as they call them, Firingi. A Siyah Posh slave is considered worth two of any other race. Wood[5] states that " they pride themselves on being, to use their own words, brothers of the Firingi ;" and the Mahometan from whom Burnes[6] derived much of his information assured him " that he had never seen people more resembling Europeans in their intelligence, habits, and appearance, as well as in their hilarious tone and familiarity over their wine." Their intelligence is displayed in the construction of their houses, which are in general of wood, several stories high, and embellished with much carving ; for the Siyah Posh are skilful carvers and joiners. They are also good smiths, and take considerable quantities of the iron of Bajour. Their silver drinking cups and bowls are worked and embossed in a very elaborate and tasteful manner.[7] The exercise of their skill in woodwork is encouraged by the abundance of timber in their country ; for though in general the Hindoo Koosh is characterized by great barrenness and want of wood, Griffith[8] found that the woody character of the Himalaya continues in the mountains as far westward as Kafiristan. The Siyah Posh appear to be scarcely under the influence of any form of government. Elphinstone observes,[9] " It is uncertain whether there are any acknowledged magistrates ; if there are, they have very little power, every thing being done by consultations among the rich men.

[2] Burnes' Siah Posh, 70.
[3] Oxus, 286.
[4] Exp. in Afg. Preface, xi.
[5] Oxus, 289.
[6] Ut supra, 72.
[7] Mass. Bal. Afg. Panj. i. 228.
[8] Jour. As. Soc. 1841, p. 801 ; Rep. on Subjects connected with Afg.
[9] Ut supra, 625.

They seem to practise retaliation like the Afghans, and I know of no other administration of justice." Elphinstone[1] gives the names of nearly forty of their tribes, but it is needless to repeat them here. Masson,[2] on the contrary, states that, "as far as regards the division of the Siyah Posh into tribes, no one knows, or pretends to know, any thing about them." This last-quoted author mentions several towns reported to have some one thousand, some two or three thousand, and one as many as six thousand houses ; the latter, if five persons be assigned to each house, containing thirty thousand inhabitants. His remarks on this point appear very just: "It may be reasonably suspected that those calculations are above the truth ; still, when it is known that there are large and populous villages in a country, it is difficult to reconcile the fact with so complete a state of barbarism as is imputed to the Siyah Posh, or to avoid the impression, that men assembled in such communities must have a certain kind of order prevalent amongst them, and be subject to some of the influences inseparable from society."[3] Elphinstone,[4] also, remarks, that " the valleys must be well peopled ; that of the Caumojee tribe contained at least ten villages, and the chief place, Caumdaish, consisted of five hundred houses." The Kafirs are a very martial race, being engaged in incessant warfare with their Mahometan oppressors by whom they are surrounded. On this point an intelligent Siyah Posh observed to Wood[5]—" The Mussulmans were responsible for the blood thus spilt, for since they hunted down the Kafirs to make them slaves, the latter had retaliated, for the loss of liberty was worse than the loss of life." They bear shields for defence, and for offensive arms, swords, spears, bows and arrows, and knives ; of late years they have begun to provide themselves with matchlocks purchased from the Afghans. In the simple language of Mohun Lal[6]—" They fight with great ferocity, gnashing their teeth, and roaring like a lion." Though making a desperate resistance when driven to extremity, they, like most semi-barbarous and undisciplined troops, prefer surprise, stratagem, and ambuscade, to open conflict.[7] Such was the information obtained by Elphinstone[8]—" Their commonest mode is by surprisals and ambushes, and they expose themselves to the same misfortunes by neglecting to keep watch by night. They often undertake remote and difficult expeditions, for which they are well suited, being naturally light and active. When pursued

[1] 619.

[2] Bal. Afg. Panj. i. 210.

[3] Masson, i. 215.
[4] 619.

[5] Oxus, 286.

[6] Jour. As. Soc. 1834, p. 77, Information respecting the Siah Posh.

[7] Wood, Oxus, 421.
[8] Ut supra, 627.

they unbend their bow, and using it as a leaping-pole, make surprising bounds from rock to rock." Though readily admitted to quarter by the Mahometans, in consequence of their marketable value as captives, they seldom spare the life of an enemy at their mercy. This want of clemency is attributable partly to their fierce hatred towards their persecutors, partly to the high honours and privileges awarded to the slayer of a Mussulman, and the slights endured by such as have not attained that distinction. The successful warrior wears a black fillet, ornamented with cowry shells, one for each slain Mussulman. For each, the victor also is allowed to fasten a small bell to his belt and to insert a feather in his turban. He is further entitled to erect a pole before the door of his house with a hole to receive a pin for every one of these detested enemies whom he has killed, and a ring for every one whom he has wounded, and none but a warrior distinguished by the possession of these privileges is allowed to flourish the war-axe over his head in their solemn dances According to Masson,[9] on the return of a party from an ex- [9] Ut supra, i. 234. pedition, those who have slain Mahometans are presented by the maidens with dried fruits, whilst those who failed in attaining this distinction are pelted with ashes and other dirt; and, at the feast of rejoicing which succeeds, the former are regaled with great honour and abundance, the latter receive a scanty portion from the hands of the manager of the feast, who delivers it to them over his shoulder. In case of marriage, a bridegroom who has not slain his enemy is, as a mark of humiliation, given his food behind his back.[1] The [1] Burnes on the female relatives of those who have slain Mahometans are al- Siah Posh, 71. lowed the exclusive use of certain honorary distinctions in dress.

The Siyah Posh have made so good use of the natural strength of their country that, as has been already observed, they have never been conquered. Tamerlane, who subdued so many kingdoms and empires, and overcame all other resistance, from the Hellespont to Central India, and from Syria to Moscow, retired baffled from his attempt to subjugate Kafiristan. One of his principal generals, to use the words of Price,[2] with "ten thousand men at his [2] Mahometan disposal, had fled ingloriously before an inferior force of bar- Hist. iii. 226. barians;" and Tamerlane, after much loss inflicted and suffered, thought it best to make his way back to his fort of Khawak and proceed on his route to India. About sixty years

ago, the adjoining Mahometan powers confederated for the purpose of waging a religious war and forcing this people to embrace

3 Elph. 627. Islamism.[3] The Khan of Badakshan, the chiefs of Kooner, of Bajour, and of several of the Eusufzai tribes, by simultaneous
marches, met in the heart of Kafiristan, but, unable to keep
their ground, were forced to evacuate the country after suffering considerable loss.   It seems strange that a people so
formidable in war have never burst from their mountain fastnesses in a career of conquest.

Our information is very limited and vague respecting the
feelings, belief, and practices which hold the place of religion

4 620. among this rude people.   According to Elphinstone,[4] they believe in one Supreme God, called by some Imra, by others
Dagun, but they also worship numerous idols, which, they
say, represent great men of former days, who intercede with
God in favour of their worshippers.   It is supposed that in
certain instances a resemblance may be traced between their
idolatry and some points of Hindoo mythology.   Thus they
venerate stone posts resembling *lingas*, and make offerings by
throwing flour, butter, and water on them; but, on the other
hand, they sacrifice various animals, not excepting kine, burning part of the flesh as an offering, and feasting on the rest.
The privilege of deification after death is generally attained, like
municipal honours with us, by plenteously regaling the community.

5 Id. Elphinstone[5] observes, " Caufirs appear, indeed, to attach the
utmost importance to the virtues of liberality and hospitality ;
it is they which procure the easiest admission to their paradise."
At their sacrifices they pray for exemption from sickness
and other afflictions, for power to kill Mussulmans, and for
admission into paradise.   They offer to their idols the arms
and clothes of Mussulmans whom they have slain, and should
any of these be made prisoners in attacks on the Siyah Posh
villages, they are sacrificed as burnt-offerings.

Though so furiously hostile to Mahometans, they hold in-

6 Masson, Bal.
Afg. Panj. I. 231 ;
Leech, App. 37. tercourse with various neighbouring tribes, called Nimchas,[6] who
profess partial Mahometanism, retaining however their original
idolatrous belief, akin to that of the Siyah Posh.   By means of
traffic with these, they supply themselves with coarse cottons,
hardware, firearms, gunpowder, salt, and a few other articles, and
in return give dried fruits, honey, wine, vinegar, slaves, and gold.

The slaves are all of their own nation, as they do not spare the lives of Mahometans. They are captives taken in their intestine wars, or even individuals of their own tribes; for Elphinstone[7] [7 624.] was informed that it was " quite common for powerful men to seize on the children of weak ones, and sell them to the Mussulmans, or keep them for their own use: a person who loses his relations is soon made a slave." The gold[8] is obtained from the [8 Masson, Bal. Afg. Panj. i. 213.] sands of their innumerable streams.

The dress of the poorer Siyah Posh is truly primitive, being composed of four goat-skins, two of which form a vest, and two a kind of petticoat. They are worn with the hair outside, and fastened round the waist with a leathern belt. The arms are left bare, as is the head; but any man who has killed a Mahometan wears a small red turban, or rather bandage, as a distinction. The Siyah Posh allow their hair to fall down in ringlets on each side of the head, and the beard of the chin to grow. Those who can afford it wear trowsers and shirts of cotton or black hair-cloth, and a blanket over the shoulder, after the manner of the Highlander's plaid; they also wear worsted stockings, and short boots of white goat-skin. The women have their hair plaited, and fastened on the top of the head, and over it a small cap, round which is a little turban ; their dress in other respects differs little from that of the men. Both sexes wear rings round the neck, bracelets, earrings, and similar trinkets, sometimes of silver, but more generally of brass or pewter. They cannot endure to sit cross-legged, like the other people of this part of Asia, but use habitually stools shaped like drums, and if forced to sit on the ground, stretch out their legs before them.[9] The new-born babe is made to choose its own [9 Masson, Bal. Afg. Panj. i. 229.] name, by means of a curious ceremony : when first applied to the breast, a number of names are repeated in succession; and that during the pronunciation of which it begins to suck, is adopted.[1] [1 Elph. 623.] The age of marriage is from twenty to thirty for men, and about fifteen or sixteen for women. The bridegroom purchases the bride, paying her father a number of kine proportionate to the extent of his means or the ardour of his love. The marriage ceremony consists in procuring two rods or twigs, of the respective heights of the bride and bridegroom, and tying them together. These are preserved by the couple as long as they choose to live together; but if desirous of separating, they break the twigs, and thus dissolve the union. The women perform not only all the work of the family, but even bear the main part of agricultural labour, and similar out-door toils. It is said that the nuptial bond is little regarded. The bodies of the dead are dressed in their best clothes, and being placed in coffins, are laid in some retired spot, where they are allowed to decay above-ground. A procession of both sexes attends the corpse to its last home, the men performing a war-dance, the women lamenting. In disposition, the Siyah Posh are a jovial race, much addicted to wine-drinking, dancing, and merry-making; and, though beyond measure murderous in hostilities, readily become reconciled to their enemies.

Of their language, according to Klaproth,[2] nothing is known. Elphinstone, however, states unreservedly, " There are several languages among the Caufirs, but they have all many words in common, and all have a near connection with the Shanscrit;"[3] and Burnes[4] observes of the specimens which he examined, that they bear an evident affinity to the Hindoo stock. There is great diversity of belief as to the parentage of this people. An opinion, perhaps first broached in the Ayecn Akbery,[5] and brought into notice by Rennell,[6] attributes their origin to colonists planted by Alexander the Great. Such a claim of descent has also been made respecting the inhabitants of Bulti,[7] of Wakhan,[8] and of various other places, and probably has arisen from some confused traditions respecting the Greco-Bactrian empire. Elphinstone[9] comes to the conclusion that " the most general and only credible story is, that they (the Siyah Posh) were expelled by the Mussulmans from the neighbourhood of Candahar, and made several migrations from place to place before they reached their present abode." Wood[1] supposes them to have been Tajiks, the aboriginal inhabitants of Badakshan, on the north of Hindoo Koosh, who retired to these fastnesses when the low country was conquered by the Mahometans. Not the least plausible opinion is that of the unpretending Mohun Lal,[2] that they are descendants of Greco-Bactrians, who survived the destruction of their empire, by taking refuge in the mountains. They are themselves fond of claiming affinity with the Feringis, or Europeans,[3] and on the invasion of Afghanistan by the British, sent a mission to express their gratification at the arrival of so many brethren.[4] In conclusion, it may be observed, that nothing cogent can be urged

[2] Asia Polyglotta, 44.
[3] 619.
[4] On the Siah Posh, 71.
[5] II. 171.
[6] As quoted in Elph. 617.
[7] Burnes' Bokh. ii. 214.
[8] Wood, Oxus, 371.
[9] 620.
[1] Oxus, 288.
[2] Jour. As. Soc. 1834, p. 78, Information respecting the Siah Posh.
[3] Wood, Oxus, 288.
[4] Burnes' Pers. Narr. 207.

against the opinion that they are the aboriginal population of the country which they now inhabit.

KAFIR KILA, in Afghanistan, a village in the Huzareh country. It is situate on a feeder of the river of Andkhoo. Lat. 36°, long. 64° 56'. *E.I.C. Ms. Doc.*

KAFIR KOTE.—See KAFR KOT.

KAFIR TUNJEE, in Afghanistan, is a foot-path collateral with the most eastern part of the Khyber Pass. It runs from the vicinity of Jamrood to the right or north of the main pass, which it joins about two miles south-east of Ali Musjid, and in consequence is of much importance when the eastern entrance of the pass is contested. It was occupied by the Khyberees when the British commenced operations to force the pass in 1839. Lat. 34° 3', long. 71° 10'. *Hough, Narr. of Exp. in Afg. 231; Mil. Op. in Afg. 134.*

KAFR KOT, or THE INFIDELS' FORT.—A huge, lofty, and massive ruin near the west bank of the Indus, and between that river and the Largee valley. It consists of a number of towers bearing every mark of extreme antiquity, rising on the very summit of the mountain chain. These are connected with the Indus by a dilapidated wall extending from them to the edge of the water. Wood, who surveyed the spot, expresses his astonishment at the toil and skill which must have been directed to the construction of this stupendous edifice, singularly contrasting with the mean mud hovels which, with this exception, are the only buildings to be found throughout this region. The time and circumstances of its erection are totally unknown. Lat. 32° 30', long. 71° 21'. *Wood, Oxus, 90; Masson, Bal. Afg. Panj. i. 102; Burnes' Pers. Narr. 96.*

KAGGALWALLA, in Afghanistan, a village in the Daman, is situate on the river Koorum, about three miles west of the place where it falls into the Indus on the right side. Lat. 32° 37', long. 71° 21'. *Elph. Acc. of Caubul, 114.*

KAHAG, in Kashmir, a village, the capital of a district of the same name. It is situate at the north-eastern base of the lofty mountain of Pir Panjal, and eighteen miles south-west of the city of Sirinagur, or Kashmir. It is remarkable for a spring of very fine water, with which the old Hindoo monarchs used to be supplied. Lat. 33° 58', long. 74° 29'. *E.I.C. Ms. Doc.; Vigne, Kashmir, II. 107.*

KAHEE.—See KAEE.

KAHEER, in Sinde, is a mouth of the Indus, by which the Moutnee, formerly a large offset of the Sata, or great eastern *E.I.C. Ms. Doc.; Carless, Official Survey of the*

indus, 2 ; Burnes'
Bokh. iii. 237. branch of that river, discharged its water into the sea. In consequence of the channel of the Moutnee having been almost
entirely deserted by the stream, the Kaheer mouth has become
little more than a salt-water creek. Lat. 23° 58', long. 67° 38'.

Elph. Acc. of
Caubul, 28.   KAHEREE, in Afghanistan, a village of the Daman, is
situate on the right bank of the Indus. Here is one of the principal ferries on that river. It is on the route from Hindostan to
Afghanistan, by Dera Ismael Khan and the Gomul or Goolairee
Pass. Elphinstone, who crossed here at the beginning of January,
when the water is lowest, found the main channel a thousand and
ten yards wide, and it is known to be much broader during the
swell. Lat. 31° 25', long. 70° 57'.

E.I.C. Ms. Doc.   KAHUN, in Afghanistan, a fort and town among the mountains inhabited by the Murrecs Belooches, and extending from
the southern extremity of the Suliman range to that of the Hala.
It is situate in an extensive valley, or rather plain, fifteen miles
long and six broad. It is tolerably well built, and is surrounded
by a thin wall, twenty-five feet high, nine hundred yards in circuit, of a hexagonal outline, with six bastions and one gateway.
The chief of the Murrees, with his immediate followers, have
usually inhabited the town, but the rest of the tribe live in huts
of mats outside the walls. The air is very pure, and the heat less
than in the plains of Sewestan or of Sinde ; but there is a scarcity
of water, the town having no supply but from rain, which is collected in a tank before the gateway. In the beginning of May,
1840, a British force, consisting of three hundred of the fifth
Bombay native infantry, two twelve-pounder howitzers, and fifty
Sinde irregular horse, was pushed forward from Poolajee, in
Sinde, to Kahun, which was found deserted, and was forthwith
paced by the invaders in charge of a garrison of a hundred and
forty men, with one gun. The remainder, having left the fort
with a return convoy for Poolajee, were cut off, except about
twelve men, who escaped by flight. At the end of the following
August, Major Clibborn marched from Poolajee, with a convoy for the relief of Kahun, and, after suffering dreadfully from
heat and thirst, reached the bottom of the Nuffoosk Pass, distant
from Kahun about four miles. The road through the pass
had been rendered almost impracticable by the Beloochees,
who, in greatly superior numbers, manned the nearly inaccessible heights which commanded it, and, rushing from various

fastnesses in rear and flank, commenced a furious and well-sustained attack, destroying with stones the party which attempted to move forward into the opposite gorge. At length the Beloochees drew off, having lost four hundred of their bravest men; but by this time the strength of the beasts of burthen was found so prostrated by the excessive heat and total want of water, that they were totally unable to move, and numbers of men were falling dead from the same causes. In consequence the force was withdrawn to Poolajee, which it reached in a state of the most deplorable exhaustion. On this disastrous occasion one hundred and seventy-nine of the British force were killed, ninety-two wounded, and one thousand and seventy-six camels, a great quantity of ammunition and stores, and three pieces of artillery, fell into the hands of the enemy. At the close of September, the Murrees offered the little garrison of Kahun an unmolested retreat to Poolajee, which place was reached without loss, the Beloochees strictly observing their promise, probably being terror-struck at the carnage of the late action. Kahun is in lat. 29° 20', long. 69° 15'.

KAILLEEAWALA, in the Punjab, a village thirteen miles E.I.C. Ms. Doc. south-west of Ramnuggur. It is situate in the level tract between the rivers Ravee and Chenaub, and six miles from the left bank of the latter. Lat. 32° 14', long. 73° 31'.

KAIMPOOR, a village in Bhawlpoor; situate on an offset of E.I.C. Ms. Doc. the Indus, and about eight miles from the main stream. Lat. 28° 38', long. 70° 15'.

KAJOOR, in Sinde, a halting-place, on the route from Kur- E.I.C. Ms. Doc. rachee to Sehwan, and fifty-eight miles south of the last-mentioned place. It is situate on the right bank of the Pakrun river, lower down called the Dhurwal. There is a good supply of water from the river, but forage is scarce. The road in this part of the route is good, though in a few parts rocky. Kajoor is in lat. 25° 40', long. 67° 53'.

KAJOOR.—See DOOBAH RIVER.

KAKA, in Sinde, a village situate on the left bank of the Ms. Map of Sinde. Indus, and six miles north-east of Sehwan. Lat. 26° 21', long. 68°.

KAKAJAN, in Afghanistan, is a village forty miles south of E.I.C. Ms. Doc. Ghuznee, on the route from it to Dera Ismael Khan, by the Goolairee Pass. The road here is good, and there is a supply of water from a kareez, or subterraneous aqueduet. Lat. 33° 4′, long. 68° 10′.

E.I.C. Ms. Doc. KAKAPORE, in Kashmir, a village situate eleven miles southeast of the town of Sirinagur, or Kashmir, near the left bank of the river Jailum. Lat. 33° 57′, long. 74° 50′

E.I.C. Ms. Doc. KAKUR, in Afghanistan, a village close to the route from Shawl to Kandahar, and forty miles north-west of the former town. It is situate in the valley of Pisheen, near the southeastern base of the Amran mountains. Lat. 30° 43′, long. 66° 40′.

¹ Elph. Acc. of Caubul, 87; Burnes' Pers. Narr. 107; Wood, Oxus, 103. Jour. As. Soc. 1838, p. 25, Mohun Lal, Acc. of Kala Bagh. KALA BAGH.¹—A town on the right or west bank of the Indus, where it finds a passage through the Salt range, which stretches from Afghanistan into the Punjab. The breadth of the stream, bounded by very lofty and steep banks, is here about three hundred and fifty yards. The road, a gallery cut in the side of the cliff, and about a hundred feet above the edge of the water, is so narrow as not to allow a laden camel to pass. A great part of this excavation is through rock-salt, extremely hard, pellucid, clear, and nearly colourless as crystal. Some specimens are so hard that they are worked into platters. The town rises as though it were stuck against the precipitous eminence overhanging the road and river, and, together with the salt rock, the stream, and the prospect over the country to the east, forms a striking scene. The heat in summer is here excessive, and the air unwholesome, as well naturally as from the effluvia of alum-works. The alum is obtained from a sort of slate, which is in vast quantities in the neighbouring mountains. This is placed in layers between wood, and the pile thus formed is set on fire.;' the residuum is boiled in iron pans, filtered, and by means of evaporation, rendered solid alum. There are fourteen manufactories for the purification of the mineral. Great quantities of salt are extracted here for the supply of Western India and Afghanistan. There is also coal in its vicinity, but of

² Journ. As. Soc. 1842, p. 2, Jameson, Letter from Kala Bagh; id. 1843, 212; Rep. on Geol. of Punj. and Afg. poor quality, and in inconsiderable seams.² The Indus is navigable to Kala Bagh at all seasons. The population probably does not exceed 2,000. Lat. 32° 57′, long. 71° 37′.

E.I.C. Ms. Doc. KALAGUR, in Afghanistan, a village and halting-place on the route from Ghuznee to Dera Ismael Khan, and eighty miles south-east of the former place. The road is indifferent, and the place owes its importance to a supply of water from a stream. Lat. 32° 32′, long. 68° 41 .

KALAICHI, a town of the Derajat, ten miles south of Dera Masson, Bal. Afg. Ismael Khan, and four miles from the west, or right bank of the Panj. i. 75. Indus, has considerable commerce, so as to be enabled to pay a tribute of about 30,000 rupees annually to the Sikhs. Lat. 31° 43', long. 70° 50'.

KALA KULLAI, in the Punjab, a village thirteen miles E.I.C. Ms. Doc. north-east of Lahore, and four miles from the right bank of the river Ravee. Lat. 31° 47', long. 74° 23'.

KALEE, CAVE OF.—See HINGLAJ.

KALEESA RABAT, in Afghanistan, a village on the route Walker's Map of Afg. from Kandahar to Khash, and thirty-five miles west of the former town. Lat. 31° 29', long. 64° 54'.

KALE SURA, in the Punjab, a village and caravanserai on E.I.C. Ms. Doc.; Hough, Narr. Exp. in Afg. 338. the route from Attock to Rawul Pindee, and thirty-two miles south-east of the former place. It is situate on the river Kalee, a tributary of the Hurroo. The Kalee, though of short course, is deep; the passage across it is effected by an old stone bridge. It is the Toomrah of Walker's Map. At a short distance to the north-west of the village is a *bauli*, or great well, the water of which is reached by a descent of a hundred steps. The surrounding country is remarkably rocky, rugged, and barren, and the roads are rough and difficult. Lat. 33° 44', long. 72° 49'.

KALLOO, in the Punjab, a village situate about sixteen E.I.C. Ms. Doc. miles west of Lahore, on the road from Ferozpoor to Ramnuggur. Lat. 31° 38', long. 74° 1'.

KALLORA,[1] in Sinde, a village on the route from Hyderabad [1] E.I.C. Ms. Doc. to Bukkur, and thirty-five miles north of the former town. It is situate twelve miles from the left bank of the Indus, in a level, uninteresting country,[2] in many places overgrown with jun- [2] Wood, Oxus, 36. gle. Lat. 25° 51', long. 68° 33'.

KALOO, in Afghanistan, is a lofty pass on one of those Jour. As. Soc. 1842, p. 69, Grif. Bar. and routes into which the Kabool road to Turkestan divides westward Ther. Meas. in of Gooljatooe, and which debouch in various parts of the valley Afg.; Burnes' Bokh. i. 182; ii. of Bamian. It has an elevation of 12,480 feet, being the highest 240; Wood, Route of Kabool of the passes, except that of Erak. The Kaloo Pass is in lat. and Toorkestan, 24; Id. Oxus, 204; 34° 40', long. 67° 48'. Moorcr. Punf.

KAMA RIVER, so called from a district of that name Bokh. ii. 395; Outram, Rough through which it passes, bears also the name of the river Kooner, Notes, 126. from a town on its eastern bank. It rises in the valley of Chitral, Baber, Mem. 144; Masson, Bal. Afg. in the Hindoo Koosh, and, flowing south-west, traverses Kafir- Panj. i. 170; Jour. As. Soc.

istan, whence it proceeds still in a south-west direction into Lughman, a province of Afghanistan, and falls into the Kabool river at its northern side, in lat. 34° 24', long. 70° 35'. Though about two hundred and twenty miles in length, it is, according to Moorcroft, of no great size.

KAMALIA,[1] in the Punjab, a small town five or six miles from the right, or west bank of the Ravee. It has an appearance of antiquity, and is built of burnt bricks. There is a fortress, constructed of the same materials, and a bazaar. Masson[2] supposes " that Kamalia may have been the fortress at which the great Macedonian hero. had nearly become the victim of his temerity." Arrian[3] distinctly states that Alexander was marching through the Doab, or peninsula between the Chenaub, or Acesines, and the Ravee, or Hydraotes; that he crossed the Hydraotes[4] in pursuit of some Indians who had fled over it; that he again crossed (recrossed) the same river in pursuit of the fugitives, and there attacked this unnamed city, in the storming of the citadel of which he received his wound. This certainly very exactly designates the country in which Kamalia is situated, and affords countenance to Masson's opinion, though he states that he had nothing to rely on but his memory. Still there is no sufficient evidence to fix this very town as the actual scene of the event. Kamalia is lat. 30° 44', long. 72° 38'.

KAMBAR, in the north of the Punjab, and among the mountains south of Kashmir, is a fort finely situated on an insulated rock to the left of the route from Lahore to Kashmir, by Kotli. At the time of Vigne's visit, it belonged to the powerful Sikh chieftain Dhihan Singh.   Lat. 33° 12', long. 73° 55'.

KANAJEE,[1] in Beloochistan, a village on the route from Sonmeanee to Kelat, and ninety miles north of the former town. It is situate in a hilly country of considerable elevation, and in consequence of this, notwithstanding the lowness of the latitude, the winters are severe.   Pottinger[2] and his party found, on the 1st of February, that "the night was piercingly cold." Kanajee is in lat. 26° 31', long. 66° 26'.

KANDAHAR,[1] the principal city of Western Afghanistan, and the capital and stronghold of the Duranis, is situate in a fertile and cultivated plain, well watered by canals from the Urghundab river, which flows about four miles to the west of it, and from the Turnak river, at a somewhat greater distance to the

east. The produce, for a small space round the city, is excellent
and abundant, consisting of grains of various kinds, the finest and
most delicious fruits, grapes, peaches, figs, apricots, nectarines,
and various others.[2] This rich tract is, however, of no great ex- [2] Forster, Jour. Beng. Eng. ii. 117.
tent, as precipitous and rocky hills rise around it at no great
distance on the west and north.[3] Though the present city was [3] Id.
built by Ahmed Shah,[4] the founder of the Durani dynasty, and [4] Masson, Bal. Afg. Panj. i.270.
hence in public documents is called Ahmed Shahi, the vicinity
has from remote antiquity been the site of a large town, and has
repeatedly suffered from the attacks of invaders. Kandahar
was taken by Tamerlane, in 1384;[5] by Sultan Baber, in 1507;[6] [5] Price, Mahomedan Hist. iii.50.
by Shah Abbas, of Persia, in 1620;[7] by Nadir Shah, in 1751.[8] [6] Memoirs, 229.
Nadir founded a new city close to that of which he had made [7] Malcolm, Hist. of Persia, i.544.
himself master, and styled it Nadirabad; but this fell into total [8] Id. ut supra, ii. 69.
decay on the foundation of Ahmed Shahi.[9] The importance which [9] Atkinson, Exp. into Afg. 104.
brought down upon the city these attacks resulted from its com-
manding the southern route from India to Persia and the west,
as Kabool does the northern. The present city is of the shape
of an irregular quadrangle, enclosed by a mud wall, twenty-six
feet thick at the bottom, fourteen and a half at the top, and
twenty-seven feet high, formed of curtains, and semicylindri-
cal bastions, fifty-four in number, strengthened by a low
fausse braye, and farther protected by a ditch from fifteen
to twenty feet wide and ten feet deep, capable of being filled
with water from the canals of the Urghundab. The western
face of this is one thousand nine hundred and sixty-seven
yards in length, the northern one thousand one hundred and
sixty-four, the eastern one thousand eight hundred and ten, the
southern one thousand three hundred and forty-five. The
circumference of the city is consequently three miles and one
thousand and six yards.[1] There is a large tower at each of the [1] Hough, Narr. Exp. in Afg. 133.
four corners, and each of the six gates is protected by double bas-
tions. The citadel containing the palace where the sovereigns resided is in the middle of the north side, near the gateway. Though
originally beautiful,[2] it is now little better than a heap of [2] Allen, March through Sinde and Afg. 193.
ruins, both within and without, the defences as well as the
enclosed houses having nearly fallen to pieces.[3] Kandahar has [3] Kennedy, Sinde and Kabool, i.252.
two principal streets which proceed from opposite gates and
cross in the middle, at right angles, under a large dome,
called Charsoo,[4] about fifty yards in diameter, and beneath [4] Havelock, War in Afg. ii.8.

which is a public market-place, surrounded by shops. The private houses are wretchedly built of mud; they are seldom more than two stories high, and, in consequence of the scarcity of timber, the roofs are made of the same material as the walls, the mud being moulded into the shape of a dome. In the few instances where timber is used the roofs are flat. The mansions of the great are enclosed with high walls, and contain three or four courts with gardens and fountains. The accommodations for the inmates generally consist of large halls, into which a number of small apartments open, the walls being ornamented with paintings and mirrors; the intervals between these are covered with a curious coating of talc, finely powdered and thickly dusted over a varnish of size whilst wet, an operation which produces a brilliant frostwork resembling silver. The ceilings are of wood, either painted or curiously carved. The houses of the poorer classes have generally only one room, with no ornament and little furniture; a coarse carpet and a few cushions of felt constituting the whole.

The town in general exhibits strong symptoms of oppression, poverty, and decay. The principal business arises from the transit trade, which brings a great number of foreigners in proportion to the resident population. Hence there is a surprising diversity of costumes in the bazaars, and the more crowded parts of the town. Even among the natives, the variations in costume are considerable. Some wear long cloaks, either of chintz or broad cloth, with huge turbans, and beards of large growth stained red with henna; others are closely shaven, and wear jackets and trousers of blue linen, or tunics of drab cloth with hanging sleeves, and skull-caps of cotton of various colours. The women, when abroad, wear the *boorka*, a long white veil from the top of the head to the feet, a piece of network before the eyes allowing them to see.

The mosques in this city are in general mean; and with the exception of the dome-shaped central bazaar, already mentioned, the only building worth notice is the tomb of Ahmed Shah, the founder of the Durani dynasty; even this, though remarkable from the paucity of architectural decoration at Kandahar, would be little regarded elsewhere. It is raised on a platform of stone, and is an octagonal building, surmounted by a cupola having minarets at the angles. It is about forty feet in diameter, and seventy feet high. The materials are mean enough, being coarse stone from the neighbouring hills, intermixed with sun-dried bricks, and having outside a coating of stucco gaudily painted red and blue, and embellished with figures of flowers and other devices. The inside is finished in a similar manner; the pavement is covered with a carpet, and the sarcophagus with a shawl. Twelve smaller tombs of the children of the deceased Shah are ranged about the principal one. Light is admitted by windows of trellis-work in stone; and many a holy text of the Koran strewed around, afford solemn impressions and associa-tions to the Mahometan visitors. An establishment of Moollas is attached to the tomb; one of their number constantly attends in the building, and reads aloud a portion of the Koran.

Kandahar is well supplied with provisions, which are both cheap and of excellent quality. There is great variety of the finest fruits, and these are purchasable at extremely low prices. Several pounds of grapes can be obtained for a sum not exceeding a halfpenny, and in quality they are considered superior even to those of Kabool. Water is excellent and in great abundance; a small watercourse passes through the courts of every residence of importance. This abundance is, however, attended by a serious evil. The site of Kandahar is very moist, and water can in most parts be obtained by digging three or four feet; in con-sequence, low fevers, dysenterics, intermittents, and liver com-plaints are very prevalent. Fuel is very scarce and dear, and this is severely felt, as the elevation above the sea being three thousand four hundred and eighty-four feet,[5] the winters are rather cold. The summers are hot, the thermometer sometimes reaching one hundred and ten in the shade.

[5] Jour. As. Soc. 1842, p. 57, Grif. Bar. and Ther. Obs. in Afg.

The amount of population is variously stated at twenty-five thousand, thirty thousand, eighty thousand, and a hundred thousand. As the greater part of the area within the walls is occupied by courts and gardens, the houses, in proportion to the extent, being few and in general small and ruinous, it is improbable that the population exceeds fifty thousand. The greater part is Afghans, the remainder a mixed multitude of Persians, Usbegs, Beloochees, Jews, Hindoos, and various other races. The commercial transactions are generally managed by Hindoos. Under Ahmed Shah, Kandahar was the seat of government, which was removed to Kabool by his successor,

Timur. On the dismemberment of Afghanistan, subsequent to the expulsion of Shah Shooja, the brothers of Dost Mahomed, by his connivance, established themselves in Kandahar, and levied contributions over the neighbouring districts. Their weak and pernicious rule was terminated by the occupation of their capital by a British force in 1839. The army of occupation, notwithstanding the frequent and desperate attacks of the natives, made good the defence until the autumn of 1842, when it finally evacuated the place, and commenced its triumphant march on Ghuznee and Kabool. When the British took possession of Kandahar, the revenue of the town and adjacent territory was estimated at 800,000 rupees. It is now suffering all the horrors of the sanguinary anarchy consequent on the murder of the Shah and the evacuation of the country by the British. Lat. 31° 37′, long. 65° 28′.

Walker's Map of N.W. Frontier.   KANDAIROH, in Bhawlpoor, a village in the desert near the south-western frontier. Lat. 28° 1′, long. 70° 15′.

E.I.C. Ms. Doc.   KANEGORUM, in Afghanistan, a village on the route from Dera Ismail Khan, by the way of Tak to Ghuznee, and sixty miles north-west of the former place. It is situate in the hilly country between the range of Suliman and the Salt range, and which, though pleasant, well watered, and rather fertile, is rendered nearly a waste by the predatory Vazerees. Lat. 32° 27′, long. 70° 21′.

E.I.C. Ms. Doc.   KANGHUR, in Sinde, a town on the route from Shikarpoor to Shahpoor, and twenty-two miles north of the former place. It is situate in a tract overrun with stunted jungle, and where the country assumes the aspect of the *Pat*, or desert stretching to the north-west. Lat. 28° 13′, long. 68° 35′.

KANHI.—See BOLAN RIVER.

E.I.C. Ms. Doc.   KANOTEH-KA-GOTE, in Sinde, a town on the route from Hyderabad to Sehwan, by way of Kotree, and twenty-six miles north of Hyderabad. It is situate close to the right bank of the Indus, in a fertile and well-cultivated country. Lat. 25° 43′, long. 68° 27′.

Vigne, Kashmir, ii. 395.   KANTAL, in the north-east of Kashmir, a lofty mountain south of the pass called Bultul by Vigne and modern geographers.* Through this pass lies one of the principal routes

Kaschmir, ii. 165.   * Hugel, however, whose opinion should have great weight, considers the

from Kashmir to Ladakh and Bultistan. Its crest forms a division between the basin of the Indus and that of the Jailum; the Dras river, which rises here, flowing northwards to the former river, and the Sinde, in a south-west direction, to the Jailum. The elevation of this pass is 10,500 feet. Lat. 34° 10′, long. 75° 15′. (See BUL-TUL.)

KANTASIR, in Sinde, a village on the route from Hyderabad E.I.C. Ms. Doc. to Lueput, in Cutch, and eighty miles south of the former place. Lat. 24° 12′, long. 68° 41′.

KAPOORTHELLA.—See KOPURTHELLA.

KAPOURDIGUERI, in Afghanistan, a village in the Eu- Jour. As. Soc. sufzai country, on the northern boundary of the plain of Pesha- 1839, p. 312, wur, and forty miles north of the town of that name. Lat. Alexander. Map. 34° 20′, long. 72° 12′.

KARA BAGH.—A town, with a large fort, on the route from E.I.C. Ms. Doc.; Kandahar to Ghuznee, and thirty-five miles south-west from the 1842, p. 60, latter place. The surrounding district, called also Kara Bagh, is Grif. Bar. and remarkably fertile, well cultivated, productive in-grain, populous, Hough, Narr. of and crowded with forts and villages, held partly by Afghan Leech, Rep. on Ghiljies, partly by Huzarehs. The elevation above the sea is Sind. Army, 89. 7,426 feet. Lat. 33° 10′, long. 67° 59′.

KARACHI.—See KURRACHEE.

KARAILA.—A village in the Punjab, situate near the right Walker's Map of bank of the Ravee river. Lat. 30° 33′, long. 72° 34′. N.W. Frontier.

KARA-SU, or BLACK RIVER, a stream which descends from Masson, Bal. Afg. the Sufeid Koh into the plain of Jelalabad, and falls into the Panj. i. 181; Soorkh Rood, a little above its confluence with the Kabool river, 1842, p. 120, in lat. 34° 24′, long. 70° 14′. MacGregor, Geog. Notice of the

KARA TUPPA FORT, in Afghanistan, a ruined fort on the Valley of Jullala- route from Herat to Mero, and sixty miles north of the former Abbot, Heraut town. Kara Tuppa (black mound) is an artificial hill, a hundred and Khiva, i. 14. and fifty feet high, crowned by ruined ramparts. It is situate near the left bank of the small river Khooshk, and in a pleasant valley, overlooked by lofty hills on the west. It is a favourite en-campment of the Jumsheedee tribe of Eimaks, who may gene-rally be observed here located with their substantial tents of black felt. Lat. 35° 16′, long. 62° 11′.

Kantal of the old maps, and described by the missionaries, to be identical with the vast bifurcated summit, Mer and Ser, situate about fifty miles east of Bultul.

Walker's Map of N.W. Frontier.   KARATUPUH, in Afghanistan, a village in the hilly country where the Huzareh mountains sink towards Bokhara. It is situate on the left bank of the river of Andkhoo, and sixty miles south-west of the town of that name. Lat. 36° 15′, long. 64° 48′.

E.I.C. Ms. Doc.   KARDO, in Sinde, a village situate on the west bank of the Koree estuary of the Indus, twenty miles from the sea. Lat. 23° 43′, long. 68° 35′.

E.I.C. Ms. Doc.   KAREEZ DOST MOHAMED, in Beloochistan, a village on the route from Quetta to Kelat, forty miles south of the former town. It is well supplied with watèr by means both of a small stream and of a *kareez*, or subterraneous aqueduct, which conducts a supply to the village from some neighbouring hills. The road in this part of the route is excellent, rising with a gentle acclivity southwards towards Kelat. The inhabitants emigrate to Cutch Gundava in winter, to avoid the cold, which is severe, the elevation of the country above the sea exceeding 5,000 feet. Lat. 29° 40′, long. 66° 34′.

[1] E.I.C. Ms. Doc.   KARMEL,[1] in the Punjab, a village on the route from Ramnuggur to Pind Dadun Khan, and six miles north-west of the former town. It is situate near the right bank of the Chenaub, and close to the ferry, which is one of great importance, as the river, [2] Hough, Nar. Exp. In Afg. 343.   when fullest, is above a mile broad,[2] and the traffic considerable. Lat. 32° 26′, long. 73° 34′.

E I.C. Ms. Doc.   KARORA, in Sinde, a village on the route from Roree to Jessulmair, and sixty miles south-east of the former town. The road in this part of the route is over a sandy surface (often rising into low sandhills), producing a scanty jungle. There are three good wells in the village. Lat. 27° 27′, long. 69° 40′.

Walker's Map of N.W. Frontier.   KARUK, in Afghanistan, a village amidst the hills of the Salt range, and on the western route from Kala Bagh to Kohat, from which last town it is distant thirty miles south. Lat. 33° 10′, long. 71° 16′.

E.I.C. Ms. Doc.   KASBAH, in Sinde, a village close to the south-eastern frontier, and about two miles from the northern boundary of the Great Western Rin. Lat. 24° 17′, long. 70° 44′.

Hough, 345.   KASEE.—A small river in the Punjab, which flows by the fort of Rotas, and falls into the river Jailum, on the right or western side, in lat. 32° 56′, long. 73° 36′. Its course, which is in general from north-west to south-east, is about thirty miles long. The bed of this river forms a road or pass into the strong country between the river Jailum and Attock.

KASHGAR.[1]—This name has been given by Elphinstone E.I.C. Ms. Doc. and Burnes to a locality in the north-eastern part of Kafiristan and the adjacent region. The eminent writer first named describes it as "an extensive but mountainous and ill-inhabited country, lying to the west of Badukshan, from which it is divided by Beloot Taugh, having Little Tibet on the east, the Pamere on the north, and the ridge of Hindoo Koosh (which separates it from the Eusofzyes) on the south."[2] This locality corresponds [2] Acc. of Caubul, closely with that which Humboldt assigns to Thsoungling, the 629. supposed junction of the Kouenlun and Bolor ranges.* Burnes[3] [3] Bokh. ii. 225. gives a very confused account of it from native report, which stated it to be situate north of Peshawur, and in high repute for coarse blankets; and Vigne,[4] in half a dozen words, tells us that [4] Kashmir, ii. 309. Chitral is "called Little Kashghar by the Patans." Wood, who has more extensively explored this region than any other European, does not notice this name in his map.[5] There seems, in [5] Accompanying fact, to be no evidence for its existence except native report, Source of the which, with inaccuracy not unusual in such a quarter, may Oxus. have assigned a locality too far south to the well-known town and territory of Kashgar, in Chinese Tartary. Such is the view of the subject taken by Klaproth,[6] who, with much vehemence, [6] Quoted by censures "the mass of absurdities received with open arms by the 225. compilers, and among which the double Kashgar holds the first rank." The question, however, is not to be considered as settled on the authority of Klaproth. Waddington,[7] whose geographical [7] Introd. to Baber, information respecting these regions is entitled to the highest xxviii. respect, distinctly recognizes the lesser or more southern Kashgar. In Walker's Map of the North-west Frontier, it is set down in lat. 35° 58', long. 71° 41'.

KASHMIR, north of the Punjab, is an elevated tract, inclosed by very lofty mountains, having in the middle a level and alluvial soil, watered by the river Jailum, and in all other parts a very uneven surface, formed by numerous ridges and gorges, extending from the plain to the culminating line of the surrounding range. The etymology of the name of this celebrated region has singularly perplexed antiquarians. Wilford[1] derives the name from [1] On Mount Cau- the *Chasas*, a very ancient and powerful tribe, who inhabited the casus, As. Re-

searches, vi. 455,
* See the hypsometrical map accompanying *Asie Centrale*. 456.

z 2

Himalaya and Hindoo Koosh, from the eastern limits of India to the confines of Persia. They are mentioned in the Institutes of Menu and other sacred books of the Hindoos, and still hold large tracts in Northern Hindostan. Baber[2] mentions them under the name of *Kas*, and is of opinion that Kashmir may have taken its name from them ; and his judicious commentator, Waddington,[3] observes on this—" The conjecture is certainly happy, and the fact on which it is founded important ;" he adds, that *mir* is still united with the name of several districts, as Jeselmir and Ajmir. According to others,[4] it is derived, by the Brahmins, from *Kas*, light, and *Mira*, sea. Humboldt[5] states that its primæval name was *Kasyapamar*, signifying " the habitation of Kasyapa," a mythological personage, by whose agency the valley was drained. Kasyapa, according to the Hindoo authorities,[6] was the grandson of Brahma, and lived as an ascetic on the mountain contiguous to the lake which originally occupied the valley. Having, by his austerities, great influence with the gods, he fervently prayed to Matta, the wife of Siva, that she would change the watery expanse into a garden. Siva, complying with the entreaties of Matta, struck his trident into the bottom of the lake, and made an opening, by which the water passed away. The city founded in the country thus drained was called after the saint, Kasyapur, or " Town of Kasyapa," converted in ordinary pronunciation into Kash- appur, and passing ultimately into Kashmir.* Hugel[7] calls the ascetic Kasha, and adds " that *Mar* signifies, according to them (the Hindoos),[8] a garden, and the name *Kaschah Mar*, ' Garden of Kasha,' which the valley thenceforward bore, was subsequently changed into Kashmir." According to Mahometan traditions, the drainage was effected by Kasheb, a *Deo* or *Genie* subject to the power of Solomon, king of Israel, at whose command he performed this work of benevolence.[1]† Vigne[2] states, " The word Kashmir is Kashuf-mir (the country of Kashuf), as Kasyapa is called by the Mahomedans,—so at least the Shah Sahib and other authorities in the village used to inform me." Abul Fazel, in his abridgement of the Raja Taringini, merely states, that Kushup, an ascetic, first brought the Brahmins to inhabit

[2] Memoirs, 313.
[3] Introd. xxvii.
[4] Von Hugel, Kaschmir, i. 6.
[5] Asie Centrale, i. 102.
[6] F. Von Hugel, i. 6; As. Research. xv. 9 ; Wilson, Hist. of Kashmir.
[7] Kaschmir, i. 6.
[8] Erdkunde von Asien, iii. 1084-1690.
[1] As. Res. xv. 9.
[2] Kashmir, ii. 47.
[1] In Conversation with Vigne, Kashmir (ii. 47).
[2] Bernier, Voyages, ii. 268. Jour. Beng. Eng. ii. 19.

* Such is the derivation given by one of the most learned inquirers into the subject—Professor Wilson.[1] It is also adopted by the Rev. Mr. Renouard,[2] and apparently by Ritter.
† Forster attributes the drainage to Solomon himself.

the country after the water had subsided.[3] Kashmir has on the [3] Ayeen Akbery, II. 157.
north, Bulti, or Little Thibet; east, the mountainous tracts of
Zanskar Kishtewar; south, Jamu, Chumba, Rajawur, and some
other small hilly districts occupying the southern declivity of the
mountains inclosing the valley in that direction, and sloping to
the plain of the Punjab; on the west is the wild unexplored
country held by the Dardus, and the remnant of that once powerful race—the Guikkers. All these, as well as Kashmir itself,
have been overrun by the Sikhs, so that the valley at present is
altogether embodied into the dominions of that upstart race. If the
limits be considered as determined by the culminating ridge of the
tortuous range of mountains which on every side inclose it, Kashmir will be found to be one hundred and twenty miles long, from the
snowy Panjal on the south-east, to the Durawur ridge in the north,
and seventy miles broad, from the Futi Panjal on the south, to
Shesha Nag at the north-east. The superficial extent is about
four thousand five hundred square miles, or a little less than
four-fifths of the size of Yorkshire.* The shape of the outline
is irregular, but has a remote resemblance to an oval. The tract
thus defined, lies between lat. 33° 15′—34° 30′, long. 73° 40′—
75° 30′. Hügel[4] estimates the plain forming the bottom of the [4] II. 152.
valley to be seventy-five miles long and forty miles broad.

The general aspect of Kashmir is simple and easily compre-
hended, it being a basin bounded on every side by lofty mountains, in the inclosing range of which are several depressions,
called popularly passes, as they afford means of communication
between the valley and the adjacent countries. In the middle is
an extensive level alluvial tract, intersected by the Jailum and its
numerous feeders, which flow down from the mountains, and are
fed by the abundant snow and rains falling in those elevated
regions. All these numerous streams find their way by the sole
channel of the Jailum, through the Baramula Pass, to the plain of
the Punjab, in their course to the ocean. With the exception
of one summit south of Bultul Pass, the elevation of the inclosing range falls far short of that attained by the summits of
the Himalaya or of the Hindoo Koosh. Thus, the elevation of the
Pir Panjal, bounding the valley on the south-west, and probably

* The extent of surface given in the text is deduced from Vigne's map,
published by Walker. Hügel makes it 5,000 square miles.   II. 151

⁵ II. 180.
the highest of the Kashmirian summits, is stated by Hügel⁵ to be
above 15,000 feet.* On the north-eastern side of the valley, the
highest summit appears to be that of Haramuk, having an elevation
⁶ Vigne, ii. 151.
of 13,000 feet.⁶ Vigne⁷ states, that when he surveyed the valley
⁷ I. 287.
from an eminence, he found it on every side to be surrounded by
snowy mountains; but as he does not mention the time of the year
when this view took place, this statement proves nothing as to the
general height of the range, or the relation which the elevation
bears to the limit of perpetual snow. In his map, however, he
distinctly states, that the Pir Panjal, there laid down 13,500 feet
high, is always covered with snow, and consequently the limit
of perpetual congelation is, on that mountain, below its position in places several degrees farther north.† The less elevation of the limit in the Kashmirian mountains results, probably, from the rapid slope southwards to the vast plain extending to the Indian Ocean, so that there is in that direction no
lofty table-land to raise the temperature by the radiation of
heat. The Panjals, or mountains forming the range which in-
closes Kashmir, appear, with little exception, to be of igneous
origin, and "basaltic, their usual formation, being a beautiful
⁸ Vigne, i. 275.
amygdaloidal trap."⁸ Vigne found rocks of this character on the
summit of almost all the passes, except that of Dras, which is
three days' journey beyond the limits of the valley, and on the
⁹ Vigne, i. 275.
crest of which slate occurs.⁹ In the north-west, in the vicinity of
Baramula, "the bare cliffs of schistoze rock rise perpendicularly
¹ Vigne, i. 278.
to the height of from five hundred to a thousand feet."¹ There
are several basaltic eminences of small elevation scattered over
the bottom of the valley.   Such a physical conformation cannot
fail to suggest the notion that this singular region was once the
crater of a vast volcano; and such was the first impression of
² I. 289.
Vigne,² on viewing from a commanding eminence the valley in its
whole extent. " There are," he observes, " many elevated points
of view from which this extraordinary hollow gave me, at first
sight, an idea of its having been originally formed by the falling

---

* Hügel elsewhere states the elevation at 14,092. (ii. 155.)
† In Pamir, for instance, in lat. 37°, or above three degrees north of the
¹ Oxus, 364.
Pir Panjal, Wood ¹ found the limit of perpetual congelation to be above seventeen thousand feet; and in Koonawur, only a degree south of the Pir Panjal,
² Koonawur, 159.
Gerard ² found the limit to be above nineteen thousand feet.

in of an exhausted volcanic region." It seems, however, at one
time to have formed the bottom of the ocean, as there are in many
places great beds of limestone containing organic remains principally marine.[5] Gypsum occurs in the north-west of this [5 Vigne, i. 276.]
region. Primary formations appear of very rare occurrence ;
erratic blocks of granite are scattered over the slopes of the Haramuk mountain, on the north-east, and in the Baramula Pass, but
this formation has nowhere been observed in situ.[6] Veins of [6 Id. i. 278.]
quartz, however, so usually accompanying schistoze formation,
have been observed of large dimensions. The subterraneous dis-
turbance, of the past activity of which the results have been just
briefly traced, continues to the present time. In June, 1828, the
city of Kashmir was shaken by an earthquake which destroyed
about twelve hundred houses and one thousand persons.[7] The earth [7 Vigne, i. 281.]
in several places opened and discharged fetid warm water from the
clefts, and masses of rock rolled from the mountains amidst repeated
explosions. For above two months, every day, from one hundred
to two hundred shocks were felt, each accompanied by an explosion. Deleterious gases appear to have been extricated on that
occasion, as the cholera then broke out and caused very dreadful
fatality.[7] Abul Fazel,[8] describing the country above two centuries [7 Id. i. 282.]
before, mentions the frequency of earthquakes. In his time the [8 Ayeen Akbery, ii. 135.]
houses were framed of timber, as a precaution against destruc-
tion by the shocks, and the same precaution is still observed.
Some years ago, at Suhoyum, near the north-western extremity
of the valley, the ground became so hot, that the sand was fused,
and appearances seemed to indicate that a volcanic eruption was
about to take place.[9] Moorcroft[1] observes, " Indications of vol- [9 Vigne, i. 280.]
canic action are not unfrequent, hot springs are numerous at par- [1 Punj. Bokh. ii. 109.]
ticular seasons, the ground in various places is sensibly hotter
than the atmosphere, and earthquakes are of common occurrence."
Vigne supposes that the great calcareous deposits have been raised
to their present position, from the bed of the ocean, by the upheaving of volcanic masses from beneath. Pebbly conglomerate,
sandstone, and clay, in many places, extensively overspread the
mountain slopes.[2] [2 Vigne, i. 280; Moorcroft, ii. 109.]
    Besides the low alluvial tract, extending along the banks
of the Jailum, and forming the greater part of the cultivable soil of the valley, there are several extensive table-lands of
slight elevation, stretching from the mountains[3] various dis- [3 Vigne, i. 277.]

tances into the plain. These *Karywas*, as they are called by the natives, are described by Vigne as " composed of the finest alluvial soil, usually free from shingle. Their surface is verdant, and generally smooth as a bowling-green, but they are divided and deeply furrowed by mountain streams." He considers the appearance which they present a strong proof of the truth of the tradition, that the whole valley was once occupied by a lake. " The flat surfaces of the Karywas, whose cliffs are from one hundred and fifty to two hundred feet above the lowest part of the valley, are attributable to their having for ages remained at the bottom of a still lake, perhaps at least three hundred feet above its present level, at the bottom of that valley."[4] Some who have viewed the scenery of the valley consider that they have found corroboration of the tradition, that it was once occupied by a lake, in a succession of horizontal stages observable on the sides of the mountains, and which apparently have been breaches formed successively by the waters of the lake in the course of subsidence.[5] The soil of the lowest part of the valley appears to have been deposited from a salt lake, as the water obtained from wells dug there is brackish,[6] and none perfectly fresh can be had, except from the river, which is of course supplied principally from the snows and rains falling on the mountains. The great opening at the north-western extremity, by which at present the aggregate waters of Kashmir escape to the lower country, has probably been coeval with the original upheaving of this region, as, though an earthquake might have caused a fissure sufficiently large to drain the supposed lake, it is more difficult to suppose such an event to have removed the enormous mass of matter requisite for filling up the space of the present valley of Baramula. Such is the view taken by Vigne, who considers the Baramula opening to have been from the first filled with submarine shingle and soft conglomerate, through which the Jailum has worked its way, assisted, in some degree, by openings resulting from earthquakes.[7] " So far," observes Rennell, " am I from doubting the tradition respecting the existence of the lake that covered Cashmere, that appearances alone would serve to convince me, without either the tradition or the history."[8] This lake, according to Kashmirian tradition, bore the name of *Satisaras*, or " the lake of the chaste woman," as it was considered peculiarly to belong to Uma, the wife of Mahadeo, one of whose

[4] Vigne, i. 280.

[5] Moorcr. ii. 109; Vigne, i. 277.

[6] Id. i. 285.

[7] Id. i 253, 286, 287.

[8] Memoir of a Map of Hindoostan, 107.

names is Sati, in the character of a chaste woman.[1] Baron Von
Hügel, however, whose opinion unquestionably merits very high
regard, is quite incredulous respecting the existence of the lake.
He observes, " There is not in the valley the slightest appearance
of its having been drained. The pass through which the Jhelum
found its way is one of the most beautiful in the world : its bed,
1,000 to 1,500 feet. I do not believe more in the traditions of
the Kashmirian Brahmins than in the fables of Manethou." [2] *

As might be expected, from the rare occurrence of primary formations in Kashmir, its mineralogy is not rich. Iron-ore, however,
abounds,[3] and Vigne[4] says, " veins of lead, copper, and, as I
was informed, also of silver, and even of gold, are known to exist
in the long grass-covered hills in the neighbourhood, but the iron
alone is worked." Such a statement is too vague to be relied
on. The iron-ore is found in the south-eastern extremity of
the valley, embedded in limestone,[5] near Shahbad. Lead-ore
was found in the same vicinity by Jacquemont,[6] and has been
worked since 1833. Hügel found copper-ore, but the mines
are not worked. He informs us that neither gold nor silver
has been found, nor do the streams bear down gold-dust, as
in the neighbouring countries. Plumbago abounds in the Pir
Panjal mountain.[7] Sulphureous springs are numerous, but the
mineral has nowhere been found in a solid state,[8] and the country
is supplied with it from the Punjab. Excellent limestone exists
in inexhaustible quantities in many places ; some kinds of it
are a fine black marble. The inclosing range bears different
names in different parts : the Snowy Panjal on the east ; the Futi
Panjal and Panjal of Banihal on the south ; the Pir on the west ;
the Durawur mountain on the north ; the Haramuk and Sonamurg mountains on the north-east.† We have no satisfactory
data to determine whether they, throughout, enter into the
limits of perpetual congelation, but it is probable that such
is generally the fact, as travellers frequently mention the striking

[1] Wilson, in As. Res. xv. 8 ; Aycen Akbery, ii. 157 ; F. Von Hugel, ii. 14.

[2] As. Jour. Oct. 1836, p. 66, xxi. N.S., Von Hugel on Kashmir.

[3] Moorcr. ii. 162 ; F. Von Hugel, ii. 244.

[4] i. 337.

[5] F. Von Hugel, ii. 244.

[6] Id. ib.

[7] Id. ii. 245.

[8] Id. ib. ; Moorcr. ii. 163.

* Could Moorcroft and Vigne have mistaken the usual appearance of trap-
rocks for beaches formed by the lake in the successive stages of subsidence ?

† The Bultul mountain, near the north-eastern boundary, is supposed by
Vigne to be the Kantal of the old maps, but Hügel considers the Kantal to [ii. 166.]
be a mountain having two very lofty summits of the same shape and
height, the one quite black, the other covered with snow of a dazzling whiteness. These summits are respectively called Mer and Ser.

effect which their snowy summits produce on the landscape.
⁹ ii. 164. The fullest information on this point is given by Hügel,⁹ who states that the mountains " form a regular oval of snowy summits, which inclose Kashmir. Only south-west of the town, and for a fifth part of the circumference, is the oval interrupted and continued by a lower range." The soft and beautiful scenery of the valley is on the southern side, where the mountains slope gently to the lower part; on the northern side, the scenery is wild and sublime, as there the mountains rise in rugged precipices of stupendous height, down the bare sides of which the numerous ¹ F. Von Hugel, ii. 181. streams rush in prolonged cataracts.¹ The scientific traveller so frequently quoted well describes this alpine region. " From the summits one can seldom see any thing of the valley, as it is concealed under the perpendicular brow which first rises from the plain. Wherever the view is directed, little can be seen but endless snow. I know scarcely any prospect more gloomy; no tree, no bird, no living creature can be beheld. On these summits reigns a terrific silence, and the name of *Raan*, ' the waste,' ² Id. ii. 183. which the natives have given it, is admirably just."²

The number of the passes into Kashmir over these mountains is ³ Ayeen Akbery, ii. 134.
⁴ Hist. iv. 440.
⁵ Acc. of Caubul, 506.
⁶ ii. 171. very variously stated; by Abul Fazel³ at twenty-six, Ferishta⁴ at three, Elphinstone⁵ at seven. Hügel⁶ mentions twelve, and adds, that the four following of these are practicable at all times of the year: 1, The Nabog, on the eastern frontier, in lat. 33° 37′, long. 75° 20′; 2, the Banihal, on the southern frontier, in lat. 33° 24′, long. 75° 8′; 3, the Baramula Pass, southwards, or Punch Pass, on the western frontier, and in lat. 34° 2′, long. 73° 54′; 4, Baramula Pass, westward, or Dub Pass, on the same frontier, and ⁷ ii. 149. in lat. 34° 10′, long. 73° 33′. Vigne⁷ enumerates twenty, and adds, that " an active mountaineer could enter the valley in many places besides the regular passes. Eleven of these passes are said to be practicable for horses; there is no carriage-way into the valley, but the Mogul emperors frequently brought elephants by the Pir Panjal Pass, or that through which the Bimber road lies. These huge animals, being wonderfully sure-footed and capable of ⁸ Bernier, Voyages, ii. 266. making their way in difficult places,⁸ were used to convey the females of the household. The Sikhs invaded the valley through ⁹ Vigne, ii. 181. the Baramula Pass, and took with them a six-pounder,⁹ slung on poles and borne by thirty-two men at a time. That European skill and perseverance could make these passes practicable for

artillery cannot be doubted. The Pir Panjal Pass is in lat. 33° 32', long. 74° 27', its elevation above the level of the sea 11,800 feet.[1] This and the passes of Baramula and Banihal, [1] Vigne, i. 264. already mentioned, are the principal between Kashmir and the Punjab. There are two other important passes, that of Bundipur,[2] on the north-east, in lat. 34° 37', long. 74° 40', through [2] Vigne, ii. 198. which lies the route to Iskardo; and that of Duras or Dras,[3] [3] Oriental Magazine, 1825, March, in the east, in lat. 34° 11', long. 75° 18'; elevation above p. 105, Izzet the level of the sea, 10,500 feet. When the Mogul emperor Ullah, Travels beyond Himalaya; Akbar visited Kashmir, in 1587, he appointed seven Maleks, Vigne, ii. 395; Moorcr. ii. 95. or chieftains, as hereditary wardens, one for each of the passes considered to be the most important,[4] and allotted to each [4] F. Von Hugel, ii. 167. a revenue, from lands and villages, proportioned to the support of an armed force deemed requisite to defend the post committed to his care. The descendants of these Maleks retain the titles, but their revenues and powers are now little more than nominal.

The grandeur and splendour of Kashmirian scenery results from the sublimity of the huge inclosing mountains, the picturesque beauty of the various gorges, extending from the level alluvial plain to the passes over the crest of the inclosing range ; the numerous lakes and fine streams, rendered often more striking by cataracts; the luxuriance and variety of the forest trees, and the rich and multiform vegetation of the lower grounds. The attractiveness of the scenery, the mildness of the climate, and the fertility of the soil, make Bernier[5] [5] Voyages, ii. 27. conclude that it was actually the site of the garden of Eden ; and Abul Fazel describes it " as a garden in perpetual spring."[6] [6] Ayeen Akbery, ii. 194. Jacquemont, on the contrary, expresses himself concerning it in very disparaging language. " The appearance of the inclosing mountains (he observes) is grand, rather than beautiful, presenting a striking outline and nothing more, as nature has done nothing to embellish the interior; so that it is a grand frame without a picture, and totally devoid of the picturesque charms of the Alps ;"[7] but Vigne, who was infinitely better acquainted with [7] Correspond. ii. 90. the scenery, and untainted by affectation, is untiring in its praise, calling to his aid the mellifluous eloquence[8] of Milton : [8] ii. 63.

———— " Sweet interchange
Of hill and valley, rivers, woods, and plains ;
Now land, now *lake*, and shores with forest crowned,
Rocks, dens, and caves."—*Par. Lost*, ix. 115.

Whilst Jacquemont accuses Moore of too high embellishment
"according to the practice of lying usual among the gentlemen of
Parnassus,"[9] Vigne [1] "thought that the departure from truth on
the score of ornament was far less wide than might have been
expected from a perusal of Mr. Moore's poem."* The extent of
the level alluvial tract in the lowest part of the valley is variously
estimated—by Hügel,[2] at seventy-five miles in length, and from
forty to six in breadth; by Vigne,[3] at ninety miles in length,
and twenty-five in breadth; by Moorcroft,[4] at fifty miles in
length, and from fifteen to five in breadth. The superficial extent is probably about two thousand square miles, of which by
much the greatest part is on the left or south-western side of the
Jailum. So flat is this alluvial tract, that the Jailum,[5] which flows
through it from south-east to north-west, is navigable for boats
of considerable burthen throughout the whole of this part of its
course, from Kaniball, within a mile of Islamabad, to Baramula;
and as its channel is very winding, scarcely any part of this
level is deprived of the benefit of inland navigation. A great
part of the alluvial tract is lower than the channel of the Jailum,
and preserved by means of embankments from being overflowed.
There are three lakes on a level with the Jailum, or Behut, and
communicating with it, gradually decreasing as the river deepens
the exit at Baramula, or sweeps into them shingle, silt, or other
deposits. Though Hügel denies that the whole valley was originally a great lake dried by a vast and rapid efflux of its contents
through the Baramula gorge, he admits that there was once a
considerable expanse of water, which has disappeared in consequence of the cavity which it occupied being silted up.[6]

The soil on the sides and at the bases of the less precipitous mountains is of clay, and in the level part of the
valley a rich vegetable mould, which, where uncultivated,
throws up a thickly-matted turf, of fiorin or other natural
grasses, unmixed with rank vegetation.[7] Hügel describes it
as a light slimy earth of a clear colour, and mixed with fine
sand, its appearance not indicating its wonderful fertility.
The most fertile part of the country is that in the vicinity of
Pampur, ten miles south-east of the capital. The soil there con-

[9] ii. 74.
[1] ii. 02.

[2] ii. 153.
[3] i. 283.
[4] ii. 112.

[5] Moorcr. ii. 111;
F.Von Hugel, ii.
101.

[6] Kaschmir, ii.
180.

[7] Moorcr. ii. 100.

---

* Those who have had occasion to direct their researches to the subjects
on which Moore's oriental fictions turn, have found that his information is both
extensive and in general accurate.

tains a large admixture of loam, and is reserved principally for
the cultivation of saffron, for which Kashmir is highly celebrated.
At the base of the Pir Panjal, on the south-west side of the valley, are several gorges, the bottoms of which are filled, to a great
depth, with rich, dark-coloured mould, the result of the decay of
leaves and other vegetable matter. Where the highlands have
mould, it consists of peat.[6] The eminences throughout the valley, [6] F. Von Hugel,
except those connected with the great inclosing range, are few
and inconsiderable. According to Vigne, Huri Purbut rises two
hundred and fifty feet above the City Lake.[7] Tukt-i-Suliman, at [7] Vigne, ii. 85.
no great distance from it, rises to the height of four hundred and
fifty.[8] The hill of Shupeyon,[9] at the south-eastern extremity, to [8] Id. ii. 42.
three hundred and fifty feet. Aha Thung, in the north-east, three [9] Id. i. 287.
hundred.[1] There is no other eminence of any importance. As the [1] Id. i. 7.
city of Kashmir is situate on the Jailum, which is navigable both
upwards and downwards from it, the elevation at that place may
be taken as the average elevation of the valley, which may be
set down at between 5,500 and 6,000 feet.*

The three principal lakes of Kashmir are on a level with the
Jailum, and communicate with it. They all are on the right, or
north-eastern side of the river, and in the following order down
the course of the stream. The City Lake,[3] generally called em- [3] F. Von Hugel,
phatically *Dal*, "the Lake," is close to the city on the north-east, ii. 193; Vigne, ii.
and communicates with the river Jailum by a channel, about two 89; Moorcr. ii.
miles in length, the lake itself being six miles long, and four broad. 112.
The Manasa Bul, the most beautiful lake in Kashmir, is a mile
and a half long, three-quarters of a mile wide, and in general
very deep. The Great, or Wulur Lake, is about twenty miles †
long, and nine wide, and is merely a shallow expansion of the river
Jailum. Between the City and Manasa lakes, on the right side

---

* Hugel states the elevation of the valley, as determined by the ther-
mometer, at 5,818 feet. He states it elsewhere at 6,300 feet.[1] Jacquemont,[2] [1] As. Jour. 1836,
at 5,350. Humboldt, in his hypsometrical map accompanying Asie Cen- Oct. p. 67.
trale, at 910 toises, or 5,733 feet. Vigne,[3] at 5,000 feet. [2] Corresp. ii. 63.
[3] i. 253.

† The editor of Moorcroft (ii. 111) states that Hügel gives the length
of this lake at thirty miles, quoting, no doubt, from a communication published in Jour. As. Soc. Beng. 1836, p. 186. But the baron, in his later and
(as may be presumed) more correct work on Kashmir,[1] states the dimensions [1] Kashmir, ii. 193.
as given above in the text. "Der Wuller-See ist der Grösste und erstreckt
sich 21 meilen, vielleicht etwas weniger von W. nach O., und 9 von N.
nach S."

⁴ Vigne, ii. 147. of the river, are two small lakes, the Opun and Wusikura.[4]
There are several small mountain-lakes, or *tarns* as they would
be called by a North Briton, as Nandan Sar, and Kosah Nag,
in the south, Shesha Nag in the east, Gunga Bul in the
north-east, and a few others not worth notice. The water-
system of the valley is very simple, consisting of several tributaries, all discharging themselves into the Jailum, by which
their aggregate contents are conveyed through the Baramula Pass
to the low country of the Punjab. They are the Breng, or
Bureng, Sandren, Lidur, Sinde, Rembeara, Chanz, Lolab, besides
a great number of small streams too inconsiderable for separate
notice. No country more perfectly enjoys the advantages of
extensive irrigation without the inconvenience of attending general
periodical inundations.

TABLE OF HEIGHTS.

		FEET.
[5] Jacquemont, Voyage Dans L'Inde. v. 310.	Mountain south of Bultul Pass,[5] lat. 34° 10′, long. 75° 5′, estimated*	19,650
[6] F. Von Hugel, ii. 180.	Pir Panjal,[6] south-west side of valley, lat. 33° 50′, long. 74° 15′	15,000
[7] Id. ii. 182; Jacquemont, v. 264.	Range[7] north side of the valley, lat. 34° 15′, long. 74° 50′	15,000
[8] Jacquemont, v. 226.	Highest Point[8] reached by Jacquemont on Pir Panjal, lat. 33° 40′, long. 74° 20′	14,300
[9] Id. 237.	Mountain east of the Pergunna of Vehi,[9] lat. 34° 5′, long. 74° 55′	13,100
[1] Vigne, ii. 151.	Haramuk Mountain,[1] lat. 34° 25′, long. 74° 40′ ...	13,000
[2] Id. l. 276.	Shesha Nag,[2] lat. 34° 7′, long. 75° 35′	13,000
	Pir Panjal Pass,† lat. 33° 30′, long. 74° 25′	12,500
[3] Vigne, i. 292.	Kosa Nag,[3] lat. 33° 25′, long. 74° 45′	12,000
[4] Id. ii. 151.	Gunga Bul,[4] lat. 34°·25′, long. 74° 42′	12,000
[5] Id. i. 212.	Nabog Nye,[5] summit of pass above, lat. 33° 45′, long. 75° 20′	12,000

* Six thousand metres, estimating the metre at 39·3 inches. See Lambton
in As. Res. xiii. p. 117.

[5] ii. 155.
[6] i. 264.
[7] v. 225.

† By Hugel,[5] 12,952; by Vigne,[6] 11,800 ; by Jacquemont,[7] 11,970.

FEET.

Crest dividing the water systems [8] of Bulti and Kashmir, lat. 34° 12', long. 75° 18' 11,708   [8] Jacquemont, v. 364.

Ratan Panjal,[9] south-west of Pir Panjal, Lat. 33° 40', long. 74° 10' 11,600   [9] F. Von Hugel, ii. 162.

Boheur, or Mirbul Pass,[1] lat. 33° 20', long. 75° 30' ... 11,400   [1] Jacquemont, v. 258.

Nunnenwarree,[2] highest point of the pass from Bundurpur to Iskardo, lat. 34° 40', long. 74° 40' 11,271   [2] F. Von Hugel, ii. 155.

Summit over Banihal Pass,[3] lat. 33° 25', long. 75° 10' . 10,807   [3] Jacquemont, v. 157.

Bultul Pass,[4] lat. 34° 10', long. 75° 15' 10,500   [4] Vigne, ii. 305.

Wurster Wun mountain,[5] lat. 33° 58', long. 74° 55' ... 10,116   [5] Jacquemont, v. 237.

Small glacier on northern slope of Futi Panjal,[6] lat. 33° 30', long. 74° 50' 9,800   [6] Id. 263.

Pass of Banihal,[7] * lat. 33° 25', long. 75° 7' 9,690   [7] Id. 256.

Bultul [8] village, lat. 34° 8', long. 75° 12' 9,660   [8] Id. 304.

Poshiana,[9] lat. 33° 33', long. 74° 23' 9,500   [9] Vigne, i. 200.

Doubjonn,[1] lat. 33° 35', long. 74° 32' 9,160   [1] Jacquemont, v. 222.

Sonamurg,[2] lat. 34° 13', long. 75° 10' 9,120   [2] Id. 303.

Duras village,[3] lat. 34° 24', long. 75° 37' 9,000   [3] Vigne, ii. 303.

Punch Pass,[4] lat. 33° 52', long. 73° 54' † 8,500   [4] Id. i. 249.

Huripur,[5] lat. 33° 40', long. 74° 40' 8,180   [5] Jacquemont, v. 222.

Height in Kol Naruwa Ridge,[6] lat. 33° 30', long. 74° 55' 8,180   [6] Id. 262.

Dudina summit,[7] lat. 33° 54', long. 75° 5' 8,100   [7] Vigne, ii. 25.

Sar-i-Bul,[8] lat. 33° 21', long. 75° 20' 8,000   [8] Id. i. 337.

Summit of Shupeyon,[9] lat, 33°. 42', long. 74° 48' ... 7,480   [9] Jacquemont, v. 219.

Tukt-i-Suliman,[1] lat. 34° 5', long. 74° 44'‡ 6,950   [1] F. Von Hugel, ii. 155.

Ilahabad, in the Punch Pass,[2] lat. 34°, long. 73° 55' ... 6,860   [2] Id. 160.

Baramgula,[3] lat. 33° 30', long. 74° 17' 6,800   [3] Vigne, i. 259.

Summit of Aha Thung,[4] lat. 34° 14', long. 74° 35' ... 6,600   [4] Jacquemont, v. 314.

Shupeyon town,[5] lat. 33° 42', long. 74° 45' 6,500   [5] Vigne, i. 271.

Suhoyum,[6] lat. 34° 16', long. 74° 4' 6,100   [6] Id. ii. 281.

Khund,[7] lat. 33° 30', long. 75° 4' 6,000   [7] Id. i. 322.

* Vigne estimates the height of the pass at 8,600 feet.   i. 332, 335.
† 8,780, by Jacquemont, p. 169.
‡ Jacquemont makes the height of Tukt-i-Suliman 6,396.   v. 219.

		FEET.
Shahbad,[8] lat. 33° 30′, long. 75° 9′		5,600
City of Kashmir, * lat. 34° 5′, long. 74° 41′		5,500
Kahouta, in Punch Pass,[9] lat. 33° 58′, long. 73° 54′ ...		4,720
Serai, in Punch Pass,[1] lat. 34° 2′, long. 73° 54′		2,734

[8] Vigne, I. 332.

[9] Jacquemont, v. 168.

[1] Id. 105.

In consequence of the great elevation of Kashmir, the cold of winter is considerable, being, on an average, much more severe than in any part of the British Isles, and this in a latitude lower than that of Sicily. Snow usually begins to fall early in December.[3] Night frosts set in as early as the middle of November, and, by the end of that month, the trees are stripped of their leaves, and all annual vegetation is cut off. A thick haze overspreads the whole valley, and the lakes and rivers send up clouds of vapour. Every movement of men or beasts raises great quantities of dust, and the haze becomes so great, that even at midday, and under a cloudless sky, no object can be seen at a mile's distance. This murky state of the air extends for about two hundred feet above the level of the valley, and those who ascend beyond that height see the snowy mountains of a dazzling whiteness, and the sun shining clearly in a cloudless sky, whilst the low country lies hidden in dim obscurity.[4] The first fall of snow restores the clearness of the air. Though snow lies to the average depth of two feet from the early part of December to the middle of April, the cold in general is a few degrees only below the freezing point. The Jailum is seldom completely frozen over, though ice invariably covers the surface of the lakes to a considerable distance from the banks. The snow begins to disappear in March. "The end of March and beginning of April are distinguished by the popular term of dirty spring or mud season, and these appellations, in regard to the mire of the surface and the rapid succession of gusts of wind and hail with short gleams of sunshine, are well deserved."[5] Up to the beginning of June much rain falls, though Kashmir is beyond the

[3] F. Von Hugel, ii. 190; Moorer. Punj. Bokh. ii. 107; Vigne, ii. 88.

[4] F. Von Hugel, ii. 190.

[5] Moorer. ii. 108.

* Hügel, in his communication in Jour. As. Soc. Beng. 1836, p. 185, states the height at 6,300 feet. He seems elsewhere to intimate it to be 5,818 (Kashmir, ii. 155). Jacquemont states it (Correspondence, ii. 65) at 5,350, and (Voyage, 219), at 1,635 metres, or 5,354 feet. Humboldt, in the hypsometrical map accompanying *Asie Centrale*, states it at 610 toises, or 5,733 feet. Vigne vaguely intimates it to be 5,000 (Kashmir, i. 253).

influence of the periodical monsoon, which so extensively deluges
parts of Asia.[6] During the April which Moorcroft passed in Kash- [6] F. Von Hugel,
mir there were only three days of sunshine, and in the following il. 103.
May scarcely a day passed without a shower. After a prolonged
residence in the very arid climate of Middle Tibet, he, on entering
Kashmir, found reason, from the contrast, to complain of the
humidity of the atmosphere, and considered it more favourable to
vegetable than to animal life.[7] Hügel,[8] on the contrary, considers [7] ii. 107.
the air dry, and supports his opinion by reference to the facts, that [8] ii. 107.
mosses and lichens are rare, and that a decayed tree is not to be
found throughout the valley. This dryness of the air he attributes
to the lightness of the soil, which quickly absorbs the rain and
melted snow, though the volume of water derived from these
sources is sometimes so considerable as to cause the Jailum to
rise thirty feet. The air of Kashmir is in general remarkable for
stillness. According to Hügel,[9] " the wind is never violent; the [9] ii. 106.
extensive surface of the Wulur lake is at no time ruffled by a
wave, and a boat passing over its mirror-like surface leaves a
trace extending for miles until lost on the distant bank." This
statement, however, must be received with considerable qualifica-
tion, as, according to Vigne,[1] " the surface of the Wulur lake, [1] ii. 150.
like every other lake surrounded by mountains, is liable to the
action of sudden and furious hurricanes, that sweep over it with
such extraordinary violence, that no boatman can be induced to
face it."* A gust of this kind, encountered by him, made the surface of the lake one sheet of foam like that of the sea under the
influence of a white squall. In the passes, the wind is in general
very violent, the cold air of the adjacent elevated tracts rushing
in to supply the place of that which ascends from the low and
warm parts of the valley. In consequence of the general stillness of the air, the heat appears much greater to the feeling than
it is ascertained to be by the thermometer. Jacquemont describes
his sufferings from this cause as excessive, and he found no relief
by immersion in the neighbouring lake, as the water gave no
sensation of coolness.[2] He remarks, however, that such high tem- [2] Corresp. ii. 141.
perature is of rather unusual occurrence in Kashmir, and was felt
so distressing and injurious by the natives, that they had recourse to religious processions and supplications to implore

* See also, with reference to gusts of wind in the spring, the quotation
from Moorcroft, supra.

a remission of it from heaven. The hottest season is from the middle of July to the middle of August, during which time the thermometer in the shade at noon ranges from 80° to 85°. In June, the average height of the thermometer at noon is about 75°. Kashmir has this great advantage respecting climate, that any depression of temperature can be obtained by a journey of a few hours in ascent of the mountains. Moorcroft[3] intimates that the climate is unwholesome; and Vigne[4] states, " though nothing can be more delicious than the air of the valley, yet in many places it is affected by a miasma from stagnant water." Yet Jacquemont[5] expresses his surprise at the extremely rare occurrence of intermittents, amidst so many causes which elsewhere invariably produce them, and Hügel styles the climate of Kashmir one of the best and healthiest in the world.[6] The remarkable fecundity[7] of marriages among the Kashmirians may perhaps be regarded as evidence of the salubrity of the climate.

The zoology of Kashmir does not appear to be rich. Bears, both brown and black, are very numerous.[8] The brown bear is between six and seven feet long, and, though a very formidable animal, does not molest man unless previously attacked, when his onset is most ferocious. The black bear, though much smaller, is far more dangerous. They are said at particular seasons to descend from the mountains and rob the fruit-trees. The wolf is rare; Vigne mentions the hyena, but doubts its existence. A panther, or sort of leopard, of a white colour with small black spots, is common in the mountains. The other beasts of prey are the jackal, fox, otter, mongoose or ichneumon, and stoat. A large and fine variety of stag occurs wild in the more retired valleys, and sometimes in severe weather great herds enter from the neighbouring wilds and commit great havoc in the cultivated grounds. The gazelle, ibex, wild goat, musk-deer, and some other species of deer frequent the wilder parts. The wild goat, though not larger than the common tame goat, has enormous horns, those of a specimen examined by Hügel being four feet long, and so heavy that the pair formed a load for an able-bodied porter. It also yields a remarkably fine wool or fur, which is wrought into highly-prized cloths. The flying squirrel, and various other sorts of that animal, some varieties of marmot, and divers marine animals, may be considered to complete the list of quadrupeds. There are no hares[9] in

Margin notes:
[3] ii. 108.
[4] ii. 88.
[5] Voyage, 322.
[6] ii. 197.
[7] Forster, ii. 25.
[8] P. Von Hugel, ii. 292; Vigne, ii. 16.
[9] P. Von Hugel, ii. 292; Vigne, i. 17.

Kashmir. Birds of prey are numerous. The highest mountains are the haunt of a huge species of vulture, according to Hügel [9] the largest in the world. As they cannot suddenly rise from the ground, the natives steal cautiously towards them, and often succeed in killing them by the throw of a cudgel. The naked skin of the breast is formed into a cap, to which the credulity of the natives attributes various marvellous qualities, and, in consequence, it is very highly valued.[1] These wild tracts are also frequented by the bearded vulture of the Himalaya, the black vulture of Hindostan, and the white-winged and black-winged vulture. Here are also a brown variety of eagle, another variety of a dark-brown colour, with white on the shoulders, and a fishing-eagle of a brown and white plumage. There are several kinds of falcons and hawks. The heron [2] is considered important, as yielding the feather-tufts worn in the turbans of the Sikh chieftains of rank. Each heron has two feathers, which grow downwards from the back of the head; and these, in the moulting-season, are carefully collected by men who watch in the heronries for this purpose. The birds are also often netted, and, after their feathers have been plucked, are set free. A fine of five hundred rupees is inflicted for killing one. The finest feathers only cost a rupee each; and the feather tuft, the badge of Sikh dignity, consists of from ten to twenty, fixed in a funnel-shaped stem, covered with gold wire, and often richly jewelled. There are two other species of herons, but they do not bear the valued feathers. The gigantic crane frequents the marshes on the banks of the Jailum. There are also various kinds of geese, ducks, divers, bitterns, baldcoots, snipes, woodcocks, and a small kind of pelican. So numerous are they, that in some places they almost hide the surface of the water on which they alight. The gallinaceous tribe contains peacocks, pheasants, partridges, both the common red-legged kind, and a gigantic species four or five times its size. The *bulbul*, or nightingale, of Kashmir is a distinct species from the genuine one of Europe, and greatly inferior in note, but amusing, on account of its bold familiar habits, taking greedily the food offered to it, and expressing its gratification by warbling. A kind of *maina* (coracias Indica), a species of jay, is very common, and being a restless, bold, turbulent bird, is the tyrant of the grove. The hoopoe is also common. A bird, resembling the thrush in size and shape, enlivens the wood with

[9] F. Von Hugel, ii. 293.

[1] F. Von Hugel ii. 293.

[2] Jacquemont, Voyage, v. 262; Vigne, ii. 306; F. Von Hugel, ii. 294.

its beautiful plumage and full melodious song. There are a vast number and much variety of the smaller kinds of birds. To this last circumstance must be attributed the paucity of insects for which Kashmir is remarkable.[2] The purple butterfly of Kashmir, introduced by Byron into one of his most beautiful similes, may be regarded as called into existence by the imagination of the poet, as Hügel found no butterfly peculiar to the valley.[3] Bees abound, and are skilfully managed so as to yield very fine honey. There are no scorpions nor poisonous centipedes; venomous serpents are rare, though the cobra di capello is sometimes found. Vigne[4] asserts that the boa constrictor is known in Kashmir, but as that terrible reptile delights in the swamps and forests of the warmest countries, it is scarcely credible that it could live in a climate so cool as that of Kashmir. Vigne[5] mentions, under the name of *aphia*, a venomous snake about a yard long, and another of a smaller size, which darts upwards to seize the throat of the person whom it attacks. Lizards are rare, but frogs are very numerous. Hügel enumerates fourteen kinds of fish found in the waters of Kashmir; of these, the largest, called *shiruh*, is often taken of the weight of twenty-four pounds: it is firm and of fine flavour. Moorcroft,[6] who, as manager of the East-India Company's studs, must be believed to be a competent judge, considers the horses of Kashmir to be but indifferent; and Jacquemont,[7] describes them as miserable ponies. The opinion of Hügel is much more favourable. By him[8] they are described as excellent; though small, strong, lively, of great bottom, and very tractable. It is represented as amusing to see one of them, mounted by a native, dash at a gallop across a shallow river, over the bed of which, covered with loose stones, no other horse could venture but with the greatest caution. Hügel has known these hardy creatures carry each a weight of three hundred pounds during the course of a day nearly forty miles across the elevated Pass of Pir Panjal. Their price is usually from two to three pounds sterling. There are very few kine, and those few are ugly, wretched animals. The natives do not like milk, and prefer vegetable oils to butter; and, as their fanatic Sikh tyrants prohibit the slaughter of kine under pain of death, there is no inducement to incur the care, trouble, and expense of keeping these animals during the long winter. Sheep are numerous,

[2] Id. ii. 299.

[3] ii. 299.

[4] ii. 21.

[5] ii. 21.

[6] ii. 152.

[7] 236.

[8] ii. 287.

and their flesh and that of goats constitute the animal diet of
the natives. Moorcroft [9] states that the mutton is well flavoured, [9] ii. 152.
and the fat particularly white ; while Hügel,[1] describing the sheep [1] ii.
as hideous, lean, and frowsy, with its neglected fleece hanging in
tatters about it, adds that the quality of the flesh is suitable
to its wretched appearance. Though the climate is so cold,
the Kashmirians unaccountably make scarcely any use of the
native wool. The *dumba*, or broad-tailed kind, in these regions,
called *hindu*, has become extinct.[2] Goats are very numerous ; [2] F. Von Hugel, ii.
of sheep the breed is small but good, and yields excellent milk ; 289.
the price of one is seldom more than two shillings. Asses and
mules abound. Dogs are abhorred, as among other Mahometans, and are in general wretched animals. The mountaineers,
however, keep a very fine breed for protection against wild
beasts. This variety is about the size of a small Newfound-
land dog, which it resembles in the head and curling tail, but
is more strongly built. It has short pricked ears, is covered
with long black hair, intermixed with tawny, and has close to
the skin a short fine fur or wool, resembling that of the shawl-
goat.[3]

[3] Vigne, ii. 149;
F. Von Hugel, ii.

The climate, in its effect on vegetation, is described by 289.
Jacquemont[4] as wonderfully resembling that of Lombardy, and [4] Corresp. ii. 80.
we consequently are not surprised at finding its flora bearing a
strong affinity to that of Europe.[5] Of the character of the vege- [5] Royle, Botany
tation, an accomplished naturalist, Dr. Royle, remarks, that there of the Himalaya.
is " so great an extension of the herbaceous parts as well as of
the flowers of plants, that many of them rival in luxuriance those
of tropical climates." Of trees, the *deodar*, or Himalayan
cedar (*cedrus deodara*), merits the first notice. Its botanical range
extends from seven thousand to twelve thousand feet above
the level of the sea, and in its most congenial locality attains
a great height and a circumference of above thirty feet.[6] [6] Royle, ut supra,
When young it closely resembles the real cedar, but never sends 245.
forth spreading branches. The cone resembles that of the cedar, 350; Hugel, ii.
and is preceded by a catkin of a bright yellow colour, so that the
tree when in full blossom appears covered with a rich mantle of
gold.[7] These catkins are loaded with a golden dust, which the [7] Id. ii. 246.
wind shakes from the branches in such quantity that the
ground, for a considerable distance about the tree, becomes
as it were sheeted with gold. So durable is its timber, that some

used in the building of one of the wooden bridges over the Jailum was found little decayed, after exposure to the weather for above [6 Moorcr. ii. 152.] four hundred years.[6] The forests of Kashmir also contain the *pinus longifolia,* and two other species of pine, a species of fir, one of yew, and one of juniper. The cypress, and a variety of *thuja,* are common in gardens, but they do not appear to be indigenous. The chunar (*platanus Orientalis*) is also considered an exotic, but is probably nowhere found more abundant or luxuriant than in Kashmir. By order of the Mogul emperors, a grove, composed of chunars and poplars, was planted in every Kashmirian village; and these, now arrived at their full growth, are among the greatest ornaments of the valley. Most of these are ascribed to the philanthropic governor of Kashmir, Ali Mirdhan Khan, who exercised his office under Shah Jehan from 1642 to 1657. So tastefully have they been disposed, that, according to Hügel, a judicious landscape-gardener could scarcely wish one to be added or removed throughout the whole valley. They are protected by a fine equal to fifty pounds sterling for each tree cut down ; but as this penalty does not reach the governor, the tasteless Sikhs have destroyed many   Hügel proves the chunar to be exotic, from the fact that it has ceased to be reproductive in this soil, and as many of the trees already exhibit symptoms of decay, the valley is likely soon to be deprived of these magnificent ornaments. The wood is highly esteemed for purposes requiring a tenacious grain. Poplars and lime-trees attain great size and luxuriance. The mountain glades produce a species of wild chesnut-tree,* which attains a size in general far exceeding that of the European variety. Hügel met with some, of which the trunk measured a hundred feet from the ground to the parting of the branches, and the total height exceeded that of the tallest pines. This author does not [1 In Vigne, ii. 458.] mention the oak. Dr. Royle[1] states, on the authority of Falconer, " that few, if any, oaks descend on the northern side of the Pir Panjal into the valley.". The maple, willow, and white thorn arc common. Birch and alder trees approach the limit of perpetual congelation, and as their trunks and branches are weighed down by deep snow for the greater part of the year, they never recede more than five feet from the surface of the steep declivities of the mountains, though their total length is generally thirty feet or more. The birch is more hardy than the

* Probably the *Castanea Indica* of Royle and Roxburgh (Royle, 345)

alder, and extends to a greater elevation. The inner bark is
called *tus*[2] by the natives, who were accustomed to write on it, [2] F. Von Hugel,
before the introduction of paper ; its present use is principally to ii. 250 ; Ayeen
furnish wrappers for packing fruit for exportation ; it is also wound Akbery, ii. 136.
round the long curved tubes of hookas. The *sanjit*, a species of
elæagnus, according to Moorcroft[3] is of "a beautiful appearance ; [3] ii. 151.
its flowers are exquisitely sweet, and its fruit, by distillation, yields
a beverage which the Chinese hold to be not inferior to that of
the grape." He states that it is plentiful in Kashmir; but
Hügel is silent on the subject, and there is reason to conclude
that it is not common. Junipers and rhododendrons grow on
the mountains at the elevation of eleven thousand feet. There
is also a species of *daphne*, and several of barberry ; one of
these last bears clusters of blue berries the size of a small plum,
and of a sweet and pleasant taste. Roses, both wild and cultivated, grow in vast profusion, besides syringa, jasmine, ivy, and a
species of smilax. Of wild plants, the most deserving of notice
are rhubarb, various kinds of *chrysanthema* and *primulæ*, and saxi-
frage, lilies, narcissuses, crocuses, irises. and a host of annuals.*
Ferns are scantily produced, but funguses abundantly, and the
edible sorts are gathered in great quantity, and form an article of
traffic. Hügel, a sound and well-informed botanist, considers Kashmir superior to all other countries in the abundance and excellence
of its fruits. Those which attain maturity are the apple, pear,
peach, apricot, plum, almond, pomegranate, mulberry, walnut,
hazel-nut, pistachio, and melon. Neither orange, lemon, nor any
other species of *citrus* arrives at maturity, though many attempts
have been made to introduce them, as .the cold of winter proves
invariably fatal to them. No mention is made by travellers of fig
or olive trees in Kashmir. The most valuable product of the uncul-
tivated vegetation is the *singhara*[2] (*trapa bispinosa*), or water-nut, [2] Royle, Botany
which grows on the bottom of the Wulur lake in such quantity that 211 ; F. Von Hu-
sixty thousand tons are raised every year, affording subsistence gel, ii. 278 ;
to twenty thousand persons. These nuts are eaten raw, boiled, Forster, Jour.
roast, or ground into flour, and made into gruel, and though in- Beng. Eng. ii. 83.
sipid, are so nutritious that those who live exclusively on them, are
in no respect inferior in strength or condition to the rest of the

---

* Much valuable information is given on this subject by Royle in his great
work on the Botany of the Himalayas, and in his Appendix to Vigne's
Kashmir.

population, and find this diet so agreeable to their constitution, that they sicken if obliged to have recourse to any other. The inhabitants consider this nut so great a blessing, that they attribute its introduction to Lacshoni, the goddess of prosperity. As the superficial extent of Wulur lake is about one hundred square miles, it supports two hundred persons to the square mile, or a number shewing a relative density of population greater than that of France. The *Nymphœa lotus*, or Egyptian water-lily (*nelumbium speciosum*), adorns the City Lake, and most other standing waters, with its foliage and large poppy-like rose-coloured flowers.[3] The beans which it bears are regarded as a delicacy when eaten unripe, and the leaf-stalks are consumed in great quantities, being boiled till tender, in which state they are both a palatable and nutritious food.[4] As the flowers and leaves are never covered by water, it is regarded by the Hindoos as a mystic emblem of the reappearance of the world after having been submerged beneath the ocean. Hence it is viewed with the utmost reverence,[5] and its introduction attributed to the deity Vishnu. Rice is the principal crop, and the staple article of diet in Kashmir. It is cultivated with great skill and corresponding success, in consequence of the fertility of the soil, the facility of irrigation, and the warmth of the summer. The returns are from thirty to forty fold, and in favourable seasons sometimes as high as fifty or sixty.[6] The other sorts of grain cultivated are wheat, barley, millet, maize; but in consequence of the scanty rains in summer, the produce is both precarious and small, being often only twofold. Gram and other kinds of pulse, buck-wheat, and amaranth (*celosia cristata*), are also extensively cultivated. Artificial floating gardens are common on the City Lake, where they produce abundant crops of fine cucumbers and melons. For forming these islands, choice is made of a shallow part of the lake, overgrown with reeds and other aquatic plants, which are cut off about two feet below the surface, and then pressed close to each other without otherwise disturbing the position in which they grew. They are subsequently mowed down nearly to the surface, and the parts thus taken off are spread evenly over the floats, and covered with a thin layer of mud drawn up from the bottom; on the level thus formed, are arranged, close to each other, conical heaps of weeds, about two feet across and two feet high, having each at top a small

[3] Royle, Botany of the Himalaya, 65.

[4] Id. 65; P. Von Hugel, ii. 284; Moorcr. ii. 137.

[5] P. Von Hugel, Ibid.; Vigne, II. 331.

[6] P Von Hugel, ii 272; Moorcr. ii 135.

hcllow filled with fresh mud. In each hollow are set three plants of cucumber or melon, and no farther care or trouble is required but to gather the produce, which is invariably fine and abundant. Each bed is about two yards wide; the length is variable; the bed is kept in its place by a stake of willow sent through it at each end and driven into the bottom of the lake. The melons produced in this way are obviously wholesome, as those who live entirely on them during the season soon become fat.[7] Tobacco is cultivated to a very limited extent;[8] cotton (*gossypium herbaceum*), more largely, for the manufacture of cloth, both for home consumption and exportation. Kashmir supplies most of Hindostan with saffron: it is produced almost exclusively in the district of Pampur, on the right bank of the Jailum, from three distinct varieties of crocus; the root of one sort continues productive for fifteen years; of another, for eight; of the third, for five.[9] As vegetable oil is a favourite article of diet with the Kashmirians, sesame, mustard, flax, hempseed, and some others, are cultivated for the purpose of obtaining it. Wild hemp, or *bang*, is used for its inebriating qualities. Those addicted to it, either smoke the dried blossoms or swallow confections or decoctions of the resinous secretion with which it abounds.[1] The climate, soil, and disposition of the surface in Kashmir, appear well suited for bringing the grape to maturity; but as the management neither of the vine nor of its produce is well understood there, the wine made is very poor.[2] This inferiority is probably the result of the prohibition of fermented beverages during the Mahometan sway, which preceded that of the Sikhs. At present, vinegar and brandy, as well as wine, are obtained from grapes. There is great variety and abundance of esculent vegetables,—the kidney-bean, turnip, cabbage, beet-root, radish, capsicum;[3] and Hugel enumerates fifteen different sorts not known in Europe.[4] Grass is stored for winter fodder by being formed into thick ropes and hung on the branches of trees.[5] The leaves and small branches of walnut, willow, mulberry, elm and many other trees, are cut in their most succulent and luxuriant state, and packed in the forks and between the large branches, and thus preserved to the severe part of winter. The cattle greedily eat this provender, which is considered more warming and nutritious than any other.[6] Clover[7] and the *prangos* are largely used for winter fodder. Though mulberry trees abound,

[7] Moorcr. ii. 144.
[8] F. Von Hugel, ii. 277.
[9] Id 275.
[1] Id. ii. 282.
[2] Moorcr. ii 151.
[3] Roylo, Botany of Himalaya, 27.
[4] F. Von Hugel, ii. 269.
[5] Moorcr. ii. 153.
[6] Id. ibid.
[7] Royle, Botany of the Himalaya, 29.

and the climate well suits the silkworm, very little silk is produced.

The most celebrated manufacture of Kashmir is that of shawls. The wool used for this purpose is of two kinds : one called *pashm shal* (or shawl wool), and obtained from the tame goat ; the other, the fleece of the wild goat, wild sheep, and other animals, named *asali tus.** In all instances it is a fine down, growing close to the skin under the common coat, and is found not only on the animals just mentioned, but also on the yak or grunting ox, and on the dog of the intensely cold and arid tracts of Tibet.[8] The greater part is supposed to be produced in Chan Than, a tract in the west of Tibet, and is in the first instance sold at Rodokh, a fort near the frontier towards Ladakh, to which it is conveyed on the backs of sheep, there usually employed as beasts of burden. It is purchased by the Kashmirians at Le, the chief place of. Ladakh, and carried thence to Kashmir, either on men's shoulders or on the backs of horses. There is also some brought by Moguls from Pamir, or from the vicinity of Yarkund.[9] About a third of the quantity imported is dark-coloured, and the price of this is little more than one-half that of the white, in consequence of the latter being better suited for dyeing. At the time of Vigne's visit, the white sort sold at the rate of about four shillings a pound. The long hairs are picked out by the hand, and this is of course a very tedious process. The residue is carefully washed, rice-flour being used as an abstergent instead of soap, and then hand-spun by women, who are stated by Moorcroft[1] not to earn more than half-a-crown a month by incessant toil. There is much division of labour in this manufacture : one artisan designs the patterns, another determines the quality and quantity of the thread required for executing them, a third apportions and arranges the warp and woof (the former of which is generally of silk) for the border. Three weavers are employed on an embroidered shawl, of an ordinary pattern, for three months; but a very rich pair will occupy a shop for eighteen months. They are dyed in yarn, and carefully washed after the weaving has been finished. The Kashmirian dyers profess to use sixty-four differ-

* Vigne, ii. 124.

9 Moorcr. ii. 166.

1 ii. 173.

1 ii. 165.
2 ii. 305.

* Such is the account of Moorcroft,[1] who must be allowed to be the highest authority on the subject. Bernier is censured by Hugel[2] for calling the wool *tour* but his criticism seems erroneous.

ent tints, and some of these are obtained by extracting the
colours of European woollens, imported for the express purpose.
The embroidered border of the finest shawls is generally made
separately, and joined skilfully by sewing to the field or middle
part. According to Hügel,[2] shawls of this description are alto- [2] ii. 310.
gether patchwork, consisting of as many as fifteen pieces, joined
by seams. The charge incurred for bringing a pair of fine
shawls to market is thus stated by Hügel — for the labour
of twenty-four artisans, for twelve months, 80*l.*; materials
and dyeing, 30*l.*; duty, 70*l.*; charges of the establishment
20*l.*; total, 200*l.* The highest price mentioned by Moor-
croft,[3] for any fabric of this kind, is 700*l.* He states the total [3] ii. 191.
annual value of the shawls manufactured in Kashmir at 300,000*l.*
The amount is now much less, the diminution having resulted
from several causes. Hügel computes that 13,000 weavers
perished, in the course of a few years, from cholera and famine.
Great numbers have emigrated to avoid the intolerable oppression
practised by the Sikhs in the valley. The demand also for shawls
has much diminished in Hindostan, where British officers have to
a great extent superseded the class of natives with whom
this sort of manufacture was in chief demand. The reduced
prosperity of the Ottoman and Persian nations has also greatly
contracted the demand from those quarters. In Europe the taste
for these costly articles is on the wane, and even in India shawls
of British manufacture are beginning to displace those of
Kashmir. To give full effect to these various causes of decay,
the Sikh governors, with short-sighted rapacity, have so completely wrung capital from the merchants and manufacturers that
they are destitute of means to carry on the process of production.
The manufacture neither of sheep's-wool, cotton, nor silk, appears at any time to have been extensive. Kashmir has been long
famous for gun and pistol barrels. The artisans employ extraordinary pains, care, and time in the process of fabricating them,
and succeed in producing work of great beauty and excellence
and of various kinds—plain, twisted, or damasked. The iron employed is that brought from Bajour, in the Eusufzai country, and,
though loaded with impurities, in consequence of the rude mode
of smelting practised in the first instance, it is sold in Kashmir [4] Jour. As. Soc. 1841, p. 83, Drummond on Min. Resources of Afg.
for three times the price of that raised in the valley, or the neigh-
bouring mountains, and by suitable processes is rendered a mate-

rial of great purity, tenacity, and strength.* This manufacture, like all others, has much decayed under the domination of the Sikhs, who are furnished with arms from Lahore. The Kashmirians manufacture excellent leather for saddlery. Moorcroft[5] describes it as " strong, solid, heavy, and pliable, without any disposition to crack ; some of the pieces had been in use eighteen or twenty years, and were none the worse for constant wear." The paper of Kashmir is the finest manufactured in India,[6] its superiority consisting in its great smoothness and whiteness. The inferior qualities are made of rags, ropes, and sacking; the finest, of the filaments of wild hemp. These materials are reduced to pulp, under hammers worked by water-power, and the sheet of paper is formed on a fine mat instead of wire-work ; it is then pumiced, receives a thin coat of rice-paste, and is finally polished very carefully with an agate. It is very dear, a quire of twenty-four sheets of the finest costing from five to six shillings. There are seven or eight hundred copiers of MSS. in Kashmir. They are wretchedly remunerated, the best not earning more than threepence per day, and the results of their labour may be had for a very low price. Thus a copy of the Shah Nameh, which contains sixty thousand distichs, costs only seven or eight pounds sterling.[7] The lacquered-ware of Kashmir is very fine, comprising bedsteads, seats of various kinds, cabinets, boxes, pencases, and similar articles, tastefully painted and ornamented with foil and overlaid with a fine hard varnish.[8] The lapidaries of Kashmir have produced specimens of their skill and taste far superior to any in Europe. They principally work in the rock crystal and chalcedony of Iskardo ; and Hügel[9] saw a vase of the former material, which four men could scarcely lift; but this branch of elegant industry is fast disappearing amidst the depression and misery produced by Sikh oppression. The essential oil, or celebrated attar, of roses,† made in Kashmir, is considered superior to any other; a circumstance not surprising, as, according to Hügel,[1] the flower is here produced of surpassing fragrance as well as beauty. A large quantity of rose-water twice distilled is allowed to run off into an open vessel, placed over night in a cool running stream, and in the morning the oil is

[5] ii. 214.

[6] Jacquemont, Voyage, 204; F. Von Hugel, 328; Moorer. ii. 217.

[7] Jacquemont, v. 211.

[8] F. Von Hugel, 328 ; Moorcroft, ii. 215.

[9] ii. 328.

[1] ii. 329.

---

* The ingenious process by which those admirable fire-arms are made is given very fully and satisfactorily by Moorcroft.

† Vulgarly called otto of roses.

ii. 195-213.

found floating on the surface in minute specks, which are taken off very carefully by means of a blade of the sword-lily. When cool, it is of a dark-green colour, and as hard as resin, not becoming liquid at a temperature below that of boiling water. Between five hundred and six hundred pounds weight of leaves are required to produce one ounce of the attar. It is never an article of commerce, being reserved for the use of the Sikh court; and that which is known in Europe under the name of Persian is a very inferior article to the produce of Kashmir. The species used for distillation is the *Rosa biflora*. Some other fragrant oils are also made in Kashmir. There is an inconsiderable manufacture of glass, producing a few bottles, small mirrors, and other trifling articles.

The Kashmirians have a strong natural bias to commerce, but this has been almost utterly crushed by their unfortunate political circumstances. Hügel estimates the total value of the exports at 400,000*l.*, which he thus apportions : woollens of all kinds, 250,000*l.* ; rice, 100,000*l.* ; other articles, 50,000*l.* The imports he values at 50,000*l.* ; of which, the value of the shawl wool is 34,000*l.* The enormous excess of exports over imports would be regarded by a political economist of the old school as evidence of great prosperity ; but it is in reality the amount wrung from the industry and talent of the natives by the rapacity of the Sikhs. The commercial intercourse is principally with Ladakh, Afghanistan, the Punjab, and the remoter parts of Hindostan. So vigorous and efficient are the measures of the Sikhs, in matters of police, that open robbery is unknown, and two or three men can conduct in safety a string of twenty ponies laden with merchandise.[1] The weights most in use are—   [1] P. Von Hügel.

1 Kurwar	... ...	= 16 Tarock.
1 Tarock	... ...	6 Pau.
1 Pau	... ...	74 Tola.

The kurwar is equal to one hundred and ninety-seven pounds twelve ounces avoirdupois.* The Kashmirians do not use either dry or liquid measures, weighing not only grain and similar articles but even fluids.†

* The weights of Kashmir do not appear to be given either by Prinsep (Tables), or Kelly (Oriental Metrology) ; the appreciation of them in the text is from Hügel.   ii. 140.

† Runjeet, in his carousals, used to drink by weight. (Burnes' Bokhara, i. 30.)

The measures of length are the—

Kro ... ... = 10 Tenab.

Tenab ... ... 400 Guz.

[2] F. Von Hügel, ii. 242. The Guz contains thirty-three inches,[2] and consequently the kro is equal to eleven thousand feet, or two miles one hundred and forty-six yards.

Superficial measures are the—

Bega... ... ... = 900 Danda.

Danda ... ... 4 Square Guz.

Calculations are universally made in the decimal notation and Arabic cipher.

The currency consists of a great variety of coins struck at different times and under various authorities. The gold *mohur* of Runjeet Singh is worth fifteen *Nanakshi rupees*, each equal to a *sicca rupee*.* The Herat *dinar* is worth six of the same denomination of rupee. The Iskardo *hun* is a small, thin, gold coin worth 1·6 sicca rupee. The Kabool rupee is equal in value to the sicca; the rupee of Hari Sing, 1·4 of the sicca. The *anna* is the money of account, and the sicca rupee is worth sixteen of them. The *anna* contains five *pau*, the *pau* twenty *ganda*, the *ganda* four *kouri;* the ganda is actually an almond, the kouri the small shell (*cypræa moneta*), so well known in semi-civilized commerce. There is the utmost confusion in the copper currency; in the names, forms, and value of which there is almost endless diversity, and coins of very remote ages and countries are found in [3] Jour. Beng. Ind. ii. 32. the bazaars. According to Forster,[3] the revenue,† in his time (1783), amounted to between 200,000*l.* and 300,000*l.* Elphin [4] Acc. of Caubul, 507. stone,[4] about thirty years after, states it at nearly 500,000*l.* [5] ii. 127. Moorcroft,[5] in 1823, estimated it at 290,000*l.*, besides a considerable sum extorted fraudulently from the people. In 1836, [6] ii. 351. Hügel[6] estimated the revenue at from 200,000*l.* to 220,000*l.* ; but adds that if the country had a short respite from oppression the amount would soon increase to 340,000*l.* from the following sources :—

Government share of the produce of the soil and
of the *singhara* nut £284,000

House-tax in Kashmir 20,000

* The sicca rupee is of the value of 2*s.* 0½*d.* (E.I.C.'s Records.)

[font] ii 240. † In the Ayeen Akbery, an account is given of the revenue, but Abul Fazel is there inconsistent with himself and altogether unintelligible.

Tax on boats		5,800
Duty on shawls and other woollens		25,000
Monopolies `		2,200
Tribute from neighbouring petty powers ...		3,000

The annual expenditure amounts to about 115,000*l*., which would consequently leave 225,000*l*. to be transmitted to the Maha Raja of the Punjab, but it is supposed that latterly he has not been able to draw 100,000*l*. annually.[7] The government of [7] Vigne. ii. 119. Kashmir, since its conquest by the Sikhs in 1819, has been conducted by an officer of that nation, as a representative of the authority of the Punjab. He has under his command two regiments amounting in the aggregate to about fifteen hundred men. The nominal pay of a private is sixteen shillings a month, with arms and ammunition and a red frock every year. A lieutenant has three pounds a month, a captain four, the commanding officer fifty.[8] [8] F. Von Hugel. The pay, however, is very irregularly disbursed; Vigne[9] men- [9] ii. 119. tions that one regiment had not been paid for fourteen years.

The greater part of the population are Mahometans, of whom the Sunis, or those considered the orthodox class, are much more numerous than the Shias, or votaries of Ali. All the Afghans, and those descended from that people, are Sunis, the Shias are generally either Persians or of Persian descent. There are also a few of the mystic Mahometan sectarians called Sufis. The Sikhs do not allow[1] the *muezzin* to [1] F. Von Hugel, intonate from the mosque the solemn call which summons the [1] ii. 382. people to prayers, in countries where the Mahometans have the supremacy. All the Hindoos of Kashmir are Brahmins, who are, in a physical point of view, distinguished from the rest of the population by darker complexions, a circumstance the reverse of that observable in other parts of India, throughout which that caste is remarkable for the comparative lightness of their hue. The native Brahmins in Kashmir informed Hügel, that subsequently to the establishment of Mahometanism, the number of their caste was by oppression reduced to eleven, and that it was recruited by the settlement of 400[2] Brahminical families from [2] Id. ii. 305. the dark-complexioned natives of the Deccan. Their number is at present estimated at 25,000. Their only visible object of worship is the *linga*, though there are various other idols in Kashmir set up by foreign Hindoo pilgrims. The Mahometan rulers prohibited *satis*, or widows from being burned with the corpses of their husband: there have been a few instances of these revolting murders since the Sikh con-

³ Vigne, ii. 151.

quest.³   The Sikh population consists almost exclusively of the troops and the followers of the governor, and the entire number does not exceed two thousand.   All classes of Kashmirians are remarkably superstitious.   They visit in pilgrimage numerous places of reputed sanctity, and they firmly believe in the existence of various supernatural beings, resembling in character the fairies, satyrs, and similar phantoms, which haunt

⁴ Id. i. 328-330;
F. Von Hugel, ii.
378-380.

the imagination of the credulous in other countries.⁴

⁵ ii. 141.

The Kashmirians probably excel all other branches of the great Indian nation in physical qualities. Vigne ⁵ describes the men as of " broad Herculean build and manly features;" Moorcroft regards the aboriginal race as in general tall and of symmetrical proportions, and adds that amongst the peasantry " are to be found figures of robust and muscular make, such as might have served for models

⁶ ii. 128.
⁷ Acc. of Caubul,
506.
⁸ Jour. Beng. Ind.
ii. 2.,.

of the Farnesan Hercules." ⁶   Elphinstone ⁷ and Forster ⁸ also bear evidence to their athletic and finely proportioned conformation. The porters in the service of Hügel carried each a burden of above a hundred pounds, besides his bed, cooking utensils, and provisions for eight or ten days; and one of them, without complaining, carried over the Pir Panjal a load considered too heavy

⁹ F. Von Hugel,
ii. 428.
¹ ii. 153.
² ii. 430.

for a mule.⁹   Forster expresses himself rather disparagingly respecting the beauty of the females; but Vigne¹ and Hügel ² represent them as having full-formed symmetrical figures, being light brunettes in complexion, with regular and beautiful features, blooming cheeks, fine white teeth, and large, clear, dark eyes. These attractions make them in great request in the Punjab and adjacent parts of Hindostan, where they are frequently found as dancing girls or inmates of the harem.   They have generally aquiline noses, and bear so strong a resemblance to the Jews, as to induce Bernier to maintain them to be sprung from the lost tribes of Israel.

Vigne, i. 325;
Moorcr. ii. 128.

Lively, ingenious, witty, and good-humoured,³ the Kashmirians are much addicted to the never-failing vices of slaves, lying and

⁴ Forster, ii. 26.

trickery, and inordinately devoted to amusement and pleasure.⁴ Moorcroft, engaged against them in a course of commercial rivalry, shews no mercy in delineating their moral qualities :—" In character, the Kashmirian is selfish, superstitious, ignorant, supple, intriguing, dishonest, and false ; he has great ingenuity as a mechanic, and a decided genius for manufactures and commerce, but his transactions are always conducted in a fraudulent spirit, equalled only by the effrontery with which he faces detection."[5] [5] Moorcr. ii. 128. Hügel[6] describes them as venal, dishonest, and dreadfully ad- [6] ii. 431-433. dicted to sexual immorality, the diseases resulting from which nowhere appear in more numerous or appalling forms.* Among their most estimable qualities is their remarkable aversion to shedding blood; and hence crimes of violence are almost unknown.[7] Though at a remote period of their history not devoid [7] F. Von Hugel, ii. 429. of martial qualities, a long course of oppression seems to have so broken their spirit, that they never entertain the notion of throwing off the foreign yoke which so frightfully afflicts them.

The dress of both sexes is very simple, consisting of a long loose wrapper and trousers, the former of woollen cloth.[8] In cold weather both sexes carry a small wicker basket, [8] Moorcr. ii. 131. containing an iron or earthenware vessel about five inches in diameter, holding lighted charcoal. This contrivance, which is called a *kangri*,[9] is carried within the dress, and applied to such [9] F. Von Hugel, ii. 397; Vigne, i. parts of the body as require to be warmed. Very severe burns 317. are sometimes caused by this practice, and invariably the skin suffers a discoloration which never can be effaced. In hot weather the whole female population repair twice a day to the nearest water, and, placing on their heads their simple costume in the form of a rude turban, bathe, without the slightest covering or precaution, before all who may happen to be in view.[1] [1] F. Von Hugel, ii. 399.

The population is calculated at present not to exceed 200,000 persons,[2] to which number it has been in twenty years reduced from [2] Id. ii. 358. 800,000 by the awful dispensations of earthquake, pestilence, and famine. In 1828 a dreadful earthquake destroyed 1,200 persons, and was in two months followed by the cholera, by which 100,000 perished in the course of forty days.[3] In 1833, an unseasonable [3] F. Von Hugel, ii. 213. fall of snow caused the failure of four-fifths of the rice crop. The roads were covered with the corpses of those who perished of want in attempting to emigrate. Parents frequently sold a child for a rupee to prolong existence for two or three days; mothers killed and devoured their own offspring. Pestilence followed; and from these successive calamities resulted the almost unexampled depopulation stated above. The population of the

* This, however, seems hardly reconcilable with the testimony borne by this author, as well as others, to the strength and beauty of the Kashmirians.

⁴ Acc. of Caubul, 507.
⁵ F. Von Hugel, ii. 221, 258.
capital, Serinagur, which was estimated by Elphinstone ⁴ at from 150,000 to 200,000, is now not more than 40,000.⁵ The other towns, besides the capital, are Islamabad, Shupeyon, Pampur, Sopur, Bijbahar, Baramula, Shahbad. The country was formerly considered to consist of two parts, Eastern Kashmir, or Merraj,
⁶ Ayeen Akbery, ii. 150.
and Western, or Kamraj ;⁶ but this division has become obsolete. It is at present subdivided into thirty-six * pergunnahs or dis-
⁷ F. Von Hugel, ii. 206 ; Moorer.
ii. 113 ; Vigne, ii. 272.
⁸ Ayeen Akbery, ii. 136 ; Adelung
Mithrirdat, i. 195 ;
Forster, Jour.
Beng. Eng. ii. 23 ;
Vigne, Kashmir,
i. 368 ; ii. 430;
Jour. As. Soc.
1841, p. 1038,
Edgworth on
Cashmiri Lan-
guage.
tricts.⁷

The language of Kashmir is a dialect of Sanscrit,⁸ and is written in the Devanagari character. It contains a large admixture of Persian, in which the records and correspondence of government are written. The pronunciation of the Kashmirians is remarkably broad, coarse, and uncouth ; and the Sikh commanders cause those who wish to enlist to pronounce certain words as a means of ascertaining whether the proposed recruits be Kashmirians, as these are rejected.

Kashmir abounds in monuments of a peculiar style, generally indicating very remote antiquity, and clearly referable to a period previous to the Mahometan invasion. Nearly all have been reduced to obscure and shapeless ruins, and the work of demolition is generally ascribed to a native of the valley, a fanatical convert from Brahminism to Islam, who was born A.D. 1350, and, in 1396, returned home with an order, as it is said,
¹ F. Von Hugel, ii. 435.
from Tamerlane ¹ to destroy all the temples which throughout Kashmir were dedicated to the worship of idols. His zeal and perseverance are recorded by the huge blocks of marble which in many places still attest the size and massive style of the edifices which he is alleged to have destroyed ; and his memory is famous among Mussulmans under the name of Secunder Budh Shikan, or Alexander the Iconoclast ; but the fact that Tamerlane was never master of Kashmir appears to throw doubt on the story of his commission and achievements. A few buildings at the south-eastern extremity of the valley escaped the general destruction, by whomsoever perpetrated ; but they have suffered so much from earthquakes, and from the removal of materials to be employed in other erections, that only one remains in sufficient per-
² Kaschmir, ii. 452.
³ i. 385.
⁴ Punj. Buᵏh. ii. 254.
Ayeen Akbery, ii. 150.
fection to give an adequate impression of the early architecture of Kashmir. This ruin, called Korau Pandau by Hügel,² the Temple of Martund by Vigne,³ Khana Panduwa by Moorcroft,⁴

* Abul Fazel states thirty-eight or forty-one.

and Srinaghur by Jacquemont,[5] is situate two miles north-east of ⁵ Voyage, v. 248. Islamabad, on an eminence rising from the surface of a *Karywah*, or elevated table-land of alluvial earth, and which, in the present depopulation of Kashmir, is nearly uninhabited. The great size of the blocks of hard black marble, from six to nine feet in length, the excellence of the cement, and general massiveness of the proportions, might seem calculated to have secured this edifice from the partial ruin to which it has been reduced, probably by earthquakes. The intelligent and well-informed travellers just referred to agree that no building ever excited in them a stronger sensation of the sublime—in this instance, unconnected with size, as the structure is not of very large dimensions. Of all orders of architecture known in Europe, it appears most to resemble the Tuscan, with perhaps some admixture of the heavy Saxon. It is briefly sketched by Vigne in the following words :— " At present all that remains of the Pandu Koru, or Temple of Martund, consists of a central and rectangular building, surrounded by a court, or quadrangle, and rectangular colonnade, facing inwards. The length of the outer side of the wall, which is blank, is about ninety yards, that of the front is about fifty-six. The remains of three gateways opening into the court are now standing." " There are twenty pillars of the colonnade along the inside of the wall now remaining out of more than double that number. The height of the shaft of each pillar is six feet, of the capital twenty inches, and of the base two feet."[6] The height of ⁶ Vigne, i. 387. this enclosing wall is about fifteen feet, the thickness six. In the middle of this court is the temple, about sixty feet long, thirty wide, and forty high. It is probable that it was formerly much higher, as there are indications of its having been surmounted by a pyramidal roof of stone, the solid fragments of which are now scattered over the ground, where they were probably thrown by an earthquake. Of the era and object of this building there is no certain knowledge ; some consider it of Buddhist, some of Hindoo, origin. Hügel supposes it to have been intended for enshrining the *Linga*.

The early history of Kashmir, which lies rather within the province of the oriental antiquarian than the limits of the present work, has been drawn from darkness and methodized by the varied learning and cultivated judgment of Professor Wilson.* Still there is much uncertainty regarding it until the reign of Shums-ud-Din, who ascended the throne in 1315,[9] and introduced Mahometanism. In 1586 † the country was conquered by the Mogul emperor Akbar, and became an integral part of his vast empire.[1] In 1752 [2] it was subjugated by the Afghan Ahmed Shah, the founder of the Durani empire, and remained under Afghan sway until 1819,[3] when it was conquered by the Sikhs, and since that time has been ruled by a governor appointed by the Maharajah of the Punjab.

KASIEN, in Afghanistan, a village on the route from Ghuznee to Kohat, and seventy-five miles east of the former town. Lat. 33° 36', long. 69° 30'.

KASIMPOOR.— A village in the Punjab, situate on the road from Ferozepoor to Ramnuggur; thirty-six miles south of the latter place, and thirty-two miles south-west of Lahore. Lat. 31° 52', long. 73° 50'.

KASON, in Sinde, a village situate nine miles from the left bank of the Indus, and twenty-six north-east of Hyderabad. Lat. 25° 42', long. 68° 32'.

KASSYE GOPANG, in Sinde, a town on the route from Hyderabad to Sehwan, by the way of Kotree, and twenty-eight miles north of Hyderabad. It is situate on the right bank of the Indus in a fertile and well-cultivated country. The road in this part of the route is occasionally cut up by water-courses, and in some parts liable to be swampy in time of inundation. Lat. 25° 46', long. 68° 22'.

KASUNKA, in Bhawlpoor, a village situate four miles from the left bank of the Ghara river. Lat. 30° 5', long. 73°.

KATACHEE, in Afghanistan, a village about eighty miles north-east of Subzawur, and nearly the same distance south-east of Herat. Lat. 33° 49', long. 63° 20'.

KATAIKE.—A village of north-eastern Bhawlpoor, situate on the left bank of the Ghara river, in lat. 30° 15', long. 73° 20'.

KATAKCHUND, or KARTAKSHE, as it is called by Moorcroft, in Bultistan or Little Tibet, is a town with a fort on

Side notes:
[9] Ferishta, iv. 451; Ayeen Akbery, ii. 155.
[1] Ferishta, iv. 530.
[2] Elph. Acc. of Caubul, 548.
[3] P. Von Hugel, ii. 151.
E.I.C. Ms. Doc.
E.I.C. Ms. Doc.
E.I.C. Ms. Doc.
E.I.C. Ms. Doc.
E.I.C. Ms. Doc.
E.I.C. Ms. Doc.
Map of N.W. Frontier.
Vigne, Kashmir, ii. 325; Moorcr. Punj. Bokh. i. 262.

* See his History of Kashmir, As. Res. xv., pp. 1—120; also Prinsep's Tables, 101—104.

† In the Ayeen Akbery this conquest is stated as having taken place under Humaion, 1570.

ii. 169.

the right or north bank of the Indus, here called the Sinh-kha-bah. Previously to the recent conquest of this country by the Sikhs, this town belonged to the raja, the nephew of the sovereign of Bultistan. The inhabitants are remarkable for their zeal as Shia Mussulmans. Lat. 34° 52', long. 76° 10'.

KATAWAS, in Afghanistan, a village situate on the route E.I.C. Ms. Doc. from Ghuznee to Dera Ismail Khan through the Gomul Pass. Lat. 33° 3', long. 68° 30'.

KATEYCHEE-KE-GHURREE, in Afghanistan, a fort in the E.I.C. Ms. Doc. mountainous tract between Hurrund and Kahun, and twenty-six miles east of the last-mentioned place. It is situate on the left bank of the torrent or river of Illiassee, and is well supplied with water and forage. Lat. 29° 14', long. 69° 44'.

KATIA, in Sinde, a village on the route from Omercote to E.I.C. Ms. Doc. Nuggur Parker, and twenty miles south-east of Omercote. Lat. 25° 7', long. 70° 2'.

KATOR, in Sinde, a town situate on the route from Bukkur E.I.C. Ms. Doc.; Corresp. on Sinde, to Omercote, near the right bank of the eastern Narra river. 498. Lat. 26° 51', long. 69°.

KAUHEE.—See BOLAN RIVER (and BOLAN PASS, p. 109).

KEDJE, or KEDGE, in Beloochistan, the capital of the pro- Belooch. 303. vince of Mekran, is situate on the Mooleanee river, which more to the north is called the Badoor, farther south the Bhugwar, and subsequently the Dustee. The river here is described by Pottinger as an abundant and never-failing stream. The fort of Kedje is built on a high precipice, on the left or eastern bank of the river, and its site is so defensible and strong by nature, that the natives consider it impregnable. The town entirely sur-rounds three sides of the base of the eminence on which the fort stands. It once contained three thousand houses, and car-ried on a brisk trade with Kandahar, Kelat, Shikarpoor, and the landing-place on the coast of Beloochistan ; but, as of late years the Khan of Kelat has failed to protect commerce and pro-perty here, the place has much decayed, and the Hindoos and other opulent traders have removed elsewhere. It is governed by a chief, who formerly was subject to the Khan of Kelat, but has for some time ceased to pay him even nominal obedience. The revenues are very trifling, and the governor's armed force consists merely of a few hundred Arabs. The adjacent district also bears the name of Kedje. Lat. 26° 20' long. 62° 15'.

KEDYWAREE, in Sinde, is the mouth of an offset from the right or western side of the Sata, or great eastern branch of the Indus. It is broad and shallow, and is little frequented except for the purpose of cutting firewood; yet is of importance, as since the closing of the Hujamree branch it appears to be the only navigable channel, except the Kookewaree, for gaining access from the sea to the main stream of the Indus. Lat. 24° 7', long. 67° 28'.

KEECHREE.—A small town of Cutch Gundava, on the route from Larkhana to Gundava. It is situated at the base of a rocky, rugged, and bare range of hills, is well supplied with water, and has a bazaar. Lat. 27° 56', long. 67° 31'.

KEEHAL, in Afghanistan, a village of the Daman, between Dera Ghazee Khan and Mittunkote, and thirty-five miles south of the former town. It is situate on the right bank of the Indus, in a tract enclosed between an offset of that river and the main channel. Lat. 29° 35', long. 70° 53'.

KEEHAL, in the Punjab, a village situate on the left bank of the Indus, about thirty miles south-east of Dera Ghazee Khan. Lat. 29° 41', long. 70° 55'.

KEER, in Sinde, a village situate on the right bank of the Indus. Lat. 27° 31', long. 68° 19'.

KEERTAR.—A range of mountains of inconsiderable height, in the western part of Sinde, being an offset of the great Hala range farther west. Their average height is probably below two thousand feet; but neither as to dimensions nor in a geological point of view have they been well explored. They lie between lat. 25° 50'—26° 40', and about the meridian line of long. 67° 40'.

KEERTEE, in Sinde, a village situate in the Little Desert, twenty miles from the north boundary of the Great Western Rin. Lat. 24° 30', long. 69° 51'.

KEEWA.—See KHEEWA.

KEHCHEE.—See KEECHREE.

KELAL, in the Punjab, a village situate about three miles from the right bank of the Chenaub river, and sixty miles north-east of Mooltan. • Lat. 30° 56', long. 71° 59'.

KELAT, a small province of Beloochistan, is bounded on the north, north-east, and west by Sarawan, and south and south-east by Jhalawan. It lies between lat. 28° 32'—29° 12' long. 65° 25'—66° 50', is a hundred miles long, forty

miles broad, and contains about two thousand square miles
of surface. Though the smallest of the provinces of Beloochistan, it is the most important, as it contains the capital
and almost the only place in the country which deserves
the name of a town. The elevation is very great, that of
the town of Kelat being 6,000[1] feet, and no part of the [1] E.I.C. Ms. Doc.
province having probably a less height than 5,000 feet;
hence the cold in winter is so severe, that the Khan and
all who can afford it migrate at that season to the low and
warm plain of Gundava.[2] Pottinger thus describes the climate [2] Pott. Belooch. 321.
of the province of Kelat: "The heat is at no time unplea-
santly great, unless it may be a few days at the close of
summer; but, on the other hand, the cold is intense during
the winter and attended by a north-easterly wind, that blowing without intermission, and sometimes with extreme violence, not only through that season, but the spring months,
brings with it heavy falls of snow, sleet, and rain."[3] During the [3] Ut supra, 319.
stay at Kelat of the traveller just cited it snowed incessantly for
fifteen days in February, and he ascertained that the frost sets in
early in October and continues to March. This surprising severity of climate takes place in a latitude nearly the same as that
of Delhi, of the Canary Islands, and of the great sultry Desert
of Africa.

KELAT, the chief place of the province of the same name,
and the capital of Beloochistan, is situate on the eastern acclivity
of a hill called Shah Mirdan. The town is in the form of an irregular quadrangle,[1] six hundred yards long from north to south, [1] Outram, Rough
three hundred yards wide from east to west, and is commanded by Notes, Plan, 186;
Masson, Bal. Afg.
the citadel, built on an eminence on the west side, and enclosed Panj. ii. 96;
Pott. Belooch. 48;
within the wall of the town. This wall is of mud, about twenty Jackson, 17.
feet high, flanked with bastions, and pierced with innumerable
loopholes for musketry, but not strong enough to be mounted
with heavy cannon. It has three gates; one on the north,
another on the east, another on the south side. The residence of
the Khan is within the precincts of the citadel, and is an irregular collection of mud buildings with flat terrace roofs. The houses
of the town are wretchedly built of mud, strengthened by wooden
frames, and the streets are filthy in the extreme. The bazaar is
well supplied with wares and provisions, which are cheap and of
excellent quality. There are two suburbs outside the walls, one

on the west, the other on the south side. Fine water is supplied
abundantly from a spring which issues in a very copious stream

from the hill over the town. The water, according to Pottinger,[2]
is warm previously to sunrise; then it becomes excessively
cold.

Kelat has some little transit and retail trade, and a few
coarse manufactures; the principal being the making of matchlocks,

swords, and spears.[3] It is the seat of the government (such
as it is) of Beloochistan. On the advance of the army of
the Indus through the Bolan Pass, in March 1839, Mehrab
Khan, the ruler of Beloochistan, was considered to evince such
hostile feeling towards the British, as required that he should
be chastised, and rendered incapable of future mischief; and
in the following November, on the return of the Bombay column
from Kabool to Sinde, Major-General Willshire was detached
from Quetta against Kelat. One of the gates was knocked in
by the fire of two of the horse-artillery guns which accompanied

the force,[4] and the town and citadel immediately stormed, the
Khan being killed fighting sword in hand, and with him above
four hundred of his troops : nearly all the rest, amounting to
about two thousand men, were made prisoners. The British
force, on this occasion, consisted of 1,261 men, and six horse-
artillery guns. Their loss was thirty-one killed, and a hundred and seven wounded. In the following year, a weak garrison of sepoys was overpowered by some insurgent Belooches,

who made themselves masters of the town,[5] deposed the Khan
placed in power by the British, made prisoner the British officer
in command, and subsequently put him to death. In the close

of the same year the place was retaken by General Nott.[6] In
1841, the British government recognized as ruler, Nasir Khan,
the youthful son of Mehrab Khan, and subsequently withdrew
their troops from his dominions. The population of the town
and its two suburbs is about 12,000. The elevation above

the level of the sea is 6,000 feet.[7] Humboldt, in the hypsometrical map accompanying *Asie Centrale*, states the elevation at
less than its real degree, as he sets it down at 903 toises, or 5,688
feet. He does not give his authority for the estimate. Lat.
28° 52′, long. 66° 29′.

KELAT-I-GHILJIE.—See KILAT-I-GHILJIE.

KEMANG, in the Punjab, a village thirty-four miles north-east of Vazeerabad, on the route from thence to Punch. Lat. 32° 59′, long. 74° 12′.

KEN, in Sinde, a village situate near the right bank of the Indus. Lat. 28° 24′, long. 69° 38′. *Walker's Map of N.W. Frontier.*

KEPRA, in Sinde, a village situate on the route from Bukkur to Omercote, and thirty miles north-west of the latter place. Lat. 25° 40′, long. 69° 33′. *E.I.C. Ms. Doc.*

KERIS, in Bulti, or Little Tibet, a small town with a fort on the right bank of the Shyhyok, or great northern feeder of the Indus, and close to the confluence. The Shyhyok here flows over more level ground, and is, in consequence, broader than the Indus, as it has a width of one hundred and fifty yards, whilst the principal stream, rushing through a rocky defile, is not more than eighty yards wide; but is of great depth and velocity. The Baltis characterize the relative importance of these rivers by styling the Shyhyok Tsuh-Mo, or female river—the Indus, Tsuh-Foh, or male river. Keris is in lat. 35° 8′, long. 75° 48′. *Vigne, Kashmir, ii. 317.*

KERKU.—A village in Little Tibet. Lat. 35° 8′, long. 76° 10′. *Walker's Map of N.W. Frontier.*

KERNASHEEN, in Afghanistan, a village situate on the left bank of the river Helmund. Lat. 30° 46′, long. 63° 10′. *Walker's Map of Afg.*

KETTAS, in the Punjab, a village situate about thirty miles west of Julalpoor. Lat. 32° 47′, long. 72° 45′. *E.I.C. Ms. Doc.*

KEYPUR, in Sinde, a village ten miles from the left bank of the Indus, and twenty-one miles north-east of Hyderabad. Lat. 25° 38′, long. 68° 33′. *E.I.C. Ms. Doc.*

KEYRA GURRIE.—See KYREE GURREE.

KHAIRABAD.—A village on the right bank of the Indus, opposite Attock, and at the Peshawur or western extremity of the ferry, or of the bridge of boats which affords the means of communication during the season of low water. It is a poor place, with a small mud fort, built, according to some, by Akbar, according to others, by Nadir Shah; but there is a good aqueduct for the purposes of irrigation. It is commanded by the high grounds on both sides of the river. Lat. 33° 54′, long. 72° 18′. *Leech, Attok, 15; Elph. Acc. of Caubul, 73; Hough, Narr. of Exp. in Afg. 334; Burnes' Pers. Narr. 118; Moorcr. Punj. Bokh. ii. 324.*

KHAIRR.—A village in Sinde, on the route from Shikarpoor to Larkhana, and twelve miles south-west of the former town. It is supplied with water from wells. The population is about 400. Lat. 27° 50′, long. 68° 40′. *E.I.C. Ms. Doc.*

KHAISA GHAR.—See TUKHT-I-SULIMAN.

E.I.C. Ms. Doc ; Conolly (A.), Jour. to India, ii. 59.

KHAJEH OURIEH, in Western Afghanistan, a ziearat, or place of pilgrimage, on the route from Kandahar to Herat, and sixty miles south of this latter place. It is a ruin strikingly situated on the summit of a rocky hill, at the base of which runs a stream slightly brackish, yet fit for drinking. Lat. 33° 29', long. 62° 17'.

E.I.C. Ms. Doc.

KHAK-I-CHAPAN, in Western Afghanistan, a halting-ground on the route from Kandahar to Herat, and fifty-one miles west of the former place. The road in this part of the route is rather level and easy for travelling, but in some places sandy. There are a few villages, considerable cultivation, and a moderate supply of water from Kareezes or subterraneous aqueducts. Lat. 31° 40', long. 64° 40'.

Wood, Oxus, Bolleau, Rajwara. Map.

KHANBAILA, in Bhawlpoor, a considerable town near the left bank of the Punjnud. The neighbouring country is very fertile, and, in the season of inundation, overspread by the waters of the river, so that the dense population, by light labour, draw from it abundant and rich crops, especially of rice, wheat, and barley. When visited by Wood, so early as the end of April "the surface was often, as far as the eye could range, one continuous corn-field. It was harvest-time, and crops of wheat and barley stood ready for the sickle, dressed in the rich livery of the season." When the waters retire, the seed is thrown down, and the farmer has no further trouble till the harvest calls him forth to husband his crops. Khanbaila is in lat. 29°, long. 70° 52'.

E.I.C. Ms. Doc.

KHANDEARAH, in Sinde, a village on the middle route from Roree to Hyderabad, and forty-two miles south of the former town. Lat. 27° 6', long. 68° 52'.

E I.C. Ms. Doc.

KHANGAUM, in Sinde, a town close to the north-western frontier, and on the south-eastern border of the Pat, or desert of Shikarpoor. Lat. 28° 11', long. 68° 35'.

E.I.C. Ms. Doc.

KHANGUR, in the Punjab, a village situate on the route from Shoojuabad to Dera Ghazee Khan, two miles from the right bank of the Chenaub river, in lat. 29° 49', long. 71° 12'.

Boileau, Rajwara and Bahawulpoor, 61.

KHANGUR, in the Punjab, a village situate on the right bank of the Punjnud river, twenty-four miles from its confluence with the Indus. Lat. 29° 10', long. 70° 48'.

Id. Map.

KHANGURH, in Bhawlpoor, a village situate in the Desert,

eighty miles south of the town of Bhawlpoor. Lat. 28° 25', long. 71° 45'.

.KHANJEE, in Afghanistan, a village a short distance to the E.I.C. Ms. Doc. north of the Pisheen valley. Lat. 30° 41', long. 67° 7'.

KHANKAIL, in Afghanistan, a village situate on the right E.I.C. Ms.Doc. bank of the Urghundab river, and on the route from Giriskh to Bamian, thirty miles north of Kelat-i-Ghiljie. Lat. 32° 32', long. 66° 57'.

KHANPOOR,[1] in Bhawlpoor, a flourishing commercial town, with a good roofed bazaar, is situate on the Ikhtiarwah, a navigable canal from the Punjnud. There is a ruinous mud fort two hundred yards long and a hundred and twenty broad. The surrounding country is populous, and, where irrigated, fertile, but in general of lighter quality than the region to the south and west, as the eastern desert here begins to be observable. The route from Islamgurh, situate fifty-five miles south, is through the sandy desert, in which the characteristic features of such frightful tracts are peculiarly striking. They are well described by Boileau:[2] " Long and lofty ridges of sandhills follow each other in ceaseless succession, as if an ocean of sand had been suddenly arrested in its progress, with intervals of a quarter or half a mile, or even more, between its gigantic billows; for, after ascending many hundred yards along a gradual slope, we would suddenly come to a steep descent, when our path lay across the line of waves; and on other occasions we would perhaps move parallel to them with a steep wall of sand on one hand, and a gentle rise on the other." Khanpoor has many symptoms of having been formerly a place of much greater importance than now. Population, 20,000.[3] Lat. 28° 38', long. 70° 39'.

[1] Masson, Bal. Afg. Panj. i. 389; Conolly(A.), Jour. to India, ii. 282.

[2] Rajwara and Bahawulpoor, 52.

[3] Hough, 13.

KHANPOOR, in the Punjab, a village situate about seven miles from the right bank of the Chenaub river, and sixteen miles north-east of its confluence with the river Jailum. Lat. 31° 19', long. 72° 19'. Burnes, Bokh. i. 70.

KHANPOOR, in the Punjab, a fort at a short distance east E.I.C. Ms. Doc. of Attock, is situated at the foot of the low range of mountains forming the first stage of the ascent from the plain to the Himalaya. It is surrounded by a fertile country, containing beautiful gardens. Lat. 33° 52', long. 73°.

KHARAN, a small district of Beloochistan, having Nooshky on the north, Jhalawan on the east, Mooshki to the south, and Masson,Kalat, 280; Pott. Belooch. 261.

Punjgoor to the west. It is, in general, arid and barren, yielding a little wheat and barley, but not sufficient for the support of the inhabitants, who barter some articles of the scanty native produce for the grain of Nooshky and other places. The principal export is a sweet gum, which exudes from a variety of the tamarisk, and is in much request in the neighbouring countries as an ingredient in sherbet. Dates and melons abound in the level country, and the hills produce Assafœtida. Kharan lies between lat. 27° 50'—28° 40', long. 64° 10'—64° 30'.

E.I.C. Ms. Doc.; Masson, Kalat,286. KHARAN, in Beloochistan, the capital of the small district of the same name, is worth notice merely as being, with the exception of Waskak, the only place which can be called a town in this part of the country. Lat. 28° 10', long. 64° 33'.

E.I.C. Ms. Doc. KHARDOO CHUMMUM, in Afghanistan, a halting-place on the route from Ghuznee to Shawl, and about a hundred miles north of the latter place. There is a good stream of water here, but the country is barren and almost uninhabited, and the road uneven and difficult. Lat. 31° 28', long. 67° 25'.

E.I.C. Ms. Doc. KHARUCK, in Western Afghanistan, a mountain on the route from Herat to Kandahar, and a hundred and ten miles south of the former place. The pass over it is rather difficult for wheel-carriages, but it may be turned by a road striking off to the south-west, about three miles north of Kharuck, and rejoining the Kharuck road fifteen miles further south. The country about the Kharuck Pass is barren and devoid of supplies, but water is fine and abundant. Lat. 32° 52', long. 62° 30.'

E.I.C. Ms. Doc.; Jour. As. Soc. 1840, p. 713, 714, Conolly (E.), Physical Geogr. of Seistan; Leech, Descrip. of Seis-than, 152. KHASH, in Afghanistan, a town with a fort near the western boundary, which separates the Afghan territory from Seistan. It is situate near the left bank of a stream, called from it the Khash Rood, or river of Khash. The population is about two thousand. Lat. 31° 36', long. 62° 40'.

KHASH RODUK.—See KHASH ROOD.

¹ E.I.C. Ms. Map; Conolly (A.), Jour. to India, ii. 78. KHASH ROOD, or RIVER of KHASH,¹ in Afghanistan, is a considerable river crossing the route from Kandahar to Herat, one hundred and fifty miles west-north-west of the former place, in lat. 32° 19', long. 63° 29'. It apparently takes its rise in a very lofty range of mountains, south of Ghore, sometimes denominated the Toot-i-Gusserman range. The source is probably not far from lat. 32° 50', long. 63° 35'. It holds a south-westerly course of about a hundred and eighty miles, and, passing

by the small town of Khash, expands into the reedy swamp of Aishkeneik,[2] near the eastern border of the lake of Hamoon, in lat. 31° 22′, long. 62° 14′. At the point where it crosses the route from Kandahar to Herat, at a distance probably of about fifty miles from its source, it was found, at the beginning of July, to be thirty-seven yards wide, eighteen inches deep, and having a current of one mile and a half per hour. It is subject to great floods, which detain caravans for weeks together. In the lower part of its course, the greater portion of its waters is drawn off for the purpose of irrigation, and in summer, water is to be met with only in artificial reservoirs, or in natural pools in the channel of the river. The Khash Rood flows through a rugged, barren, desolate country, rising into hills of conglomerate, among which numeous torrents wind. It forms the boundary between the territories of Kandahar and Herat.

[2] Jour. As. Soc. 1840, p. 713, Conolly (E.), Sketch of the Seistan.

KHATIAN, in Sinde, a village situate near the left bank of the Indus, seven miles east of Sehwan. Lat. 26° 19′, long. 68°.

Ms. Map of Sinde.

KHAWAK, the most eastern of the explored passes over Hindoo Koosh, forms the communication between the head of the Punchshir valley and the valley of Inderab. In consequence of the sanguinary hostilities of the Kafirs and of the inhabitants of Punchshir, it is scarcely frequented, though, from Wood's account, it may be considered the most practicable of all the lines of communication between Kunduz and Afghanistan. It was in consequence chosen by Tamerlane, in his march on Hindostan, at the close of the fourteenth century. On that occasion, he made an unsuccessful attack on the Kafirs, and retreating precipitately from their country, resumed his route southwards, having repaired the fort of Khawak, which he found in ruins. The Pass of Khawak has an elevation of 13,200 feet. Lat. 35° 42′, long. 69° 53′.

Wood, Oxus, 416; Price, Mahomedan Hist. iii. 222.

KHEDAREE, in Afghanistan, a village in the valley of Pisheen, and on the route from Shawl to Kandahar, and thirty miles north of the former place. It is situate in a well-cultivated country, having numerous villages. The elevation above the sea is 5,063 feet. Lat. 30° 33′, long. 66° 50′.

E.I.C. Ms. Doc.; Hough, Narr. of Exp. in Afg. 77.

KHEDIWAREE MOUTH.—One of the mouths of the Indus. Lat. 24° 9′, long. 67° 29′.—See INDUS.

KHEEWA, or KEEWA, in the Punjab, a village situate

E.I.C. Ms. Doc.

three miles from the left bank of the Chenaub river. Lat.
31° 21', long. 72° 33'.

E.I.C. Ms. Doc.;   KHEIL-I-AKHUND, in Afghanistan, is a village containing
Hough, Narr. of
Exp. In Afg. 145. the mausoleum of an *akhund*, or Mahometan pastor, whence it
has its name. It is situate near the right bank of the Turnak
river, on the route from Kandahar to Ghuznee, and twenty-nine
miles north-west of the former place. The Turnak is here a
clear, rapid river, from five to eight yards wide. The valley
through which it flows is fertile and well cultivated. The elevation above the sea is 4,418 feet. Lat. 31° 41', long. 65° 59'.

KHELAT-I-GHILJIE.—See KILAT-I-GHILJIE.

E.I.C. Ms. Doc.   KHENGUNPOOR, in the Punjab, a small town situate on
the road from Ferozpoor to Mooltan, thirty-five miles south-west
of the former, and ten miles from the right bank of the Ghara
river. Lat. 30° 45', long. 73° 57'.

Walker's Map of   KHENJ, on the northern frontier of Afghanistan, a village
Afg.
in the Punchshir valley, which furrows the southern declivity of
Hindoo Koosh. Lat. 35° 25', long. 69° 38'.

E.I.C. Ms. Doc.   KHEORAH, in the Punjab, a village twenty-six miles north-
west of Julalpoor, and six miles north of Dadun Khan Pind.
Lat. 32° 42', long. 72° 49'.

E.I.C. Ms. Doc.   KHER.—A village of the valley of Suwat, in Northern Afghanistan, about three miles from the left bank of the river
Suwat. Lat. 34° 44', long. 71° 59'.

E.I.C. Ms. Doc.   KHEWA.—A village in Afghanistan, situate on the right
bank of the river Kooner, twenty-two miles north of Jelalabad.
Lat. 34° 38', long. 70° 40'.

Walker's Map of   KHIMPOOR, in the Punjab, a village situate about five
N.W. Frontier.
miles from the right bank of the Ghara river. Lat. 29° 44',
long. 72° 6'.

E.I.C. Ms. Doc.   KHIRPOOR, in the Punjab, a village situate on the river
Indus, seventeen miles north of the confluence with the Punjnud
river. Lat. 29° 10', long. 70° 40'.

E.I.C. Ms. Doc.   KHIRPOOR, in the Punjab, a village situate six miles from
the right bank of the river Punjnud. Lat. 29° 19', long. 70° 51'.

Hough's Narr. of   KHOAR.—A small town of the Punjab, on the route from
Exp. in Afg. 351. Jailum to Ramnuggur, and near the left or eastern bank of the
river Jailum. There is here a small mud fort. Lat. 32° 49
long. 73° 37'.

KHODABAD,[1] in Sinde, is a ruined town, thirty miles north [1] E.I.C. Ms. Doc. of Hyderabad, and ten miles east of the Indus. Little more than thirty years ago it rivalled Hyderabad in size and population, yet now not one habitable dwelling remains. The ruins cover two square miles. On this Wood[2] remarks, " How perishable must [2] Oxus, 38. be the architecture of Sinde !" It had been a favourite residence of the Talpoor chiefs of Sinde, and here the remains of several of them rest in tombs of neat but plain construction. Lat. 25° 48', long. 68° 32'.

KHODAD KHAN, in the Punjab, a village situate about E.I.C. Ms. Doc. nine miles from the left bank of the Indus, and thirty miles south of Attock. Lat. 33° 28', long. 72° 12'.

KHOJA AMRAN.—See AMRAN.

KHOJA KHIDREE JULGHA, in Afghanistan, a collection of forts in a grassy tract in the Khoja Kedari, a district on the eastern boundary of the *dasht*, or plain of Begram. Here, to use the words of Masson, " are numerous castles, much cultivated Bal. Afg. Panj. land, and, as the name Julgha implies, a large extent of pasture." iii. 153. It is situate on the banks of the Punchshir river, forty-five miles north-east of Kabool. Lat. 34° 57', long. 69° 33'.

KHOJUCK.—See KOJUK.

KHOLOO CHOYTYALLY.—See CHOTYAALI.

KHOOD ZYE, in Afghanistan, a village situate on the right E.I.C. Ms. Doc. bank of the Indus, ten miles south-west of Kala Bagh. Lat. 32° 53°, long. 71° 30'.

KHOOSH-AB.—A small town of Afghanistan, on the route E.I.C. Ms. Doc.; from the Kojuk Pass to Kandahar. It is situate in a well-culti- Hough, Narr. of Exp. in Afg. 93; vated country, very productive of grain, especially wheat; has a Havelock, War in Afg. i.328; Atkin- good supply of excellent water; and is surrounded by a mud wall. son, Exp. into Lat. 31° 30', long. 65° 34'. Afg. 160.

KHOOSHK-I-SUFAID,—See KOOSHK-I-SAFFEED.

KHOOSHK NAKHOOD, in Western Afghanistan, a halt- E.I.C. Ms. Doc.; ing-place on the route from Kandahar to Herat, and forty miles Conolly, Jour. to India, ii. 92. west of the former place. The road in this part of the route is level, hard, and good; there is abundance of water, and the neighbourhood is highly cultivated, containing numerous groves and orchards, especially of pomegranates. About two miles west are the ruins of a large fort called Killa-i-Nadir. Lat. 31° 33', long. 64° 54'.

KHOOTPOOR, in the Punjab, a village on the route from E.I.C. Ms. Doc.

Lahore to Mooltan, and twenty-eight miles south-west of the former town. It is situate on the left bank of the Ravee river. Lat. 31° 22′, long. 73° 55′.

Vigne, Kashmir, ii. 317.

KHOPALU, in Bultistan or Little Tibet, a fort built on the summit of a rock, nearly isolated in an expanse, on the left bank of the Indus. This open space is described by Vigne as a sloping bank " of two or three miles in extent, and exhibiting a green and shady confusion of stone walls, cottages, and fruit-trees." The eminence on which the fort stands is more than a thousand feet above the Indus, and commands a very grand view. Lat. 35° 3′, long. 76° 13′.

E.I.C. Ms. Doc.

KHORZANA KOTUL, in Afghanistan, a pass on the route from Kandahar to Ghuznee, and distant fifty-five miles north-east from the former place. The road in this part of the route, though stony, presents no great difficulty, there being only a moderate ascent of two furlongs, and a descent of about the same length. There is abundance of water, and supplies may be obtained in considerable quantity. Lat. 31° 54′, long. 66° 15′.

Walker's Map of Afg

KHOWALI SYAKUK.—A village in Northern Afghanistan, on the road from Bamian to Siri Pool. Lat. 35° 29′, long. 66° 22′.

Masson, Bal. Afg. Panj. ii. 41 ; Pott. Belooch. 36.

KHOZDAR, in Beloochistan, a small town in the province of Jhalawan, of which it is considered the chief place. It is situate in a narrow, fertile, well-watered, and highly-cultivated valley, amidst gardens and orchards. When Pottinger visited it, about thirty years ago, it contained five hundred houses, inhabited chiefly by Hindoos, who had here a temple, dedicated to Kalee, the goddess of fate. Masson found it, a few years ago, greatly decayed, not having above sixty mud-built houses, of which three only belonged to Hindoos. It is enclosed by a mud wall, and close to it is a ruinous mud fortress. The neighbouring hills abound in rich lead ore. Lat. 27° 50′, long. 66° 23′.

Vigne, Kashmir, i. 322.

KHUND, or KOOND, in Kashmir, a valley furrowing the northern side of the Panjal, or mountain Barichal. It is three miles long, displays great picturesque beauty, is well cultivated, and contains some villages. The less cultivated part is covered with wild apricot-trees, " whose blossom," Vigne observes, " in the early spring, yields a perfume so fragrant and powerful, that the Kashmirians come far and near to inhale it." So romantic a spot could scarcely be without one of those legends so rife in Kashmir ; accordingly, Vigne was informed, "that the place was infested by a serpent, so long, that his tail was perceived at the bottom of a hill when his head might be seen moving on the top of it." It is so embosomed in lofty mountains that its climate is said to be the coolest in the lowlands of Kashmir. Vigne estimates its elevation above the level of the sea at 6,000 feet. Lat. 33° 30', long. 75° 2'.

KHURBUZY SERAI, in the Punjab, a halting-place situate E.I.C. Ms. Doc on the road from Attock to Ramnuggur, forty miles south-east of the former place. Lat. 33° 41', long. 72° 57'.

KHURD KABOOL, or Little Kabool, a village sixteen miles E.I.C. Ms. Map; south-east of Kabool, situate in a pleasant valley on the south- Masson, Bal. Afg. Panj. i. 188; ern route through the Kurkutcha ranges, just after it emerges Hough, Narr. Exp. in Afg. 295; from the Boothauk defile, and before it enters that of Tangee Sale, Dis. in Afg. Turkai. Here, the British troops, in their attempted retreat to 234; Eyre, Mil. Op. at Ka- Jelalabad from Kabool, in 1841, became totally disorganized, and bool, 250; Jour. As. Soc. 1842, yielded themselves up without resistance to the butchery by the p. 73; Grif. Afghans. Here, also, the British army, under General Pollock, Bar. and Ther. Meas. in Afg. ; encamped in September 1842, on the night after the decisive de- Mil. Op. in Afg. feat of the Afghans at Tezeen. The elevation of Khurd Kabool 396. above the sea is 7,466 feet. Lat. 34° 21', long. 69° 18'.

KHURTOOT, in Afghanistan, a village on the route from Map of Afg. Giriskh to Bamian, and fify miles north of Kandahar. Lat. 32° 15', long. 65° 54'.

KHURWAR PASS, in Afghanistan, fifty miles south of E.I.C. Ms. Doc. Kabool. Lat. 33° 47', long. 68° 51'.

KHUT-I-KHURGA OONA, in Afghanistan, a village situate E.I.C. Ms. Doc. on the Gomul Pass, and near the Gomul river. Lat. 31° 58', long. 69° 29'.

KHYBER MOUNTAINS,[1] in Eastern Afghanistan, rise [1] E.I.C. Ms. Map; Leech, Descrip- west of the plain of Peshawur, and connect the most southern tion of Khy- and lowest range of Hindoo Koosh with the Sufeid Koh, the ber Pass, 8; Wood, Khyber Salt range, and the Suliman mountains. They, at first sight, Pass, 3; Lord, Koh-i-Damun, present the appearance of a mass of hills irregularly grouped, but 45; Elph. Acc. of a careful observer will find the distinct arrangement of a chain Caubul, 356; Masson, Bal. Afg. separating the plain of Peshawur on the east from the plain of Panj. i. 162; Jelalabad and the uneven surface of Nungnehar on the west. Moorcroft, Punj. Bokh. ii. 353; They generally consist of slate and primary limestone, with a Jour. As. Soc. 1842, p. 79. Grif. small proportion of overlying sandstone. The sanguinary and ra- Bar. and Ther. pacious character of the population has prevented their mineral Obs. in Afg.

deposits from being explored; they are, however, known to abound in antimony, which so strongly impregnates the water at Ali Musjid, as to render it highly deleterious. The Tatara summit is the most elevated in the range, being 3,500 feet above the plain of Peshawur, and 5,100 above the sea. The breadth of the Khyber range may be stated at about twenty miles; the length, from the base of the nearest and lowest range of the Hindoo Koosh to the Sufeid Koh and Salt range, at about fifty. It is cross cut by two great natural channels—the Khyber ravine or pass, and, further north, the channel of the Kabool river. These, in the opinion of Lord, drained a vast lake, which once occupied the extensive valley of Kabool, an opinion strengthened by the nature of the soil of Peshawur, which, near the pass, for a great depth, consists of fragments of slate and limestone, the constituent substances of the Khyber range. Griffith,[2] however, urges some forcible objections to this hypothesis of Lord. The Khyber mountains are supposed to be so called from the Khyber tribe who inhabit them, and these are divided into the Afreedees, Shainwarries, and Oruk Zais. As this range is lower than the Hindoo Koosh to the north, and the Sufeid Koh, the Salt, and the Suliman ranges to the south, the most practicable passes from Hindustan to Northern Afghanistan lie through it. There are four of these passes, leading from east to west, and lying in the following order from south to north :—First, the Khyber Pass, the most level and the only one practicable for cannon. Second, the Tatara Pass, commencing near the eastern entrance of the Khyber Pass, taking a circuit northwards, and then running in some degree parallel to it, and finally rejoining it at Duka, at the entrance of the valley of Jelalabad. Third, the Abkhana Pass, by which the Abkhana route proceeds. This crosses the Kabool river at Muchnee, and recrosses it at Abkhana, where it enters the Khyber mountains, and proceeds along the southern bank of the river to Duka, joining the Tatara and Khyber Passes. Fourth, the Carapa route, which crosses the Kabool river above Dobundee, then crosses the Lundye from east to west, and proceeding nearly due west to Lalpoor, recrosses the Kabool river, and joins the main road proceeding westward. The Khyber range lies between lat. 33° 30'—34° 20', and long. 71° 10'—71° 30'.

KHYBER PASS,[1] the principal pass in the north between Afghanistan and Hindustan, as the Bolan is in the south ; hence

[2] Jour. As. Soc. 1841, p. 806, Rep. on Subjects connected with Afg.

[1] Same authorities as on Khyber Mountains.

it is called the Key of Afghanistan. It commences at Kadam, a remarkable collection of caves, about ten miles west of Peshawur, and extends about thirty miles in a tortuous, but generally north-westerly course, to Duka, at the entrance of the plain of Jelalabad. Havelock, considering the pass to commence at Huzarnow on the west, estimates its entire length at fifty miles.[2] It lies for the most part through slate rock, and along the bed of a torrent, liable to be filled with a sudden fall of rain, and then so violent as to sweep away every thing in its course. At other times the bed is dry, or the water shrunk to a small rill, sometimes disappearing under the gravel, or running on one side. There are two peculiarly difficult portions of the pass. One of these is close to Ali Musjid, where the road is merely the narrow bed of a rivulet, enclosed on each side by precipices, rising to the height of six or seven hundred feet, in some places to a thousand or twelve hundred, at an angle of seventy or eighty degrees, and overhung by the small fort of Ali Musjid. This petty fort occupies the summit of a peaked rock, but is of small value as a military position, from want of water, and from being commanded by adjacent heights. Its possession was obstinately contested during the late military operations in Afghanistan. The Afghans in garrison evacuated it as soon as they found it commanded by the hostile artillery, and the British occupied it, but being ultimately in peril from the Khyberees, retreated, though with considerable loss. The air in this gorge, though dry, has been considered remarkably deleterious, as most of the troops posted in it perished by disease. Some, however, with more reason, attribute the mortality to the poisonous nature of the water, which is impregnated with antimony.[3] At Lalabeg, about midway through, the pass expands into a small valley, in which is a great tope, or artificial mound, on the north side of the road.—(See LALABEG.) Near Landee Khana,[4] the road is for a great distance a gallery of about twelve feet wide, having on one side a perpendicular wall of rock rising to a great height above, and on the other a deep precipice. The pass rises gradually from the eastern entrance, but has a steep declivity westward, though the descent is not so great in that direction, as the plain of Jelalabad is more elevated than that of Peshawur. The height of the summit of the pass is 3,373 feet above the sea,[5] and about 2,300 above Peshawur. As the Khyberees are a predatory

[2] War in Afg. ii. 187

[3] Hough, Nar. of Exp. to Afg. 315.

[4] Havelock, War in Afg. ii. 189.

[5] Jour. As. Soc. 1842, p. 78, Grif., Bar. and Ther. Meas.

and ruthless race, well armed with long rifled matchlocks, jez-zails, or jingels, which take effect at greater distance than mus-kets, it is necessary that those who have occasion to use the pass should purchase their forbearance, and for this purpose, the Du-rani monarchs paid them 130,000 rupees annually. The slender resources of Dost Mahomed Khan obliged him to reduce this al-lowance to 20,000 rupees, distributed among 26,000 fighting men.

[6] Hough, Narr. of Exp. in Afg.
[7] Bal. Afg. Panj. i. 162.

Nadir Shah,[6] is said to have disbursed a sum equal to 100,000*l.* for an unmolested march through the pass ; but, according to Masson,[7] he turned it by taking a southern route through Tira. The Khyber Pass was the scene of obstinate and sanguinary con-flicts during the war in Afghanistan. It was forced by the British after their first occupation of Kabool.[8] A similar attempt, made after the disastrous retreat from Kabool, failed, with great loss, but subsequently, though obstinately defended by a large body of men, it was again forced in April, 1842. The eastern entrance of the Khyber Pass is in lat. 33° 58′, long. 71° 30′.

[8] Hough, 219, 228 ; Havelock, ii. 191 ; Mil. Op in Afg. 130, 237.

[1] E.I.C. Ms. Doc.

KHYERPOOR,[1] a town of Sinde, is situated about fifteen miles east of the Indus, in a country of alluvial formation, but in which, as bordering on the Thurr, or eastern desert,[2] sand is largely intermixed with the clay deposited by the river. A large canal, called the Merwah, from the Indus, yields water both for irrigation and drinking, that obtained from wells being in general brackish, unpalatable, and unwholesome. One well in the palace yields very fine water. The canal receives its water a few miles below Roree, and in time of inundation, by means of numerous ramifications, overspreads the country. Part of the water finds its way back, in many small streams, to the Indus, in the lower part of its channel; the rest is finally lost by absorption and evaporation. When the river is very low, the canal is some-times destitute of water. The town,[3] originally a military canton-ment, has grown into its present importance in consequence of having been selected as the residence of the chief Ameers of Northern Sinde. But notwithstanding this, it is but a large col-lection of mud hovels, with a few houses of a better description scattered about ; destitute of fort or defence, unless the embattled mud-wall, enclosing the residence of the Ameer, can be deemed such. This palace is situate amidst the bazaars, and presents little worth notice, except a mosque crowned with a cupola covered with gaudy lackered tiles of various hues. The town

[2] Lord. Med. Rep. on the Plain of the Indus, 68 ; Jour. As. Soc. 1840, p. 1187, Westmacott, Acc. of Khyrpoor.

[3] Masson, Bal. Afg. Panj. i. 363; Conolly, Jour. to India, ii. 255 ; Burnes, Bokh. iii. 273 ; Havelock, War in Afg. i. 130.

is very filthy; from this cause, together with the heat of the climate, and the deleterious influence of the stagnant marshes around, it is unhealthy. The population is estimated at 15,000.[3] There is no manufacture, except to a very small extent in weaving and dying coarse cottons. During the Talpoor dynasty, the Ameers of Khyerpoor held the northern and finest part of Sinde, but as it was much inferior in size to the dominions of their kinsmen, the Ameers of Hyderabad, the former were subordinate, though allowed an influential voice in all questions considered to affect the general welfare. The territory subject to the Ameers of Khyerpoor was one hundred and twenty miles long, and of the same breadth. The government, it need scarcely be added, was a military despotism; the power, military resources, and revenue being divided in various proportions between a great number of the ruling Belooche family of Talpoor, of whom the eldest in lineage was regarded as the chief. Though mild as affecting life, the rule of this multitude of chieftains was in all fiscal matters so oppressive and rapacious as to be productive of rapidly progressive ruin and desolation. The revenue of the Khyerpoor Ameers was estimated at 120,000*l.* per annum.[4] * The military force appears to have been based on a rude and ill-compacted feudal system; the chiefs having allotments of lands on condition of bringing forward and supporting a proportionate force of armed men, who were paid partly in money, partly in grain. The number of men which might be raised on emergencies was from 10,000 to 12,000. Khyerpoor is about seventeen miles south-west of Roree, the road from which place is good. Lat. 27° 31′, long. 68° 45′.

[3] Mohun Lal on the Trade of Khyrpoor, 36.

[4] Westmacott, 1098; Burnes states 100,000*l.*, Bokh. iii. 213.

E.I.C. Ms. Doc.

KHYRABAD.—See Khairabad.

KHYRABAD, in Afghanistan, a village in that part of the Huzareh country where the mountains slope downwards to Bokhara. It is situate on a feeder of the river of Andkhoo, near its confluence with the main stream. Lat. 36° 12′, long. 64° 49′.

E.I.C. Ms. Doc.

KHYREE DEREE.—See Kyree Dera.

KHYRGAON, in Sinde, a town on the west bank of the Koodun, a branch of the western Narra, the great offset leaving the Indus near Bukkur and terminating in lake Manchur, from which this town is distant about thirty miles north. Though, as

* Pottinger (400) states the revenue at 70,000*l.*, and the military force between 4,000 and 5,000 men.

Acc. of Khyrpoor, in Jour. As. Soc. 1840, p. 1207. Westmacott observes, it has not yet found a place in the map, it is of considerable importance, having seven mosques, and between 2,000 and 3,000 inhabitants, of whom a fifth part are Hindoos. It has a handsome bazaar, well supplied with cottons. Lat. 26° 55′, long. 67° 50′.

Ms. Map.   KHYROODDEN, in the Punjab, a halting-place on the route from Loodiana to Lahore, and twenty miles south-east of the latter town. Lat. 31° 31′, long. 74° 47′.

Jour. As. Soc. 1837. p. 107, Mackeson's Jour. of Wade's Voyage. KHYRPOOR, in Bhawlpoor, a town situate a mile from the left bank of the river Ghara. The sand-hills of the Thurr, or great sandy desert, are, on the east, so close to the town, that the extremities of the streets in that direction open on a dreary waste of sandhills, ruined houses, and walls half buried by the sand, which is continually encroaching on the cultivated ground along the river. The rapidity of the encroachment may be estimated from the fact that a few years ago the boundary of the desert was two miles east of the town. In time of inundation, the town only intervenes between the water's edge and the desert. The houses are built of unburnt brick, which are found to last long, as rain seldom falls; the round domes of the mosques are generally built of the same material, the great mosque alone being constructed of burned brick. This last edifice is embellished with tiles, varnished, of various colours, but has been allowed to fall greatly into decay. There is a tolerable bazaar, containing about four hundred shops; but the number of these was greater formerly, all trade having here, of late years, fallen away considerably. It is, however, still a small mart for cafilas, or caravans, resorting from the desert to obtain various articles of commerce. The neighbourhood abounds in small, ruined, mud forts, formerly held by petty chiefs, who resisted the authority of the ancestors of the present Bhawl Khan. Khyrpoor is in lat. 29° 34′, long. 72° 7′.

        KHYRPOOR DAHR, in Sinde, a town between Subzulcote and Roree, and fifty miles north-east of the latter place. It is of Masson, Bal. Afg Panj. i. 376. considerable size, and has a good bazaar. The surrounding country consists of fine gardens and richly-cultivated land, irrigated by water-courses from the Indus, distant twelve miles to the north-west, or from wells. Lat. 28° 6′, long. 69° 34′.

        KIDUR, in Kashmir, a village fourteen miles north-east of Islamabad. Lat. 33° 53′, long. 75° 9′.

KIJREEAREE, in Sinde, a village in the desert, eight miles south of the fort of Oomereote. Lat. 25° 15′, long. 69° 48′.

KILA AMEER KHAN, in Afghanistan, a fort in the hilly country north-east of Furrah, and thirty miles distant from this town. Lat. 32° 30′, long. 62° 40′. E.I.C. Ms. Doc. Walker's Map of Afg.

KILA BUDUL, in Afghanistan, a fort situate on the bank of a feeder of the river Moorghab. Lat. 35° 43′, long. 63° 56′. Map of Afg.

KILA HAJEE, in Afghanistan, a fort in the Koh-i-Damun, ten miles north of the city of Kabool. It is situate on a small stream, a feeder of the Punchshir river. Lat. 34° 40′, long. 69° 5′. E.I.C. Ms. Doc.; Masson, Bal. Afg. Panj. iii. 146.

KILAH DOLLAH, in the Punjab, a fort twenty miles north-east of the town of Bukkur. Lat. 31° 45′, long. 71° 29′. E.I.C. Ms. Doc.

KILAKAZEE, in Afghanistan, a fort twenty miles north of Kabool, and five miles east of Istalif. Lat. 34° 48′, long. 69° 2′. E.I.C. Ms. Doc.

KILA KHARZAR, in Afghanistan, a fort on the route from Kabool to Bamian, twenty-eight miles south-east of the latter. It is situate at the eastern base of the Hajeguk ridge, in the fork formed by two small streams which, uniting, constitute the nascent river Helmund. Lat. 34° 34′, long. 68° 4′. E.I.C. Ms. Map.

KILA NOW, in Afghanistan, a fort sixty-three miles north-east of Herat, on the route from thence to Bamian, through Siri Pool. Lat. 34° 52′, long. 63° 5′. E.I.C. Me. Map.

KILAT-I-GHILJIE,[1] or "Fort of the Ghiljies," on the route from Kandahar to Ghuznee, and eighty-four miles north-west from the former place, was, when the British army arrived there in its progress to Kabool, completely in ruins. The site is admirable, occupying a conical and very steep hill about three hundred feet high, having on its summit space for a considerable fortress, and two abundant springs of water. Close to it, on the north-west, are two small walled villages. The fort was repaired and garrisoned by ‑the British, who successfully resisted all attempts to dislodge them, and were withdrawn without loss on the evacuation of the country in 1842. The evil reputation of this place and its neighbourhood has caused the use of the high road on which it is situate to be in a great degree discontinued, it being scarcely possible for travellers to escape being plundered by the Ghiljie chiefs or their emissaries. Kilat-i-Ghiljie was, in 1505, taken by Sultan Baber.[2] Elevation, 5,773 feet. It is eight miles and a half from Azcree Chukee. Lat. 32° 8′, long. 66° 45′. [1] E.I.C. Ms. Doc.; Hough, Narr. Exp. in Afg. 148; Havelock, War in Afg. ii. 45; Kennedy, Sinde and Kabool, ii. 8; Mil. Op. in Afg. 313. [2] Memoirs, 171.

Walker's Map of Afg.

KILA TUKUH, in Afghanistan, a fort forty-two miles south of Siri Pool. Lat. 35° 34', long. 65° 46'.

E.I.C. Ma. Doc.; Hough, Narr. of Exp. into Afg. 78; Atkinson, Exp. into Afg. 143, Kennedy, Sinde and Kabool, I. 234.

KILLA ABDALLA, in Afghanistan, a village with a fort two or three miles left of the route from Shawl to Kandahar, and forty-eight miles north-west from the former place. Here is a good stream, a feeder of the river Lora : the fort is in good repair, is strengthened with bastions, and well supplied with water from a tank. The adjacent country is a plain broken by small hills, and the beds of mountain streams, but tolerably fertile and well cultivated. Lat. 30° 42', long. 66° 30'.

E.I.C. Ms. Doc.; Wood, Oxus, 170.

KILLA ASSEEN, in Afghanistan, a fort on the route from Kabool to Jelalabad, by the Kurkutcha Pass, the most southern of the four collateral routes crossing the Kurkutcha range. It is thirty-three miles south-east of Kabool, and has the elevation of 8,000 feet. Lat. 34° 17', long. 69° 36'.

E.I.C. Ms. Doc.

KILLAEE TILLA.—A village in Afghanistan, forty miles west of Ghuznee, and situate on the route from Giriskh to Bamian. Lat. 33° 27', long. 67° 33'.

E.I.C. Ms. Doc; Jour. As Soc. 1842, p. 58, Grif. Bar. and Ther. Meas.; Hough, Exp. into Afg. 144; Atkinson, Exp. into Afg. 181.

KILLA-I-AZIM KHAN, in Afghanistan, is a fort surrounded by a village on the route from Kandahar to Ghuznee, and fourteen miles in a direction nearly east from the former place. The fort is built of mud, and is of a square form with a round tower at each angle. There are several streams, some of good and some of brackish water. The neighbouring country is fertile and well cultivated. The elevation above the sea is 3,945 feet. Lat. 31° 38', long. 65° 47'.

E.I.C. Ms. Doc.

KILLA-I-BUKSHEE, in Afghanistan, is a collection of walled villages on the route from Ghuznee to Shawl, and thirty-six miles south-west from the former place. It is situated in a fertile and extensive valley, bounded on the north by a high range of mountains, and on the south by another of inferior elevation. The road in this part of the route is good, save that it is crossed by several water-courses. Lat. 33° 8', long. 67° 55'.

E.I.C. Ms. Doc.; Jour. As. Soc. 1841, p. 321, Conolly (E.), Jour. in Seistan.

KILLA-I-DOOKTER, or "Maiden's Castle," in Afghanistan, a small ruined fort on the left bank of the Adruscund river, and on the extremity of a spur proceeding from the Subzawur mountains. Opposite to it is a fort, also in ruins, called Killa-i-Pisr, or "the Youth's Fort." Both are much celebrated in the fables and traditions of the inhabitants. Lat. 33° 19', long. 62° 10'.

E.I.C. Ms. Doc.

KILLA-I-HAJEE, in Afghanistan, a village on the route

from Ghuznee to Kabool, and seven miles west from the latter place. The surrounding country is an expanse of groves, gardens, and orchards, watered by channels drawn from the Kabool river. Lat. 34° 27', long. 68° 56'.

KILLA-I-JAFFREE, in Afghanistan, a fort on the route E.I.C. Ms. Doc. from Kandahar to Ghuznee, and one hundred and thirty miles north-east of the former place. It is situate near the left bank of the river Turnak, in a fertile and well-cultivated country. Lat. 32° 34', long. 67° 20'.

KILLA-I-KHALEKDAD KHAN, in Afghanistan, a ruinous E.I.C. Ms. Doc. village on the route from Kandahar to Ghuznee, and thirteen miles east of the former place. It is situated in an open, level, but ill-cultivated country, through which the road is good. Lat. 31° 38', long. 65° 48'.

KILLA-I-KHUROTEE, in Afghanistan, a village on the E.I.C. Ms. Doc. road from Ghuznee to Dera Ismael Khan, by the Gomul Pass. Lat. 32° 32', long. 68° 48'.

KILLA-I-LUNGUR, in Afghanistan, a fort on the road from E.I.C. Ms. Map. Ghuznee to Dera Ismael Khan, twenty-five miles north-east of Lake Abistada. Lat. 32° 51', long. 68° 29'.

KILLA-I-MURGHA, or NOWA MURGHA,[1] in Afghanistan, [1] E.I.C. Ms. Doc. was a fort, the residence of Abdul Rehman Khan, the principal chief of the Ghiljies. So powerful was the father of this chieftain, that at the head of fifty thousand men, he contested the sovereignty with Shah Zeman, the brother of Shah Shooja. Abdul Rehman having shewn the most inveterate enmity against both Shah Shooja and his British auxiliaries, Major Outram, in 1839, invested Killa-i-Murgha, in which he had taken refuge. It is described as " a well-constructed fort, possessing a high citadel and a wet ditch,"[2] which [2] Outram, Rough had defied the power of Shah Shooja, who twice besieged it Notes. 150; Jackson, Views in without success. Abdul Rehman had eighty chosen horsemen, Afg. and expected a large reinforcement promised by another chieftain, who did indeed arrive at the head of his troops, but immediately joined the besiegers. In the ensuing night the little garrison forced its way through the British lines, and escaped without loss, carrying with them the three wives and the sister of their leader. The deserted fort was then totally destroyed by mines exploded under the citadel, towers, and gateway. Killa-i-Murgha is in lat. 32° 18', long. 67° 30'.

KILLA-I-NADIR, in Afghanistan, a ruined fort of great E.I.C. Ms. Doc.

dimensions, situate on the route from Kandahar to Herat, and forty-two miles west of the former place. There is a good supply of water, and the adjacent country is well cultivated. l ı t. 31° 23′, long. 64° 48′.

E.I.C. Ms. Doc.   KILLA-I-RAMAZAN KHAN, in Afghanistan, a small fort in the valley of the Turnak river, on the route from Kandahar to Ghuznee, and distant from the former place ninety-one miles north-east. The road in this part of the route is stony, running among low hills, but is practicable for artillery. Lat. 32° 2′, long. 66° 45′.

E.I.C. Ms. Doc.   KILLA-I-SHA MEER, in Afghanistan, a fort between Kandahar and Khash, and fifty miles south-west of the former town. It is situate on the left bank of the Urghundab river. Lat. 31° 30′, long. 64° 42′.

E.I.C. Ms. Doc.   KILLA-I-SOBHA, in Afghanistan, a fort thirty miles north-east of Kandahar, on the route from thence to Kilat-i-Ghiljie. Lat. 31° 44′, long. 65° 56′.

E.I.C. Ms. Doc.;
Atkinson, Exp.
Into Afg. 860.   KILLA KASSIM, in Afghanistan, an old, deserted fort on the route from Kabool to Ghuznee, and thirteen miles west of the former place. It is situate in a beautiful and highly-cultivated valley near the bank of a feeder of the Kabool river. Lat. 34° 28′, long. 68° 50′.

E.I.C. Ms. Doc.   KILLA RAHIM KHAN, in Afghanistan, a fort on the route from Ghuznee to Shawl, by the western shore of Lake Abistada, and sixty miles south of Ghuznee. Lat. 33°, long. 68° 10′.

Walker's Map of
N.W. Frontier.   KILLAWALLA, in the Punjab, a village seven miles from the right bank of the Ravee river. Lat. 30° 49′, long. 72° 48′.

Jour. As. Soc.
1840, p. 724,
Conolly (E.),   KIMBULDAI, in Afghanistan, a village thirteen miles north of Khash. Lat. 31° 48′, long. 62° 41′.

Phys. Geogr. of
Seistan.
E.I.C. Ms. Doc.   KINJIR, in the Punjab, a village situate three miles from the left bank of the Indus. Lat. 29° 52′, long. 71° 1′.

KINJORE, in Sinde, a lake, or, as it is vernacularly called, a

[1] E.I.C. Ms. Doc.;
Wood, Oxus, 12.   dund [1]—an extensive and permanent piece of stagnant brackish water, left by the Indus after it has retired to the channel to which

[2] Burnes' Pers.   it is confined in the season when it is lowest.[2] The dund of Kinjore is about three miles westward of the channel, and is a beautiful expanse of water. It is one of three which extend north and

[3] Wood, 23.   south about twenty miles,[3] and swarm with fine fish, caught with much skill and in great abundance by the fishing population on

the banks, and forming their principal subsistence. Lat. 24° 51′, long. 68° 8′.

KIRKUNEE, in Afghanistan, a village situate on the Suli- E.I.C. Ms. Doc. man mountains. Lat. 32° 20′, long. 70°.

KIRMAN, in Afghanistan, a village about twenty miles south Walker's Map of of the Sufeid Koh mountains. Lat. 33° 39′, long. 70° 17′. Afg.

KIRTA or KISTA.—See BOLAN PASS.

KIRTARPOOR, in the Punjab, a small town about twenty Moorcr. Punj. miles east of the river Beas, and near the southern base of the Bokh. i. 118. Himalaya. Lat. 31° 30′, long. 75° 35′.

KISHAN, in Beloochistan, a village on the route from Kelat[1] [1] E.I.C. Ms. Doc. to Beebee Nanee, in the Bolan Pass, and eighteen miles north- east of Kelat.[2] The road has a considerable descent from that [2] Jour. As. Soc. placc, falling four thousand three hundred and five feet, between 1842, p. 54, Grif. Bar. and Ther. it and Beebee Nanee, a distance of eighty miles. It is passable Obs. in Afg. for horses and camels, but by no means for wheel-carriages. It is locally important, as being a great channel of the emi- gration which yearly, on the approach of winter, takes place from the cold highlands of Kelat to the warm plain of Cutch Gundava. The village of Kishan scarcely contains one hundred inhabitants. It is supplied with water from a stream, and there is some cultivation in the vicinity. Lat. 28° 58′, long. 66° 42′.

KISHANEE, in Afghanistan, a collection of villages on the E.I.C. Ms. Doc. route from Ghuznee to Shawl, and one hundred and seventeen miles south-west of the former. The road northward of this place is good, but southward very bad, so as to be with difficulty prac- ticable for wheel-carriages. Lat. 32° 13′, long. 67° 35′.

KISHENGUNGA, in the Punjab, a large river, which, Moorcr. Punj. Bokhara, ii. 307 ; rising in the mountains forming the north-eastern boundary of Vigne, Kashmir, Kashmir, sweeps round the north of that valley, and, after a ii. 184, 206 ; P. Von Hugel, ii. course of about one hundred and twenty miles, falls into the Jai- 117 ; iv. 133 ; Oriental Mag. lum at Mazufurabad, in lat. 34° 11′, long. 75° 25′, being little 1825, p. 105, Izzet inferior there to the principal stream. It was formerly crossed by Ullah, Travels beyond the Hima- a wooden bridge, but this has been destroyed, and the communi- laya. cation is now kept up by a ferry. E.I.C. Ms. Doc. ; Jour. As. Soc.

KISHT, in Afghanistan, a village on the route from Kanda- 1840, p. 724, Conolly (E.), har to Khash, ten miles east of the latter town. Lat. 31° 40′, Sketch of Phys. long. 62° 52′. Geog. of Seistan. Map.

KISHTAWAR, in the north of the Punjab, and on the south- Vigne, Kashmir, ern slope of the Himalaya. It is situated in a small plain near i. 292 ; F Von Hugel, Kaschmir, i. 35.

the left bank of the Chenaub, which here rushes through a ravine
having precipitous sides of gneiss rock about a thousand feet
high. A little up the river, and on the opposite side from the
town, is the confluence of the Muru Wurdwun, a considerable
river from the north. It is a small town of ill-built flat-roofed
houses, with an insignificant bazaar and a fort. There are trifling
manufactures of shawls of inferior quality and of coarse woollens.
The population, mixed, of Mahometans and Hindoos, are at
present proverbially poor, the place having suffered excessively
from the oppression of the Sikhs since the expulsion of the right-
ful rajah, who ruled over the surrounding territory, which bears
the same name, and whose power extended northwards as far as
Ladakh. Kishtawar is situated five thousand feet above the sea,
and in lat. 33° 15′, long. 75° 46′.

KISTA.—See Bolan Pass.

E.I.C. Ms. Doc. KOBUL, a village in North-eastern Afghanistan, situate
on the right bank of the Indus, thirty miles north-east of Attock. Lat. 34° 16′, long. 72° 40′.

Leech, Rep. on
Manufacturing
Towns of Sinde,
32. KODA, a town of Sinde, situate twenty-three miles south-
west of Khycrpoor. Population 2,200. Lat. 27° 25′, long. 68°
52′.

E.I.C. Ms. Doc. KOHARE, in Sinde, a village on the route from Larkhana to
Jull, and eight miles north-west of the former town. It is
situate on a torrent, which, flowing from the Hala mountains,
discharges itself, in time of inundation, into the water-courses in
the vicinity of Larkhana. Lat. 27° 36′, long. 68° 9′.

KOHAT.—A valley in Afghanistan.—See the succeeding
article.

Wood, Oxus, 141;
Elph. Acc. of
Caubul, 40;
Lord, Koh-i-
Damun, 44;
Masson, Bal.Afg.
Panj. i. 113. KOHAT.—A town in the hilly tract north of the Salt range
of mountains, and in the valley of Kohat, which is about seven
miles in diameter, populous, fertile, well watered by the river Teo
and by numerous springs. The town, which is surrounded by
a wall, is meanly built, but has a good bazaar and a fine
mosque. Its beautiful situation, and the luxuriant vegetation of
the surrounding country, render it a delightful place, though it
has suffered much from the devastation of the Sikhs, who have
cut down its fine groves and orchards for fuel. These invaders,
to control the population, have erected a triangular fort two
hundred yards long and fifty wide. The great route from Peshawur to Kala Bagh passes through Kohat, as does also westward

an important route by Bungush to Khorasan. Kohat is the capital, not only of the village of the same name, but of the extensive and fertile valley of Bungush. At Sheikh, which is situate a few miles east of the town, are springs of naphtha and very rich and extensive deposits of sulphur. Kohat is in lat. 33° 31', long. 71° 29'.

KOHEE.—See KAHEE.

KOHEE MERWITTY, in Afghanistan, a village twenty- five miles west of the Suliman mountains. Lat. 32° 31', long. 69° 40'. ^{Walker's Map of N.W. Frontier.}

KOH-I-BABA,[1] in Afghanistan, a lofty mountain at the south- western extremity of Hindoo Koosh, with which it is connected by the transverse ridges of Kaloo and Hajeguk. Its appearance is very sublime when viewed from the east; its extremity in that direction presenting the form of a vast rounded mass, and the culminating ridge rising above it in a succession of lofty peaks stretching westward as far as the eye can reach. Still farther to the west it sinks into the mazy mountains of inferior height, forming the Huzareh highlands. If viewed from the north, it appears surmounted by three vast snowy peaks, the upper parts of which are reported to be inaccessible. Griffith, who, in August, ascended this mountain to the height of 13,500 feet, found patches of snow at that elevation lying in the more sheltered spots, and saw it also occurring in various places towards the summit, the more exposed points being free. " The upper portion of the range," he observes, " appeared entirely bare." Lady Sale[2] also saw it without snow in the end of August. This circumstance leads to the conclusion that it does not rise beyond the limit of perpetual congelation ; but this limit is very variable and anomalous in the mountains of Central Asia. Lord[3] states the limit to be as high as fifteen thousand feet on the neighbouring Hindoo Koosh ; and if it be assumed at the same elevation at Koh-i-Baba, which is a full degree lower in latitude, it follows that the height of the latter mountain does not exceed fifteen thousand feet. All, however, who have made conjectures as to its elevation have concluded it to be higher than this. Burnes[4] and Lady Sale[5] give eighteen thousand feet; Outram,[6] twenty thousand ; but such estimates, formed with the nerves disturbed by the intense cold of those elevated regions and the eyes dazzled by vast expanses of snow, can be little depended on. As its summit is

[1] E.I.C. Ms. Map; Jour. As. Soc. 1841, p. 803, Grif. Rep. on Subjects connected with Afg.; Masson, Bal. Afg. Panj. ii. 333 ; Moorcr. Punj. Bokh. ii. 386 ; Eyre, Mil. Op. in Afg. 357.

[2] Dis. in Afg. 419.

[3] Koh-i-Damun, 48.

[4] Bokh. ii. 241.

[5] 419.

[6] Rough Notes, 127.

regarded as inaccessible, barometrical measurement is not available ; and it does not appear that any trigonometrical observations have been made on this point. The elevation may perhaps with some probability be stated at sixteen thousand feet. Humboldt, in the hypsometrical map accompanying *Asie Centrale*, states the height at 2,800 toises, or 17,640 feet, but does not give the grounds of this estimate. The range of Koh-i-Baba, about sixty miles long, extends along lat. 34° 30', and between long. 67° 30' and 68° 30'.

F.I.C. Ms. Doc.;
Lord, Koh-i-
Damun;
Masson, Bal. Afg.
Panj. iii. 120;
Burnes, Pers.
Narr. 120;
Baber, Memoirs,
147.

KOH-I-DAMAN, or the Mountain-skirt, an elevated tract north of Kabool, extends over the eastern declivity of the Pughman range of mountains. It slopes towards the north-east, the numerous small streams by which it is intersected flowing in that direction, and falling into the Punchshir river. The elevation in general exceeds seven thousand feet, and the climate in consequence is severe in winter and rather cool in summer, though sufficiently genial to mature the fruits of the finest part of the temperate zone, and for productions of this kind its rugged surface is much more suitable than for the growth of grain. In consequence of the scarcity of corn, the population is largely supported on mulberries, dried, and either eaten without further preparation, or ground and made into bread. This diet is considered very heating, and the inhabitants attribute their own irritable and sanguinary character to this quality. The population consists for the most part of Tajeks, who are generally in rebellion against the government of Kabool. In summer, the purity of the air, the scenery, in some places sublime, in others soft, and everywhere highly picturesque, and the luxuriant groves and orchards, render this one of the most delightful regions in the world. The principal towns are Istalif, one of the largest in Afghanistan, Charikar, and Isturgeteh. The Koh-i-Daman is about twenty miles long and fifteen broad, and lies between lat. 34° 40'—35° 5', long. 68° 50'—69° 10'.

F.I.C. Ms. Doc.;
Conolly (A.),
Jour. to India,
ii. 77.

KOH-I-DOOZD, or "Thieves' Mountain," in Western Afghanistan, on the south of the route from Herat to Kandahar, and one hundred and fifty miles north-west of the latter place. Its name has been given in consequence of the predatory Afghans taking post on it to look out for travellers. Lat. 32° 15', long. 63° 12'.

KOH-I-KHARUK.—See KHARUCK.

KOHOO, or KOHOW.—See Moola Pass.

KOHUK, in Western Beloochistan, a town fifty miles north- E.I.C. Ms. Doc.
west of Punjgoor. Lat. 27° 38′, long. 61° 56′.

KOHUK, in Afghanistan, a village six miles west of Kan- E.I.C. Ms. Doc.
dahar, near the right bank of the Urghundab river. Lat. 31° 38′,
long. 65° 22′.

KOJUK PASS,[1] in Afghanistan, crosses the Amran moun- [1] E.I.C. Ms. Doc.;
tains, from the valley of Pisheen on the east, to the plains of Hough, Narr. of
Kandahar on the west. There are two ridges * traversed in tra- Exp. in Afg. 79;
velling by this pass. The ascent of the first, from the eastward, Havelock, War in
is gradual for six miles six furlongs; the road then contracts to Atkinson, 144;
a width of from twelve to twenty feet, and for six furlongs be- Outram, Rough
comes steeper, then still more so for two furlongs, and steeper Notes, 83; Ken-
still for forty yards, near the top. A spring of water crosses the nedy, Sinde and
road half-way up the steep part of the ascent. The descent, on Kabool, I. 235.
the other side, is almost as steep as the ascent. A good stream
of water here crosses the road, and another road joins from the
left, by which part of the baggage was conveyed during the
advance of the British army in 1839. The ascent of the next
ridge is nearly as steep as that of the first, and extends two furlongs and a half. About half-way up, the best road for camels
turns off to the left from the gun road. It holds its way
along a small water-course, but admits only one camel at a time.
A path turns off to the right, but should be carefully avoided,
as it is very difficult, and numbers of the British force fell
in attempting to proceed by it. The road from the summit
descends for three furlongs and a half, and is here steeper
than in the other parts of the pass, turning sharp round a
point near the top, on the brink of a precipice. As no cattle
could be employed in such a situation, the battering and field-
train and carriages of the British army, in its progress through
this pass, were dragged up and lowered down by the astonishing
exertions of parties of European infantry. It is said that a better
road than that above described runs off to the right, after passing
the stream of water at the foot of the first descent, and rejoins it
at a distance of two miles and a half beyond the bottom of the
last descent by a more gradual slope. This pass was found to
offer much greater obstruction to the passage of troops than the

* Havelock mentions three (War in Afg. i. 297, 298).

Bolan Pass, which was surmounted without much difficulty : the British army was five days in making the passage through it. The eastern brow of the pass is 6,848 feet[2] above the level of the sea ; the summit, 7,449. The mountains are in general of slate and overlying sandstone, and, where not too steep and bare of earth for vegetation, are covered with grass, flowering shrubs, and a great variety of fragrant and beautiful plants. Wild rhubarb, here called *ruwash*, is peculiarly abundant, and is eaten in great quantities by the inhabitants. The main road from Sinde to Kandahar by the Bolan Pass lies through the Kojuk ; that to Ghuznee turning off northwards, about thirty miles south-east of the pass. The difficulties of the Kojuk Pass were again overcome by a British army in April, 1842, when General England,[3] having forced it, formed a junction with General Nott at Kandahar ; and on the final evacuation of Afghanistan, the pass was once more traversed by General England,[4] in his march from Kandahar into Sinde. The Kojuk Pass is in lat. 30° 45′, long. 66° 30′.

Jour. As. Soc. 1842, p. 50, Grif. Bar. and Ther. Meas. in Afg.

Mil. Op. in Afg. 260.

Id. 420.

E.I.C. Ms. Doc.   KOKARAN, in Western Afghanistan, a village at a ford over the Urghundab, on the route from Kandahar to Herat, and seven miles west of the former place. The river is here about forty yards wide and two feet and a half deep, when not in inundation. The water is drawn off in numerous channels to irrigate the country, which is fertile and well cultivated. Lat. 31° 37′, long. 65° 21′.

Vigne, Kashmir, i. 339.   KOKER NAG, in Kashmir, a celebrated spring at the northern base of the Panjal of Banihal, bounding the valley on the south. It gushes with a copious volume of water out of six orifices at the bottom of a limestone cliff. A considerable stream is thus formed, which flows into the Bureng river. The water is celebrated for its excellence, and the Afghan court, when established in Kashmir, drank no other. Koker Nag is in lat. 33° 30′, long. 75° 12′.

E.I.C. Ms. Doc.   KOL, in Kashmir, a village fifteen miles south-west of the town of Islamabad. Lat. 33° 31′, long. 74° 54′.

E.I.C. Ms. Doc.   KOLALGOO, in Afghanistan, a village thirty-two miles east of Ghuznee. Lat. 33° 29′, long. 68° 49′.

Walker's Map of N.W. Frontier.   KOLBEE, in the Punjab, a village situate on the left bank of the river Jailum. Lat. 32° 28′, long. 72° 32′.

KOLEEGRUM, in Northern Afghanistan, a village situate E.I.C. Ms. Doc.
on the right bank of the Kooner river, sixty miles north-east of
Jelalabad. Lat. 35° 8′, long. 70° 56′.

KOLGUI, in Northern Afghanistan, a village situate on the E.I.C. Ms. Doc.
left bank of the Alishang river. Lat. 35° 29′, long, 70° 27′.

KOL NARAWA.—A pass into Kashmir, over the Banihal Vigne, i. 304.
mountain, lies at the base of the Kol Narawa summit. The elevation of this summit is 12,500 feet. The pass is in lat. 33° 28′,
long. 75° 2′.

KONDILAN.—See Bolan Pass.

KOOBREE, in Sinde, a village near the south-western Map of Sinde.
frontier, and eight miles from the border of the *Rin*, or Salt
Desert of Cutch. Lat. 24° 43′, long. 70° 58′.

KOOCHEN, in Afghanistan, a village in the desert which Walker's Map of
extends over the south-western part of the country. Lat. 29° N.W. Frontier.
56′, long. 63° 19′.

KOOCHLAK, in Afghanistan, a small mud-built town situate E.I.C. Ms. Doc.;
in the Pisheen valley, two or three miles south of the base of Mil Op. in Afg.
222; Havelock,
Tukatoo mountain, and on the route from Shawl to Kandahar, War in Afg. i.
282; Leech, Rep.
being eleven miles north of the former place. Here, in April, on Sind. Army,
1842, a skirmish took place between the Afghans and the British 89.
army under General England, on his retreat to Shawl, after the
reverse which he suffered at Hykulzye. Lat. 30° 16′, long. 66°
51′.

KOOJLA, in the Punjab, a village on the route from Va- E.I.C. Ms. Doc.
zeerabad to Julalpoor, and distant twenty-nine miles from the
latter town. Lat. 32° 34′, long. 73° 50′.

KOOKEWAREE, in Sinde, is the principal mouth for the dis- Carless, Official
charge of the water of the Sata, or great eastern branch of the Rep. on the Indus,
2-9.
Indus, and consequently for that of the main stream itself. The
width at the mouth is eleven hundred yards. Lat. 24° 2′, long.
67° 32′.

KOOKSHEH, in Afghanistan, a village situate on the Furrah E.I.C. Ms. Doc.
river, eighteen miles below the town of Furrah. Lat. 32° 13′,
long. 61° 59′.

KOOLAJ, in Beloochistan, a town forty-eight miles south of E.I.C. Ms. Map.
Kedje, and eight miles east of the river Dustee, in lat 25° 42′,
long. 62° 2′.

KOOLAZY, in Afghanistan, a large village lying immediately E.I.C. Ms. Doc.

to the left of the route from Shawl to Kandahar, and forty-two miles north-west of the former place. The surrounding district being part of the valley of Pisheen, is fertile and well cultivated. Lat. 30° 37', long. 66° 42'.

Walker's Map of Afg. KOOLOOKAIL, in Afghanistan, a village situate on the left bank of the Urghundab river. Lat. 32° 23', long. 66° 48'.

E.I.C. Ms. Doc. KOOLY WALLEE, in Afghanistan, a village situate on the right bank of the Indus, and six miles north-east of Dera Ghazee Khan. Lat. 30° 9', long. 70° 52'.

KOOND.—See KHUND.

Walker's Map of N.W. Frontier. KOONDEEAN, in the Punjab, a village situate on an offset of the Indus, two miles from the left bank of the main stream. Lat. 32° 28', long. 71° 31'.

Walker's Map of Afg. KOONDUL, in Afghanistan, a village in the Daman, is situate on the right bank of the Indus. Lat. 32° 34', long. 71° 24'.

KOONER.—See KAMA.

E.I.C. Ms. Doc. Masson, Kalat, 315, 316. KOOR, in Beloochistan, a small town, the principal place of a petty district of the same name. It is situate twenty miles north-west of the town of Kelat. Lat. 28° 59', long. 66° 9'.

E.I.C. Ms. Doc. KOORANIA, in Sinde, a village on the route from Sehwan to Larkhana, and twenty-one miles north of the former place. It is situate a mile and a half from the right bank of the Indus, in a level, fertile country, mostly covered with grass, but diversified by occasional patches of cultivation. The road in this part of the route is in general good, though in a few places rough ; but everywhere practicable for wheel-carriages. Lat. 26° 38', long. 67° 55'.

E.I.C. Ms. Doc. KOORD, in the Punjab, a village situate eighteen miles north-east of Julalpoor. Lat. 32° 53', long. 73° 27'.

Jour. As. Soc. 1840, p. 724, Conolly (E), Phys. Geogr. of Seistan. KOORHI MADALI, in Afghanistan, a village on the route from Kandahar to Khash, and a hundred and five miles west of the former town. Lat. 31° 40', long. 63° 45'.

E.I.C. Ms. Doc.; Jour. As. Soc. 1840, p. 724, Conolly (E.), Phys. Geog. of Seistan. KOORKEE TAGRISH, in Afghanistan, a village on the route from Kandahar to Khash, and a hundred and fifty miles west of the former town. Lat. 31° 34', long. 63° 11'.

E.I.C.Ms. Doc. KOORUM, in Afghanistan, a halting-place in a district of the same name, and on the route from Kandahar to Ghuznee, and one hundred and ten miles north-east of the former place. It is situate two or three miles from the left bank of the Turnak. Here is some scanty cultivation, and a supply of water from a subterraneous aqueduct. Lat. 32° 14′, long. 67° 7′.

KOORY, in Afghanistan, a village of the Daman, between Walker's Map of Kala Bagh and Dera Ismael Khan, and thirty-five miles north-east Afg. of the latter town. It is situate on the right bank of the Indus, where the Largee range closes down on the river. Lat. 32° 15′, long. 71° 19′.

KOOSHAB.—See KHOOSH-AB.

KOOSHAK, in the Punjab, a village situate near the left bank E.I.C. Ms. Doc. of the river Jailum. Lat. 32° 3′, long. 72° 11′.

KOOSHAK, in Beloochistan, a village situate on the route from E.I.C. Ms. Doc. Kelat to the munzilgah, or halting-place, at the western extremity of the Bolan Pass, and sixty miles north of the former place. The road is level and good in this part of the route. The village is supplied with water from wells. As, in consequence of the great elevation above the sea, the cold is very severe in winter, the inhabitants at that season emigrate to Cutch Gundava. Lat. 29° 37′, long. 66° 51′.

KOOSHK, in Afghanistan, a small fort and village on the E.I.C. Ms. Doc.; route from Herat to Merve, and forty-five miles north of the former Abbott, Herant and Khiva, i. 9. town. It is situate at the north-western base of the Kytoo mountain, and on a small river, which hence is called the river of Kooshk. The village consists of a few mud huts, and the fort is described by Abbott, as " resembling a dilapidated farm-yard." It is inhabited by the Teimunee tribe called Jumsheedee. Lat. 34° 54′, long. 62° 25′.

KOOSHK.—A river of Afghanistan, which rises in lat. 34° Id. i. 9-20 52′, long. 62° 38′, and falls into the river Moorghab, or Awb-i-Moor, in lat. 36° 16′, long. 62° 32′, after a course of about one hundred and thirty miles, in a direction generally from south to north.

KOOSHK-I-SAFFEED, in Western Afghanistan, a village E.I.C. Ms. Doc. on the route from Kandahar to Herat, and one hundred and thirty miles north-west of the former place. There is an abundant supply of water from subterraneous aqueducts. The road westward, for above ten miles, is broken and stony, winding among hills of gravel and rock, rising in some places nearly one thousand feet above the adjacent country. In some places the breadth of the path scarcely allows the passage of a laden camel ;

and travelling by it is altogether toilsome and tedious. There is some cultivation, and some scanty supplies may be obtained. Lat. 32° 18′, long. 63° 48′.

Von Hugel, lil. 410.
KOPURTHELLA, a town in the Punjab, about ten miles from the left bank of the Beas, and on the route from Loodiana to Lahore. Here Futteh Sing, the half-brother of Runjeet, built a magnificent street, a palace, and a temple, and near the town commenced and almost completed a mansion, in so massive a style that he incurred the suspicions of the Maharajah, and was in consequence obliged to fly. Lat 31° 24′, long. 75° 21′.

Westmacott on Khyrpoor; Jour. As. Soc. 1840, p. 1189, Leech, Visit to Manuf. Towns of Khyrpoor, 37.
KORA, in Sinde, a small town about fifteen miles south of Khyerpoor, and on the great route from that town to Hyderabad. The population consists generally of weavers engaged in the manufacture of loongees, or scarfs, and of coarse cotton cloths. Lat. 27° 12′, long. 68° 30′.

E.I.C. Ms. Doc.
KORAEEN, in Sinde, a village on the route from Subzulcote to Shikarpoor, and twenty-three miles west of the former town. It is situate in a low, level country, overflowed extensively, in time of inundation, by the Indus, from the left bank of which the village is three miles distant. The road here is tolerably good, though jungle and water-courses occasionally cause obstructions. Koraeen is in lat. 28° 11′, long. 69° 21′.

E.I.C. Ms. Doc.
KORAEJEE NA GOTE, in Sinde, a town on the route from Hyderabad to Sehwan, by the way of Kotree, and twenty-two miles north of Hyderabad. It is situate about a mile from the right bank of the Indus. The road in this part of the route lies through a shikargah, or hunting-preserve, lately belonging to one of the Ameers of Hyderabad, and is in many parts heavy, from the yielding nature of the soil. The town is in lat. 25° 42′, long. 68° 19′.

Carless, Official Rep. of the Indus, 2; Burnes' Bohk. lil. 238, 315, 316.
KOREE, in Sinde, at the south-eastern extremity of the sea-coast of that country, is an arm of the sea, supposed to have been formerly the estuary of the most eastern branch of the Indus, and still receiving part of its waters during high inundations. At Cotasir, twenty miles from the open sea, it is seven miles wide. The Koree mouth is in lat. 23° 30′, long. 68° 25′.

E.I.C. Ms. Doc.
KOREH, in Sinde, a town eight miles from the left bank of the Indus, and fourteen miles east of Larkhana. Lat. 27° 28′, long. 68° 28′.

Vigne, Kashmir, I. 292, 206.
KOSAH NAG, in Kashmir, a mountain lake on the north

side of the Futi Pañjal, one of the mountains bounding the valley on the south. It is three-quarters of a mile long, and five hundred yards broad, and is replenished from the melted snows of the neighbouring summit ; the supply from which is sometimes so abundant as to raise the surface of the water forty feet above its level in the lowest state. It gives rise to the Veshau, one of the principal feeders of the Jailum, which last river is also known in some parts of its course by the name of the Veshau. Vigne thus describes its efflux :—" Its full strong torrent is suddenly seen gushing out from the foot of the last and lofty eminence that forms the dam on the western end of the lake, whose waters thus find an exit not over, but through, the rocky barrier with which it is surrounded." The enclosing rock is a beautiful amygdaloid, containing spots of quartz in a dull dark purple-coloured matrix. The lake is held in great veneration by the Hindoos, who call it Vishnu Paudh (the foot of Vishnu), in consequence of a legend that the deity produced it by stamping the ground with his foot. It is, in consequence, visited in pilgrimage by devotees, for the purpose of performing ceremonial ablutions. The elevation above the level of the sea is estimated by Vigne at twelve thousand feet. Lat. 33° 26′, long. 74° 45′.

KOSHAUB, in the Punjab, a village situate seven miles from E.I.C. Ms. Doc. the right bank of the river Jailum. Lat. 32° 16′, long. 72° 10′.

KOT, in Afghanistan, a fort on the route from Dera Ismael E.I.C. Ms. Doc. Khan to Ghuznee, and fifty miles south-east of the latter place. Lat. 33° 7′, long. 68° 58′.

KOT, in the Punjab, ten miles east of the Indus, is a Von Hugel, iii. small and poor town. It contains one spacious and fine house 70. belonging to a fakir, or religious mendicant. This holy man was the pauper of thirty different villages, the inhabitants of which prided themselves on their benevolence in maintaining their mendicant in such state. Von Hügel met him clothed in silk, and borne in a palanquin. Kot (the fort) is in lat. 33° 59′, long. 72° 48′.

KOTANA, in the Punjab, a village situate eight miles E.I.C. Ms. Doc. from the left bank of the Indus, on the route from Leia to Mooltan. Lat. 30° 28′, long. 71° 4′.

KOT BUXADA, in the Punjab, a village, situate three miles Walker's Map of from the right bank of the Ghara river. Lat. 30° 10′, long. N.W. Frontier. 73° 1′.

E.I.C. Ms. Doc.   KOTE, in Afghanistan, a fort on a small stream, which, flowing from the northern declivity of Sufeid Koh, falls into the river of Kabool. The fort is in lat. 34° 8′, long. 70° 41′.

E.I.C. Ms. Doc.   KOTE, in the Punjab, a village situate on the right bank of the Chenaub river, and twenty-two miles north-east of Mooltan. Lat. 30° 25′, long. 71° 38′.

Walker's Map of N.W. Frontier.   KOTE BELOCHWALA, in the Punjab, a village situate about ten miles east of the Indus. Lat. 31° 50′, long. 71° 16′.

E.I.C. Ms. Doc.   KOTE BHAT, in the Punjab, a village situate on the left bank of the river Jailum. Lat. 32° 14′, long. 72° 20′.

Walker's Map of N W. Frontier.   KOTE ISASHAH, in the Punjab, a village situate near the left bank of the river Jailum. Lat. 31° 40′, long. 72° 4′.

Vigne, Kashmir, i. 143.   KOTELI, in the Punjab, a town on the route from Nadaun to Nurpur, and in the lower and southern part of the Himalaya. It has a good bazaar, and a fort built by one of the Mogul emperors on a precipitous sandstone rock. Lat. 32° 7′, long. 75° 38′.

KOTH.—See KOTLI.

KOTIAH.—See KOTTAI.

Walker's Map of N.W. Frontier.   KOTKABOO, in the Punjab, a village situate on the left bank of the Chenaub or Acesines river. Lat. 31° 32′, long. 72° 42′.

Moorcr. Punj. Bokh. i. 129 ; Vigne, Kashmir, i. 140 ; Forster, Jour. Beng. Eng. 241 ; Masson, Bal. Afg. Punj. i. 429 ; F. Von Hugel, Kaschmir, i. 79 ; iv. 125.   KOT KANGRA, in the north-east of the Punjab, among the mountains in the lower ranges to the south of the Himalaya, is an extensive hill fort, situated on the top of an eminence, about a hundred and fifty feet above the Ban Gunga, near its confluence with the Beas. The eminence is about three miles in circuit, bounded for the most part by precipices nearly perpendicular, and, in places of less declivity, rendered inaccessible by masonry and ramparts. Its position is in all respects such, that Vigne considers that by European engineers it might be rendered impregnable. About the beginning of the present century, it belonged to Sansa-Chand, who, being attacked by the Goorkhas, defended it for four years against them, but finally gave it up to Runjeet Singh, who expelled the invaders ; from that time it has remained in possession of the Sikh government. Kot Kangra is famous for what Butler calls, " supplemental snouts," there being practitioners here celebrated for carving from the skin of the forehead, new noses for those who have suffered mutilation of that organ ; and they are applied to by the afflicted from all parts of India. Kot Kangra is in lat. 31° 57′, long. 76° 4′.

KOTKEE, in Afghanistan, a village situate on the river Go- Walker's Map of mul. Lat. 32° 2', long. 69° 39'. Afg.

KOT KUMALIA.—See KUMALIA, or KAMALIA.

KOTLEE, in the Punjab, a town on the route from Am- E.I.C. Ms. Doc. ritsir to Vazeerabad, and forty miles north-west of the latter town. Lat. 32° 1', long. 74° 15'.

KOTLI, in the north of the Punjab, a small town among the Vigne, i. 247. mountains south of Kashmir, and on the route from Lahore to Kashmir, by the town of Punch. It contains a hundred and fifty houses, and is the post for levying the duties on goods introduced into Kashmir through the Punch Pass. Lat. 33° 29', long. 73° 47'.

KOTRDEE, in Sinde, a village on the middle route from Roree E.I.C. Ms. Doc. to Hyderabad, and ninety miles north of the latter place. Lat. 26° 28', long. 68° 20'.

KOTREE, in Sinde, a station on the right, or western, side Burnes (James), of the Koree estuary of the Indus. It is the place of embarkation 33. Mission to Sinde, and disembarkation on the line of communication between Cutch and Hyderabad. Lat. 23° 52', long. 68° 50'.

KOTREE, in Sinde, a village on the right bank of the Indus, E.I.C. Ms. Doc.; nearly opposite Hyderabad, from which it is distant four miles Notes, 39; Ken- south-west. It is important in a military point of view, as here nedy, Sinde and Kabool, i. 143. is the junction of the routes from Kurrachee, from the Delta, and from Sehwan to Hyderabad. It consequently commands, in a great measure, the southern part of Sinde west of the Indus. Here, in the beginning of 1839, was encamped the Bombay division of the British army advancing towards Afghanistan. Kotree is in lat. 25° 22', long. 68° 20'.

KOTREE, in Sinde, a village on the eastern route from Roree E.I.C. Ms. Doc. to Hyderabad, and ninety miles north of the latter town. Lat. 26° 30', long. 68° 48'.

KOTREE, in Beloochistan, a town of Cutch Gundava, is E.I.C. Ms. Doc.; situate on the plain, a short distance from the eastern entrance of 330. Masson, Kelat, the Moola Pass. It is one of the largest towns in the province, and has a good bazaar. There is also a fort built by the Eltarzai, a branch of the reigning family of Kelat. The Eltarzai are able to protect it from the oppression generally practised by the officers of the Khan of Kelat. Hence Kotree has become a place of refuge for the Hindoos, who are the class most liable to oppression. These refugees, here, as elsewhere in this country, principally manage the commercial transactions. Elevation above the sea, 600 feet. Lat. 28° 24′, long. 67° 27′.

E.I.C. Ms. Doc. KOTTAI, in Sinde, an encamping-ground on the route from Hyderabad to Sehwan, by the way of Kotree, and two miles and a half south of Sehwan. It is situate about a mile from the right bank of the Indus, and a mile and a half north of the pass formed by the approach of the Lukkee mountains to that river. Its site is important, as being the only place where an army can encamp between the pass and Sehwan. The road in this part of the route generally consists of heavy sand. Kottai is in lat. 26° 18′, long. 67° 57′.

E.I.C. Ms. Doc. KOTTANGA, in Sinde, a village on the route from Hydera-bad to Sehwan, by the way of Kotree, and eight miles south-east of Sehwan. It is situate near the right bank of the Indus, and close to the southern extremity of the pass formed by the approach of the Lukkee mountains to the river. Here travellers generally encamp to prepare for making their way through the pass. Kottanga is in lat. 26° 18′, long. 67° 56′.

E.I.C. Ms. Doc. KOTUL-I-TUCHT, in Afghanistan, a custom-house and military post on the route from Kandahar to Kabool, seven-teen miles south-west of the latter place. Lat. 34° 25′, long. 68° 49′.

[1] E.I.C. Ms. Doc. KOUSHAN,[1] in Afghanistan, the most frequented of those passes over Hindoo Koosh which lie to the east of Bamian. It forms a communication with Turkestan, and is called emphati-[2] Hindoo Koosh. cally the Pass of Hindoo Koosh, according to Leech,[2] because the most frequented, in consequence of the protection afforded to travellers by the governments of Kabool and Kunduz; the former of which held the southern, the latter the northern portion of the pass. It is, however, more probable that it was so called from its highest part lying over the eastern declivity of the vast peak called properly Hindoo Koosh. There are three entrances to the pass from the Kohistan of Kabool. Of these the principal lies along the bed of the Ghorbund river, and in consequence is impassable when the river is swollen. The road, which is very steep, proceeds up a deep and narrow valley, cross-cutting alternating veins of mica-slate, clay-slate, gneiss, and granite, which last ex-tends through the highest part of the pass for six miles. The elevation of the summit of the pass is estimated by Leech [3] Koh-i-Damun, and Lord[3] at fifteen thousand feet, but does not appear to
48.

have been ascertained by actual measurement. The general direction is from north to south: the inclination of the northern slope is much steeper than that of the southern, in consequence of the adjacent part of Turkestan having a far lower elevation than the Kohistan of Kabool; still, even on the southern side, the upper part of the pass is steep, difficult, and dangerous. Lord states that "it is for wheeled carriages perfectly impassable." Leech,[4] on the contrary, states that the Meer Timur (meaning Timur Leng, or Tamerlane) brought guns by it; but it is well known that cannon were not used by that prince; * and though Prinsep[5] assumes that Alexander marched from Afghanistan to Turkestan by this pass, the account given by Arrian is too general to warrant such a conclusion.† The Koushan Pass appears to be that called by Baber[6] the Pass of Kipchak. The summit is in lat. 35° 57', long. 68° 55'.

[4] Koushan Pass, 29.

[5] Jour. As. Soc. 1842, p. 564, Passes into Hindoostan from the West and North-west. (Signed) H.T.P.

[6] Memoirs, 139.

KOW.—See ALINGAR.

KOWALSIR, in Afghanistan, eight miles west of the city of Peshawur, is a place near the eastern entrance of the Khyber Pass. Here, in 1842, the British army was encamped, previously to the forcing of the pass by General Pollock. Lat. 34°, long. 71° 27'.

Mil. Op. in Afg. 177; Hough, Narr. of Exp. in Afg. 320.

KOWRANEE, in Sinde, a village situate on the route from Kurrachee to Hyderabad, and thirty-five miles south-west of the latter town. Lat. 25° 8', long. 67° 51'.

E.I.C. Ms. Doc.

KRISHNA GURH, in the Punjab, a strong fort, about ten miles east of the Indus, and on the route to Kashmir through the Dub Pass. It is of a quadrangular form and regularly built, though the walls are only of mud. Vigne observes, " Krishna Gurh is the finest specimen of a regular square mud fort that I have seen in the Punjab." Lat. 34° 4', long. 72° 53'.

F. Von Hugel, Kaschmir, iii. 65; Vigne, Kashmir, ii. 187.

KUBBUR-I-JUBBAR, a village on the route from Kabool to Jelalabad, twenty-four miles east of Kabool. Here, great

Eyre, Mil. Op. at Kabool, 237.

---

* Timur's march on India took place in 1498; four years later he succeeded in storming Smyrna, which was one of his most arduous exploits, and on that occasion he proceeded by mining. No mention is made in the accounts of the siege of the use of cannon. Von Hammer, Geschichte des Osmaneschen Reiches, i. 332.

† There can be no reasonable doubt that Timur advanced by the Khawak Pass, as he marched on Kafiristan from Inderab, which lies at the north-western foot of that pass.

Price, Mah. Hart. iii. 222; Wood's Oxus, 412, 413.

numbers of British were slaughtered in the attempted retreat from Kabool to Jelalabad in 1842. Lat. 34° 21', long. 69° 27'.

KUBBUR JABBAR.—See KUBBUR-I-JUBBAR.

KUBOOLA, in the Punjab, a village eight miles from the right bank of the river Ghara. Lat. 30° 10', long. 72° 51'.

KUBURMACH, in Afghanistan, a village among the Huzareh mountains, and in lat. 35° 42', long. 63° 31'.

KUCHEEREE, in Sinde, a village on the route from Kurrachee to Tatta, and eighteen miles west of the last-mentioned town. Lat. 24° 46', long. 67° 42'.

KUCHLAK.—See KOOCHLAK.

KUDDEEN, in Sinde, a village on an offset of the Goonee, or lower part of the Fulailee branch of the Indus, and near the western edge of the *Run*, or great salt marsh of Cutch. It lies on the route from Hyderabad to Cutch. Lat. 24° 24', long. 68° 53'.

KUDJAH, a village in Afghanistan, situate on the route from Kabool to Peshawur. Lat. 34° 15', long. 70° 14'.

KUDMEH KA TULAO, in Sinde, a large tank or artificial piece of water in the Delta of the Indus, twenty miles south-west of Tatta. Lat. 24° 40', long. 67° 36'.

KUDUN.—See KUDDEEN.

KUDUNEE, in Afghanistan, a halting-place on the route from Ghuznee to Shawl, and one hundred and five miles north of the latter place. It is situate on the Kudunee river, at the southern base of a range of hills. Lat. 31° 19', long. 67° 20'.

KUDUR, in Kashmir, a village thirteen miles north-east of Islamabad, in lat. 33° 52', long. 75° 10'.

KUKEE, in the Punjab, a village situate in the *Doab* between the Ravee and Chenaub, and ten miles from the left bank of the latter river. Lat. 30° 46', long. 72° 9'.

KUKIWAREE.—See KOOKEWAREE.

KUKUR, in Sinde, a village situate on the right bank of the Western Narra river. Lat. 26° 56', long. 67° 46'.

KULAIREE,[1] in Sinde, a considerable water-course, which parts from the right side of the Indus three miles due east of Tatta, and in lat. 24° 44', long. 68° 2'. It holds a circuitous course, first north, then west, and then south; and, in times of inundation, has so great a body of water as to insulate Tatta. At such times as the torrents flow down from the hilly country

to the north-west, several of them empty themselves into the
Kulairee. At the season of low water in the Indus, the Kulairee
becomes completely dry. Its course is very imperfectly explored,
but it probably rejoins the Indus at a short distance below Tatta.
Burnes [2] inadvertently states that it is the first offshoot of the [2] Pers. Narr. 18.
Indus on its right bank; but the Western Narra and many others
leave the right bank far above this place.

KULAN COTE, or KULIA KOTE (the Great Fort), in Wood's Oxus, 19;
Sinde, is situate near the north or right bank of the Buggaur, or Narr. 16;
western branch of the Indus, and three miles south of Tatta. To Outram, Rough Notes, 16;
the west are the remains of a suburb, and on the other side the Kennedy, Sinde
ruined fort is washed by a lake of considerable extent, communicat- Macmurdo in
ing with the Indus. The site is on a hill of limestone abounding in Jour. As. Soc.
marine shells, and everywhere honeycombed with natural cavities. De La Hoste, in
The walls are of mud, faced with kiln-burned brick, and enclose same, 1840, p.913.
an area three-quarters of a mile long and five or six hundred
yards broad. It appears to have been constructed with much
care and skill, and has numerous massy round towers, connected
by curtains: among other remarkable ruins, are those of a
mosque of spacious dimensions. In a large building is a great quantity of grain burned to charcoal; and this, as well as the vitrified
state of the brickwork in many places, indicates that the place
must have been destroyed by fire. Lat. 24° 42', long. 67° 56'.

KULCHA, in Afghanistan, a halting-place on the route from Pott. Belooch.
Nooshky to Herat, and one hundred and thirty miles west of the 405.
former town. Here is a well of excellent water, much venerated
because produced, according to tradition, by a Mahometan *Pir*,
or saint, who opened the rock with a blow of the point of his
spear, and caused the water to rush out. Lat. 30° 2', long. 63° 3'.

KULEEL KHAN.—See KULUL KHAN.

KULIAKOTE.—See KULAN COTE.

KULIGAM. in Kashmir, a town, the capital of the district of Vigne, Kashmir,
Dessir, is situated near the left bank of the river Jailum, here l. 148, 272, 305.
called the Veshau. The road from the Punjab, by the Col Nar-
rawa Pass, debouches by Kuligam, and hence is sometimes
called the Kuligam Pass. Kuligam is in lat. 33° 37', long. 74°
55'.

KULIGAM, in Kashmir, a village at the head of the Lolab Id. l. 100.
valley, and near the source of the river of that name, a small tributary of the Jailum. It is situate at the southern base of the

Green Mountains, bounding the valley of Kashmir on the north-west. Close to it on the east is a circular valley, five miles and a half in diameter, enclosed on every side by a verdant range, and having a morass in the centre. Here every evening an incredible number of birds, of the *corvus* genus, assemble from all parts of Kashmir to pass the night in the sheltered and warm valley. Kuligam is in lat. 34° 30′, long. 74° 23′.

Abbott, Heraut and Khiva, i. 20.

KULLA MOWR.—A ruined fort on the north-western frontier of Afghanistan, and at the line of division between it and the kingdom of Khorasan. Abbott found it so dilapidated that only one cell remained capable of affording shelter. It is situate on the left bank of the river Khooshk, in a fine valley containing a large *kareeze*, or subterraneous aqueduct, indicating its former populous and highly-cultivated state. At present the valley is totally uninhabited. Kulla Mowr is in lat. 35° 48′, long. 62° 26′.

E.I.C. Ms. Doc.

KULLAR, in Sinde, a village situate on the right bank of the Goonnee, or Fulailee, a great branch of the Indus, and forty-two miles south-east of Hyderabad. Lat. 24° 52′, long. 68° 40′.

E.I.C. Ms. Doc.

KULLER KAHAR, in the Punjab, a town in that part of the Salt range extending from the Indus to the Jailum. Lat. 32° 50′, long. 72° 29′.

E.I.C. Ms. Doc.

KULLOOR, a village in the Punjab, situate on an offset of the Indus, four miles from the main stream. Lat. 32° 7′, long. 71° 24′.

Pott. Belooch. 131-145.

KULLUGAN, in Beloochistan, a town in the province of Mekran, close to the frontier of Afghanistan, and on the route from Noshky to Bunpoor. It is situate in a narrow and most romantic valley, amidst stony hills, and close to the great sandy desert of Southern Afghanistan. It contains one hundred and fifty houses of two or three stories, which are built in this way to enable the inhabitants to take refuge in the upper part from the robbers who frequently attack them. The town is built on one side of a narrow grove of date-trees, in a fertile valley, productive of rice and other grain, and irrigated by a rivulet flowing down the middle, between rows of lofty spreading trees with rich and luxuriant foliage. The eminences which overhang the valley are covered with verdure ; and Pottinger thus describes the impression produced on the spectator : " On the whole, I thought it more embellished by Nature with her various beauties than any place I had ever seen." Kullugan is in lat. 28° 16', long. 62°.

KULORA, in Sinde, a village on the western route from E.I.C. Ms. Doc. Roree to Hyderabad, and sixty miles south-west of the former town. It is situate four miles from the left bank of the Indus, in an alluvial country much intersected by water-courses, dug for the purposes of irrigation. Lat. 27° 11', long. 68° 13'.

KULORAH, in Sinde, a village on the western route from E.I.C. Ms. Doc. Sehwan to Larkhana by way of the Arul river, and seven miles south-west of Larkhana. It is situate on the Cheela, a water-course from the Western Narra river. The road in this part of the route is in general good, though occasionally traversed by small water-courses. Kulorah is in lat. 27° 24', long. 68° 12'.

KULU, a small *raj*, or state, in the north-east of the Punjab, Moorcr. i. 170-consists of a few rugged valleys on the southern slope of the 182. Himalaya, together with the enclosing ridges. It is consequently rough, barren, and thinly peopled. The chief is a Rajpoot, who suffers much from the tyranny of the Sikh government. The capital is sometimes called Kulu, but is better known by the name of Sultanpoor. Kulu lies between lat. 30° 50'—32° 10', long. 70° 20'—70° 40'.

KULUL KHAN, in Afghanistan, a fort and village, in the E.I.C. Ms. Doc. mountainous tract south of Ab-istada lake, and situate thirty miles south of the southern shore of the lake. Lat. 32° 4', long. 67° 35'.

KULUNG, in Beloochistan, a village situate on the route from E.I.C. Ms. Doc. Kohuk to Punjgoor. Lat. 27° 27', long. 62° 22'.

KULUTZI, or KHALETSE, in Ladakh, one of the largest Vigne, Kashmir, villages in that country, is situate on the right or north bank of ii. 334; Moorcr. the Indus, which has here a rocky channel only twenty-five yards Punj. Bokh. ii. 8. wide. The site is elevated considerably above the stream. Moorcroft observes : " At first sight the situation appears unfavourable, presenting to the southward a line of towering rocks, and encircled nearly from east to west by a ridge of brown and barren hills. The cultivated ground is, however, of good quality, though rather incommodiously laid out in terraces. The grain sown here ripens in three months, and a second crop of buck-wheat, or turnips, is obtained from the same soil." The population, for the most part, are Buddhists, votaries of the Grand Lama of Tibet. At the time of Moorcroft's visit, there was a *sanga*, or wooden bridge, across the river, three-quarters of a mile from the village. It was "substantially constructed, resting on two scarped rocks, and was about thirty yards long. The river was not more than twenty yards broad, and was rolling, black and impetuously, about twelve feet below it." The depth at this time must have been very great, as, during the season of low water, a few months after, the surface of the stream was forty-five or fifty feet below the bridge. Kulutzi is in lat. 34° 20′, long. 76° 44′.

Walker's Map of Afg. KULYPUT, in Afghanistan, a village situate on the right bank of the Helmund river. Lat. 30° 47′, long. 62° 20′.

E.I.C. Ms. Doc. KUMAIKE, in the Punjab, a village forty miles west of Julalpoor, from whence there is a road through Dadun Khan Pind. Lat. 32° 47′, long. 72° 36′.

E.I.C. Ms. Doc. KUMBUR, in Sinde, a large town, with good wells, on the road from Larkhana to Gundava. Lat. 27° 33′, long. 68° 2′.

[1] Vigne, Kashmir, i. 111. KUMLA GURH, or *the Fool's Fortress*, in the north-east of the Punjab, and near the left or south bank of the Beas, a range of forts, constructed partly out of the natural rock, and partly of masonry. They are built on several sandstone peaks, which extend, north and south, a distance of about three miles.* The principal stronghold among them is an isolated rock, with precipitous sides rising about a hundred and fifty feet above the other peaks, about fifteen hundred feet above the Beas, and having an elevation of three thousand feet above the sea. This range of forts is situated on the summit of a mountain about eight miles long and five broad, surrounded by deep ravines, with precipitous sides, eighty, a hundred, or a hundred and fifty feet high. These strongholds belong to the ruler of Mundi. Sansar Chand, the powerful Rajah of Tira, and once the rival of Runjeet Singh, attacked them in vain; and they were considered by the [2] Vigne, i. 130. people of the country to be impregnable, until[2] taken by the Sikhs under Ventura. Kumla Gurh is in lat. 31° 41′, long. 76° 37′.

Walker's Map of N.W. Frontier. KUMMARA, a village in Bhawlpoor, situate on the left bank of the Ghara river. Lat. 29° 51′, long. 72° 35′.

E.I.C. Ms. Doc. KUMMEESA-KA-GOTE, in Sinde, a village on the route from Subzulcote to Shikarpoor, and six miles west of the former

* Moorcroft (i. 66) states twelve coss. It is, indeed, impossible to reconcile his account of this fortress with that of Vigne.

town   It is seven miles from the left bank of the Indus, which here extensively overflows the country in seasons of inundation. The road in this part of the route is in general good, though in a few places slightly obstructed by jungle. Lat. 28° 12', long. 69° 25'.

KUMMUR, in Afghanistan, a village situate where the Salt range closes down on the right bank of the Indus. Lat. 33° 30', long. 72° 1'. E.I.C. Ms. Doc.

KUMUR, in Afghanistan, a village on the route from Dera Ismail Khan to Kala-Bagh, and eighteen miles south-west of the latter town. It is situate at the northern extremity of the valley of Largee, on an offset of the Indus, and three miles from the right bank of the main channel. Lat. 32° 50', long. 71° 26'. E.I.C. Ms. Doc.

KUNDARA, in Sinde, a village situate on the western route from Bukkur to Hyderabad, and one hundred and twenty miles north of the latter town. Lat. 26° 28', long. 68° 9'. E.I.C. Ms. Doc.

KUNDYE, or KONDILAN, or KOONDELAUNA, in Bolan Pass. See p. 109.

KUNGHAL.—A village five miles north-east of Astor in Bulti. Lat. 35° 18', long. 74° 46'. Walker's Map of
N.W. Frontier.

KUNNA KHYLE, in Afghanistan, a village in the mountains bounding the plain of Peshawur on the east, and eighteen miles south-east of the town of Peshawur. Lat. 33° 49', long. 71° 54'. E.I.C. Ms. Doc.

KUNUK, in Beloochistan, a village on the route from Shawl to Kelat, and twenty-two miles south of the former town. The road in this part of the route is excellent, and rises gradually on the south or Kelat side. The country has a very great elevation, in no part less than five thousand feet above the sea, and in consequence the cold is severe in winter. Lat. 29° 55', long. 66° 41'. E.I.C. Ms. Doc.

KURAEE KILLA, in Afghanistan, a walled village on the route from Ghuznee to Shawl, and sixty miles south-west from the former place. The road in this part of the route is in general good, though sometimes crossed by ravines. The surrounding country is fertile, and cultivated to a considerable extent. Lat. 32° 50', long. 67° 40'. E.I.C. Ms. Doc.

KURAZEE, in Afghanistan, is a large village on the route from Shawl to Kandahar, and five miles east of the latter place. It is surrounded with gardens and much cultivation, and yields abundant supplies. Lat. 31° 33', long. 65° 30'. E.I.C. Ms. Doc.

Vigne Kashmir, i. 304.

KURI.—A small town of Kashmir, situated in a beautiful and fertile spot at the northern foot of Futi Panjal, a mountain forming part of the range bounding Kashmir to the south. Lat. 33° 35′, long. 74° 48′.

Masson, Bal. Afg. Panj. i. 40.

KURJAH.—A town of the Derajat, ten miles north-west of Dera Ismael Khan. It has a bazaar and a fort. Lat. 31° 56′, long. 70° 53′.

[1] Elph. Acc. of Caubul, 106; Conolly, Jour. to India, ii. 218.

KURKLEKKEE,[1] in Beloochistan, close to the southern border of Afghanistan, is a part of the great Hala range of mountains. The name is applied to that part of the range which rises on each side of the Bolan Pass, and has its greater elevation on the west, where it bounds the table-land of the Dusht-i-Be-daulet, and the valley of Shawl, and on the north, where it

[2] Ut supra, ii. 218.

adjoins the Tukatoo mountain. Conolly[2] describes it " as the first of a close and high series, that cover the country as far as the plain of Dauder, and which have a general inclination up to the Tukatoo chain." Their elevation above the level of the sea must be considerable, as that of the crest of the Bolan Pass,

[3] Jour. As Soc. 1842, p. 55, Grif. Bar. and Ther. Obs. in Afg.; Wood, Khyber Pass, 3.

which intersects them, is 5,793 feet.[3] Lat. 29° 20′—30° 10′, long. 67°—67° 30′.

KURKUTCHA.—A range of mountains in Afghanistan, running north and south, connecting the Hindoo Koosh with the Sufeid Koh, and separating the valley or basin of Kabool from the plain of Jelalabad. There is, however, an interval between its northern extremity and the southern base of the Hindoo Koosh, and through this the Kabool river flows. The range is for the most part of primary formation, consisting of dense slate. At its highest point it has an elevation of eight thousand feet. It is in general very rugged and rocky, but where there is any soil, it is covered with large and flourishing timber. There are four several routes over this range. First, that known as the pass of the Kurkutcha, the most southern. This first pass is impracticable for wheel-carriages, dangerous for camels, and difficult for laden horses or mules. Second, one immediately north of this, and leading from Tezeen to Jugduluk. Third, a circuitous route still further north, and, like that last mentioned, leading from Tezeen to Jugduluk. And, fourth, the Luttarbund Pass, the most northern of all. The cold on these mountains is intense in winter, the frost splitting the rocks and causing them to roll down the precipices in huge shattered fragments. The route from

Tezeen to Jugduluk was that taken by the British in their attempted retreat from Kabool in 1842, in the course of which the whole British force, amounting to 3,909 regular troops, of whom 1,139 were Europeans, were so completely cut off that only one man escaped; about 100 being made prisoners, and subsequently liberated. Lat. 34° 25′, long. 69° 30′.

KURMPOOR, in Sinde, a village on the route from Sehwan E.I.C. Ms. Doc. to Larkhana, and three miles north of the former place. It is situate half a mile from the right bank of a considerable offset of the Indus, and near the south-eastern edge of a large *dund*, or piece of stagnant water. The surrounding country is low, level, and fertile. The road in this part of the route is in general good. Lat. 26° 25′, long. 67° 56′.

KURNEE, in Afghanistan, a fort in the mountainous tract E.I.C. Ms. Doc. lying between the valley of Pisheen and Ab-istada lake, being sixteen miles south-west of the south-western angle of the lake. Lat. 32° 26′, long. 67° 37′.

KURPA, in the Punjab, a village situate about ten miles E.I.C. Ms. Doc. north-west of Ferozpore, and near the right bank of the Ghara river. Lat. 30° 59′, long. 74° 20′.

KURRAMKA, in Sinde, a village between Tatta and Hy- E.I.C. Ms. Doc. derabad, and twenty-seven miles north-east of the first-mentioned place. It is situate two miles from the right bank of the Indus, and close to a *shikargah*, or hunting-preserve, formerly belonging to one of the Ameers of Hyderabad. Kurramka is in lat. 25° 2′, long. 68° 10′.

KURRACHEE[1] is a sea-port of Sinde, near the north- [1] E.I.C. Ms.Doc.; western extremity of the coast of that country. It is situate Dir. I. 492. near the base of the southern extremity of the Pubb or Brahooic mountains, on a level space,[2] intervening between them and the [2] Hart, Jour. sea, and is the only sea port in Sinde for vessels drawing more As. Soc. 1840, p. 134. than ten feet of water.[3] The port is protected from the sea and [3] Carless, Survey bad weather by Munorah, a bluff, rocky headland, projecting of the Indus, 7; Wood on the In- south-eastward from the mainland, and leaving a space of about dus, in Burnes' two miles between the extreme point and the coast to the east. Pers. Narr. 366. In the harbour and within the entrance are some rocky islets,[4] [4] Pott. Belooch. which are seen from sea over the low isthmus connecting the 232; Kennedy, Sinde and Kabool, point of Munorah with the coast to the west. There is a good ii. 219. roadstead outside Munorah, except during May,[5] June, July, and [5] Postans. Obs. on the Com. of the part of August, when the south-west monsoon blows with such Indus, 8.

violence as to render anchoring there impracticable. At the entrance of the harbour is a bar, having one fathom and a quarter of water when the tide is out, and two and a half or three fathoms at high-water spring tides; it consequently cannot be safely crossed by ships the draught of which exceeds sixteen feet.[6] About a mile inside the bar there is an extensive bank, dry at low water, and between this and the western shore is the channel up the harbour. The general depths in the fair tract along that side of the bay are from two to four fathoms at low water. The harbour[7] is spacious, extending about five miles northward from Munorah point, and about the same distance from the town on the eastern shore to the extreme western point; but a small part only of this expanse admits large ships.* The point of Munorah terminating to the eastward the promontory, which landlocks the harbour on the south, is rocky, and about one hundred and fifty feet high. On it a fort[8] was built in 1797, which has been said to be so placed, that the fire of ships could have no effect on it, because their guns would require to be so greatly elevated, to avoid striking the brow of the hill, that most of the shot must pass over and fall into the sea at the opposite side ; while at the same time the vessel must approach the headland so close, that musketry, protected by the rocks, could clear the decks. This opinion, however, was disproved, and that of Lord,[1] that the eleven guns on the fort, owing to their partial depression, could produce no effect on shipping, corroborated, by what occurred in the beginning of 1839,[2] when the fire of the Wellesley, 74 guns, in an hour dismantled the fort, which was forthwith occupied by the British troops.

The town, which is three miles from the landing-place when the tide is out, is at that time difficult of access, as there is no hard road over the part left dry by the sea. Before the occupation by the British troops, the fortifications were very mean and irregular, being composed chiefly of mud and straw, and in many parts[3] so dilapidated that a horseman might ride to the top of them. In a few places they were found in good repair, and

Side notes:
[6] Pottinger, 343; Horsburgh, i. 492.
[7] Masson, Bal. Afg. Panj. i. 470
[8] Leech, Rep. on Sind. Army, 78.
[1] As quoted by Leech, 78.
[2] Hough, Narr. Exp. in Afg. 5, 24; Kennedy, i. 152.
[3] Pottinger, 343.

* Writers of reputation and of general accuracy have given much more favourable statements of the depth of water, and the capability of the harbour for receiving ships of large tonnage, than those contained in the text ; but the latter have been collected with scrupulous care from the best sources, and may be relied on.

partially faced with masonry. The town, with its extensive
suburbs, consisting for the most part of straggling huts,[4] was [4] Masson, i. 470.
ascertained, by census, in 1813, to contain 13,000 persons,[5] [5] Pottinger, 344.
and its population and prosperity are regarded as on the
increase. Burnes,[6] in 1830, estimated the population at 15,000, [6] Bokh. iii. 227.
about one-half of them Hindoos, who here carry on an ex-
tensive commerce. When Pottinger wrote (about 1815), the
annual revenue drawn by government from this port was
15,375l.; and in 1840,[7] it was estimated at a lac of rupees, [7] De La Hoste, in Jour. As. Soc.
or 10,000l. The native exports[8] are camels, saltpetre, salt, rice 1840, p. 909.
and other grain, ghee or clarified butter, hides, tallow, oil, oil- [8] Pott. 344; Burnes' Rep. on
· seeds, fish, bark for tanning, alkalies, indigo, cotton cloths, cotton, the Com. of Sinde, 21.
loongees, and carpets. The transit exports from the adjoining
countries are assafœtida, opium, and various other drugs ; madder, and other dyes ; alum, wool, silk, Kashmir shawls, dried
fruits, lapis lazuli, gems of various kinds, the precious metals,
and horses. The imports are metals, hardware, ivory, glass,
chinaware, fine cottons and silks, fruits and groceries, slaves,
shields of the hides of the rhinoceros and other animals, dried
fruits, and a few others of minor value.

Kurrachee is a position of very great importance, whether
regarded in a commercial, a political, or a military point of
view.[9] It has been laid down that a force stationed here, [9] E.I.C. Ms. Doc.
with detachments at Sehwan and Bukkur, might hold Sinde
in complete subjection. Kurrachee is the only safe port of
Sinde, and has acquired increased importance in this respect,
from the obstruction of the Hujamree mouth of the Indus,
which took place in 1839.[1] It has a good route[2] west- [1] Kennedy, ii. 220 [2] Hart, in Jour.
ward to Sonmeeanee, and consequently ready access to Beloo- As. Soc. 1840, p.
chistan. To the east there is a route to Tatta, along the sea- 134 ; Masson, Kalat, 8 : Leech,
coast, as far as Garrah creek, then along the course of the 95.
Garrah stream,[3] and from the small town of that name directly to [3] Kennedy, ii. 214; Outram, 5; Pot-
Tattah. There is another route from Kurrachee, directly through tinger, 346.
the hilly country to Tattah. Another route conducts to Kotree,[4] [4] De la Hoste, in Jour. As. Soc.
on the Indus, opposite Hyderabad ; another, westward of these, 1840, p. 914.
through the Lukkee hills, to Sehwan ;* another, still farther west,
through the same hills to Shikarpoor.[5] [5] Leech, Rep. on Sind. Army, 85.

* The distance from the gardens south of Sehwan to Kurrachee, by the
direct route, is one hundred and forty-six miles one furlong.

Burnes and Carless state that there is an inland navigation,

6 Burnes, on the
Navig. of the
Indus, 4; Carless,
Official Rep. on
the Indus, 6.
7 ii. 216.

by means of cross channels, from Kurrachee [6] to the Indus ; but there is little doubt that this is an error, as Kennedy [7] who went down the creek in a boat, found that it debouched into the sea nine miles east of the mouth of the harbour of Kurrachee, and in this he is borne out by the manuscript map of the Quarter-master-General. The ground, however, between the creek and the port is quite level, so that a canal could, without much difficulty, be made, connecting the two waters. The Garrah creek is navigable as far as Garrah village, about forty miles from the sea, and the land intervening between this last place and the Indus, abreast of Tatta, is level, low, of a soft nature, and only twenty-five miles across, so that the great river might, with little labour and a moderate outlay, be thus rendered accessible from the sea for large vessels. The climate of Kurrachee is cool in proportion to its latitude, and, under British protection, it bids fair speedily to become a very prosperous and important place. Lat. 24° 51', long. 67° 2'.

E.I.C. Ms. Doc.

KURRA KHAN, in Western Afghanistan, a halting-place on the route from Kandahar to Herat, and one hundred miles north-west of the former place. It has a supply of water. Lat. 32° 11', long. 63° 58'.

E.I.C. Ms. Doc.

KURRAMNOER, in the Punjab, a village situate on the route from Mooltan to Ferozpoor, three miles from the right bank of the Ghara river. Lat. 29° 51', long. 72° 13'.

Kennedy, i. 75.

KURREEMPOOR, in Sinde, a village in the Delta, on the left or eastern bank of the Buggaur, or great western branch of the Indus. Lat. 24° 39', long. 67° 41'.

E.I.C. Ms. Doc.

KURU, in Bultistan, a village thirty miles east of Iskardoh. Lat. 35° 8', long. 75° 57'.

Macartney in
Elph. 658; Wood,
Oxus, 99.

KURUM, a river of Eastern Afghanistan, rises on the eastern slope of the Suliman mountains, and fertilizes the fine valleys of Marwat and Banoo. After a south-easterly course of one hundred and fifteen miles, it falls into the Indus on the western side, in lat. 32° 37', long. 71° 25'. Its water is of a bright red colour from the hue of the earth suspended in it.

E.I.C. Ms. Doc.

KUSAB, in Afghanistan, a village situate on the right bank of the Indus, where the Salt range closes down on the river. Lat. 33° 23', long. 71° 56'.

KUSMORE, in Sinde, a village on the right bank of the E.I.C. Ms. Doc. Indus, between Mittunkote and Shikarpoor, and sixty miles south-west of the latter place. Lat. 28° 26', long. 69° 43'.

KUSRAON, in the Punjab, a village situate thirty miles E.I.C. Ms. Doc. south of Attock, and about twenty miles east of the Indus. Lat. 33° 29', long. 72° 26'.

KUSSOOR, in the Punjab, a large town near the right or Hough, 360. western bank of the Ghara. It is a place of great antiquity, is enclosed with a wall, and has several divisions, each surrounded by a separate wall strengthened with bastions. According to tradition, there were formerly twelve of these divisions, corresponding to the number of the twelve sons of the founder, who assigned one to each. There are several mosques and palaces. The surrounding country abounds in gardens and other well-cultivated spots. The inhabitants are all Mahometans. Hough observes, that at this place " an army might make a good stand, as not only are there heights, but each division of the town might be turned into a fortified position." Lat. 31° 9', long. 74° 27'

KUTCHA.—See Kulcha.

KUTTAJEE, a small river of Sinde, rises in the hilly tract E.I.C. Ms. Doc. between Kurrachee and Sehwan, and in lat. 25° 6', long. 67° 42'. After a course of twenty miles in a north-westerly direction, it falls into the river Goorban. Though so inconsiderable in point of size, it is in this arid country important for affording a constant supply of good water, as, even when it has ceased to run, the pools in its bed contain considerable quantities.

KUTTAJEE MUKAM, in Sinde, a halting-place on the E.I.C. Ms. Doc. route from Sehwan to Kurrachee, and forty miles north-east of the latter town. It is situate near the confluence of the Kuttajee and Goorban rivers, and has a constant supply of water from these streams. The road in this part of the route is in general good, though occasionally stony. Lat. 25° 8', long. 67° 34'.

KYE BADANEE, in Sinde, a village situate near the right E.I.C. Ms. Doc. bank of the Indus, on the route from Sukkur to Mittunkote, and sixty miles north-east of the former town. Lat. 28° 19', long. 69° 28'.

KYODAH, in Beloochistan, a village situate near the right E.I.C. Ms. Doc. bank of the Mooleanee river, on the road from Kedge to Punjgoor. Lat. 26° 59', long. 62° 40'.

KYRA-KA-GURREE.—See Keyra Gurrie.

E.I.C. Ms. Doc.   KYREE DERA, in Sinde, a village on the route from Lark-hana to Bagh, and fifteen miles north of the former place. There is a good supply of water from wells and pools about the village. The road in this part of the route lies through thin jungle, and presents little difficulty. Lat. 27° 40′, long. 68° 12′.

E.I.C. Ms. Doc.   KYREE GURREE, in Sinde, a town on the route from Larkhana to Bagh, and forty-eight miles north of the former place. It is situate on the south-eastern border of the *Pat*, or desert of Shikarpoor, is surrounded with a wall, and is supplied with water from wells. The road in this part of the route is level and good. Lat. 28° 1′, long. 68° 8′.

KYSUR, in Beloochistan, a small river, which, rising in the hilly country north of the town of Sarawan, flows northward, and

Belooch. 102.   is lost in the desert of Shorawuk. Pottinger, who crossed it in lat. 29° 35′, long. 65° 14′, found it, at the beginning of March, with a stream two or three feet deep and six or seven yards wide. He was informed that it is deep and rapid during wet weather, but quite dry in the months of May, June, and July.

KYTOO, on the north-western border of Afghanistan, a lofty mountain about fifty miles north-east of Herat. Its altitude is

Herat and Khiva, i. 8.   probably very great, as, according to Abbott, it " holds awful pre-eminence over the solitude," while the crest of the pass at its base is six thousand feet above the level of the sea, and travellers are every year lost in the snow. Kytoo is in lat. 34° 40′, long. 62° 35′.